Data Structures in
JAVA™

*From Abstract Data Types to the
Java Collections Framework*

Simon Gray

PEARSON

Addison
Wesley

Boston   San Francisco   New York
London   Toronto   Sydney   Tokyo   Singapore   Madrid
Mexico City   Munich   Paris   Cape Town   Hong Kong   Montreal

Executive Editor, Computer Science	*Michael Hirsch*
Assistant Editor	*Lindsey Triebel*
Senior Marketing Manager	*Michelle Brown*
Marketing Assistant	*Sarah Milmore*
Associate Managing Editor	*Jeffrey Holcomb*
Senior Manufacturing Buyer	*Carol Melville*
Composition	*Gillian Hall, The Aardvark Group*
Proofreading	*Holly McLean-Aldis*
Text Design	*Sandra Rigney*
Cover Design	*Night & Day Design*
Cover Image	*©2006 Roberto Adrian, iStockphoto*

Many of the designations used by manufacturers and sellers to distinguish their products are claimed as trademarks. Where those designations appear in this book, and Addison-Wesley was aware of a trademark claim, the designations have been printed in initial caps or all caps.

Library of Congress Cataloging-in-Publication Data

Gray, Simon (Simon James McLean)
  Data structures in Java : from abstract data types to the Java Collections Framework / Simon Gray.-- 1st ed.
    p. cm.
  ISBN 0-321-39279-5
  1. Java (Computer program language) 2. Data structures (Computer science) I. Title.
  QA76.73.J38G734 2007
  005.13'3--dc22

                              2006000295

ISBN 0-321-39279-5
1 2 3 4 5 6 7 8 9 10—CS—00 09 08 07 06

To my parents, Dora and Bruce
To my wife, Pam
To my children, James and Selena

for their love and support,
and for making this possible

Preface

Data Structures in Java: From Abstract Data Types to the Java Collections Framework is intended for a one-semester or two-quarter course that introduces data structures and abstract data types (ADT). It is expected that students will have completed an introductory programming course using an object-oriented language prior to using this book, though not necessarily Java. This book is appropriate for use in courses CS102 (I/OO versions), CS103 (I/OO versions), and CS111 (A version) as described in IEEE/ACM Computing Curricula 2001. It also fits the CS2 course in ACM Computing Curriculum 1978.

■ The Approach of this Book

This book combines the use of the Java Collections Framework (JCF) with development "from scratch."

Students are introduced to the Java Collections Framework (Sun's library of collection types). Collections from the JCF are used in examples and design issues raised by the JCF are discussed throughout the book. All collection types are also developed from scratch, but *within* the framework philosophy. This gives students' programming experience a positive practical flavor. They get to see and use an industry-standard library, while also developing an understanding of what goes into *creating* such a library. Moreover, the collections developed in the text and those the students are asked to develop in the exercises are designed to work within the JCF.

Develops Strong Problem-Solving Skills

The consistent approach in this book provides an effective model for students to develop their problem-solving skills. This approach also illustrates the book's philosophy—that construction of high-quality software requires careful planning. The book provides a consistent and coherent approach to introducing each collection type.

1. Description of the ADT's purpose including essential properties the ADT possesses

2. Specification of the ADT's behavior

3. Use of the ADT in an application

4. ADT implementation (including alternatives)

5. Analysis of the implementation

Uses Applications of Design and Object-Oriented Concepts

In this book, we explain and apply OO concepts so students have working examples they can use as models. Concepts such as encapsulation and inheritance are explained both textually and visually with illustrations. Then, numerous code examples show how the concepts work within Java and provide effective and consistent models. Importantly, the concepts are revisited many times throughout the book.

Integrates Software Testing

Students know that their code should be bug free and provide the functionality outlined in a specification. Since testing is intellectually demanding, students don't always understand or apply it. In this book, we bring the importance of software testing to the front. Unit testing is an integral part of the book and is described in detail, including how to implement unit tests in JUnit. Unit tests are developed for each collection type *prior* to presentation of the implementation under the philosophy that if you can't say how you would verify a collection's behavior through testing, you aren't yet in a position to implement that behavior.

■ Organization

This book was written in a way that allows the instructor to choose the ordering of the topics to best fit the course. Chapters 1-4 develop fundamental concepts that are explored in later chapters in the context of specifying and implementing common collection types and the algorithms that manipulate them. We recommend that these topics are covered first.

Chapter 0: Introduction to What We Will be Studying

This chapter provides an overview of the topics that will be presented in the rest of the book. The idea is to start with the "big picture" so students have a sense of where they will be going during the course and, roughly, how all the parts fit together. This includes the fundamental notion of abstraction used throughout the text; the software development cycle with emphasis on specification, design, and testing; the UML which is used to visualize the relationships that exist between classes we will develop; and the JCF, Sun's library of collection types.

Chapter 1: Object-Oriented Programming and Java

The chapter begins with application of the notion of abstraction to the specification of data types. This is followed by a presentation of fundamental concepts in object-oriented programming, including classes and objects, and code reuse through composition, inheritance, and polymorphism. ADTs and OO concepts are then applied in the development of a hierarchy of shapes (circle, rectangle, box, etc.).

Chapter 2: Error Handling, Software Testing, and Program Efficiency

Three characteristics of applications are presented: robustness, correctness, and efficiency. First, robustness has to do with a program's ability to spot and handle exceptional conditions gracefully. We look at Java's exception handling mechanisms and how to use them to make software more robust. Next, we'll show how to test a program using unit testing, specifically using a Java testing framework called JUnit. Finally, we examine mechanisms for determining the resource (time and space) usage of an algorithm or collection implementation. Students will do this using asymptotic analysis (theta and big-Oh notation) and will also learn how to time an algorithm. Throughout the text as we develop containers and algorithms that manipulate them, we ask, "Okay, but what does it cost?" This chapter provides the tools to answer that question.

Chapter 3: Fundamental Data Structures: The Array and Linked Data Structures

The specification of an ADT includes a description of the kind and range of values to be supported by the new type. What the specification won't necessarily tell us is how those values are to be stored. In this chapter we look at the two fundamental data structures used to store the elements of a collection: arrays (a random access data structure) and linked structures (a sequential access data structure). We compare them in terms of their coding complexity and, especially, their access characteristics. Later chapters build on this material by using arrays and linked structures to implement various container types. The Focus on Problem Solving section applies the Model-View design pattern to develop a system for tracking jobs for the Acme Courier Company using an array to store the courier slips that describe the deliveries to be made.

Chapter 4: A Basic Collection Class

We begin our exploration of collection types by building a simple collection class, `BasicCollection`, within the JCF. This introduces interfaces and abstract classes in Java and additional notation in support of Java generic types. We present the Iterator design pattern. We also develop our first full test plan and see how to implement it in JUnit.

Chapter 5: The List Abstract Data Type

This chapter continues the material from Chapter 4. Here we specify the List ADT, a linear collection, and look at its place within the JCF. We develop a test plan for the List ADT, then implement it using a linked List to store the collection's elements. The implementation is tested using the test plan previously developed. Finally, we look at the time and space complexity of our implementation, and following up on Chapters 2 and 3, compare the linked List implementation with an array-based implementation. This chapter's Focus on Problem Solving section revisits the Acme Courier problem from Chapter 3, using a List to store the courier slips. Because the Model-View design pattern was used to develop the original solution, we'll see that only a single class needs to be modified and all the others will work "as is"; a neat example of the power of thoughtful design.

Chapter 6: The Stack Abstract Data Type

A Stack is a linear collection type that stores its elements in a Last-In-First-Out (LIFO) order. We use the Adapter design pattern to implement the Stack using a List to store the Stack's elements. The Focus on Problem Solving section applies a Stack to the evaluation of postfix expressions. The infix expression a*b–c is represented in postfix as ab*c–.

Chapter 7: The Queue Abstract Data Type

A queue is also a linear collection. It stores its elements in a First-In-First-Out (FIFO) order. Two implementations are presented in this chapter: one using an array to store the queue's elements and a second using the Adapter design pattern again with a List providing element storage. This chapter's Focus on Problem Solving section uses a queue in the simulation of the normalization of traffic flow in a computer network.

Chapter 8: Recursion

A recursive definition is one that reapplies itself to a smaller instance of the problem input. This may sound unpromising, but it is very powerful (in fact, some languages rely almost entirely on the use of recursion.) Recursive definitions have many applications. This chapter explores their use in the specification of programming languages, data structures, and functions, where we see that recursion is another way to do iteration. In later chapters we will see that recursion provides elegant and intuitive solutions to sorting algorithms (Chapter 9) and traversals of Trees (Chapters 10 and 11) and graphs (Chapter 13). Recursion is implemented in the game of MineSweeper in this chapter's Focus on Problem Solving section.

Chapter 9: Sorting and Searching

Sorting is an important topic in computing, so we devote an entire chapter to evaluating algorithms to sort a collection of elements. We'll also look at creating generic sorting algorithms in Java using the Comparable and Comparator interfaces. Recursion is revisited when we look at two powerful sorting algorithms, quick sort and merge sort. The merge sort algorithm is applied in the Focus on Problem section when we look at the problem of sorting very large data sets, in this case security log files, using external sorting.

Chapter 10: Trees

The introduction of Trees takes us from the linear collections to hierarchical collections. We start with general tree terminology and quickly move to a discussion of the Binary Tree ADT. We look at array- and linked-based implementations and present several recursive algorithms for iterating over the elements of a Binary Tree. Iteration using "visitors" is discussed. The Heap ADT is introduced and implemented using a Binary Tree to store the heap elements. Heaps and Binary Trees are used in the chapter's Focus on Problem Solving section, which develops an application to do data compression using Huffman Trees.

Chapter 11: Binary Search Trees

This chapter extends the material from Chapter 10 by looking at Binary Trees specialized for searching, Binary Search Trees (BSTs). A goal of searching is to find the target element as quickly as possible. We'll see that maintaining the optimum organization of a BST is prohibitively expensive, so we'll settle for a close approximation to the optimum called an AVL Tree. We'll also examine a very different approach to BSTs called a Splay Tree. We use a BST implementation to store the vocabulary of a modifiable spell checker in the chapter's Focus on Problem Solving section.

Chapter 12: The Map ADT

A Map is an unordered collection that stores <key, value> pairs. Given a key, a Map produces the associated value from the pair. The important topic of hashing is presented and the Map ADT is implemented using a hash table. Two variations on the Map ADT, OrderedMap and MultiMap, are presented. A pizza delivery system is developed in the Focus on Problem Solving section. A Map stores information about delivery clients with the phone number acting as the key.

Chapter 13: The Graph ADT

Like a tree, a graph is a hierarchical collection type. We will look at directed, undirected and weighted graphs, and a number of important algorithms for traversing graphs and exploring the properties of a graph. Since there are several kinds of graphs that are useful, designing a hierarchy of related graph types presents an interesting problem in design.

■ Features

Investigate

Almost every chapter includes an *Investigate* section in which the student can further explore a topic from the chapter through self-discovery while developing independent problem-solving skills. Typically this involves reading documentation, doing some design, developing a test plan to verify the design, and then doing an implementation. There is also some analysis done at the end to evaluate the implementation, perhaps in terms of its coding complexity in comparison to alternatives, its use as an application of an OO concept, or its runtime and space complexities. The *Investigate* sections help students build confidence in their ability to tackle problems whose solution is not known in advance.

Example Programs

The text has a large number of complete programs, each designed to highlight the topic currently being studied. In most cases, the programs are practical, real-world examples with clear explanations. Visualization is used extensively to help clarify difficult concepts.

CheckPoints

CheckPoint exercises at the end of sections allow students to test their understanding of important concepts and terms to better prepare for subsequent sections. Answers to all CheckPoints are available at www.aw.com/cssupport.

Exercises

Each chapter presents a thorough and diverse set of review questions. These include:

- Paper and Pencil exercises strengthen students' familiarity with the material through simple application of the concepts.
- Testing and Debugging exercises require students to develop their program reading, testing, and analysis skills.
- Modifying the Code exercises require students to develop their program reading skills while specifying, designing tests for, and implementing extensions to code presented in the chapter or developed in other exercises.

Bonus Material on the Web

The following items are available online at www.aw.com/cssupport to further enrich students' experience with this material:

- Source Code for all example programs in the book.
- Focus on Problem Solving sections in which a problem is presented, analyzed, a solution planned, and implemented. An important aspect of these sections is that students see the process of working from a problem statement through to a solution.
- A chapter on the Graph ADT. Some instructors may choose not to cover this material in their course, but it is there if the student wants it.
- Additional exercises for many chapters, similar in style and level to those in the book.
- Study Guide exercises have students reflect on the chapter's material, further developing familiarity with the concepts and terms.

■ Instructor Supplements

The following supplemental material is available to qualified instructors from Addison-Wesley's Instructor Resource Center. Visit www.aw.com/irc for access:

- Solutions to the end-of-chapter exercises
- All the material from www.aw.com/cssupport is posted for instructors as well

■ Acknowledgements

There have been many helping hands in the development and publication of this text. I would like to thank the following faculty reviewers, in alphabetical order, for their helpful suggestions and expertise during the preparation of this manuscript:

Ijaz Awan, *Savannah State University*
David Boyd, *Valdosta State University*
Roelof Brouwer, *University College of the Cariboo (Canada)*
Peter Casey, *Central Oregon Community College*
Norm Cohen, *SUNY, Morrisville State College*
James Comer, *Texas Christian University*
Herb Dershem, *Hope College*
Dan Everet, *University of Georgia*
Mario Garcia, *Texas A&M University, Corpus Christie*
Adrian German, *Indiana University*
Teofilo Gonzalez, *University of California, Santa Barbara*
Dennis Higgins, *SUNY, Oneonta*
Norman Jacobson, *University of California, Irvine*
Bruce Johnston, *University of Wisconsin, Stout*
Cary Laxer, *Rose-Hulman Institute of Technology*
Blayne Mayfield, *Oklahoma State University*
Jonathan Mohr, *Augustana University*
Bina Ramamurthy, *SUNY, Buffalo*
Dale Skrien, *Colby College*
Carolyn Schauble, *Colorado State University*
William Shay, *University of Wisconsin, Green Bay*
David Sykes, *Wofford College*
Deborah Trytten, *University of Oklahoma*

Special thanks go to Jackie Middleton (College of Wooster) for her good humor and assistance in preparing the figures in this book, Ken Fogel (Dawson College) for his help in developing some of the Focus on Problem Solving sections, and Chris Haynes (University of Indiana) and Martine Ceberio (University of Texas, El Paso) for their technical edit prior to publication.

I would also like to thank the excellent team at Addison-Wesley for making this book a reality. In particular Richard Jones for getting me started, then keeping me going, and Michael Hirsch, Pat Mahtani, Lindsey Triebel, Michelle Brown, Sarah Milmore, Holly McLean-Aldis, Gillian Hall, and Kathleen Cantwell for their support and guidance in seeing me to the finish.

Most of all, I want to thank my family, Pam, James, and Selena, for their tremendous patience and support while I finished this book, and, of course, to the founding members of Barking Dogs Software: Ginger and Blue.

Contents

3

Fundamental Data Structures: The Array and Linked Structures   163

4 A Basic Collection Class 217

5 The List Abstract Data Type 285

6 The Stack Abstract Data Type 339

7 The Queue Abstract Data Type 369

13 Graphs (located on the Web at www.aw.com/cssupport)

Introduction to What We Will Be Studying

0

CHAPTER OUTLINE

Suzi and Gopal, two young programming consultants, are relaxing after completing their part of their first significant programming project at a small software company. They talk about the experience, comparing it to the work they did as students. In their student days

- The programs were pretty straightforward and usually small enough to be easily understood, designed, and implemented by a single student.
- Once completed, a program was rarely looked at again.
- The work was done quickly with the focus on getting the program to compile and produce plausible output by the deadline.
- Design and debugging were done somewhat haphazardly.
- Each program was only a small percentage of the final course grade.

Their new experience as paid programmers was quite different:

- The program their team just completed was about 60,000 lines long and was too complex to be understood by a single programmer. The application's design and development were handled by a team of five programmers.

- The application will remain in use for a long time and will be revised by programmers not involved in its original design and implementation.

- The focus was on providing the requested functionality on time, within budget, and with demonstrable assurances regarding reliability, functionality, and usability.

- Design, implementation, and testing were approached methodically to produce a better product, faster.

- Promotions and job security depend on results.

To a large extent, Suzi and Gopal's successful transition from student to professional depended on their problem-solving skills. The main goal of this book is to show you how to design, implement, and use a number of common **collection types** that are building blocks in many applications. In the process, you will develop effective problem-solving techniques that will move you further along the path to being an effective software developer. The rest of this chapter introduces you to the topics we will cover in this book, and how they are related.

■ 0.1 Abstraction

We start with the concept of abstraction, a simple, but very powerful tool that will be used extensively in this text and that was fundamental to the techniques used successfully by our two consultants.

0.1.1 Managing Complexity

We use complex systems every day—cars, CD players, cell phones, computers—it is a long list. What these systems have in common is that each presents us with an "interface" (buttons, knobs, dials, pedals, etc.) that allows us to focus on the system's purpose while hiding "irrelevant" details (such as what components were used to make the system and how they work). This technique of highlighting some features of a system while suppressing the details is called *abstraction* and is an important tool in managing complexity.

Abstraction involves focusing on the aspects of a system most relevant to its use while hiding the details of how the system accomplishes its tasks.

Abstraction is a tool for managing complexity

It is usually the case that the details of *how* something is done are unimportant to the action you want to perform. Indeed, if you were required to understand such details before acting, you would not get very much done. Instead, you want to use an object through a straightforward interface that presents its capabilities (the operations it can perform) in an *intuitive* way that matches your expectations of the object's purpose and behavior. Consider these examples:

- When programming a CD to record some music, you don't need to know how the electronics of the CD drive works, or how the music will be stored and transferred to the CD. You only need to know how to use the recording interface to execute the commands for music recording.

- When searching on the Web, you need to know how to select a search engine, how to enter a search phrase, and how to click a "Start search" button. You do not need to know the details of how HTTP and TCP/IP are used to transmit your request to the search site, how the search is actually done, or how the response is returned to your workstation.

- Using a graphical user interface (GUI), you can perform the file delete operation by selecting the icon representing a file and dragging it to the trash icon. The physical act of deletion is modeled by the manipulation of visual symbols on a screen. You don't need to know about disk drives, file systems, how files are stored, or how they are removed from a file system. Your idea of files can be blissfully simple and you can still manipulate them meaningfully.

You also expect that similar things will behave in similar ways and have a set of similar operations. So you expect that all time-programmable devices will support operations such as "set current time," "set start time," and "set stop time." A VCR is a time-programmable device that would *also* have the operation "set channel to record," while an oven would also have "set baking temperature."

Similar things should behave in similar ways

How does this relate to software development? You relied on abstraction when you used existing software libraries to write your programs. Java has a large collection of classes to support commonly needed capabilities. To output information to the console, for example, you used methods from the `PrintWriter` class of the `java.io` package or `Formatter` from the `java.util` package.[1] To get a random number you used the `Math` class from the `java.lang` package.

```
System.out.println("A random number: " + Math.random());
```

Your use of these classes was based on your understanding of their interface (the abstraction) as described by the class documentation (the "user's manual" for the class). You did not need to know how these methods were implemented to make use of them. In fact, having to know the details would only slow you down and interfere with your programming responsibilities.

The interface to a thing is an abstraction of it

Similarly, as our young consultants discovered, most applications are far too large—tens or hundreds of thousands, or even millions, of lines long—for a single person to understand in their entirety, not to mention completing in a reasonable amount of time. Instead, the software is designed as a collection of components, each of which has a well-defined role within the complete system, and that role is presented to the other components through a well-defined interface.

Different members of the programming team will work on different components and will make use of components from existing libraries and those built by other team members based solely on each component's interface and accompanying documentation. The complexity of those other components will be hidden

---

[1] A package is a collection of related classes.

behind (abstracted by) their interfaces. Just as you have used the standard libraries without ever looking at their implementation, you would have no knowledge about how the teams responsible for implementing the other components will implement them, and you don't need to know those details.

Abstraction will be your first and most important tool for managing complexity.

0.1.2 Abstraction and Abstract Data Types (ADTs)

Let's follow up on this idea of using abstraction in programming with a simple example. Consider the following code fragment.

```
int a = 5, b = 17, c;
c = a + b;
```

Before reading on, try to answer these questions (really!).

■ What is the data type of the variables a, b, and c and what values can these variables store?

■ What operations can you perform on int values?

■ What does the statement on the second line do? What is its meaning?

■ How are integers stored in the memory of the computer?

■ How is the addition operation from the second line done? How is this assignment done?

The declaration of a, b, and c tells us that these are integers. Specifically, ints are one of the primitive data types defined by Java, and Java documentation will tell us the range of values that can be assigned to these variables. We know there is a set of arithmetic operations, also specified by the language, that are defined on ints. Armed with this information, we know that the result of the operation on the second line is to assign the value 22 to the integer variable c. You probably have little idea about the answer to the last two questions (how ints are stored and how the arithmetic operators are implemented), but that did not prevent you from answering the other questions and has never stopped you from using ints!

A **data type** is defined by a set of:

■ Data values and their representation.

■ Operations defined on the data values and the implementation of these operations as executable statements.

Okay, now consider another code fragment.

```
String str;
str = "Ginger" + "Dog";
System.out.println("length of str is " + str.size());
```

String is not a primitive type in Java. It is a class defined in the java.lang package. A class defines a data type and we can declare variables of the type. A String object can store a certain kind of data (a collection of characters) and provides a set of operations for manipulating that data. So it makes sense that we can

A Java class defines a data type

ask questions of this code similar to those we asked of the `int`-based code. You would get the answers to all but the last two questions by looking at the description of the `String` class in a textbook or by going to the Java online documentation (JavaDocs).

The point, again, is that it is possible to write code that uses a type (primitive or class) based on its interface (the type's public side), as described in the documentation and with no knowledge of the implementation details behind the interface (the type's private side). In fact, you have been doing this in all the programs you have written.

Types have public and private sides

As our two brief examples suggest, a data type can be viewed from two perspectives.

1. Specification or model of a data type, defining the set of values (its domain) that instances of the type can take on and the operations that can be performed on those values (the type's interface). The specification is given independently of its implementation. This is the perspective of a user of the type (referred to here as a *client* of the class) who wants to know how to use the type. This is the public side of a data type.

Specification view of a data type

2. Implementation of the type, including a language-specific representation for the type's domain and executable statements for the type's operations. The implementer is concerned with the details behind the type's interface. This is the private side of a data type.

Implementation view of a data type

The application of abstraction to the definition of a data type is called **data abstraction**. An **abstract data type (ADT)** defines a model for a new data type, providing the *specification* view of a data type.

ADT = data type model

An ADT specification is abstract because it does not specify how values of the type are actually represented or how the operations on the type are implemented. These are details that a client of the ADT does not need to know to be able to use it, just as you don't need to know how the electronics of a remote control work to be able to use one.

Throughout the book we will alternate between wearing our user's hat when we are interested in what an ADT is to do and how to use it in a program, and our implementer's hat when we are interested in turning an ADT specification into a data type in Java and need to provide the implementation details for how the ADT will meet its responsibilities. The format for an ADT specification is presented in Chapter 1.

■ 0.2 Algorithms

Many years ago (by computing standards), Niklaus Wirth characterized a program as data plus algorithms. The data is the information we want to manipulate and the algorithms provide the mechanisms to do the manipulation.

An **algorithm** is a finite sequence of steps that solves some well-defined problem. The user's guide to my cell phone, for example, includes an entry "To save a phone number," which is followed by step-by-step directions on how to do this. The

Algorithm

bicycle we purchased recently for our daughter included instructions for its assembly (which, remarkably, I managed to do without any parts left over). These instructions are examples of algorithms. In terms of an ADT, an algorithm specifies how an operation will meet its responsibilities.

0.2.1 Algorithm Development

You will develop algorithms through three levels of abstraction. At the highest level, you are specifying what the algorithm will do and the context under which it will run. This is a very abstract representation of the algorithm and is equivalent to the specification of an ADT operation. No implementation details are provided at this level.

Level	Activity
Highest	Algorithm specification
	Pseudocoding
Lowest	Code in a programming language

At the lowest level, the details of how the algorithm will meet its responsibilities are expressed in a programming language. In other words, you have working code that can be compiled and executed on a machine. This is clearly a concrete representation of the algorithm.

There is also an intermediate level we will use that bridges the abstract specification and the concrete implementation. This is the pseudocoding level, in which you outline the steps the algorithm will take.[2]

Pseudocode is a set of natural language-like statements that describe, at various levels of detail, the steps an algorithm must take to solve a problem and the order in which those steps should be taken. Pseudocoding is a tool you use to take you incrementally from the abstract specification level to the concrete implementation level.

Pseudocoding is like writing a rough draft of a paper—you are getting your ideas down on paper

I approach pseudocoding in much the same way I approached writing papers when I was an undergraduate. Knowing my paper's theme (the algorithm's purpose), I first identified the major ideas my paper would develop (roughly equivalent to a high-level view of the major steps of the algorithm) and I would put them in an order that made sense. In part, my goal was just to get started and to get ideas flowing—I knew I could smooth out the rough spots later. My next step was to begin to fill in the details for each of my major ideas—identify the substeps to take for each major step in the algorithm. This is called **stepwise refinement**. Occasionally I would look through what I had and, if necessary, rearrange parts. I continued the process, providing more detail at each step until I felt I had enough to write the paper with complete sentences (translate the pseudocode into a programming language).

---

[2]Arguably there is another level of development in which we test the algorithm. This topic is important enough that it gets its own section in this chapter.

0.2.2 Determining the Cost of an Algorithm

When you want to buy something, you can often choose from among several products. This applies to everything from shoes and CD players to cars and homes. To make an informed choice you need criteria by which you can evaluate the products. Generally, you want the least expensive item that meets your needs.

So it is with algorithms (and many other things in computing). You will almost always find that there are a variety of ways you can solve a programming problem. The issue then becomes how you determine which of the possibilities is "best" for your situation. What you need are *criteria* by which you can compare the different algorithms. Every algorithm has a cost in:

- *Time.* How long will it take the algorithm to complete?
- *Space.* How much additional memory will it need?

We refer to these as the **time complexity** and the **space complexity** of the algorithm.

Typically, the time and space complexities are a function of the size of the input to the algorithm. Using time as an example, we would expect that the time it takes to sort 100 integers into ascending order will be less than the time it takes to sort 10,000 integers into ascending order. But how long will this actually take?

You could code the algorithm and run it, measuring how long it takes to run. The downside of this is that the performance of an algorithm (the time it actually takes to run) depends on factors that are independent of it, such as the speed of the processor, involvement of the cache, and other programs running. If wall clock time is your metric, then a fast algorithm running on a slow machine could be made to look slower than a slow algorithm running on a fast machine.

A better, *independent* measure of time is to count "representative operations" in the algorithm (arithmetic operations, comparisons, and data movement operations are typical examples). The number of such operations will give you a good idea about the *theoretical* time complexity of the algorithm.

Chapter 2 describes how we will estimate the time and space complexities of algorithms. As each ADT is implemented, we will discuss its cost so that you have some sensible criteria by which to compare them.

> Algorithms can be evaluated based on their time and space complexity

> Wall clock time won't do for measuring an algorithm

> Independent measure: count the number of operations needed

0.2.3 Living with Tradeoffs

At the outset of this section we talked about the decision-making you do when buying something. Often tradeoffs are involved—this item is more expensive, but has more uses and will last longer than the cheaper, poorly made brand; on the other hand, buying in bulk may save you multiple trips to the store (time) and money, but you'll need lots of storage space. Living with tradeoffs is also a regular part of computing.

For example, another "cost" of an algorithm is its coding complexity (by which I mean its difficulty or trickiness). The more complicated an algorithm is, the more difficult it is to code correctly. Algorithms that have better time complexities tend to also be trickier to code. So one tradeoff that programmers will sometimes make is running time for coding simplicity—all things being equal, it is often worth it to choose the simplest algorithm.

Another common tradeoff is space for time or time for space. We will look at alternative implementations for some ADTs that trade additional space for greater flexibility at the cost of additional time, and others that choose speed at the cost of reduced flexibility. It is important that you be aware of the costs involved when you make these tradeoffs, so that you are making an informed decision.

0.2.4 Generic Algorithms

An inconvenience you have probably already experienced is having to write different versions of a method to handle different data types. This is called **type-specific code**. As a simple example, consider the swap method used as part of a sorting algorithm. The code in Listing 0.1 is type-specific and only works for `Rational` objects. What if we wanted to swap two `Integer` or two `BankAccount` objects? We would have to write two more `swap()` methods.

There is a better way. One of the advantages of object-oriented programming is that it makes it possible to write a single piece of code that applies to more than one data type. This is done in Java by writing a **generic method**.

This is done in Java by writing a generic method that takes a **type argument** that can be used to specify the types of the method's parameters, local variables, and the method's return type. The generic version of `swap()` is shown in Listing 0.2. The type parameter `<T>` that appears before the method return type is matched by a specific type when `swap()` is invoked. Thus if `swap()` is called with an array of `Rationals`, T will be `Rational`. If it is called with an array of `BankAccounts`, T will be `BankAccount`. Thus `swap()` can swap two of *any* kind of object.

The beauty of this is that we can get away with writing less code because the generic code applies to more situations than the type-specific code. Sometimes, as

Listing 0.1 A `swap()` method to swap `Rational` objects in an array.

```
1    void swap( Rational[] theArray, int i, int j ) {
2        Rational t = theArray[i];
3        theArray[i] = theArray[j];
4        theArray[j] = t;
5    }
```

Listing 0.2 A generic `swap()` method for an array.

```
1    <T> void swap( T[] theArray, int i, int j ) {
2        T t = theArray[i];
3        theArray[i] = theArray[j];
4        theArray[j] = t;
5    }
```

in our `swap()` example, it is as easy to write generic code as it is to write type-specific code. But usually writing generic code is more difficult and requires careful attention to design.[3] We will use generic methods in many places.

■ 0.3 Object-Oriented Programming

An **object-oriented program** seeks to model the structure and behavior of a real-world system (a university enrollment management system, a banking system, a video rental system, etc.) through the interaction of software objects, each of which represents an entity from the problem domain.

Objects are constructed in the memory of the computer. They store data relevant to the real-world entity they are modeling and they provide methods (operations) that can be applied to that data. These methods define the **Application Programmer Interface (API)** of the object. The objects of an OO program interact by sending **messages** to one another. The kinds of messages an object can receive are determined by the operations in the object's API.

Objects interact by sending messages to one another

Here is a short story to illustrate the OO ingredients presented so far. Suzi and Gopal received bonuses for their work on the recently completed project. They head to the bank. There are two tellers at the drive-up windows, Teller A and Teller B. When a teller starts work for the day, he or she logs into the bank's computer system, which creates a `Teller` object for that teller. The `Teller` object logs the teller's activities and allows the teller to provide banking services to customers. Each teller will be represented in the bank's software system by his or her own `Teller` object, which will look something like Figure 0.1.

Figure 0.1 Human tellers and `Teller` objects.

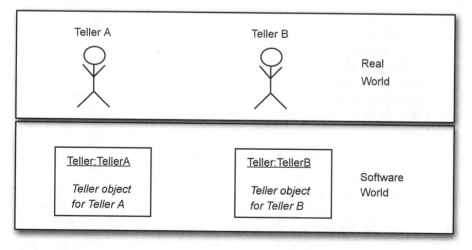

---

[3]In fact, as the book progresses, getting the most out of many of the most powerful features of OO languages such as Java requires great foresight.

Figure 0.2 Interacting bank system objects.

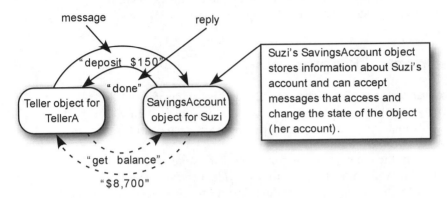

Suzi gets in the lane handled by Teller A and first asks to deposit her bonus ($150) into her *savings* account. She then asks for the current balance on her savings account. As shown in Figure 0.2, the `TellerA` object first sends a "make deposit" message to the object representing Suzi's savings account. Since making a deposit is one of the operations that a savings account object can perform, it accepts the message and Suzi's savings account is updated accordingly. Then the `TellerA` object sends a "get balance" message to Suzi's savings account object. This is also an operation a savings account object can perform, so it accepts the message and returns the balance of the account to the `TellerA` object, which displays the information on a screen for the human Teller A to see and pass on to Suzi.

Gopal gets in the lane with Teller B and deposits his bonus ($150) into his *checking* account. He then asks for the balance in his checking account. The `TellerB` object first sends a "make deposit" message to the object representing Gopal's checking account. Since making a deposit is one of the operations that a checking account object can perform, it accepts the message and Gopal's checking account is updated accordingly. Then the `TellerB` object sends a "get balance" message to Gopal's checking account object and the balance of the account is returned to the `TellerB` object, which displays the information on a screen for the human Teller B to see and pass on to Gopal—same operations (make a deposit, get a balance), different, but related, kinds of accounts (savings and checking).

> Similar things should behave in similar ways

0.3.1 Enforcing Abstraction: Classes, Encapsulation, and Information Hiding

In Java, the data stored by an object (such as Suzi's savings account object and Gopal's checking account object) and the operations it provides are implemented in a **class** definition. This is called **encapsulation**. It is helpful to think of a class definition as a blueprint and an object as the thing that is constructed in the memory of the computer based on that blueprint, just as we would use a blueprint of a house to construct an actual house. Also, just as we can build many homes from a single blueprint, so we can create many objects from the same class definition. The

> Encapsulation: a class is a language construct that contains (encapsulates) data and operations on that data

`TellerA` and `TellerB` objects, for example, would be created from a single `Teller` class definition. They would have the same structure, but the data they store would be unique to the two tellers.

A class definition is the Java language implementation of an ADT. Thus, classes provide the **implementation view** of an ADT. Whereas an ADT describes what a type can do, but says nothing about how it does these things, a class definition says both what the type can do (its public side or API) and internally provides the details (implementation) of how the operations will be carried out.

Java class = ADT implementation

However, a class hides these implementation details (its private side) from its clients. This is called **information hiding** and is completely within the spirit of ADTs and abstraction—clients can use an object through its API without needing to know how the ADT is implemented.

Information hiding: A class can hide information meant to be private and release information meant to be public

One really wonderful advantage of this is that we can change the implementation of a class without affecting either the interface of the class or the clients who rely on that interface. In fact, if I have two different classes with exactly the same interface but different implementations, I can swap them in an application and the clients who use the interface need not know a switch has been made.

0.3.2 Creating the New from the Old: Inheritance and Composition

As you program, you will have to design new classes. Fortunately you don't have to make them all from scratch. Instead, you can treat existing classes as building blocks to create new classes. There are two powerful mechanisms in OOP to do this: inheritance and composition.

Inheritance in OOP behaves much the way it does in the biological world. A parent class (also called a **superclass**) has characteristics, which it passes on to all of its children (**subclasses**). Each child class will provide a specialization that distinguishes it behaviorally from its parent and its siblings.

Consider the `SavingsAccount` and the `CheckingAccount` classes that were used to create the savings and checking account objects from our story. You may have noticed that Suzi's savings account object and Gopal's checking account object were accepting the same messages ("make deposit" and "get balance"). That is because these kinds of accounts have characteristics in common, which could be extracted and moved into a parent class (`BankAccount`), as shown in Figure 0.3. The `SavingsAccount` and `CheckingAccount` subclasses would inherit these things from the more general `BankAccount` parent class and then provide specializations unique to their needs. For example, a checking account may charge a fee for each transaction on the account.

Inheritance defines what is called an "is a kind of" relationship. A savings account "is a kind of" bank account and a checking account "is a kind of" bank account. But a savings account behaves differently than a checking account, so you would not say that a savings account "is a kind of" checking account.

Inheritance defines an "is a kind of" relationship

Composition is also pretty intuitive. It simply means that one class may contain (be composed of) one or more other classes. This is called a "has a" relationship. For example, the `BankAccount` class will need a name field to store the name of the account holder. This can conveniently be stored using an instance of the

Composition defines a "has a" relationship

Figure 0.3 UML class diagram for a simple bank account class hierarchy. A `SavingsAccount` "is a kind of" `BankAccount`, and a `CheckingAccount` "is a kind of" `BankAccount`.

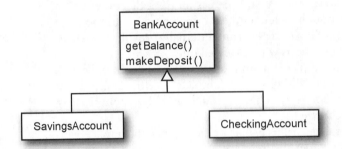

`String` class. The mailing address of the account holder could be stored in an instance of an `Address` class. The date the account was opened could be stored in an instance of the `Date` class, and so on. In this example, a `BankAccount` class is composed using `String`, `Address`, and `Date` classes (among others). So a `BankAccount` "has a" `String`, an `Address`, and a `Date` within it (Figure 0.4).

0.3.3 Plugging in Related Objects: Polymorphism

Another advantage of OOP is that we can write polymorphic code. **Polymorphism** means "many forms." In OOP, this means that I can write one piece of code that sends the same message to different, but related, objects, and those objects will react to the message in a way that is appropriate for the kind of real-world thing they represent. For example, "make deposit" and "get balance" messages were sent to Suzi's "*savings account*" object and Gopal's "*checking account*" object, and each reacted in a way that was appropriate to the kind of object it is.

Here is a more dramatic example illustrating the same principle. Picture a football game. The players line up for a play. What they have in common is that they are

Figure 0.4 UML class diagram showing composition of classes in defining `BankAccount`. A `BankAccount` "has a" `String`, "has a" `Date`, and "has an" `Address`.

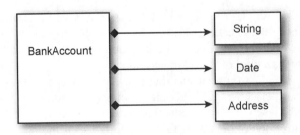

all football players, but they each have different roles to play. When the ball is snapped, each player receives the same message: "start the play." But what each player does will depend on the *kind of* football player he is; that is, by position. This is polymorphism: one message sent to multiple (similar) objects producing multiple behaviors. This is a very powerful idea and is what makes it possible to write generic code.

Chapter 1 gives you an overview of OOP, including inheritance, composition, and polymorphism. These are all topics we will revisit many times and they will become an integral part of your OO problem-solving toolkit.

■ 0.4 The Software Life Cycle

Large applications are very complex and, as Suzi and Gopal quickly realized, their construction is not to be approached in a carefree manner. The discipline of **software engineering** researches methods to manage this complexity. One outcome of this research has been the realization that all software goes through a software life cycle with five phases.[4]

1. *Analysis and Specification.* Carefully examine the problem you are given and produce a clear, complete, and unambiguous statement of the problem to be solved.

   Be clear about what you are to solve

   You cannot begin to solve a problem until you have a clear idea about what it is you are to solve. Frequently, the problem to be solved is not described clearly enough for you to think of a solution right away. There may be missing information, ambiguities, and even contradictory information in the problem statement. A very important part of problem solving is developing a clear statement of the problem to be solved. You should expect to have to ask questions about the problem before you can solve it.

   Ask questions!

   A useful tool here is to imagine using the software. What does the input look like (e.g., the type of the data, its format, and the order of the data items)? What should the output look like (e.g., should there be a particular format such as a table or chart, and what labeling should there be)? Remember that you aren't paid to produce the software you want; you are paid to produce the software the client wants. One possibility is to quickly develop a prototype of the system highlighting the user interface the system will have (with little or no functionality behind the interface), and let the client react to it. Early feedback is important because often the client's own idea of what the software is to do is vague, and seeing something concrete helps clarify the picture for them, which means you have a more accurate idea of what you need to build.

   Determine input and output formats

   Visually oriented software design notations such as the Unified Modeling Language (UML is introduced in Section 0.6) provide an intuitive tool that designers and clients alike can use to characterize important aspects of a system. Different parts of UML support different parts of the software development cycle.

---

[4]There are, of course, variations on this that you would study in depth in a software engineering course. The phases presented here are typical.

The output of the first phase is a written document that has been approved by the client and the software developer. This document serves a couple of purposes. First, it forms a contract between the client and the developer and will be used during the acceptance-testing portion of phase 4. Second, it is provided to the software design team for use in the design phase.

2. *Design.* In the design phase, the solution is decomposed into a collection of modules, each of which has a well-defined responsibility within the entire system. In OO design, this decomposition involves identifying discrete components in the problem domain that are to be modeled by objects in the resulting software system (e.g., `Teller`, `BankAccount`, `SavingsAccount`, `CheckingAccount`, `Date`, `Address`, and `Transaction` from our simple banking system). For our purposes, the design of these modules corresponds to the design of ADTs. In addition to specifying each module, you need to specify how the modules would interact to provide a solution to the client's problem.

> **Identify objects in the system and their responsibilities**

Before moving to the next phase, you should do a **walk-through** of your design. In a walk-through, the designer of a component presents the design to other members of the team. The designer explains the problem the module is to solve, the module's interface, and the role played by each operation in the module's interface. Other members of the team ask questions and critique the design. An advantage of walk-throughs is that the other team members can provide some objectivity and may see problems you missed because you were too close to the design.

> **Verify your design before implementing it**

It is also a good idea to identify points in your solution that are especially sensitive to the data and are possible fail points. You will use this information when you develop a plan for testing your solution.

> **Begin thinking about testing now**

The output of this phase is a clearly specified solution to the problem identifying the modules that will make up the solution, the responsibilities and constraints on each module, the input expected by each module, and the results to be returned.

3. *Implementation.* Translate the design developed in phase 2 into code in an implementation language such as Java. With the clear description of the solution developed in phase 2, members of a programming team can work independently on different components.

Two bits of advice can be offered here. First, methods that are more than a few lines long or that involve control structures (e.g., selection or iteration) should be pseudocoded first and then desk-checked before being coded. This is only "extra" work in the short term. By reducing the number of errors you introduce into your code, you are reducing debugging time (which has a much higher frustration factor than coding) in the long run. Second, unless the program is very small, don't try to code it all at once. Identify the classes that have to be built first.

> **Pseudocoding saves time by shortening debugging time**

> **Do the implementation in increments, testing each part as it is done**

Within each class, identify the methods that must be coded first and work on them, providing empty bodies for the other methods so the class will compile. Make sure each method works properly before writing more code. A **test program** is a program that creates instances of the classes you want to test and invokes methods from them, sending various sets of test data and producing output to be checked. Once this is done to your satisfaction, implement other methods or classes of the program and test them by expanding your test program.

4. *Testing and Debugging.* There are several kinds of testing that can be done at different points in the life cycle. The next section looks at testing in more detail.

5. *Maintenance.* Provide updates and continued bug fixes. Most of the lifetime of a piece of commercial software is spent in the maintenance phase. During this time the software may be updated to meet new needs, additional features may be coded and obsolete features deleted, and bugs are fixed as they are discovered. The bulk of the cost of a piece of software is spent in the maintenance phase. That cost can be reduced if the original program was coded with maintenance in mind. Readability and modularity are important characteristics of a program that simplify maintenance.

   Readability refers to how easy it is to read a piece of code and understand what it does. Consistent use of a sensible programming style (good identifier names, formatting, and comments) enhances readability. A program that is easy to read and understand is easier to change and to debug. Modularity also simplifies maintenance by isolating behavior within well-defined classes.

A readable program is easier to update and debug

0.4.1 The Classic Waterfall Model

There are several models for the development of software based on the phases of the software life cycle. In the classic waterfall model (see Figure 0.5), the phases are visited sequentially and, ideally, a new phase is not begun until the previous phase is complete.

Figure 0.5 The waterfall model of software development.

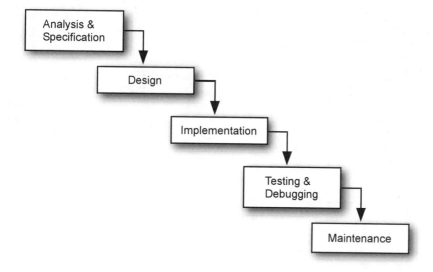

This model is rigid and unforgiving, and tends to increase the cost of mistakes made earlier in the development process.

0.4.2 The Object-Oriented Spiral/Incremental Model

A more flexible model and one more suited to OOP is the spiral/incremental model (see Figure 0.6) in which the software is built in iterations, with each iteration incrementally adding parts to the system (the area within the spiral indicates the amount of effort spent so far).[5] Each iteration repeats, to various degrees, the first four phases of the life cycle. The last iteration should produce the "final" product with the complete functionality requested by the client. At that time the maintenance phase begins.

There are four advantages to this approach for small projects. Large projects typically require more advance planning.

1. It encourages rapid development of prototypes that the client can actually use to provide quick feedback about the initial design.

2. Incremental development allows the most essential features to be built first and even for a working subset of the final application to be used under real working conditions. This adds business value to the software (which makes the client happy) and provides more feedback (which increases the likelihood that the final product really meets the client's needs).

Figure 0.6 The spiral/incremental model of software development.

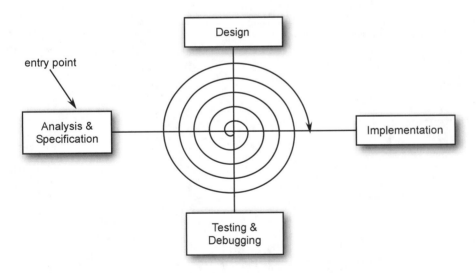

---

[5]An alternative version has the spiral moving from the outside in, reflecting that each iteration moves closer to the center, the final, released product.

3. The experience gained from each iteration brings a better understanding of the problem and how to go about solving it. Incremental development makes it easier to adapt to the improved understanding each iteration brings.

4. Incremental development fits very nicely with the testing philosophy we will embrace.

■ 0.5 Software Testing

We were given a problem and we created a solution. So how do we know that our solution is correct? In the absence of a formal proof of correctness, we cannot *know* the solution is correct (and proofs may be difficult even for small programs). Instead, we rely on testing to find bugs and to establish confidence in the design and the code. Testing generally means applying input to your solution and comparing the *actual* output against the *expected* output. If they match, the test passes, otherwise we have at least one bug to track down.

Of course there is more to it than this and doing a good job of testing requires good problem-solving skills. Here is our philosophy on testing:

Testing philosophy

■ Testing should be done throughout the software development process and not treated as an afterthought once all the coding is done. The three points of interest are:

□ *After the analysis and design are complete.* The design should be critically examined within the context of the problem to be solved. Does it look like the proposed solution will solve the problem?

□ *During the implementation.* As code is completed, its correctness should be tested. This is called **verification** and helps catch problems early and gives you confidence that you are building on a solid code foundation.

□ *After the implementation is complete.* The components should work together as expected and the completed system should meet the client's needs.

■ Developing tests for code can be painless (even fun!) and is an intellectually challenging part of the software development process that reaps benefits *before* coding has begun. In OOP, **unit testing** exercises individual methods of a class and the class as a whole. Developing such test plans can begin once the design is complete (before coding has begun). This provides a nice check on the design because developing a good test for an operation forces you to be clear about what the operation is supposed to do. If you don't know enough to ask probing questions of your design, it is probably because your specification lacks clarity and/or you don't know enough. This is a clear message that you have more design work to do before you should invest time in implementation.

■ Frequent testing will reduce debugging time and give you increased confidence in your code as you develop it. Test plans will be implemented using the JUnit testing framework, which is presented in Chapter 4. JUnit makes it easy to execute some or all of your tests whenever you need them and will tell you which tests passed and which failed.

Remember: think twice, code once

We will apply testing strategies frequently throughout this text.

■ 0.6 The Unified Modeling Language: Using Pictures to Express Design

Another important tool we will use in this book is the Unified Modeling Language (UML). UML is a notation that *visually* describes the components of a software system and their interrelationship. For example, Figure 0.3 used UML to show the inheritance relationship among the `BankAccount` superclass and the `CheckingAccount` and `SavingsAccount` subclasses.

UML is a visual design notation

The purpose of a modeling language is to bring clarity and precision to the description of the components of the system being designed. UML does this by providing notation to clearly identify and label components of the system and the static and dynamic nature of their interaction. Furthermore, UML notation provides different views (or perspectives) of the same entity, with the goal being that each view will bring something new to the developer's understanding of the requirements of the system.

UML grew out of a number of competing notations and, with its adoption by the Object Management Group, has become an industry standard. Like all languages, UML has both syntax and semantics. The syntactic elements include diagrams, lines and arrows connecting diagrams, and some accompanying text. Each syntactic element has a well-defined meaning. Our use of UML will be basic, being restricted largely to class, object, and collaboration diagrams to supplement our descriptions of the classes we develop (which is precisely what a modeling language should do). UML diagrams will be introduced gradually as they are needed.

■ 0.7 Software Design Patterns: Applying Proven Solutions to New Problems

A **software design pattern** is an *abstraction* of a software solution to a commonly encountered software engineering problem. The general idea will be familiar to you from your own life experiences. We each develop experience over the years that allows us to more quickly recognize and solve reoccurring problems. In many disciplines, it is possible to capture that experience so that it can be shared with less-experienced practitioners. This is the case with object-oriented software and design patterns.

Software design pattern = reusing solutions

The idea is that if we encounter a problem and recognize it as one described by a software pattern, instead of solving the problem from scratch, we use the associated design pattern solution as a guide to solve the problem. Each pattern is described by the following.

A ***name*** *by which the pattern is known.* This may include a list of alternative names used to identify the pattern.

Description of a design pattern

A *description of the* **context** *in which the pattern applies.* That is, the problem it solves—including a list of requirements that the solution must meet.

An **outline** *of the solution to the problem the pattern is meant to solve.* The description is abstract, allowing it to be readily adapted to solve the programmer's particular problem. Our descriptions will be accompanied by UML diagrams to help clarify the relationships between the pattern's components.

A set of **consequences** *of using the pattern.* This can include a description of what we can expect to gain by using the pattern, what our responsibilities are in using it correctly, and the cost of using the pattern, including issues such as space-time tradeoffs and dependencies between classes.

There are a growing number of catalogs of such patterns. An important part of becoming adept in OOP is learning how to use design patterns effectively. Specific design patterns will be presented as we have a need for them. In each case, we will present the design pattern using the above format, then customize the pattern to the particular problem to be solved and explain how it works.

■ 0.8 Collections and the Java Collections Framework

A **collection** is a group of elements that can be treated as a single entity. A collection that requires all of its elements be of the same type is called **homogeneous**, while one that allows the elements to be of different types is called **heterogeneous**. Some collections allow the element type to be a primitive type or an object, while some are more restrictive. Some collections allow duplicate elements and others do not; some allow `null` elements and others do not.

If you have worked with arrays or the `List` type in Java before, then you are already familiar with the idea of a collection. Most of the ADTs we will develop in this book describe a collection type.

0.8.1 Collection Categories

Collections can be categorized by how the elements they contain are organized. Different organizations produce different characteristics, have different uses, and apply to different kinds of problems. Four categories of collections covered in this text are described next along with the ADTs we will develop in each category.

Linear Collections

In a linear collection, the elements are arranged in sequence such that all elements except the first have a unique predecessor and all except the last have a unique successor. In Figure 0.7, element E3's predecessor is E2 and its successor is E4. E1 has no predecessor and E4 has no successor.

Note that there are two ends to every linear collection. Linear collections may or may not allow null or duplicate entries. Here are some examples of linear collections.

- *List.* A list maintains a notion of position, so that we can talk about "the element at position 6" in a list. Accesses (insertions, deletions, and retrievals) can be done at any position in a list. A list is also known as a sequence. (Chapter 5)

Figure 0.7 An example of a linear collection.

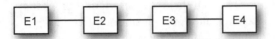

- *Stack.* A stack is a linear collection in which all accesses are restricted to one end, which is called the top of the stack. The trays stacked in a cafeteria are an example of a stack. The "Back" button of a browser makes use of a stack. (Chapter 6)
- *Queue.* A queue is a linear collection in which all insertions are done at one end, called the rear, and all deletions are done at the other end, called the front. A line of people waiting to use an ATM machine is an example of a queue. (Chapter 7)

Hierarchical Collections

Hierarchical collections are also called **trees**. The elements of a tree are called **nodes**. A nonempty tree has a special node called the **root**, which has no predecessors (called **parents**) and zero or more successors (called **children**). Elements called **leaves** have one parent and no children. All other elements reside in the **interior** of the tree and have one parent and one or more children. An essential characteristic of a hierarchical collection is that it cannot contain a **cycle**. As shown in Figure 0.8, a tree is drawn upside down, with the root (E1) at the top and the leaves (E5, E6, E7, E8) at the bottom. E1 is the parent of E2, E3, and E4; conversely, E2 is a child of E1. E2, E3, and E4 are called **siblings** because they have a common parent. Hierarchical collections may or may not allow null or duplicate entries.

Here are some examples of hierarchical collections.

- *Tree.* A tree is a general hierarchical collection that does not specify how many children an element may have. Figure 0.8 is an example of a general tree. (Chapter 9)

Figure 0.8 An example of a hierarchical collection.

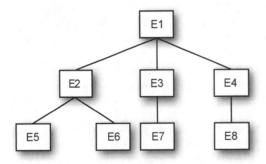

- *Binary Tree.* A binary tree is one in which a node can have no more than two children. A strict binary tree is a binary tree in which each node has zero or two children. (Chapter 10)

- *Binary Search Tree.* A binary search tree is a binary tree that orders its elements to facilitate searching. We will look at several implementations of this collection type. (Chapter 11)

Graph Collections

A graph collection is quite similiar to a hierarchical collection, but allows cycles, so an element can have zero or more predecessors and zero or more successors. The elements of a graph are called **vertices** and the connections between them are **edges**. The topology of a computer network is an example of a graph, as is a roadtrip. A graph may or may not allow duplicate entries.

The edges of a **weighted graph** may have a weight associated with them. This weight can represent metrics such as distance, time, money, etc. In an **undirected graph**, two elements that are connected by an edge are both successor and predecessor to one another. In a **directed graph**, the edges clearly specify which mode is the predecessor and which the successor. In Figure 0.9(b), the direction of the edge is from E2 to E3, so E2 is a predecessor to E3, and E3 is a successor to E2. (Chapter 13)

Nonpositional Collections

An unordered collection does not recognize successors or predecessors, so there is no notion of a position or sequencing in an unordered collection. Instead, elements are inserted, found, and removed based on some unique identifying value. See Figure 0.10 for an example of an unordered collection.

- *Collection.* A `Collection` is the most basic of collection types. Duplicates are allowed. We will use this class in Chapter 4 as an introduction to collection ADTs. (Chapter 4)

Figure 0.9 Examples of undirected and directed graphs.

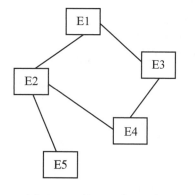

(a) An undirected graph.

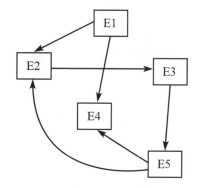

(b) A directed graph.

Figure 0.10 An example of an unordered collection.

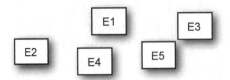

- *Map.* A map associates an entry with some unique, identifying value. Your student record is one example. Another example would be a definition (the value) in a dictionary, found using the word (the key) being defined. Another name for a map is **dictionary**. (Chapter 12)

0.8.2 Collection Operations

While there are obviously important differences between kinds of collections, they all support many of the same operations. A collection may also, of course, support other operations that are unique to its needs. Here we describe in very general terms the operations that most collections support. The names can differ from collection to collection. For example, the operation to add an element to a collection is called `add()` for a list, `push()` for a stack, `enqueue()` for a queue, and `put()` for a map.

Adding an Element

Depending on the kind of collection, we may be restricted in where we can add a new element to a collection. Collections supporting the notion of a position may allow insertions by position. In a value-oriented collection, where a new element is placed depends on the element's value and the values already in the collection. Some collections allow duplicates; others do not. Most collections can grow and shrink as the application requires, but some have a fixed capacity and attempts to add an element once the collection is full will generate an error.

Removing an Element

The element to be removed from a collection may be identified by its position in the collection (if the collection type supports the notion of a position) or by passing in a target element which, if found in the collection, is removed from the collection. Trying to remove an element from an empty collection may generate an error.

Replacing an Element

An element in a collection can be replaced with a different element, given a position or a target element.

Retrieving an Element

An element can be retrieved from a collection given a position or a target element. The retrieved element remains in the collection, unchanged.

Determining Whether an Element Is Contained in a Collection

A boolean operation will return true if the target element is contained in the collection and false otherwise.

Determining the Size of a Collection

The number of elements stored in a collection can be determined. Collections that have a fixed capacity will also have an operation that returns the capacity of the collection—that is, how many elements *could be* stored in it.

Testing to See Whether the Collection Is Empty

A test to determine whether a collection is empty will return true if the collection currently stores no elements. Collections that have a fixed capacity will also support an operation to determine whether the collection is full—that is, when size is equal to capacity.

Traversal

Also known as iteration, traversal provides a way to visit the elements of the collection in sequence (one element at a time), the order of which is determined by the collection. An element may be accessed (read) and/or modified (written) during a traversal. Some collections may also allow add and/or remove operations to be performed during a traversal.

Equality

A boolean operation can determine whether two collections are equal. The simplest notion of "equals" says that two collections are equal if they contain the same number of elements and each element from the first collection is equal to one element from the other collection. Collections that are ordered will also require that the elements be in the same respective positions in the two collections. Note that equality at the collection level relies on the ability to test for equality of elements.

Cloning

Producing a copy of the collection is called cloning. There are two levels of cloning. A **shallow copy** duplicates only the structure of the original collection, but not the elements contained in the collection, so that both the original and the copy share access to the original elements. In a **deep copy**, both the structure and the elements are duplicated.

Serialization

The collection can be written to disk in a format that is suitable for retrieval later on. Most applications require the ability to store the data from a collection so that it can be reloaded when the application is run next (think of a game in which you want to save the current scenario before quitting so that you can resume the game later). This is known as **persistence**, because the data persists beyond the run time of the application that manipulates it, and the process of writing the data to disk is called **serialization**.

0.8.3 The Java Collections Framework (JCF)

A **collection framework** is a software architecture consisting of the following:

- A hierarchy of `interfaces`[6] that define various kinds of collections and specifies how they are related

- A set of **abstract classes** that provide partial implementations of the interfaces and serve as the foundation for constructing **concrete classes**

- A set of concrete classes based on different underlying data structures (sometimes referred to as backing stores) that offer different runtime characteristics

- A set of algorithms that works with collections

Collection framework

The **Java Collections Framework**, introduced with the Java 2 platform, provides implementations for a number of common collections, including lists, maps, sets, stacks, and vectors. It also provides mechanisms to extend these types to create new types (classes) that are also part of the framework. There are several advantages to working with a collections framework:

Java Collections Framework

- *It promotes code reuse.* Rather than write classes from scratch, we can use the existing classes, which will enable us to concentrate on other aspects of the problem to be solved.

- *It increases robustness and decreases debugging effort.* Any time we can use a class that already has extensive use and can be regarded as bug free, we are making our program more robust and reducing the amount of code we will need to debug.

- *It provides a mechanism for passing collections of objects among unrelated, and possibly independently written, components.* The only requirement is that the collection object being passed around is descended from `Collection`, the root of the collections hierarchy.

0.8.4 How We Will Use the Java Collections Framework

Describing the JCF in an introductory book on abstract data types presents two somewhat competing goals. On the one hand, since code reuse is an important aspect of OOP, it is important to learn to work within an existing framework, rather than always designing classes from scratch. Since the JCF provides ready-made implementations of most common kinds of collections, looking at them will give your learning experience an important practical flavor. On the other hand, it is equally important to understand the *design* and *implementation* issues involved in creating these collection ADTs.

We will balance these competing goals by using some of the classes defined in the JCF (promoting the first goal) *and* by defining some of our own implementations (promoting the second goal). But when possible, we will create our implementations following the collection framework philosophy so that our classes can be

---

[6]An interface only specifies an API. It does not provide any implementation of the methods, leaving that to classes that implement the interface.

used interchangeably with other classes in the JCF. This is a valuable lesson in and of itself and will allow us to look at the design choices (such as space-time and code complexity-time tradeoffs) that arise with different implementations for common ADTs. Finally, the JCF itself raises several design issues (some good, some debatable), which are instructive to discuss. We look at the Java Collection Framework in detail in Chapter 4, right after discussing some fundamental data structures in Chapter 3.

0.8.5 The JCF Collection Hierarchy

The two JCF interface inheritance hierarchies are shown in Figure 0.11. The relationships between the interfaces is somewhat different from the classical relationships described above (this is one of those design decisions we could debate):

- `Collection` provides the most general way to access a collection of elements; duplicate elements within a collection are allowed. The elements are unordered, so there is no notion of the position of an element.
- `List` extends `Collection`; it allows duplicate elements and introduces an ordering by supporting positional indexing.
- `Stack` implements `List`; a stack allows accesses and deletions only at its top.
- `Queue` extends `Collection`; a queue allows insertions at one end (its rear) and deletions from the other (its front).
- `Set` extends `Collection`; an unordered collection that does not allow duplicates.
- `SortedSet` extends `Set`; a `Set` whose elements are sorted.
- `Map` is the root of a separate hierarchy in the JCF. Maps deal with ⟨key, value⟩ pairs instead of single elements, so they are treated in the JCF as different from `Collections`.
- `SortedMap` extends `Map`; a `Map` whose elements are sorted.

Figure 0.11 The Java Collection Framework interface hierarchy (UML inheritance diagram).

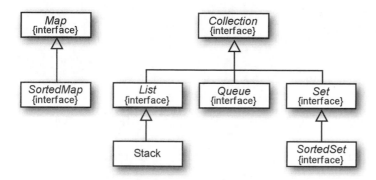

ON THE WEB

Additional study material is available at Addison-Wesley's Website at http://www.aw.com/cssupport. This material includes the following:

■ Study Guide Exercises

Object-Oriented Programming and Java

1

CHAPTER OUTLINE

■ **1.1** Abstraction and Abstract Data Types

Abstraction is a tool we commonly use to manage complexity, allowing us to focus on those aspects of a system that are most relevant to us.

What is abstraction?

- When programming a CD to record some music, I don't need to know how the electronics of the CD drive work, how the music will be stored, transferred to the CD, and so forth. I only need to know how to use the recording interface to execute the commands for music recording.

- When searching on the Web, I need to know how to select a search engine, how to enter a search phrase, and how to click on a "Start search" button. I do not need to know the details of how HTTP and TCP/IP are used to transmit my request to the search site, how the search is actually done, or how the response is returned to my workstation.

■ Using a graphical user interface (GUI), I can perform the file delete operation by selecting the icon representing a file and dragging it to the trash icon. I don't need to know about file systems or disk drives; I just drag and drop.

It is usually the case when using a system that the details of *how* something is done are unimportant to the action we want to perform. Indeed, if we were required to understand such details before acting, we would not get very much done. Instead, we want to use a thing through a straightforward interface that presents its capabilities (operations) in a way that matches our expectations of the thing's purpose and behavior. Furthermore, we expect that *similar things* will behave in *similar ways* and have a set of *similar operations*. So all time-programmable devices would support operations such as "set time," "set start time," and "set stop time" operations. A VCR is a time-programmable device that would also have the operation "set channel to record," while an oven would add "set baking temperature."

Data abstraction is the application of abstraction to the definition of a data type. A data type can be viewed from two perspectives.

Data abstraction

1. *Specification* or *model* of the type, defining the domain of values that instances of the type can take on and the operations that can be performed on those values. This view emphasizes external appearance and behavior, and says nothing about the implementation.

Two perspectives on data types

2. *Implementation* of the type, including a language-specific representation for the type's domain and executable statements for the type's operations.

An **abstract data type (ADT)** defines a model for a new data type. As such, an ADT provides the specification view of a data type. An ADT is abstract because it does not specify *how* values of the type are actually represented or *how* the operations on the type are implemented. These are details that a client of the ADT does not need to know to be able to use it.

ADT = data type model

Figure 1.1 diagrams a portion of a List ADT. As you can see, the List can be *implemented* using any of a number of different data structures–we look at these in detail in Chapter 3. But just as the implementation details of your television remote control are hidden from you, the List implementation details are hidden from the List user, who just sees the ADT's public interface, sometimes called its **application programmer interface (API)**.

Application Programmer Interface (API)

Hiding the details of how a data type is implemented is known as **information hiding**. Working with an ADT is useful for programmers for the same reasons abstracted models are useful in everyday life—it allows a programmer to design using only the ADT's documented syntax and semantics, leaving the details of the ADT's implementation for later. This is shown in Figure 1.2, where we see two possible uses for a List (there are literally thousands of uses). An AddressBook could use a List to store AddressBookEntries. A course management system could use a List to store information about the sections of the courses that are offered. But note that in both cases the clients are relying on nothing more than their understanding of what a list is as defined by the List API. The figure also highlights another important aspect of ADTs (and object-oriented programming!): Once designed and implemented, a List can be *reused* wherever there is a need for its services. We invent the wheel once and just keep making copies of it as needed.

Why design with ADTs?

Figure 1.1 Possible implementations of the List ADT. The implementation details are hidden from the user of the List, who relies on the List's public interface.

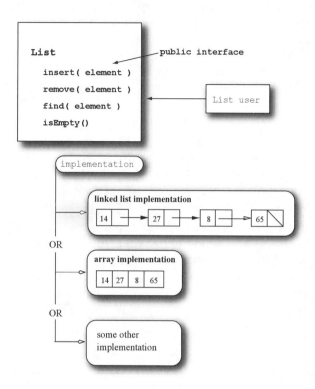

Figure 1.2 A List has many uses. A client (user) accesses a List through its public interface.

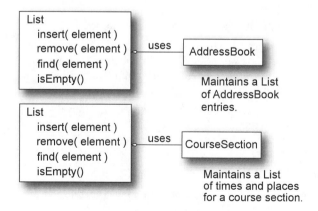

1.1.1 Specification of ADTs

A goal of this book is to learn how to design and implement ADTs and accompanying algorithms within the object-oriented programming (OOP) paradigm using Java. In particular, this book focuses on the design and implementation of collection ADTs. These are also commonly referred to as containers for the obvious reason that they contain a number of elements.

An ADT specification contains several entries. Here I present the approach we will take to specify ADTs. The format is described below and summarized in Table 1.1.

ADT name. A descriptive name we will give the ADT. Abbreviations should be avoided unless they are obvious and/or well known. An ADT for rational numbers would be called Rational. In some cases a generic name will suit, but in others, the name should reflect something distinctive about the ADT. For example, ADTs for bank accounts and checking accounts would be BankAccount and CheckingAccount, and not merely Account.

ADT description. A brief description of the type's characteristics and purpose. For an ADT for Rational numbers, for example, you would describe what a rational number is and the role of the numerator and denominator.

ADT invariants. Also called *class invariants* in OOP, an invariant is a condition that must be true before an ADT operation begins and after the operation completes. Invariants might include constraints on the values that can be held by

> **Class invariant—a property of the state of an object that must always be true**

Table 1.1 The format for an ADT specification.

ADT name	The name of the ADT.
ADT description	A brief description of the type.
ADT invariants	Characteristics that must always be true of an instance of this type.
ADT attributes	Represent the state of an instance of the ADT.
ADT operations	Define the behavior of the ADT and the interface available to clients.

Include the following for each operation

responsibilities:	The purpose of the operation—its intended semantics.
pre-conditions:	The conditions assumed to be true on entry to the operation if the operation is to execute successfully. This may include assumptions about the state of the object on entry, assumptions about the parameters passed in, and so on.
post-conditions:	What the operation guarantees to be true on exit and how the operation changed the state of the object. On exit from the operation, no change to the object's state may violate any of the ADT's invariants.
returns:	The type of value, if any, returned by the operation.
exceptions:	A description of the exceptions an operation may generate and the circumstances under which exceptions may be generated.

the ADT's attributes. For example, if we were defining an ADT to represent rational numbers, we would include a property saying the denominator can never be 0 because division by 0 is undefined. Another property might be that all rationals must be stored in reduced form, so ⁶⁄₈ would be stored as ¾.

It is possible that *during* an operation an invariant may be violated, but the operation must restore the property before the operation ends. When multiplying the rational ¾ by ²⁄₁ for example, we initially produce the rational ⁶⁄₄ which is not reduced. However the multiplication operation would see to it that the reduced form ³⁄₂ is returned, preserving the "minimized rational" invariant.

ADT attributes. An attribute is a piece of information that must be available for the ADT to work properly. The numerator and denominator would be attributes of a rational ADT. An ADT for a bank account would include attributes such as the client's name and address, the account number and the balance (just to mention a few). The specification may say something about an attribute's type, but it says nothing about how the values of attributes are to be represented in a computer. This is up to the implementation.

ADT operations. The operations define the *behavior* of the ADT and the interface available to clients. Operations in the Rational ADT would include all the arithmetic operations (+, −, *, /) and operations to see if the rational number is zero, is negative, to compare two rationals, and so on. Operations in a Bank Account ADT would include those to make a deposit, make a withdrawal, get the account balance, and so on.

The description of an operation is frequently referred to as a **contract** because it lays out the responsibilities each operation agrees to take on, which, in turn, defines the behavior it agrees to provide to a client. The terms of the contract are laid out in several additional entries for *each* operation.

- *Responsibilities.* The purpose of the operation—its intended semantics. This may be given as a list of responsibilities the operation is obligated to meet. There should be no discussion of implementation issues (*how* the responsibilities will be met).

- *Pre-conditions.* An operation typically requires that certain conditions be met for the operation to execute properly. For example, the division operation for the Rational ADT would have a pre-condition saying that the divisor cannot be zero since division by zero is undefined. Similarly, the "make withdrawal" operation from the BankAccount ADT might require that the amount of the withdrawal be less than or equal to the current balance.

A key issue in system design is determining who has the responsibility to verify that the pre-conditions of an operation have been met. On the one hand, by its very nature, a *pre*-condition is something the operation *assumes* the caller has checked and thus is true on entry to the operation. On the other hand, if a pre-condition is not met, the operation may fail outright or, worse, return an invalid, but plausible, result.[1] To ensure the integrity of an

Who should check pre-conditions?

---

[1]The advantage of a spectacular failure (a program that exits with lots of serious-looking error messages) is that you know there is a problem and thanks to the messages have a clue about what and where it is. Silent failures, on the other hand, may go unnoticed for quite a while, making it more difficult to trace the problem to its source.

instance of an ADT, any operation that changes the state of any of the ADT's attributes should take the responsibility of verifying that its pre-conditions have been met.

For example, the division operation for the Rational ADT might throw an illegal argument exception if the divisor is zero. The "make withdrawal" operation from BankAccount can throw an insufficient funds exception (and hit your account with a service charge too) if the withdrawal amount exceeds the current balance.

□ *Post-conditions.* A post-condition is a statement about the state of the ADT's attributes on exit from the operation. This could include a list of which attributes are changed and their new status. A post-condition of the make withdrawal operation would be that the current balance has been reduced by the amount of the withdrawal (assuming this doesn't produce a negative balance) and that the transaction was logged in the customer's activity file. The post-conditions should *not* be a reiteration of the responsibilities of the operation.

Since it is always assumed that the ADT invariants are true, it is not necessary to list them among the pre- and post-conditions. On the flip side, it should be obvious that the pre- and post-conditions of an operation cannot be in violation of any ADT invariant.

Pre- and post-conditions must be consistent with the ADT's invariants

If an operation has no pre/post-conditions, return value, etc., you can either put "none" or leave the field blank in the operation description.

□ *Returns.* A description of the value returned by the operation. This can include its type, if known. If nothing is returned, you can either put "nothing" or leave the field blank.

□ *Exceptions.* An operation may generate an exception if an error occurs during its execution. An exception is a language-defined indication that something unexpected has occurred. The description should include which exceptions could be thrown and under what circumstances. In practice, this is a list of the pre-conditions the operation agrees to check.

Generating an ADT specification might seem like a lot of unnecessary work, but consider that if you cannot clearly express in a natural language what an operation is to do, how can you possibly express it in a programming language? Many, many mistakes arise from starting to code without having a clear idea about *what* you need to code.

A thread you will see running throughout this book is the importance of providing carefully thought out descriptions of what we are going to do before putting anything into code. Our mantra will be "Think twice, code once." It cannot be emphasized enough that diligence in observing this principle will lead to better code and higher productivity. Remember, time you spend fixing mistakes is time you are not spending doing other, more interesting things (like writing more code!). Later we will present a defensive programming strategy designed to help you catch bugs before they can become really costly.

Think twice, code once

Finally, the ADT specification is just an agreement about how a type is *supposed* to behave. It is up to the implementation of the ADT to *fulfill* the terms of the contract.

The implementation must honor the contract

Thus documented pre- and post-conditions become something you need to validate with tests so you can be sure that you have met the terms of the ADT's contract with its clients.

Validate the implementation with testing

CHECKPOINT

1.1 Abstraction is such a common part of our everyday lives that we take it for granted. Identify and describe a few examples from your everyday life, explaining the nature of the abstraction.

1.2 Are there times it would be useful to know something about the details of how a type is represented or how an operation is done?

1.3 What is the relationship between class invariants and an operation's pre- and post-conditions?

1.4 Legal contracts are very specific. Why is this? Relate this to the notion of contract as it is applied to ADTs.

1.1.2 Example: a Rectangle ADT

So that we can concentrate on the concepts, our first example is familiar and quite simple. But be careful: Although the invariants in our first example are almost trivial given the ADT description, do not underestimate the importance of being complete and accurate, even with something that appears to be "obvious".[2] Particularly as the problem domain becomes more complex, precision in the description becomes essential.

Precise specifications are important

A specification should be clear, complete, and unambiguous so that if two programmers are given the same ADT specification, their implementations, although probably not identical, must be interchangeable in terms of the interface (API) supported. Also, precision in the specification will be an important element in developing a test plan for the implementation. (*Note*: The Rectangle ADT description is incomplete—some parts have been left as exercises.) We will return to the Rectangle example a couple of times in this book.

Partial Specification of the Rectangle ADT

Description
A rectangle is a four-sided shape in which opposite sides are parallel and equal in size. The length of a side must be greater than 0. A rectangle has four right angles.

Invariants
1. Opposite sides are of equal size.
2. Length and height must be greater than 0.

---

[2]How many times have you debugged a program only to discover, perhaps after hours of frustrating searching, that the bug was "obvious" (simple, silly, etc.)?

Attributes

DEFAULT_SIZE	a constant, the default size for the dimensions
length	size of the "top" and "bottom" sides
height	size of the "left" and "right" sides
surface area	the surface area of the rectangle
perimeter	the perimeter of this rectangle

Operations

constructor()

pre-condition:	none
responsibilities:	default constructor—creates a rectangle with *length* and *height* set to *DEFAULT_SIZE*
post-condition:	the rectangle is initialized to the default values
returns:	nothing

constructor(length, height)

pre-condition:	none
responsibilities	creates a rectangle with *length* length and *height* height; if a dimension is invalid, the default size is used
post-condition:	the rectangle is initialized to client-supplied values, if valid, or the default values otherwise
returns:	nothing

getLength()

pre-condition:	none
responsibilities	returns this rectangle's *length*
post-condition:	the rectangle is unchanged
returns:	the *length* of the rectangle

setLength(newLength)

pre-condition:	none
responsibilities	resets *length* to newLength if newLength is valid; otherwise does nothing
post-condition:	rectangle's *length* field is updated if newLength is valid
returns:	nothing

getSurfaceArea()

pre-condition:	none
operation:	compute the surface area of this rectangle
post-condition:	the rectangle is unchanged
returns:	the surface area of the rectangle

Two comments on our first ADT are in order. First, you may have noticed that we have not specified a data type for the data field's *length* and *height*, leaving that up to the implementation to decide. They could be represented by a primitive type such as an int or float in Java, or a user-defined type such as a Rational. If, on the other hand, we *know* what we want the types to be, we put it in the specification.

Second, as you were looking through the ADT, you may have found yourself saying, "That isn't how I would have done it." When you design an ADT there are a lot of decisions to be made and some of them will not be easy. You do what you believe will solve the problem and what makes sense to you at the time, keeping in mind that design is an iterative process and you will have a chance to make changes later as your understanding of the problem grows.

Design is an iterative process

A constructor operation is invoked when an instance of the type is created. Its purpose is to construct a new instance (called an object) in the computer's memory, initializing the object so that it is guaranteed to begin with meaningful values for its attributes. The state of an object is defined by the values of these attributes.

Constructor method

We should take a moment to convince ourselves that, so far as we can tell from the pre- and post-conditions, the invariants are never violated. It is very important to understand that the notion of software testing begins not with compiled code, but with reviews of the initial design. Typically, the earlier an error is caught, the simpler and less expensive it is to correct.

***Verify* that the design maintains the class invariants**

For our simple example this is straightforward. Because the ADT stores the size of the two sides in a single attribute (height) and the size of the top and bottom in another attribute (length), we are guaranteed to always maintain Invariant 1. The constructors and the setLength() operation never allow length or height to be invalid (less than or equal to 0), thus maintaining Invariant 2.

Finally, a few comments about naming. You will see naming styles when you look at different texts and programs. The style generally used here is to preface accessor operations with "get," mutator operations with "set," and predicate operations with "is".[3] While some texts might prefer length() to getLength(), there is a very nice symmetry between getLength() and setLength() that is lost when length() is used for the accessor. The symmetry helps make naming intuitive and consistent, simplifying the learning curve and cutting down on errors.

Naming conventions

SUMMING UP

Abstraction is a tool for managing complexity. It allows us to use something without having to think about how things are actually done. Using a remote control is a good example.

Data abstraction is the application of abstraction to the definition of a data type. The specification view of a data type defines the domain of values a type can represent and the operations defined on those values. The specification view provides no implementation details. The details are left to the implementation view of a type, which uses information hiding to hide implementation details from the user.

A new data type should be specified before being implemented. The invariants of a type are conditions that must always be true about the state of an object at the

---

[3]An accessor returns ("accesses") the value of an attribute of an object (more on this shortly). A mutator can change ("mutate") the value of an attribute of an object (more on this shortly). You will see examples where we do not follow this convention. But in looking at the name adopted in those cases you will see that it would have been very artificial to have enforced this style. While following a style is good, we don't want to be pedantic about it. Common sense should prevail.

beginning and end of an operation. An operation pre-condition describes what must be true before an operation executes if it is to execute successfully. An operation post-condition states what must be true on completion of an operation. These must always be consistent with the type's invariants.

Before implementing a type, you should verify that the invariants are sound and that all operations defined on the type honor the invariants. A test plan for an ADT can be written based on the ADT specification.

CHECKPOINT

1.5 The `Rectangle` ADT is not fully specified. Using the format shown in Table 1.1, add descriptions to `Rectangle` for the following:

    a. an accessor operation to get the Rectangle's perimeter.

    b. an accessor operation to get the Rectangle's height.

    c. a mutator operation to set the height of the Rectangle.

    d. a predicate operation to see whether a Rectangle is a square.

1.6 Why must we check the validity of the input value in setLength()?

1.7 Would it be useful to add a mutator operation setSurfaceArea()? Explain.

■ 1.2 The Object-Oriented Approach

Figure 1.2 illustrated a simple example of the use of a List. Of course real problems are much more complex and involve many more components that interact in diverse and complicated ways. Fortunately, abstraction is more powerful than we have shown so far and can be applied at many levels. A key feature of the object-oriented approach is that it tries to model both the static and dynamic aspects of the problem domain as they exist in the real world. The static aspect identifies the components of the system (represented as objects in a program) and the dynamic aspect is the behavior resulting from the interaction of the components.

OO programs model the problem domain

Object-oriented programming involves writing programs in which software objects interact by sending messages to each other requesting that some action be taken by the receiving object. A software object represents an entity from the problem domain that we need to model in the program. The exchange of messages between objects models the behavior of the components found in the problem domain. This helps explain the appeal of the OO method—it works at an intuitive level because the objects manipulated in the program appear and behave like their real-world counterparts. More formally we would say that with OOP, the solution space models the problem space because it preserves both the structure and the behavior of the problem space.

Objects interact through messages

You can get a taste of this by considering the kinds of interactions you have with a university and the requirements placed on an enrollment management system that handles almost every aspect of your official involvement with a university. The top of Figure 1.3 shows a familiar scenario—a student submitting a list of the

Figure 1.3 Modeling student registration.

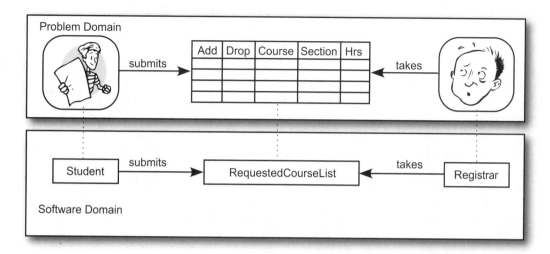

courses he would like to take in the upcoming semester. The bottom of the figure shows the corresponding objects that would exist in the enrollment management program and identifies the actions (behavior) the objects would take for this scenario. Of course, students do more than enroll in classes, and registrars do more than take course requests. Figure 1.4 shows a student interacting with a different part of the university, this time the business office, where he is making a tuition pay-

Figure 1.4 Modeling tuition payment.

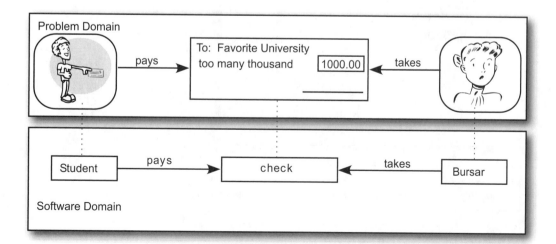

ment. We could draw other pictures for the student in which he interacts with the housing office, financial aid, dining services, parking services (!), and so on. These are all things students do at a university and are things that an enrollment management system would track, hence these are all actions we would expect a student software object to be able to "know how to do" within the application.

There are several points you should glean from this example:

1. A software object models an entity from the world of the problem domain.

   Objects model entities and their behavior

2. A software object does not exist in a vacuum; it is part of a larger system of *interacting* objects.

3. An object may play several *roles* in an application. The scenarios depicted in the figures show a student from *different perspectives*, with each perspective reflecting a different role that a student plays at a university and which the corresponding student object must play in the program. An advantage of OOP is that it encourages and benefits from repeatedly looking at a problem from different perspectives. This is part of the iterative nature of software development that is typical of OO-designed software.

4. Finally, an object may represent something tangible that in the real world you could see and touch, such as a programmable heat sensor attached to a piece of equipment, a student, or an office manager, or it may be more abstract, such as a course schedule, a task to be completed by a worker, or a bank transaction (Figure 1.5).

   Objects model tangible and intangible "entities"

Figure 1.5 Objects can represent tangible and intangible things.

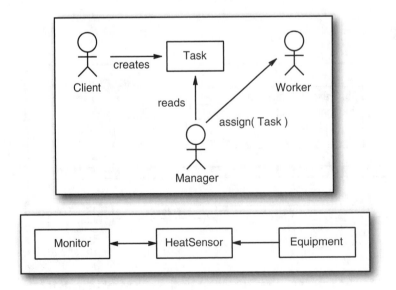

1.2.1 A First Look at the Unified Modeling Language

We will be using a software design notation called the Unified Modeling Language (UML) to visually represent program elements and their interrelationships. The purpose of a software design notation is to bring clarity and precision to the description of the elements of the system under design. It does this by providing notation to clearly identify and label components of the system and the nature of their interaction (the static and dynamic aspects of the system). As you will see, UML notation provides several views of (perspectives on) the same entity, with the goal being that each view will bring something new to your understanding of the requirements of the system.

UML grew out of a number of competing notations and is an industry standard. Like all languages, UML has both a syntax and a semantics. The syntactic elements include diagrams, lines and arrows connecting diagrams, and some accompanying text. Each syntactic element has well-defined semantics. Our use of UML will be fairly elementary and UML elements will be introduced gradually as needed. Here is a brief description of the UML diagrams we will be using.

Class Diagrams. Show the classes that make up the system and how they are related. This is the *static* structure of the system. UML has notations for several kinds of interclass relationships that frequently occur in practice. These are described in Section 1.3. A class diagram can include information about the class's data and method fields.

Object Diagrams. Are much like class diagrams. An object diagram represents an *instance* of a class diagram (just as objects are instances of classes). While class diagrams can illustrate the relationship between *classes* in general, object diagrams can illustrate these relationships in particular scenarios. So instead of talking about some student submitting a course schedule to someone in the registrar's office, we would take a specific case of, say, Anne, submitting a schedule with course conflicts to registrar Bob. Clearly there will be several such diagrams illustrating, concretely, the possibilities a single general scenario can produce.

Sequence Diagrams. Provide another perspective on the interaction between objects in a particular scenario. Here the focus is on the *order* (sequence) in which messages are sent between objects to achieve the desired behavior.

1.2.2 Characteristics of an Object

The examples given so far should give you an idea of what an object is, but we need to be more precise if we are to understand some of the more powerful OO concepts presented later. Every object has three characteristics: state, behavior, and identity. (See Figure 1.6)

What is an object?

State

A software object stores information, referred to as **attributes**, in **data fields**. Some attributes may be read-only, meaning they cannot be set directly, and others may be

Figure 1.6 Characteristics of an object.

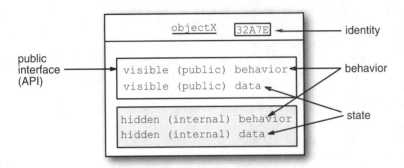

constants, meaning that once they are set, their value cannot change. Typically, though, the attributes are variables whose values change through time as the result of the object's behavior. For example, a heat sensor's state includes the temperature of the last reading, the range of temperatures the sensor should regard as safe, and so on. A student's state would include his academic year, his GPA, the courses he has taken and is currently taking, the number of hours attempted and the number passed, home address, campus address, and so on.

The values of an object's attributes define its **state**. We say that an object is in a **stable state** when the values of its attributes make its invariant properties true (see Section 1.1.1 for a discussion of class invariants). Some attributes may actually be other objects. For example, a student's address information is probably stored in an `Address` object. So, an object's state is composed of the state of its simple attributes (`int`s, `float`s, etc.) and its structured attributes (other objects).

> **State = value of an object's attributes**

The example in Figure 1.7 shows the UML diagram for an object. The top compartment identifies the type of the object and has the format *identifier* ":" *type* (all underlined) where *identifier* is optional (and not included in this figure). The lower compartment contains the attributes (and possibly their values) that we are interested in seeing at this point of the analysis. A `Student` object will certainly have other attributes, but we only need to show the attributes that are relevant to the aspect of the problem we are currently trying to solve. Again, UML allows us to view a component of a system from whatever perspective is of interest at the time.

The rectangle with the folded corner is the UML notation for an explanatory comment. The figure shows how the state of an object can change with time. At the beginning of a student's first semester, she has a GPA of 0 and 0 class hours passed. This continues until the end of the semester, when the registrar will update each student's record to reflect the number of hours passed and the GPA earned.

Behavior

The behavior of an object is defined by the set of operations it can perform. The object's visible operations define its public interface, or API. An operation in an object executes when the object receives a message that matches that operation's sig-

> **Behavior = operations**

Figure 1.7 Object state and state change (UML object diagram with a comment).

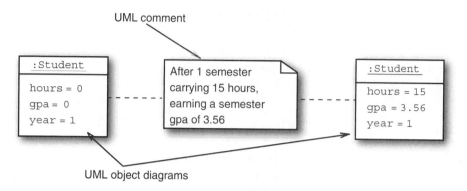

UML comment

UML object diagrams

nature. The **signature** of a method is the method name and the types of its arguments. The object that receives the message and will execute the operation is called the target.

In this example, the `selena` object will execute its `setHoursAttempted()` operation. The effect will be to change the state of the `selena` object (look at Figure 1.7 again).

Clearly there is an important relationship between an object's state and its behavior. The state of an object is the result of the sequence of messages it has received so far. Your checkbook balance, for example, is the result of the sequence of `deposit()` and `withdraw()` messages it has received. Similarly, the behavior of an object may be affected by the object's state. For example, a student whose `hoursPassed` field shows she is still a sophomore, would not be allowed to successfully register for a seminar restricted to seniors. So the `selena.register ( seniorSeminar )` operation would not complete successfully for the `selena` object, because according to Figure 1.7, she is still a sophomore. Similarly, the effect of a `withdraw()` message sent to a checking account will depend on whether there are sufficient funds to cover the check. If so, the balance is just reduced by the amount of the check and, if not, the balance is reduced by both the amount of the check (giving you a deficit!) *and* the amount of an insufficient funds penalty. In short, the *same* message may cause *different* behaviors depending on the receiving object's current state.

The kinds of messages an object can receive correspond, naturally, to the kinds of operations it can execute. The main categories of messages are:

■ *Constructor.* Constructs an object from a class definition, initializing all the object's state variables to meaningful initial values so that it always starts out in a stable state.

> **Behavior can affect state and vice-versa**

> **There are four kinds of messages**

■ *Accessor.* Retrieves information about the object. This information may be part of the object's data fields or it might be *synthesized* from the object's data fields.

■ *Mutator.* Changes the state of the object by changing one or more of the object's attributes.

■ *Finalizer.* Performs cleanup operations just prior to the object being reclaimed by the garbage collector. This is not used often in Java.

Identity

Every object has an identity that is unique among all objects and that cannot change during the object's lifetime. This identity is created from an *object reference*, which is established by the runtime system and assigned to the object when it is constructed. One possibility for the value of an object reference is the address in memory where the object resides. Unless you fancy looking at memory dumps, you will never see an object's identity, nor do you need to. As you will see later, the runtime system is responsible for binding an access to an object to the correct object reference. Figure 1.8 shows the result of creating two `Student` objects:

Identity = object reference

```
Student selena = new Student("Selena McLean");
Student gopal = new Student("Gopal Nayar");
```

Clearly there is an association between an object variable (e.g., `selena`) and an object's identity (e.g., 74392), and from this example it would appear that the iden-

Figure 1.8 Object identity.

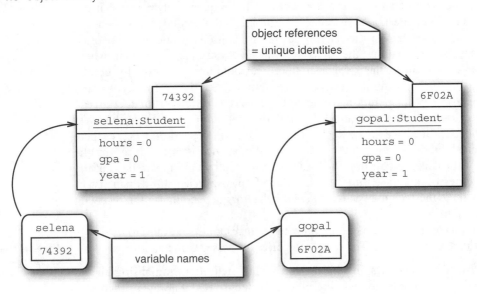

tity of an object is the name of the *variable* that references it. However, unlike an object's identity, the value of a variable can change. If we mistakenly did

Identity ≠ identifier

```
gopal = selena;
```

we would have both variables referencing the object with identity 74392 and would lose access to the object previously referenced by gopal. But, as shown in Figure 1.9, object 6F02A has not lost its identity (it still has object reference 6F02A). However, object 6F02A is now unreachable from any variable in the program, becoming **garbage**, and it will eventually be reclaimed by the garbage collector.

CHECKPOINT

1.8 What is the relationship between class invariants and an object being in a stable state?

1.9 How does the state of an object change?

1.10 Identify some static and dynamic aspects of the systems shown in Figures 1.3 and 1.4.

1.11 How are an object's state and behavior related?

1.12 What is the relationship between a variable pressureMonitor, which refers to a Monitor object, and the identity of this object?

1.2.3 Classes and Objects

Figure 1.10 shows three UML class diagrams. The simple form on the left is just a box with the class name inside it. The extended class diagram in the middle has three compartments and lists some of the class's attributes and operations. The top compartment holds the class name. The middle compartment lists the class's data fields and the bottom compartment lists its method fields and their return types. The diagram on the right is another view of the same class this time including the method parameter types. The notations in Table 1.2 are used to indicate the visibil-

---

Figure 1.9 Object identity versus an object identifier.

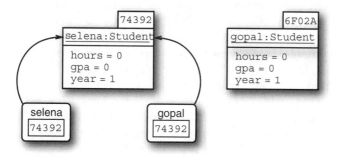

Figure 1.10 Simple and extended UML class diagrams.

Rectangle

Rectangle
-length:double -height:double
+setLength:void +getLength:double +setHeight:void +getHeight:double

Rectangle
-length:double -height:double
+setLength(newLength:double):void +getLength():double +setHeight(newHeight:double):void +getHeight():double

Table 1.2 UML class visibility notation.

Notation	Visibility
+	public
#	protected
–	private

ity of the fields. As a shorthand device, we commonly leave out the visibility notation and, unless otherwise specified, assume that data fields are private and method fields are public.

The construction of an object based on a class definition is called **instantiation** (because we are creating an *instance* of the class). The relationship between the class definition and the instantiated object is quite basic: The class definition is the blueprint that guides the construction of the object. A popular analogy is that a class definition is like a cookie cutter and the objects created from a class definition are like the cookies cut out of the dough by the cookie cutter. You don't eat the cookie cutter, you eat the cookies; you don't use the class, you use the objects created from the class.

Instantiation

A program can construct as many instances of a class as it needs. We would expect, for example, that a successful business would need many instances of a Client class and a bank would have many instances of a SavingsAccount class. Figure 1.11 shows more concretely the relationship between a class definition and the objects created through instantiation. Objects are created by invoking a constructor from the class definition, whose job is to initialize the object's data fields. In the example, each Rectangle variable is actually a reference to a unique object in memory and each object has a unique identity. The fact that all the objects are unique in memory is apparent from the layout of the figure (there are separate rectangles for each of the objects) and from their unique identities.

Class variables and **class methods** are shared among all instances of the class (there is only a single physical copy of them made) and can be accessed without creating an instance of the class. **Instance variables** and **instance methods**, on the other hand, are created for *each* instance of the class and are *only* accessible through

Figure 1.11 Object instantiation.

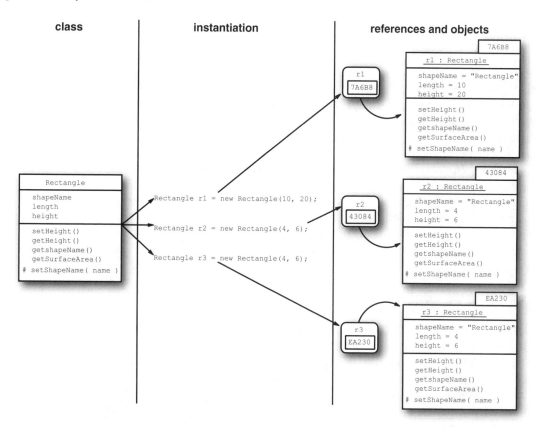

instances. While each object will always have distinct copies of the instance variables, in practice, to conserve memory, there is only a single copy of the instance methods created and they are shared by all instances of the class.

1.2.4 Characteristics of Good Class Design

Deciding what should go in a class is sometimes easy and sometimes difficult. Consideration of the class's purpose and how it is to interact with other classes will provide important guidance. Two general characteristics possessed by a well-designed class also provide some guidance.

Cohesion

A class with high **cohesion** has a single, well-defined purpose presented through a public interface. A class with low cohesion attempts to fill too many roles and/or reveals too many details about how it is implemented. A `CircleRectangle` class that stores a circle, a rectangle, or possibly both, is doing too much and has low cohesion—it does not have a single well-defined purpose. Similarly, a `SavingsAccount` class that shows *how* interest is accrued (as opposed to accruing the interest "behind the scenes" and informing a client of *how much* has accrued) is revealing too much.

Coupling

Coupling refers to the degree to which a class depends on other classes to perform needed operations. The fewer such dependencies there are, the looser the coupling. A class is tightly coupled if it must call a large number of methods from other classes to fulfill its purpose. The disadvantage of tight coupling is that it creates dependencies between classes so that if one class is changed, we may be forced to change all the classes with which it is tightly coupled. An expansion of a class's available operations would be regarded as a benign change from the perspective of a client because all the older operations still exist and are accessed in the way they were originally provided. Also, a change in the way a service is *implemented* is not a problem so long as the method's syntax and semantics remain the same (this the whole point of abstraction and information hiding!). However, dropping a method from a class's public interface or a change in an operation's syntax or semantics will require changes in the clients who use the affected methods.

SUMMING UP

OO programs model static (components) and dynamic (behavior of interacting components) aspects of the problem domain. The Unified Modeling Language is a graphical notation used to visually describe static and dynamic elements of a system. There are notations for all phases of software development.

An object has state (the values of its attributes), behavior (the set of operations it can perform), and identity (unique for each object within the system). The operations of an object can be affected by the object's state, and an object's state can be modified by operations.

An object is an instance of a class. An object is constructed (instantiated) by executing one of the constructors for its type. The `class` construct is Java's linguistic mechanism for providing encapsulation—data and operations are defined within a class. Information hiding is provided through access modifiers (`public`, `private`, `protected`, and the default package access) that control what access a client has to a class's fields. We'll look at access modifiers in this chapter's *Investigate*.

A well-designed class has high cohesion (a single, well-defined purpose) and low coupling (does not rely on many other classes). When possible, a class should also be general so that it can easily be reused in a variety of applications.

CHECKPOINT

1.13 Which message category is involved in instantiation (refer back to Section 1.2.2 for a list of the message categories)?

1.14 How are class variables and instance variables different?

1.15 Give an example of poor cohesion.

1.16 Describe changes to a class that would affect clients of the class.

1.17 Describe changes to a class that would *not* affect clients of the class.

■ 1.3 Code Reuse through Composition and Inheritance

There are two common mechanisms to accomplish code reuse in OO programs: composition and inheritance.

1.3.1 Composition

The idea of composition is quite familiar to you – one thing is composed of several other things. A car is composed of a chassis, an engine, a transmission, and so on. Thus, composition defines a "has a" relationship between two classes. So we would say that a car "has a" chassis, "has an" engine, "has a" transmission, and so on. We can also say that composition defines a whole-part relationship. The car is the "whole" and the engine, chassis, transmission, and so on are "parts" that belong to the whole.

Classes can work in much the same way. Consider the UML class diagram in Figure 1.12 (a). It says that a `BankAccount` is composed of a `Client` and 0 or more `BankTransactions`.[4] It also says that a `Client` is composed of a `Name` and an `Address`. Thus in OOP, a class can be composed of other classes.

Figure 1.12 A composition relationship between classes (UML class diagram).

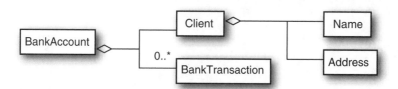

(a) Using composition to define a `BankAccount`

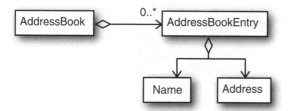

(b) Using composition to define an `AddressBook`

---

[4]A bank account would contain other information, but this is enough to get the feel of composition.

In the UML diagram for composition, the class diagrams are connected with a solid line and a hollow diamond adjacent to the class taking the role of the "whole". Each association can be labeled, typically with a verb, giving more information about the nature of the association. The *ranges* at the ends of the connecting lines indicate how many instances of the class participate in the association. For example, the 0..* notation means "0 or more instances of".

Figure 1.12 (b) shows the makeup of an AddressBook. It is composed of 0 or more AddressBookEntrys. An AddressBookEntry is composed of a Name and an Address.

How Does Composition Promote Code Reuse?

The code reuse is pretty clear from the examples. A class defines a new type and once implemented, can be reused anywhere appropriate. In the examples in Figure 1.12, we see Name and Address being reused.

How Is Composition Done in Java?

The composing class (the "whole") has data fields corresponding to its "parts." If the cardinality of a part allows for multiple instances (as it does for BankTransactions and AddressBookEntrys), the data field will be some collection type. Here are the code fragments for the examples from Figure 1.12 (a). In this example, the BankTransaction objects are stored in a List, which is one of the collection types we'll be examining in this book.

```java
public class BankAccount {
    private Client client;
    private List<BankTransaction> transactions;
    // other fields
    ...
}
public class Client {
    private Name name;
    private Address address;
    // other fields
    ...
}
```

In a UML diagram, the line connecting two classes in a composition relationship can also show directionality indicating the direction in which messages can travel. Typically, composition relationships are unidirectional from the whole to its parts. For example, we would expect an AddressBook to send messages to an AddressBookEntry and not the other way around. This is indicated by the directions of the arrows in Figure 1.12 (b). Similarly, an AddressBookEntry would send messages to a Name and an Address, but not the other way around.

In a more general form of the composition relationship (also called an "association"), two classes may contain references to each other. This is the situation in Figure 1.13. According to the diagram, a student can take zero to five courses. From the code skeleton we see that a Student object would store references to these courses (the student's courseSchedule—in this case, implemented using an array)

Figure 1.13 An association relationship (UML class diagram).

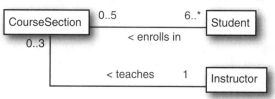

in a `private` data field. Similarly, each section must have a minimum of six students to avoid being cancelled. This is suggested by the range given next to the `Student` class diagram (6..*) and is clarified in the **adornment** that appears above it between the braces. The diagram also tells us that each section is taught by one instructor and that an instructor will teach zero to three sections of a course. The code skeleton shows that each `CourseSection` object would store a list of the students enrolled in the course section and a reference to an instructor object responsible for teaching the course.

```
public class Student {
    private CourseSection[] courseSchedule;
    // other data and method fields ...
}
public class CourseSection {
    private Student[] sectionRoster;
    private Instructor instructor;
    // other data and method fields ...
}
public class Instructor {
    private CourseSection[] sectionsTaught;
    // other data and method fields ...
}
```

CHECKPOINT

1.18 How does composition provide code reuse?

1.19 Write the class skeletons corresponding to Figure 1.12 (b).

1.20 How is bidirectional composition different from unidirectional composition?

1.21 Using a UML diagram, show the composition relationships for the following classes: `Name`, `BillOfSale`, `Address`, `Item`, `Client`.

1.3.2 Inheritance

Inheritance is an important OOP concept, providing a mechanism for both the organization of related classes and the construction of new classes.

Let's approach inheritance through the example in Figure 1.14. Banks manage many kinds of accounts, but all accounts will have several characteristics in common. For example, all accounts will have an account ID, a balance, a history of transactions, a creation date, a client name and address, and so on, as well as operations for these fields.

Different *kinds* of accounts will have *additional* needs that are unique to those kinds of accounts. For example, banks offer savings accounts, checking accounts, mortgage accounts, and so on. A savings account will need to store an interest rate and provide operations to set/get that rate as well as to calculate the interest for an account.

A checking account has different needs. It will have to keep track of whether a client wants their cancelled checks sent each month with a statement, how many

Figure 1.14 A hierarchy of accounts. Remember, + means public and – means private.

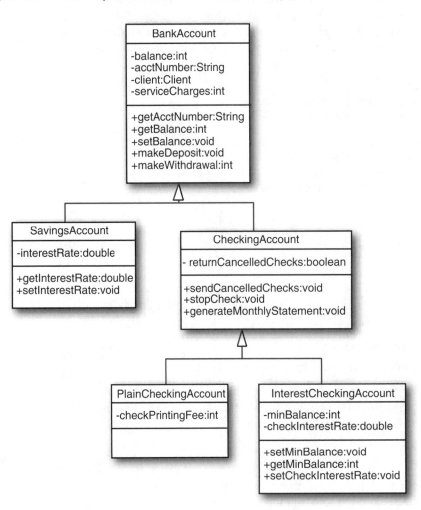

checks have been written, whether the balance dropped below a minimum, and so on. Furthermore, banks offer a wide array of checking accounts, including checking accounts that accrue interest and those that do not.

It would be very handy if we could put the characteristics (attributes, operations, and constraints) that are common to all bank accounts into one place and then *reuse* them as we create specific kinds of accounts. Similarly, we would like to put the characteristics common to all checking accounts into a single class and allow special kinds of checking accounts to have access to (reuse) it.

This is precisely what inheritance lets us do. Broadly, we can say that a subclass (child) inherits the characteristics of its superclass (parent). Thus, in Figure 1.14 class `BankAccount` is the superclass (parent) of `SavingsAccount` and `CheckingAccount`. `SavingsAccount` and `CheckingAccount` are siblings since they have a common parent. Class `CheckingAccount` is the superclass (parent)[5] of classes `PlainCheckingAccount` and `InterestCheckingAccount`. `PlainCheckingAccount` and `InterestCheckingAccount` are related to `BankAccount` through `CheckingAccount`.

How Is Inheritance Done in Java?

Remember that a subclass *extends* its superclass by providing additional features that are unique to the subclass's specialization. In fact, a subclass extends a superclass using the keyword `extends`. Look at the inheritance hierarchies in Figure 1.14 as you look at the following class headers.

```
public class CheckingAccount extends BankAccount {
    // class body goes here
}
public class InterestCheckingAccount extends CheckingAccount {
    // class body goes here
}
```

Where Is the Code Reuse through Inheritance?

A subclass inherits everything defined in its superclass and has *direct* access to all the superclass's `public` and `protected` fields. Figure 1.15 illustrates this for `BankAccount` and `CheckingAccount` and this chapter's *Investigate* has you explore this in more depth. Since `CheckingAccount` extends `BankAccount`, it is as if `CheckingAccount` has an instance of `BankAccount` embedded in it. All `public` and `protected` fields in `BankAccount` are *directly* accessible from code within `CheckingAccount`. All `private` fields within `BankAccount` are still private and cannot be *directly* accessed from within `CheckingAccount`, but can be accessed *in*directly via `BankAccount`'s accessor and mutator methods.

From a *client's* perspective, all `public` fields in `BankAccount` *and* `CheckingAccount` are accessible through a reference to a `CheckingAccount` object. This is illustrated in Figure 1.15 by the two messages sent to the `CheckingAccount` object referenced by `chkacct` (the client). The first message is made to a public

---

[5]In the rest of the book I will use superclass and parent, and subclass and child interchangeably.

Figure 1.15 What `CheckingAccount` inherits from `BankAccount`.

```
public BankAccount {
    private int balance;
    private String acctNumber;
    private Client client;
    private int serviceCharges;

    public String getAcctNumber();
    public int getBalance();
    public void setBalance();
    public void makeDeposit();
    public int makeWithdrawal();
}
```

```
CheckingAccount chkacct;

. . .

chkacct.getBalance();

chkacct.stopCheck( check );
```

```
public CheckingAccount extends BankAccount {

    private boolean returnCancelledChecks;

    public String getAcctNumber();
    public int getBalance();
    public void setBalance();
    public void makeDeposit();
    public int makeWithdrawal();

    public void sendCancelledChecks();
    public void stopCheck();
    public void generateMonthlyStatement();
}
```

method defined in `BankAccount` and inherited by `CheckingAccount`. From a client's perspective, it is as if `getBalance()` was defined in `CheckingAccount`. The second message is to a public method defined in `CheckingAccount`.

What Have We Done So Far?

We have abstracted a set of characteristics (attributes, behaviors, and constraints) shared by all `BankAccounts` to define the general class `BankAccount`. For example, all `BankAccounts` have an account number, a client name and address, a balance, and so on, and have the shared behavioral characteristics that they can `getAccountNumber()`, `getBalance()`, `getClientName()`, and so on. Then, we identified subclasses that all share the characteristics of the superclass, but each subclass added characteristics that distinguished it from both its superclass and its "sibling" classes.

We say that moving from a superclass to a subclass defines a **specialization**. A `SavingsAccount` is a kind of `BankAccount` specialized for saving money that accrues interest and can be drawn on (a withdrawal operation) or added to (through interest and deposits). This distinguishes `SavingsAccounts` from the general class of `BankAccounts` as well as from its sibling class `CheckingAccount`.

Specialization

Similarly, a superclass is a **generalization** of its subclasses, thus `BankAccount` is more general than `SavingsAccount` and `CheckingAccount`, and `CheckingAccount` is more general than either `RegularCheckingAccount` or `InterestCheckingAccount`.

Generalization

Single versus Multiple Inheritance

The language C++ allows multiple inheritance, in which a subclass is extended from more than one superclass (it has multiple parents), which is a very powerful mechanism. The cost of this power and flexibility is increased complexity. Java's simpler inheritance mechanism only allows single inheritance (a subclass can extend only a single superclass). The consequent loss in expressive power is partially made up through Java's `interface` mechanism, which is explained later.

Single and multiple inheritance

Where composition defined a "has a" relationship between two or more classes—a Car is composed of/"has an" Engine—inheritance defines an "is a kind of" relationship between two classes—an `InterestCheckingAccount` "is a kind of" `CheckingAccount`, and a `CheckingAccount` "is a kind of" `BankAccount`. This is also called an "is a" relationship. When designing classes, it is not always clear whether composition or inheritance is the best choice, but the "is a kind of" test is a valuable, if somewhat subjective guide.

An **inheritance hierarchy** forms a class tree from superclass/subclass relations. An important implication of the structure of a hierarchy is that a class can be both a subclass and a superclass. For example, `CheckingAccount` is a subclass of `BankAccount` and is a superclass of `InterestCheckingAccount`. Note that the inheritance relationship is transitive, but not symmetric. So we can say that, if an `InterestCheckingAccount` "is a kind of" `CheckingAccount` and a `CheckingAccount` "is a kind of" `BankAccount`, then, an `InterestCheckingAccount` "is a kind of" `BankAccount` (transitivity: if A=B and B=C, then A=C). But we cannot say that if an `InterestCheckingAccount` "is a kind of" `CheckingAccount`, then a `CheckingAccount` "is a kind of" `InterestCheckingAccount` (not symmetric: A=B, but B=A).

Inheritance hierarchy

The classes shown in Figure 1.16 offer another intuitive example of the generalization/specialization relationships found in an inheritance hierarchy. A rectangle "is a kind of" shape, as are circles and triangles. So we could define a `Shape` superclass that holds the features common to all shapes and define subclasses for each of the different *kinds* of shapes (`Rectangle`, `Circle`, and `Triangle`, for example) that extend, in unique ways, the more general superclass. We develop a version of this hierarchy in Section 1.5.

SUMMING UP

Two common OO mechanisms for code reuse are composition and inheritance. With composition, a class is composed of references to instances of other classes. Composition defines a "has a" relationship between two classes. With inheritance, a subclass (child) inherits the `public` and `protected` fields of its superclass (parent) and has direct access to them. Inheritance defines an "is a kind of" relationship between a subclass and a superclass, so that you can say for subclass `Dog` and super-

Figure 1.16 A hierarchy of shapes.

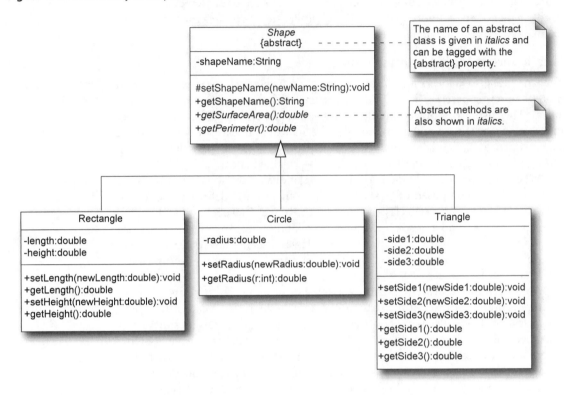

class Animal that Dog "is a kind of" Animal. An inheritance hierarchy is a collection of classes related through inheritance. Inheritance also defines a generalization/specialization relationship. A superclass is a generalization of all its subclasses (and all its descendants), and a subclass is a specialization of its superclass (and all its ancestors). C++ allows multiple inheritance in which a subclass can have more than one parent. Java allows only single inheritance (a subclass can have only a single parent), but gets some of the power of multiple inheritance by allowing a subclass to implement more than one interface.

CHECKPOINT

1.22 What do the subclasses of BankAccount inherit from it?

1.23 Organize the following into an inheritance hierarchy. Identify features belonging to the root of the inheritance hierarchy and to the subclasses.

Secretary, Faculty, Employee, Instructor, Registrar, Staff, Professor

1.24 Show the class headers for SavingsAccount and PlainCheckingAccount from Figure 1.14.

INVESTIGATE Inheritance, Packages, and Access Modifiers

Description

We know that inheritance provides a form of code reuse because a child inherits things from its parent, but what roles do packages and access modifiers play in inheritance? In this *Investigate*, we explore the answers to these questions. We'll also look at the effect of method overriding.

Objectives

- Determine what a subclass inherits from its ancestors.
- Create and use packages.
- See how inheritance and packages affect field access.
- See how access modifiers interact with inheritance and packages.
- Override inherited methods.

Background

Packages. A package is a collection of related classes. When you install the Java SDK, you get a wide assortment of ready-made classes grouped into packages, some of which you will have already used. You can think of a package as a reusable library. Table 1.3 gives examples of a few standard Java packages.

A package is a collection of related classes

It is also possible for you to create your own packages. A class is made part of a package through the `package` statement, which must be the first non-comment line in the file (that is, it comes before your import lines at the beginning of the class definition). A class can only be part of one package. As an example, to create a class `Client1` within `pkg1` you could write the following lines:

Table 1.3 Some standard Java packages.

Package	Description	Example Classes
`java.awt`	The Abstract Windowing Toolkit provides support for developing Graphical User Interfaces (GUIs).	`Dialog, Frame, Button`
`javax.swing`	A newer collection of packages and classes for building GUIs.	`JFrame, JButton, JDialog`
`java.util`	Support for the event model, collections framework, date and time facilities, and other utility classes.	`Date, List, Map`
`java.io`	System input and output through data streams, serialization, and the file system.	`File, BufferedReader, BufferedWriter`
`java.net`	Support for networking applications.	`Socket, ServerSocket, URLConnection`

```
package pkg1;

public class Client1 {
    // rest of class goes here
}
```

The account classes from Figure 1.14 could be made part of a bank.account package if you put the following at the top of each of the source files:[6]

```
package bank.account;
```

The package name is part of a class's **fully qualified name**. Client1's full name is pkg1.Client1. The fully qualified names for the bank.account classes from Figure 1.14 are:

```
bank.account.BankAccount
bank.account.SavingsAccount
bank.account.CheckingAccount
bank.account.PlainCheckingAccount
bank.account.InterestCheckingAccount
```

As you might have guessed, class names within a package must be unique. However it *is* possible for two packages to have a class with the same name, such as java.lang.Object and org.omg.CORBA.Object. The fully qualified names are used to disambiguate the classes in this situation.

If you use the fully qualified name, you don't need to import the package. So, instead of writing

```
import java.util.ArrayList;

public class AddressBook {
    // use just the class name
    private ArrayList<AddressBookEntry> addressBookEntries;
    ...
}
```

you could write

```
public class AddressBook {
    // fully qualified name
    private java.util.ArrayList<AddressBookEntry> addressBookEntries;
    ...
}
```

The package name plays another role. It defines the directory structure where the .class files are to go. Each dot-separated identifier in a package name is the name of a folder (directory). Figure 1.17 shows the folder arrangement for the inheritance hierarchy of Figure 1.14 (assuming they are part of package bank.account).

---

[6]If you are wondering about the "." in bank.account, we will get to that shortly.

Figure 1.17 The file structure where the bank account class files will be stored when they are part of package `bank.account`.

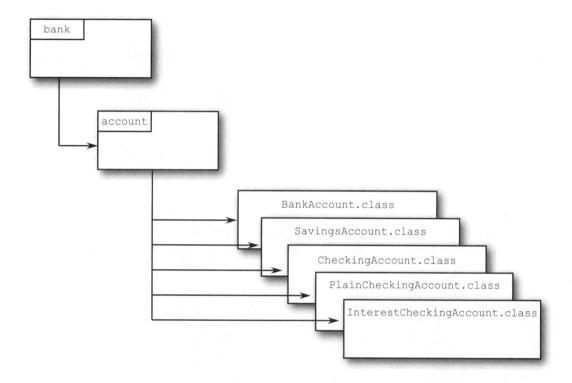

As you accumulate your own packages, you will find it convenient to keep them in a single place. I have a folder called `javalib` that is the root of all my packages. Once I'm confident a package is ready for "release," I put the package's class files under `javalib`. Most IDEs today will do much of this work for you.

The Java compiler knows where to look for the packages that are part of every standard Java environment. If you want the compiler to find your library of packages, you need to tell it where they are. How you do this will depend on how you are doing the compilation—through an IDE or from the command line. You can also set the `CLASSPATH` environment variable, which stores a list of paths to libraries. How you do this depends on your system. Your instructor or TA can tell you the specifics.

There is also an anonymous package to which all classes that lack an explicit package statement belong. There is only one anonymous package.

Access Modifiers Revisited. You will have used the `public` and `private` access modifiers in your class definitions. There are two other access levels: `protected` and package.

The `protected` access modifier provides access rights somewhere between public and private. A protected data field or method field of a `public` class is accessible in

- the defining class, and
- all its subclasses, and
- all classes that are part of the same package as the class containing the `protected` definition.

If no access modifier is given for a data or method field, the default access is called "package." A package access field is accessible in

- the defining class and
- all classes that are part of the same package as the class containing the definition.

Visualization

On the Web site for this text, in the folder holding the resources for Chapter 1, you will find a folder called `Investigate` that contains the starter files you will use for this *Investigate*. Copy the folder to your workspace. Open the `.java` files and look at them carefully.

1. Draw the UML diagram showing the inheritance relationships between the classes.
2. Draw a picture similar to that of Figure 1.15 showing the inheritance relationship between classes A and B, and A and D.
3. Give the fully qualified names for the four classes.
4. Show the directory structure where the corresponding class files would be stored.

The Experiment

You will learn more about access under packages and inheritance by modifying, compiling, and running the starter code provided and examining the results. Use those results to fill out the following table below. Put a checkmark in a box if access is permitted or an X if it is not permitted.

Access Level	Subclass in the Same Package	Subclass in a Different Package	Client in the Same Package	Client in a Different Package
Public				
Private				
Protected				
Package				

You will do the experiment in three parts. The first part looks at package and superclass access from the perspective of a subclass, and the second part looks at package and superclass access from the perspective of a client class. The final part has you experiment with method overriding.

PART 1 Access and Inheritance from the Perspective of a Subclass

From the sample code for this *Investigate* you will have noticed that class A has two subclasses, class B, which is in the same package (pkg1) as A, and class D, which is in a different package (pkg2). Take the following steps to look at how package identity affects what is inherited by a subclass.

1. Add a constructor to B that includes code to invoke the four methods defined in its superclass, A. Compile B.

   Note: You might try accessing the superclass methods in different ways. For example, if class A had a public method foo(), it could be accessed from B using foo(), super.foo(), or this.foo(). Try it!

2. Add a main() method to class B that invokes the constructor created in step 1. Recompile.

3. Was the compilation successful? If not, what error message did you get?

4. Comment out the offending code, and recompile and run the program. What output do you get?

5. Now add code to B.main() to *directly* access the *data* fields of A. You can just print out their values. Recompile B.

6. Was the compilation successful this time? If not, what error message did you get? What does this have in common with the results of step 2? What does this tell you about filling in the first column of the table?

   Now we want to look at access when the subclass is in a different package from its superclass.

7. Repeat steps 1 through 6 for class D. You should now be able to fill in column two of the table.

PART 2 Access and Inheritance from the Perspective of a Client Class

1. Create a client class, Client1, in package pkg1. In the main() method of Client1, declare a variable b of type B and create an instance of B. Now write code in main() to invoke the four methods defined in class B. Compile Client1.

2. Did Client1 compile successfully? If not, what error messages did you get?

3. If you received a compiler error, comment out the offending code, and recompile and run B. What output did you get this time?

4. Would you expect to get different results if Client1 attempted to *directly* access the data fields of object b?

   Test your hypothesis by writing output statements in Client1's main() method to print the values of each of the data fields of object b. Recompile Client1.

5. Did `Client1` compile successfully? If not, what error message did you get? What does this tell you about column three of the table? If you received a compiler error, comment out the offending code.

    Now we want to look at access when the client is in a package different from the class it is accessing.

6. Create another client class, `Client2`, that is in a different package, `pkg3`. Now repeat steps 1 through 5 of Part 2 for class `Client2`. You should now be able to fill in column four of the table.

PART 3 Overriding Inherited Methods

In the final part of this *Investigate* we look at clients, inheritance, and method overriding.

1. Modify `Client1` so that it tries to invoke the four methods class B inherits from class A. Recompile B.

2. Was the compilation successful? If not, what error message did you get? Explain the error. Comment out the offending code.

3. Recompile and run `Client1`. What output do you get?

    Recall that we said that inheritance hierarchies form a generalization and specialization relationship – superclasses are more general than their specialized subclasses. Occasionally this means that a subclass inherits a method that is too general for its needs. The solution is to allow the subclass to provide its own definition of the method. This is called **method overriding**—the subclass's version of the method overrides that of the superclass (or some other ancestor). The requirement is that the method header in the subclass must have the same return type and signature as the method it is overriding from the superclass.

    Method overriding

4. Provide an overridden version of `publicInA()` in class B (you can just copy and paste the method from A to B then edit it). Change the output line to say "overridden version of `publicInA()` in class B". Recompile class B. You should have no error messages.

5. Rerun `Client1`. How does the output differ from what you got in step 3? Which version of `publicInA()` was executed?

    Finally, we need to look at how access is affected when the client is not part of the same package as the class it is trying to access.

6. Repeat steps 1 through 5 for `Client2`.

SUMMING UP

A package is a collection of related classes. A class becomes part of a package by using the `package` keyword followed by the package name. The package name specifies a directory hierarchy where the corresponding `.class` files will be stored. Protected access lies between public and private. A `protected` field is directly accessible in the defining class, all subclasses of the defining class, and all classes that are in the same package as the defining class. If no access modifier is given with a field, the default **package access** is used. A package access field is accessible in all classes in the same package.

▪ **1.4** Polymorphism and Generic Programming

Another important aspect of OOP is **polymorphism**. Polymorphism means that a single thing can take on more than one form. There are two kinds of polymorphism. The first is **static polymorphism** and is implemented as method overloading. In this sense of polymorphism, a single method name can have several implementations within the *same* class and different (but presumably related) meanings, depending on its parameters. For example, constructors are commonly overloaded. So the `Rectangle` class would have

Static polymorphism

```
public Rectangle()            // default constructor
public Rectangle ( double theLength, double theHeight )
```

The more interesting type of polymorphism is **dynamic polymorphism**, which is based on inheritance and the **substitution principle**. The substitution principle says that when writing code based on the set of operations defined in a superclass, we should be able to substitute instances of a subclass for instances of its superclass in the code. With dynamic polymorphism, a single variable (called a **polymorphic variable**) can refer to objects of *different* classes. The key that makes this possible is that the classes are related through inheritance—they have a common ancestor. Consider the hierarchy shown in Figure 1.18. The substitution principle says that if you write an application in terms of the operations found in the `Monitor` class, you should be able to substitute a reference to a `Monitor` object with a reference to an object *descended from* `Monitor`. How is this possible? Recall that through inheritance, a subclass inherits all the characteristics (attributes, operations, and constraints) of its superclass (and all the superclass's ancestors). So all the `Monitor`

Dynamic polymorphism

Substitution principle

Figure 1.18 A hierarchy of monitors.

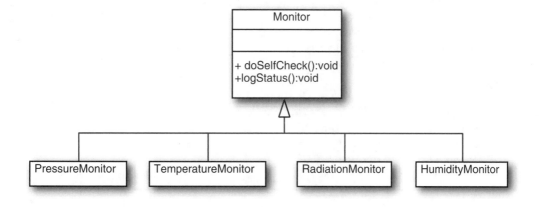

methods are also defined in its subclasses, hence *objects of the subclasses can accept the same messages as the superclass.* For dynamic polymorphism to work, each subclass must either leave the inherited method unchanged or must override it while being consistent with the intended semantics of the superclass.

A common application of polymorphism is to access a collection of related classes to perform the same operation on each of them. Rather than write type-specific code for each subclass, we write a *generic* piece of code that is written in terms of operations found in the superclass (this is the polymorphism). As an example, let's assume there is a central monitor that is responsible for monitoring a collection of diverse kinds of monitors and periodically sends each of them messages to do a diagnostic check and to log their current status.

Clearly each kind of monitor will go about doing a self-check differently and will have different status information to log, so each subclass of Monitor will have overridden the doSelfCheck() and logStatus() methods to handle its unique monitoring responsibilities.

Look at the code in Listing 1.1. When monitor[i].doSelfCheck() on line 13 is executed for different values of i, how do we guarantee that the doSelfCheck() message is received by the right kind of monitor? For example, since monitor just stores references to Monitor objects and not any particular kind of monitor, when i is 0, how can we be sure that the doSelfCheck() method from PressureMonitor is called and not the same method by that name from Monitor or one of its other subclasses? This is handled by the runtime system using **dynamic binding** (also called **late binding** in the programming language literature), which binds an object reference to a specific object *at the time of the method call.* This is possible because each object stores information about its actual type that is accessed by the runtime system to resolve the generic superclass reference into a reference to the specific sub-

Dynamic (late) binding

Listing 1.1 An example of polymorphism using different kinds of monitors.

```
1    // create N monitor references
2    Monitor [] monitor = new Monitor[ N ];
3
4    // populate array with instances of particular Monitors
5    monitor[0] = new PressureMonitor();
6    monitor[1] = new TemperatureMonitor();
7    monitor[2] = new RadiationMonitor();
8    monitor[3] = new HumidityMonitor();
9    // and so on...
10
11   // now have each one do a regular checkup
12   for ( i = 0; i < monitor.length; i++ ) {
13       monitor[i].doSelfCheck();
14       monitor[i].logStatus();
15   }
```

class object being accessed. Thus, when you compile the code in Listing 1.1, the compiler is satisfied with the statement `monitor[i].doSelfCheck()` because it knows from looking at all the class definitions that such a method exists in the superclass `Monitor` and, therefore, is available in all of `Monitor`'s subclasses through inheritance. It then becomes the responsibility of the runtime system to make the proper reference when the method is actually invoked.

Polymorphism is powerful, allowing us to do more with less code. Part of "thinking OO" is looking for opportunities to use polymorphism. We will see many opportunities to use polymorphism throughout the book, sometimes in surprising places. We will develop a complete example of polymorphism in the next section.

Polymorphism naturally is related to writing **generic code**. Most code is writ- **Generic code** ten with a specific data type in mind. Polymorphic code is written for a type representing a family of related classes (in our example, the set of classes descended from the `Monitor` class). Generic code takes this a step further to produce code that would work for several families of related classes. A generic sort method, for instance, could sort any kind of object (monitors, geometric shapes, tasks, bank accounts, etc.) through polymorphism and the substitution principle.

SUMMING UP

Polymorphism allows a single thing to take on more than one form. Static polymorphism is method overloading—two or more related methods in the same class can have the same name, but with different parameters.

Dynamic polymorphism relies on inheritance and the substitution principle and allows a polymorphic variable to refer to objects of different classes that are related through inheritance. Polymorphic code is written in terms of the methods defined in the class at the root of the inheritance hierarchy. Subclasses can override these method definitions to provide type-specific behavior. At run time, the polymorphic variable references instances of the subclasses and the runtime system dynamically bind an object reference to a specific object at the time a method is called, thus ensuring that the desired method implementation is executed.

CHECKPOINT

1.25 What is the difference between static and dynamic polymorphism?

1.26 Explain the benefit of static polymorphism and give some convincing examples to reinforce your argument.

1.27 What does the substitution principle say? How can it be used?

1.28 How does dynamic polymorphism make use of inheritance and the substitution principle?

1.29 Why can static polymorphism be handled by the compiler, but dynamic polymorphism cannot? How are the references by polymorphic variables resolved?

■ **1.5** Case Study: a Shapes Hierarchy

In this section we make the OO concepts presented in this chapter more concrete by writing the Java classes for most of the Shape hierarchy shown in Figure 1.16. In doing this, we will look at abstract classes, concrete classes, and interfaces.

1.5.1 Abstract Shape

Look at the shapes in Figure 1.16 again. Shape is at the top of the hierarchy. What should be in it? As you might suspect, the trick in designing a class hierarchy is to determine what can be put in the superclass at the root of the hierarchy and what should be left for its subclasses. If there are multiple levels to the hierarchy, you have to repeat this decision-making process for each level.

Recall that a superclass is always more general than its subclasses, so there should not be anything in a superclass that cannot be used directly or overridden in all its subclasses. So, to develop the Shape ADT, we need to identify the features we want to have shared by the various *kinds* of shapes we want to represent. For this example, we decide that every shape has a name, a surface area, and a perimeter, so these are the attributes common to all shapes. What can we say about common operations? It is reasonable to provide accessor methods to return the values for a shape's attributes. A protected mutator method is provided to change a shape name. The reason the method is protected and not public is that we do not want to allow random shape shifting; if a client creates a Rectangle, we do not want to allow the client to change the shape's name and say it is now a Circle![7] Why not provide mutators for the surface area or the perimeter attributes? These are values that are *synthesized* from other attributes of a shape (e.g., *length* and *height* for a Rectangle object), so they are read-only attributes. Mutator methods are not provided for synthesized attributes.

Synthesized attributes = read-only attributes

The Shape ADT

Description
A shape object represents a geometric shape. Every shape has a name (the kind of shape it is), a surface area, and a perimeter. Surface area and perimeter are determined by characteristics particular to a kind of shape. An object created to be one kind of shape cannot become another kind of shape. The dimensions of a shape must be greater than 0.

Invariants
  1. Every shape has a name. The default name is "Unknown."
  2. The dimensions of a shape must be greater than 0. The default size for a dimension is 1.0.

---

[7]The assumption here is that those classes with restricted access to the protected field will behave themselves.

Attributes

Class variables
    DEFAULT_SIZE   a constant, the default size for a shape is 1.0
    DEFAULT_NAME String   the default shape name is "Unknown"

Instance variables
    shapeName String   the name of this type of shape

Operations

constructor()
pre-condition:	none
responsibilities:	default constructor - initialize *shapeName* to *DEFAULT_NAME*
post-condition:	the shape is initialized
returns:	nothing

constructor(String name)
pre-condition:	name is not null or empty
responsibilities:	initialize *shapeName* to name, if name is valid, otherwise use *DEFAULT_NAME*
post-condition:	the shape is initialized
returns:	nothing

getShapeName()
pre-condition:	none
responsibilities:	return the name of this shape
post-condition:	the shape is unchanged
returns:	String – the name of this shape

setShapeName(String newName)
pre-condition:	newName is not null or empty
responsibilities:	reset *shapeName* to newName, if newName is valid, otherwise make no change
post-condition:	this shape's name is set to newName, if valid
returns:	nothing

getSurfaceArea()
pre-condition:	none
responsibilities:	compute the surface area of this shape
post-condition:	the shape is unchanged
returns:	the surface area of this shape

getPerimeter()
pre-condition:	none
responsibilities:	compute the perimeter of this shape
post-condition:	the shape is unchanged
returns:	the perimeter of this shape

Abstract Classes

The Java implementation of the Shape ADT is given in Listing 1.2 and follows in a straightforward fashion from the description. The package statement on line 1 names the Java package to which this class will be added.

Listing 1.2 The Shape abstract class.

```
1    package gray.adts.shapes;
2
3    public abstract class Shape {
4        /**
5         * The default size used in constructing a shape.
6         */
7        protected static final double DEFAULT_SIZE = (double) 1.0;
8        protected static final String DEFAULT_NAME = "Unknown";
9        private String shapeName;
10
11       /**
12        * Construct a generic instance of unknown shape type.
13        */
14       public Shape(){
15           this.shapeName = DEFAULT_NAME;
16       }
17
18       /**
19        * Construct a <tt>Shape</tt> whose type is specified in
20        * the argument.
21        * @param name the name of this kind of shape
22        */
23       public Shape( String name ){
24           setShapeName( name );
25       }
26
27       /**
28        * Reset the shape name for this <tt>Shape</tt>.
29        * @param name the name of this kind of shape
30        */
31       protected void setShapeName( String name ) {
32           if ( name.trim().length() == 0 )
33               shapeName = DEFAULT_NAME;
34           else
35               shapeName = new String( name );
36       }
37
```

```
38        /**
39         * Get the name of this kind of shape.
40         * @return the name of this shape
41         */
42        public String getShapeName() {
43            return shapeName;
44        }
45
46        /**
47         * Get the surface area of this <tt>Shape</tt>.
48         * @return the surface area of this <tt>Shape</tt>
49         */
50        public abstract double getSurfaceArea();
51
52        /**
53         * Get the perimeter of this <tt>Shape</tt>.
54         * @return the perimeter of this <tt>Shape</tt>
55         */
56        public abstract double getPerimeter();
57    }
```

The keyword abstract in the class header on line 3 tells us that this is an abstract class. A class must be declared abstract if one or more of its methods is declared to be abstract. In a very real sense you can think of *abstract* as meaning "not completely implemented" or "some details to be filled in later." The methods on lines 50 and 56 of Listing 1.2 are abstract.

An abstract method is one that has an *intended* semantics as described by its documentation, but no implementation that concretely defines those semantics[8] All we are given is the documentation describing the method's intended semantics, the method's return type, and the argument list. The method is included in the abstract class because it is required by the ADT specification and will be of use in classes that extend Shape, using it as the basis for defining classes for different kinds of shapes (rectangles, circles, triangles, etc). Related to this is the notion, mentioned at the beginning of the chapter, that similar things should behave in similar ways. By specifying the syntax and semantics of the abstract methods in Shape, we are guaranteeing some uniformity in the interface of all its subclasses (without even knowing in advance what they will be). In this way, we are ensuring that various kinds of shapes can be accessed and will behave in similar ways. Remember, this is a precondition for writing polymorphic code.

The abstract modifier

---

[8]As pointed out earlier, we can say anything we want about what a method is supposed to do, but it is the code in the method's body that defines what the method really does (its actual semantics). This is often the reason we find it difficult to debug our own code; we confuse what we intended the code to do with what the code actually does.

The reason we cannot provide a body for some of the methods is that their implementation is specific to the unique needs of a subclass. How we go about getting "surface area," for example, clearly depends on the kind of shape we are talking about—you compute the area of a circle differently from that of a rectangle. This example reaffirms the value of abstraction. In creating our design, we can talk about "surface area" and provide a method description for getting it without worrying (yet) about the details of how the method is to be implemented.

Abstraction (again)

The instance variable `shapeName` is declared to be `private` (line 9) to `Shape` and can be set through `Shape`'s constructors and the protected `setShapeName()` method, and it can be read through the accessor method `getShapeName()`. We can provide an implementation for `getShapeName()` in `Shape` because it does not require any special knowledge of a particular shape. Every shape has a name, which is stored in `shapeName`, so we have all the information we need to complete the definition of the method.

We cannot create instances of an abstract class, because an abstract class is not completely defined (its abstract methods have no implementation). A **concrete class** is one that provides implementations for *all* its methods, so it *can* be instantiated. If a subclass provides implementations for all the abstract methods inherited from its superclass, it is a concrete class, otherwise the subclass must *also* be declared abstract.

Concrete classes

Since `Shape` is abstract, we cannot create instances of it. Rather, what we must do is to *extend* the `Shape` class to define concrete classes for some specific shapes, which is what we do next.

1.5.2 Inheritance and Concrete Classes
`Rectangle` and `Circle`

`Shape` was designed to be very general. Our goal now is to extend `Shape` to define the specialized classes `Rectangle` and `Circle` from the inheritance hierarchy shown in Figure 1.16.

The `Rectangle` Class

We begin with the definition of the `Rectangle` class whose description was given in Section 1.1.2 in the `Rectangle` ADT. The implementation is shown in Listing 1.3. Recall that a subclass extends a superclass by using the `extends` keyword (line 3). Figure 1.19 illustrates the effect inheritance has on the `Rectangle` class. The fields in the shaded boxes inside `Rectangle` are inherited from `Shape` and so are available in `Rectangle`. Remember that with the exception of the two abstract methods `getSurfaceArea()` and `getPerimeter()`, which `Rectangle` must implement if it is to be a concrete class, the fields in the shaded boxes are *not* redeclared inside `Rectangle`. Rather, `Rectangle` gets them automatically because an instance of `Shape` (the shaded boxes) will be found inside each instance of `Rectangle`. Examination of the code for `Rectangle` in Listing 1.3, and similarly for `Circle` in Listing 1.4 as well as the sample program in Listing 1.5 that uses `Rectangle` and `Circle`, will confirm this.

extends and subclassing

The constructors for `Rectangle` (lines 7–15 and 17–35) invoke the constructor for `Shape`, its superclass, using the keyword `super` (lines 12 and 27). This initializes

Superclass access through super

Listing 1.3 The Rectangle class.

```
1    package gray.adts.shapes;
2
3    public class Rectangle extends Shape {
4       private double length;
5       private double height;
6
7      /**
8       * Construct a <tt>Rectangle</tt> object
9       * using the default size for its dimensions.
10      */
11      public Rectangle() {
12         super("Rectangle");
13         setLength( super.DEFAULT_SIZE );
14         setHeight( Shape.DEFAULT_SIZE );
15      }
16
17     /**
18      * Construct a <tt>Rectangle</tt> object using the arguments.
19      * If an argument is <= 0, the default size specified in
20      * <tt>Shape</tt> is used instead.
21      * @param theLength the length of this <tt>Rectangle</tt>;
22      *         must be > 0
23      * @param theHeight the height of this <tt>Rectangle</tt>;
24      *         must be > 0
25      */
26      public Rectangle( double theLength, double theHeight ) {
27         super("Rectangle");
28         if ( theLength < 0 )
29            setLength( Shape.DEFAULT_SIZE );
30         else setLength( theLength );
31
32         if ( theHeight < 0 )
33            setHeight( Shape.DEFAULT_SIZE );
34         else setHeight( theHeight );
35      }
36
37     /**
38      * Get the surface area of this <tt>Rectangle</tt>.
39      * @return the surface area of this <tt>Rectangle</tt>;
40      */
41      public double getSurfaceArea() {
42         return this.length * this.height;
43      }
44
45     /**
```

```
46        * Get the perimeter of this <tt>Rectangle</tt>.
47        * @return the perimeter of this <tt>Rectangle</tt>;
48        */
49       public double getPerimeter() {
50           return 2 * this.length + 2 * this.height;
51       }
52
53       /**
54        * Get the length dimension of this <tt>Rectangle</tt>.
55        * @return the length of this <tt>Rectangle</tt>;
56        */
57       public double getLength() {
58           return this.length;
59       }
60
61       /**
62        * Get the height dimension of this <tt>Rectangle</tt>.
63        * @return the height of this <tt>Rectangle</tt>;
64        */
65       public double getHeight() {
66           return this.height;
67       }
68
69       /**
70        * Set the length dimension of this <tt>Rectangle</tt>.
71        * If <tt>theLength</tt> is <= 0, the dimension is unchanged.
72        * @param theLength new length of this <tt>Rectangle</tt>;
73        *        must be > 0
74        */
75       public void setLength( double theLength ) {
76           if ( theLength <= 0 )
77               return;
78           this.length = theLength;
79       }
80
81       /**
82        * Set the height dimension of this <tt>Rectangle</tt>.
83        * If <tt>theHeight</tt> is <= 0, the dimension is unchanged.
84        * @param theHeight the new height of this <tt>Rectangle</tt>;
85        *    must be > 0
86        */
87       public void setHeight( double theHeight ) {
88           if ( theHeight <= 0 )
89               return;
90           this.height = theHeight;
91       }
92   }
```

Figure 1.19 What `Rectangle` inherits from `Shape`.

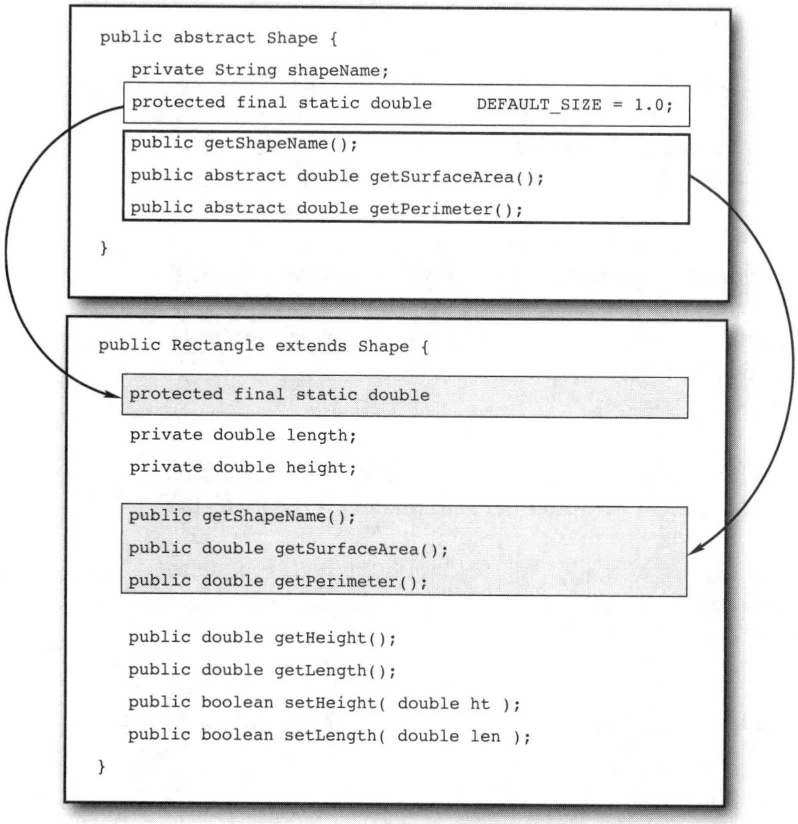

```
public abstract Shape {
    private String shapeName;
    protected final static double     DEFAULT_SIZE = 1.0;

    public getShapeName();
    public abstract double getSurfaceArea();
    public abstract double getPerimeter();

}
```

```
public Rectangle extends Shape {
    protected final static double

    private double length;
    private double height;

    public getShapeName();
    public double getSurfaceArea();
    public double getPerimeter();

    public double getHeight();
    public double getLength();
    public boolean setHeight( double ht );
    public boolean setLength( double len );
}
```

the `Shape` object that is a part of every `Rectangle` object. If a superclass constructor is invoked in a *subclass* constructor, it must be the first thing done in the subclass constructor. Recall that any visible method or data field of the superclass can be accessed in a subclass using the form `super.fieldname`. This is illustrated in the default constructor for `Rectangle` with

```
setLength( super.DEFAULT_SIZE );
```

However, the preferred approach is to use the class name, as follows:

```
setHeight( Shape.DEFAULT_SIZE );
```

This is valid because `DEFAULT_SIZE` is a *class* variable—it is declared `static` in `Shape`. Recall that a class variable is accessible by using the class name without creating an instance of the class. This is a common way to access constants. Another example is the public constant for π in the `Math` class—`Math.PI`.

Returning to the constructors, you should note that they use methods defined in `Rectangle`'s interface to set the length (lines 13, 29, 30) and height (lines 14, 33, 34) of the rectangle rather than duplicating the code from those methods.

If you have a method that performs a generally useful operation and you have other methods that also have to perform this operation, then do the common work in one method (perhaps a private utility method) and invoke that method in all the places it is needed inside the class. Unless efficiency considerations dictate otherwise, do this even when the task requires only a line or two of code. This provides a form of encapsulation *within* the class by isolating how the class's data fields are accessed and updated.

Implementation note

Lastly, if `Rectangle` is to be a concrete class that can be instantiated, it must provide definitions for the two abstract methods it inherited from `Shape`: `getSurfaceArea()` on lines 37 through 43, and `getPerimeter()` on lines 45 through 51. You cannot change the headers of the inherited methods—you just have to provide the implementations. `Rectangle` also provides data fields (lines 4 and 5) and method fields that are *unique* to rectangles (lines 53–91). It is the implementation of the abstract methods and the inclusion of the fields that are unique to rectangles that extends a `Shape` into a `Rectangle`.

The `Circle` Class

Like `Rectangle`, the `Circle` class extends `Shape`, so must provide implementations for the abstract methods `getSurfaceArea()` and `getPerimeter()`. Of course, the implementations in `Circle` are specific to the meaning of "surface area" and "perimeter" for a circle. `Circle` must also add data fields and methods unique to circles—again, these are the features that differentiate circles from shapes and rectangles. `Circle`'s Java definition is in Listing 1.4.

Listing 1.4 The `Circle` class.

```
1    package gray.adts.shapes;
2
3    public class Circle extends Shape {
4        private double radius;
5
6        /**
7         * Construct a <tt>Circle</tt> object using the default size
8         * for its radius.
9         */
10       public Circle() {
11           super( "Circle" );
12           setRadius( super.DEFAULT_SIZE );
13       }
14
15       /**
16        * Construct a <tt>Circle</tt> object using the argument
17        * for the radius. If <tt>r</tt> is <= 0, the default size
18        * specified in <tt>Shape</tt> is used for radius instead.
19        * @param theRadius the radius of this <tt>Circle</tt>;
```

```
20          *     must be > 0
21          */
22         public Circle( double theRadius ) {
23             super( "Circle" );
24             if ( theRadius <= 0.0 )
25                 setRadius( Shape.DEFAULT_SIZE );
26             else
27                 setRadius( theRadius );
28         }
29
30         /**
31          * Get the surface area of this <tt>Circle</tt>.
32          * @return the surface area of this <tt>Circle</tt>
33          */
34         public double getSurfaceArea() {
35             return this.radius * this.radius * Math.PI;
36         }
37
38         /**
39          * Get the perimeter of this <tt>Circle</tt>.
40          * @return the perimeter of this <tt>Circle</tt>
41          */
42         public double getPerimeter() {
43             return 2 * this.radius + Math.PI;
44         }
45
46         /**
47          * Get the radius of this <tt>Circle</tt>.
48          * @return the radius of this <tt>Circle</tt>
49          */
50         public double getRadius() {
51             return this.radius;
52         }
53
54         /**
55          * Set the radius of this <tt>Circle</tt>.
56          * If <tt>r</tt> is <= 0, the radius is unchanged.
57          * @param theRadius the new radius of this <tt>Circle</tt>
58          *     must be > 0
59          */
60         public void setRadius( double theRadius ) {
61             if ( theRadius <= 0 )
62                 return;
63             this.radius = theRadius;
64         }
65     }
```

Using Rectangle and Shape

The program in Listing 1.5 confirms what was shown pictorially in Figure 1.19 and discovered experimentally in the *Investigate* section—that the `public` and

---

Listing 1.5 Demonstrating inheritance using the `Rectangle` and `Circle` classes.

```
1    package shapeExamples;
2
3    import gray.adts.shapes.*;
4    import javax.swing.JOptionPane;
5    /**
6     * Illustrate inheritance in a simple shapes hierarchy.
7     */
8    public class ShapeEx1 {
9
10      public static void main ( String [] args ) {
11         Rectangle r = new Rectangle();
12         Circle c = new Circle();
13         String output;
14
15         // use methods defined in Rectangle and Circle
16         r.setLength( 4 );
17         r.setHeight( 5 );
18         c.setRadius( 6 );
19
20         // use method inherited from Shape
21         output = r.getShapeName() + ": length = " + r.getLength()
22                         + " height = " + r.getHeight() + "\n";
23         output += c.getShapeName() + ": radius = " +
24                         c.getRadius() + "\n";
25
26         JOptionPane.showMessageDialog( null, output,
27                           "Shape inheritance example",
28                           JOptionPane.INFORMATION_MESSAGE );
29         System.exit( 0 );
30      }
31    }
```

OUTPUT

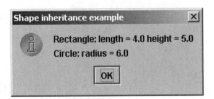

protected fields of Shape are accessible in its subclasses and that the public fields of Shape can be accessed through instances of its subclasses. The output of this code is shown at the end of the listing.

The example program creates instances of Rectangle and Circle (Listing 1.5, lines 11 and 12) using their default constructors and then uses mutator methods unique to the two classes to set their data fields (lines 16–18). For a rectangle this means setting its length and height fields, and for a circle we set the radius. Lastly, information about the two shape objects is displayed. We get each shape's name (lines 21 and 23) using getShapeName(), which was inherited from the Shape class.

CHECKPOINT

1.30 What happens if we changed the method header for getSurfaceArea() from Shape to, say, getArea() or getSurfaceArea()?

1.31 How can a subclass access a method from its superclass?

1.32 What makes an abstract class abstract?

1.33 Where is a protected field visible?

1.5.3 Overriding Object Methods toString() and equals()

The approach we used to output information about the shapes in Listing 1.4 was lengthy and awkward.

```
output = r.getShapeName()
            + ": length = " + r.getLength()
            + " height = " + r.getHeight() + "\n";
```

It would be more convenient if there were a method that converted the value of an object into a string, allowing us to use the much simpler statement:

```
output = r.toString();
```

The toString() method is one of several useful methods defined in the Object class. Because Object is at the root of the Java class hierarchy, it is an ancestor for *all* other classes, including Rectangle. Figure 1.20 shows this inheritance hierarchy. The principles of inheritance we observed in our simple Shape hierarchy apply for all inheritance hierarchies. Since Object is at the root of the Java class hierarchy, the methods defined in Object are inherited by *every* other class. Specifically,

■ The public and protected fields of Object are inherited by Shape.

■ The public, protected, and package fields of Shape (including fields inherited from Object) are inherited by Rectangle and Circle.

■ A subclass of Rectangle will inherit all of Rectangle's public and protected fields as well as anything Rectangle inherited from its ancestors.

■ and so on down to the bottommost classes in the inheritance tree.

Figure 1.20 `Rectangle` in the inheritance hierarchy from `Object`.

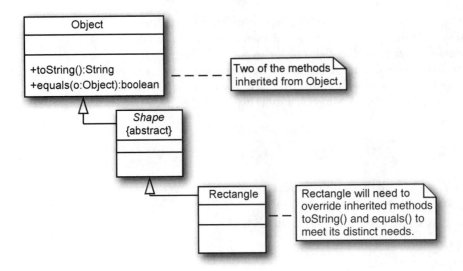

This means that the `toString()` method defined in `Object` is available in `Rectangle`. Unfortunately, the implementation provided by `Object` is very general and simply outputs the name of the class followed by '@' and the object's identity. This is illustrated by the program in Listing 1.6.

The generality of this is understandable when you consider that `Object` could not possibly know what is appropriate to print out for every class *descended* from it (e.g., `Circle`, `Rectangle`). Instead, recall that subclasses are expected to **override** inherited methods to provide more appropriate implementations. To override a method you must provide

The `toString()` method from `Object`

Method overriding

■ The method header *exactly* as found in the ancestor class from which you are inheriting it.

■ An implementation that is tailored to the needs of the inheriting class.

Listing 1.6 Using the `toString()` method.

```
1    package shapeExamples;
2
3    import gray.adts.shapes.*;
4    import javax.swing.JOptionPane;
5
6    /**
7     * Illustrate the use of the overloaded toString() method.
8     */
9    public class ShapeEx2 {
```

```
10
11        public static void main ( String [] args ) {
12            Rectangle r = new Rectangle();
13            String output;
14
15            // use methods defined in Rectangle and Circle
16            r.setLength( 4 );
17            r.setHeight( 5 );
18
19            output = "Class name is " + r.getClass().getName() + "\n";
20            output += "r.toString() produces " + r.toString() + "\n";
21
22            JOptionPane.showMessageDialog( null, output,
23                               "overridden toString() example for Rectangle",
24                               JOptionPane.INFORMATION_MESSAGE );
25            System.exit( 0 );
26        }
27    }
```

OUTPUT

To override the toString() method inherited from Object, you would include the method definition in Listing 1.7 in the Rectangle class. Figure 1.21 shows the output generated when we use this overridden toString() method.

Listing 1.7 The toString() method as overridden in Rectangle.

```
1    /**
2     * Returns a <tt>String</tt> object representing this
3     * <tt>Rectangle</tt>'s value.
4     * Overridden from <tt>Object</tt>.
5     * @return a string representation of this object
6     */
7    public String toString() {
8        return this.getShapeName() + ": this.length = " + length +
9                " height = " + this.height;
10    }
```

Figure 1.21 Output of the *overridden* `toString()` method in `Rectangle` (code is in Listings 1.6 and 1.7).

Another useful method inherited from `Object` is `equals()`, whose purpose is to determine whether one object is "equal" to another. For example, `obj1.equals ( obj2 )` tests to see if `obj1` is "equal to" `obj2`. If so, `true` is returned, otherwise `false` is returned. The default implementation provided by `Object` merely tests to see if two *references* are to the same object. Let's look at an example.

The `equals()` method from `Object`

In the program shown in Listing 1.8, the `Rectangle`'s `r1` and `r3` (lines 11 and 13) have the same dimensions, so we would say they are equal. `Rectangle r2` (line 12) has different dimensions, so is not equal to `r1` or `r3`. `Rectangle r4` is a reference to the same object referenced by `r2` (line 14), so clearly `r2` and `r4` have the same dimensions. Figure 1.22 shows the resulting objects and references.

Listing 1.8 Using the `equals()` method.

```
1    package shapeExamples;
2
3    import gray.adts.shapes.*;
4    import javax.swing.JOptionPane;
5    /**
6     * Illustrates the use of the equals() method.
7     */
8    public class ShapeEx3 {
9
10       public static void main ( String [] args ) {
11           Rectangle r1 = new Rectangle(3, 4);
12           Rectangle r2 = new Rectangle(1, 2);
13           Rectangle r3 = new Rectangle(3, 4);
14           Rectangle r4 = r2;
15           String output;
16
17           // use methods inherited from Object
18           output = "r1 = " + r1.toString() + "\n";
19           output += "r2 = " + r2.toString() + "\n";
20           output += "r3 = " + r3.toString() + "\n";
21           output += "r4 = " + r4.toString() + "\n";
```

```
22            output += "r1.equals( r2 ) is " + r1.equals( r2 ) + "\n";
23            output += "r1.equals( r3 ) is " + r1.equals( r3 ) + "\n";
24            output += "r2.equals( r4 ) is " + r2.equals( r4 ) + "\n";
25
26            JOptionPane.showMessageDialog( null, output,
27                               "generic equals() example for Rectangle2",
28                               JOptionPane.INFORMATION_MESSAGE );
29            System.exit( 0 );
30         }
31    }
```

OUTPUT

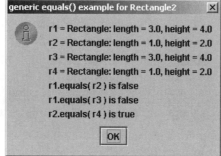

Figure 1.22 The `Rectangles` created in the code in Listing 1.8.

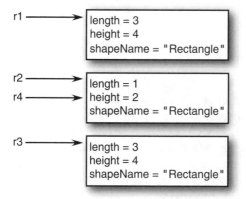

The output for Listing 1.8 does not match our expectations—the only `Rectangles` found to be equal are `r2` and `r4`, which reference the *same* `Rectangle` object. To be fair, this is the best that the `equals()` implementation from `Object` can be expected to do since, as we saw with `toString()`, `Object` can't be expected to know about the unique characteristics of its descendants. The `equals()` method as implemented in `Object` looks at the only piece of information it has about the objects being compared—their references. This explains why r2 and r4, which reference the same object, are found to be equal, but r1 and r3, which reference *different*, but "equal" Rectangles are not found to be equal.

What we need to do is have Rectangle provide its *own* definition of equals(). That is, Rectangle must override equals().

The contract for equals(), taken from the Java 2 Platform Standard Edition version 1.5 API Specification, is quite specific. The equals() method implements an equivalence relation:

- It is *reflexive*: for any reference value x, x.equals(x) should return true.
- It is *symmetric*: for any reference values x and y, x.equals(y) should return true if and only if y.equals(x) returns true.
- It is *transitive*: for any reference values x, y, and z, if x.equals(y) returns true and y.equals(z) returns true, then x.equals(z) should return true.
- It is *consistent*: for any reference values x and y, multiple invocations of x.equals(y) consistently return true or consistently return false, provided no information used in equals comparisons on the object is modified.
- For any non-null reference value x, x.equals(null) should return false.

What is the basis for equality for a rectangle? It could be surface area, however it is possible for two rectangles to have different heights and lengths, but have the same area. However, two rectangles that have the same height and length *must also* have the same surface area, so this is the better choice. The overridden method is shown in Listing 1.9.

Overridden equals() in Rectangle

You should note that the parameter passed in on line 10 is of type Object and *not* of type Rectangle. Let's consider why this is because it is a powerful idea that is used a lot in Java.

Listing 1.9 The overridden equals() method in Rectangle.

```
 1    /**
 2     * Returns <tt>true</tt> if and only if the argument is not
 3     * <tt>null</tt> and is a <tt>Rectangle</tt> object that
 4     * represents the same rectangle value as this object. The
 5     * comparison is done based on the dimensions length and height.
 6     * @param o the object to compare with
 7     * @return <tt>true</tt> if the <tt>Rectangle</tt> objects represent
 8     * the same value; <tt>false</tt> otherwise.
 9     */
10    public boolean equals( Object o ) {
11        if ( ( o == null ) || ( !( o instanceof Rectangle ) ) )
12            return false;
13        return (   (((Rectangle)o).getLength() == this.getLength() ) &&
14                   (((Rectangle)o).getHeight() == this.getHeight() ) );
15    }
```

Recall that every object has an instance of Object inside it because Object is at the root of Java's inheritance hierarchy (look again at Figure 1.20). A Rectangle "is a kind of" Object, so you can pass Rectangle references around as Object references (remember the substitution principle?). This is *very* convenient. Consider the following code fragment:

```
1    Rectangle r1 = new Rectangle( 5, 10 );
2    Rectangle r2 = new Rectangle( 10, 15 );
3    Circle c1 = new Circle( 5 );
4
5    System.out.println( "r1.equals( r2 ) is " + r1.equals( r2 ) );
6    System.out.println( "r1.equals( c1 ) is " + r1.equals( c1 ) );
```

On line 5, an equals() message is sent to Rectangle object r1, with Rectangle object r2 as the argument. The line is asking "Is r1 equal to r2?" The equals() method in Rectangle expects an Object as the argument. This is okay. Since class Rectangle has Object as an ancestor we can pass Rectangles around as Object references.

Thus Rectangle's equals() method gets a reference to a Rectangle through a generic Object reference, o (line 10 of Listing 1.9). Before you can treat o as a Rectangle though, you first must check to see that it is, in fact, a reference to an object of type Rectangle. This is done on line 11 in equals() using the instanceof operator. The rationale is simple—you can't compare apples and oranges, or, as we try to do on line 6 in the code fragment above, compare a Rectangle and a Circle. Such a comparison will always return false.

Since we are passing in an Object, but want to compare instances of the Rectangle class, we will need to first cast the parameter o into a reference to a Rectangle object so that we can invoke the argument's accessor methods for the length and height fields. Pay particular attention to the placement of the parentheses.

```
((Rectangle)o).getLength() == this.getLength()
```

The inner set of parentheses surround the name of the target class to which we want to cast o, and the outer parentheses bind the target class name (Rectangle) to o. This combination of parentheses is necessary because the member selection operator (.) has higher precedence than the type cast. If we forget to include the outer set of parentheses and did

```
(Rectangle)o.getLength() == this.getLength()
```

the compiler will complain that

```
"Rectangle.java": cannot resolve symbol: method getLength() in class
java.lang.Object
"Rectangle.java": operator == cannot be applied to
gray.adts.shapes.Rectangle,double
```

What is going on here? Because of the precedence of the operators, the equivalent expression is

```
( (Rectangle)(o.getLength()) ) == this.getLength()
```

Figure 1.23 Output of the overridden `equals()` method in `Rectangle` (code is in Listings 1.8 and 1.9).

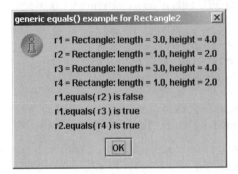

This grouping makes it plain that the compiler will treat o as a reference to an instance of `Object` and consequently become agitated because it cannot find a method called `getLength()` in `Object`. This generates the first compiler error above. The second error occurs because the left side of the equality operator is cast to be of type `Rectangle` while the method call on the right side of the equality operator produces a `double`. Since `Rectangles` and `doubles` cannot be meaningfully compared, we get the second compiler error.

The output using the overridden method is shown in Figure 1.23.

CHECKPOINT

1.34 What is method overriding and why do we use it?

1.35 Name and briefly describe two methods other than `toString()` and `equals()` from the `Object` class.

1.36 Why is the contract for `equals()` so precise?

1.5.4 3D Shapes, Interfaces, and the `ThreeD` Interface

Earlier we saw how to extend abstract classes to create concrete classes. Here we continue to develop our shape hierarchy by extending the concrete class `Rectangle` to create `RectangularPrism`.

Our first two shapes (`Rectangle` and `Circle`) existed in two dimensions, while our new shape will exist in three dimensions. Figure 1.24 makes the notion of "extension" here seem very literal. The visualization also helps us to identify the additional field we have to provide for the new classes—each new shape needs an instance variable `depth` to store the extra dimension. At a minimum this requires an accessor method for each class to get the depth, and, since we provided mutator methods for the other dimensions, we probably should provide one here as well. Finally, we need a method to get the 3D shape's volume.

How is Rectangular Prism different from its parents?

Figure 1.24 Extending 2D shapes to 3D shapes.

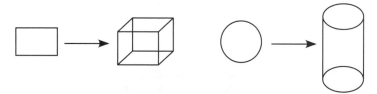

The **ThreeD** Interface

We would like to guarantee that all 3D shapes perform the 3D operations using the same syntax. We don't want, for example, one class using getVolume() and another using calculateVolume(). We know that defining abstract methods in abstract classes has the effect of forcing subclasses to adopt the syntax of these methods and provide implementations for them, forcing uniformity in the method interface across the subclasses (and their descendants).[9] It would be convenient to define a new abstract class ThreeD and have it define the syntax for these methods. Unfortunately, since Java does not support multiple inheritance, we cannot use this approach because RectangularPrism is already extending one class (Rectangle), so cannot extend another class.

Enforcing consistent interfaces

Java doesn't support multiple inheritance

We mentioned this problem in Section 1.3.2 and pointed out that Java's interface construct provides some of the power of multiple inheritance. A class can extend only one class or one abstract class, but it can implement as many interfaces as it needs. A Java interface can contain only class variables and abstract methods, so it cannot contain any instance variables or implemented methods.

Java's interface construct

Thus, the purpose of an interface is to specify the syntax and semantics for a set of operations and to ensure that the implementing classes provide these operations using exactly the same syntax. It is up to the class that uses an interface to implement the interface's methods with the intended semantics.

An interface defines a new type, just as a class does, and can appear in declarations and parameter lists. But an interface cannot be instantiated for the same reason an abstract class cannot—it is not fully implemented. A class that implements an interface becomes a subtype of the interface.

Occasionally an interface may have no body at all (!), in which case it is called a **marker interface** and its purpose is simply to act as a collection point for the methods of two or more interfaces or to state that the implementing class has a particular capability (the Cloneable and Serializable interfaces are examples).

Marker interface

Our solution to the 3D problem, then, is to define an interface containing the methods that our three-dimensional shapes will implement. Interface ThreeD is shown in Listing 1.10. All methods are automatically considered to be abstract, so do not need to be explicitly declared as such. The inheritance hierarchy of Figure 1.25 shows the UML notation for an interface. The dotted line with the hollow

---

[9]A related idea: manufacturers may make the specifications for a part in a system (a car, air conditioner, or computer for example) publicly available, allowing other companies to make the part. So long as a company follows the specifications, its part should be interchangeable with the same part made by other companies.

Listing 1.10 The `ThreeD` interface.

```
1    package gray.adts.shapes;
2
3    public interface ThreeD {
4       /**
5        * Get the depth of this <tt>ThreeD</tt> object.
6        * @return the depth of this <tt>ThreeD</tt> object
7        */
8       double getDepth();
9
10      /**
11       * Set the depth of this <tt>ThreeD</tt> object.
12       * If the argument <tt>theDepth</tt> is <= 0.0, it is ignored and
13       * the <tt>ThreeD</tt> object is unchanged.
14       * @param theDepth the new depth of this <tt>ThreeD</tt> object;
15       * must be > 0.0
16       */
17      void setDepth( double theDepth );
18
19      /**
20       * Get the volume of this <tt>ThreeD</tt> object.
21       * @return the volume of this <tt>ThreeD</tt> object
22       */
23      double getVolume();
24   }
```

Figure 1.25 The complete `Shape` inheritance hierarchy starting from `Object`.

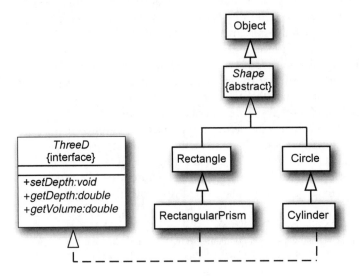

arrow represents a "realizes" relationship, which means that `RectangularPrism`
provides a realization (implementation) of the methods in the `ThreeD` interface.

The `RectangularPrism` Class

The definition of `RectangularPrism` is found in Listing 1.11. We don't anticipate
extending `RectangularPrism` to create any new classes, so it is tagged as `final`

Listing 1.11 The `RectanglularPrism` class.

```
1    package gray.adts.shapes;
2
3    /**
4     * A <tt>RectangularPrism</tt> has three dimensions: length,
5     * height and depth.
6     */
7    public final class RectangularPrism extends Rectangle          A class marked final
8                            _ implements Cloneable, ThreeD {       cannot be extended
9
10       private double depth;
11
12       /**
13        * Construct a <tt>RectangularPrism</tt> object using the
14        * default size for its dimensions.
15        */
16       public RectangularPrism() {
17          this(Shape.DEFAULT_SIZE, Shape.DEFAULT_SIZE,
18             Shape.DEFAULT_SIZE);
19       }
20
21       /**
22        * Construct a <tt>RectangularPrism</tt> object using the
23        * arguments. If an argument is <= 0, the default size
24        * specified in <tt>Shape</tt> is used instead.
25        * @param theLength length of this <tt>RectangularPrism</tt>;
26        *        must be > 0
27        * @param theHeight height of this <tt>RectangularPrism</tt>;
28        *        must be > 0
29        * @param theDepth depth of this <tt>RectangularPrism</tt>;
30        *        must be > 0
31        */
32       public RectangularPrism(  double theLength, double theHeight,
33                                 double theDepth ) {
34          setShapeName( "Rectangular Prism" );
35          if ( theLength <= 0.0 )
36             setLength( Shape.DEFAULT_SIZE );
```

```
37                  else
38                     setLength( theLength );
39
40                  if ( theHeight <= 0.0 )
41                     setHeight( Shape.DEFAULT_SIZE );
42                  else
43                     setHeight( theHeight );
44
45                  if ( theDepth <= 0.0 )
46                     setDepth( Shape.DEFAULT_SIZE );
47                  else
48                     setDepth( theDepth );
49         }
50
51         /**
52          * Get the surface area of this <tt>RectangularPrism</tt>.
53          * Overridden method inherited from Rectangle.
54          * @return the surface area of this <tt>RectanglularPrism</tt>
55          */
56         public double getSurfaceArea() {
57             return   super.getSurfaceArea() * 2          // front and back
58                         + this.depth * getHeight() * 2      // sides
59                         + this.depth * getLength() * 2;     // top and bottom
60         }
61
62         /**
63          * Get the perimeter of this <tt>RectangularPrism</tt>.
64          * Overridden method inherited from Rectangle.
65          * @return the perimeter of this <tt>RectanglularPrism</tt>
66          */
67         public double getPerimeter() {
68             return 2 * super.getPerimeter() + 4 * this.depth;
69         }
70
71         /* methods unique to RectPrism */
72
73         /**
74          * Get the volume of this <tt>RectangularPrism</tt>.
75          * @return the volume of this <tt>RectanglularPrism</tt>
76          */
77         public double getVolume() {
78             return this.depth * getLength() * getHeight();
79         }
80
81         /**
82          * Get the depth of this <tt>RectangularPrism</tt>.
83          * @return the depth of this <tt>RectanglularPrism</tt>
```

```
84        */
85       public double getDepth() {
86           return this.depth ;
87       }
88
89       /**
90        * Reset the depth of this <tt>RectangularPrism</tt>.
91        * If <tt>theDepth</tt> is <= 0, the dimension is unchanged.
92        * @param theDepth the new depth of this
93        *          <tt>RectangularPrism</tt>; must be > 0
94        */
95       public void setDepth( double theDepth ) {
96           if ( theDepth <= 0 )
97               return;
98           this.depth = theDepth;
99       }
100
101      /**
102       * Returns a <tt>String</tt> object representing this
103       * <tt>RectangularPrism</tt>'s value. Overridden from
104       * <tt>Object</tt>.
105       * @return a string representation of this object
106       */
107      public String toString() {
108          return super.toString() + ", depth = " + getDepth();
109      }
110
111      /**
112       * Returns <tt>true</tt> if and only if the argument is not
113       * <tt>null</tt> and is a <tt>RectangularPrism</tt> object that
114       * represents the same rectangular prism value as this object.
115       * The comparison is done based on the dimensions length,
116       * height and depth.
117       * @param o the object to compare with
118       * @return <tt>true</tt> if the <tt>RectangularPrism</tt>
119       * objects represent the same value; <tt>false</tt> otherwise.
120       */
121      public boolean equals( Object o ) {
122          if ( ( o == null ) ||
123                  ( !( o instanceof RectangularPrism ) ) )
124              return false;
125          return super.equals( o ) &&
126                  ((RectangularPrism)o).getDepth() == this.getDepth();
127      }
128  }
```

(Listing 1.11, line 7). The meaning of `final` is very straightforward: The entity to which `final` is applied cannot be modified in any way. Thus

The `final` modifier

- The value of a `final` variable cannot be changed once initialized.
- A `final` method cannot be overridden in a subclass.
- A `final` class cannot be extended to create a subclass.

The default constructor for `RectangularPrism` (lines 12–19) simply invokes the overloaded constructor, passing it the default value for the dimensions. The overloaded constructor (lines 21–49) uses the `protected` method `setShapeName()` inherited from `Shape` to set the shape name. This is necessary because `RectangularPrism`'s superclass constructor (from `Rectangle`) will set the shape name to "`Rectangle`" (which is close, but not quite right) and we cannot invoke the `Shape` constructor with the "`RectangularPrism`" shape name. So we need a way to directly set the name, but this is not a capability we want to give to clients of the class, so the method is designated `protected`, which excludes clients of `RectangularPrism`.

Methods `getSurfaceArea()`, `getPerimeter()`, `toString()` and `equals()` need to be overridden, but notice how we rely on the superclass methods by the same name to do part of the work (lines 57, 68, 108, and 125).

Finally, methods specified in the `ThreeD` interface (which distinguishes `RectangularPrism` from its superclass) are implemented: `getDepth()`, `setDepth()`, and `getVolume()` (lines 73–99).

Using `RectangularPrism`

The program in Listing 1.12 illustrates using the `RectangularPrism` class. To demonstrate, once again, the effect of inheritance, the program creates an instance of the `RectangularPrism` class (line 10) and uses it to access methods defined (or specified) in abstract class `Shape` (lines 19 and 25), class `Rectangle` (lines 14 and 15), and the interface `ThreeD` (lines 16 and 27), as well as an overloaded method inherited originally from `Object` and overridden in each of the `Shape` classes (line 23). The output generated by the program is shown in Figure 1.26.

Listing 1.12 Using the `RectangularPrism` class (output is Figure 1.26).

```
1    package shapeExamples;
2
3    import gray.adts.shapes.*;
4    import java.text.DecimalFormat;
5    import javax.swing.JOptionPane;
6
7    public class ShapeEx4 {
8
9        public static void main ( String [] args ) {
10           RectangularPrism rp1 = new RectangularPrism();
11           DecimalFormat prec3 = new DecimalFormat( "#0.000" );
```

```
12            String output;
13
14            rp1.setHeight( 5.3 );  // method from Rectangle
15            rp1.setLength( 6.6 );  // method from Rectangle
16            rp1.setDepth( 7.2 );   // method from RectangularPrism
17
18            // getShapename() is inherited from Shape
19            output = "rp1 is a " + rp1.getShapeName() + "\n\n";
20
21            // toString() is originally from Object and overridden
22            // in the various shape classes.
23            output += "rp1 = " + rp1.toString() + "\n";
24            output += "rp1 surface area = "
25                    +  prec3.format( rp1.getSurfaceArea() ) + "\n";
26            output += "rp1 volume = "
27                    +  prec3.format( rp1.getVolume() ) + "\n\n";
28
29            JOptionPane.showMessageDialog( null, output,
30                                    "3D shape example",
31                                    JOptionPane.INFORMATION_MESSAGE );
32            System.exit( 0 );
33        }
34    }
```

Figure 1.26 Using the `RectangularPrism` class (code is in Listings 1.10, 1.11, and 1.12).

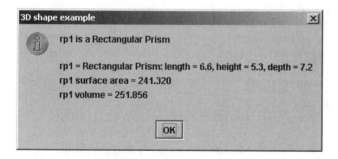

SUMMING UP

An abstract class is a class that has the `abstract` keyword in the class header. Typically this means that one or more of the class's methods are not implemented and so are also declared to be `abstract`. An abstract class cannot be instantiated because it is not completely defined (its abstract methods have no implementation). The expectation is that subclasses of an abstract class will provide definitions for the inherited abstract methods. Making the methods abstract in the abstract class allows subclasses to provide their own type-specific implementations, but guarantees that all implementing subclasses adhere to the same syntax for the inherited methods. A concrete class is one that provides implementations for *all* its methods, so *can* be instantiated.

An interface is like an abstract class except that *none* of the methods in an interface are implemented. An interface defines a new type, just as a class does, but an interface cannot be instantiated. The type defined by an interface can appear in declarations and parameter lists. A class that implements an interface becomes a subtype of the interface. A marker interface has no methods at all and simply indicates that an implementing class has a certain capability; java.io.Serializable is an example. In Java, one class may extend only one other class or abstract class, but may implement more than one interface.

CHECKPOINT

1.37 How are an interface and an abstract class similar and different?

1.38 Since a square is a specialization of a rectangle and a cube is a specialization of a rectangular prism, it seems logical to extend the shape hierarchy in Figure 1.25 with the classes Square and Cube.

    a. Draw a UML diagram similar to that in Figure 1.25 for this new hierarchy.

    b. Why should we resist the temptation to add these new classes?

1.39 Add an isSquare() method to the Rectangle class.

1.5.5 Polymorphism with Shapes

Our last experiment with shapes provides another look at polymorphism. In Section 1.4 we said that, using the substitution principle, if we write generic code in terms of a class that is at the root of a hierarchy of related classes, then we can substitute instances of the subclasses for instances of the superclass (root), and the code will work properly.

If we need to write a polymorphic piece of code dealing with shapes, we must look at the root of our shapes hierarchy—the abstract class Shape.[10] The methods available to us are those found in Shape and those inherited from Object. The program in Listing 1.13 makes use of several of these methods. It begins by creating instances of four kinds of shapes (lines 10–14)[11] and an array of Shapes (line 15) that is then populated (lines 20–23) with the four kinds of shapes. Assignments such as

```
bunchOshapes[1] = circle;
```

---

[10]Phrased another way, if I want to talk about all kinds of shapes, I must do so through their common denominator, which, in an inheritance hierarchy, will always be the class from which all the classes of interest are descended. In this case, that is Shape.

[11]The Cylinder class used in the example is another 3D shape. It extends Circle and implements ThreeD. You are asked to provide the implementation as an exercise.

Listing 1.13 Polymorphism with the **Shapes** hierarchy of classes.

```
1    package shapeExamples;
2
3    import gray.adts.shapes.*;
4    import java.text.DecimalFormat;
5    import javax.swing.JOptionPane;
6
7    public class PolyEx {
8
9        public static void main ( String [] args ) {
10           Rectangle rectangle = new Rectangle( 3.4, 4.5 );
11           Circle circle = new Circle(4.2);
12           RectangularPrism rectPrism =
13                             new RectangularPrism( 5.3, 6.6, 7.2 );
14           Cylinder cylinder = new Cylinder(3.5, 19.5 );
15           Shape [] bunchOshapes = new Shape[4];
16           DecimalFormat prec3 = new DecimalFormat( "#0.000" );
17           String output = "\n";
18
19           // populate the array of shapes with some real shapes
20           bunchOshapes[0] = rectangle;
21           bunchOshapes[1] = circle;
22           bunchOshapes[2] = rectPrism;
23           bunchOshapes[3] = cylinder;
24
25           for ( int i = 0; i < bunchOshapes.length; i++ ) {
26               output += bunchOshapes[i].toString() + "\n";
27               output += "\tsurface area = "
28                       + prec3.format( bunchOshapes[i].getSurfaceArea() )
29                       + "\n";
30               output += "\tperimeter = "
31                       + prec3.format( bunchOshapes[i].getPerimeter() )
32                       + "\n\n";;
33           }
34
35           JOptionPane.showMessageDialog( null, output,
36                                 "Polymorphic shapes example",
37                                 JOptionPane.INFORMATION_MESSAGE );
38           System.exit( 0 );
39       }
40   }
```

OUTPUT

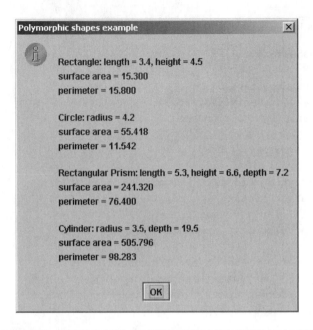

Polymorphic shapes example

Rectangle: length = 3.4, height = 4.5
surface area = 15.300
perimeter = 15.800

Circle: radius = 4.2
surface area = 55.418
perimeter = 11.542

Rectangular Prism: length = 5.3, height = 6.6, depth = 7.2
surface area = 241.320
perimeter = 76.400

Cylinder: radius = 3.5, depth = 19.5
surface area = 505.796
perimeter = 98.283

OK

---

are syntactically correct and meaningful because a `Circle` "is a kind of" `Shape`. As this example illustrates, assigning a reference of a subclass to an instance of a super-class requires no special notation. This is often referred to as an **upcast** because you are moving "up" the type hierarchy. Upcasts do not require explicit casts. Going the other direction, from a superclass to a subclass is called a **downcast** and requires an explicit cast, as we saw in the implementation of the `equals()` method for `Rectangle` and `Circle` in Section 1.5.3. Downcasts always involve a runtime check that the cast is appropriate. These casts may fail, resulting in a runtime error.

The `for` loop (lines 25 to 33) indexes through the array, collecting the general information about each shape provided by the `toString()` method, as well as its surface area and perimeter. This works for two reasons. First, the methods being invoked are defined in each of the shape classes. For example, `Circle` implements the `getSurfaceArea()` method, so `Circle` objects can accept `getSurfaceArea()` messages (as can the other specific shapes we implemented). Second, each object stores information about its true type, which the runtime system can access when a message is to be sent to the object. So the runtime system is able to dynamically bind a reference to the correct target object. In the example, when `i` is 2, `bunchOshapes[i]` on line 26 actually references a `RectangularPrism` object (see line 22). The runtime system will determine this by examining the object at execution time and will send the `getSurfaceArea()` message to that specific object. The output of our sample polymorphic program is shown at the end of Listing 1.13.

Why does this work?

Why can't we use any of the "specialized" methods from the subclasses (such as `getLength()` from `Rectangle`, `getRadius()` from `Circle`, or `getVolume()` from `RectangularPrism`) in the loop? The answer is that these methods are indeed special to the particular classes where they are defined and so are not found in *all* shape classes. We cannot send a `getRadius()` message to a `Rectangle` object, because a `Rectangle` object does not have a method to receive such a message. Of course, this is because rectangles don't know about radii! Similarly, two-dimensional shapes don't have a volume, so it would be pointless to have a call to `getVolume()` in the loop. What would the `Circle` and `Rectangle` objects do with it?[12]

CHECKPOINT

1.40 Add a constructor to the `RectangularPrism` class that initializes a `RectangularPrism` object given a `Rectangle` object and a depth. The constructor header would look like this:

```
public RectangularPrism ( Rectangle r, double d )
```

1.41 Add a call to `bunchOshapes[i].getLength()` to the for loop of Listing 1.13. Try to recompile and run the program. When is the error caught? What is the error?

■ 1.6 Java Generic Types

We have said that a class or interface defines a new data type and that you can declare variables of this new type. Java generic types take this a step further, allowing you to parameterize a type. Consider a class `Pair<T>` that stores a pair of elements of some yet to be specified type `T`. We say that `Pair<T>` is the **generic type** (also called a parameterized type), `<T>` is the **formal type parameter list** for `Pair`, and `T` is the **type variable** (see Figure 1.27), which acts as a type placeholder and will be replaced by a type argument when the generic type is instantiated. We say that `Pair<T>` is generic because the actual type stored by `Pair` is left unspecified until an actual `Pair` is declared.

Generic type

Figure 1.27 Format for a generic (parameterized) type and instantiation of a generic type.

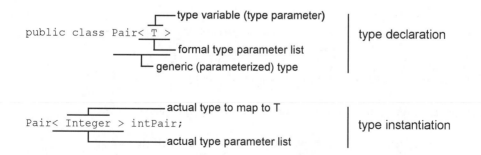

---

[12]Technically this is a moot point since the compiler will quickly inform you that there is no method `getVolume()` defined in `Circle` or `Rectangle` or their ancestors, so this is an error.

The advantage of using generic types is that it allows the compiler to do more thorough type checking on your code, which cuts down on the type errors you can get at run time when a class stores elements of one type and your code attempts to access them as elements of some other type. This also cuts down on the number of explicit type casts you have to do. We will use generics quite a bit when we look at collection types in the rest of the book. Additional features of generic types will be presented as we need them.

Generic types allow the compiler to do better type checking

1.6.1 Using a Generic Type

Listing 1.14 illustrates how `Pair<T>` can be used. When you declare a variable to be of a generic type, you supply actual data types to map to the type variables in the generic type's formal type parameter list. Since `Pair<T>` has a single type variable, we must supply a single reference type (the actual type cannot be a primitive type). For example, to declare a `Pair<T>` variable that stores a pair of `Integer` objects, you would do:

```
Pair<Integer> intPair; // intPair can store a pair of Integers
```

Listing 1.14 Using `Pair<T>` to create a pair of `Integer`s and a pair of `String`s.

```
1    /**
2     * Illustrate the use of a generic type.
3     */
4    public class GenericsEx {
5        public static void main ( String args[] ) {
6            Pair<String> stringPair = new Pair<String>( "string", "Pair" );
7            Pair<Integer> intPair;
8
9            intPair = new Pair<Integer>( new Integer( 1 ), new Integer( 2 ));
10
11           System.out.println( "intPair is: " + intPair );
12           System.out.println( "stringPair is: " + stringPair );
13
14           intPair.swapElements();
15           System.out.println( "\nAfter swapping elements, intPair is " +
16                               intPair );
17
18           intPair.setFirstElement( new Integer( -1 ) );
19
20           stringPair.setSecondElement( "Generic types are useful" );
21
22           System.out.println( "\nThe pairs after some resetting: " );
23           System.out.println( "\tintPair is: " + intPair );
24           System.out.println( "\tstringPair is: " + stringPair );
25
```

```
26          Integer intElement1 = intPair.getFirstElement();
27          String stringElement1 = stringPair.getFirstElement();
28
29          System.out.println( "\nintElement1 is " + intElement1 +
30                              " and stringElement1 is " + stringElement1 );
31      }
32  }
```

OUTPUT

```
intPair is: < 1, 2 >
stringPair is: < string, Pair >

After swapping elements, intPair is < 2, 1 >

The pairs after some resetting:
   intPair is: < -1, 1 >
   stringPair is: < string, Generic types are useful >

intElement1 is -1 and stringElement1 is string
```

Here `Integer` is the **actual type parameter** since it is the actual type that will be stored by this instance of `Pair<T>`. Variable `intPair` doesn't reference anything yet, so we have to instantiate a `Pair<Integer>` object. To instantiate a generic type you need to provide the actual type parameters again when applying the new operator to one of the type's constructors (the definition of `Pair<T>` is in Listing 1.16). For the `Pair<Integer>` example from above, the instantiation would be done as follows:

Actual type parameter

```
intPair = new Pair<Integer>( new Integer( 1 ), new Integer( 2 ) );
```

This creates an instance of `Pair<Integer>` that stores two `Integer` objects. We could combine the two lines:

```
Pair<Integer> intPair = new Pair<Integer>( new Integer( 1 ), new Integer( 2 ) );
```

Note that once a variable of a generic type has been declared and instantiated (lines 6, 7, and 9 in Listing 1.14), you use the variable in the same way you would any other object (see lines 11, 14, and 18 for example).

It is important to understand that `stringPair` (line 6) and `intPair` (line 7) are of *different types*: `intPair` is of type `Pair<Integer>` and `stringPair` is of type `Pair<String>`. Forgetting this can lead to writing code that will not compile (recall I said generics allow for stronger type checking by the compiler). Listing 1.15 illustrates some type errors:

- *Line 6–7.* `stringPair` is declared to be of type `Pair<String>`, but is instantiated as `Pair<Integer>`. The two type parameters do not match.

Listing 1.15 One advantage of generic types is that the compiler can do a better job of type checking. This example is rife with type errors, which the compiler will catch.

```
1     /**
2      * Illustrate type checking with generic types.
3      */
4     public class GenericsTypeCheckingEx {
5         public static void main ( String args[] ) {
6             Pair<String> stringPair =
7                         new Pair<Integer>( "string", "Pair" );  // ERROR
8             Pair<Integer> intPair;
9             intPair = new Pair<Integer>( "a string!",           // ERROR
10                                        new Integer( 2 ) );
12            intPair.setSecondElement( new Date() );             // ERROR
13
14            StringBuffer sb = stringPair.firstElement();        // ERROR
15        }
16    }
```

- *Lines 8–10.* intPair is declared to be of type Pair<Integer>, so both arguments to the constructor need to be of type Integer.
- *Line 12.* Since intPair was declared to store Integers (line 8), its mutator methods expect an Integer as the argument type.
- *Line 14.* stringPair stores instances of type String, so its accessor methods will return String references, but sb is of type StringBuffer, generating another type error.

1.6.2 Defining a Generic Type

As you might expect, the definition of a generic type is a little different from that for a nongeneric type. Let's start by looking at where the type variable, T, appears in Pair<T>'s definition in Listing 1.16:

- Class header (line 6): when instantiated, the client must provide a single reference type to map to T
- Data field declarations (lines 7 and 8): Pair<T> stores two elements of the same data type, identified as T
- Parameter types in method headers (lines 18, 48, and 61)
- Method return type (lines 29 and 37)
- Local variable within a method (line 71)

Listing 1.16 The generic type `Pair<T>`.

```
1    /**
2     * A pair consists of two elements of the same type. This class
3     * illustrates the definition of a generic type with type
4     * parameter <tt>T</tt>.
5     */
6    public class Pair<T> {
7        private T firstElement;
8        private T secondElement;
9
10       /**
11        * Construct an instance of a <tt>Pair</tt> initialized to the
12        * given elements.
13        * @param e1 the first element of this pair
14        * @param e2 the second element of this pair
15        * @throws NullPointerException if either <tt>e1</tt> or
16        * <tt>e2</tt> is <tt>null</tt>.
17        */
18       public Pair( T e1, T e2 ){
19           if ( ( e1 == null ) || ( e2 == null ) )
20               throw new NullPointerException();
21           this.firstElement = e1;
22           this.secondElement = e2;
23       }
24
25       /**
26        * Return the value of the first element of this pair.
27        * @return the first element of this pair
28        */
29       public T getFirstElement(){
30           return this.firstElement;
31       }
32
33       /**
34        * Return the value of the second element of this pair.
35        * @return the second element of this pair
36        */
37       public T getSecondElement(){
38           return this.secondElement;
39       }
40
41       /**
42        * Set the first element of this pair to the new value.
43        * @param newFirst the new value for the first element of
```

```
44          * this pair
45          * @throws NullPointerException if <tt>newFirst</tt> is
46          * <tt>null</tt>.
47          */
48         public void setFirstElement( T newFirst ){
49             if ( newFirst == null )
50                 throw new NullPointerException();
51             this.firstElement = newFirst;
52         }
53
54         /**
55          * Set the second element of this pair to the new value.
56          * @param newSecond the new value for the second element of
57          * this pair
58          * @throws NullPointerException if <tt>newSecond</tt> is
59          * <tt>null</tt>.
60          */
61         public void setSecondElement( T newSecond ){
62             if ( newSecond == null )
63                 throw new NullPointerException();
64             this.secondElement = newSecond;
65         }
66
67         /**
68          * Swap the two elements.
69          */
70         public void swapElements(){
71             T temp = this.firstElement;
72             this.firstElement = this.secondElement;
73             this.secondElement = temp;
74         }
75
76         /**
77          * Returns a string representation of the object: this is
78          * the string representation of element 1 followed by the
79          * string representation of element 2.
80          * @returns a string representation of the object.
81          */
82         public String toString(){
83             return "< " + this.firstElement + ", "
84                     + this.secondElement " >";
85         }
86     }
```

1.6.3 Generic Types and Erasure

In instantiating `Pair<Integer>`, it is convenient to think of all appearances of `T` within `Pair<T>` as being replaced by `Integer`. As we will see in a moment, this is *not* what the Java compiler does, but this mental model provides an intuitive way to think about the semantics of generic types. For example, because `intPair` in Listing 1.14 is of type `Pair<Integer>`, you can imagine that the `firstElement` field of Listing 1.16 (line 7) will be of type `Integer`, so on line 26 of Listing 1.14, when `intPair` is sent a `getFirstElement()` message, it will return a reference to the `Integer` object stored in the `firstElement` field, and if we wanted to change what is stored as `intPair`'s first element, we would have to provide an `Integer` reference as the parameter to `setFirstElement()` (see line 18 of Listing 1.14 and lines 41–52 of Listing 1.16).

So, what does the Java compiler do with the type parameter in a generic class? Through a process called **erasure**, the type parameter is removed and all occurrences of the formal type parameter in the class are replaced by what is called the **upper bound** of the actual type parameter. By default, the upper bound is the class `Object`; we'll see a more sophisticated example in Chapter 4. So, in the case of `Pair<T>`, the compiler will actually remove the type parameter section and substitute `Object` wherever it finds `T` in `Pair`. Listing 1.17 shows a portion of `Pair<T>` once this substitution has been made (the substitutions are in **boldface**).

Type erasure

Listing 1.17 A portion of `Pair<T>` with the type variable `T` substituted with `Object` as the result of erasure.

```
1    /**
2     * A pair consists of two elements of the same type. This class
3     * illustrates the definition of a generic type with type
4     * parameter <tt>T</tt>.
5     */
6    public class Pair {
7        private Object firstElement;
8        private Object secondElement;
9
10       /**
11        * Construct an instance of a <tt>Pair</tt> initialized to the
12        * given elements.
13        * @param e1 the first element of this pair
14        * @param e2 the second element of this pair
15        * @throws NullPointerException if either <tt>e1</tt> or
16        * <tt>e2</tt> is <tt>null</tt>.
17        */
18       public Pair( Object e1, Object e2 ){
19           if ( ( e1 == null ) || ( e2 == null ) )
```

```
20              throw new NullPointerException();
21          this.firstElement = e1;
22          this.secondElement = e2;
23      }
24
25      /**
26       * Return the value of the first element of this pair.
27       * @return the first element of this pair
28       */
29      public Object getFirstElement(){
30          return this.firstElement;
31      }
32
33      /**
34       * Return the value of the second element of this pair.
35       * @return the second element of this pair
36       */
37      public Object getSecondElement(){
38          return this.secondElement;
39      }
40
41      /**
42       * Set the first element of this pair to the new value.
43       * @param newFirst the new value of the first element of
44       * this pair
45       * @throws NullPointerException if <tt>newFirst</tt> is
46       * <tt>null</tt>.
47       */
48      public void setFirstElement( Object newFirst ){
49          if ( newFirst == null )
50              throw new NullPointerException();
51
52          this.firstElement = newFirst;
53      }
    . . .
```

Why does this work? Recall that Object is at the root of the inheritance hierarchy—*all* classes can claim Object as an ancestor and through the substitution principle can be referenced using an Object reference. So I can store an Integer reference or a String reference (or any kind of reference) in firstElement and secondElement of type Object.

The next question is how does erasure affect the code that *uses* a generic class? What does the compiler do there? First, the extra type information is used to do type checking. You saw an example of the kinds of type errors the compiler can catch in Listing 1.15. Once the type checking is done, the generic syntax is no longer needed and is stripped out by the compiler. For example, Listing 1.18 shows the result of erasure on GenericsEx from Listing 1.14 (the affected lines are shown in boldface). Note the declaration and instantiation of stringPair and intPair on lines 6, 7, and 9. Also, remember that after erasure is done on Pair<T>, it is storing Object references, so when an element is retrieved via getFirstElement() or getSecondElement(), it will always be an *Object* reference that is returned.

Listing 1.18 GenericsEX with the generic types stripped away by the compiler.

```
1    /**
2     * Illustrate the use of a generic type.
3     */
4    public class GenericsEx {
5        public static void main( String args[] ) {
6            Pair stringPair = new Pair( "string", "Pair" );
7            Pair intPair;
8
9            intPair = new Pair( new Integer( 1 ), new Integer( 2 ));
10
11            System.out.println( "intPair is: " + intPair );
12            System.out.println( "stringPair is: " + stringPair );
13
14            intPair.swapElements();
15            System.out.println( "\nAfter swapping elements, intPair is " +
16                                intPair );
17
18            intPair.setFirstElement( new Integer( -1 ) );
19
20            stringPair.setSecondElement( "Generic types are useful" );
21
22            System.out.println( "\nThe pairs after some resetting: " );
23            System.out.println( "\tintPair is: " + intPair );
24            System.out.println( "\tstringPair is: " + stringPair );
25
26            Integer intElement1 = (Integer) intPair.firstElement();
27            String stringElement1 = (String) stringPair.firstElement();
28
29            System.out.println( "\nintElement1 is " + intElement1 +
30                                " and stringElement1 is " + stringElement1 );
31        }
32    }
```

This reference must be cast back to its original type before it can be used as an instance of that type. This is seen on line 26, where the first element of `intPair` must be cast back to an `Integer`, and on line 27, where the first element of `stringPair` must be cast to a `String`. Now, the neat part is that the compiler does all this for you. It is essential that you understand that you would write the code in Listing 1.14 and the *compiler* would produce the "erased" version in Listing 1.18.

Casting Object references

SUMMING UP

A generic type (parameterized type) allows you to specify what actual type of data a container will hold. A generic type definition includes a formal type parameter list that contains one or more type variables. These type variables act as placeholders for the actual type, which is specified when the generic type is instantiated. Type variables may appear as the data field for the class, in method parameters and return types, and as local variables to methods.

Through a process called erasure, the formal type parameter is removed and all occurrences of it in the class are replaced by the upper bound of the actual type parameter supplied where the generic type is instantiated. By default this upper bound is `Object`.

CHECKPOINT

1.42 Identify and describe the type errors in the following code.

```
1    public class GenericsTypeCheckingEx {
2        public static void main ( String args[] ) {
3            Pair<Date> dPair = new Pair<Date>( "10/1/2004", new Date() );
4            Pair<Item> itemPair new Pair( new Item(), new Item() );
5
6            dPair<Date>.swapElements();
7            System.out.println( "item elements are " + itemPair.toString() );
8
9            dPair.setFirstElement( new Circle() );
10           Object o = itemPair.getSecondElement();
11       }
12   }
```

1.43 Give the statement to declare a variable `twoRectangles` that stores a pair of `Rectangles`, then show how to instantiate `twoRectangles` to store a pair of `Rectangles`.

1.44 What is the advantage of generic types?

EXERCISES

Paper and Pencil

1. Show the class skeletons similar to those given in Section 1.3 for the class diagram in Figure 1.28.

2. Give a UML diagram for a `Clock` class that has a `Button` to set the hour, another `Button` to set the minute, and a `DigitalDisplay` to display the time.

3. What does the `InterestCheckingAccount` class of Figure 1.14 inherit from the `Account` class?

4. What do you expect will be output by the program below (available on the book's Website)? Run the program. What is actually output? If there is a difference between what you expected and what was generated, explain the difference.

```
import java.text.DecimalFormat;
import javax.swing.JOptionPane;
import gray.adts.shapes.*;

public class ShapeQ1 {
    public static void main ( String [] args ) {
        DecimalFormat p3 = new DecimalFormat( "#0.000" );
        String output;
```

Figure 1.28 Two composition classes.

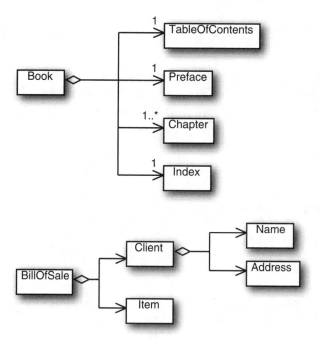

```
    RectangularPrism rp1 = new RectangularPrism( 4, 5, 6 );
    Rectangle rect1 = rp1;
    // getShapename() is inherited from Shape
    output = "rp1 is a " + rp1.getShapeName() + "\n";
    output += "rect1 is a " + rect1.getShapeName() + "\n\n";
    // toString() is originally from Object & overridden
    // in the various shape classes.
    output += "rp1 = " + rp1.toString() + "\n";
    output += "rp1 surface area = "
            +  p3.format( rp1.getSurfaceArea() ) + "\n";
    output += "rp1 volume = "
            +  p3.format( rp1.getVolume() ) + "\n\n";
    output += "rect1 = " + rect1.toString() + "\n";
    output += "rect1 surface area = "
            +  p3.format( rect1.getSurfaceArea() ) + "\n";
    JOptionPane.showMessageDialog( null, output,
                            "Rectangle-RectangularPrism exercise",
                            JOptionPane.INFORMATION_MESSAGE );
    System.exit( 0 );
    }
}
```

Testing and Debugging

1. What is wrong with overriding Object's equals() method in the Circle class as follows?

```
public boolean equals ( Circle c ) {
    // body goes here
}
```

2. The program below is available on the Website for this book. What do you expect will be output by the program? Run the program. What is actually output? Why is the cast in the assignment to c2 necessary? Why don't we need a cast for the assignment to s?

```
import javax.swing.JOptionPane;
import gray.adts.shapes.*;

public class ShapeCylEx {
    public static void main ( String [] args ) {
        String output;
        Cylinder c1 = new Cylinder( 3.5, 7.2 );
        Cylinder c2;
        Shape s = c1;
        c2 = (Cylinder)s;
        output = "c1 = " + c1.toString() + "\n";
        output += "c2 = " + c2.toString() + "\n";
```

```
        JOptionPane.showMessageDialog( null, output,
                              "shape-cylinder cast exercise",
                              JOptionPane.INFORMATION_MESSAGE );
        System.exit( 0 );
    }
}
```

3. Identify and describe the type errors in the following code.

```
1    public class GenericStuff {
2        public static void main ( String args[] ) {
3            Pair<Player> pPair = new Pair<Player>( new Player( "Tom" ),
4                                          new Player( "Rohal" ) );
5            Pair<Rental> rentalPair new Pair<Item>( new Rental(), new Item() );
6            Rental r1 = Rental(), rental2 = new Rental();
7
8            pPair.swapElements();
9            System.out.println( "Rental elements are " +
10           rentalPair<Rental>.toString() );
11           rentalPair.swapElements( rental1, rental2 );
12           Object o = rentalPair.getFirstElement();
13       }
14   }
```

Modifying the Code

1. Create a `Cylinder` class that extends `Circle` following the model of `RectangularPrism`.

2. Add an `isACube()` method to the `RectangularPrism` class.

3. Add a method to `Pair<T>` that implements the following description.

```
/**
 * Determine if either element of this <tt>Pair</tt> is equal to the argument.
 * @param e the object to compare to the elements of this <tt>Pair</tt>
 * @return the first element of this <tt>Pair</tt> found equal to <tt>e</tt>,
 *     <tt>null</tt> if neither element is equal to <tt>e</tt>.
 */
T elementEqualTo( T e )
```

ON THE WEB

Additional study material is available at Addison-Wesley's Website at http://www.aw.com/cssupport. This material includes the following:

- Study Guide Exercises
- Answers to CheckPoint Problems
- Additional exercises

Error Handling, Software Testing, and Program Efficiency

2

CHAPTER OUTLINE

2.1 Error Handling with Exceptions
2.2 Software Testing
2.3 Analysis and Measurement of Algorithms
Exercises
On the Web: Study Guide Exercises; Answers to CheckPoint Problems; Additional Exercises

This chapter introduces three characteristics of applications of interest to us: robustness, correctness, and efficiency. By **robustness** I mean the program's ability to spot exceptional conditions (problems) at runtime and either deal with them so that the program can continue, or it can shutdown gracefully with an explanation for the early and unexpected termination. Java's approach is to throw an **exception** when a problem is encountered at runtime. Section 2.1 introduces Java's exception-handling mechanism. We'll look at the conditions under which exceptions can occur, how to throw and handle exceptions, how to use exceptions to improve the error checking and reporting your code does, and how to create your own exception classes.

The word **correctness** can have many meanings; here I use it loosely to mean that a program does what it is intended to do. Section 2.2 introduces the very important area of software testing as a way of verifying that actual behavior matches intended behavior. This discussion will dovetail nicely with the presentation of exception handling. Despite sincere effort, a program can still contain logic errors (bugs). With good error checking and reporting, exceptions can be used at runtime to handle some of those errors. We will see how to produce **test plans** (also called

oracles) for your classes, then how to implement them using a Java testing framework called JUnit.

The **efficiency** of a program is a measure of its time and space requirements. Understandably, if we have our 'druthers, we would choose more efficient code over less efficient code. In Section 2.3 we look at how to determine the space and time complexities of algorithms using asymptotic analysis. As we look at the implementations of collections and associated algorithms in the remaining chapters, we will always consider the question: What is the cost? We'll also look briefly at how we can time our algorithms. Actual time measurements will provide insights into the choices we have for implementing collection types.

■ 2.1 Error Handling with Exceptions

2.1.1 What Can Go Wrong with Your Program?

Successful compilation of a program only indicates that the program is syntactically correct. What can go wrong at runtime? Some of the problems a program can encounter at runtime are internal to the program and are under the control of the programmer. Others, though, belong to the environment in which the program runs and are outside programmer control. A third area that can produce problems is at the boundary between a program and the outside world, that is, input and output (I/O). This is summarized in Table 2.1.[1]

Table 2.1 Categories of problems that a program can experience at runtime.

Problem	Description
Logic error	The program does something unintended, such as allow an array index to go beyond the bounds of the array or try to reference a null pointer. The worst kind of logic error goes undetected by either the Java Virtual Machine (JVM) or your code, producing incorrect results, which may or may not be easily identifiable ("Mr. Snively, here are the budget projections you asked for. They look right to me.") Of course this isn't supposed to happen and with good design, careful programming, and thoughtful testing, you can reduce the likelihood of these bugs entering your code. Section 2.2 looks at software testing.
Environment error	Programs run in an environment supplied by the operating system. This includes memory and, in the case of Java, the Java Virtual Machine, which executes the Java byte code from the compiled version of your application. Problems in the environment are outside the programmer's control and there is not much a program can do to correct them.
Input/output errors	Applications can get their input from a variety of sources (mouse, keyboard, network, disk, etc.) and can send their output to a variety of destinations (terminal, disk, network, etc.). An I/O resource can malfunction while being used (the network goes down, a server or disk crashes, etc.) or access to a resource may be denied (resource may be unavailable or protected). Sometimes a program can recover from these kinds of problems and go on to do useful work.

---

[1]There are, of course, other kinds of problems that can arise at runtime.

Let's look at an example to get a feel for what can go wrong. The program in Listing 2.1 simply computes the quotient of two integers and outputs the result. The program creates a `Scanner` object (line 18) to read from standard input (the keyboard). The main loop (lines 23–34) reads in two integers (lines 25–26) from the keyboard and calls `computeQuotient()`. There are a couple of places where things can go wrong.

Listing 2.1 An illustration of code that can generate exceptions. Sample output for `ArithmeticException` is in Figure 2.1 and `InputMismatchException` is in Figure 2.3.

```
1    import java.util.Scanner;
2
3    /**
4     * Illustration of the use of exceptions.
5     */
6    public class ExceptionEx {
7
8      /**
9       * Computer the quotient of numerator / denominator. Assumes
10      * denominator is not 0.
11      */
12     public static int computeQuotient( int numerator,
13                                        int denominator ) {
14        return numerator / denominator;
15     }
16
17     public static void main( String []args ) {
18        Scanner kbd = new Scanner( System.in );
19        int x, y, result;
20        boolean done = false;
21        String answer;
22
23        while ( !done ) {
24           System.out.print( "\nEnter two integers:" );
25           x = kbd.nextInt();
26           y = kbd.nextInt();
27           result = computeQuotient( x, y );
28           System.out.printf( "%d / %d = %d\n\n", x, y, result );
29
30           System.out.print( "Execute again? (y/n): " );
31           answer = kbd.next();
32           // we are done if user gives us anything but y or Y
33           done = !( answer.equals( "y" ) || answer.equals( "Y" ) );
34        }
35     }
36  }
```

First, consider what happens when the divisor is 0. The introductory comment (lines 8–11) for `computeQuotient()` says quite plainly that the method assumes that denominator is *not* 0, but it does not check that this is so. This is of some concern because integer division by zero is illegal in Java and can generate an exception, as shown in the output in Figure 2.1. The user enters the values 8 and 0, which are passed to `computeQuotient()`. The JVM will detect the attempt to divide by 0 on line 14 and will report the error by throwing an `ArithmeticException`.

When an exception occurs, an exception object is created, which stores information about the nature of the exception—which exception occurred and where it occurred. The JVM then looks for a block of code to catch and handle the exception (we'll see how to do this in Section 2.1.3). If there is no such block in the method that threw the exception, that method is exited immediately (it does *not* run to completion) and the JVM looks for an exception-handling block in the method's caller. This continues until either an exception-handling block is found within the program or the exception gets all the way back to the JVM. Figure 2.2 illustrates this behavior.

> When the JVM encounters a problem it creates an exception object describing the problem

By default, a program terminates when an exception occurs, displaying some information about the exception that was thrown and the place of the infraction.

Figure 2.1 `ArithmeticException` is thrown as a result of an attempt to divide by 0. User input is given in **boldface**.

```
Enter two integers: 8 0
Exception in thread "main" java.lang.ArithmeticException: / by zero
        at ExceptionEx.computeQuotient(ExceptionEx.java:14)
        at ExceptionEx.main(ExceptionEx.java:27)
```

Figure 2.2 When an exception occurs, the JVM searches back through the method call chain for a handler for the exception.

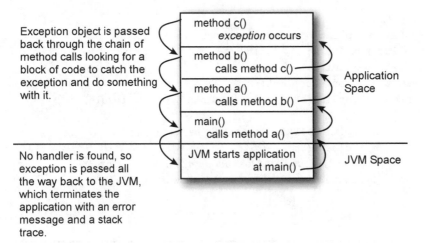

Exception object is passed back through the chain of method calls looking for a block of code to catch the exception and do something with it.

No handler is found, so exception is passed all the way back to the JVM, which terminates the application with an error message and a stack trace.

method c()
exception occurs

method b()
calls method c()

method a()
calls method b()

main()
calls method a()

JVM starts application at main()

Application Space

JVM Space

We will see shortly how to alter the default behavior, but, for now, our program makes no attempt to recover from such errors, so the program is terminated and a **stack trace** is generated, telling us what happened and where.

A stack trace is simply a trace of the method calls that were made up to the method that generated the exception, including the line number (when known) where the method calls were made and the line number of the statement that generated the exception. So, reading the output in Figure 2.1 from top to bottom, you see that the program generated an arithmetic exception (with a detail message "/ by zero" at the end of the line indicating the specific nature of the problem) where the error was generated (line 14 in computeQuotient() in file ExceptionEx.java), and where computeQuotient() was called in main() (line 27). Pretty cool!

The JVM generates a stack trace when an exception occurs

Figure 2.3 gives the output generated for a second problem. This time the problem is that on lines 25 and 26 of Listing 2.1, the Scanner expects to read in character sequences from the keyboard that it can convert into ints. What happens when the user supplies non-numeric input? There is a mismatch in the input between what is expected and what is given, generating an InputMismatchException. The stack trace is shown in Figure 2.3. As you can see, the JVM does not know the line number where several of these methods were called, so it marks them "Unknown source." However, it knows that the call to nextInt() that generated the exception occurred on line 26 of main() in file ExceptionEx.java.

Exception detail messages provide additional information about the cause of the exception

So, how do you know what statements might generate exceptions? Some of it you learn by reading books, some of it you learn from experience, but most of it you learn by reading the documentation for a class. A method should indicate what exceptions it throws and under what conditions it throws them. There should be few surprises!

Document the use of exceptions in the javadoc comments

Lastly, you need to learn how to look at stack traces to help develop your debugging skills.

2.1.2 The Java Exception Hierarchy

Java defines a number of exception classes. A portion of the Java exception hierarchy is shown in the UML class diagram in Figure 2.4. Later we'll see how to extend this hierarchy by defining our own exception classes.

Throwable is at the root of this hierarchy and defines several methods that its

---

Figure 2.3 InputMismatchException is thrown when the type of input expected by Scanner doesn't match the input provided. User input is given in **boldface**.

```
Enter two integers: 1 a
Exception in thread "main" java.lang.InputMismatchException
        at java.util.Scanner.throwFor(Unknown source)
        at java.util.Scanner.next(Unknown source)
        at java.util.Scanner.nextInt(Unknown source)
        at java.util.Scanner.nextInt(Unknown source)
        at ExceptionEx.main(ExceptionEx.java:26)
```

Figure 2.4 A portion of the Java exception class hierarchy.

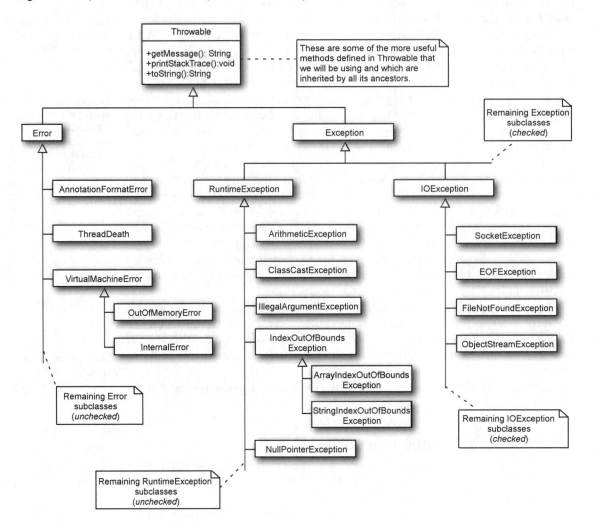

descendants inherit. The meaning of some of the commonly used methods is given in Table 2.2. Also, as you can see in the class diagram in Figure 2.4, exceptions fall into two categories: checked and unchecked exceptions.

Checked exceptions are descended from class `Exception`, but are outside the hierarchy rooted at `RuntimeException`. Checked exceptions are so named because the compiler will check to see that you either catch or rethrow them (we'll deal with these issues shortly). That is, the compiler will not let you simply ignore the possibility that such an exception can be thrown by your program. Why not? Because it is possible that your program could recover from these errors and do some useful work.

Unchecked exceptions typically represent the kinds of things your program

Table 2.2 Some commonly used methods inherited from `Throwable`.

Method	Description
String getMessage()	Return a string containing a detail message about this exception. The detail message is supplied at the time the exception is thrown.
void printStackTrace()	Print to `system.err` the trace of the method calls leading to this exception.
String toString()	Return a string containing this exception's name plus the detail message for the exception.

can avoid through careful programming (e.g., logic errors such as dividing by 0, accessing a null pointer, allowing an array index to go out of bounds). The compiler does not check that your code is handling these errors. In a sense, the compiler expects that you will have been careful enough that such problems don't arise!

The exception classes in the hierarchy rooted at `Error` represent problems that are usually fatal to a program and that are outside the programmer's control. They are included among the unchecked exceptions because there really is little you can do about them. For example, if a `VirtualMachineError` occurs there is a problem with the JVM—what could your program possibly do to recover?

2.1.3 Try-Catch Blocks

As you saw in Figures 2.1 and 2.3, the default behavior when an exception is thrown is for the program to terminate with an error message. It is possible, however, for you to have the program catch and handle an exception, so that the program can either continue to execute or terminate gracefully (release resources, provide an informative message, etc.).

Exceptions are handled in **try-catch blocks** whose format is shown in Figure 2.5. The statements that appear in a try block are considered part of the normal flow of execution. Any statement that might throw an exception that you want to handle must appear in a try block. In a very real sense, you are going to try to execute the code, recognizing that one or more statements in the block *might* throw an exception.

Try blocks

A try block is followed by one or more catch blocks. Each catch block has a header that identifies the kind of exception it catches. The idea here is that you have a catch block for each kind of exception that could be thrown by the statements in your try block that you want to catch.

Catch blocks

If an exception is thrown by a statement in the try block, an object of the corresponding exception type is instantiated and the rest of the try block is skipped. The JVM will search through the catch blocks *in the order that they appear*, searching for the first `ExceptionTypeX` (see Figure 2.5) that either exactly matches the type of exception thrown or is an ancestor (supertype) of the exception thrown. For example, if `IllegalArgumentException` is thrown, it can be caught by `IllegalArgumentException` (exact match) or `Exception` (ancestor—see Figure 2.4 again). If a matching catch block is found, the statements in that catch block

Throwing an exception creates an exception object

Figure 2.5 The format for try-catch blocks.

```
try {
  program statements; some of which may throw an exception
}
catch ( ExceptionType1 exception ) {
    program statements to handle exceptions of type
    ExceptionType1 or any of its subclasses
}
catch ( ExceptionType2 exception ) {
    program statements to handle exceptions of type
    ExceptionType2 or any of its subclasses
}

. . . // other catch clauses

catch ( ExceptionTypeN exception ) {
    program statements to handle exceptions of type
    ExceptionTypeN or any of its subclasses
}
finally {
  this block is optional;
  program statements to execute after the try block or a
  catch block has executed;
  this block will execute whether an exception is thrown
  or not
}
```

are executed. Control does *not* return to the try block. Assuming the catch block doesn't throw another exception, control is then transferred to the finally block or the first executable statement beyond the last catch block. If no exception is thrown in the try block, the catch blocks are skipped. If there is a finally block, its statements will be executed before the method returns whether an exception was thrown or not.

Finally block

Listing 2.2 shows the program from Listing 2.1 redone with the appropriate try-catch blocks. Note that not all the statements in the try block on lines 25–31 are potential troublemakers. As indicated earlier, code in a try block is part of the normal flow of execution. The two catch blocks are on lines 31–34 and 35–38. Since `ArithmeticException` and `InputMismatchException` are siblings (see the exception inheritance hierarchy in Figure 2.4 again), their order here is unimportant—their catch blocks could have been reversed. The finally block on lines 39–45 executes whether an exception is thrown or not. Its responsibility is to prepare for another set of inputs. The exercises have you look at the effect of different orderings of the catch blocks.

The output for Listing 2.2 shows that this program behaves much better than

Listing 2.2 The program from Listing 2.1 redone with try-catch blocks.

```
1    import java.util.Scanner;
2    import java.util.InputMismatchException;
3
4    /**
5     * Example illustrating catching exceptions.
6     */
7    public class ExceptionCaughtEx {
8
9       /**
10       * Computer the quotient of numerator / denominator. Assumes
11       * denominator is not 0.
12       */
13      public static int computeQuotient( int numerator,
14                                         int denominator ) {
15         return numerator / denominator;
16      }
17
18      public static void main( String []args ) {
19         Scanner kbd = new Scanner( System.in );
20         int x, y, result;
21         boolean done = false;
22         String answer;
23
24         while ( !done ) {
25            try {
26               System.out.print( "\nEnter two integers: " );
27               x = kbd.nextInt();
28               y = kbd.nextInt();
29               result = computeQuotient( x, y );
30               System.out.printf( "%d / %d = %d\n\n", x, y, result );
31            } catch ( ArithmeticException e ) {
32               System.err.printf( "Error: %s\n", e );
33               System.out.println( "The denominator cannot be 0.\n" );
34            }
35            catch ( InputMismatchException e ){
36               System.err.printf( "Error: %s\n", e );
37               System.out.println( "The inputs must be integers.\n" );
38            }
39            finally{
40               kbd.nextLine(); // clear out the line for next input
41               System.out.print( "Execute again? (y/n): " );
42               answer = kbd.next();
43               // we are done if user gives us anything but y or Y
44               done = !( answer.equals( "y" ) || answer.equals( "Y" ) );
45            }
```

The try block includes code that is part of the normal flow of execution

The catch block only executes if an exception of the catch type or one of its descendants is thrown

The finally block executes whether or not an exception occurred

```
46                 }
47         }
48     }
```

OUTPUT

```
Enter two integers: 8 0
Error: java.lang.ArithmeticException: / by zero
The denominator cannot be 0.

Execute again? (y/n): y

Enter two integers: 1 a
Error: java.util.InputMismatchException
The inputs must be integers.

Execute again? (y/n): y

Enter two integers: 12 3
12 / 3 = 4
Execute again? (y/n): n
```

our original version. It catches both division by zero and mismatched input, tells us what the problem is, then continues executing. This is the advantage of exception handling—it gives you the opportunity to recover from errors.

An advantage of exception handling is that it lets you recover from some errors

As a second example, the program in Listing 2.3 does a simple file copy of text files. Opening and accessing files can generate a variety of I/O exceptions. Recall that IOException and its descendants are checked exceptions, so the compiler is going to check that the code catches or rethrows the appropriate exceptions. The input file is opened in openInputFile() (lines 23–31). If the file to open for reading cannot be found, an exception is thrown on line 25. The catch block (lines 26–30) lets the user know what the problem is, then exits the program.

The output file is opened in openOutputFile() (lines 33–47). Checking the Java documentation for Formatter(String), we see that two exceptions can be thrown. Note that the corresponding catch blocks close the *input* file (lines 39 and 44), which will have been opened by this point, before exiting the program.

The actual file copying is done in copyFile() (lines 49–60). If something goes wrong at this point, the method generates an error message, then returns to the constructor, which closes the files (lines 19–20).

IOException and its subclasses are all checked exceptions, so the compiler checks that your code either catches the exceptions or *rethrows* them. Listing 2.4 is the file copy program redone to ignore unchecked exceptions and to rethrow the checked exceptions. One of the first things you note is that the program is shorter by almost half—exception handling can really expand and clutter up the code. The second thing you notice is that the header to main() (lines 19–20) now says the

Rethrowing an exception

Listing 2.3 A simple text file copier that catches various I/O exceptions.

```
1    import java.io.File;
2    import java.io.FileNotFoundException;
3    import java.util.Formatter;
4    import java.util.FormatterClosedException;
5    import java.util.NoSuchElementException;
6    import java.util.Scanner;
7
8    /**
9     * Copy a text file to another file.
10    */
11   public class TextFileCopier {
12      private Scanner infile;
13      private Formatter outfile;
14
15      public TextFileCopier( String src, String dest ){
16         openInputFile( src );
17         openOutputFile( dest );
18         copyFile();
19         infile.close();
20         outfile.close();
21      }
22
23      private void openInputFile( String infileName ) {
24         try {
25            infile = new Scanner( new File( infileName ) );
26         } catch ( FileNotFoundException e ) {
27            System.err.printf( "Error opening input file: %s\n%s",
28                               infileName, "Exiting application." );
29            System.exit( 1 );
30         }
31      }
32
33      private void openOutputFile( String outfileName ) {
34         try {
35            outfile = new Formatter( outfileName );
36         } catch ( FileNotFoundException e ) {
37            System.err.printf( "Error opening output file: %s\n%s",
38                               outfileName, "Exiting application." );
39            infile.close();
40            System.exit( 1 );
41         } catch ( SecurityException e ) {
42            System.err.printf( "Error insufficient write access to " +
43                               "create file: %s\n", outfileName  );
44            infile.close();
45            System.exit( 1 );
```

If the output file cannot be opened, processing cannot continue, so release input resources before exiting

```
46            }
47        }
48
49      private void copyFile() {
50          try {
51              while ( infile.hasNext() ) {
52                  String line = infile.nextLine();
53                  outfile.format( "%s\n", line );
54              }
55          } catch ( FormatterClosedException e ) {
56            System.err.println( "Error writing to output file; " +
57                                    "copying terminated" );
58              return;
59          }
60      }
61
62      public static void main( String []args ){
63          if ( args.length != 2 ) {
64              System.err.println( "usage: TextFileCopier src dest" );
65              System.exit( 1 );
66          }
67          if ( args[0].equals( args[1] ) )
68              System.err.println( "Source file and destination file " +
69                                    " can't be the same." );
70          else
71              new TextFileCopier( args[0], args[1] );
72      }
73  }
```

Listing 2.4 A simpler version of the text file copier program that rethrows the I/O exceptions. Compare with Listing 2.3.

```
1    import java.io.File;
2    import java.io.FileNotFoundException;
3    import java.util.Formatter;
4    import java.util.Scanner;
5
6    /**
7     * Cheap version of text file copier. This version
8     * does no exception handling if anything goes wrong.
9     */
10   public class TextFileCopier2 {
11
12     private static void copyFile( Scanner in, Formatter out ) {
13         while ( in.hasNext() ) {
```

```
14                  String line = in.nextLine();
15                  out.format( "%s\n", line );
16              }
17          }
18
19      public static void main( String []args )◄──────────
20                          throws FileNotFoundException {
21          if ( args.length != 2 ) {
22              System.err.println( "usage: TextFileCopier src dest" );
23              System.exit( 1 );
24          }
25          if ( args[0].equals( args[1] ) ) {
26              System.err.println( "Source file and destination file " +
27                              " can't be the same." );
28              System.exit( 1 );
29          }
30
31          Scanner infile;
32          Formatter outfile;
33
34          infile = new Scanner( new File( args[0] ) );
35          outfile = new Formatter( args[1] );
36          copyFile( infile, outfile );
37          infile.close();
38          outfile.close();
39      }
40  }
```

main() rethrows the checked exception *instead of* handling it

method throws FileNotFoundException. This means that one or more statements in main() can throw a FileNotFoundException (opening the files on lines 34 and 35). Instead of handling the problem internally, the program passes it off to the JVM, which will unceremoniously terminate the program.

2.1.4 Throwing Exceptions

In the examples we've seen so far, *the JVM* has detected the error and thrown the exception. Here we look at how your code can take on that responsibility and why you would want to.

In the last chapter we said that a method's pre-conditions state what must be true on entry to the method for the method to honor its contract (that is, for it to execute successfully). What obligation does the method have to make sure the pre-conditions are met? The approach we take here is "trust, but verify"—a method must make an earnest attempt to verify that its pre-conditions were honored by the caller.

Method pre-conditions—"trust, but verify"

This raises the question of what should be done when the pre-conditions are not met. We need to inform the caller that there is a problem. How? By throwing an exception!

Exceptional conditions are handled by throwing an exception

As an example, let's revisit the `Rectangle` class from Chapter 1. An invariant of `Rectangle` is that its attributes `height` and `length` must be greater than 0. The simple implementation of the overloaded constructor and the mutator `setLength()` in the last chapter (shown again in Listing 2.5(a)) assigned a default value if an argument was illegal (lines 13 and 17). As you can see, the documentation warns the programmer about illegal input and what will happen when it is supplied, but we could be more proactive and inform the client at runtime when an invariant is violated.

The updated code in Listing 2.5(b) uses `IllegalArgumentException` to alert the client to a problem. The documentation for the overloaded constructor now indicates (lines 7 and 8) that an exception is thrown if the pre-conditions aren't met. Note, however, that the exception isn't originally thrown in the constructor. Instead, the constructor calls the mutator methods `setLength()` and `setHeight()` to do the initialization (lines 12 and 13), relying on the parameter validation in those methods to catch any problems.

Method `setLength()` (lines 15–27) is shown as an example; `setHeight()`

Listing 2.5 Using exceptions to notify the caller that an error has occurred (see the **boldface** lines in part b).

(a) The original overloaded constructor and `setLength()` methods from `Rectangle` (implemented in Chapter 1).

```
 1    /**
 2     * Construct a <tt>Rectangle</tt> object using the arguments.
 3     * If an argument is <= 0, the default size specified in
 4     * <tt>Shape</tt> is used instead.
 5     * @param theLength the length of this <tt>Rectangle</tt>;
 6     *          must be > 0
 7     * @param theHeight the height of this <tt>Rectangle</tt>;
 8     *          must be > 0
 9     */
10    public Rectangle( double theLength, double theHeight ) {
11        super("Rectangle");
12        if ( theLength <= 0 )
13            setLength( Shape.DEFAULT_SIZE );
14        else setLength( theLength );
15
16        if ( theHeight <= 0 )
17            setHeight( Shape.DEFAULT_SIZE );
18        else setHeight( theHeight );
19    }
        .
        .
        .
```

Original version: assign a default value if the pre-condition is not met

```
54    /**
55     * Set the length dimension of this <tt>Rectangle</tt>.
56     * If <tt>theLength</tt> is <= 0, the dimension is unchanged.
57     * @param theLength the new length of this <tt>Rectangle</tt>;
58     *          must be > 0
59     */
60    public void setLength( double theLength ) {
61        if ( theLength <= 0 )
62            return;
63        this.length = theLength;
64    }
```

(b) The overloaded constructor and `setLength()` methods modified to throw an
`IllegalArgumentException`.

```
1     /**
2      * Construct a <tt>Rectangle</tt> object using the arguments.
3      * @param theLength the length of this <tt>Rectangle</tt>;
4      *          must be > 0
5      * @param theHeight the length of this <tt>Rectangle</tt>;
6      *          must be > 0
7      * @throws IllegalArgumentException if either <tt>theLength</tt>
8      *            or <tt>theHeight</tt> are <= 0.
9      */
10    public Rectangle( double theLength, double theHeight ) {
11        super("Rectangle");
12        setLength( theLength );
13        setHeight( theHeight );
14    }
          .
          .
          .
15    /**
16     * Set the length dimension of this <tt>Rectangle</tt>.
17     * @param theLength the new length of this <tt>Rectangle</tt>;
18     *          must be > 0
19     * @throws IllegalArgumentException if <tt>theLength</tt> is <= 0
20     */
21    public void setLength( double theLength ) {
22        if ( theLength <= 0 )                              ◄──────────── New version: throw
23            throw new IllegalArgumentException(                          an exception if the
24                          "Illegal Rectangle length (" +                pre-condition is not
25                          theLength +"): must be > 0 ");                 met
26        this.length = theLength;
27    }
```

would be almost identical. The Java documentation for `setLength()` is updated (line 19) to reflect the use of exceptions—again, it is important that you let the client know what might happen. The test to see if the pre-condition is met is done on line 22. Lines 23 through 25 illustrate how your code can throw an exception.

An exception is thrown with the reserved word `throw`. The argument to `throw` is an exception object. In our case we want to throw `IllegalArgumentException`, so we must create an instance of the class, which, of course, we do by applying `new` to one of the class's constructors. Typically an exception class includes an overloaded constructor that takes a string providing a detail message about what caused the exception. After all, if we just throw `IllegalArgumentException`, we wouldn't be giving the user much information about what went wrong. So on lines 24 and 25 we provide a detailed message telling the user why the exception was thrown. This also tells the user how to fix the problem, which is pretty handy.

Throwing an exception

To show you the effect, the code in Listing 2.6 creates two `Rectangle` objects. The first has legal inputs, so is created without incident, but as you can see, the `Rectangle` created on line 10 has an illegal argument. The output generated is shown at the end of Listing 2.6. Note that the detail message is very helpful in figuring out what went wrong and the stack trace leads us to the offending line.

Listing 2.6 Sample code that creates a `Rectangle` object with legal arguments, and one that has illegal arguments and will generate an exception.

```
1    import gray.adts.shapes.Rectangle;
2
3    /**
4     * Illustrate the information provided by the detail message and
5     * the stack trace when an exception is thrown.
6     */
7    public class RectangleExceptionEx {
8        public static void main( String []args ){
9            Rectangle r1 = new Rectangle( 4, 5 );      // this is okay
10           Rectangle r2 = new Rectangle( -1, 5 );     // this is NOT okay
11           // once the exception is thrown by the constructor, the
12           // program will exit since we don't make any attempt to
13           // catch the exception.
14       }
15   }
```

OUTPUT

```
Exception in thread "main" java.lang.IllegalArgumentException:
Illegal Rectangle length (-1.0): must be > 0
    at gray.adts.shapes.Rectangle.setLength(Rectangle.java:91)
    at gray.adts.shapes.Rectangle.<init>(Rectangle.java:41)
    at RectangleExceptionEx.main(RectangleExceptionEx.java:10)
```

2.1.5 Defining Your Own Exception Class

It is occasionally useful to be able to create your own exception type. This turns out to be very easy to do. As an example, we will create an *un*checked exception, ShapeException, which our shape classes could throw whenever they encounter a problem.

Building a custom exception class

Since our class will be unchecked, it will extend RuntimeException. All the really useful methods we will need are inherited from Throwable (see the UML class diagram in Figure 2.4), so all we need to do is provide constructors. As shown in Listing 2.7, we provide a default constructor and an overloaded constructor that takes a string providing a detail message. Both constructors simply call their super constructor counterparts. That's it!

Listing 2.8 shows how we would use our custom exception class in the Rectangle class. This is just Listing 2.5(b) with IllegalArgumentException replaced by ShapeException. Figure 2.6 shows the output that would be produced by the sample program in Listing 2.6 with this change.

SUMMING UP

Java's mechanism for dealing with exceptional situations at runtime is to throw an exception. This causes an exception object describing the problem to be created.

The Java exception hierarchy is split into checked and unchecked exceptions. A checked exception represents an unexpected condition outside the programmer's control (such as a lost network connection) that the program might be able to recover from. Checked exceptions are so called because the compiler checks to see

---

Listing 2.7 The ShapeException class is an unchecked exception.

```
1    package gray.adts.shapes;
2
3    /**
4     * The exception that is thrown whenever an operation on a
5     * shape is in violation of a method pre-condition.
6     */
7    public class ShapeException extends RuntimeException {
8
9        public ShapeException() {
10           super();
11       }
12
13       public ShapeException( String errMsg ) {
14           super(" " + errMsg );
15       }
16   }
```

Listing 2.8 The `setLength` method from `Rectangle` modified to throw `ShapeException`. Compare with Listing 2.5(b).

```
33    /**
34     * Set the length dimension of this <tt>Rectangle</tt>.
35     * @param theLength the new length of this <tt>Rectangle</tt>;
36     *          must be > 0
37     * @throws ShapeException if <tt>theLength</tt> is <= 0
38     */
39    public void setLength( double theLength ) {
40        if ( theLength <= 0 )
41            throw new ShapeException(
42                                      "Illegal Rectangle length (" +
43                                      theLength +"): must be > 0 ");
44            this.length = theLength;
45    }
```

Figure 2.6 Output produced by Listing 2.6 if `Rectangle` throws a `ShapeException`.

```
Exception in thread "main" gray.adts.shapes.ShapeException: Illegal Rectangle
length (−1.0): must be > 0
        at gray.adts.shapes.Rectangle.setLength(Rectangle.java:91)
        at gray.adts.shapes.Rectangle.<init>(Rectangle.java:41)
        at RectangleExceptionEx.main(RectangleExceptionEx.java:10)
```

that the program either catches the exception or rethrows it. There are two categories of unchecked exceptions. The first represents problems beyond the programmer's control that are usually unrecoverable (e.g., running out of memory). The second includes logic errors the programmer can fix. The compiler does not check that the code handles unchecked exceptions.

Exceptions can be caught using try-catch blocks. The try block contains code that is part of the normal flow of execution including statements that might throw an exception. The catch block identifies the type of exception it can catch and handle. The exception type appearing in a catch phrase matches exceptions of that type and all its descendants. Uncaught exceptions are handled by the JVM, which terminates the program.

The hierarchy of exception types can be extended with user-defined exceptions.

CHECKPOINT

2.1 What exceptions can be thrown by `java.text.Format.format(Object)`? You will need to look at the Java documentation for the class. Are any of these exceptions checked?

2.2 Assume an exception of type `NullPointerException` is thrown in a try block. What types of exceptions can be used in a catch block to catch this exception? That is, what types of exception will "match" `NullPointerException`?

2.3 Revise the implementation of `Rectangle.setHeight()` to throw an `IllegalArgumentException` when the argument violates the method's pre-conditions. Be sure to update the JavaDocs!

■ 2.2 Software Testing

You were given a problem and you created a solution. So how do you know whether your solution is correct? Our philosophy on testing was presented in the book's introduction.

- Testing should be done *throughout* the software development process and not treated as an afterthought once all the coding is done.

  Testing philosophy

- Developing tests can be painless (even fun!) and is an intellectually challenging part of the software development process that reaps benefits *before* coding has begun.

  Remember: think twice, code once

- Frequent testing will reduce your debugging time and give you increased confidence in your code as you develop and build on it.

In this section we make the components of this philosophy more concrete by talking about strategies for testing, developing test plans, and implementing those test plans using a testing framework called JUnit.

2.2.1 Testing Throughout the Software Development Process

A common misconception is that testing does not begin until the code compiles and can be run. In fact, testing should be an integral part of the entire software development process. The three points of interest are

When do you test?

1. after the analysis and design is complete
2. during the implementation
3. after the implementation is complete

Given that testing is not going to prove that your software is completely bug-free, it is reasonable to ask, "How much is enough?" By what metric do you decide that no more testing is needed? The nature of the problem allows no precise answer. A rule of thumb is that if all your tests pass, you are done (for now). A more formal testing regime would use the percentage of possible test cases actually tested as a metric and require documentation showing which tests were done, what they tested, and their results.

How much do you test?

2.2.2 Checking the Specification

Although it is early in the development of a piece of software, the time to begin "testing" is the design phase with the specification of the ADTs. At this stage you should do three checks.

First, check that the ADT's API contains all the operations clients will need and that the names are consistent and meaningful. This may seem a really dumb thing to have to do, but it is a common mistake to *think* you have done something, when, in fact, you haven't. It pays to be meticulous about this. There should be

Check the API

- Operations providing the main behavior to be offered by the ADT.

- Accessor and mutator operations for ADT attributes to which the clients can have access.

- Accessor operations for read-only attributes. A read-only attribute is one that a client can read, but not write (change), so no mutator method is provided.

It is good to have an independent observer help with this to provide some objectivity. Ironically, it is notoriously difficult for the author to see obvious problems because he or she is too close to the design. You are probably familiar with this phenomenon from your debugging experience and it is also true when developing specifications.

Second, check that the specification is internally consistent. If the blueprint isn't correct, it would be a miracle if what is constructed from it is correct. You should carefully check the ADT's invariants to be sure that

Check the ADT invariants

- They are consistent with one another. If two or more invariants are contradictory, it is not possible for all the ADT invariants to be true at the same time!

- The pre- and post-conditions of the ADT's operations are consistent with the ADT's invariants.

- Post-conditions are consistent with the responsibilities of each operation.

Third, design a **test plan** to be used during the implementation phase. You should develop a plan for testing each operation specified in an ADT. Once the ADT has been coded as a class in the implementation phase, it can be tested in isolation before being integrated into the rest of the system. In OOP, **unit testing** exercises individual methods of a class and the class as a whole.

Design a test plan

But if no code has been written yet, how can you possibly know what to test? Well, you know the *expected* behavior of each of the operations in the ADT's API and the pre- and post-conditions tell you something of the state of the object before and after each operation executes. For a given input, you know what the expected output is. So you have enough information to develop test cases for each operation in the API.

Start with writing the test plan during the design phase

Developing a test plan at this point in the development process provides another check on the specification because developing a good test for an operation forces you to be clear about what the operation is supposed to do. If you don't know enough to ask probing questions of the ADT you are designing, it is probably because your specification lacks clarity and/or you don't know enough yet. If this is the case, keep rewriting the specification until you know enough to have concrete ideas about how to test it.

Writing a test plan adds clarity to the design

A test plan is composed of a collection of test cases. Each test case is written as a table with four columns.

Operation	Purpose	Object State	Expected Result
A call to an operation of the ADT to be tested.	The role the operation plays in the test case.	The expected state of the test object once the operation is complete.	The expected output (if any).

Test plans will be implemented using a testing framework called JUnit. Once coded, the tests can be run as often as needed and will tell you whether or not all the tests passed. JUnit will tell you which tests failed, the expected output, and the actual output generated. JUnit is introduced in Section 2.2.6.

Testing based solely on the expected behavior (interface) of an operation is called **black-box testing** because the unit to be tested (method, class, etc.) is viewed as a black box whose implementation is hidden from you (which is indeed the case, since in the design phase, there is no implementation yet—see Figure 2.7). We know the box's purpose, what data inputs are legal and illegal, and the expected outputs for the inputs—that's all.

Black-box testing

There are several ways to approach black-box testing. In **exhaustive testing**, you would test using *all* legal inputs (and some illegal input as well), comparing the output generated to the expected output. Except for fairly simple pieces of code, exhaustive testing is not practical.

A reasonable alternative to exhaustive testing is to carefully examine the operations to be tested and identify groups of values with similar characteristics, then test with representative values from each group. How do you identify the groups?

1. *Determine what data are legal and what are illegal.* You need a clear idea about which input values are legal and should be processed, and which input values are illegal and should be rejected. It is worth pointing out that if you have no clue what the output is supposed to be for a given input, testing with that input is of very little use. Looking at the output and saying "That looks about right" does *not* count as testing!

2. *Identify the ranges of legal data values.* Knowing the range of legal inputs allows you to identify the values at the *boundaries* of the range. Test with legal input at the bounds of the range(s) of legal values. For example, if an operation processes temperatures in the range of 100 to 200 inclusive, then values of 100 and 200 are right at the bounds for *legal data* and you would test using these values. This kind of test checks for those pesky off-by-one errors that are so easy to make.

Figure 2.7 Black-box testing.

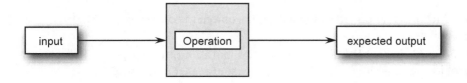

3. *Test with values just inside the legal range* (101 and 199 in our temperature range example).

4. *Frequently values **between** the bounds can be treated as a single group* and you can choose a few randomly from within that group (125, 150, or 175 from our example problem would work), under the assumption that if one value from that group passes, they all will.

5. *Test with illegal data that is just **outside** the range of legal values* (this would be the values 99 and 201 from our example).

6. *Finally, treat values well outside the range of legal inputs as a group* and randomly pick a few values from this group to test. Obviously the operation should reject them. From our example, the values –45, 0, and 298 are well outside the range of legal inputs and could be used. Again, the assumption is that if your operation rejects these values, it will reject similarly illegal data.

It may seem a bit odd to be testing with data that is known to be illegal, but consider that a program that accepts illegal data is as bad as a program that rejects legal data. Testing with illegal data also lets you exercise your exception handling.

Accept valid data; reject bad data

A third possibility for black-box testing is to write the test using either actual data supplied by the client or simulated data. It is important to test with the kinds of values the application is most likely to see. It would be embarrassing if your solution did a brilliant job of handling the pathological (rare and really evil) cases, but failed when given a common case.

2.2.3 Writing Test Cases for Unit Testing

A test plan consists of a set of test cases. Each test case focuses on a part of the class being tested. Earlier we discussed software testing in general terms, looking at the format of a test plan and the kinds of tests that are especially useful (e.g., boundary tests). Here we discuss how to develop a test plan to unit test the `Rectangle` class. Testing in later chapters will be more sophisticated than what is presented now, but will follow the same pattern.

A test plan can be developed as soon as the API is known. We do not have to wait until there is an actual implementation of the class. Again, the advantage of developing the plan before implementing the class is that it forces you to think carefully about what each method is supposed to do. A clear understanding of the expected behavior of a method is essential before trying to implement it!

The goal of a unit test is to test the methods of a class individually and, where sensible, in combination to confirm that the class behaves as promised in its contract. Developing a test plan to achieve this goal may sound difficult, but actually relies mostly on common sense. We'll start by separating the methods from `Rectangle` into two categories.

Unit testing

1. *Mutator Methods.* Methods that can affect the state of the object: the constructor, `setLength()`, and `setHeight()`.

2. *Accessor and Predicate Methods.* Methods that report on, but cannot change, the state of the object: `getLength()`, `getHeight()`, `getSurfaceArea()`, and `getPerimeter()`.

I will use the accessor and predicate methods to verify the state changes made by the mutator methods. For each of the mutator methods, I ask the simple question: "How will this operation change the state of the object?" If I can't answer this question correctly, I can't design a test case *and* I have no business trying to implement the method. Let's develop a few test cases to see how this works.

Test Case 2.1 simply verifies that the default constructor properly initializes the length and height attributes to 1.0. A boldface entry in the Object State column indicates a change in state. A blank entry in the column means there was no change in state. Let's be clear about this. How do I know what the state of the newly constructed object will be in Test Case 2.1? I didn't make it up! The ADT description tells me!

Test Case 2.2 verifies that the overloaded constructor properly initializes the attributes when given legal data.

Test Case 2.3 checks that the overloaded constructor correctly validates its length argument and Test Case 2.4 does the same for the height argument. Why are

Test Case 2.1 Instantiation of a `Rectangle` object using default values for the attributes.

Operation	Purpose	Object State	Expected Result
Rectangle r1 = new Rectangle()	To create a rectangle using the default values.	*length* = *1.0* *height* = *1.0*	A new Rectangle object with default values for the attributes.
r1.getLength()	To verify instantiation and accessor method.		1.0
r1.getHeight()	To verify instantiation and accessor method.		1.0

Test Case 2.2 Instantiation of a `Rectangle` object with legal, client-supplied values for the attributes.

Operation	Purpose	Object State	Expected Result
Rectangle r1 = new Rectangle(2.0, 3.0)	To create a rectangle with client-supplied values.	*length* = *2.0* *height* = *3.0*	A new Rectangle object with client-supplied values for the attributes.
r1.getHeight()	To verify instantiation and accessor method.		2.0
r1.getLength()	To verify instantiation and accessor method.		3.0

Test Case 2.3 Instantiation of a `Rectangle` object with an illegal, client-supplied value for the length attribute.

Operation	Purpose	Object State	Expected Result
Rectangle r1 = new Rectangle(−3.0, 5.0)	To create a rectangle with an an illegal length value—verify pre-condition validation.		IllegalArgumentException

Test Case 2.4 Instantiation of a `Rectangle` object with an illegal, client-supplied value for the height attribute.

Operation	Purpose	Object State	Expected Result
Rectangle r1 = new Rectangle(3.0, −5.0)	To create a rectangle with an illegal height value—verify pre-condition validation.		IllegalArgumentException

these distinct tests? Why not test with new `Rectangle(-5.0, -4.0)`? Because I want to be sure that both arguments are validated and I can't be sure of that without explicitly testing for each.

Test Case 2.5 verifies that the `setLength()` mutator works for legal input and Test Case 2.6 verifies that illegal input is rejected. Since we have seen the implementation of these methods in Listing 2.5, we know that the constructor relies on the mutators to do the attribute assignment, so it would seem sufficient to just test the

Test Case 2.5 Mutator to change a `Rectangle`'s length: legal input.

Operation	Purpose	Object State	Expected Result
Rectangle r1 = new Rectangle(1.0, 2.0)	To create a rectangle with client-supplied values.	*length = 1.0* *height = 2.0*	A new Rectangle object with client-supplied values for the attributes.
r1.setLength(5)	To test mutator with legal input.	*length = 5.0* *height = 2.0*	
r1.getLength()			5.0

Test Case 2.6 Mutator to change a `Rectangle`'s length: illegal input.

Operation	Purpose	Object State	Expected Result
Rectangle r1 = new Rectangle(1.0, 2.0)	To create a rectangle with client-supplied values.	*length = 1.0* *height = 2.0*	A new Rectangle object with client-supplied values for the attributes.
r1.setLength(0)	To test length mutator with illegal input.		IllegalArgumentException

Test Case 2.7 Accessor for a `Rectangle`'s perimeter attribute.

Operation	Purpose	Object State	Expected Result
Rectangle r1 = new Rectangle(6.7, 5.3)	To create a rectangle with client-supplied values.	*length = 6.7* *height = 5.3*	A new Rectangle object with client-supplied values for the attributes.
r1.getPerimeter( )	To test accessor method.		24.0

mutators. However, if I am creating test cases prior to implementation, I won't know this, so would devise separate tests. More importantly, the implementation *could* change in the future such that the constructors actually do the check and the work.

CHECKPOINT

2.4 Create a test plan for mutator `setHeight()`.

2.5 Create a test plan for accessor `getSurfaceArea()`.

2.2.4 Testing During the Implementation

The first step in implementing an ADT operation is to develop pseudocode based on the operation's responsibilities and pre- and post-conditions. At this point you can perform a **desk check** of the pseudocode by "executing" it by hand using the test cases from the test plan. The idea is that desk checking will catch errors with the pseudocode and the design before you commit your ideas to code. Desk checking may also suggest additional test cases, which you would add to your test plan.

In unit testing, we test a class in isolation from the other components of the system. This is done by creating a test program that constructs an instance (object) of the class to test, then sends it messages corresponding to the test cases from the test plan.

It is not necessary to code and test all the methods from a class at once. As recommended earlier, with the incremental approach you code *and test* methods one at a time. A distinct advantage of this is that you catch bugs before moving on and can confidently build on top of the code just written and tested. Since you only coded a method or two since your last successful unit test, you know the bug is related to the code you just wrote. This greatly reduces the time it takes to locate a bug and since the offending code is fresh in your mind, you end up spending less time trying to understand the code to fix the problem.

Frequent testing cuts down on debugging time

Also, now that the implementation details are known, there may be special cases you want to test. In **clear-box testing**, the internals of the box are revealed to you. Now you can test specific code points in the implementation. This may lead to development of additional test cases.

Clear-box testing

A **path** through a method is a particular sequence of statements that are executed from the method's entry to its exit. In **path coverage** you test all possible paths through a method. Figure 2.8 illustrates a section of code that has two paths that are easy to see from the diagram on the right hand side of the figure.

If a is less than 0, the left path is taken; otherwise the right path is taken. Presumably the different paths produce different behavior, so ideally both paths should be tested. Looping constructs and switch statements also produce alternate paths. In the example in Figure 2.8, we would certainly want to test using −1, 0, 1, and a selection of other positive and negative values for a. Providing values right around the testing point (a < 0) is a good way to catch off-by-one errors.

Code coverage

The problem with path coverage is that the number of paths is exponential in the number of branches that can be taken. The compromise is to identify the most

Figure 2.8 Execution paths.

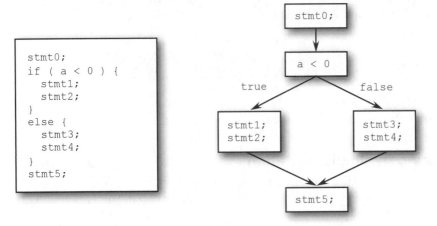

```
stmt0;
if ( a < 0 ) {
    stmt1;
    stmt2;
}
else {
    stmt3;
    stmt4;
}
stmt5;
```

important and problematic paths and test them. Earlier we asked how much testing is enough. You could say that you have done enough when some percentage of the possible paths have been *successfully* tested. Another criteria commonly used is **statement coverage**, in which every statement is executed at least once.

2.2.5 Testing After the Implementation Is Complete

Unit testing applies to individual classes tested in isolation. As classes are built and pass their unit tests, they are integrated with other classes to create components of the overall system. At that point **integration tests** are done to verify that the classes work correctly in combination with other classes in the system.

Integration testing

Once the integration tests have passed, the software is ready for close inspection by the client. **Acceptance testing** is done by the client and is largely a comparison of what the system does against the requirements laid out in the requirement specification document produced in the first phase of the development process (the analysis phase). Integration and acceptance testing are covered in greater detail in a course on software engineering and will not be discussed further in this text.

Acceptance testing

2.2.6 Testing with JUnit[2]

In Section 2.2.3 we began developing a unit-level test plan for `Rectangle`. It is time now to look at implementing that test plan.

The traditional approach to unit testing has been to write a testing program that implements a test plan, sending messages to the methods of a class and outputting the results to the screen or a file so that the *programmer* could compare the actual results returned against the expected results from the test plan. Understandably, programmers regard this as a boring task and find various reasons to avoid it.

---

[2]Source, executables, and documentation for JUnit can be found at http://www.junit.org/.

JUnit is a framework for testing Java classes at the unit level that not only makes testing simpler, it makes it fun! Its chief features are

1. *Test Cases.* A test case runs a single test from a test plan such as the ones developed in Section 2.2.3. Each test case may test a single method from the class under test or a small combination of methods from the class.

2. *Assertions and **Self-Reporting** of Test Results.* Using tools from the JUnit framework, each test case will make assertions about the method results and will report whether those assertions passed or failed, relieving the programmer of the need to do this checking manually. When a test fails, you will know precisely which test failed and why it failed, providing valuable feedback for locating the source of the bug. (Quite often the bulk of the time spent debugging is devoted to *finding* the bug.)

3. *Test Suites and Testing Hierarchies.* Test cases can be grouped into test suites. Typically a test suite represents a complete unit test of a class. Test suites can be collected into a testing hierarchy for testing a complete system, with different branches of the hierarchy responsible for testing different components (classes or groups of classes) of the system.

4. *Running Tests.* Running a single test case, a group of test cases or test suites is done easily within the framework and provides instant feedback on which tests passed and which failed. Because the tests are so easy to run, programmers can feel comfortable making it a regular part of the software development process.

A really good way to approach testing with JUnit is to code the test plan, then implement the class one method at a time starting with the most fundamental methods, and run the test case(s) for those methods. Once these tests pass, you can move on to the other methods, confident that you are building on a solid (bug-free) foundation.

The JUnit testing framework is a Java application and is run like any other Java application. At a command prompt, type

```
java RectangleTester
```

Assuming you have the JUnit jar file in your CLASSPATH, this runs the GUI version of the `RectangleTester` class we are going to implement (see Figure 2.9). To rerun the entire suite of tests from the test program, simply click on the topmost "Run" button (the test-suite run button).

If all the tests pass, the success/failure bar will be green. A red bar indicates one or more tests did not pass. After the full test suite has been run once, click on the Test Hierarchy tab to see all the test cases that are part of the test suite. The tests are identified by their `testXXX()` name (explained shortly). A green checkmark appears next to the tests that passed. A failed test will have a red X next to it and additional information will appear in the message window (we'll do an example later). To rerun a single test, select it with the mouse (click on the name) and then click on the test case run button (the lower "Run" button).

In the rest of this section we look at JUnit's components and how to build a testing program within the JUnit framework. We'll use the partial test plan developed for `RectangleTester` as the running example.

Figure 2.9 A successful run of a JUnit test program.

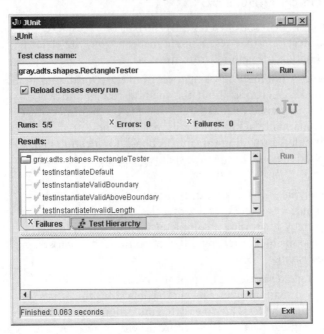

2.2.7 Creating a Test Program Using the JUnit Framework

There are several classes and interfaces within the JUnit framework. Fortunately, we need only look at a few of them to use JUnit. Also, most integrated development environments for Java provide tools to help construct JUnit test programs. In this section we'll look at some of the methods from some of these classes and develop a working example for testing the `Rectangle` class. You should use the test program developed here as a model for future test programs.

Every testing class should extend `TestCase`, one of the classes from the JUnit framework. Here's the start to our own test class, `RectangleTester`.

```
import JUnit.framework.*;       // JUnit stuff
import JUnit.extensions.*;      // JUnit stuff
import gray.adts.shapes.Rectangle;   // the class to test
public class RectangleTester extends TestCase {
```

Within your test class, you need to define one or more instances of the class you will test. These objects are called the **test fixture**. The number of instances you have depends on the class under test, the methods to be tested, and the test cases. Most of our needs here will be met by two `Rectangle` objects.

Test fixture is the object(s) under test

```
private Rectangle r1, r2; // stores the Rectangle objects under test
```

You might have noticed that for each of the test cases developed in Section 2.2.3, we created a test object (the test fixture) and put it in a state suitable for the test to be done (see the first line of Test Cases 2.1, 2.2, and 2.3 for example). The setUp() method from TestCase removes the toil of doing this manually for each test case.

The test fixture is initialized in the method setUp(), which is called automatically by JUnit before each testXXX() method is invoked. This prevents side effects between the test methods that make up your testing application by guaranteeing that each testXXX() method begins from the same starting point (just as we did in the test cases we developed in Section 2.2.3). Here is the overridden setUp()method for our test program. It creates a Rectangle object using the default values and a second one with client-supplied values.

```
/* Called automatically BEFORE EACH testXXX() method is run. */
protected void setUp() {
    r1 = new Rectangle();
    r2 = new Rectangle( 2.0, 3.0 );
}
```

After each testXXX() method returns, the JUnit framework automatically invokes the tearDown() method to perform housecleaning on the test fixture. This may include releasing memory and closing I/O streams, among others. An example is shown below, but the garbage collector should take care of memory cleanup by itself, so unless you have something like I/O streams to close, you can safely leave this method out and rely on the default implementation of tearDown() inherited from TestCase.

```
/* Called automatically AFTER EACH testXXX() method is run. */
protected void tearDown() {
    r1 = null;
    r2 = null;
}
```

A testing class such as RectangleTester will contain a number of test cases, each of which implements part of the test plan developed for the class under test. Generally, a test case will make some change to the test fixture using mutator methods from the class being tested, then examine the state of the test object using accessor and predicate methods, just as we did in the test plan developed earlier. The actual results returned by these method calls are compared to the expected results from the test plan. If the actual result matches the expected result, the test passes; otherwise it fails. The Assert class from the JUnit framework provides a number of utility methods used to compare expected and actual results.

The most basic method from Assert is assertTrue(condition), where condition is a boolean expression that you expect (assert) will evaluate to true. If the condition evaluates to true, the test passes. If the condition evaluates to false, an AssertionFailedError exception is thrown, the test fails, and JUnit reports the failure by making the success/failure bar red and marking the failed test with an X in the test hierarchy window.

A variation of assertTrue() allows you to supply a String message to be output if the assertion fails: assertTrue(String msg, boolean condition). Most of the methods in Assert provide these two forms: one with a message argument and one without.

Another commonly used method is assertEquals(expectedValue, actualValue). The assertEquals() method is overloaded to support testing equality between values of the primitive types and between two objects using their equals() method. Read the online documentation for Assert for details. If expectedValue is equal to actualValue, the test passes; otherwise it fails. This is ideal for coding our test cases.

Let's look at an example. The following test method implements Test Case 2.2, developed in Section 2.2.3. It demonstrates the two versions of assertEquals() just described.

Note the name of the test case, testInstantiateLegal(). All JUnit test cases follow the format testXXX(), where XXX is the name you want to give the test. The name should be descriptive and typically is related to the methods being tested. I have also included the caption of the test case as a reminder to myself about the test's purpose.

JUnit test method naming convention

```
/**
   Test Case 2.2: Instantiation of a Rectangle object with legal
   client-supplied values for the attributes.
 */
public void testInstantiateLegal() {
    assertEquals( 2.0, r2.getLength() );
    assertEquals( "Argh! Constructor didn't set height properly!",
                  3.0, r2.getHeight() );

}
```

You might be wondering where r2 was instantiated. Remember that for each testXXX() method called, the JUnit framework automatically does the following:

```
setUp();        // establish the test fixture
testXXX();      // run the test
tearDown();     // do house cleaning
```

So before testInstantiateLegal() is invoked, the Rectangle object r2 will have been instantiated by setUp().

The first assertEquals() in testInstantiateLegal() verifies that the overloaded constructor properly set the length attribute. The second assertEquals() verifies that the height attribute was set properly. As you can see, the implementation of a testXXX() method from a test case is very straightforward.

How did I know to test that the length was 2.0 and the height was 3.0? This isn't magic! I wrote the setUp() method that created r2, so I know what is in r2. When you write your own test program, all your testXXX() methods will make use of the environment established by setUp(), which *you* will write, so you will know what the test fixture looks like. What goes in setUp() will be determined by the test cases in your test plan.

Once the test cases are coded as testXXX() methods, you need to gather them into a test suite. This will allow JUnit to run all the tests at once, while also giving you the flexibility to run individual tests as needed.

Creating a test suite

A test suite is represented in JUnit by a TestSuite object. The tests added to a TestSuite object are either instances of TestCase (such as our RectangleTester, which is a subclass of `TestCase`), or other `TestSuite` objects. It is through the latter mechanism that a hierarchy of test suites can be built.

The easiest way to add tests to a `TestSuite` object is to just provide the test class as the argument to the `TestSuite` constructor and leave it to JUnit to extract and identify the individual tests.[3]

You can have JUnit locate and load a `TestSuite` automatically by creating and loading the `TestSuite` object in a static `suite()` method, as follows.

```
public static Test suite() {
    // The simplest approach is to let JUnit do all the work using
    // Java's reflection mechanism.
    return new TestSuite( RectangleTester.class );
}
```

Note the argument to the constructor for `TestSuite`. It is just the name of the testing class, `RectangleTester`, with ".`class`" appended to it.

Finally, we need a `main()` method to get everything going. It gets the name of the test class, which is stored in an array of `String` objects. This is passed to the test runner within JUnit.

```
public static void main (String[] args) {
    // Use reflection to get the name of this class.
    String[] TestCaseName = { RectangleTester.class.getName() };
    junit.swingui.TestRunner.main( TestCaseName );
}
```

2.2.8 Putting It All Together

Here is a simple algorithm for writing a test class within the JUnit framework. The sample code in Listing 2.9 identifies each of these steps with comments that provide additional details.

1. Create a testing class that extends (is a subclass of) `TestCase`. This will be the testing application run within JUnit. Remember that by extending `TestCase` you will give your testing class access to all the public and protected methods of `TestCase` and its superclass, `Assert`.

2. Declare the instance variables to reference the objects to be used in the test. This is the test fixture.

3. Define a constructor for the test class that invokes the `TestCase` constructor. The constructor should not perform any initialization of the instance variables declared in step 2.

4. Override the `setUp()` method from `TestCase` to instantiate and initialize the test fixture that will be used for the individual test cases. The `setUp()` method is invoked before *each* `testXXX()` method to prevent side effects among the tests (see step 6).

---

[3]JUnit does this using Java's reflection capability. Reflection just means that a class is able to provide information about itself, including its name, data, and method fields, return and argument types for each method, and so on. This is a very cool and powerful tool.

Listing 2.9 The complete code for `RectangleTester`.

```
1    package gray.adts.shapes;
2
3    import junit.framework.*;
4    import junit.extensions.*;
5
6    //  Step 1. Create a testing class that extends TestCase.
7    public class RectangleTester extends TestCase {
8        // Step 2: Declare variables for the objects to be
9        //          tested.
10       private Rectangle r1, r2;
11
12       // Step 3: Create a constructor that invokes the
13       //          super constructor. The name argument is the name
14       //          of a test case (see the suite() method).
15       public RectangleTester(String name) {
16           super( name );
17       }
18
19       // Step 4. Create a setUp() method to instantiate and
20       //          initialize the objects under test. This method
21       //          is invoked before EVERY test case.
22       protected void setUp() {
23           r1 = new Rectangle();
24           r2 = new Rectangle( 2.0, 3.0 );
25       }
26
27       // Step 5. Create a tearDown() method to clean up after
28       //          EACH test case. Unless you need something more than
29       //          general garbage collection, such as closing I/O
30       //          streams, you can leave this method out.
31       protected void tearDown() {
32           r1 = null;
33           r2 = null;
34       }
35
36       // Step 6. Create the test cases. Each test case should follow
37       //          the pattern:   void testXXX()
38       //          where XXX is the name of the test to perform.
39       /**
40          Test Case 2.1: Verify that instantiation was done
41          properly using default values for the Rectangle's
42          dimensions.
43        */
44       public void testInstantiateDefault() {
45           assertEquals( 1.0, r1.getLength() );
```

```
46            assertEquals( 1.0, r1.getHeight() );
47        }
48
49        /**
50            Test Case 2.2: Instantiation of a Rectangle object
51            with legal user-supplied values for the attributes.
52         */
53        public void testInstantiateLegal() {
54            assertEquals( 2.0, r2.getLength() );
55            assertEquals( 3.0, r2.getHeight() );
56        }
57
58        /**
59            Test Case 2.3: Instantiation of a Rectangle object
60            with an illegal user-supplied value for the length
61            attribute.
62         */
63        public void testInstantiateIllegalLength() {
64            try {
65                new Rectangle( -3.0, 5.0 );
66                fail( "Should raise IllegalArgumentException");
67            } catch ( IllegalArgumentException e ) {
68                assertTrue(true);
69            }
70        }
71
72        /**
73            Test Case 2.5: Mutator to change a Rectangle's
74            length: legal input.
75         */
76        public void testLengthMutatorLegal() {
77            r2.setLength( 5.0 );
78            assertEquals( 5.0, r2.getLength() );
79            assertEquals( 3.0, r2.getHeight() );
80        }
81
82        /**
83            Test Case 2.7: Accessor for a Rectangle's perimeter
84         */
85        public void testGetPerimeter() {
86            r2.setLength( 6.5 );
87            r2.setHeight( 5.3 );
88            assertEquals( 23.6, r2.getPerimeter(), 0.01 );
89        }
90
91        // Step 7: Create a suite of test cases.
92        public static Test suite() {
```

Should throw an exception here

Exception not thrown, so the test fails

We expected an exception, so the test passes

Use a delta for comparison of real numbers

```
93          // The simplest approach is to let JUnit do all the work
94          // using Java's reflection mechanism.
95          return new TestSuite( RectangleTester.class );
96
97          // Alternatively, you can create a TestSuite object and
98          // add the tests manually. But this shows the purpose
99          // of the String arg in the RectangleTester constructor.
100   /*
101          TestSuite suite = new TestSuite();
102          suite.addTest(
103              new RectangleTester( "testInstantiateDefault" ) );
104          suite.addTest(
105              new RectangleTester( "testInstantiateLegal" ) );
106          suite.addTest(
107              new RectangleTester( "testInstantiateIllegalLength" ) );
108          suite.addTest(
109              new RectangleTester( "testLengthMutatorLegal" ) );
110          suite.addTest( new RectangleTester( "testPerimeter" ) );
111          return suite;
112   */
113      }
114
115      // Step 8: Define a main() method that invokes JUnit to run
116      //         the test application.
117      public static void main (String[] args) {
118          // Use Java's reflection mechanism to get the name of
119          // this class.
120          String[] TestCaseName = {RectangleTester.class.getName()};
121          junit.swingui.TestRunner.main( TestCaseName );
122      }
123   }
```

5. Override the `tearDown()` method from `TestCase` to do any housecleaning following the execution of a test case. The `tearDown()` method is invoked at the conclusion of *each* `testXXX()` method. An example of `tearDown()` is given in Listing 2.9, but generally it can be left out. It is useful, for example, when I/O streams were opened in `setUp()` and need to be closed.

6. Define the test case methods following the format: `testXXX()`, where XXX is the name of the test. For example, to test the `setLength()` method for an illegal value, you could create a method called `testSetLengthIllegal()`. It is a good idea to provide comments with each test method briefly describing what it is testing.

7. Define a method `suite()` that creates and returns a `TestSuite` object that contains all the `testXXX` methods created in step 6.

8. Define a `main()` method that runs the JUnit framework.

Two of the test methods deserve extra attention. In Section 2.1.4 we modified the `Rectangle` class so that its constructor would throw an exception if it received illegal input. We need to verify that, in fact, the exception in thrown under the correct circumstances. Test Case 2.3 in Section 2.2.3 does this and is implemented as `testInstantiateIllegalLength()` (lines 58–70) of Listing 2.9.

Note the use of the try-catch block. If we did not handle the exception in the test method, the exception would terminate the testing program. That would be an expensive and irritating way of verifying the constructor properly checks its parameters.

An exception *should* be thrown by the constructor call on line 65 (we don't need to assign the resulting object reference to a `Rectangle` variable because we will never use it and, if all goes as expected, it won't be created anyway). If the exception is thrown as expected, the catch clause will handle it. The catch clause merely executes `assertTrue(true)`, which is our way of indicating that the test method expected an exception to be thrown and the test passed.

If an exception is *not* thrown on line 65, the `fail()` statement on line 66 will execute, marking the test as having failed.

The other method to look at is `testGetPerimiter()` (lines 82–89). It uses a variation of `assertEquals()` specialized to deal with the inaccuracy of representation of real numbers. The third argument to `assertEquals()` on line 88 is a delta and the assertion is true if the actual and expected values differ by no more than the delta.

2.2.9 When a Test Fails

Eventually a test will fail. To illustrate a failed JUnit test, let's make a change to `Rectangle` and rerun the test suite. The `getPerimeter()` method from `Rectangle` only has one line in it.

```
return 2 * this.length + 2 * this.height;
```

We'll change this to produce an incorrect result.

```
return this.length + 2 * this.height; // INTENTIONALLY WRONG!
```

You'll need to recompile `Rectangle` before rerunning the test program. Since we didn't change the test program, `RectangleTester`, it does *not* need to be recompiled. The result of rerunning the test suite is shown in Figure 2.10. The bar across the top is red, indicating a test failed. The middle portion of the window shows an X next to `testGetPerimeter()`, telling you this was the test method that failed. The text window at the bottom provides more information, telling you which line generated the failure (line 92) and that 23.6 was expected, but 17.1 was returned. From this it should be pretty easy to figure out where the problem is.

> Only recompile the test program if it was changed

When a test fails, you have to

1. Find and fix the bug that caused the test to fail.
2. Recompile the class (remember you do not need to recompile your JUnit testing class unless you changed its code).
3. Rerun the test. You can retest at first by selecting only the test that failed from the test case window and clicking on the lower "Run" button. In regression testing you rerun the entire suite of tests to make sure that your bug fix did not

> Regression testing: verify that the code has not regressed to an earlier, more "buggy" state

Figure 2.10 A run of a JUnit test program with a failed test.

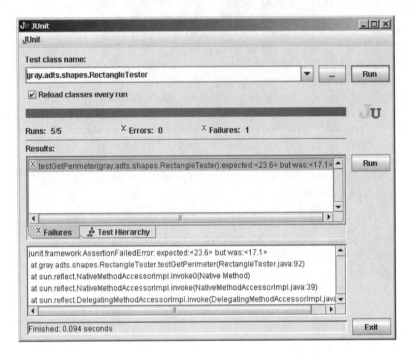

introduce a new bug or reintroduce an old bug; that is, you are checking that your code has not regressed to a more "buggy" state. But rerunning the entire test suite is as easy as clicking on a button, so you can't complain that it is hard work.

Remember, you aren't done testing until *all* the tests pass!

SUMMING UP

Testing should be done throughout the software development process. Test plans can be developed as soon as the interface for a class is known. Developing test plans at this point promotes a deeper understanding of the expected behavior of the classes to be implemented and provides insight into the quality (usefulness) of the interface.

In black-box testing the implementation details are hidden and testing is based on the described behavior of the class. In clear-box testing, the implementation details are revealed, which usually suggests additional tests.

JUnit is a unit-testing framework for Java programs. A test method is an implementation of a test case and uses assertions to verify that the actual behavior of a class matches its expected behavior. Test methods can be run as a group or individually.

CHECKPOINT

2.6 What is an assertion? What role does it play in JUnit testing?

2.7 What is a test fixture?

2.8 Write the JUnit test methods for the test cases you developed for CheckPoint questions 2.4 and 2.5.

∎ 2.3 Analysis and Measurement of Algorithms

Performance is an important characteristic of a system in many areas of engineering and so it is with software. An algorithm's performance can be described by its

- *Time Complexity.* How long it takes to execute. In general, our preference is for shorter execution times rather than longer ones.
- *Space Complexity.* How much additional space the algorithm needs. If the amount of additional memory needed is a function of the algorithm's input size, we prefer "smaller" functions.

Data structures also have a space complexity. As we will see, each collection type we will examine can have any of several implementations. The choice of internal organization, or backing store, affects the collection's space complexity.

Knowing these two characteristics allows us to compare different algorithms that solve the same problem. Naturally, when given a choice, we want the algorithm with the greatest speed and the lowest space requirements, but occasionally we need to trade one for the other. We could throw algorithm complexity (how difficult the algorithm is to code correctly) into this mix. Often we can get better performance at the cost of increased complexity. So, in choosing an algorithm to solve a problem we need to know what we are paying for.

Making tradeoffs

In this section we look at these performance issues from two perspectives. First, how can we determine an algorithm's time and space complexity? Second, how can we use that information to make decisions about which algorithms to use for a particular problem?

First we consider time complexity. What factors influence an algorithm's run time? Perhaps the most obvious answer is the number of instructions that execute and how long an individual instruction takes.

Time = number of instructions × time per instruction

However, as indicated in Chapter 0, wall clock time is not a good measure for objectively comparing algorithms (however, we revisit this idea in Section 2.3.3). I could make a fast algorithm look slow by running it on a slow machine and a slow algorithm look fast by running it on a fast machine. What we need is an objective measure that is independent of the hardware on which the algorithm will run.

Wall clock time is not a good way to compare algorithms

Since we want a measure that is independent of its implementation on any particular machine, we'll concentrate on the number of instructions from the algorithm that execute.

Time ≈ number of instructions that execute

What factors influence the number of instructions that execute? The size of the input is a pretty obvious one—the number of instructions that execute to calculate the mean of 100 grades will be less than that for 500 grades. We'll see later that some algorithms are also sensitive to the order of the data.

If we let n represent the size of the input, then $T(n)$ will be the time required for some algorithm to execute with input size n. In **asymptotic analysis** we want to capture an algorithm's *rate of growth* as n gets very large. We will use asymptotic notation to describe an algorithm's time and space complexity.

> Use asymptotic analysis to describe an algorithm's rate of growth

Listing 2.10 gives a method to calculate the average of an n-element array. If we are interested in assessing the "cost" of this method, it is pretty evident that the statements on lines 2, 3, and 8 through 11 don't contribute much. They are each executed once, no matter how big the array is. Individually, the statements on lines 4 through 6 also don't contribute much. What makes lines 4 through 6 significant is that they are repeated. The combination of the initialization of count on line 3 and the loop entry test on line 4 tell us how many times the loop will execute (the test on line 4 will pass n times and fail once, giving a total of $n + 1$ executions). Thus, for this example, the bulk of the time is spent in the loop, so *that* is what we want to reflect in our estimate of the cost of findAvg1D(). The number of instructions that will execute is $3n + 5$. As n becomes large, the coefficient 3 and the constant 5 play a diminishing role in determining the function's magnitude. We can capture this idea using asymptotic analysis.

2.3.1 Theta (θ) Notation

A function $f(n)$ is $\theta(g(n))$ if there are positive constants c_1, c_2, and n_0 such that $0 \leq c_1 g(n) \leq f(n) \leq c_2 g(n)$ for all $n \geq n_0$. This means that for all $n \geq n_0$, the graph of $f(n)$ falls between $c_1 g(n)$ and $c_2 g(n)$.

Listing 2.10 The number of statements executed to calculate the average of an array with n elements.

	Statements	Cost
1	`float findAvg1D( int []a, int n ) {`	
2	`    float sum = 0;`	1
3	`    int count = 0;`	1
4	`    while ( count < n ) {`	$n + 1$
5	`        sum += grades[count];`	n
6	`        count++;`	n
7	`    }`	
8	`    if ( n > 0 )`	1
9	`        return sum / n;`	
10	`    else`	1
11	`        return 0.0f;`	
12	`}`	
		$\overline{}$
		$3n + 5$

We start by describing the runtime of `findAvg1D()`.

$$T_{findAvg1D}(n) = \theta(n), \text{ for } c_1 = 2, c_2 = 4, n_0 = 5$$

As shown in Figure 2.11, the graph of $3n + 5$ falls between $2n$ and $4n$ for all values of $n \geq 5$.

There may be many choices for constants that will satisfy the inequality. For example, we also have

$$T_{findAvg1D}(n) = \theta(n), \text{ for } c_1 = 1, c_2 = 5, n_0 = 3$$

What matters to us is that we can find some combination that works. Finally, note that the number of statements executed for the algorithm is independent of the particular *values* in the array—all possible input combinations for an n element one-dimensional array will have a cost of $3n + 5$. Let's make sure we understand why this is so, because we will see examples where characteristics of the input such as range or ordering *do* have an impact on an algorithm's cost. To find the average of n numbers, we *have* to sum *all* of them, but the actual values being summed don't matter.

Input ordering can affect time complexity

Figure 2.11 A graph showing that $3n + 5$ is $\theta(n)$ for $c_1 = 2$, $c_2 = 4$, and $n_0 = 5$.

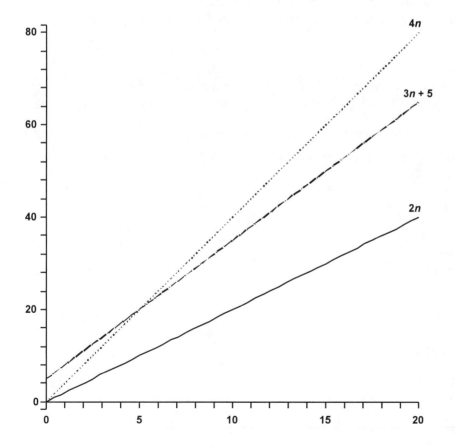

As a second example, consider a two-dimensional version of find average, shown in Listing 2.11. Again, there are statements that will only be executed once, no matter how big the input array is. Clearly it is the loops on lines 4 through 11 (particularly the nested loop on lines 6–9) that will dominate the runtime cost of this method. For each iteration of the outer loop, the inner loop will execute n times. The outer loop also executes n times; thus lines 7 and 8 will each execute $n \times n$ times. The total cost of the method is $3n^2 + 4n + 5$. Focusing on the high-order term, we see that this method has a quadratic growth rate.

As in the one-dimensional version, the number of statements that execute in the two-dimensional version is dependent on the size of the input and not on the particular values passed in the array. Thus

$$T_{\text{findAvg2D}}(n) = \theta(n^2), \text{ let } c_1 = 2, c_2 = 3, n_0 = 6$$

The graph in Figure 2.12 shows that $3n^2 + 4n + 5$ lies between $2n^2$ and $4n^2$ for all values of $n \geq 6$.

Bounded above and below by a multiple of $g(n)$, $\theta(g(n))$ provides what is called a *tight bound* on an algorithm's growth rate.

2.3.2 Big-Oh (O) Notation

Let's consider an algorithm for which the number of statements that execute can vary from instance to instance and so cannot be described using θ notation. As an

---

Listing 2.11 The number of statements executed for calculating the average value of a two-dimensional array with $n \times n$ elements.[4]

	Statements	Cost
1	`float findAvg2D( int [][]a, int n ) {`	
2	`    float sum = 0;`	1
3	`    int i = 0;`	1
4	`    while ( i < n ) {`	$n + 1$
5	`        int j = 0;`	n
6	`        while ( j < n ) {`	$n \times (n + 1)$
7	`            sum += a[i];`	$n \times n$
8	`            j++;`	$n \times n$
9	`        }`	
10	`        i++;`	n
11	`    }`	
12	`    if ( n > 0 )`	1
13	`        return sum / n;`	
14	`    else`	1
15	`        return 0.0f;`	
16	`}`	
		$3n^2 + 4n + 5$

Figure 2.12 A graph showing that $3n^2 + 4n + 5$ is $\theta(n^2)$ for $c_1 = 2$, $c_2 = 4$, and $n_0 = 6$.

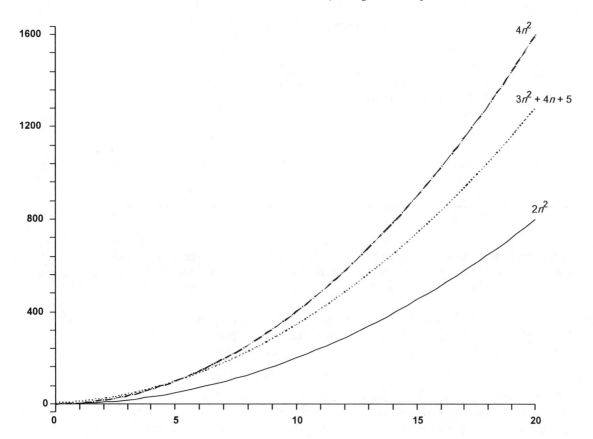

example, Listing 2.12 presents a simple linear search algorithm for searching an n element array for some target.

In the best case our target is in the first position of the array and we find it immediately. This is nice, but we aren't usually interested in the best case. It isn't that we are pessimists, but we don't expect the best case to happen all that often *and* we need to make sure that we can live with the resource requirements when the *worst* case happens.[4] However, in Chapter 11 we will look at an approach to organizing data that does expect the best case to happen often and whose runtime complexity is based on a cost that is amortized over time.

The worst case for `linearSearch()` occurs when we are forced to look at all n elements of the array. This happens when the target is either not in the array or is

---

[4]Typically you would write this code using nested for loops, but while loops are used here to make it easier to see the execution count for individual statements. The total count would be the same for the for loop implementation, but it would be harder to see how we arrived at it.

Listing 2.12 A simple linear search algorithm on an unsorted array.

	Statements	Cost
1	`int linearSearch( int []a, int n, int target ) {`	
2	`    int i = 0;`	1
3	`    while ( i < n ) {`	$n + 1$
4	`        if ( target == array[i] )`	n
5	`            return i;`	1
6	`        i++;`	n
7	`    }`	
8	`    return −1;`	1
9	`}`	
		$3n + 3$

in the last position of the array. So the cost column in Listing 2.12 represents the *maximum* number of times the line can execute. This introduces the notion of an *upper bound* on the amount of work that can be done, which we describe using big-Oh (O) notation. **Upper bound on growth rate**

A function $f(n)$ is $O(g(n))$ if there are positive constants c and n_0 such that $f(n) \leq cg(n)$ for all $n \geq n_0$. What we are saying is that $f(n)$ *will grow no faster* than a multiple of $g(n)$; hence $g(n)$ is an upper bound on the growth rate of $f(n)$.

$T_{linearSearch}(n) = 3n + 3 = O(n)$ for $c = 3$ $n_0 = 3$, in the worst case.

The graph in Figure 2.13 illustrates this idea. It also shows that $T_{linearSearch}(n)$ is $O(n^2)$ for $c = 2$ and $n_0 = 3$. But, we would not regard this as being honestly descriptive of `linearSearch()`'s run time. That is, saying that $3n + 2$ is $O(n^2)$ is an abuse of asymptotic notation.

We might also be interested in the average case, but the average case is usually difficult to determine and is often as expensive asymptotically as the worst case. For example, in `linearSearch()` we would expect that if the target is in the array and if every position in the array has the same probability of holding the target, then, on average, we would have to look at approximately half the elements before finding the target. But $1/2n = O(n)$ for $c = 1$ and $n_0 = 1$, so the average and worst cases are the same, $O(n)$. Consequently, we will typically present an algorithm's performance in terms of its worst case.

Before moving on we need to look at one more case. The method in Listing 2.13 returns the median of values from three positions in an array (we'll use this in Chapter 9). In the best case only statements 2 through 7 would execute (six statements). In the worst case, we take the longest path through the method, executing statements 2 through 5, 9, and 13 through 15 for a total of eight statements, so we could say that the method is $O(8)$. However, what is important here is that the number of statements that execute is *independent* of the size of n. We say that algorithms whose runtime is independent of the size of their input run in *constant time* and have a time complexity of $O(1)$. **Constant time algorithms are O(1)**

Figure 2.13 A graph showing that $T_{linearSearch}(n)$ is both $O(n)$ and $O(n^2)$.

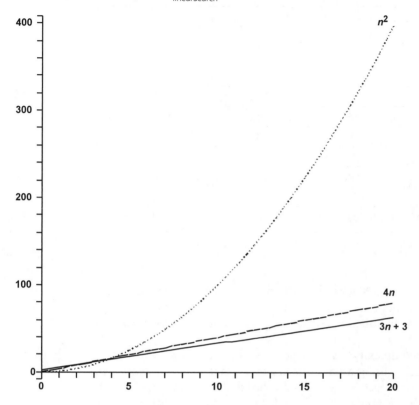

Listing 2.13 Finding the median value from three postions in an array.

```
1    int medianOf3( int []a, int n ) {
2        int v1 = a[0];
3        int v2 = a[n/2];
4        int v3 = a[n-1];
5        if ( (v1 < v2 ) && ( v1 < v3 ) )          // v1 is smallest
6            if ( v2 < v3 )
7                return n/2;                        // middle position
8            else return n - 1;                     // last position
9        else if ( ( v2 < v1 ) && ( v2 < v3 ) )     // v2 smallest
10           if ( v1 < v3 )
11               return 0;                          // first position
12           else return n − 1;                     // last position
13       else                                       // v3 is smallest
14           if ( v1 < v2 )
15               return 0;                          // first position
16           else return n / 2;                     // middle position
17   }
```

Table 2.3 Computing times for some common functions.

$\log_2 n$	n	$n \log_2 n$	n^2	2^n
1	2	2	4	4
2	4	8	16	16
3	8	24	64	256
4	16	64	256	65,536
5	32	160	1,024	4,294,967,296
6	64	384	4,096	1.84×10^{19}
7	128	896	16,384	3.40×10^{38}
8	256	2,048	65,536	1.16×10^{77}
9	512	4,608	262,144	1.34×10^{154}
10	1,024	10,240	1,048,576	1.80×10^{308}

In this book we will look at algorithms with different time complexities. Table 2.3 gives you a good idea about the computing times for some common functions. As you can see, slow growing functions such as $\log_2 n$ are much preferable to fast-growing functions such as 2^n.

What about **space complexity?** We can describe the space complexity of an algorithm or data structure using asymptotic analysis. What we are interested in knowing is how much *extra* space is needed to get the job done. So, for example, in the algorithms used in this section we don't include the arrays themselves since they represent the data to be manipulated. Rather, we look at the space required to run the algorithm. This includes, for example, the variables declared locally to the algorithm. So far, all of our examples have a space complexity of O(1) since the amount of extra space needed is independent of the input size. This won't always be the case.

As we look at the implementation of collection types, we will consider the space complexity implications of our choice of backing store.

SUMMING UP

Algorithms require resources (time and space) to run. Asymptotic analysis provides a way to measure the cost of an algorithm in a machine-independent way. Frequently, the cost of an algorithm is a function of the size of its input, often represented as n. Asymptotic analysis considers the cost of an algorithm as n gets large. Theta notation gives a tight bound on the cost of an algorithm, while big-Oh notation specifies an upper bound on cost.

CHECKPOINT

2.9 Determine the time complexity for the following method.

```
1      void doubleIt( int []a, int n ) {
2          int i = 0;
3          while ( i < n )
4              a[i] = 2 * a[i];
5      }
```

2.10 Determine the time complexity for the following method.

```
1      boolean find2D( int [][]a, int n, int target ){
2          int i = 0;
3          while ( i < n ) {
4              int j = 0;
5              while ( j < n )
6                  if ( a[i][j] == target )
7                      return true;
8          }
9      }
10         return false;
11     }
```

2.11. Express the following using big-Oh notation.

    a. $3n + 6n^2 + 200$

    b. $10\log_2 n + 2n$

    c. $21n + 14n + 7n^3$

2.3.3 Algorithm Measurement

Asymptotic analysis gives us an objective way to compare the "time cost" of algorithms based on the number of instructions that execute. While useful, this assumes that all "instructions" take the same amount of time to execute. This convenience breaks down in two instances: when instructions involve additional memory references and when an algorithm is affected by optimizing hardware (e.g., caching and processor pipelining). We will look at an example of each and in the process will see how we can explore performance differences in the implementations of the algorithms we will look at in the rest of the book.

The first problem we consider is finding the maximum integer in an array of integers. The pseudocode and asymptotic cost analysis for algorithm `findMax` is shown in the following pseudocode.

Algorithm findMax

We will create two versions of `findMax`: one for an array of `int`s (a Java primitive type) and another for an array of `Integer` objects (a Java reference type). Figure 2.14 illustrates the difference between these two arrays and hints at which version will be slower and why.

Figure 2.14 Layout for an array of `ints` and an array of `Integer` objects.

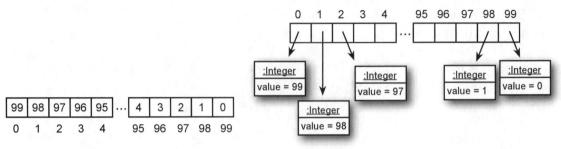

(a) An array of `ints`—each cell of the array stores an `int` primitive.

(b) An array of `Integer` objects—each cell of the array stores a *reference* to an `Integer` object.

Pseudocode: findMax(array of length *n*)

max = first element of the array	*1*
i = 1	*1*
while i is less than n	*n*
if the ith element of the array is greater than max	*n*
max = the ith element of the array	*n*
return max	*1*

$$3n + 3 = \theta(n)$$

Accessing an element of the `int` array requires a single memory reference to get to a value in a cell of the array, while accessing an element of the `Integer` array requires a memory reference to get to the cell, a second memory reference to get to the `Integer` object and a third to get the `int` stored in the object's `value` field. Memory accesses are expensive, so, although asymptotic analysis tells us these two algorithms are $\theta(n)$, we hypothesize that the `int` array version will be faster.

The general design for timing an algorithm is shown in the following pseudocode. We'll now develop the steps and apply them to our `findMax` problem.

Pseudocode: for timing an algorithm

initialize the data structure
for n *iterations*
    get the starting time
    run the algorithm
    get the finish time
    total time = total time + (finish time – start time)
average time = total time / n

Since we want to see the effect of `int` array access versus `Integer` array access, it is important that the two findMax algorithms execute the same number of instructions (see Table 2.4). This is accomplished by initializing the two arrays to

Make sure the test environment is controlled

Table 2.4 Time to run findMax on an array of length 4,000,000 (times are in milliseconds).

Array Type	Time 1	Time 2	Time 3	Time 4	Time 5
int	15	16	16	0	15
Integer	16	15	31	16	32

the same values and in the same order (Listing 2.14: lines 24–25 and 48–49). Furthermore, the initialization places the largest value in position 0, guaranteeing that lines 33 and 57 will execute the same number of times for both versions of the algorithm.

Listing 2.14 FindMaxTimed.java—a class to time searching for the largest element in an int and an Integer array.

```
1    import java.util.*;
2
3    public class FindMaxTimed {
4        private static int[] intArray;
5        private static Integer[] intObjArray;
6        private static final int NUM_ITERATIONS = 20;
7
8        public static void main( String[] args ){
9
10           long start, finish, total;
11
12           if ( args.length == 0 ) {
13               System.err.println( "array size missing" );
14               System.exit( -1 );
15           }
16
17           int SIZE = Integer.parseInt( args[0] );
18           float intArrayTimeTotal = 0, intObjArrayTimeTotal = 0;
19
20           System.out.println( "Array size is " + SIZE );
21           // allocate and initialize the int array with
22           // values from SIZE - 1 to 0
23           intArray = new int[SIZE];
24           for ( int j = 0, i = SIZE - 1; i >= 0; j++, i-- )
25               intArray[j] = i;
26
27           // find the largest value in the int array
28           for ( int i = 0; i < NUM_ITERATIONS; i++ ) {
29               int largest = intArray[0];
30               start = System.currentTimeMillis();
31               for ( int j = 1; j < SIZE; j++ )
```

```
32                  if ( intArray[j] > largest )
33                      largest = intArray[j];
34                  finish = System.currentTimeMillis();
35                  intArrayTimeTotal += finish - start;
36              }
37          System.out.println( "Done timing int array" );
38
39          // force cleanup to prevent it happening while
40          // looking for the largest in the Integer array
41          intArray = null;      // make the array garbage
42          System.gc();          // invoke the garbage collector
43
44          System.out.println( "Timing Integer array now" );
45          // allocate and initialize the Integer array with
46          // values from SIZE - 1 to 0
47          intObjArray = new Integer[SIZE];
48          for ( int j = 0, i = SIZE - 1; i >= 0; j++, i-- )
49              intObjArray[j] = new Integer( i );
50
51          // find the largest value in the Integer object array
52          for ( int i = 0; i < NUM_ITERATIONS; i++ ) {
53              Integer largest = intObjArray[0];
54              start = System.currentTimeMillis();
55              for ( int j = 1; j < SIZE; j++ )
56                  if ( intObjArray[j] > largest )
57                      largest = intObjArray[j];
58                  finish = System.currentTimeMillis();
59              intObjArrayTimeTotal += finish - start;
60          }
61
62          System.out.println( "Avg int array time            = " +
63                              ( intArrayTimeTotal / NUM_ITERATIONS ) );
64          System.out.println( "Avg Integer object array time = " +
65                              ( intObjArrayTimeTotal / NUM_ITERATIONS ));
66          System.out.println();
67      }
68  }
```

OUTPUT

```
java -verbose:gc -XX:+AggressiveHeap FindMaxTimed 8000000
Array size is 8000000
Done timing int array
[Full GC 31506K->98K(936064K), 0.0069578 secs]
Timing Integer array now
Avg int array time            = 22.65
Avg Integer object array time = 43.0
```

Java provides `System.currentTimeMillis()` to get the current time in milliseconds (there are 1,000 milliseconds in a second). The timing algorithm uses it to get the starting times (lines 30 and 54) and finish times (lines 34 and 58).

Unfortunately, what we are measuring here is elapsed time. This means that anything else your computer is asked to do while running the timing algorithm is "charged" to the computation time for `findMax`. This is evidenced in Table 2.5 where you can see that the time to find the maximum value in an array of 4,000,000 `ints` can range from 0 to 16 milliseconds, and the time to find the maximum value in an array of 4,000,000 `Integers` ranges from 15 to 32 milliseconds. What should we make of this?

First, measuring execution time is limited by the resolution of the clock. If the event we are measuring occurs faster than the clock can measure it, the event's time will appear to be 0.

Second, the variation in the non-zero times is due to other things the operating system and the JVM are doing while `findMax` is executing. For example, the operating system may be responding to requests from hardware devices (network, disks, the mouse) or from programs (i.e., your instant messenger window or an automatic page update to your browser). Consequently you should close all other applications when timing and don't jiggle the mouse! Also, the JVM can do garbage collection at any time. If that occurs while `findMax` is running, the execution time of `findMax` will appear to be longer than it really is. This is partially controlled in our experiment by allocating the arrays just before they are needed (lines 23 and 47) and releasing the `int` array when it is no longer needed and forcing garbage collection (lines 41–42) so it (hopefully) won't occur while timing `findMax` on the `Integer` array. Lastly, we time the algorithm several times (see line 2 of the pseudocode for timing algorithms and lines 28 and 52 of Listing 2.14 for examples) and take the average.

The output shows a sample run. The first line shows how the program was launched. The first argument tells the JVM to output information about garbage collection events. You can see in the output that, as planned, garbage collection is done on the `int` array between running the `int` and `Integer` versions of `findMax`. The second argument is needed to ensure the heap is large enough to allocate each array. Try running the timing algorithm without it and you receive an `OutOfMemoryError` when the heap runs out of memory.

The timings are shown in Table 2.5. They confirm our hypothesis that the extra memory references needed to access `Integers` cause a performance hit, so the $\theta(n)$ runtime doesn't tell the full story in this case. Having said that, you should note something else about Table 2.5. Algorithm `findMax` has a time complexity of $\theta(n)$, so if we double the size of the input, we expect that the execution time should

Table 2.5 Timings for `findMax` on an array of `ints` and an array of `Integers` (times are in milliseconds).

n	Array of `int`	Array of `Integer`
4,000,000	11.363	21.739
8,000,000	22.727	42.958
800,000	2.314	4.329

Table 2.6 Pseudocode for `twoDimensionArrayCopy` for an n by n array

Copying row by row	Copying column by column	$2n^2 + 3n + 2$
let row = 0	let col = 0	1
while row < n	while col < n	$n + 1$
let col = 0	let row = 0	n
while col < n	while row < n	$n(n + 1)$
arraycopy[row][col] = twoDArray[row][col]	arraycopy[row][col] = twoDArray[row][col]	n^2

double, which is (almost exactly) what happens for both versions of the algorithm.

As a second example we look at the effect of processor cache on algorithm performance. The problem we will explore is making a copy of an $n \times n$ array. Table 2.6 shows two pseudocode versions—one makes the copy row by row and the other column by column.

Before timing the algorithms, we have to look at how two-dimensional arrays are laid out in memory and how a processor cache works.

Two-dimensional arrays are laid out in memory using one of two organizations: row major order or column major order. As shown in Figure 2.15(a), when using row major order, we simply start with the first row of the array, follow it with the second row, then the third and so on. Similarly, for column major order, we start with the first column, followed by the second column, and so on (see Figure 2.15(b)). Java stores two-dimensioned arrays using row major order.

The second background topic we need to cover is how **cache** on a processor works and what it does.[5] Cache is a form of very fast memory that resides on the processor. As shown in Figure 2.16(a), the cache is composed of some number of blocks of memory called **slots** each with room for m words of data. From the per-

A cache slot stores a copy of a memory block

Figure 2.15 Layout of a two-dimensional array in memory using row major order and column major order.

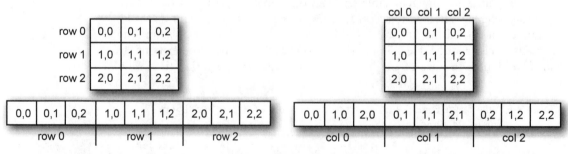

(a) Layout of a two-dimensional array using row major order.

(b) Layout of a two-dimensional array using column major order.

---

[5]The presentation here is quite basic and leaves out many details you will get in a computer organization course.

Figure 2.16 The result of a cache miss—loading a block into a cache slot.

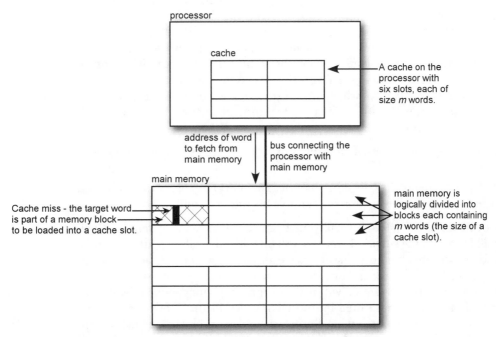

(a) An address generated by the processor is not found in the cache, generating a cache miss.

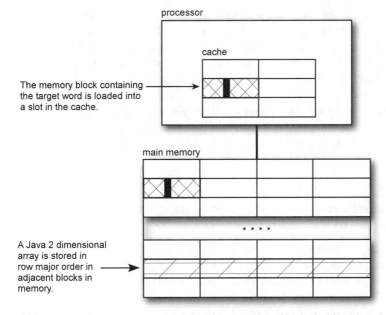

(b) The block from memory containing the target word is copied into a cache slot.

spective of the cache, main memory is composed of a collection of **memory blocks**, each of size *m* words (to match the size of a cache slot). Each slot in the cache holds a *copy* of a block from main memory that has been accessed recently.

Here is how it works. When the processor generates the address of a data item it needs to access, it first asks the cache if it contains a copy of the data for the given address. If the answer is yes we have a **cache hit** and the cache provides the data to the processor very quickly (avoiding an expensive memory reference). If the answer is no, we have a **cache miss** (see Figure 2.16(a)). On a miss, main memory is accessed and the *entire block* of which the target address is a part is loaded into a slot in the cache (see Figure 2.16(b)). There are two concepts that explain how a cache can provide a performance boost.

Temporal locality. An accessed element is likely to be accessed again in the near future.

Spatial locality. Items close together in space (memory) are likely to be accessed close together in time—our array example fits this description.

Because the cache is quite small (much smaller than main memory), it will eventually run into the situation where it will be full and a subsequent cache miss will load a block from memory into the cache, displacing a block already loaded.

We learned in the findMax example that memory accesses are slow. The two-dimensional array copy example will reaffirm this in a roundabout way. A two-dimensional array in Java is stored in row major order. Picture a two-dimensional array laid out in memory, occupying a number of adjacent blocks (see the bottom of Figure 2.16(b)). When accessed in row major order, when we access the first cell of the first row, we'll load the entire block of which that word is a part. This means that it is likely that the next couple of array cells from the first row will have been loaded into the cache and when the processor generates addresses to access them, the cache will be able to supply them quickly, avoiding an additional memory access. Thus, an algorithm that copies a two-dimensional Java array in row order (lines 27–35 of Listing 2.15) will benefit from a succession of cache hits as sections of each row are accessed and loaded into the cache. Conversely, an algorithm that performs the copy in column major order (lines 37–45 of Listing 2.15) will be accessing elements that are *not* adjacent in memory and so will suffer from a succession of cache misses. Consequently, entire blocks will be loaded into the cache, but only a single word from the block will be used in the near future. Worse, it is

---

Listing 2.15 ArrayCopyTimed.java—a class to time copying a two-dimensional int array using row order and column order access.

```
1    public class ArrayCopyTimed {
2        private static int[][] intArray, copy;
3        private static final int NUM_ITERATIONS = 20;
4
5        public static void main( String[] args ){
6
```

```
 7          long start, finish;
 8          float rowCopyTime = 0, columnCopyTime = 0;
 9
10          if ( args.length == 0 ) {
11              System.err.println( "array size missing" );
12              System.exit( -1 );
13          }
14
15          int SIZE = Integer.parseInt( args[0] );
16          intArray = new int[SIZE][SIZE];
17          copy = new int[SIZE][SIZE];
18
19          System.out.println( "Array size is " + SIZE );
20
21          // initialize the matrix
22          for ( int i = 0; i < SIZE;   i++ ) {
23              for ( int j = 0; j < SIZE; j++ )
24                  intArray[i][j] = i + j;
25          }
26
27          // get a copy going row by row
28          for ( int i = 0; i < NUM_ITERATIONS; i++ ) {
29              start = System.currentTimeMillis();
30              for ( int r = 0; r < SIZE;   r++ )
31                  for ( int c = 0; c < SIZE; c++ )
32                      copy[r][c] = intArray[r][c];
33              finish = System.currentTimeMillis();
34              rowCopyTime += finish - start;
35          }
36
37          // get a copy going column by column
38          for ( int i = 0; i < NUM_ITERATIONS; i++ ) {
39              start = System.currentTimeMillis();
40              for ( int c = 0; c < SIZE; c++ )
41                  for ( int r = 0; r < SIZE;   r++ )
42                      copy[r][c] = intArray[r][c];
43              finish = System.currentTimeMillis();
44              columnCopyTime += finish - start;
45          }
46
47          System.out.print( "array copy time (row-column):      " +
48                              ( rowCopyTime / NUM_ITERATIONS ) );
49          System.out.print( "\narray copy times (column-row):      " +
50                              ( columnCopyTime / NUM_ITERATIONS ) );
51          System.out.println( "\n" );
52      }
53  }
```

Table 2.7 Timings for `ArrayCopyTimed` using row order and column order access (times are in milliseconds).

n	Row Order Access	Column Order Access
500	.75	7.05
1,000	5.5	21.05

possible that the block might be replaced by a new block before it can be accessed again.

The timings in Table 2.7 show how significant this difference is for the two array access orders. Again, the two copy algorithms execute the same number of instructions (they are both $\theta(n^2)$). In this case, it is optimizing hardware support (the processor cache) that affects the algorithm's actual performance.

SUMMING UP

Asymptotic analysis provides a way to compare algorithms based on the objective measure of instruction count. However the actual runtime behavior of different implementations of the same algorithm may be quite different. The cost of memory accesses and the effect of optimizing hardware are two examples that can affect runtime that aren't accurately represented by asymptotic analysis.

`System.currentTimeMillis()` can be used to get the current time in milliseconds. Using this method provides a total elapsed time, which includes any time the computer is busy with tasks unrelated to timing the algorithm. Care must be taken to reduce the number of other tasks the computer is asked to do while timing an algorithm and you must take the average of several timings.

EXERCISES

Paper and Pencil

1. Using some graphing/plotting software, draw the graphs of the functions from Table 2.3.

2. Express the following using big-Oh notation
   a. $3\log_2 n + 4n\log_2 n + n$
   b. $546 + 34n + 2n^2$
   c. $2^n + 14n^2 + 4n^3$

3. What does the following algorithm do? What is its time complexity?

```
public static int doSomething( int array[], int n ) {
    int k = 0;
    for ( int i = 1; i < n; i++ )
```

```
      if ( array[i] > array[k] )
      k = i;
   int temp = array[0];
   array[0] = array[k];
   array[k] = temp;
      k = 1;
   for ( int i = 2; i < n; i++ )
      if ( array[i] > array[k] )
         k = i;
   return array[k];
}
```

4. Write a test plan to test the method in the previous problem.

5. Reimplement method doSomething() so that it doesn't modify the array. What is the cost of this new algorithm?

Testing and Debugging

1. Roland suspects that a block of code he has written could generate a bunch of exceptions, and he just doesn't want to deal with it. Here is how he ended up handling it. What does this do? Is it a good idea?

```
try {
    // lots of lines of code
}
catch ( Exception e )
{
    // do nothing
}
```

2. Ben initially coded the openOutputFile() from Listing 2.3 as follows. What do you think of this implementation?

```
33    public void openOutputFile( String outfileName ) {
34       try{
35          outfile = new Formatter( outfileName );
36       } catch ( FileNotFoundException e ) {
37          System.err.printf( "Error opening output file: %s\n%s",
38                            outfileName, "Exiting application." );
39       } catch ( SecurityException e ) {
40          System.err.printf( "Error insufficient write access to " +
41                            "create file: %s\n", outfileName  );
42       }
43       finally {
44          infile.close();
45          System.exit( 1 );
46       }
47    }
```

ON THE WEB

Additional study material is available at Addison-Wesley's Website at http://www.aw.com/cssupport. This material includes the following:

- Study Guide Exercises
- Answers to CheckPoint Problems
- Additional exercises

Fundamental Data Structures: The Array and Linked Structures

3

CHAPTER OUTLINE

The specification of an ADT includes a description of the kind and range of values to be supported by the new type. What the specification won't necessarily tell you is how those values are to be represented. It is up to you as the implementer of the ADT to choose a suitable representation in the implementation language for the new type's values. A **data structure** provides a concrete representation for the data values specified by a collection ADT, often referred to as the backing store.

In this chapter we look at two very basic data structures that have wide application: the array and linked data structures. Since the operations of an ADT will be implemented using the operations of the data structure, it is important to understand how these operations work and what they cost.

■ **3.1** The Array Data Structure

The array is a very common data structure found in many programming languages. While arrays can be created in several dimensions (two dimensions produces a table or matrix, three dimensions produces a cube), we will concentrate on one-dimensional arrays here.

3.1.1 Memory Allocation: Static versus Dynamic Arrays

Some programming languages require that the programmer say how big an array is to be when the program is being *written*. These are called **static arrays** and have the following characteristics:

- The size of the array must be given by the time the program is compiled.
- The memory allocated for the array is permanently bound to the array variable name.
- The size of the array is fixed for the duration of the program, so the array cannot shrink or grow to meet the application's needs.

The inflexibility of static arrays is apparent from this description. The programmer must make a best guess on the *upper bound* of the size of the array. If it turns out the application needs more space, too bad; all the application can do is exit gracefully with an error message saying that demand for the application's resources exceeded capacity.

On the other hand, if the application turns out to need only a small portion of the allocated space, then the unused portion of the array is wasted space. For many applications this isn't a problem, but for some it is, and you do not want to get in the habit of assuming there will always be such an abundance of resources that you can be carefree about their use.

Java supports **dynamic arrays**. Arrays in Java are objects, and, like all objects in Java, are created using the new operator. Dynamic arrays have the following characteristics:

- The size of the array can be given at compile time or at runtime, so an application can begin execution and wait until it has a better idea of its space needs before allocating the array.
- The memory that is allocated is *not* permanently bound to the array variable. It is perfectly legal to assign a different block of memory to the array variable.
- The size of the block that is allocated is fixed, but it is possible to allocate a *new* block of memory that is smaller or larger than the original block.

These characteristics of dynamic arrays provide a great deal of flexibility and allow you to resize your arrays as needed, making them smaller if your needs have shrunk or larger if you have reached the capacity of the current array and need more space. The implementation details of array resizing are given in Section 3.2.2.

3.1.2 Storage and Access Characteristics

The memory that is allocated for an array is composed of a block of *contiguous* locations in the computer's memory. The data-bearing portion of an array has the layout shown in Figure 3.1 as follows:

- *Length* is the number of data cells allocated to the array.
- A *data cell* stores a single value of the array's type. The size of each cell will depend on the type of data stored in each cell.

The number of bytes allocated for an array depends on the number of cells in the array and the size of each cell.

number of bytes of data = number of cells × size of each cell

Here are some examples.[1]

Array Declaration	Data Size Computation
`short[] s_array = new short[100];`	$100 \times 2 = 200$ bytes for the data
`double[] d_array = new double[100];`	$100 \times 8 = 800$ bytes for the data
`String[] str_array = new String[100];`	$100 \times 4 = 400$ bytes for references to the `String` objects

Java arrays can store either primitive types (`int`, `float`, `char`, etc.) or *references to* objects. This distinction is important because while s_array stores 100 `short` values, str_array does *not* store or allocate memory for 100 `Strings` (see Figure 3.2(b)). Instead, it stores 100 *references to* `Strings`. In this example we assume the size of an object reference is 4 bytes. When an array is created, its cells are automatically initialized to 0 for numeric primitive types, `false` for `booleans`, and `null` for objects.

The range of indices that can be accessed in an array is always 0 to `length` −1. The bounds for all three of the arrays we just created is 0 to 99. In Java, attempting to access an indexed position outside the bounds of an array produces an `IndexOutOfBoundsException`, so it is important to know what the bounds are and to make sure your indices never stray from them.

Figure 3.1 The memory layout of a one-dimensional array.

data cell 0	data cell 1	data cell 2	. . .	data cell *length*-1

---

[1]These computations do not include the overhead of the tag and length fields that all Java arrays have.

To access a cell of an array, the computer needs to know its address in memory. Because the cells of an array are adjacent in memory, the computer can easily calculate the address of any cell in the array. Consequently, an array is a **random access** data structure.[2] The time to access an element with random access is independent of the element's location in the data structure—accessing the cell at index `length` − 1 is as efficient as accessing the cell at index 0. Consider the `short` array declared earlier and look at Figure 3.2. The address of cell *i* can be calculated as follows:

Arrays provide random access

array base address + (*i* × cell size)

For example, assuming the array starts at address 200, the address of s_array[41] is 200 + (41 × 2).

The cost to calculate an address is constant because there are a fixed number of operations involved in the calculation. This is independent of how big the array is and which cell of the array is to be accessed. So the time to access an array element is O(1), which is the cost of the address calculation plus the cost of a memory access to fetch the array element from memory.

Address calculation is a constant cost – O(1)

Figure 3.2 Layout of s_array and str_array.

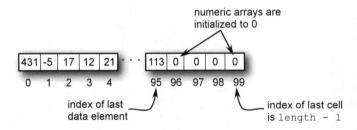

(a) A partially populated array of shorts.

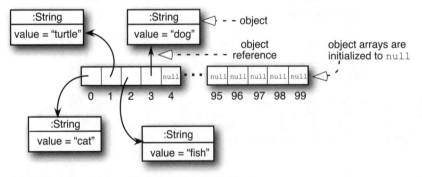

(b) A partially populated array of String objects.

---

[2]Random access is also referred to as direct access. Some texts reserve direct access to refer to magnetic disk accesses where we can move the disk's read/write head directly to the desired track, then wait for the target sector to rotate beneath the head.

3.1.3 Size versus Capacity of an Array

Each array stores the number of cells that are allocated to the array in a `length` field that is part of the data structure. This is an upper bound on the number of elements that can be stored in the array at one time and represents the *capacity* of the array. Unfortunately the array data structure does not keep track of how many of those cells actually store data. This is the program's responsibility. Look at Figure 3.2(a) again.

The `length` field gives the array's capacity

Why is this important? Imagine you have created a 100-element array of `shorts` to store test scores and the array is populated with 47 test scores, so the indices 0 to 46 hold valid data and cells 47 to 99 store junk (as far as your program is concerned). If you are asked to write an algorithm to determine the average test score, which cells do you want to examine? Only those that store data (indices 0 to 46). Including any values from indices 47 to 99 of the array in your computation would produce an incorrect result.

CHECKPOINT

3.1 What does it mean to say that the cells of an array are contiguous in memory?

3.2 What does `int[] zample = new int[50];` do? How is that different from `int[] foo;`?

3.3 What is the cost of the following operation: `zample[5] = 10;` Explain.

3.4 Is the following legal in Java? Draw two diagrams to illustrate what is happening.

```
int[] fluffle = new int[50];   // Diagram (a)
fluffle = new int[100];        // Diagram (b)
```

■ 3.2 Array Operations

Basic array operations include the following:

- Traversing, or walking through, the array structure
- Resizing the array
- Replacing an element
- Inserting an element
- Deleting an element

3.2.1 Traversing an Array (Bidirectional)

A fundamental operation on arrays is traversal.

- A traversal can begin anywhere in the array and can be bidirectional—you can move either "up" to the last indexable position or "down" toward index 0.

■ The traversal can move in increments of 1 or any number that is appropriate, so long as the resulting index remains within the bounds of the array.

■ Any of a number of operations can be done with an array element during the traversal: compute with it, examine it, delete or move it, and so on.

Here is the pseudocode for a generic array traversal. A *cursor* is a variable used to walk through the data structure and marks the current position in the traversal.

> **Cursor: a variable that marks a position in a traversal of a data structure**

Pseudocode: generic array traversal
set the cursor to the starting point for the traversal
while there are still cells to examine
  process the cell referenced by the cursor
  move the cursor to reference the next cell to be examined

Let's look at two examples. First, the code fragment in Listing 3.1 computes the average test score from an array of test scores. For this problem we must access all the cells of the array that hold test scores and sum them. The summing could be done with a while loop, as suggested by the pseudocode above. However, for loops are ideal for walking through arrays.

You will note that the pseudocode for the traversal doesn't look exactly like the code produced from it, but they are semantically equivalent. When I write pseudocode, I am more concerned with *what* needs to be done in each step than with *how* I am going to do it in some language. The pseudocode statement *while there are still cells to examine* captures the essence of *what* the loop must do. If you look closely at the for loop, you will see that it is just a rearrangement of the pseudocode statements. Trying to figure out *what* and *how* at the same time is often more than I can do well, and I have learned to stop trying to force it. When I get to the coding part, I think carefully about how to best express the pseudocode in the implementation language.

> **Pseudocoding shows what needs to be done**

Listing 3.1 Calculating the average test score from an array of test scores.

```
1    static final int MAX_GRADES = 100;        // array capacity
2    short[] grades = new short[MAX_GRADES];
3    short numGrades = 0;                       // # data elements in array
4    float sum = 0.0, avg = 0.0;
5
6    numGrades = getGrades(grades);   // populate array with test scores
7    // post-conditions: numGrades <= grades.length and
8    // valid grades are in positions 0 to numGrades − 1
9
10   for (int i = 0; i < numGrades; i++)        // i is the cursor
11       sum += grades[i];
12       // loop invariant: sum = sum of all cells from grades[0]
13       // to grades[i]
14
15   if ( numGrades > 0 )
16       avg = sum / numGrades;
```

In our second example, we are looking for the *first* occurrence of a target object in an array of objects starting at index 0. This is written as a method as shown in Listing 3.2.

As in the first example, i plays the role of the cursor used to access individual cells of the array. The method assumes that the objects have provided a meaningful implementation of the equals() method inherited from the Object class (see Chapter 1 for an example of overriding the equals() method).

This method is known as a linear search—start at one end of a linear data structure and walk through it until you either find what you are looking for or have looked at all the elements and not found the target. The cost of this algorithm is linear in the length of the array, so is characterized as O(n). In Listing 3.2, n is numElements.

Linear search is O(n)

3.2.2 Expanding the Capacity of an Array

An array needs to be expanded when you want to insert an element, but the array is already full. Listing 3.3 gives the pseudocode to increase the array size by 50% and the equivalent Java code.

Listing 3.2 A method for finding an object in an array of objects.

```
1   /**
2    * Find the first occurrence of an object in an array of objects.
3    * @param array — the array of objects.
4    * @param numElements — the number of elements in the array;
5    *   assume the elements are in positions 0 to numElements — 1
6    * @param target — the object we are seeking.
7    * @returns index of the object if found, -1 otherwise.
8    */
9   int find( Object[] array, int numElements, Object target ) {
10      for (int i = 0; i < numElements; i++)
11          if ( array[i].equals( target ) )
12              return i;                          // success
13      return —1;                                 // failure
14  }
```

Listing 3.3 Code to resize an array to 150% of its original size.

Allocate memory for a new array that is 50% larger than the old array
```
int new_length = array.length + array.length / 2;
Object[]temp = new Object[new_length];
```
Copy the contents of the old array to the new array
```
System.arraycopy(temp, 0, array, 0, array.length);
```
Assign the new array to the old array variable
```
array = temp;
```

The cost of this algorithm would seem to be determined by the `arraycopy()` method that copies all the elements from the old array into the new array. This has a cost of θ(`array.length`) because that is the number of elements that will be copied. However, the default initialization of the array created in step 1 means walking through the new array cell by cell, so the actual cost is dominated by the initialization at a cost of θ(`temp.length`).

After the assignment on line 4, the memory block previously referenced by the `array` variable becomes garbage and can be collected by the garbage collector (assuming there are no other references to it).

One issue is how much bigger the new array should be. At the low end, you could just increase it by 1 to accommodate the single new element to be inserted. This approach has the advantage that it does not allow any wasted space, since you allocate *only* what you can use. However, this becomes expensive if there will be several insertions, since *each* insertion will require a resizing of the array.

Alternatively you could increase the capacity of the array so that there is room to make additional insertions before incurring the cost of enlarging the array again. However, the extra space is wasted if you end up not needing it. This is one of those space-time tradeoffs mentioned in Chapter 0.

3.2.3 Replacing an Element in an Array

Replacing an element at a position *p* in an array is a simple two-step process:

Replace by position

Pseudocode: replace an array element by position
Verify p *is in the bounds of the array (0 to array.length – 1)*
Assign the new element to position p *in the array*

The cost of this is O(1) because the number of steps is constant and an array access has a cost of O(1).

Instead of identifying the element to be replaced by its position, you can supply a target element to be replaced. That is, instead of saying, "Replace the element in position 7 with Y," you can say "Replace element X with element Y." However, you don't know X's position in the array, so you have to find it. The pseudocode shows the steps to take and makes use of the `find(Object)` method created earlier.

Replace by target element

Pseudocode: replace an array element by value
p = *find(array, numElements, target)*
if the search was successful   *// p not equal to –1*
    assign new element to position p *of the array*

The cost of this replacement is dominated by the `find()` method, which we determined has a cost of O(*n*). The other steps have a constant cost.

3.2.4 Inserting an Element into an Array

Unfortunately, the characteristic that makes array access fast (cell adjacency and calculation of the address of an array cell) can make insertions expensive. Consider

Figure 3.3(a) where `numElements` is the number of data elements stored in the array. If the insertion is done in position p in the range 0 to `numElements` $- 1$, you will have to shift all the elements from cell p to cell `numElements` $- 1$ "up" one position to make room for the new element.

An insertion at the logical "end" of the array (position `numElements`) is inexpensive, O(1), if the array is not full, since the address of this cell can be easily calculated and no elements need to be moved (see Figure 3.3(b)). Inserting an element into an array at a position p requires the steps shown in Listing 3.4.

The method `enlargeArray()` is not shown, but would look much like the code from Listing 3.3. The cost of the algorithm is determined by lines 1 and 3. The cost of enlarging the array is linear in the length of the new array if implemented following Section 3.2.2, so it is O(n). Line 3 is also O(n) since, in the worst case, `numElements` is equal to `array.length`. From Chapter 2 we know that the resulting time complexity is still O(n).

If increasing the capacity of the array is not an option, line 2 would be replaced by code that throws an exception when the array is at its capacity.

3.2.5 Deleting an Element from an Array

Deleting the element in position p can be done two ways. First, assume that we want the data elements of the array to be adjacent—that is, we don't want any gaps in the array. If p is in the interior of the array *and* we don't care about the ordering of the

---

Figure 3.3 Inserting an element into an array.

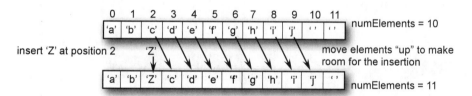

(a) Inserting in the interior of the array requires shifting elements.

(b) Inserting at the "end" of the array can be done in constant time (no element shifting is required).

Listing 3.4 Inserting an element into an array.

If the array is full, increase its capacity

```
if (numElements == array.length)
    enlargeArray(array);    // see Listing 3.3
```

Ensure that p is within the array bounds

```
if ((p < 0) || (p > array.length))
    throw new IndexOutOfBoundsException();
```

Make room for the new element by shifting "up" all the elements from p to the end of array

```
for (int i = numElements; i > p; i--)
    array[i] = array[i - 1];
```

Insert the new element at position p

```
array[p] = new_element;
```

Increment the count of the number of elements in the array

```
numElements++;
```

array's elements, the simplest solution is just to move the last data element into position p. This has an O(1) cost and is shown in Figure 3.4(c).

If the ordering of the elements cannot be disturbed, we cannot use our simple trick of moving the last element into position p. Instead, we need to shift all the elements above position p down one cell to close the gap created by the removal of p's element (Listing 3.5). This has a cost of O(n) in the worst case (when p is 0 and the array is full) and is shown in Figure 3.4(a). As Figure 3.4(b) shows, deleting the *last* element in an array can be done efficiently with an O(1) cost. (This is not a theoretical curiosity; we will use it later.)

SUMMING UP

Arrays are commonly used as the storage data structure for many kinds of collections. Arrays in Java are objects and are dynamically allocated using the new operator. The cells of an array are contiguous in memory and are indexed from 0 to length −1, where length is a data field in the array object storing the number of cells allocated to the array. Attempting to access an index outside this range produces an IndexOutOfBoundsException. The adjacency of cells makes it easy to calculate the address of any cell in an array and the time to access an element is independent of its position in the array. Consequently an array is referred to as a *random access* data structure.

Arrays are homogeneous data structures—the elements stored in each cell must be the same data type. Since all objects are related under the rules of inheritance (all objects are descended from Object), an array of Object references can store objects of different types.

Figure 3.4 Deleting an element from an array.

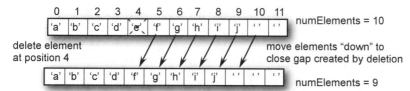

(a) Closing the gap created by a deletion by shifting elements. This is the most expensive approach, but keeps the elements in their original order.

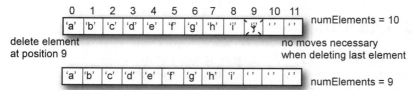

(b) No data movement is necessary when the last element is deleted.

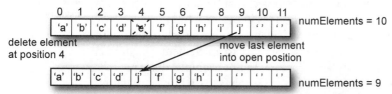

(c) Closing the gap created by a deletion by moving the last element into position of the deleted element. This is the most efficient approach, but changes the ordering of the elements.

Listing 3.5 Deleting the element in position *p* from an array, when the element ordering cannot be disturbed.

Ensure that p *is within the array bounds.*
```
if ((p < 0) || (p >= array.length))
    throw newIndex OutOfBoundsException();
```
Close the gap in the array created by the deletion by shifting "down" all elements from p + 1 to the last data element in the array.
```
for (int i = p; i < numElements; i++)
    array[i] = array[i + 1];
```
Decrement number of elements in the array.
```
numElements--;
```

Typical array operations include inserting, replacing and deleting an element, traversal, and resizing.

CHECKPOINT

3.5 Why are insertions and deletions at the logical end of the array more efficient than insertions and deletions in the interior of the array?

3.6 What will happen if the following code fragment were to execute?

```
int[] hmm = new int[50];
hmm[50] = 13;
```

3.7 Why would you want to minimize the number of times you have to resize an array?

■ 3.3 The Linked Data Structure

Linked data structures can provide the same functionality as arrays, but in many important respects are quite different from arrays and are more convenient for some applications. Linked structures avoid some of the problems arrays have, but, of course, have their own problems.

A **linked structure** is composed of a collection of **nodes**, which are individually allocated on an as-needed basis. Each node is an object that has a field to store data and one or more **links** that connect it to other nodes in the structure.

The nodes are not adjacent in memory

A node in a linked structure is *logically* equivalent to an array cell in that both a node and an array cell store an element (or a reference to an element). Figure 3.5 illustrates this similarity for a singly linked structure. In this example, the array cells and node element fields store references to a `String` object. I will use a stylized UML object diagram to illustrate linked data structure concepts.

The nodes can be linked together in a number of configurations, as shown in Figure 3.6.

In this section and the next we will explore the singly and doubly linked linear structures, often referred to as linked lists.[3] The nonlinear configurations (tree and graph) from Figure 3.6 are variations on the configurations presented here. The operations that can be performed on linked structures are largely the same as those for an array: traversal, replacement, insertion, and deletion.

3.3.1 Memory Allocation: Dynamic Allocation of Nodes

First, a refresher on objects and references. The new operator

- ■ creates an instance of an object in the computer's memory and
- ■ returns a reference to that object.

Consider the following declaration:

```
String str = null;
```

---

[3]A linked list is just one way to represent a collection of elements. Arrays are another. Linked lists get their name from the fact that they are somewhat list-like in their behavior, but they should not be confused with the List ADT presented in Chapter 5. Linked lists, like arrays, can be used as the data structure to implement many different collection ADTs.

Figure 3.5 Comparison of the array and singly linked data structures. SLNode stands for Singly Linked Node.

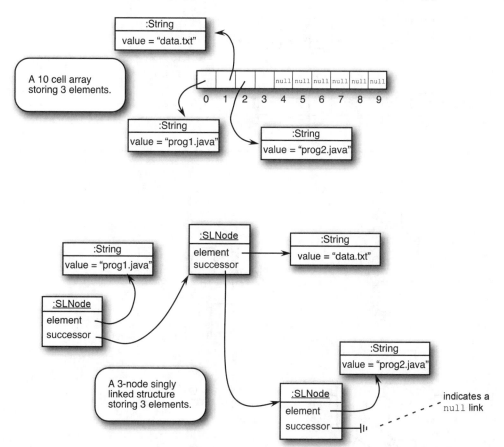

The variable `str` is of type `String`, which means it can store a *reference to* a `String` object. In the declaration, `str` is initialized to the special value `null`, saying that, at this point, `str` doesn't reference anything, so no object is accessible through `str`. Trying to access an object through a `null` reference will generate a `NullPointerException`.

Now we construct a `String` object using `new` and have `str` reference that object.

```
str = new String("a String object");
```

The reference returned by `new` is stored in the variable `str`, through which the `String` object is now accessible. Note the direction of the arrow from the variable to the object—this indicates the direction in which messages can flow. As a UML object diagram, we put `str` in the top compartment next to its type, as shown in Figure 3.7.

Like the `String` object we just created, each node of a linked structure is an object and is allocated dynamically using the `new` operator at the time it is needed. The system allocates a block of bytes for the node in the computer's memory and

Figure 3.6 Configurations for linked data structures.

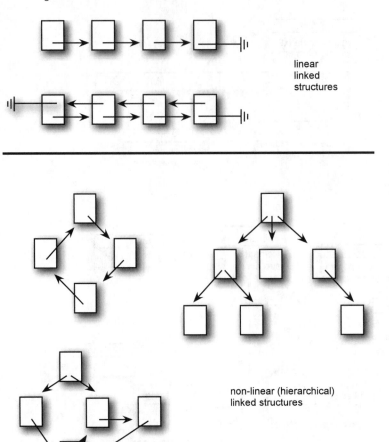

linear
linked
structures

non-linear (hierarchical)
linked structures

Figure 3.7 UML diagram of `String` object.

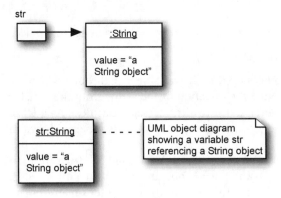

returns a *reference* to that block. The reference is stored in a variable and the object is referenced through that variable. What makes a linked node different from the other objects in the example (such as the `String` object) is that each node contains a reference to another node (in this sense they are recursive, or self-referential). These references are often called "links" because they link together the nodes of a linked data structure.

3.3.2 Storage and Access Characteristics

There are three important characteristics of linked data structures that distinguish them from arrays.

Array and linked data structure differences

1. Nodes in a linked structure are allocated individually, so the number of nodes in the linked structure can grow and shrink as needed. In contrast, with the array data structure you allocate resources (array cells) in advance of their use and may never use them all. Figure 3.5 illustrates this important difference.[4]

2. The nodes of a linked structure are not necessarily adjacent in memory. The memory manager is free to allocate a node from any block of memory that is available, and this block is chosen independently of the locations of the other nodes in the structure.

3. Because the nodes of a linked structure are not necessarily adjacent in memory, the computer cannot *calculate* the address of a node as it could for a cell in an array, so each node must *store* the location of node in the structure—this reference is the link.

These characteristics make a linked structure a sequential access data structure. With **sequential access**, the access time for an element depends on the location of the element in the structure. Videotapes provide a good analogy. If you want to locate a particular frame on a tape, you cannot jump directly to that frame. Instead, you must sequentially access all frames from your current location on the tape to the location of the target frame. Similarly, finding an element in a linked structure requires traversing the structure one element at a time until the target is found.

Linked lists provide sequential access

As a practical matter, because the address information (reference) is stored as a field of a node, an additional memory reference is necessary to retrieve the stored address, and that is going to be much slower than getting an address through calculation.

Memory references are expensive

Linked structures replace the calculation done for arrays with a memory reference stored in each node's linked field.

3.3.3 Size versus Capacity

Because we allocate nodes as they are needed, the size of a linked structure (the number of nodes storing data) should always be equal to its capacity (the number of nodes available to store data). As we will see, when a data element is no longer needed, it is a simple matter to unlink its node from a linked structure. Thus a

---

[4]You could start with an empty array and resize it to add one cell each time you wanted to insert a new element, but this would get expensive quickly and is not practical.

linked structure can grow and shrink dynamically so that you always have exactly the amount of storage your application needs. However, a linked structure is still responsible for keeping track of the number of nodes it contains.

SUMMING UP

A **linked structure** is composed of a collection of **nodes**, which are individually allocated. Each node is an object that has a field to store data and one or more **links** that connect it to other nodes in the structure.

A linear linked list may be unidirectional, with each node containing a single link that references its successor, or be bidirectional, with each node storing a pair of links, one to the node's successor and one to its predecessor.

From a storage perspective, a node is like the cell of an array in that they both store a data element. However, the nodes of a linear linked list are not guaranteed to be stored in contiguous memory locations, hence the link field of a node is needed to get to "adjacent" cells. For this reason, linked structures are called *sequential access* data structures – to get from one position in the linked structure to another you must follow the links in the intervening nodes individually.

CHECKPOINT

3.8 What is the relationship between a link and a reference?

3.9 Why is a linked structure a sequential access data structure?

3.10 What is an important difference between a `string` object and a node object in a linked structure?

■ 3.4 A Generic Singly Linked Data Structure

In this section we look at the singly linked data structure. First, we look at the definition of a generic node, class `SLNode<E>`, which stores an element of some client-specified type `E`, and the operations defined for `SLNode`.[5] Then we see how to put `SLNodes` together to make a singly linked data structure and look at the operations defined on that collection of nodes.

3.4.1 A Generic Singly Linked Node: The `SLNode<E>` Class

Each node in a singly linked data structure is a *separate* instance of the `SLNode` class, whose definition is given in Listing 3.6. As we did with `Pair<T>` in Chapter 1, we specify the type the node is to store as a type parameter in the class header (line 7). Here the identifier `E` is used (think of `E` for *element type*). It could just as easily have been `T` (think of `T` for *type*).

---

[5]Unless I want to remind you that a type is generic, I'll drop the type parameter from the text (but not from the code listing). Thus SLNode<E> and SLNode refer to the same class definition.

SLNode has two data fields.[6] The first (line 8) is of generic type E and will hold a reference to the element that is to be stored in this node. As we saw with Pair<T> in Chapter 1, when we create an instance of SLNode<E>, we will have to specify the type of the data to be stored (examples are coming up shortly).

The second field in SLNode (line 9) is called successor and is of type SLNode<E>. The self-referential (recursive) nature of this declaration arises from the need to store a reference to another instance of the same class (see the UML class diagram in Figure 3.8; recursive data structures are discussed in more depth in Chapter 8); that is, to a node's successor in the linked structure. As illustrated in Figures 3.5 and 3.6, the *last* SLNode object in the linked structure will store null in its successor field to indicate that there are no more nodes after it (no successors).

> A null successor field marks the end of the data structure

3.4.2 Basic Operations on a Singly Linked Node

Before looking at the definition of a class that uses SLNode to create a basic collection data structure, we'll present the operations that can be performed on singly linked nodes.

Constructing a Node

There are two constructors for SLNode<E>. The default constructor (lines 11–17 of Listing 3.6) takes no arguments and assigns a default value of null to the object's two data fields. A node is instantiated the way any other object would be instantiated, with the new operator.

The second constructor (lines 19–29) takes two arguments. The first is a reference to an element of generic type E, to be stored in the node, and the second is a reference to the new node's successor in the linked structure. Either or both of these values can be null.

Figure 3.9(a) shows the result of constructing a node using the default constructor. Figure 3.9(b) illustrates the overloaded constructor. Remember that you need to specify the actual type that is to be stored in the node. Here we are creating two nodes that each can store a reference to a Circle object. The type must appear in both the type declaration and the constructor invocation.

```
Circle circle1 = new Circle( 15.0 );
SLNode<Circle> node2 = new SLNode<Circle>();                // all fields null
SLNode<Circle> node1 = new SLNode<Circle>( circle1, node2 ); // create & connect
```

Figure 3.8 SLNode is recursive—it contains a reference to an instance of itself (UML class diagram).

---

[6]There can be other fields, but there have to be at least two fields: one to store data and a link field. A link node with only a link field would have few uses!

Listing 3.6 The `SLNode<E>` class stores a data element of a yet to be specified type E and a link to its successor.

```
1    package sgray.ch3;
2
3    /**
4     *    The structure of a node in the singly linked list
5     *    introduced in Fundamental Data Structures chapter.
6     */
7    public class SLNode<E> {
8        private E element;              // the data field        ◄──── The self-referential
9        private SLNode<E> successor;    // link to successor           (recursive part of the
                                                                        definition)
10
11       /**
12        * Create an empty <tt>SLNode</tt> object.
13        */
14       public SLNode() {
15           this.element = null;
16           this.successor = null;
17       }
18
19       /**
20        * Create an <tt>SLNode</tt> that stores
21        * <tt>theElement</tt> and whose successor is
22        * <tt>theSuccessor</tt>.
23        * @param theElement    the element to store in this node
24        * @param theSuccessor  this node's successor
25        */
26       public SLNode( E theElement, SLNode<E> theSuccessor ) {
27           this.element = theElement;
28           this.successor = theSuccessor;
29       }
30
31       /**
32        * Return the element stored in this <tt>SLNode</tt>
33        * object.
34        * @return the element stored in this node
35        */
36       public E getElement( ) {
37           return this.element;
38       }
39
40       /**
41        * Set the element field for this node.
42        * @param newElement the new element to be stored in
43        * this node
44        */
```

```
45        public void setElement( E newElement ) {
46            this.element = newElement;
47        }
48
49        /**
50         * Return this node's successor.
51         * @return this node's successor
52         */
53        public SLNode<E> getSuccessor( ) {
54            return this.successor;
55        }
56
57        /**
58         * Set the successor to this node in the list.
59         * @param newSuccessor this node's new successor
60         */
61        public void setSuccessor( SLNode<E> new successor ) {
62            this.successor = newSuccessor;
63        }
64    }
```

Figure 3.9 SLNode construction (default and overloaded constructors).

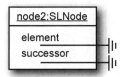

(a) SLNode<Circle> node2 = new SLNode<Circle>();

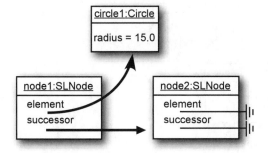

(b) SLNode<Circle> node1 = new SLNode<Circle>(circle1, node2);

Accessing a Node's `element` Field

`SLNode<E>`has accessor and mutator methods for its `element` field. The mutator method takes a reference to an object of type `E` and sets the `element` field to reference that object. Continuing from Figure 3.9(b) we do

    setElement()

```
Circle circle2 = new Circle( 4.75 );   // Figure 3.10(a)
node2.setElement( circle2 );            // Figure 3.10(b)
```

Check the definition of `SLNode<E>` again and you will see that the `element` field is of generic type `E`. As explained earlier, the reason for doing this is to make `SLNode<E>` generic so that it can store references to any kind of object we might need to store, but still allow the compiler to type check your code. The accessor method `getElement()`returns a reference to an object of type `E` because that is `element`'s generic type. For example, continuing the mutator example from Figure 3.9, if you retrieve the `element` field of node2, you get a `Circle`.

    getElement()

```
Circle aCircle = node2.getElement();   // get the Circle that
                                       // node2 stores
```

Accessing a Node's Successor

Given a reference to a node in a singly linked structure, we can get to its successor by "following" the node's successor link. We do this by sending a message to the node's accessor method, `getSuccessor()`, which returns the value of the node's successor field.

    getSuccessor()

Figure 3.10 Changing the element field of an `SLNode` object.

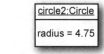

(a) `Circle circle2 = new Circle(4.75);`

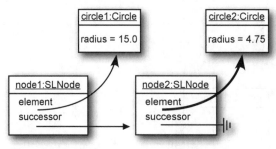

(b) `node2.setElement(circle2);`

In Figure 3.11(a), assume we have

```
SLNode<Circle> temp = null;      // see bottom of Figure 3.11(a)
```

To get `temp` to reference node1's successor, we would write

```
temp = node1.getSuccessor();     // make temp reference node1's successor
                                 // see Figure 3.11(b)
```

The value returned by `node1.getSuccessor()` is the value of node1's successor field, which is a reference to the node that follows it in the linked structure, giving us the situation shown in Figure 3.11(b).

You should note the direction of the arrows in the figure. Our singly linked structure is unidirectional because each node contains a single link that points to its *successor*. Given a reference to a singly linked node, it is not possible to get directly to the node's *predecessor* simply because there is no link to it (we'll take care of this problem with a second link in Section 3.5). Consequently, it is not possible to easily travel "backward" through a singly linked structure.

Figure 3.11 Accessing the successor field of an `SLNode<Circle>` object.

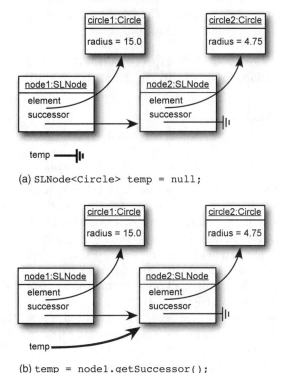

(a) `SLNode<Circle> temp = null;`

(b) `temp = node1.getSuccessor();`

Changing a Node's Successor

You *change* a node's successor by changing the node's successor field so that it stores a reference to a different node. This is done by sending a setSuccessor() message to the node with a reference to the new successor as the argument.

As an example, assume we have the situation shown in Figure 3.12(a) and we want to insert temp between node1 and node2. This is accomplished by updating the successor fields of temp and node1 (in that order).

```
temp.setSuccessor( node1.getSuccessor() );
node1.setSuccessor( temp );
```

The step-by-step results are shown in Figures 3.12(b) and (c). Before moving to the next section, you should look at the figures again and determine what would happen if the order of the successor updates were reversed.

3.4.3 The SinglyLinkedList<E> Class

To give us something concrete to work with, we will present linked structures within the context of two very useful and common data structures, singly and doubly linked lists that can be used to implement a variety of ADTs. We will implement a singly linked structure as a class. The lessons we learn here will also apply to the non-linear linked structures we will study later.

A SinglyLinkedList is composed of a *collection* of individual SLNode objects that are linked together through their successor fields. The exercises explore an alternative implementation in which SLNode is made an **inner class** of SinglyLinkedList.

SinglyLinkedList provides operations you would expect of a collection data structure: traversal, replacement, insertion, and deletion. The SinglyLinkedList class uses three data fields.

```
public class SinglyLinkedList<E> {
    SLNode<E> head;        // access point to the linked list
    SLNode<E> tail;
    int       length;      // # of data nodes in the linked list
```

The head field is the access point to the linked list and the tail field identifies the end of the linked list. There are two approaches we can take to using head and tail. First, we can let head reference the first data node in the list and tail the last.

If the list is empty, head and tail are null, as shown in Figure 3.13(a). When the list is not empty, head references the first node in the list and tail the last (Figure 3.13(b)). When the list has only a single element, head and tail reference it. It is very important to be clear about what empty and non-empty lists look like since all methods that access the list must guarantee that they honor this protocol.

Alternatively, we can create **dummy nodes** referenced by head and tail; dummy nodes *store no data element*. When the list is empty the successor field of the head dummy node references the tail dummy node, as shown in Figure 3.13(c). When the list is not empty, the head's successor field references the first data-bearing node in the list (Figure 3.13(d)). The successor field of tail will *always* be null because there should *never* be any nodes that follow it in the linked list.

Linked list dummy nodes store no data element

Figure 3.12 Change a node's successor by updating its **successor** field.

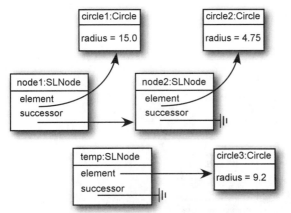

(a) Initial configuration before updating the **successor** fields of **temp** and **node1**.

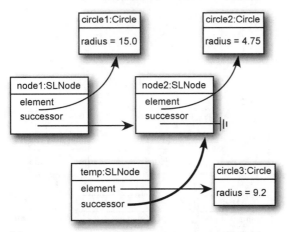

(b) `temp.setSuccessor( node1.getSuccessor() );`

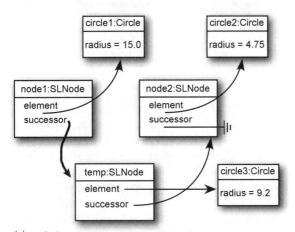

(c) `node1.setSuccessor( temp );`

Figure 3.13 Alternatives for the head and tail references of a singly linked list.

(a) Head and tail are null when the list is empty.

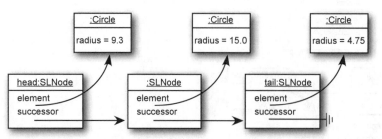

(b) Using head and tail as references to the first and last nodes of a non-empty linked structure.

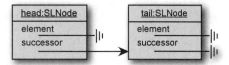

(c) An empty linked list using dummy nodes (shown shaded).

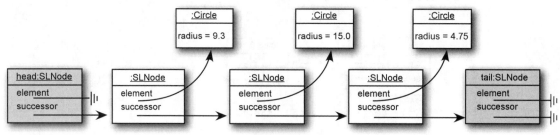

(d) Using dummy nodes for the head and tail of a non-empty linked structure.

The advantage of using the dummy nodes at the head and tail of the linked list is that they will simplify the logic of some of the linked-list methods. The dummy nodes are **administrative overhead** and are an example of trading space (the dummy nodes) for less complexity in how some operations are done. We will justify this with an example shortly.

Trade-off—space for less complexity

For consistency, we'll adopt some of the terminology and perspective of arrays. The length field keeps track of the number of *data* nodes in the linked list (the dummy nodes don't count toward the length), the first node in a linked list will have index 0, and the last will have index length − 1.

3.4.4 Creating an Instance of the `SinglyLinkedList<E>` Class

The constructor's code is straightforward—it just initializes the object's data fields.

```
public SinglyLinkedList() {
    tail = new SLNode<E>();              // the tail dummy node
    head = new SLNode<E>( null, tail );  // the head dummy node
    length = 0;
}
```

By using the default constructor for `SLNode`, we guarantee that the `element` and successor data fields for the `tail` node are `null`. Note the order in which the dummy nodes are created. The `head` dummy node is created with its `successor` field referencing the `tail` node, which is precisely what we need for a linked list that is empty. The result would look like the empty linked list shown in Figure 3.13(c).

3.4.5 Traversing a Singly Linked List (Unidirectional)

Because linked structures are sequential access structures, traversals are part of many linked structure operations. In a traversal of a singly linked structure, you "walk" through and visit the nodes one-by-one.

The algorithms for traversal developed here follow the general outline first presented for arrays in Section 3.2.1. You can determine the end of a traversal of a linked list in two ways: count-controlled or sentinel-controlled.

1. If the length of the linked list is known, you count the nodes as they are visited and when the count reaches length, you are done.

   Count-controlled traversal

   Pseudocode: count-controlled iteration of a singly linked list.
   let cursor reference head's successor
   count = 0
   while count is less than length of the list
   *   visit the node referenced by cursor*
   *   advance cursor to the next node*
   *   increment count*

2. Use the tail dummy node as a sentinel to mark the end of the traversal, as shown in Listing 3.7.

   Sentinel-controlled traversal

Listing 3.7 Sentinel-controlled iteration of a singly linked list.

let cursor reference head's successor
```
SLNode<E> cursor = head.getSuccessor();
```
while cursor is not at tail
```
while ( cursor != tail ) {
```
visit the node referenced by cursor
```
    visit( cursor );
```
advance cursor to its successor
```
    cursor = cursor.getSuccessor();
}
```

The cost of the traversals is $\theta(n)$ because all n nodes are examined. While this is also the cost of a traversal of an array of length n, in practice the cost of traversing a linked list will be higher because

Linked list iterations will be slower than array iterations

1. The adjacency of array cells in memory allows for address *calculation*, which is fast, followed by a single memory access to fetch the data element.

2. Following link fields in a linked structure requires two memory accesses per node: one to fetch the node and a second to fetch the link field of the node. Memory accesses are slow.

3.4.6 Finding a Position or an Element in a Singly Linked List

A commonly needed operation is finding a particular node in a linked list. We can search either *by position* (find the node at position p) or *by value* (find the node whose element field equals a value).

The steps for finding the node in position p are shown in Listing 3.8. To be consistent with arrays, we start the indexing of positions at 0. This method is `private` in this sample class because it will be used as a utility method in support of other singly linked list operations.

When we designed this algorithm for arrays, we first verified that the position we wanted was, in fact, within the data structure's bounds. Step 1 of `find(int)` does this. If we did not have this check and the target position were greater than the length of the linked list, the traversal would attempt to walk *beyond* the last node in the linked list and would produce a `NullPointerException` when it tried to access

---

Listing 3.8 Finding the node at position p in a singly linked list.

```
private SLNode<E> find( int p ) {
```
1. Verify that p is within the linked list bounds
```
    if ( ( p < 0 ) || ( p >= this.length ) )
        throw new IndexOutOfBoundsException();
```
2. Let cursor reference head's successor
```
    SLNode<E> cursor = head.getSuccessor();
```
3. Start i at 0
```
    int i = 0;
```
4. Walk through the linked list, advancing cursor and incrementing i until i == p
```
    while ( i != p ) {
        cursor = cursor.getSuccessor();
        i++;
    }
```
5. Return cursor
```
    return cursor;
}
```

---

the "object" referenced by `tail`'s `successor` field (which is `null`, so there is nothing there to access, hence the exception). Also, performing this check at the beginning of the method relieves step 4 in the pseudocode of having to do it.

Because step 4 is a loop which could execute many times, it is important to the algorithm's performance to keep it as simple as possible.

Minimize the work done in loops

Step 2 positions the `cursor` at the first node in the linked list that stores data, which is `head`'s successor. Remember that the `head` node is a dummy node that stores no data.

Step 3 initializes the position counter used to determine when the cursor has arrived at the target position.

Step 4 simply advances through the linked list one node at a time by following each node's successor field until it arrives at the node in position p. Remember that linked lists are *sequential access data structures* and, unlike with arrays, we cannot jump directly to the position we want in the data structure.

Instead of searching for a node by position, we may need to search for a node by its contents; that is, a node whose `element` field matches some target object. This will require walking through the linked list, extracting the element from each node and comparing it to the target. Our stroll through the linked list stops when either we have found the target or we have reached the end of the structure. Listing 3.9 shows the pseudocode and Java implementation as a method from the `SinglyLinkedList` class.

Find a node by target element

Listing 3.9 Finding a node in a singly linked list whose element field equals some target.

```
private SLNode<E> find (E target) {
```
Let cursor reference head's successor
```
    SLNode<E> cursor = head.getSuccessor();
```
while cursor isn't at end of the list
```
    while (cursor != tail) {
```
if cursor's element field matches target
```
        if(cursor.getElement().equals(target))
```
return cursor
```
            return cursor;    // success
```
else
```
        else
```
advance cursor to its successor
```
            cursor = cursor.getSuccessor();
    }
```
return null indicating failure
```
    return null;              // failure
}
```

This code uses two notions of equality.

- Test to see if two variables reference the *same* object. The test to see if the end of the linked list has been reached on line 4 compares cursor to tail using the inequality operator (!=). Here we are testing to see if cursor and tail reference the same object.

- Test to see if two variables reference *equivalent* objects on line 5. The test of the loop to see if the element in the current node matches the target node uses the equals() method overloaded from the Object class (as discussed in Chapter 1) and is testing to see if the two *objects* are equal.

3.4.7 Replacing an Element in a Singly Linked List

Replacing an element in a node of a linked structure is a two-step process.

> **Pseudocode: Replacing an element in a node in a singly linked list**
> 1. *Let cursor reference the node whose element field is to be replaced*
> 2. *Replace cursor's element field with the new element*

Step 1 is handled using one of the two find() methods developed earlier. Step 2 is accomplished easily using the setElement() method from SLNode. The cost of replacement is dominated by the time it takes to find the target node in Step 1. This is the cost of find(), which is O(n).

3.4.8 Inserting an Element at the Head of a Singly Linked List

The characteristic of linked structures that makes accessing them slow (the *lack* of adjacency) makes inserting and deleting at any point in the structure efficient because it is not necessary to shift the other elements in the structure either to make room for an insertion or to fill the gap created by a deletion. Instead we just update the successor fields to reflect the change.

Insertions and deletions on a linked list don't require moving elements

Adding a node at the head of the linked list can be done very efficiently because we already have a reference it. The pseudocode and Java code are shown in Listing 3.10. The first step is to create a new SLNode object that will store the element to be added to the linked list. Then we must link the new node in. Finally, we need to update length to reflect that the list is now larger by 1 element. The steps in the pseudocode and the code correspond to the parts of Figures 3.14. and 3.15.

The constructor for SLNode in step 1 will create a new node and initialize its element field to reference the element passed in. It will also initialize the new node's successor field to null. We could have compressed the first two steps into one step by writing

```
SLNode<E> newnode = new SLNode<E>(theElement, head.getSuccessor());
```

One of the advantages of using the dummy nodes is that it helps to eliminate special cases the code must check. For example, with the dummy nodes, inserting at the head of an *empty* list is exactly the same as inserting at the head of a nonempty list. Compare (a) and (b) of Figure 3.14 to (a) and (b) of Figure 3.15.

Justification for using the dummy nodes

Listing 3.10 Inserting an element at the head of a singly linked list.

```
public void addAtHead(E theElement) {
```
1. *Create the new SLNode*   *Figures 3.14–3.15(a)*
```
    SLNode<E> newnode = new SLNode<E>(theElement, null);
```
2. *Set the new node's next field to be the same as head's next field*   *Figures 3.14–3.15(b)*
```
    newnode.setSuccessor(head.getSuccessor());
```
3. *Set head's next field to reference the new node*   *Figures 3.14–3.15(c)*
```
    head.setSuccessor(newnode);
```
4. *Increment length by 1*
```
    length++;
}
```

Figure 3.14 Adding a node at the head of an empty linked list.

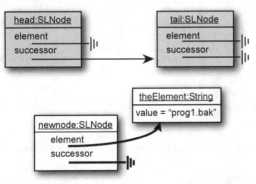

(a) `SLNode<E> newnode = new SLNode<E>( theElement, null);`

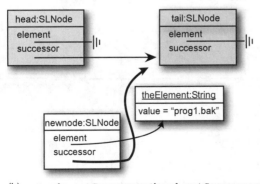

(b) `newnode.setSuccessor(head.getSuccessor());`   *(continues)*

Figure 3.14 (continued) Adding a node at the head of an empty linked list.

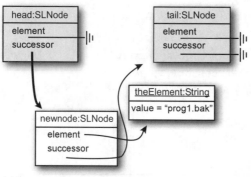

(c) `head.setSuccessor(newnode);`

Figure 3.15 Adding a node at the head of a non-empty linked list.

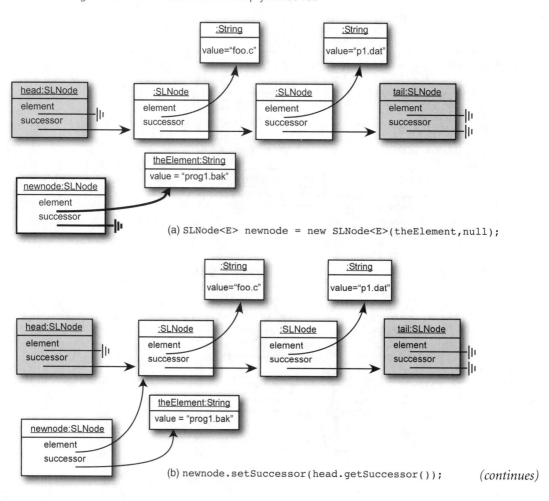

(a) `SLNode<E> newnode = new SLNode<E>(theElement,null);`

(b) `newnode.setSuccessor(head.getSuccessor());`   *(continues)*

Figure 3.15 (continued) Adding a node at the head of a non-empty linked list.

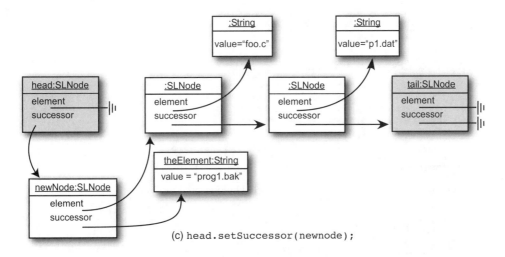

(c) `head.setSuccessor(newnode);`

were empty, in which case the `tail` reference would need to be updated too. Some other methods would be similarly affected. Here is the additional code for comparison.

```
// special test required when dummy nodes aren't used
if ( head == null ) {  // the list is empty
    head = newnode
    tail = newnode;
}
else                   // the list is NOT empty
    // do the regular insertion
```

Inserting without dummy nodes

When a node is inserted or deleted, the order in which the links are updated is important. The danger is that a portion of the linked list will become unlinked and lost forever. To show how easily this can happen, consider the following (incorrect!) version of `addAtHead()` in Listing 3.11 and illustrated in Figure 3.16.

The order of link updates is important

As a result of the update to `head`'s `successor` field in step (b), we have lost our

---

Listing 3.11 Incorrect version of `addAtHead()`.

```
public void addAtHead(E e) {                          // WARNING! BAD CODE!
    SLNode<E> newnode = new SLNode<E>(e, null);       // Okay      Figure 3.16(a)
    head.setSuccessor(newnode);                       // WRONG!    Figure 3.16(b)
    newnode.setSuccessor( head.getSuccessor() );      // WRONG!    Figure 3.16(c)
    length++;
}
```

Figure 3.16 Updating links in the wrong order results in a broken list.

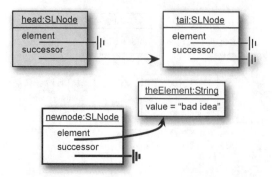

(a) `SLNode<E>newnode = new SLNode<E>( theElement,null );`

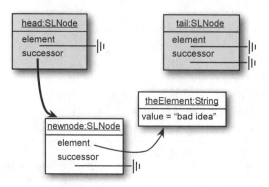

(b) `head.setSuccessor( newnode ); // WRONG!`

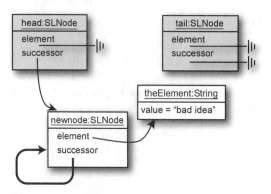

(c) `newnode.setSuccessor( head.getSuccessor() ); // WRONG!`

As a result of the update to head's successor field in step (b), we have lost our access to the remainder of the linked list. Because of this, after step c, newnode's successor field references itself instead of its successor in the linked list. This is bad.

As a side note, I want to stress that visualization is a very useful tool. It helps you to understand the objects being manipulated, the actions that have to be performed, and the order of those actions. When creating diagrams like these, you will find it helpful to label your diagram using the fields you will be manipulating in your code and to number the operations in the order your code must carry them out. While this might seem like a lot of work with limited value, you will find from (painful) experience that your coding will go faster and more smoothly if you spend a little extra time on its planning, particularly when you are learning something new. Writing correct code from scratch is almost always easier than fixing code that is wrong, especially if it is very wrong.

Visualization is a very useful tool!

3.4.9 Inserting a Node at an Indexed Position in a Singly Linked List

A more general `add()` method will allow us to insert a new node in any position in the linked list in the range 0 to `length`, inclusive. This allows insertion at position 0, at any position in the interior of the linked list, and at the very end of the linked list (see Figure 3.17). Any position outside this range is illegal.

`add(E, int)`

The pseudocode and corresponding Java code to insert a new node in position *p* are shown in Listing 3.12. The first step, as always, is to ensure that the given position is within the range of the linked list. The second step is to traverse the linked list to find the node *before* the position where you will insert the new node. The last step is to insert the node (also see Figure 3.12) and to increment `length`. The actual insertion is done with the utility method `addAfter()`. You should note that the utility method does no error checking on its pre-conditions; it assumes that the caller has taken care of them.

If the insertion position *p* is out of range, an `IndexOutOfBoundsException` is thrown (lines 2 and 3 in Listing 3.12). If this test passes, we can create the node that will store the element (lines 4 and 5). There is no need to create the node before this point since the node won't be needed if the range check fails.

Figure 3.17 Insertion points in a linked list.

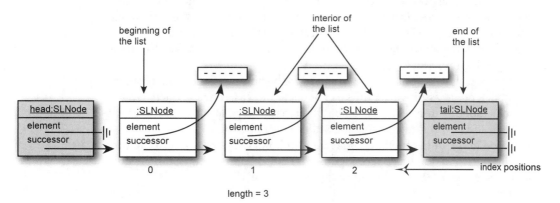

Listing 3.12 A more general add() method.

```
public void add( E theElement, int p ) {
```

verify that p is within the linked list bounds

```
    if (( p < 0 ) || ( p > length ) )
        throw new IndexOutOfBoundsException();
```

create a new SLNode

```
    SLNode<E> newnode = new SLNode<E>( theElement, null );
```

traverse linked list to node at (p – 1)

```
    SLNode<E> cursor = head; // good for p == 0
    if ( p > 0 )
        cursor = find( p - 1 );
```

insert the new node

```
    addAfter( cursor, newnode );
```

increment length by 1

```
    length++;
}
/** utility method:
 * pre: p and newnode are not null
 * post: newnode is inserted after p
 */
private void addAfter( SLNode<E> p, SLNode<E> newnode ){
    newnode.setSuccessor( p. getSuccessor() );
    p.setSuccessor( newnode );
}
```

A node inserted at position *p* will become the new successor to the node at position *p* – 1. The node *currently* occupying position *p* will be logically "shifted" up one to position *p* + 1, becoming the new node's successor in the linked list. Logically, this also "shifts" all nodes above the insertion point up one position, adding 1 to their positions (see Figure 3.18).

When *p* is 0, the insertion is being done at the beginning of the linked list and the new node's predecessor will be the head node. In this case, cursor is left at head and the new node is inserted after head. Otherwise, the position where the new node is to be inserted is located using the utility find() method.

The code in the utility method addAfter() follows the steps taken in the first addAtHead() method developed (see Figures 3.14 and 3.15). Indeed, using the utility method, the addAtHead() method could be rewritten as:

Figure 3.18 Logical shifting of positions when adding to a linked list.

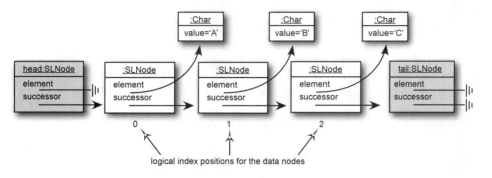

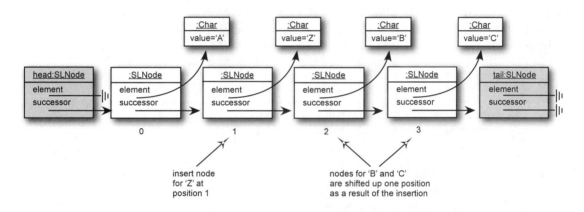

```
// insert at head of list
public void addAtHead(E theElement) {
    SLNode<E> newnode = new SLNode<E>(theElement, null);   // Figures 3.14–3.15(a)
    addAfter( head, newnode );                             // Figures 3.14–3.15(b, c)
    length++;
}
```

Finally, you will probably have noted that addAtHead(theElement) is semantically equivalent to add(0, theElement).

3.4.10 Deleting a Node from a Singly Linked List

Removing a node from a linked list means unlinking it and reforming the linked list by linking the removed node's predecessor to its successor to close the gap created by the node's removal. As with the other methods developed, removal can be done by specifying the position of the node to be removed or by supplying a target element.

remove (int)

A requirement for removing a node from a singly linked list is that we have a reference to the target node's *predecessor* in the linked list. This requirement arises from the fact that singly linked lists are unidirectional—given a reference to a node, we have no easy way of getting to its predecessor since the node has no reference to it. Doubly linked structures, which are studied in the next section, solve this problem at the cost of the space for an extra link.

First we look at removing a node at some position *p* (Listing 3.13). As with adding an element at *p*, the first step is to verify that *p* is valid—in this case, it must be in the range 0 to length − 1.

Remove by position

To completely remove the target node from the linked list, you need to make sure that the target's predecessor (referenced by cursor) is updated (done on line 11) *and* that target's successor field is set to null (line 15). We also need to make cursor's element field null (line 16). Why? For the garbage collector to consider an object to be garbage, there mustn't be any references to it. So good memory management practice dictates that when you are done with an object, all references involving it should be set to null. Finally, note that the logical positions of the nodes above the target were all "shifted" down one position.

Listing 3.13 Removing the node at position p of a singly linked list. (The letters in parentheses in the pseudocode refer to the parts of Figure 3.19.)

```
1    public E remove ( int p ) {
```
Verify that p is within the linked list bounds
```
2        if (( p < 0) || ( p >= this.length ) )
3            throw new IndexOutOfBoundsException();
```
Move cursor to node in position p − 1   *Figure 3.19(a)*
```
4        SLNode<E> cursor = head;      // good for p == 0
5        if ( p > 0 ) cursor = find( p ? 1 );
```
Let target = cursor's successor; the node to remove   *Figure 3.19(b)*
```
6        SLNode<E> target = cursor.getSuccessor();
```
Link cursor to target's successor   *Figure 3.19(c)*
```
7        cursor.setSuccessor ( target.getSuccessor() );
```
Get the target's element
```
8        E element = target.getElement();
```
Unlink target from the linked list for garbage collection   *Figure 3.19(d)*
```
9        target.setSuccessor( null );
10       target.setElement( null );
```
Decrement length
```
11       length--;
```
Return the element stored in the target node
```
12       return element;
13   }
```

Figure 3.19 Removing a node from a linked list by position—removing the node at position 1.

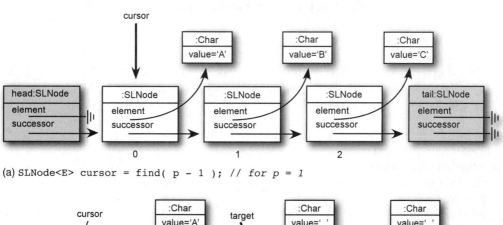

(a) `SLNode<E> cursor = find( p - 1 ); // for p = 1`

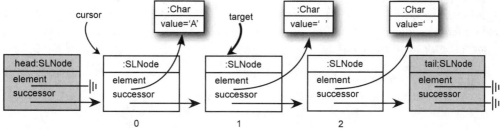

(b) `target = cursor.getSuccessor();`

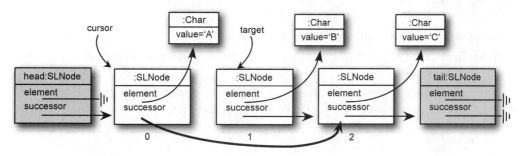

(c) `cursor.setSuccessor( target.getSuccessor() );`

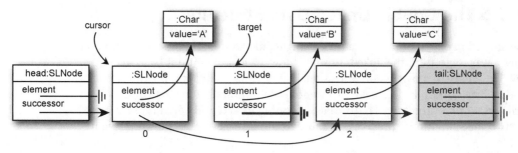

(d) `target.setSuccessor( null );`

Removing by a target element is slightly trickier than removing by position. The `find(target)` method would easily locate the target in the linked list, if it exists, but, as we just saw, what we really need is a reference to the target's *predecessor* in the linked list.

Remove by target element

The solution is to maintain two reference markers. One marker, `target`, is used to locate the target and the other, `cursor`, always references `target`'s *predecessor* so that when `target` eventually references the target node to remove, `cursor` references `target`'s predecessor in the linked list. Figure 3.20 shows the process of walking the two reference markers through the linked list to delete the node storing 'C'.

Pseudocode: remove the node containing targetElement
let cursor reference head
let target reference head's successor
while target is not at the tail and the targetElement has not been found
   advance target
   advance cursor
// loop has terminated, check for success
if the targetElement was found
   link cursor to target's successor
   unlink target from the linked list
   decrement length

CHECKPOINT

3.11 What is the purpose of the `successor` field in `SLNode`?

3.12 What happens in Figure 3.15 if the links are updated in the order shown in Figure 3.16. Why?

3.13 Traversing a linked list of n nodes has the same time complexity, $\theta(n)$, as traversing an array of n cells. Which do you think will give better performance? Why?

■ 3.5 The Doubly Linked Data Structure

The singly linked structure only stores a single link, so it is unidirectional. It provides a way to go from the linked list's head toward its tail, but not back the other way. The ability to move in both directions can be quite useful and is easily accommodated by adding a link field to the node definition that references a node's *predecessor* in the structure. This is called a **doubly linked node** because each node has two links: one to its predecessor and one to its successor, as shown in Figure 3.21.

Figure 3.20 Removing a node from a linked list by target.

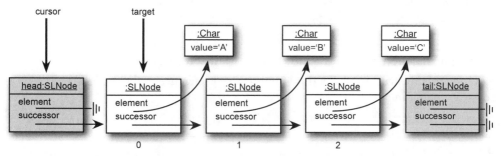

(a) Initialize `cursor` and `target` element ('C') (steps 1 and 2 of the pseudocode).

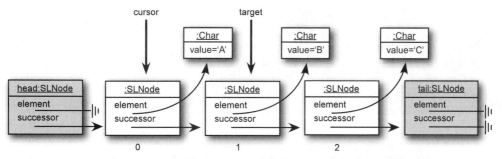

(b) Advance `cursor` and target in search of the `target` element ('C') (steps 3–5 of the pseudocode).

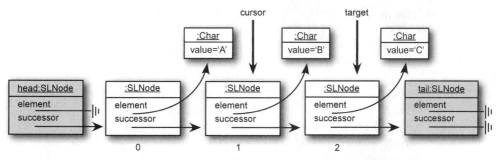

(c) `target` arrives at the target node—updating of links can occur as done for removing by position. Compare this to Figure 3.19 (b–d).

Figure 3.21 A doubly linked node.

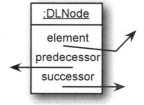

3.5.1 Defining a Doubly Linked Node: The DLNode<E> Class

The doubly linked node class, DLNode<E>, is shown in Listing 3.14. As you can see, it is implemented as a subclass of SLNode<E>. The additions are minor:

- A predecessor field of type DLNode<E> is added to link a node to its predecessor.
- Accessor and mutator methods are added to support the predecessor field.
- The overloaded constructor takes a third argument—a reference to the predecessor node to link in.

Listing 3.14 The DLNode class.

```
1    package gray.adts.ch3;
2
3    /**
4     * The structure of a node in the doubly linked
5     * list.
6     */
7    public class DLNode<E> extends SLNode<E> {
8        private DLNode<E>  predecessor;
9
10       /**
11        * Constructor. Create an empty <tt>DLNode</tt> object.
12        */
13       public DLNode() {
14           super();
15           this.predecessor = null;
16       }
17
18       /**
19        * Constructor. Create a <tt>DLNode</tt> object that
20        * stores <tt>theElement</tt>, whose predecessor is
21        * <tt>predecessor</tt> and whose successor is
22        * <tt>successor</tt>.
23        * @param theElement the element to be stored in this node
24        * @param thePredecessor  this node's predecessor
25        * @param theSuccessor  this node's successor
26        */
27       public DLNode(E theElement, DLNode<E> thePredecessor,
28                       DLNode<E> theSuccessor) {
29           super(theElement, theSuccessor);
30           this.predecessor = thePredecessor;
31       }
32
33
```

```
34      /**
35       * Return the predecessor to this node.
36       * @return this node's predecessor
37       */
38      public DLNode<E> getPredecessor( ){
39          return this.predecessor;
40      }
41
42      /**
43       * Set the predecessor to this node in the list.
44       * @param thePredecessor  this node's new predecessor
45       */
46      public void setPredecessor ( DLNode<E> thePredecessor ){
47          this.predecessor = thePredecessor;
48      }
49  }
```

Manipulation of the fields of a doubly linked node is much like for singly linked nodes, so we won't spend time on them. Instead we will look at how the operations of interest to us are affected by the addition of the predecessor link to the node definition.

We will again assume that there is a pair of administrative dummy nodes marking the head and tail of the linked list. The empty linked list shown in Figure 3.22 would be created as follows.

```
this.tail = new DLNode();
this.head = new DLNode( null, null, this.tail );
this.tail.setPredecessor( head );
```

Note that head's predecessor link and tail's successor link are always null, as are their element fields, since these nodes serve a purely administrative role.

Figure 3.22 An empty doubly linked list using dummy nodes for head and tail.

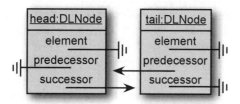

3.5.2 Traversing a Doubly Linked List (Bidirectional)

The predecessor link was added to the node definition to allow access to a node's predecessor in a linear linked structure. This makes it possible to traverse a doubly linked structure in both directions: from the head toward the tail, and from the tail back to the head.

A forward traversal on a doubly linked structure is done in exactly the same fashion as in a singly linked structure, so the code from Section 3.4.5 applies here.

Traversals from the tail to the head follow the same approach. Here is the pseudocode for a sentinel-controlled backward traversal.

> **Pseudocode: a sentinel-controlled backward traversal of a doubly linked list**
> *let cursor reference tail's predecessor*
> *while cursor is not at head*
>   *visit the cursor node*
>   *move cursor to its predecessor*

Moving backward through a doubly linked structure is no more expensive than moving forward, so the cost is $\theta(n)$.

3.5.3 Finding a Position or Element in a Doubly Linked List

Because a doubly linked list is a sequential access data structure, finding the node in position p requires traversing the linked list (just as it did for singly linked lists).

However, we can take advantage of the bidirectionality of a doubly linked list to minimize the cost. The idea is very simple: Establish if p is in the lower or upper half of the linked list, then begin the traversal at the end that is closest to p.

With this little trick we never need to traverse more than length/2 links to find the target. Asymptotic analysis tells us that the time to find the indexed node is O(length), which is true, but this hides the real performance improvement of our optimization for long linked lists. Recall that following a link requires two memory references, one to get the node and the other to get the successor/predecessor field. Because memory references are expensive in terms of time, reducing the number of references we have to do can positively affect the runtime performance of an application.

Note the casts on lines 8 and 10 in Listing 3.15. DLNode is a subclass of SLNode. Consequently, the successor link for every DLNode is actually inherited from SLNode, where it is declared as type SLNode<E>, so must be cast here before we can treat it as a reference to a DLNode<E>.

Finding a node in a doubly linked list given a target element is no different than for a singly linked list. In the worst case, finding the *first* occurrence of a particular element still requires a full traversal of the linked structure, just as we did for a singly linked list. A doubly linked list cannot improve on this. **Find a node by target element**

However, the bidirectionality of the doubly linked list makes it simpler to find the *last* occurrence of an element in a linked list. You just begin the traversal at the tail and move backward until either the head node is found (indicating failure) or the target element is found (indicating success).

Listing 3.15 Finding a node by position in a doubly linked list.

```
1    // precondition: 0 <= p < length
2    private DLNode<E> find ( int p ) {
3        if ( ( p < 0 ) || ( p >= this.length ) )
4            throw new IndexOutOfBoundsException();
5
6        DLNode<E> cursor = null;
7        if ( p < (length / 2 ) ) {                // p is in first half
8            cursor = (DLNode<E>)head.getSuccessor();
9            for ( int i = 0; i != p; i++ )
10               cursor = (DLNode<E>)cursor.getSuccessor();
11       }
12       else {                                    // p is in second half
13           cursor = tail.getPredecessor();
14           for ( int i = length - 1; i != p; i-- )
15               cursor = cursor.getPredecessor();
16       }
17       return cursor;
18   }
```

Pseudocode: finding the last occurrence of an element in a doubly linked list
set cursor to tail's predecessor
while the cursor is not at the head node
> *if the element field of the cursor node matches the target element*
>> *return a reference to cursor node*   *// success!*
>> *else move cursor to its predecessor*   *// follow the predecessor link*
return null   *// indicate failure*

3.5.4 Inserting an Element into a Doubly Linked List

Inserting an element into a doubly linked list is similar to insertion into a singly linked list. In the following pseudocode and in the code in Listing 3.16 we take advantage of the link to the node's predecessor.

Pseudocode: inserting into a doubly linked list
create the new node
let cursor reference the predecessor to the position where the insertion is to be done
link the new node after cursor

Step 1 can be done using the traversal techniques already presented and covers the following:

■ Insertion at a position *p* (advance cursor to position *p* – 1)
■ Insertion in the position after some element in the linked structure (advance cursor to the node storing element)

Listing 3.16 The link updates to insert `newnode` *after* cursor. (The letters in parentheses refer to the parts of Figure 3.23.)

make cursor the predecessor for newnode	*Figure 3.23(b)*
`newnode.setPredecessor( cursor );`	
make cursor's successor be newnode's successor	*Figure 3.23(c)*
`newnode.setSuccessor( cursor.getSuccessor() );`	
make the new node the predecessor of cursor's successor	*Figure 3.23(d)*
`cursor.getSuccessor().setPredecessor( newnode );`	
make the new node cursor's successor	*Figure 3.23(e)*
`cursor.setSuccessor( newnode );`	

Step 3 inserts the new node into the linked list right after `cursor`. This requires four substeps corresponding to the four links that must be updated. Each of these substeps is illustrated in Figure 3.23.

Figure 3.23 Inserting a node into a doubly linked list.

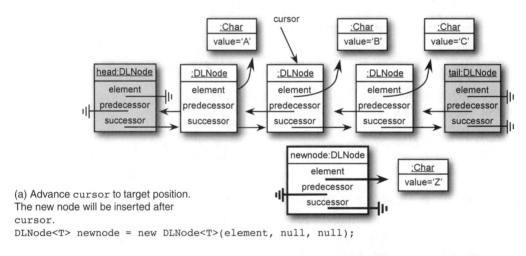

(a) Advance `cursor` to target position. The new node will be inserted after `cursor`.
`DLNode<T> newnode = new DLNode<T>(element, null, null);`

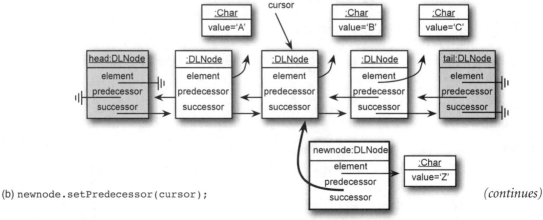

(b) `newnode.setPredecessor(cursor);`

(continues)

Figure 3.23 (continued) Inserting a node into a doubly linked list.

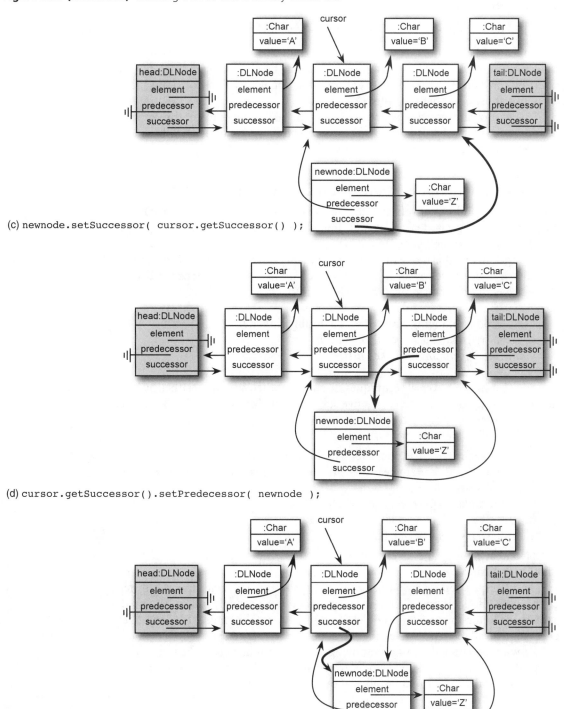

(c) `newnode.setSuccessor( cursor.getSuccessor() );`

(d) `cursor.getSuccessor().setPredecessor( newnode );`

(e) `cursor.setSuccessor( newnode );`

These four substeps can be shortened by doing (b) and (c) together when creating the new node.

```
DLNode<T> newnode = new DLNode<T>(element, cursor, cursor.getSuccessor());
```

You should also note that with the inclusion of the dummy nodes to mark the head and tail of the linked list, insertions at the head and tail are no different from insertions anywhere else in the list. This removes the need to test for those special cases and, thus, simplifies your life.

The cost of the insertion is dominated by the time it takes to get the cursor to the desired node, which is **O**(n). The actual insertion operation is **O**(1) because it requires a constant number of operations (4) to update the links.

3.5.5 Removing an Element from a Doubly Linked List

Although more links are involved, removing a node from a doubly linked list is simpler than removing a node from a singly linked list because we needn't worry about maintaining the extra reference to cursor's predecessor as we traverse the linked list to the target. Again, this is due to the bidirectionality of doubly linked lists—the reference to a node's predecessor is built into each node as the predecessor field, so all we need is a reference to the node to be deleted.

> **Pseudocode: removing a node from a doubly linked list**
> *let cursor reference the target node to be deleted*
> *unlink the target from the linked list*

Step 1 uses the traversal techniques discussed earlier, searching either by position or by target element. Step 2 has five substeps, one for each link involved. Each of these substeps is illustrated in Figure 3.24.

Step 2 *unlink the target from the linked list*

a. set the successor field of cursor's predecessor to reference cursor's successor
b. set the predecessor field of cursor's successor to reference cursor's predecessor
c. set the cursor's predecessor field to null
d. set the cursor's successor field to null
e. set the cursor's element field to null

Note that steps 2a and 2b can safely be reversed, but both must be done before steps 2c and 2d. Why?

Another question is why bother with setting the cursor's fields to null in steps 2c through 2e? As we saw when removing a node from a singly linked list, for the garbage collector to consider an object to be garbage, there mustn't be any references to it. So all references involving the node to be removed should be set to null.

As with insertion, the cost of removing a node is dominated by the time it takes to get the cursor to the desired node, which is O(n). The actual removal is O(1) because it requires a constant number of operations (5) to update the links.

Figure 3.24 Removing a node from a doubly linked list.

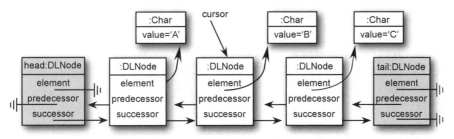

(a) After positioning `cursor` to the node to be removed.

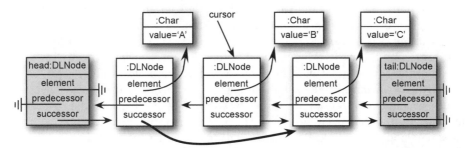

(b) Step 2a `cursor.getPredecessor().setSuccessor(cursor.getSuccessor());`

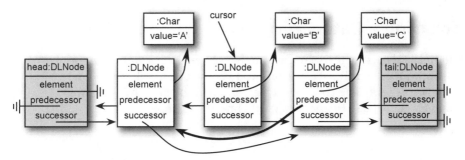

(c) Step 2b `cursor.getSuccessor().setPredecessor(cursor.getPredecessor());`

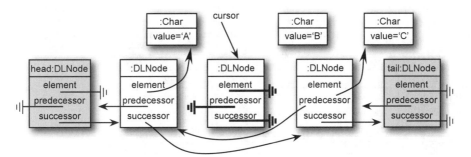

(d) Steps 2c–2e `cursor.setSuccessor( null ); cursor.setPredecessor( null );`
`cursor.setElement( null );`

CHECKPOINT

3.14 What makes bidirectional traversal of a doubly linked list possible?

3.15 What does the following do?

```
p.getSuccessor().setPredecessor(p.getPredecessor());
```

3.16 What optimization do doubly linked lists provide for finding the eighth node? How is this made possible?

■ 3.6 The Circular Linked List

Having the two dummy nodes, `head` and `tail`, simplified the logic and coding for many of the operations defined for linear linked structures, so we wouldn't want to get rid of them without good reason.

While the dummy nodes save us time and trouble, they do represent space overhead. Can we gain the advantage of dummy nodes with less space overhead? An alternative to having two dummy nodes is to have a single dummy node that plays the role of both `head` and `tail`. It does this simply by wrapping the list around the head dummy node, forming a circular linked list. The `predecessor` link of `head` references the last data node in the linked list and the `successor` link of the last data node references `head`, as shown in Figure 3.25.

■ 3.7 Selecting a Data Structure

The array and linked data structures are commonly used as the backing store for collections. As we will see, which data structure you choose to use will depend on the unique characteristics of the collection type you are implementing. Here we provide a summary of characteristics of arrays and linked structures.

Figure 3.25 A circular linked list with one dummy node.

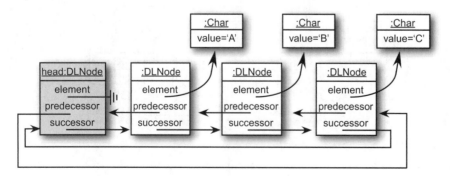

An array is a direct access data structure. The timing complexities assume the array is unsorted. (See Table 3.1)

The space complexity of an array is $O(n)$. Arrays have low administrative overhead, needing only the type tag and the length fields in addition to the space for the data. However, typically more cells are allocated than will be used, leading to wasted space. In general, arrays are easier to code with than linked structures.

A linked structure is a sequential access data structure. The timing complexities assume that the linked lists are unsorted. (See Table 3.2)

The space complexity of a linked list is also $O(n)$, but with a higher constant factor due to the links that are stored in each node. On the plus side, only as many nodes as are needed must be allocated, so an application's data space requirements can be met exactly by a linked data structure. Because of the links, linked data structures are typically more difficult to code than arrays.

Table 3.1 Time complexity for array data structure operations (n = # of occupied cells)

Operation	Cost
read (anywhere in the array)	$O(1)$
add/remove (at the logical end of the array)	$O(1)$
add/remove (in the interior of the array)	$O(n)$
resize	$O(\text{length of new array})$
find by position	$O(1)$
find by target	$O(n)$

Table 3.2 Time complexity for the linked data structure operations (n = # data-bearing nodes)

Operation	Cost	
	Singly Linked	**Doubly Linked**
read (anywhere in the linked list)	$O(n)$	$O(n)$
add/remove (at the head)	$O(1)$	$O(1)$
add/remove (at the tail)	$O(n)$	$O(1)$
add/remove (in the interior of the structure)	$O(n)$	$O(n)$
resize	N/A	N/A
find by position	$O(n)$	$O(n)$
find by target	$O(n)$	$O(n)$

EXERCISES

Paper and Pencil

1. Determine the number of bytes allocated for each of the following arrays.

   a. `float[] sngWeights = new float[50];`
   b. `byte[] rimValues = new byte[20];`
   c. `boolean[] primes = new boolean[1000];`
   d. `long[] salePrices = new long[MAX_ITEMS];`

2. Assuming the arrays from the previous problem are all allocated starting at address 100 in memory, determine the address in memory for the following array cells.

   a. `sngWeights[20]`
   b. `rimValues[9]`
   c. `primes[525]`
   d. `salePrices[0]`

3. Draw illustrations for the following operations:

   ```
   Date d = null;
   Date d = new Date();
   ```

4. Draw an illustration for a linked list resulting from the following code.

   ```
   SLNode<String> Anode = new SLNode<String> ("Ginger", null);
   SLNode<String> Bnode = new SLNode<String> ("Blue", null);
   SLNode<String> Cnode = new SLNode<String> ("Pepper", Anode);
   Bnode.setSuccessor(Cnode);
   ```

5. Write the code necessary to create a new `SLNode` whose element field references the string "Persian II" and link it into the linked list created in the previous problem in front of the "Ginger" node. What will "Persian II"'s predecessor in this new linked list be? Draw an illustration of the resulting linked list.

6. Using Figure 3.23 as an example, illustrate the sequence of actions needed to insert a new node, whose `element` fields stores "Coffee Bean," *after* the node containing "Cocoa" in the doubly linked list in Figure 3.26.

Figure 3.26 A sample doubly linked list.

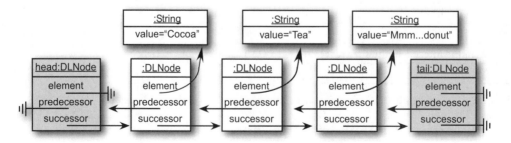

7. Using Figure 3.24 as an example, illustrate the sequence of actions to remove the node whose element fields stores "Tea" from the doubly linked list in Figure 3.26.

8. Redraw the linear linked list from Figure 3.26 as a circular linked list.

Testing and Debugging

1. Rick prepared the following pseudocode for the count controlled iteration of a singly linked list using head and tail dummy nodes. In what way is this potentially misleading?

Pseudocode: count controlled iteration of a singly linked list w/dummy nodes
let cursor reference the first data node
count = 0
while count is less than length of the list
    visit the node referenced by cursor
    advance cursor to the next node
    increment count

2. Suzi coded a method to delete a target element (without returning it) as follows. What is wrong with this code? Hint: There is more than one issue.

```
1    void delete(Object[] array, int numElements, Object target){
2        int i;
3        for (i == 0; i <= numElements; i++)
4            if ( array[i].equals( target ) )
5                break;
6        for ( ; i <= numElements; i++)
7            array[i] = array[i+1];
8    }
```

3. The following code fragment is an implementation of the count-controlled traversal of a singly linked list from Section 3.4.5. Does it work? If not, explain the problem and how to fix it. (*Note*: this.length is the number of data nodes in the linked list and assume the visit() method is implemented and works properly.)

```
SLNode<E> cursor = head.getSuccessor();
for ( int count = 0; count <= this.length; count++ ) {
    visit(cursor);
    cursor = cursor.getSuccessor();
}
```

4. Here is a simpler version of the add(Object, int) method from Section 3.4.9. Under what circumstances will it fail? How do you fix this problem?

```
1    public void add( E e, int p ) {
2        if (( p < 0 ) || ( p > length ) )
3            throw new IndexOutOfBoundsException();
4        SLNode<E> newnode = new SLNode<E> ( e, null );
```

```
5       SLNode<E> cursor = find( p - 1 );
6       addAfter( cursor, newnode );
7       length++;
8   }
```

5. The following code fragment is a variation of the code given in Section 3.5.4 for updating the links when inserting a node into a doubly linked list. Provide an illustration similar to that of Figure 3.23 to determine if these updates are done in the correct order.

```
cursor.getPredecessor().setSuccessor( newnode );
newnode.setPredecessor( cursor.getPredecessor() );
cursor.setPredecessor( newnode );
newnode.setSuccessor( cursor );
```

If this code fragment would work, provide a sequence of link updates that will not work.

Modifying the Code

1. As another possibility, if SLNode and SinglyLinkedList are classes kept in separate files and are in the same package, as done in this chapter, how would changing the data fields in SLNode to protected change things? Implement this change.

2. Insertions and deletions on doubly linked lists are error prone due to the link updates. A redesign of the DLNode class could solve this by replacing the link mutator fields with two methods that do all the linking for you:

```
void linkInBefore( DLNode<E> node )    link the argument node in before this node
void linkInAfter( DLNode<E> node )     link the argument node in after this node
```

Code these methods and recode the add and remove operations for a doubly linked list. Provide a paragraph describing which approach you favor and why.

Design and Code

1. Provide pseudocode to find the *last* occurrence of a target element in a *singly* linked list and compare it to the pseudocode given for this method for a doubly linked list.

2. Code the method whose header is given below. The method replaces a target element in an array. The pseudocode was given in Section 3.2.3.

```
void replace(Object[] array, Object target, Object replacement)
```

3. Provide code that shrinks an array when the percentage of array cells actually in use falls below the constant SHRINK_THRESHOLD . Use the code for expanding an array from Section 3.2.2 as a model. Assume the name of the array is array and the new array will have length SHRINK_THRESHOLD.

4. Code a method that finds the last occurrence of an object in an array. The method should return the index of the object if found and −1 if not found.

```
int findLast(Object[] array, Object target)
```

5. Implement the pseudocode from Section 3.5.3 that finds the *last* occurrence of a target in a doubly linked list.

ON THE WEB

Additional study material is available at Addison-Wesley's Website at http://www.aw.com/cssupport. This material includes the following:

- Focus on Problem Solving: The ACME Courier Company (preview below)

    Problem: The ACME Courier Company wants to modernize their paper-based system of keeping track of their deliveries. Currently, when a call is received for a pickup, a slip of paper is filled out that includes: the item to be picked up, where the pickup is to be made, and where the item is to be delivered. The slip is then pinned to a bulletin board next to a number giving its priority. During the course of a working day these slips of papers are moved around on the board. When a delivery is completed, the slip is removed and all pending pickups below it are moved up. Occasionally a customer will request an immediate pickup, so that slip must be placed on the board between other pickups and again the slips are rearranged. Occasionally a pickup will be cancelled, so the corresponding slip must be removed from the board and all slips below it moved up a position. Barking Dogs Software has been asked to create a Java application that implements ACME's dispatch system. It needs to function similarly to the paper-based system so that the dispatcher can learn to use it quickly.

    Solution: The solution uses the Model-View design pattern to separate how the slips are stored (the Model) from how they are viewed (the View). UML is used to visualize the solution's design. An array is used in the Model to store the courier slips. We revisit this problem in Chapter 5 and the chapter exercises have you use a linked list structure in the Model to store the courier slips.

- Study Guide Exercises

- Answers to CheckPoint Problems

- Additional exercises

A Basic Collection Class

4

CHAPTER OUTLINE

Very generally, a **collection** is a group of elements that can be treated as a single entity. We have seen that there are several categories of collections, each with distinctive characteristics; now we will look at several aspects of building and using collections that are shared. The goal for this chapter is to introduce several important topics that we will need later, including building with interfaces and abstract classes; iterators; Java generics (wildcards and generic methods); and online documentation. We will explore these topics while building a simple collection class, `BasicCollection`, within the Java Collections Framework (JCF). We will also design a test plan for unit testing `BasicCollection` and look at its JUnit implementation.

■ 4.1 The `Collection` Interface in the Java Collections Framework

The **Java Collections Framework** (JCF) provides the `Collection` interface as the root of its collection interface hierarchy. As you might expect, the methods specified in `Collection` are those that are common to most kinds of collections. Recall that a Java `interface` cannot have instance variables and provides no method implementations. It only specifies the API for a data type (this is the specification view of a type).

The methods specified in the `Collection` interface are described briefly in Table 4.1 (the full contract for `Collection` can be found in the JDK online documentation). The interface introduces several new areas for us to investigate.

1. The division of the methods of `Collection` into "required" methods and "optional" methods is covered in the rest of this section.

2. The introduction of the `Iterator` interface, returned by a call to `iterator()` is covered in Section 4.2.

3. New syntax for generic types: The unbounded wildcard ('?') in `containsAll()`, `addAll()`, and `removeAll()`; the bounded wildcard ('? extends E') in `addAll()`); and a generic method (`<T> T[]toArray( T[] a)`) are covered in Section 4.7. *Note*: As you can see, `Collection<E>` is a generic type. When I want to emphasize the generic nature of a type I'll include the type section (e.g., `Collection<E>`); otherwise I'll drop it to avoid clutter (e.g., `Collection`).

As you can see in Table 4.1, the methods in `Collection` are split into two groups: required methods and optional methods.

- A JCF **required method** is one whose implementation provides the behavior described in the documentation. A concrete class implementing `Collection` *must* provide implementations for all the required methods. Note that none of the required methods modify a collection object. They are accessors, not mutators.

- A JCF **optional method** need not be fully implemented by an implementing class. Instead, an optional method is given a default implementation consisting of a single line that throws an `UnsupportedOperationException` (a complete example is given later). The optional methods are all mutators.

Which of the optional methods are fully implemented in a concrete class depends on the needs of the class. For example, a mutable collection might support the `add()` method by providing an implementation that inserts an element into the collection. A collection that is read-only (immutable), however, would not support any of the mutator operations. So invoking `add()` on an immutable collection would result in an `UnsupportedOperationException` being thrown.

Mutable object—one whose state can be changed

Immutable object—one whose state cannot be changed

Table 4.1 The `Collection<E>` interface.

Required Methods

`boolean contains(Object target)`	Returns true if this collection contains the target element.
`boolean containsAll(Collection <?> c)`	Returns true if this collection contains all of the elements in the collection c. The unbounded wildcard is presented in Section 4.7.
`boolean isEmpty()`	Returns true if this collection contains no elements.
`int size()`	Returns the number of elements stored in this collection.
`Iterator<E> iterator()`	Returns an iterator over the elements in this collection. Iterators are discussed in Section 4.2.
`Object[] toArray()`	Returns an array containing all of the elements in this collection. The behavior of `toArray()` is explored in this chapter's *Investigate*.
`<T> T[] toArray(T[] a)`	Returns an array containing all of the elements in this collection with runtime type `T`. Generic methods are presented in Section 4.7. The method is also explored in this chapter's *Investigate*.

Optional Methods

All optional methods not fully supported by an implementing class must throw an `UnsupportedOperationException`.

`boolean add(E element)`	Adds `element` to this collection. Returns true if the collection is modified.
`boolean addAll(Collection<? extends E> c)`	Adds all of the elements from the collection c to this collection. Returns true if the collection is modified. The bounded wildcard, `<? extends E>`, is presented in Section 4.7.
`boolean remove(Object element)`	Removes a single instance of `element` from this collection, if it is present. Returns true if the collection is modified. This method relies on the `equals()` method defined in the runtime class of `element`.
`boolean removeAll(Collection<?> c)`	Removes all the elements found in the collection c from this collection. Returns true if the collection is modified.
`boolean retainAll(Collection<?> c)`	Retains only the elements in this collection that are also contained in the collection c. Returns true if the collection is modified.
`void clear()`	Removes all of the elements from this collection.

By supporting different mixes of the optional methods from `Collection`, we can create specialized collections. For example,

- Mutable and immutable collections that allow duplicates
- Mutable and immutable collections that do not allow duplicates
- A mutable collection that only supports adds
- A mutable collection that only supports removes
- A mutable collection that supports adds and removes (the `BasicCollection` class we will develop falls into this category)

From Chapter 1 you learned that the creation of specialized classes is done through inheritance—an interface would inherit all the methods of its ancestors and would specify additional methods that make it more specialized than its ances- **Why design with** tors. However, that is not the approach the JCF designers took, so it is instructive to **optional methods?** consider their motivation.

The bulleted list above hints at the heart of the problem—there are a number of legitimate variants of collections that could be created. As suggested, one way to support this variety of collections is with a larger and more complex collection interface hierarchy that defines these specializations through *different* subinterfaces. However, as the number of variations grows, the size and complexity of the inter- face hierarchy also grows, but with the distinct possibility that some obscure (but useful) variation gets left out. With this in mind, the JCF designers preferred to keep the hierarchy small and give the programmer the flexibility to tailor a subclass by choosing which optional operations would be supported, so long as the unsup- ported optional methods were clearly documented and their default implementa- tions throw an exception. This comes at the cost of having to work with the exceptions generated by the unsupported methods.

The moral to the story is that sometimes a really clean design is not possible, and painful tradeoffs need to be made. In such cases, it is essential that you docu- ment the class's behavior; it would also be useful to describe how you arrived at the design decisions adopted.

As its name implies, the sample collection class we will implement, `BasicCollection`, is a basic implementation of the `Collection` interface and will have the following characteristics:

- Allows duplicate elements—there can be two or more instances of the same element.
- Disallows `null` elements—trying to add a `null` element will generate an exception.
- Is nonpositional—insertions and deletions are element-based; elements are inserted wherever is convenient.
- Has no fixed capacity—the collection can grow beyond the initial storage pro- vided.

`BasicCollection` will provide implementations for the following:
- All of the *required* methods from `Collection`
- The `add()` and `remove()` optional methods from `Collection`

The inheritance relationships between the Java components involved are shown in Figure 4.1. Remember that every class has `Object` as a superclass, so all the methods from `Object` are available in `BasicCollection`. The `Iterable` interface is discussed in Section 4.3.

SUMMING UP

The `Collection` interface is at the root of the inheritance hierarchy that includes most of the collection types found in the Java Collection Framework (JCF). The methods defined in `Collection` are classified as required or optional. Classes implementing `Collection` must provide an implementation for the required methods that matches their description. Optional methods can be implemented as dictated by the needs of the implementing class. Unsupported optional methods throw an `UnsupportedOperationException` when invoked.

CHECKPOINT

4.1 Why can't you create an instance of an interface?

4.2 What is the difference between a required method and an optional method?

4.3 Is a class that implements `Collection` and supports the `add()` optional method a mutable collection or an immutable collection?

■ **4.2** Iterators and the Iterator Design Pattern

The need to iterate over a collection of elements is so common that the general mechanism for it has been captured in a design pattern. A design pattern provides

Figure 4.1 Inheritance relationships for `BasicCollection` (UML class diagram).

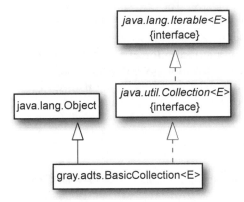

the outline of a solution to a common problem. Specific instances of the problem can adapt the general solution rather than trying to solve the problem from scratch.

4.2.1 The Iterator Design Pattern[1]

Name

Iterator

Problem

A common operation to perform on a collection of elements is to traverse, or iterate through, the collection element by element. This is useful, for example, if you want to display the contents of the collection or to examine each element to see whether it possesses some property and, if so, to perform some operation on it. Furthermore, it would be very convenient if iteration could be done in a way that is completely independent of how the collection is represented (array, linked structure, etc.).

One solution to this problem would be to have each kind of collection independently include a set of methods in its API to support iteration, but this approach has a few disadvantages. The first is that it does not *guarantee* that the APIs will all provide iteration in the same way, since different kinds of collections could use different syntax and semantics for the iteration methods. For example, the operation to get the next element in the iteration sequence might be called `next()` by one collection type, `getNext()` by another, `nextElement()` by another, and so on. This diversity in naming is confusing and unnecessary. Indeed, it would be very useful if we could make iteration **polymorphic**, so that iteration over different kinds of collections is handled in *exactly* the same way (you will see an example shortly and we will rely on this polymorphic capability). A second problem is that having the collection object handle the traversal itself makes it difficult to support multiple *simultaneous* iterations through the collection because each iteration must keep track of its own state information (which element is next in the iteration, which elements are still to be iterated over, etc.).

Make iteration polymorphic

Solution

The Iterator design pattern addresses these problems. The central idea behind the Iterator pattern is to move the responsibility for iteration from the collection object itself into a *separate* iterator object that implements an Iterator interface.

Specifying the methods for iteration in an interface enforces a uniform way of accessing the elements of a collection. This makes iteration polymorphic. Also, providing iteration through a separate object allows simultaneous iterations over the collection because each object maintains its own state.

Create a separate Iterator object

An iterator object has responsibility for the following:

■ Encapsulating the collection's implementation details

---

[1] *Design Patterns: Elements of Reusable Object-Oriented Software* by Erich Gamma, Richard Helm, Ralph Johnson, John Vlissides. Addison Wesley Professional, 1994.

- Providing access to the collection's elements without revealing what backing store is used to store the elements
- Providing access to the collection's elements one by one, in a sequential order that is defined by the underlying collection
- Keeping track of which element in the collection should be provided to the client next
- Knowing whether any elements in the collection are still to be traversed

The static structure of the solution is shown in Figure 4.2.

Collection—An interface for some collection type. Included in this interface is the `iterator()` method, which returns an instance of an iterator object.

Iterator—The interface that specifies methods for sequentially accessing the elements stored in a collection.

AClient—A client class will create a collection object of type `Collection` and will use objects of type Iterator to iterate over the collection object.

Figure 4.2 The structure of the Iterator design pattern (UML class diagram).

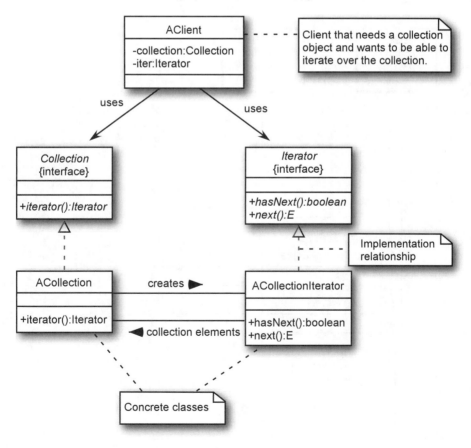

ACollection—A concrete class that implements the `Collection` interface and encapsulates a collection of elements. This includes a method to create an Iterator object to be used by a client.

ACollectionIterator—A concrete class that implements the Iterator interface and is returned as the value of a call to a collection object's `iterator()` method. The iterator gets elements from the collection and provides them to a client in a sequence that is independent of how those elements are stored in the collection.

The UML sequence diagram in Figure 4.3 nicely illustrates the dynamic relationships between objects of type `AClient`, `Collection`, and `Iterator`. Reading from top to bottom, the chronology of events is as follows:

■ The client object sends an `iterator()` message to the collection object. (Arrows moving from left to right represent method calls.)

■ The collection object creates an `Iterator` object and returns it to the client. The `Iterator` object has access to the collection's elements. (Dashed arrows moving from right to left represent returns and return values.)

Figure 4.3 Iterator behavior (UML sequence diagram).

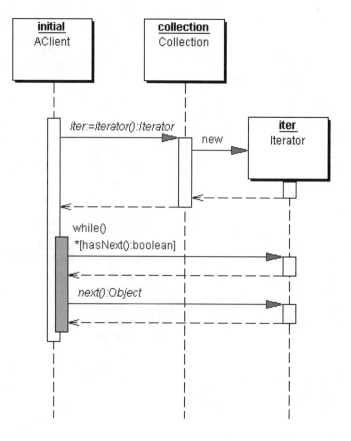

■ The client then sends messages directly to the iterator object (`hasNext()` and `next()` in the diagram) to access the elements in the collection to do something with them.

The corresponding Java code would look something like this.

```
Iterator iter = collection.iterator(); // create the iterator
while ( iter.hasNext() )    // while there are more elements in the sequence
  doSomething( iter.next() );           // get next element; do something with it
```

Consequences:

■ Through an iterator object, the elements of a collection can be accessed independently of the backing store the collection uses to store the elements.

■ It is possible for a specialized implementation of the iterator to provide different traversals of the collection. A list, for example, can be accessed by position and has a notion of predecessor and successor, so a list iterator could begin at any position in the list and allow both forward and backward traversals. (We'll see this in the next chapter.)

■ Simultaneous iterations can be done on the same collection object because each iterator object maintains its own information regarding the state of its traversal.

■ An iterator implementation must deal with the problem of **concurrent modification**—changes made to the underlying collection while an iteration is in progress.

Concurrent modification poses a problem

4.2.2 The `java.util.Iterator` Interface

The JCF provides an `Iterator<E>` type in the `java.util` package that provides the behavior described by the Iterator design pattern (see Table 4.2).

Let's consider in more detail what the iterator must do. We can logically view the sequence of elements to be provided by an iterator as shown in Figure 4.4. When developing logical (mental) models, it is important to focus on behavior and not try to pin it to implementation. The danger, as we will see, is that it is easy to confuse aspects of the implementation with their intended purpose.

Table 4.2 The `Iterator<E>` interface.

Required Methods	
`boolean hasNext()`	Returns true if the iteration has more elements.
`E next()`	Returns the next element in the iteration.

Optional Methods

All optional methods not fully supported by an implementing class must throw an `UnsupportedOperationException`.

`void remove()`	Removes from the underlying collection the element returned by the last call to `next()`. Once an element has been removed, `remove()` cannot be called again until another call to `next()` has been made.

Figure 4.4 A logical model of the elements in an iteration sequence and the gaps between the elements of the iteration sequence (cursor begins in the first gap).

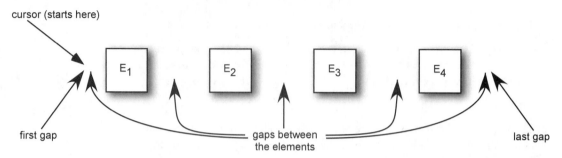

A **cursor** is a position marker used by the iterator to keep track of where it is in the iteration. This is part of the iterator's state. The iterator makes use of the notion of a gap between the elements of the sequence such that the iterator's cursor is always in the gap *before* the element to be returned by next(). For example, if the cursor were in the gap between E_1 and E_2, a call to next() would return E_2 and the cursor would advance to the gap between E_2 and E_3.

When an iterator object is created, the cursor starts out in the gap before the first element (the first gap). When the cursor is in the gap after the last element (the last gap), hasNext() should return false, since there are no more elements left in the iteration sequence; otherwise hasNext() should return true. A full example is presented in the next section.

A cursor is a position marker

Iterator gaps

SUMMING UP

The Iterator design pattern describes a way to iterate through the elements of a collection in a way that is independent of the collection type. A collection supporting iteration provides an iterator() method that returns an instance of an object implementing the java.util.Iterator interface. Specifying the iteration operations in an interface enforces a uniform way of accessing a collection's elements, making iteration polymorphic. Providing iteration through an iterator object separate from the collection object allows simultaneous iterations over the same collection.

CHECKPOINT

4.4 How does the Iterator design pattern guarantee that iteration can be done the same way for different kinds of collections?

4.5 Why *must* the remove() method from the Iterator interface be optional?

4.6 How does an iterator conceal the actual data structure used to store a collection's elements?

■ 4.3 Collection Basics: Objects, Casting, Operations, and Iterators

In this section the behavior and use of operations from `BasicCollection` are illustrated. First, we look at the basic behavior of collection operations, concentrating on general issues that will arise again. Then, because it is important that you become comfortable using iterators, a sample program is included to further illustrate their use and behavior.

Table 4.3 illustrates the behavior of most of the methods from `BasicCollection`. This format was introduced in Chapter 2 when we discussed the oracle for unit testing and will be used in the rest of the book. The Method column shows how some method or constructor would be invoked. The Purpose column describes what the method is to do. The Object State column indicates the state of the object after the method has returned—that is, how the method changes the object's state. If the entry is blank, the method does not change the object's state. The last column shows the value that would be returned by the method. If the entry is blank, the method returns nothing.

Format for examples of class behavior

The rows showing the behavior of an iterator use the Δ symbol to indicate the position of the cursor in the iteration sequence. Recall that the cursor starts in the gap before the first element of the sequence. A call to `next()` returns the element to the immediate right of the cursor and advances the cursor to the next gap (going left to right).

Listing 4.1 gives a complete example that focuses on the use of iterators. It creates a `BasicCollection` object and adds some elements to it (lines 12–15), uses an iterator to traverse and print out the elements of the collection (lines 19–21), uses another iterator to make changes to the collection (lines 25–30), and another to print out the modified collection (lines 34–35). The output from the program is shown at the bottom of the listing.

The iterator sequences on lines 19–21 and 25–30 make explicit use of the methods in the `Iterator` interface. By contrast, the iteration on lines 34–35 uses Java's enhanced `for` loop, which hides the `Iterator` details. The syntax is

Java's enhanced `for` loop

```
for ( Type Identifier : Expression )
        Statement
```

where *Type* is the element type of *Expression*, and *Expression* is an instance of the `java.lang.Iterable` interface. As shown in Figure 4.1, `Collection` extends `Iterable`. This interface specifies a single method, `iterator()`, which returns an instance of an iterator to be used to do the iteration. In fact, the `for` loop on lines 34–35 will be expanded by the compiler to create an appropriate `Iterator` object and use the iterator methods, resulting in something very much like the Iterator sequence on lines 19 through 21.

In the example, on lines 34 through 35, movies, of type `BasicCollection<String>`, is the *Expression*, and the *Type* is `String`, the element type of `movies`.

Table 4.3 The behavior of `BasicCollection`'s methods.

Operation	Purpose	Object State	Expected Result

`Collection<String>`
`c1 = new BasicCollection`
`<String>()`
	To create an empty collection c1	c1.size= 0	A BasicCollection object for Strings

`c1.add("A")`	To add "A" to the collection c1	c1.size= 1 "A"	true
`c1.add("B")`	To add "B" to the collection c1	c1.size= 2 "A" "B"	true
`c1.contains("A")`	To determine whether "A" is in the collection c1		true
`c1.add("C")`	To add "C" to the collection c1	c1.size= 3 "A" "B" "C"	true

`Collection<String>`
`c2 = new BasicCollection`
`<String>()`
	To create a second collection object c2	c2.size = 0	A BasicCollection object for Strings

`c2.add("A")`	To add "A" to collection c2	c2.size= 1 "A"	true
`c2.add("C")`	To add "C" to collection c2	c2.size= 2 "A" "C"	true
`c1.containsAll( c2 )`	To determine whether all of c2 is in collection c1		true
`c2.remove("D")`	To try to remove an element from c2		false
`c2.remove("A")`	To remove "A" from collection c2	c2.size= 1 "C"	true
`Iterator<String> iter =` `c1.iterator()`	To get an iterator for collection	Δ "A" "B" "C" c1	An iterator object
`iter.hasNext()`	To determine whether there are more elements in this iteration		true
`String s = iter.next()`	To get next element in the iteration	"A" Δ "B" "C"	"A"
`iter.hasNext()`	To determine whether there are more elements in this iteration sequence		true
`s = iter.next()`	To get next element in the iteration	"A" "B" Δ "C"	"B"
`iter.remove()`	To remove element returned by last call to `next()` To change the underlying collection object c1	c1.size= 2 "A" Δ "C"	
`iter.remove()`	Try to remove another element		InvalidState-Exception
`iter.hasNext()`	To determine whether there are more elements in this iteration sequence		true
`s = iter.next()`	To get the next element in the iteration	"A""C" Δ	"C"
`iter.hasNext()`	To determine whether there are more elements in this iteration sequence		false

Listing 4.1 An example of the use of Iterators.

```java
1    import java.util.*;
2    import gray.adts.collection.*;
3
4    /**
5     * Illustrate the use of an iterator on a BasicCollection object.
6     */
7
8    public class IteratorEx {
9
10       public static void main( String[] args ) {
11
12          Collection<String> movies = new BasicCollection<String>();
13          movies.add( "Cinema Paradiso" );
14          movies.add( "Lilies of the Field" );
15          movies.add( "In the Heat of the Night" );
16
17          System.out.println( "Here are the film titles in " +
18                              "the collection:" );
19          Iterator<String> iter;
20          for ( iter = movies.iterator(); iter.hasNext(); )
21             System.out.println("    " + iter.next() );
22
23          // use iterator's remove() method to remove all titles
24          // containing "of"
25          iter = movies.iterator();    // need to get another iterator
26          while ( iter.hasNext() ) {
27             String str = iter.next();
28             if ( str.indexOf( "of" ) != -1 )
29                iter.remove();
30          }
31
32          System.out.println("\nAfter removing all titles " +
33                             "containing \"of\", here is what is left:");
34          for ( String movie: movies )
35             System.out.println( "    " + movie );
36       }
37    }
```

OUTPUT

```
Here are the film titles in the collection:
   Cinema Paradiso
   Lilies of the Field
   In the Heat of the Night
After removing all titles containing "of", here is what is left:
   Cinema Paradiso
```

■ 4.4 Developing a Test Plan for `BasicCollection`

We discussed software testing in general terms in Chapter 2, looking at the format of a test plan and the kinds of tests that are especially useful (e.g., boundary tests). Here we discuss how to develop a test plan to unit test the `BasicCollection` class. We'll implement this plan using JUnit in the next section.

Unit testing

The goal of a unit test is to test the methods of a class to confirm that the class behaves as promised in its contract. We'll start by separating the methods from `BasicCollection` into two categories:

- The mutator methods are those that can affect the state of the object: the constructor, `add()`, and `remove()`.

- The accessor and predicate methods are those that report on, but do not change, the state of the object: `size()`, `isEmpty()`, `contains()`, `containsAll()`, `iterator()`, and `toArray()`.

We use the accessor and predicate methods to verify the state changes made by the mutator methods. For each of the mutator methods, ask the simple question: "How will this operation change the state of the object?" If you can't answer this question correctly, you can't design a test case *and* you have no business trying to implement the method. Let's develop a few test cases to see how this works.

Testing object instantiation

When a `BasicCollection` object is first created, what do you know about it? You can say that the collection is empty and its size is 0, so you would expect that `isEmpty()` would return true and that `size()` would return 0. This is shown in Test Case 4.1. This is admittedly simple, but it gives you an idea of what we want to do.

How will the `add()` method affect the state of a `BasicCollection` object?

Testing add( )

- For each element that is added, the *size* attribute should increase by 1, which can be verified using `size()`.

- The collection is no longer empty, so `isEmpty()` should return false.

- Because a `Collection` is unordered, there is no need to verify that an element is stored in any particular location in the collection (this will be different when we look at other types of collections). However, it would be a good idea to confirm that, in fact, an element inserted with `add()` actually is contained in the collection (`size()` only reports that *something* was inserted). The `contains()` method can be used to confirm this.

Test Case 4.1 Creating a collection.

Operation	Purpose	Object State	Expected Result
`Collection<String> c = new BasicCollection <String>()`	To create an empty collection	`c.size`= 0	A BasicCollection object for Strings
`c.size()`	To verify initial collection state		0
`c.isEmpty()`	To verify initial collection state		true

Looking carefully at the documentation for `add()`, we see that the method returns `true` when an element is added to the collection, so we should check for that too.

At this point you might have a sneaky feeling that our approach to testing begs the question. After all, we are using some methods from the API to verify others. For example, it was just suggested that we use `contains()` to verify that `add()` really did add an element to the collection, but this assumes that `contains()` works properly! This is a legitimate concern. We can, however, increase our comfort level by checking whether `contains()` returns false when given an argument we know is *not* in the collection. We also have the information from `size()` to confirm that an element was added to the collection. So, by combining information from several operations, we gain confidence that all the methods behave as advertised. The resulting test is shown in Test Case 4.2.

The consequences of the `remove(Object element)` method are pretty straightforward. If `element` is in the collection

- `remove()` should return true.
- `size()` should report that the size of the collection is smaller by 1.
- `contains(element)` should return false, assuming there weren't any duplicates of the element in the collection. This raises an important point—you really need to be clear about the conditions of a test.

Additionally, if the collection stored more than one element (`size() > 1`) prior to the call to `remove()`, then `isEmpty()` should still return false. If, on the other hand, the element removed was the only element in the collection, then `isEmpty()` should return true. This gives us Test Cases 4.3 and 4.4.

Test Case 4.2 Adding to an empty collection.

Operation	Purpose	Object State	Expected Result
`Collection<String> c = new BasicCollection <String>()`	To create an empty collection	`c.size= 0`	A BasicCollection object for Strings
`c.add("A")`	To add to the collection	`c.size= 1` "A"	true
`c.add("B")`	To add to the collection	`c.size= 2` "A" "B"	true
`c.add("C")`	To add to the collection	`c.size= 3` "A" "B" "C"	true
`c.size()`	To verify collection state		3
`c.isEmpty()`	To verify collection state		false
`c.contains("A");`	To verify collection state		true
`c.contains("B");`	To verify collection state		true
`c.contains("C");`	To verify collection state		true
`c.contains("Missing");`	To verify contains operation		false

Test Case 4.3 Removing an element from the collection.

Operation	Purpose	Object State	Expected Result
Collection<String> c = new BasicCollection <String>()	To create an empty collection	c.size= 0	A BasicCollection object for Strings
c.add("A")	To add to the collection	c.size= 1 "A"	true
c.add("B")	To add to the collection	c.size= 2 "A" "B"	true
c.add("C")	To add to the collection	c.size= 3 "A" "B" "C"	true
c.remove("B")	To test remove op	c.size= 2 "A" "C"	true
c.size()	To verify collection state		2
c.contains("B")	To verify collection state		false
c.isEmpty()	To verify collection state		false

Test Case 4.4 Creating an empty collection with `remove()`.

Operation	Purpose	Object State	Expected Result
Collection<String> c = new BasicCollection <String>()	To create an empty collection	c.size= 0	A BasicCollection object for Strings
c.add("A")	To add to the collection	c.size= 1 "A"	true
c.add("B")	To add to the collection	c.size= 2 "A" "B"	true
c.add("C")	To add to the collection	c.size= 3 "A" "B" "C"	true
c.remove("A")	To test remove op	c.size= 2 "B" "C"	true
c.remove("B")	To test remove op	c.size= 1 "C"	true
c.remove("C")	To test remove op	c.size= 0	true
c.isEmpty()	To verify collection state		true

What else could we check that involves `remove()`? According to the contract for `remove()`, removing an element that is not in the collection should have no effect on the collection, so

- `size()` should report no change.
- `remove()` should return false.

This is shown in Test Case 4.5.

We should also consider what happens when there are duplicates in the collection, say two instances of "A," and one of the instances is removed. This is left as an exercise, as are the test cases for the remaining methods.

SUMMING UP

It has been said before, but bears repeating. Developing test cases can (should) begin as soon as the interface (syntax and semantics) is known. A collection's accessor methods can be used to verify the behavior of the collection's mutator methods. A very productive approach is to write test cases for the methods you will implement next, implement the methods, and not move on to the next bit of code until all your test code passes. JUnit provides a convenient and intuitive framework for implementing and running suites of test cases.

CHECKPOINT

4.7 What is the minimum information needed to write a test plan for a class?

4.8 Do the test plans here follow a black box or clear box approach to testing? Explain.

4.9 Describe the state of a `BasicCollection` object after each of the following operations:

```
Collection<String> c = new BasicCollection<String>();
c.add( "Flying Tofu" );
c.remove( "Headless Cabbage" );
```

Test Case 4.5 Attempting to remove an element *not* in the collection.

Operation	Purpose	Object State	Expected Result
`Collection<String> c = new BasicCollection <String>()`	To create an empty collection	`c.size`= 0	A BasicCollection object for Strings
`c.add("A")`	To add to the collection	`c.size`= 1 "A"	true
`c.add("B")`	To add to the collection	`c.size`= 2 "A" "B"	true
`c.add("C")`	To add to the collection	`c.size`= 3 "A" "B" "C"	true
`c.remove("Missing")`	To test remove op		false
`c.size()`	To verify collection state		3

■ 4.5 Testing with JUnit

In Section 4.4 we began developing a unit-level test plan for BasicCollection. It is time now to look at implementing that test plan. JUnit is a framework for testing Java classes. Its chief features are:

1. Test cases—A test case runs a single test from a test plan such as the ones developed in Section 4.4. Each test case may test a single method from the class you want to test or a small combination of methods from the class.

2. Assertions and *self-reporting* of test results—Using tools from the JUnit framework, each test case will make assertions about the method results and will report whether those assertions passed or failed. When a test fails, you are told which test failed and *why* the test failed.

3. Test suites and testing hierarchies—Test cases can be grouped into test suites. Typically a test suite represents a complete unit test of a class. Test suites can be collected into a testing hierarchy for testing a complete system, with different branches of the hierarchy responsible for testing different components (classes or groups of classes) of the system.

4. Running tests—Running a single test case, a group of test cases, or test suites is done easily within the framework and provides instant feedback on which tests passed and which failed. Because the tests are so easy to run, you can easily make testing and *re*testing a regular part of your software development process.

A *really* good way to approach testing with JUnit is to code the test plan, *then* implement the class one method at a time starting with the most fundamental methods, and run the test case(s) for those methods. Once these tests pass, you can move on to the other methods, confident that you are building on a solid (bug-free) foundation.

4.5.1 Creating a Test Program Using the JUnit Framework

Every testing class should extend TestCase, one of the classes from the JUnit framework. Here's the start to our test class, BasicCollectionTester.

```
import JUnit.framework.*;
import JUnit.extensions.*;
import java.util.Collection<E>;
import gray.adts.collection.BasicCollection;
public class BasicCollectionTester extends TestCase {
```

Within your test class, you need to define one or more instance variables for the objects you will test. These objects are called the **test fixture.** Our needs will be met by a single BasicCollection variable. Since the test cases developed in the last section used Strings, that is what we will do here.

Test fixture—the object(s) under test

```
// stores the collection object under test
    protected BasicCollection<String> c;
```

You might have noticed that for most of the test cases developed in Section 4.4, we created a test object (the test fixture) and put it in a state suitable for the test to be done (see the first four lines of Test Case 4.2, for example). The setUp() method from TestCase removes the toil of doing this manually for each test case.

The test fixture is initialized in the setUp() method, which is called automati- **setUp()** cally by JUnit before each testXXX() method is invoked. Here is the overridden setUp()method for our test program. It creates an empty BasicCollection object, then adds three elements to it. This is how most of the test cases in Section 4.4 began.

```
/* Called automatically BEFORE EACH testXXX() method is run. */
protected void setUp() {
    c = new BasicCollection<String>();
    c.add( new String("A") );
    c.add( new String("B") );
    c.add( new String("C") );
}
```

After each testXXX() method returns, the JUnit framework automatically invokes the tearDown() method to perform housecleaning on the test fixture. This **tearDown()** may mean releasing memory, closing I/O streams, and so on. An example is shown below, but the garbage collector should take care of memory cleanup by itself. You can usually leave this out and rely on the default implementation of tearDown() inherited from TestCase.

```
/* Called AUTOMATICALLY AFTER EACH testXXX() method is run. */
protected void tearDown() {
    c = null;
}
```

A testing class such as BasicCollectionTester will contain a number of test cases, each of which implements part of the test plan developed for the class under test. Generally, a test case will make some change to the test fixture using mutator methods from the class being tested, then examine the state of the test object using accessor and predicate methods from the class under test, just as we did in the test plan developed earlier. The actual results returned by these method calls are compared to the expected results from the test plan. If the actual result matches the expected result, the test passes; otherwise it fails. The Assert class from the JUnit framework provides a number of utility methods to compare expected and actual results.

Let's look at an example. The following test method implements Test Case 4.2 **assertTrue** developed in Section 4.4. It demonstrates two versions of assertTrue(). **(boolean)**

Note the name of the test case, testAddToEmptyCollection(). All JUnit test cases follow the format testXXX(), where XXX is the name you want to give the test. **JUnit test method** The name should be descriptive and typically is related to the methods you are **naming convention** testing.

```
//Test Case 2: Verifies the three add() ops done in setUp() and that
// contains() returns false when we look for something not in the collection
```

```
public void testAddToEmptyCollection() {
    assertTrue( "verify size after the 3 add ops", c.size() == 3 );
    assertTrue( !c.isEmpty() );
    assertTrue( c.contains("A") );
    assertTrue( c.contains("B") );
    assertTrue( c.contains("C") );
    assertTrue( !c.contains("Missing") );
}
```

Remember that for each testXXX() method called, the JUnit framework automatically does the following:

```
setUp();          // establish the test fixture
testXXX();        // run the test
tearDown();       // do house cleaning
```

So before testAddToEmptyCollection() is invoked, the BasicCollection object c will have been instantiated and three elements will have been added to it by setUp().

The first assertTrue() in testAddToEmptyCollection() verifies that there are three elements in the collection. The second assert() verifies that the collection is not empty. The three assertTrue()s that follow verify that the elements added by setUp() are actually in the collection, and the final assertTrue() provides further evidence that contains() works properly. As you can see, the implementation of a testXXX() method from a test case is *very* straightforward.

How did I know to test that the size is 3 and to look for elements "A", "B" and "C"? This isn't magic! I wrote the setUp() method that created c, so I know what is in c. When you write your own test program, all your testXXX() methods will make use of the environment established by setUp(), which *you* will write, so you will know what the test fixture looks like. What goes in setUp() will be determined by the test cases in your test plan.

How do you know what to test for?

It is also possible to make assertions about the equality of two entities using one of the many assertEquals() methods found in Assert. For example, assertEquals(int expected, int actual) is true and the test passes if the integer expected is equal to the integer actual. The test method below implements Test Case 4.3 and uses assertEquals(). So, you see, there are often many ways you can test for something.

assertEquals(expected, actual)

```
// Test Case 3: Verifies removing a unique element from the collection.
public void testRemoveUniqueElement() {
    assertTrue( c.remove("B") );
    assertEquals( 2, c.size() );
    assertTrue( "Argh! Removed element is still in the collection!",
                    !c.contains("B") );
    assertTrue( !c.isEmpty() );
}
```

The assertEquals() method is overloaded to support testing equality between values of the primitive types and between two objects (using their equals() method).

Once the test cases are coded as `testXXX()` methods, you need to gather them into a test suite. This will allow JUnit to run all the tests at once, while giving you the flexibility to run individual tests as needed.

Creating a test suite

The easiest way to add tests to a `TestSuite` object is to just provide the test class as the argument to the `TestSuite` constructor and leave it to JUnit to extract and identify the individual tests.

You can have JUnit locate and load a `TestSuite` automatically by creating and loading the `TestSuite` object in a static `suite()` method, as follows.

```
public static Test suite() {
    // The simplest approach is to let JUnit do all the work using
    // Java's reflection mechanism.
    return new TestSuite( BasicCollectionTester.class );
}
```

Finally, we need a `main()` method to get everything going. It gets the name of the test class, which is stored in an array of string objects. This is passed to the test runner within JUnit.

```
public static void main ( String[] args ) {
    // Use reflection to get the name of this class.
    String[] TestCaseName = {BasicCollectionTester.class.getName()};
    junit.swingui.TestRunner.main( TestCaseName );
}
```

4.5.2 Putting It All Together

The sample code in Listing 4.2 implements some of the test cases from this chapter and includes comments describing the steps for creating a JUnit test program.

Remember, you aren't done testing until *all* the tests pass!

Listing 4.2 The complete code for `BasicCollectionTester`.

```
1     package gray.adts.collection;
2
3     import junit.framework.*;
4     import junit.extensions.*;
5     import java.util.Collection;
6     import gray.adts.collection.*;
7
8     //  Step 1. Create a testing class that extends TestCase.
9     public class BasicCollectionTester extends TestCase {
10        // Step 2: Create the test fixture. Declare the instance variables
11        //           to references the objects to be used in the test methods.
12        protected BasicCollection<String> c;
13
```

```
14      // Step 3: Create a constructor that invokes the super constructor.
15      //          The name argument is the name of a test case (see the
16      //          suite() method).
17      public BasicCollectionTester(String name) {
18          super(name);
19      }
20
21
22      // Step 4. Create a setUp() method to instantiate and initialize
23      //          the objects under test. This method is invoked before
24      //          EVERY test case.
25      protected void setUp() {
26          c = new BasicCollection<String>();
27          c.add(new String("A"));
28          c.add(new String("B"));
29          c.add(new String("C"));
30      }
31
32      // Step 5. Unless you need something more than general garbage,
33      //          collection such as closing I/O streams, you can leave
34      //          this method out.
35      protected void tearDown() {
36          c = null;
37      }
38
39      // Step 6. Create the test cases. Each test case should follow the
40      //          pattern void testXXX() where XXX is the name of the test
41      //          we want to perform.
42
43      /**
44          Test Case 1: Verify that instantiation was done properly. Note
45          that setUp() is called before this method, but isn't needed.
46      */
47      public void testInstantiate() {
48          Collection cEmpty = new BasicCollection();
49          assertEquals( cEmpty.size());
50          assertTrue( cEmpty.isEmpty() );
51      }
52
53      /**
54          Test Case 2: Verify the three add() ops done in setUp() and
55          that contains() returns false when we look for something not
56          in the collection.
57      */
58      public void testAddToEmptyCollection() {
59          assertEquals( "verify size after the 3 add ops", 3, c.size());
```

```
60          assertTrue( !c.isEmpty() );
61          assertTrue( c.contains("A") );
62          assertTrue( c.contains("B") );
63          assertTrue( c.contains("C") );
64          assertTrue( !c.contains("Missing") );
65      }
66
67      /**
68          Test Case 3: Verify removing a unique element from the collection.
69       */
70      public void testRemoveUniqueElement() {
71          assertTrue( c.remove("B") );
72          assertEquals(2, c.size());
73          assertTrue( "Argh! Removed element is still in the collection!",
74                      !c.contains("B") );
75          assertTrue( !c.isEmpty() );
76      }
77
78
79      // Step 7: Create a suite of test cases.
80      public static Test suite() {
81          // The simplest approach is to let Junit do all the work using
82          // Java's reflection mechanism.
83          return new TestSuite(BasicCollectionTester.class);
84
85          // Alternatively, you can create a TestSuite object and add the
86          // tests manually - ugh! But this shows the purpose of the String
87          // arg in the BasicCollectionTester constructor.
88      /*
89          TestSuite suite = new TestSuite();
90          suite.addTest(new BasicCollectionTester("testInstantiate"));
91          suite.addTest(new BasicCollectionTester("testAddToEmptyCollection "));
92          suite.addTest(new BasicCollectionTester("testRemoveUniqueElement "));
93          return suite;
94      */
95      }
96
97      // Step 8: Define a main() method that invokes JUnit to run the test
98      //          application.
99      public static void main ( String[] args ) {
100         // Use Java's reflection mechanism to get the name of this class.
101         String[] TestCaseName = {BasicCollectionTester.class.getName()};
102         junit.swingui.TestRunner.main ( TestCaseName );
103     }
104 }
```

CHECKPOINT

4.10 What class do you extend to create a testing program within the JUnit framework?

4.11 When are the setUp() and tearDown() methods called?

4.12 What is another way to express the following:
```
assertTrue( c.size() == 5 )?
```

■ 4.6 The `java.util.AbstractCollection` Abstract Class

There are a fair number of methods in the `Collection` interface that need to be implemented. Fortunately, the JCF provides a partial implementation for us. `AbstractCollection` is an abstract class in the JCF, provided as a building block to simplify the construction of concrete classes based on `Collection`. Recall that an abstract class is a class that has the modifier `abstract` in its class header and usually has one or more methods that are also declared to be `abstract`. An abstract method has no implementation. Abstract classes and interfaces cannot be instantiated. Figure 4.5 shows our expanded view of the inheritance relationships. Using abstract classes in this way is a common OO technique.

> Abstract classes simplify building concrete classes

    `AbstractCollection` provides implementations for all the required methods from `Collection` (see Table 4.1) except `size()` and `iterator()`, which are left abstract. The nonabstract methods can be overridden by subclasses of `AbstractCollection`. This might be done, for example, to provide more efficient implementations.

Figure 4.5 The inheritance relationship between `Collection` and `AbstractCollection` (UML class diagram).

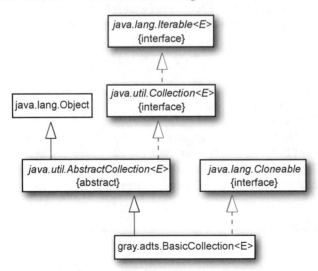

The optional methods in `AbstractCollection` all have the same implementation, which just throws `UnsupportedOperationException`. As an example, here is the implementation for `add()`:

```
public boolean add( E o ) {
    throw new UnsupportedOperationException();
}
```

The bodies of `AbstractCollection`'s other optional methods would be the same. A concrete class that needs to support an optional method simply overrides the default implementation provided by the abstract class.

How is it possible that `AbstractCollection` can provide implementations for some methods from `Collection`, but has to leave others abstract? The answer to the first part of the question is elegant and pretty neat: The nonabstract methods can be implemented using *other* methods from the class's API. Here is a very simple example from `AbstractCollection`.

Build methods using other methods

When is a collection empty? When its size is 0. How do we get the size of a collection? Using the `size()` method!

```
public boolean isEmpty() {
    return size() == 0;
}
```

The `contains()` method provides a more sophisticated example. It takes an element as an argument and returns true if the element is found in the collection, otherwise it returns false. A simple way to do this is to iterate through the collection, comparing each element to the target. Here is the implementation of `contains()` from `java.util.AbstractCollection` with my comments added.

```
public boolean contains( Object o ) {
    Iterator<E> e = this.iterator();    // get an iterator for this collection
    // if o is null, it would be catastrophic to try to do o.equals()
    if ( o == null ) {
        while ( e.hasNext() )           // look for the first null entry
            if ( e.next() == null )
                return true;            // success: o was found
    } else {                           // o is an object & implements equals()
        while ( e.hasNext() )
            if ( o.equals( e.next() ) )
                return true;            // success: o was found
    }
    return false;                       // failure: o wasn't found
}
```

What is particularly interesting about these examples is that they rely on methods that have not yet been implemented—`size()` and `iterator()` are abstract in `AbstractCollection` and there isn't even the shell of an implementation for the `Iterator` class. *But*, we know their syntax and semantics from the API and can *use* them based on that. This is a wonderful example of abstraction—using a method without any knowledge of how it will be implemented.

Hey! An application of abstraction

Now we can answer the second part of the questions—why `size()` and `iterator()` are left abstract in `AbstractCollection`. Why don't they have default implementations? `AbstractCollection` does not commit to a backing store for the collection's elements; it leaves that to the subclass. From Chapter 3 we know of two possibilities: an array and a linked structure. The methods left abstract in `AbstractCollection` rely on details about the backing store, so their implementation must be delayed until that decision has been made.

SUMMING UP

An abstract class is designated abstract by the keyword `abstract`. Typically one or more of the methods in an abstract class is designated `abstract`, which means it provides no implementation (only syntax, through the method header, and semantics, through its Javadocs). A nonabstract method can be implemented using abstract methods.

`AbstractCollection` provides a partial implementation of the methods specified in `java.util.Collection`. `AbstractCollection` does not commit to a backing store for the `Collection`'s elements, leaving that to subclasses to decide. Consequently, methods whose implementation relies on knowledge of the backing store must be left abstract in `AbstractCollection`.

CHECKPOINT

4.13 What is the distinction between an abstract class and a concrete class?

4.14 How is an abstract class able to provide implementations for some methods, but not others?

4.15 Why doesn't `AbstractCollection` commit to a data structure to store the collection's elements?

■ 4.7 More Java Generics: Inheritance, Wildcards, and Generic Methods

4.7.1 Generics, Type Parameters, and Inheritance Hierarchies

Generic types were introduced in Chapter 1 when we looked at class `Pair<T>`, which stores a pair of elements of type `T`. It will be helpful if we examine the semantics of generic types in more depth before moving on to the more sophisticated aspects of generics that appeared in Table 4.1.

Specifically, we need to look at the effect of inheritance on the type variable of a generic type. Consider the `Shape` hierarchy developed in Chapter 1 and shown again in Figure 4.6. Recall that all the methods defined in `Shape`, the root of this inheritance hierarchy, are available in its subclasses and that each subclass is expected to provide specialized implementations of the inherited methods (e.g.,

Figure 4.6 The Shape hierarchy from Chapter 1 (UML class diagram).

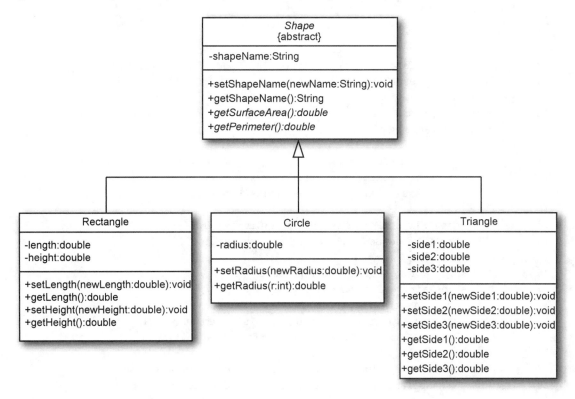

getSurfaceArea() and getPerimeter()) as well as additional methods unique to their needs (e.g., getHeight() in Rectangle and getRadius() in Circle).

Let's create shapePair, a Pair of Shapes as follows:

```
Pair<Shape> shapePair = new Pair<Shape>();
```

You can store a Shape or *any* of Shape's subclasses in shapePair.[2] For example, on line 13 of Listing 4.3 we set shapePair's first element to be a Circle and on line 14 its second element to be a Rectangle. This is valid because, as you can see in Figure 4.6, Circle and Rectangle are subclasses of Shape.

However, the attempts on lines 16 and 17 to set the fields of shapePair will generate type check errors. Line 16 generates an error because Object is not of type Shape, nor is it a subclass of Shape. In fact, Object is an *ancestor* of Shape. So, trying to set an element field of Pair<Shape> to an Object must fail. Line 17 generates a type check error because Date isn't at all related to Shape.

Since Pair<Shape> stores Shapes in its two element fields, its accessor methods will return Shape references. You can see an application of this on lines 18 and 23. On line 18 the accessor is used to get the Shape stored in the first element of the pair.

---

[2]You could also store a Shape if it weren't for the fact that Shape is abstract and cannot be instantiated.

Listing 4.3 ShapePairEx.java–an illustration of the effect of inheritance on a type variable of a generic type.

```
1   /**
2    *  An example to illustrate the effect of inheritance on the
3    *  type variable of a generic type. The code that is commented
4    *  out generates compiler errors.
5    */
6   import gray.misc.Pair;
7   import gray.adts.shapes.*;
8
9   public class ShapePairEx {
10      public static void main( String args[] ) {
11          Pair<Shape> shapePair = new Pair<Shape>();
12
13          shapePair.setFirstElement( new Circle( 5.0 ) );
14          shapePair.setSecondElement( new Rectangle( 10, 20 ) );
15
16  //      shapePair.setFirstElement( new Object() );      // ERROR!
17  //      shapePair.setSecondElement( new Date() );       // ERROR!
18          Shape shape = shapePair.getFirstElement();
19          System.out.printf( "Area of the 1st element = %.1f\n",
20                              shape.getSurfaceArea() );
21
22          System.out.printf( "Area of the 2nd element = %.1f\n",
23              shapePair.getSecondElement().getSurfaceArea() );
24
25  //      System.out.printf( "Radius of the Circle = %.1f\n",
26  //          shapePair.getFirstElement().getRadius()); // ERROR!
27          Circle circle = (Circle)shapePair.getFirstElement();
28          System.out.printf( "The radius of the Circle is %.1f\n",
29                              circle.getRadius() );
30      }
31  }
```

This reference is then used on line 20 to get the Shape's surface area. Line 23 uses method chaining to do the same thing for the second element field—the call to shapePair.getSecondElement() returns a Shape reference, to which the getSurfaceArea() message is sent. These lines are accepted by the compiler because the getSurfaceArea() method is specified in Shape. (Look at Figure 4.6 again to see this.)

Let's look some more at what we *can't* do with shapePair. First, we have established that we can only make Shape calls on the objects returned by shapePair's accessor methods. It is for this reason that the compiler will complain about the chained call on line 26. As before, shapePair.getFirstElement() returns a Shape object, but the compiler cannot find method getRadius() in class Shape. This makes sense—getRadius() is defined in Circle, a *subclass* of Shape. However, since we know that shapePair's first element really is a Circle, we can cast the more general Shape reference we get from getFirstElement() back into a Circle (line 27). Once we have done this, we can make Circle-specific method calls on it, as done on line 29.

Listing 4.4 gives us a second example, this time using our first collection class, BasicCollection, and the Number hierarchy. Number is defined in java.lang and, as shown in Figure 4.7, has several subclasses. On line 14 we create numbers of type Collection<Number>. This allows us to store various kinds of Numbers in it (lines 16–21). On line 26 we create ints of type Collection<Integer>. Since Integer has no subclasses (it is marked final), we can only put Integers in it. The attempts to add Byte and Float on lines 29–30 fail because they are siblings of Integer, not children of Integer. Lastly, an attempt to add an Object (line 31) fails because Object is a superclass, not a subclass, of Integer.

CHECKPOINT

4.16 Using Listing 4.4 as a model, create a collection of Shapes and populate it with different kinds of Shapes. Iterate through the collection to display the surface area of each shape in the collection.

4.7.2 Unbounded Wildcards

Now let's build on what we have done and consider the "simple" problem of using a method to print out the elements in a Collection of Shapes. An earnest first attempt is method printShapeCollection() on lines 10 through 16 of Listing 4.5. Here is the method header:

```
void printShapeCollection( Collection<Shape> collection )
```

We want to print information about a bunch of Shapes, so it seems intuitive that Shape is the type variable for the Collection in the method's parameter. The method body simply iterates through collection, printing out the elements. Because we know that the element type of the Collection is Shape, we can make

---

Figure 4.7 The Number inheritance hierarchy from java.lang (UML class diagram).

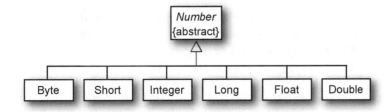

Listing 4.4 `NumberCollectionEx.java`—a second illustration of the effect of inheritance on a type variable of a generic type.

```
1   /**
2    *  Another example illustrating the effect of inheritance on the
3    *  type parameter to a generic type.
4    */
5
6   import java.util.Collection;
7   import gray.adts.collection.BasicCollection;
8
9   public class NumberCollectionEx{
10      public static void main( String args[] ) {
11          // We can add any subclass of Number to numbers. This
12          // includes all the wrapper classes for Java's numeric
13          // types.
14          Collection<Number> numbers = new BasicCollection<Number>();
15
16          numbers.add( new Byte( (byte)5 ) );
17          numbers.add( new Integer( -5 ) );
18          numbers.add( new Short( (short)10 ) );
19          numbers.add( new Long( 100200300 ) );
20          numbers.add( new Float( -125.123 ) );
21          numbers.add( new Double( 100200300.003002001 ) );
22          System.out.printf( "numbers: %s\n\n", numbers );
23
24          // Integer has no subclasses, so only Integers can be
25          // stored in ints.
26          Collection<Integer> ints = new BasicCollection<Integer>();
27          ints.add( new Integer( -5 ) );
28          ints.add( new Integer( 100 ) );
29          // ints.add( new Byte( (byte)5 ) );      // ERROR!
30          // ints.add( new Float( -125.123 ) );    // ERROR!
31          // ints.add( new Object() );             // ERROR!
32          System.out.printf( "ints: %s\n", ints );
33      }
34  }
```

the loop variable `shape` to be of type `Shape` (line 14). Lines 26–29 create and populate shapes, a `Collection` of `Shapes`. Then on line 31 we use `printShapeCollection()` to print out the elements of shapes. This works as expected, as the output for Listing 4.5 shows.

However, we get into trouble when we create circles, a `Collection` of `Circles` (lines 33–36), and try to get `printShapeCollection()` to print out its contents.

Here is what the compiler has to say about line 37 (before it was commented out!). Look at the error message carefully (the especially relevant parts are in **boldface** and *italics*).

```
UnboundedWildcardEx.java:37:
printShapeCollection(java.util.Collection<gray.adts.shapes.Shape>) in
UnboundedWildcardEx cannot be applied to
(java.util.Collection<gray.adts.shapes.Circle>)
        printShapeCollection( circles );
```

The problem is that although `Circle` is clearly a subclass of `Shape`, `Collection<Circle>` is *not* considered a subclass of `Collection<Shape>`. Why not? The reason is that by the rules of the relationship between a superclass and a subclass, if `Collection<Shape>` is considered a superclass of `Collection<Circle>`, then anything that you can do with `Collection<Shape>` you should to be able to do with `Collection<Circle>`. But while you can insert a `Rectangle` into `Collection<Shape>`, you *cannot* insert a `Rectangle` into `Collection<Circle>`.

Collection<Circle> is not a subclass of Collection<Shape>

What we need is some flexibility in the type parameter. That is, instead of specifying the exact type of the collection, we want to accept a collection storing a *family* of types. Java's solution is the type wildcard, `?`, which, because it matches anything, is called an **unbounded wildcard.** More formally, `?` is said to be an "unknown type"; thus `Collection<?>` is a "collection of unknown type."

The unbounded wildcard?

The result is method `printAnyCollection()` on lines 18 through 23. The unbounded wildcard in the method header

```
printAnyCollection( Collection<?> collection )
```

says that the type of the `Collection`'s elements is not known and so will match a collection of any type, which is just what we want. `printAnyCollection()` is used on lines 41 and 45 to print out the `shapes` and `circles` collections. We could have just as easily printed a collection of `Numbers` or anything else.

Let's be clear about why this works. Consider the method body (lines 21–22) for a moment. If the collection's element type is not known within the method body, what can we do with the elements? Well, no matter what the actual element type turns out to be, we know that it must be descended from class `Object` because *all* Java reference types are descended from `Object`, so all the methods defined in `Object` are available to us. This explains why we can make the `for` loop variable on line 21 of type `Object`. This is sufficient for our purposes, because all we want to do is to print out the elements and that just requires `toString()`, which is inherited from `Object`.

Remember, Object is the ancestor of all classes

The implementation of `containsAll()` in `AbstractCollection` shown in Listing 4.6 provides a second example of the usefulness of the unbounded wildcard. The method's purpose is to see whether the collection receiving the message contains all the elements found in the `Collection` parameter, c. The `contains()` method (lines 11–23 of Listing 4.6), called on line 5 of `containsAll()`, simply iterates through the collection looking for the `target`. The only method invoked on `target` is `equals()`, which is guaranteed to exist since it, like `toString()` in our last example, is inherited from `Object`.

Listing 4.5 An example of the unbounded wildcard.

```
1    /**
2     * An illustration of the need for and use of unbounded wildcards.
3     */
4    import gray.adts.shapes.*;
5    import gray.adts.collection.BasicCollection;
6    import java.util.Collection;
7
8    public class UnboundedWildcardEx {
9
10       // This method is specific to a collection of Shape objects.
11       // Note the variable type in the for loop.
12       static void printShapeCollection(
13                               Collection<Shape> collection ){
14          for ( Shape shape : collection )
15             System.out.println( shape );
16       }
17
18       // The most general print method. It will print collections of
19       // any kind of type. Note the variable type in the for loop.
20       static void printAnyCollection( Collection<?> collection ){
21          for ( Object element : collection )
22             System.out.println( element );
23       }
24
25       public static void main( String args[] ){
26          Collection<Shape> shapes = new BasicCollection<Shape>();
27          shapes.add( new Circle( 5.0 ) );
28          shapes.add( new Rectangle( 4.5, 21.2 ) );
29          shapes.add( new Cube() );
30          System.out.printf( "From printShapeCollection( shapes )\n");
31          printShapeCollection( shapes );
32
33          Collection<Circle> circles = new BasicCollection<Circle>();
34          circles.add( new Circle( 5.0 ) );
35          circles.add( new Circle( 15.0 ) );
36          circles.add( new Circle( 25.0 ) );
37          //printShapeCollection( circles );         // ERROR!
38
39          System.out.println(
40                      "\nFrom printAnyCollection( circles ): " );
41          printAnyCollection( circles );
42
43          System.out.println(
44                      "\nFrom printAnyCollection( shapes ): " );
```

```
45              printAnyCollection( shapes );
46      }
47  }
```

OUTPUT

```
Calling printShapeCollection( shapes )
Circle: radius = 5.0
Rectangle: length = 4.5, height = 21.2
Cube: length = 1.0, height = 1.0, depth = 1.0
Calling printAnyCollection( shapes ):
Circle: radius = 5.0
Rectangle: length = 4.5, height = 21.2
Cube: length = 1.0, height = 1.0, depth = 1.0
Calling printAnyCollection( circles ):
Circle: radius = 5.0
Circle: radius = 15.0
Circle: radius = 25.0
```

Listing 4.6 The `containsAll()` and `contains()` methods from `AbstractCollection`.

```
1    public boolean containsAll( Collection<?> c ) {
2        Iterator<?> e = c.iterator();
3        while ( e.hasNext() )
4          // does this collection contain the next element from c?
5          if( !contains( e.next() ) )
6              return false;     // nope, c has an element we don't have
7        return true;            // yep, we have all the elements c has
8    }
9
10
11   public boolean contains( Object target ) {
12       Iterator<E> e = iterator();
13       if (target == null ) {
14          while ( e.hasNext() )
15              if ( e.next() == null )
16                  return true;
17       } else {
18          while ( e.hasNext() )
19              if ( target.equals( e.next() ) )
20                  return true;
21       }
22       return false;
23   }
```

4.7.3 Bounded Wildcards

Occasionally we want to place some constraints on the types that are accepted by a type parameter. This idea may be familiar to you from command line processing. If you entered dir * under the Windows operating system or ls * under the UNIX operating system, you will get a listing of *all* files in the directory. This is equivalent to our use of ? with data types in the last section. But if you wanted to see, say, just the Java source files in the directory, you would need to restrict the wildcard by doing dir *.java, which matches only files that have the java extension. The notion of a bounded wildcard for a generic type is quite similar.

Again AbstractCollection provides us with a practical example. The class header for AbstractCollection (shown below) tells us that the collection is to store elements of type E.

```
public abstract class AbstractCollection<E> implements Collection<E>
```

As we saw in Section 4.7.1, this really means that we can store elements of type E or any of E's subclasses (also called subtypes) in the collection. For example, in Listing 4.5 we created Collection<Shape> and stored a Circle, a Rectangle, and a Cube in it. Similarly, in Listing 4.4 we created Collection<Number> and stored objects of type Byte, Short, Float, and so on, in it.

We could *not* have stored a Shape of any kind in a Collection<Number> collection (a Shape isn't related to a Number), nor could we have stored a Number of any kind in a Collection<Shape> collection for the same reason.

Now consider the problem of adding the elements of one collection to another. This is the purpose of addAll() in Collection<E>. How do we specify the *family* of types that can be added to a collection?

First,

```
public boolean addAll( Collection<E> c )
```

is too restrictive. As we saw in Section 4.7.2 and Listing 4.5, this would preclude adding a Collection<Circle> to a Collection<Shape> or a Collection<Integer> to a Collection<Number>.

Similarly,

```
public boolean addAll( Collection<?> c )
```

is not restrictive enough. It would allow you to add a Collection<Shape> to a Collection<Number>!

What we need is a flexible mechanism that will allow us to specify a family of types constrained by some "upper bound" on the type family. Java's bounded wildcard does just this. The syntax for the bounded wildcard is illustrated in the implementation of addAll() from AbstractCollection<E>, shown in Listing 4.7. The bounded wildcard in the parameter type means that the Collection type is unknown but is bounded by type E. That is, *the element type must be E or one of its subclasses.*

The bounded wildcard ? extends *someType*

Listing 4.8 illustrates bounded wildcards through the use of addAll() to add a collection of Circles to a collection of Shapes (line 27).

Listing 4.7 The addAll() method from AbstractCollection.

```
1   // method from AbstractCollection<E>
2   public boolean addAll(Collection<? extends E> c) {
3      boolean modified = false;
4      Iterator<? extends E> e = c.iterator();
5
6      while ( e.hasNext() ) {
7         if ( add( e.next() ) )
8            modified = true;
9      }
10     return modified;
11  }
```

Listing 4.8 An illustration of bounded wildcards using Collection.addAll(Collection<? extends E> c).

```
1   /**
2    * An illustration of the need for and use of bounded wildcards.
3    */
4   import gray.adts.shapes.*;
5   import gray.adts.collection.BasicCollection;
6   import java.util.Collection;
7
8   public class BoundedWildcardEx {
9
10     public static void printAnyCollection(
11                            Collection<?> collection ){
12        for ( Object o : collection )
13           System.out.println( o );
14     }
15
16     public static void main( String args[] ){
17        Collection<Shape> shapes = new BasicCollection<Shape>();
18        shapes.add( new Circle( 5.0 ) );
19        shapes.add( new Rectangle( 5, 10 ) );
20        shapes.add( new Cube( ) );
21
22        Collection<Circle> circles = new BasicCollection<Circle>();
23        circles.add( new Circle( 4.0 ) );
24        circles.add( new Circle( 6.0 ) );
25        circles.add( new Circle( 8.0 ) );
26
27        shapes.addAll( circles );
28        System.out.println( "\nCombined shapes collection: " );
29        printAnyCollection( shapes );
30     }
31  }
```

CHECKPOINT

4.17 Using Listing 4.8 as a model, create a collection of Numbers and populate it with different kinds of Numbers (e.g., Integer, Float, Short). Create a collection of some subclass of Number. Try adding the two collections to each other. Look carefully at the compiler messages and explain what is happening.

4.18 Give two examples of collections that can be printed with the following method. Give two examples of collections that *cannot* be printed with the method. In each case, explain the situation.

```
static void printShapesWithWildcard(
                    Collection<? extends Shape> collection ){
    for ( Shape shape : collection )
        System.out.println( shape );
}
```

4.19 Write a method, calculateTotalSurfaceArea(), that calculates and returns the total surface area of a collection of Shapes. You should be able to pass in any kind of Collection of Shapes (e.g., Collection<Shape>, Collection<Circle>, Collection<Rectangle>, etc.).

4.7.4 Generic Methods

First, a short refresher. Here is the header of the Pair<T> class developed in Chapter 1:

```
public class Pair<T>
```

Recall that the <T> part is the formal type parameter list and T is the type variable. When a Pair<T> object is instantiated, an actual type will be supplied for T. For example, in

```
Pair< Integer > intpair = new Pair<Integer>();
```

Integer is the actual type that will be mapped to T. As we saw in the definition of Pair<T>, the type parameter T can appear in data fields, method parameters, and return types, and within methods as the type for local variables.

Just as classes can be generic (parameterized), so can methods. Like a generic class, a generic method has a formal type parameter section. As shown in Figure 4.8, the parameter section precedes the method return type and contains one or more type variables. The type variables act as type placeholders for the actual types provided when the method is invoked. These type variables can be used to specify the method's return type, the type of one or more of its parameters and the type of variables local to the method.

As a first example, consider method copy() on lines 11 through 16 of Listing 4.9. The purpose of the method is to produce and return a copy of the Collection supplied in the parameter. The formal type parameter section, <T>, precedes the method return type. The type variable T appears in the method's return type and parameter type, both of which are of type Collection<T>, as well as in the method body (lines 12 and 13). Leaving out the type parameter section will generate a syntax error—the compiler will tell you that it cannot find the symbol represented by the formal type variable (T in our case).

Figure 4.8 Format for a generic method header.

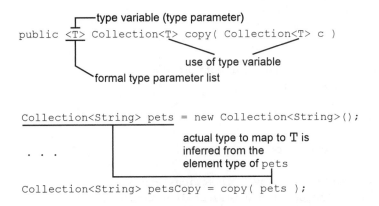

A generic method is invoked in the same manner as a nongeneric method. In Listing 4.9, a `Collection<String>` object is created and populated (lines 33–38), then copied to another collection on line 40. Note there is no special syntax in the call—it really does look like any other method call. The compiler will infer the element type (`String`) of `pets` and will map it to the type variable in the generic method `<T>` `copy()`. Consequently, the call `copy( pets )` on line 40 will produce a copy of a `Collection` of `Strings`.

As another example there are two implementations of generic method `reverseCopy()` (lines 18–23 and 25–30). The first version takes an `Iterator<T>` over a `Collection<T>` as its argument and uses that to iterate through the `Collection<T>` to copy its elements to the destination (lines 20–21). The overloaded `<E>reverseCopy()` on lines 25–30 takes a `Collection<E>` as an argument, and also uses iteration (lines 27–28) to get the elements from the source.

From the three methods you can see that the name used for the formal type variable can differ from method to method—`T` is used in `<T>` `copy()` and `<T>` `reverseCopy()`, while `E` is used in the overloaded `<E>` `reverseCopy()`. We could just as easily use `R` or `Q`. The only requirement is that the type variable that appears in the method's definition (return type, parameter list, and body) be the same as the type variable in the method's formal type parameter section. For example, the following will just upset the compiler because we say we will use type variable `Q` in the formal type parameter section but use `T` instead throughout the method definition. The compiler will complain that it doesn't know anything about the symbol `T`.

```
1    // WRONG!—type variable in the method definition must match the
2    // type variable appearing in the formal type parameter section
3    static <Q> Collection<T> reverseCopy( Iterator<T> source ) {
4        LinkedList<T> theCopy = new LinkedList<T>();
5        while ( source.hasNext() )
6            theCopy.addFirst( source.next() ); // add at front of list
7        return theCopy;
8    }
```

Listing 4.9 An illustration of the definition and use of generic methods. Also, note that reverseCopy() is overloaded.

```
1    /**
2     *  Example illustrating the definition and use of generic methods.
3     */
4    import gray.adts.collection.BasicCollection;
5    import java.util.Collection;
6    import java.util.Iterator;
7    import java.util.LinkedList;
8
9    public class GenericCopyMethodEx {
10
11       static <T> Collection<T> copy( Collection<T> c ) {
12          Collection<T> theCopy = new BasicCollection<T>();
13          for ( T element : c )
14             theCopy.add( element );
15          return theCopy;
16       }
17
18       static <T> Collection<T> reverseCopy( Iterator<T> source ) {
19          LinkedList<T> theCopy = new LinkedList<T>();
20          while ( source.hasNext() )
21             theCopy.addFirst( source.next() ); // add at front of list
22          return theCopy;
23       }
24
25       static <E> Collection<E> reverseCopy( Collection<E> source ) {
26          LinkedList<E> theCopy = new LinkedList<E>();
27          for ( E element : source )
28             theCopy.addFirst( element ); // add at front of list
29          return theCopy;
30       }
31
32       public static void main( String args[] ) {
33          Collection<String> pets = new BasicCollection<String>();
34
35          pets.add( "Ginger Puppy" );
36          pets.add( "Pepper Kitty" );
37          pets.add( "Blue Dog" );
38          pets.add( "Tense Turtle" );
39
40          Collection<String> petsCopy = copy( pets );
41          System.out.println( "Here is the copy: ");
42          for ( String pet : petsCopy )
43             System.out.print( pet + "  " );
44
```

```
45          petsCopy = reverseCopy( pets );
46          System.out.println( "\n\nHere is the reversed copy: " );
47          for ( String pet : petsCopy )
48              System.out.print( pet + "   " );
49
50          petsCopy = reverseCopy( petsCopy.iterator() );
51          System.out.println( "\n\nHere is the UN-reversed copy: " );
52          for ( String pet : petsCopy )
53              System.out.print( pet + "   " );
54      }
55  }
```

OUTPUT

```
Here is the copy:
Ginger Puppy     Pepper Kitty     Blue Dog     Tense Turtle

Here is the reversed copy:
Tense Turtle     Blue Dog     Pepper Kitty     Ginger Puppy

Here is the UN-reversed copy:
Ginger Puppy     Pepper Kitty     Blue Dog     Tense Turtle
```

It is reasonable to ask whether these generic methods could be written as non-generic methods using wildcards. That is, can we drop the type parameter section and substitute ? for T in the method body? Here is an attempt at it. Before reading on, what do you think? Will this work?

```
1   //  WRONG!—attempt to rewrite the generic method using wildcards
2   static Collection<?> badCopy( Collection<?> c ) {
3       Collection<?> theCopy = new BasicCollection<?>();
4       for ( ? element : c )
5           theCopy.add( element );
6       return theCopy;
7   }
```

The compiler will reject this for a number of reasons, but the heart of the problem is that the ? wildcard represents an "unknown type" and Java will not let you instantiate a Collection<?> of unknown type (line 3 of badCopy()), nor will it let you add an element to such a collection (line 5). Recall that one of the advantages of generic types is that they allow the compiler to do additional type checking, but how can the compiler ensure that line 5 is safe if it has no usable information about the element type of theCopy? The answer is that it can't do type checking, so it rejects the code.

The motivation for presenting generic methods here is that Collection<E> includes one generic method <T> T[] toArray(T[] array) which converts a collection into an array of type T. The *Investigate* section in this chapter further explores the use and semantics of this method. Listing 4.10 illustrates its use.

Listing 4.10 Illustration of the use of generic method `<T> toArray()` from `Collection<E>`.

```
1    /**
2     * Example illustrating the use of the generic method toArray()
3     * specified in <tt>Collection</tt>.
4     */
5    import gray.adts.collection.BasicCollection;
6    import java.util.Collection;
7
8    public class GenericMethodEx {
9
10       public static void main( String args[] ) {
11          Collection<String> pets = new BasicCollection<String>();
12
13          pets.add( "Ginger Puppy" );
14          pets.add( "Pepper Kitty" );
15          pets.add( "Blue Dog" );
16          pets.add( "Tense Turtle" );
17
18          // the array needs to exist prior to the call
19          String[] petNames = new String[ pets.size() ];
20          pets.toArray( petNames );
21
22          for ( String pet : petNames )
23             System.out.println( pet + " " );
24       }
25    }
```

SUMMING UP

Inheritance relationships affect the interpretation of a formal type parameter to a generic type. A `Collection<T>` object can store references to `T` or any of `T`'s subclasses.

Wildcards allow you to specify a family of related types. The unbounded wildcard, "`?`", represents the family of all types and as a formal type parameter will allow a "match" on any actual type. Occasionally we need to restrict which types are accepted. The bounded wildcard, "`? extends someType`", provides this service. Here `someType` is a reference type that plays the role of an upper-bound of the family of types that will be accepted. It will allow a match on `someType` or on any subclass (subtype) of `someType`. Thus, only the `someType` family of types are acceptable.

Java supports generic methods as well as generic classes. A generic method has a formal type parameter section that identifies one or more type variables. A formal type variable may be used in the method's return type, parameter list, and body.

CHECKPOINT

4.20 In Listing 4.8, why couldn't we do the following:
```
circles.addAll( shapes );
```

4.21 Redo the sample code in Listing 4.9 for a `Collection` of `Shapes` or a `Collection` of `Numbers`.

■ **4.8** Implementation of the `BasicCollection` Class

The collection class we will implement, `BasicCollection`, will extend `AbstractCollection`. Note that in the declaration of the class, we must have the *same* type variable in the formal type parameter section of both `BasicCollection` and the class it extends, `AbstractCollection`.

```
public class BasicCollection<E> extends java.util.AbstractCollection<E>
```
same type variable

From the last two sections we know that `AbstractCollection` provides implementations for many of the methods from `Collection`. To finish the implementation of `BasicCollection` we create a list of tasks to be completed:[3]

BasicCollection task list

1. Define attributes, including deciding on the backing store for the collection's elements.
2. Provide implementations for the methods left abstract in `AbstractCollection<E>`: `size()` and `iterator()`.
3. Define `BasicIterator<E>` that implements the `Iterator<E>` interface.
4. Provide overridden implementations for the optional methods `add()` and `remove()`.

Table 4.4 lists the methods defined in the `Collection` interface and where they are implemented. The table uses the following key:

■ *Abstract.* The method is not implemented in this class.
■ *Concrete.* The method is implemented and requires no additional work.
■ *Inherited.* The implementation is inherited from a superclass and used as is.
■ *Optional.* The method is an unsupported optional method that throws `UnsupportedOperationException`.
■ *Overridden.* The class provides its own implementation of the method, overriding the implementation provided by a superclass.

---

[3]I find creating such a list helpful in organizing my thoughts and creating a plan of action. Like you, I don't want to spend any more time on this than I have to.

Table 4.4 Where the methods from `Collection` are implemented.

	Implementing Classes	
Collection Methods	AbstractCollection<E>	BasicCollection<E>
`boolean contains(Object)`	concrete	inherited
`boolean containsAll(Collection<?> c)`	concrete	inherited
`boolean isEmpty()`	concrete	inherited
`Object[] toArray()`	concrete	inherited
`<T> T[] toArray(T[] a)`	concrete	inherited
`int size()`	*abstract*	concrete
`Iterator<E> iterator()`	*abstract*	concrete
`boolean add(E o)`	optional	overridden
`boolean addAll(Collection<? extends E> c)`	optional	inherited
`boolean remove(Object o)`	optional	overridden
`boolean removeAll(Collection<?> c)`	optional	inherited
`boolean retainAll(Collection<?> c)`	optional	inherited
`void clear()`	optional	inherited

Note that the two overridden methods in `BasicCollection` are the optional methods we want to support, so we must override the default implementations provided by `AbstractCollection`, which throw an `UnsupportedOperationException`. The complete code is given in Listing 4.11.

4.8.1 `BasicCollection` Task 1: Define `Collection` Attributes as Data Fields

We will use an array as the backing store and make use of the code developed in the previous chapter. Remember that the `length` attribute of an array gives the array's *capacity*. From the contract for `Collection`, we know that the *size* attribute is the number of elements actually stored in the collection. As discussed in Chapter 3, since an array does not store that information for us, we must do it ourselves. So we will store the *size* attribute in a private `size` data field. The fields of our class are:

```
// BasicCollection data fields
private E[] collection;  ◄─────────────────────────────
private int size;
```

Note the use of the formal type parameter as the element type of the array.

4.8.2 `BasicCollection` Task 2: Implement the Abstract Methods `size()` and `iterator()`

The `size()` method simply needs to return the value of the `size` data field (line 156 of Listing 4.11).

The `iterator()` method is also quite simple. It just instantiates and returns an object of type `Iterator` (line 166). This requires a class that implements the `Iterator` interface, which is our next, and most challenging, task.

4.8.3 `BasicCollection` Task 3: Define the `Iterator` Class: `BasicIterator`

The tricky (interesting!) part is defining a class that implements the `Iterator` interface.

Since the iterator object must provide the elements of the collection as a sequence, it needs *internal* knowledge about how the collection is actually implemented. For this reason, we will implement `BasicIterator` as an **inner class** of `BasicCollection`. `BasicIterator` will support the required methods from the `Iterator` interface, `hasNext()` and `next()`, as well as the optional `remove()` method.

> An inner class is one that is defined inside another class

The first step is to determine the order in which the elements of the collection are to be returned by the iterator. Because the elements are stored in an array, it makes sense to start at 0 and index through the array.

> Establishing the element sequence

Our second step is to map the components of our logical model from Table 4.3 onto the concrete implementation of the collection as an array. Our logical view of the iteration sequence had gaps in it, with a *cursor* residing in the gap before the element to be returned by `next()`. Since arrays don't have gaps between their elements, we need to establish a software equivalent. Table 4.5 gives this mapping and Figure 4.9 is a visualization of the mapping at the beginning of an iteration. This mapping is not arbitrary and has implications for the implementation of the `Iterator` methods, as you will see very shortly.

> Moving a cursor between the "gaps"

With the table and accompanying illustration, we can confidently implement the iterator methods following the understanding developed using the logical model. This is important because there is a lot of coordination between the iterator methods and it is *very* easy to make a mistake which is costly to identify.

As the table and diagram indicate, the iterator will maintain a variable `cursor` that will always store the index of the element to be returned by `next()`. Since we have established that the iteration sequence will begin at 0, `cursor` should be initialized to 0 by the `BasicIterator` constructor. A call to `next()` should get the element in the cursor's position, *then* increment `cursor` so that it is in the correct position for the next call to `next()`.

How does the iterator know whether there are more elements in the sequence? This is easy—there are still elements in the iteration sequence as long as `cursor` is not in the last gap, which we see in Table 4.5 is at array index `size`.

Table 4.5 Mapping of components of the `Iterator<E>` logical model to the concrete implementation.

Logical Model	Concrete Implementation
first gap	array index 0
last gap	array index `size`
cursor	$0 \leq$ cursor $\leq$ size

There are two further problems to consider in designing `BasicIterator`. The first arises from the fact that when an iteration is in progress, there are two objects that have access to the collection's elements: the collection object itself and the iterator object. An interesting question is: What happens if the collection is modified while an iteration is in progress? This problem is called **concurrent modification** and occurs when the collection is **structurally modified** *through the collection object* while an iteration is in progress. This problem was first mentioned as a consequence of the iterator design pattern. Here are a few scenarios that might be problematic.

> **Concurrent modification: a structural modification made through the collection object while an iteration is in progress**

- An element is added to the collection and is placed before `cursor`'s position in the current iteration sequence, so will be missed by the iterator.
- The last element of the iteration sequence is removed so that `cursor` is now in the last gap, perhaps confusing `hasNext()`.
- The element returned by the *last* call to `next()` is removed using `Collection.remove()`. This will cause problems for `Iterator`'s `remove()` method, which expects the element returned by the last call to `next()` to be available.

> **Structural modification: any operation that changes the collection's size or alters the ordering of the collection's elements**

The designers of `Iterator` foresaw these problems, so the contract for `Iterator` states that the behavior of an iterator is undefined if the collection is modified while an iteration is in progress. In our implementation we will make the stronger statement that concurrent modifications are illegal and will generate a `ConcurrentModificationException`.

How can we enforce this? Concurrent modification can be detected by having the collection object maintain a variable `modCount` (line 37) that is incremented each time the collection object is structurally modified via an add or remove operation from `Collection`.[4] When a `BasicIterator` object is created, it copies the collection's `modCount` variable into a local variable called `expectedModCount` (line 217). The iterator methods can now easily check for concurrent modification by seeing if `expectedModCount` is equal to `modCount`. If there have been no structural changes to the collection, the two count variables should be equal, otherwise a concurrent modification has been detected and the iterator can throw a `ConcurrentModificationException`. Every `Iterator` method should check for concurrent modification (see lines 242 and 275). Figure 4.10 illustrates the use of

> **Detect concurrent modification by keeping track of structural modifications**

Figure 4.9 Iterator components at the beginning of an iteration.

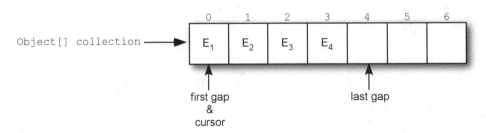

---

[4]We need to add `protected int modCount` to the data fields of `BasicCollection`.

the count variables to detect concurrent modification. Remember, modCount is the count of the number of modifications made to the collection and is *not* the number of elements the collection stores. So in Figure 4.10, modCount is two after the two add() operations, then goes to three after the remove() operation—that is three *modifications* to the collection. The fourth column will be explained shortly.

Iterator's remove() method is the second problem to consider. It has two tricky bits. First, the contract for Iterator.remove()[5] stipulates that the element to be removed is the element returned by the last call to next(). Look again at Figure 4.10 for an example. Furthermore, Iterator.remove() can be called only once per call to next(). According to the contract, two calls to Iterator.remove() without an intervening call to next() should generate an IllegalStateException. To help us reason this out, we will answer two questions:

1. When is it okay to call Iterator.remove()? When next() has been called.

2. When is it *not* okay to call Iterator.remove()? Either when next() has *not* been called at all or when the last element returned by next() has already been removed by Iterator.remove().

So we need to know when it is okay to remove an element. We can decide this by maintaining a flag okToRemove as follows:

■ that is initialized to false

■ that is set to true by next() and set to false by Iterator.remove(). This will guarantee that each call to remove() will be paired with a call to next(). The fourth column of Figure 4.10 illustrates this check.

Figure 4.10 Detect concurrent modifications and determine when it is valid to remove an element via the Iterator object.

Operation	BasicCollection modCount	BasicIterator expectedModCount	BasicIterator okToRemove
Collection<String> c = new BasicCollection<String>()	0	—	—
c.add("A")	1	—	—
c.add("B")	2	—	—
Iterator<String> iter= c.iterator()	2	2	false
iter.next()	2	2	true
iter.remove()	3	3	false
c.remove()	**4**	3	false
iter.next()	ConcurrentModificationException		

---

[5]To avoid confusion, a method will be preceded by the defining class when two or more classes define a method of the same name; for example, Iterator.remove() and Collection.remove(). When the defining class is clear from the context, I'll just use the method name.

The second tricky aspect of remove() has to do with the role played by cursor. Remember that in our implementation, cursor is the *index of* the element to return by next(). Consider the iterator sequence shown in Figure 4.11.

In Figure 4.11(a), the iterator has been created and the cursor is initialized to 0. In (b), we get the first element via a call to iter.next(). This advances cursor to index 1, so that the next element to get is E₂. In (c), we remove the element returned by the last call to next() (that is, element E₁). Note that all the array elements are shifted down a position *and* that cursor is decremented so that E₂ is still the element returned by iter.next(). See the definition of Iterator.remove() on lines 262–298 of Listing 4.11.

The moral to the story is that you *really* have to understand the role played by each component of your solution *and* how they interact. The cursor is logically associated with a gap in the sequence, not an index. If we become sloppy and think of the terms *element, gap,* and *index* as synonymous (which is easy to do), we will end up with a puzzling off-by-one error.

Figure 4.11 Updating cursor when using Iterator.remove().

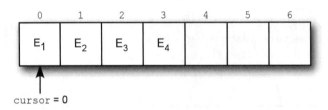

(a) Iterator iter = c.iterator();

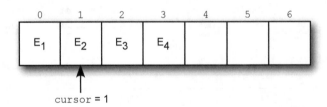

(b) Object o = iter.next();   // *gets E1*

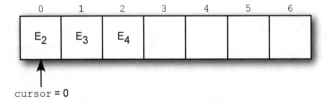

(c) iter.remove();   // *removes E1*

Listing 4.11 The BasicCollection<E> class.

```
1    package gray.adts.collection;
2    import java.util.*;
3    /**
4     * A collection represents a group of objects, known as its
5     * <i>elements</i>. <code>BasicCollection</code> is a simple
6     * implementation of the <code>java.util.Collection</code>
7     * interface and has the following characteristics. It
8     * <UL> <li> allows duplicate elements</li>
9     *         <li> disallows <code>null</code> elements</li>
10    *         <li> is unordered</li>
11    *         <li> has no fixed capacity</li>
12    * </UL>
13    */
14   public class BasicCollection<E> extends AbstractCollection<E>
15                                   implements Cloneable {
16
17     private static final int DEFAULT_SIZE = 100;
18     /**
19      * The array buffer into which the elements are stored.
20      * The array is resized when an add() occurs and the
21      * capacity of the array has been reached.
22      */
23     private E[] collection;
24
25     /**
26      * The number of elements contained in this collection.
27      */
28     private int size;
29
30     /**
31      * The number of add and remove operations performed on
32      * this collection. This information is used by the iterator
33      * to provide a fail-fast iterator. Any operation that changes
34      * the size of this collection should add 1 to
35      * <code>modcount</code> for <it>each</it> change made.
36      */
37     protected transient int modCount;
38
39     /**
40      * Constructs an empty collection.
41      */
42     public BasicCollection() {
43       collection = (E[])(new Object[DEFAULT_SIZE]);
44       size = 0;
45       modCount = 0;
```

```
46          }
47
48          /**
49           * Constructs a collection containing the elements of the
50           * specified collection.
51           *
52           * @param c the collection whose elements are to be placed
53           *           into this collection.
54           * @throws IllegalArgumentException - if <code>c</code>
55           *           is <code>null</code>.
56           */
57          public BasicCollection( Collection<? extends E> c ) {
58              if ( c == null )
59                  throw new java.lang.IllegalArgumentException();
60              int size = c.size() > DEFAULT_SIZE ?
61                               (c.size()*110)/100 : DEFAULT_SIZE;
62              collection = (E[])new Object[size];
63              c.toArray( collection );
64              modCount = 0;
65          }
66
67          /**
68           * Ensures that this collection contains the specified
69           * element. The collection does not support <code>null</code>
70           * elements.
71           * <p>
72           * Returns <code>true</code> if the collection is changed as
73           * a result of the call.
74           *
75           * @param element the element whose presence in this collection
76           *           is to be ensured.
77           * @return <code>true</code> if the collection changed as a
78           *           result of the call.
79           * @throws IllegalArgumentException if the argument is
80           *           <code>null</code>.
81           */
82          public boolean add( E element ) {
83              if ( element == null )
84                  throw new java.lang.IllegalArgumentException();
85              // if the collection is at capacity, make it bigger by 50%
86              if ( this.size == collection.length )
87                  resize(this.size + this.size / 2 );
88              collection[size] = element;
89              size++;
90              modCount++;
91              return true;
92          }
```

```
 93
 94      /**
 95       * Removes a single instance of the specified element from this
 96       * collection, if it is present.
 97       *
 98       * @param <code>element</code> the element to be removed from
 99       *          the collection.
100       * @return <code>true</code> if this collection changed as a
101       *          result of the call (this can only be true if there
102       *          was at least one instance of <code>element</code>
103       *          in this collection).
104       * @throws IllegalArgumentException if <code>element</code>
105       *          is <code>null</code>.
106       */
107      public boolean remove ( Object element ) {
108          if ( element == null )
109              throw new IllegalArgumentException();
110          int p = find( element );
111          if ( p == -1 ) return false;
112          for (int i = p; i < size - 1; i++)
113              collection[i] = collection[i + 1];
114          collection[size - 1] = null;   // be neat!
115
116          // Comment out the next line to illustrate
117          //  the behavior of JUnit when a test fails.
118          size--;
119          modCount++;
120          return true;
121      }
122
123      /**
124       * Creates and returns a copy of this object.
125       *
126       *  The following is true of the clone and the original:
127       * <blockquote><pre>
128       * x.clone() != x
129       * x.clone().getClass() == x.getClass()
130       * x.clone().equals(x)
131       * </pre></blockquote>
132       *
133       * @return       a clone of this instance.
134       * @exception    OutOfMemoryError if there is not enough memory
135       * @see          java.lang.Cloneable
136       */
137      public Object clone() {
138          BasicCollection c = null;
139          // 1. clone the entire collection object
```

```
140          try {
141              c = (BasicCollection) super.clone();
142          }catch( CloneNotSupportedException e ) {
143              // shouldn't get here, so don't do anything
144          }
145          // 2. clone the collection array
146          c.collection = (Object[])this.collection.clone();
147          return c;
148      }
149
150      /**
151       * Returns the number of elements in this collection.
152       *
153       * @return the number of elements in this collection.
154       */
155      public int size() {
156          return this.size;
157      }
158
159      /**
160       * Returns an iterator over the elements contained in
161       * this collection.
162       * @return an iterator over the elements contained in
163       *          this collection.
164       */
165      public Iterator<E> iterator() {
166          return new BasicIterator();
167      }
168
169      private void resize( int new_length ) {
170          E[] temp = (E[])new Object[new_length];
171          for ( int i = 0; i < collection.length; i++ ) {
172              temp[i] = collection[i];
173              collection[i] = null;   // cleanup
174          }
175          collection = temp;
176      }
177
178      private int find( Object element ) {
179          for (int i = 0; i < size; i++)
180              if ( element.equals(collection[i]))
181                  return i;
182          return -1;   // failure
183      }
184
185      private class BasicIterator implements Iterator<E> {
186      /**
```

```
187        * cursor is used to access the next element in the
188        * sequence. In its implementation, cursor is always
189        * the index of the next element to return. So cursor
190        * should be incremented _after_ retrieving the next
191        * element in the sequence.
192        */
193       private int cursor;
194
195       /**
196        * Provides fail-fast operation of the iterator. For each
197        * call to an iterator method, expectedModcount should be
198        * equal to the collection's modCount, otherwise an
199        * intervening change (concurrent modification) to the
200        * collection has been made and we cannot guarantee that
201        * the iterator will behave correctly.
202        */
203       private int expectedModcount;
204
205       /**
206        * the contract of remove() says that each call to
207        * remove() must have been preceded by a call to next()
208        * (they are paired). So if there has been NO call to
209        * next() prior to a remove() or if there were two remove()
210        * calls without an intervening next() call, it is NOT OK
211        * to try to remove an item.
212        */
213       private boolean okToRemove;
214
215       public BasicIterator() {
216           cursor = 0;
217           expectedModcount = modCount;
218           okToRemove = false;
219       }
220
221       /**
222        * Determine if there are more elements in the iteration
223        * sequence.
224        * @returns boolean <code>true</code> if there are more
225        *                  elements in the iteration sequence.
226        */
227       public boolean hasNext() {
228           return cursor != size;
229       }
230
231       /**
232        * Returns the next element in the iteration sequence.
233        *
```

```
234          * @returns Object next element in the iteration sequence
235          * @throws ConcurrentModificationException if this
236          *          collection has been modified by a method outside
237          *          of this iterator.
238          * @throws NoSuchElementException if hasNext() is false
239          */
240         public E next() {
241             // check for concurrent modification
242             if ( expectedModcount != modCount )
243                 throw
244                     new java.util.ConcurrentModificationException();
245
246             // check that there are more elements in the iterator
247             // sequence
248             if ( !hasNext() )
249                 throw new java.util.NoSuchElementException();
250
251             // indicate that we have met the contract
252             // requirements for remove()
253             okToRemove = true;
254
255             // there are more elements to retrieve, so
256             // 1. get the element in cursor's position
257             // 2. advance the cursor to the next element
258             E element = collection[cursor];
259             cursor++;
260             return element;
261         }
262         /**
263          * remove the element returned by the last call to
264          * <code>next()</code>.
265          * @throws ConcurrentModificationException if this
266          *          collection has been modified by a method
267          *          outside of this iterator.
268          * @throws IllegalStateException if there has been no
269          *          call to next() for this iteration or if two
270          *          calls to remove() have been made with no
271          *          intervening call to next().
272          */
273         public void remove() {
274             // check for concurrent modification
275             if ( expectedModcount != modCount )
276                 throw
277                     new java.util.ConcurrentModificationException();
278
279             // check that there has been a next() message to
280             // provide an element to remove
```

```
281             if ( !okToRemove )
282                 throw new IllegalStateException();
283
284                 okToRemove = false;
285
286                 // Use BasicCollection's remove() method to do the
287                 // actual removal. Need to predecrement cursor to
288                 // get to the LAST element returned by next(). After
289                 // the removal, this will be the value cursor should
290                 // have for the next call to next().
291                 --cursor;
292                 BasicCollection.this.remove( collection[cursor] );
293
294                 // increment expectedModcount since the remove()
295                 // message above to the collection object will
296                 // have incremented modCount
297                 expectedModcount++;
298             }
299         }
300     }
```

4.8.4 BasicCollection Task 4: Implement the Collection Mutator Methods: add() and remove()

add(E)

Since BasicCollection is an unordered collection, we are free to insert a new element anywhere that is convenient. We know from the last chapter that insertions into an array are done most efficiently at the logical end of the array, so that is what we will do. We have the following other considerations, as specified in BasicCollection's contract:

■ null elements are not allowed. If the argument is null, the method should throw an IllegalArgumentException.

■ The collection can grow, so if the array is at its capacity when an add() is attempted, it must be resized.

■ If the state of the collection was changed, the method returns true and increments modCount.

The implementation of add() (lines 67–92) follows from this and the code developed in Section 3.2.4.

remove(Object)

The remove operation takes as an argument the element to be removed. We cannot know where the target element is in the collection, so we must search for it. The simplest approach is to use an iterator to walk through the collection, comparing each element returned by next() with our target. If the target element is found, we can use the iterator's remove() method to do the actual work of removing the element (lines 94–121). This is a neat bit of code reuse: Why duplicate the work of removing an element in `Collection.remove()` when we can use an existing implementation in `Iterator.remove()`? We'll make further use of this idea in the next chapter.

Finally, if the `add` or `remove` is successful, `modCount` must be *incremented*, since the collection will have been structurally modified.

■ 4.9 Analysis of the Implementation

The cost of the operations in `BasicCollection` is determined by our understanding of the following:

- The cost of the basic array operations presented in Chapter 3
- The implementation details of `BasicCollection`'s methods

The `add()` operation, for example, takes advantage of the fact that insertions at the logical end of the array are $O(1)$ because no elements need to be moved, as we learned in Chapter 3. When the array is at capacity, the cost jumps to Θ(size of the new array), due to the resizing (see Table 4.6).

Similarly, from Chapter 3 we know that the cost of the `remove()` method is $O(n)$, owing to the need to shift the array elements to close the gap created by the deletion. As mentioned in Chapter 3, if we are not concerned about keeping the order in which the elements were inserted, we could decrease the cost of `remove()` to $O(1)$ by swapping the element in the last occupied position with the element to be removed.

The `contains()` method is $O(n)$ since, in the worst case, it requires a full traversal of the collection's n elements. Note that the $O(n)$ cost assumes that the cost of invoking the `equals()` method on each element of the collection is constant, $O(1)$.

The `size()` and `isEmpty()` methods have a cost of $O(1)$ because they execute a fixed (constant) number of operations.

The cost of the `iterator()` method is $O(1)$ because it "just" creates an iterator object. The cost of iterating through a collection is $O(n)$ because all the elements are visited.

Table 4.6 The cost of methods from `BasicCollection`.

Method	Cost
`add()`	$O(1)$
`remove()`	$O(n)$
`contains()`	$O(n)$
`size()`	$O(1)$
`isEmpty()`	$O(1)$

`equals()`, `hashCode()`, and `toArray()`

Description

In this section you will investigate the behavior of four methods from `BasicCollection` that we have not yet discussed. Two of these methods—`equals()` and `hashCode()`—are inherited from the `Object` class and the other two—`toArray()` and `toArray(T[])`—are defined in `Collection`. As you investigate these methods, you will uncover several topics that will be revisited in other parts of this book.

This *Investigate* is split into two parts. Part A examines `equals()` and `hashCode()`, and Part B looks at the two `toArray()` methods.

Approach

You will do your investigation by looking at the online documentation for these methods, writing code and answering some questions based on the documentation and code output. When you aren't sure how a method works, try writing some code that uses the method. This is an excellent way to learn and should become part of your problem-solving toolbox.

When experimenting like this, it is really important to do as follows:

■ Comment your code, saying what you are trying and why
■ Clearly label all output to minimize the possibility of misinterpretation of the results

Objectives

■ Gain experience reading documentation carefully.
■ Use iterators to examine the elements of a collection object.
■ Use type casting on `Object` references.
■ Examine the contracts for `equals()` and `hashCode()` to understand the relationship between them.
■ Understand the behavior of the default implementations of `equals()` and `hashCode()` from the `Object` class.
■ See the effect of shallow copying of objects.

Part A: `equals()` and `hashCode()`

One principle of inheritance in OOP is to put the most general methods in a superclass and let its subclasses either use those methods as is or override them with implementations that are specific to the needs of the subclass.

A good example of this is the `Object` class, which is at the root of the Java inheritance hierarchy, so that every other class inherits `Object`'s methods. Java's designers included methods in `Object` they thought every class could use. `Object` provides implementations for these methods but expects that subclasses with more discriminating needs will provide their own specialized implementations. We saw this in Chapter 1 when we overrode `toString()` and `equals()` for some shape classes. Consistent with the contract of `Collection` (see its online description), `BasicCollection` does not override `equals()` or `hashCode()`; instead it uses the implementations from `Object`.

The purpose of the `equals()` method seems pretty straightforward: You want to know whether one object is "equal" to another. The problem is that the notion of equality will depend on the type of the objects being tested. You would expect that how a `Date` will check for equality is different from how a `String` would check.

1. The contract for `equals()` in `Object` is pretty detailed. From the Javadocs for `Object`, give four requirements for the `equals()` method.

2. `BasicCollection` is an implementation of `Collection`, so must meet the contract requirements laid out in `Collection`. What does `Collection` say about the `equals()` method?

3. The implementation of `Object.equals()` in `Object` is as general as it can be and still meet the requirements of its contract. On what basis does `Object`'s implementation say two objects are equal?

4. Write a program to investigate the behavior of `equals()`. Create a class, `Investigate4_PartA`, with a `main()` method.

   a. Create and initialize three `String` objects with the values "One," "Two," and "Three."

   b. Create two `BasicCollection<String>` objects, `c1` and `c2`, and add the three `String` objects from step 4(a) to each of them in the order given.

   c. Draw a picture of what you think `c1` and `c2` look like. Be sure to include the variables `c1` and `c2` in your picture.

   d. Use an iterator to display the contents of the two collections. Be sure to label your output so you can easily interpret what you are seeing.

   e. Based on your understanding of the behavior of `Object.equals()`, are `c1` and `c2` equal? Verify your answer by writing a line of code that sends an `equals()` message to the `c1` object with `c2` as the argument, and output the result.

   f. According to the contract, you should get the same answer if you send an `equals()` message to the `c2` object with `c1` as the argument. Verify this by writing a line of code that does this, and output the result.

   g. Now declare a third collection variable, `c3`, and assign `c2` to it (`c3= c2;`). Add the variable `c3` to the picture you created in step 4(c).

   h. Based on your understanding of `equals()`, are `c1` and `c3` equal? Explain. What about `c2` and `c3`? Explain. Verify your answers by adding two lines of code that test for equality between `c1` and `c3`, and `c2` and `c3`. Output the results to the screen.

We look at hash tables and hashing in detail in Chapter 12. Briefly, a **hash table** is another data structure that can be used to store the elements of a collection. Where an element is stored in the hash table is determined by an integer **hash code**.

The hash code for an element is generated based on the element's value, so two elements with the same value should generate the same hash code. Ideally, elements with different values will generate unique hash codes, but this need not be the case. The `Object.hashCode()` method returns an integer hash code for an object.

1. The contract for `Object.hashCode()` describes a close relationship with `equals()`. Based on that contract, what can you predict about the hash codes for c1, c2, and c3?

2. To verify this, add code to your program to send a `hashCode()` message to the three `BasicCollection<String>` objects and output the results. What are the hash codes for c1, c2, and c3?

3. What is the relationship between these hash codes and the results of the equality tests between the three `BasicCollection<String>` objects?

4. If a subclass of `Object` chooses to provide its own `equals()` method, why should it also provide its own `hashCode()` method?

Part B: `toArray()` and `<T>toArray(T[])`

In this part of the *Investigate* you will look at the two `toArray()` methods specified in `Collection` and implemented in `AbstractCollection`. Very simply, these methods return a copy of the collection's elements stored in an array. What makes these methods interesting (tricky) is the meaning of "copy." Investigating this will further clarify the distinction between objects and references to objects and will serve as an introduction to the next section, which looks at cloning a collection.

As before, you will write a small program to investigate the behavior of the methods. This time we will use a collection of `Point` objects. The `Point` class is found in the `java.awt` package (so you will have to import `java.awt.Point`). A `Point` object has two *public* data fields, x and y of type `int`, which store the coordinates of the point.

Create a class, `Investigate4_PartB`, with a `main()` method.

1. In `main()` create a `BasicCollection<Point>` object, c.

2. Create three `Point` objects using the following pairs of points: (1, 2), (3, 4), (5, 6).

3. Add the `Point` objects to c.

4. Using an iterator, display the contents of c, one `Point` per line.

5. Create an `Object` array by sending a `toArray()` message to c:

   ```
   Object[] points = c.toArray();
   ```

6. Write a `for` loop to walk through the `points` array and display its elements, one element per line.

7. How many elements are there in `points`?

8. Are the contents of `points` and c the same?

9. Get a reference, p, to the first `Point` object from `points`. What do you have to do to extract a *Point* reference from the `points` array? Why did you have to do this?

10. Change the x coordinate of Point p to 57. Because the x and y data fields of Point are public, you can do this directly (p.x = 57;). Allowing a client direct access to the object's data fields like this is not considered good OO practice. Why do you think they did this? What is a another approach?

11. Display the contents of the collection c and the points array again. What has happened?

    When c.toArray() created the Object array, it populated it with *references to* the elements stored in c. It *did not* copy the Point objects themselves, only the *references* to the Point objects. This is made clear in Figure 4.12, which shows that points and c have references to the same set of *shared* objects. If a change is made to a Point object through either structure (points or c), the other structure also "sees" that change. This kind of copying is referred to as **shallow** because only the *references* are copied.

12. A subtle, but really important point is that the array and collection structures are physically separate in memory as shown in Figure 4.13. This means that you can change the structure of one of them without changing the structure of the other. To confirm this, use the remove() method to remove the Point (3, 4) from c. This changes the *structure* of c by removing an element from it. The new situation is shown below. Notice that c no longer has a reference to Point (3, 4), but Point (3, 4) still exists because there is a reference to it from the points array. Now redisplay the contents of points and c. Do points and c still have the same contents?

    In step 10 you needed to cast the Object reference back to a Point reference before you could use the object as a Point. This is because toArray() returns an array of Object references. The overloaded <T>toArray(T[ ]) method allows you to specify the *type* of the array into which the collection's elements will be copied. To see how this works, you will add a few more lines of code to the program developed for Part B.

Figure 4.12 A shallow copy created using toArray().

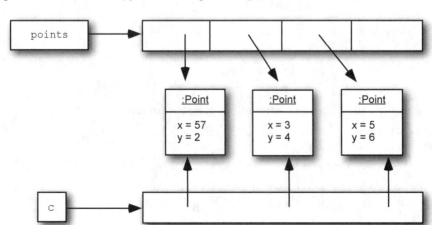

Figure 4.13 After `c.remove( new Point(3, 4) );`.

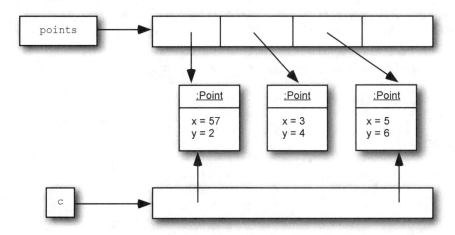

13. Create an array of `Point` objects, `pts_array1`, which has enough room to store all the elements of c.

    `Point[] pts_array1 = new Point[c.size()];`

14. Use `<T>toArray(T[])` to populate `pts_array1`.

15. Now use a `Point` variable to extract the first element of `pts_array1`. Did you have to use casting this time? Explain why or why not.

16. Create a second array of `Point` objects, `pts_array2`, *with room to store only one element* and use `<T>toArray(T[])` to populate it. How many `Point`s are stored in it after the call? What happened?

17. Now declare a third variable, `pts_array3`, of type array of `Point` objects, but *don't allocate it*. Try to use `<T>toArray(T[])` to populate it. How many `Point`s are stored in it after the call? What happened?

    You may have noticed that the type variable for `Collection<E>` is `E`, but that the type variable for `<T>toArray(T[])` is `T`. Let's investigate the meaning of this. Create a class `InvestigateGenericToArray` with a `main()` method.

18. In `main()` create shapes, a `Collection<Shape>` object; circles, a `Collection<Circle>` object; shapeArray, a `Shape[]` object; and circleArray, a `Circle[]` object. You will need to import the shape package.

19. Add three different kinds of shapes to the shapes collection and three different `Circle`s to circles.

20. Use `<T>toArray(T[])` to copy shapes to shapeArray and print out the elements of shapeArray. What do you get as output?

21. Add statements to use `<T>toArray(T[])` to copy circles to circleArray and print out the elements of circleArray. What do you get as output?

    In the last two steps you were moving elements between collections of the *same* type—a `Collection` of `Shape`s to an array of `Shape`s and a `Collection` of

Circles to an array of Circles. Now let's see what happens when we try to move between collections of different, but related, types.

22. Add statements to use `<T>toArray(T[ ])` to copy `circles` to `shapeArray` and print out the elements of `shapeArray`. What happens? Why does this work?

23. Add statements to use `<T>toArray(T[ ])` to copy `shapes` to `circleArray` and print out the elements of `circleArray`. What happens? Why does this not work?

■ 4.10 Cloning

The `clone()` method is defined in the `Object` class. Its purpose is to make a "copy" of an object. However, as seen in the *Investigate* from this chapter, the meaning of "copy" is a bit slippery.

The `clone()` method is declared `protected` in `Object`, which means that it can be used in `Object`'s descendants, but not elsewhere. Because `clone()` is not public in `Object`, it is not available to *clients* of `Object`'s subclasses. In short, you cannot send a `clone()` message to an instance of the `Object` class. Here is what the compiler has to say when I try to compile a program that has the following in it.

```
Object o = new Object();
Object oclone = o.clone();
```

method clone() has protected access in class java.lang.Object

If a class wants to support cloning, it must do two things.

1. Implement the `Cloneable` interface. This is a marker interface that defines no methods and simply indicates that the implementing class has a certain capability (in this case cloning).

```
public class BasicCollection<E> extends AbstractCollection<E>
                              implements Cloneable
```

2. Provide an overridden public `clone()` method. The particulars of the implementation will depend on the depth to which we want the cloning to extend. The rest of this section explores the issues, many of which were discussed in the previous *Investigate*.

A **shallow clone** copies only the structure so that, like the array we created in the *Investigate* section, the clone contains only *references* to shared objects. Figure 4.14 shows a `BasicCollection` object.

Object.clone() provides a shallow clone

Listing 4.12 shows a simple implementation of `clone()` for `BasicCollection`. It uses `Object.clone()` to make a shallow clone of the `BasicCollection` object (remember that `Object.clone()` is protected, so is available for internal use by all descendants of `Object`).

With this implementation of `clone()` in `BasicCollection` we can make a shallow clone of a `BasicCollection` object, c, as follows.

```
BasicCollection<String> shallowClone = (BasicCollection<String>)c.clone();
```

Figure 4.14 A `BasicCollection` object before cloning.

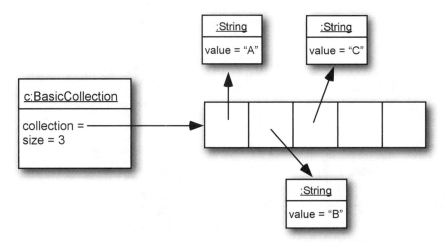

The contract for `Object.clone()` specifies that the method return an `Object` reference, so you have to cast the `Object` reference to the type of the object being cloned.

This method produces the situation shown in Figure 4.15. As you can see, `clone()` copies the *structure* of an object and not its content—shallowClone has the same structure as c and its data fields store the same values as c so that the `size` field in each is 3 *and* the `collection` field stores the same reference in each. Consequently, the array data structure that is used by `BasicCollection` to store a collection's elements is *shared* by the two collection objects.

This can lead to some very undesirable behavior. For example, if you do

```
c.remove( "A" );
```

the string object "A" will be removed from the shared array, the remaining elements will be shifted down a position, and c's `size` field will be updated to reflect the

Listing 4.12 Overridden `clone()` providing a shallow clone.

```
1    // override Object.clone()
2    public Object clone() {        // note the accessor is public
3        Object result = null;
4        try {
5            result = super.clone();
6        } catch( CloneNotSupportedException e ){
7            // shouldn't get here, so don't do anything
8        }
9        return result;
10   }
```

Figure 4.15 A shallow copy of a `BasicCollection` object.

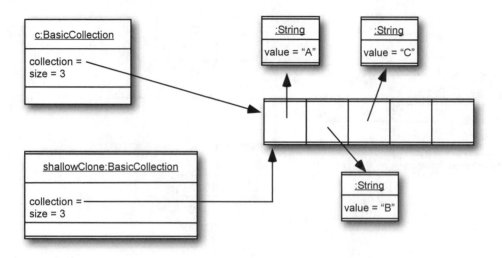

removal. Unfortunately, as Figure 4.16 shows, the `shallowClone` object still believes there are three elements in its collection. Oops!

At the other end of the cloning spectrum is a **deep clone** in which the clone is a complete copy of the original with no shared references. Figure 4.17 illustrates what this would look like.

Unfortunately, deep cloning is difficult to do and is beyond the scope of this book. Instead, we will have to settle for an intermediate clone. The version of

Figure 4.16 The problem with shallow clones.

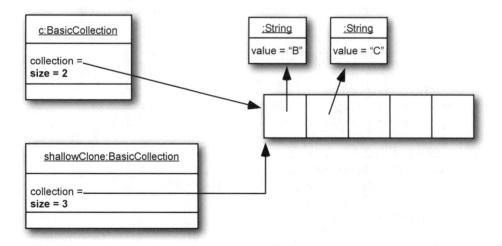

Figure 4.17 A deep copy of a `BasicCollection` object.

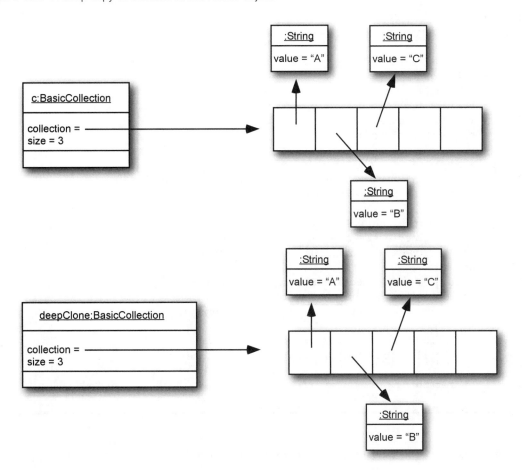

`clone()` in Listing 4.13 is the one that appears in `BasicCollection`. It does the cloning in two steps. The contract for `clone()` in `Object` says that no constructors should be called in the creation of a clone.

1. A clone of the entire object is made using `Object.clone()`, just as our shallow version of `clone()` did above.
2. A clone is made of the collection field using the array `clone()` method.

The clone that is produced is illustrated in Figure 4.18.

Now removing an element from one collection doesn't have the undesirable behavior of the shallow clone (see Figure 4.16). However, if a change is made to any object from one collection, the other collection will also "see" that change since they share access to the elements.

Listing 4.13 The overridden `clone()` method.

```
 1   /**
 2    * Creates and returns a copy of this object.
 3    *
 4    * The following is true of the original and the clone:
 5    * <blockquote><pre>
 6    * x.clone() != x
 7    * x.clone().getClass() == x.getClass()
 8    * x.clone().equals(x)
 9    * </pre></blockquote>
10    *
11    * @return     a clone of this instance.
12    * @exception  OutOfMemoryError if there is not enough memory
13    * @see        java.lang.Cloneable
14    */
15   public Object clone() {
16       BasicCollection<E> c = null;
17       // 1. clone the entire collection object
18       try {
19           c = (BasicCollection<E>) super.clone();
20       }catch( CloneNotSupportedException e ) {
21           // shouldn't get here, so don't do anything
22       }
23           // 2. clone the collection array
24           c.collection = (E[])this.collection.clone();
25
26           return c;
27   }
```

Figure 4.18 The result of cloning a `BasicCollection` object using `clone()` from Listing 4.13.

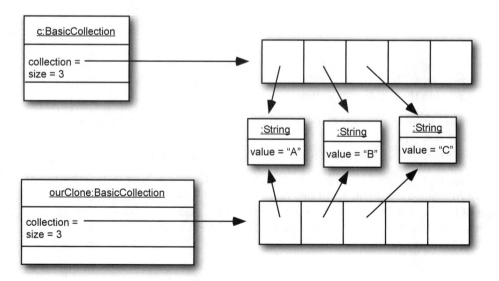

SUMMING UP

A shallow clone of a collection simply provides a copy of the structure such that if either the original or the copy is changed, the other will see the change. A deep clone duplicates the structure and the elements stored in it so that changes to the original collection would have no effect on the clone and vice versa.

EXERCISES

Paper and Pencil

1. Consider the bullet list of possible specialized collections from Section 4.1. Draw a UML diagram showing the inheritance relationships between four or five of these specialized collections. Write a paragraph comparing the complexity of your inheritance hierarchy with the optional method approach taken by the JCF designers.

2. Which optional methods would you support for a collection that can have elements added but none removed?

3. Prepare a test case for the `containsAll()` method. What is the time complexity of the `containsAll()` operation?

4. Does it make sense in an unordered collection to have a method `removeFirst(Object target)`? Explain.

5. Fill in the blank entries for the following table.

Method	New Object State	Returned Value
`c = new BasicCollection<String>()`		
`c.add ("peach")`		
`c.add("apple")`		
`c.contains("orange")`		
`c.isEmpty()`		
`c.add("banana")`		
`c2 = new BasicCollection<String>()`		
`c2.add("peach")`		
`c2.add("orange")`		
`c2.containsAll( c )`		
`c2.remove("apple")`		
`c2.remove("peach")`		
`Iterator<String> iter = c.iterator()`		
`iter.hasNext()`		
`String s = iter.next()`		
`s = iter.next()`		
`iter.remove()`		
`iter.hasNext()`		
`c.remove("peach")`		
`s = iter.next()`		

6. Draw a picture illustrating the result of the following:

```
BasicCollection<String> c = new BasicCollection<String>();
c.add("sheep");
c.add("pigs");
c.add("horses");
BasicCollection<String> dolly = (BasicCollection<String>)c.clone();
```

Testing and Debugging

1. The companion disk for this text includes a class `BuggyCollection`. Run the test cases against `BuggyCollection` to find the bugs in it. Fix the bugs. Remember, you aren't done until all the tests pass.

2. The following JUnit test method purports to test the `add()` method from `BasicCollection`. Assume the `setUp()` method from `BasicCollection-Tester` is used. Are there problems?

```
public void testAdd() {
    assertTrue( c.isEmpty() );
    assertTrue ( c.contains("B") );
    assertTrue ( c.contains("C") );
    assertTrue ( c.contains("A") );
    assertEquals( c.contains("Missing"), false );
}
```

3. Consider the following alternative implementation of the `addAll()` method. Does it have the same behavior as the implementation shown in Section 4.7.3?

```
1    // method from AbstractCollection<E>
2    public boolean addAll(Collection<?> c) {
3        boolean modified = false;
4        Iterator<? extends E> e = c.iterator();
5
6        while ( e.hasNext() ) {
7            if ( add( e.next() ) )
8                modified = true;
9        }
10       return modified;
11   }
```

4. Jodi is new to Java generics. She has proposed the following method. Will it work? If not, what has to be changed to make it work?

```
1    // method to compute total perimeter of a collection of Shapes
2    public double totalPerimeter( Collection<?> c ) {
3        double total = 0.0;
4
5        for( Shape s : c )
6            total = total + s.getPerimeter();
7        return total;
8    }
```

Modifying the Code

1. Modify `BasicCollection` to disallow duplicates. How does this affect the `add()` operation? What is its time complexity now? Write a test case for this change (you should write this *before* changing the code).

Design and Code

1. Add the following optional methods from the `Collection<E>` interface to `BasicCollection<E>` (see the online documentation for `Collection<E>` and/or Table 4.1 for descriptions):

```
boolean addAll( Collection<? extends E> c )
boolean removeAll( Collection<?> c )
boolean retainAll( Collection<?> c )
void clear()
```

Write test cases for these methods and add them to the JUnit test program from the chapter.

2. The `remove(Object target)` method described in `Collection` removes a single instance of `target` from the collection object. Write a `removeAll(Object target)` method which removes all instances of `target` from the collection. Write a test case for this method and add it to the JUnit test program from the chapter.

3. Create a class `BasicLinkedCollection<E>` that extends `Abstract-Collection<E>` and uses a linked list as the backing store.

ON THE WEB

Additional study material is available at Addison-Wesley's Website at http://www.aw.com/cssupport. This material includes the following:

■ Study Guide Exercises

■ Answers to CheckPoint Problems

■ Additional exercises

The List Abstract Data Type

5

CHAPTER OUTLINE

5.1 List Description
5.2 The List ADT
5.3 The `List` Interface in the Java Collections Framework
5.4 Designing a Test Plan
Investigate: The `Serializable` Interface—Adding Persistence to the Courier Application
5.5 A Linked List Implementation of the List ADT
5.6 Implementing the Test Plan
5.7 Analysis and Measurement
Exercises
On the Web: Focus on Problem Solving: *CourierModel Revisited*;
Study Guide Exercises; Answers to CheckPoint Problems; Additional exercises

---

The notion of a list is very familiar to us. We regularly make lists of things to buy at the store and jobs to be done. In computing, a list is a very general collection type with a wide variety of uses—applications maintain lists of recently accessed documents or recently accessed URLs, operating systems maintain lists of time-sensitive events, a handheld device might use a list to keep track of incoming messages over a wireless network. As we will see in the next chapter, a list can also be used as the backing store for other ADTs.

Lists have many uses

We begin this chapter with a general description of the List ADT and its specification. We then look at support for lists in the Java Collections Framework (JCF) and develop a test plan for the class we will implement. To illustrate how lists can be used, we will re-implement `CourierModel` from Chapter 3 using `ArrayList` from the JCF. This is followed by an implementation of `List` using a sequential access data structure (linked list). After a discussion of testing the implementation, the chapter concludes with a comparison of the array and linked list implementations in terms of their time and space requirements, giving you a guideline for matching implementation characteristics to application needs. We will make use of this in the next two chapters.

■ 5.1 List Description

A list is a **linear** collection of elements. Each element is associated with an *indexable* position in the list, such that every position except the first has a unique predecessor and every position except the last has a unique successor. From this perspective, a list "is a kind of" collection that is specialized to support indexing of its elements. As you might expect, this specialization will be reflected in List's API. I will refer to the first position in the list through an attribute called **head** and the last position as attribute **tail**. The *size* of the list is the number of elements stored in it.

> A list is a linear collection that supports indexing of its elements

If there is no relationship between an element and its position in the list, the list is **unordered**. Alternatively, a list may be **ordered**, in which case there is an important relationship between an element and its position in the list determined by an element's **key**. If each element of the list is a simple type, such as an integer, the element's value is the key. But if the elements are of a composite type (a type composed of multiple fields), then one of the fields is identified as the key and the ordering is based on it. For example, when you display the contents of a folder sorted by file size, the key is the size of the file. You could change the key to be the file name and display the files accordingly. In fact, this idea was introduced in the Focus on Problem Solving section for Chapter 3 when we discussed the Model-View design pattern. In a more sophisticated ordering, you would use primary and secondary keys. The files might be sorted first by file type (the primary key) and files of the same type would then be sorted lexicographically by name (the secondary key).

> A list may be ordered based on an element's key

You can define lists with different properties. A read-only (immutable) list would be useful for a data object that is to be shared by many users or if the data is not to be altered. An append-only list would only allow additions to the list at the end, which is what you need to support log files.[1] A list that doesn't allow duplicates would be useful when generating mailing labels. This chapter looks at unsorted lists. Chapter 9 examines sorting algorithms and ordered structures, including sorted lists.

> There are different kinds of lists: mutable, immutable, append only, etc.

■ 5.2 The List ADT

We can use the description above to help identify a set of properties every list will have. These properties will help us specify the behavior of the List ADT's operations and will suggest some test cases.

As you will discover when you create your own ADTs, there is a set of operations which clearly needs to be in your specification, but after that you have some

---

[1] A log file logs events, putting the most recent event at the end of the log file. The *Investigate* in Chapter 9 looks at an external sorting algorithm to sort log file entries for large log files.

flexibility in deciding what to include. The set of operations described here is typical for a List. Since a List "is a kind of" Collection, typical Collection operations such as size(), isEmpty(), contains(), and so on are not shown. In fact, we will say that List is an extension of Collection from the last chapter, so it inherits all the methods specified in Collection.

A List "is a kind of" Collection

The List ADT

Description
A List is a linear collection that supports indexing of its elements. The list is mutable, unordered, has no fixed limit on size, and allows duplicates. The list element type is unspecified.

Properties
1. Empty list: *size* is 0; *head* and *tail* reference null, a special value indicating they don't reference a list position.
2. Nonempty list:
   a. List has one element: *size* is 1; *head* and *tail* refer to the same position.
   b. List has more than one element: *size* is the number of elements in the list, *head* refers to the first element, *tail* refers to the last element, and these elements are in different positions.
3. All elements in the list must be in adjacent positions. Thus every position in the list except the *head* has a unique predecessor and every position in the list except the *tail* has a unique successor.
4. The index of the first position is 0 and the index of the last position is *size* -1; every indexed position refers to a list element.

Attributes

size:	The number of elements in the list; *size* ≥ 0 at all times, the range of occupied positions is 0 to *size* -1.
head:	The first element of the list; null if the list is empty.
tail:	The last element of the list; null if the list is empty.

Operations

List ()

pre-condition:	none
responsibilities:	constructor initializes the list attributes
post-condition:	*size* is 0
	head and *tail* reference null (a special value not part of the list)
returns:	nothing

add (int index, *Type* element)

pre-condition:	$0 \leq$ index $\leq$ *size*
responsibilities:	insert element into the list at the specified location

post-condition: element is inserted in the list at position index
size is incremented by 1
tail references the element in the first position if the list was previously empty, otherwise *tail*'s position is advanced by 1
head references the new element only if the list was previously empty, otherwise *head* is unchanged
throws: index out of bounds exception if pre-condition is not met
returns: nothing

get (int index)
pre-condition: $0 \leq$ index $<$ *size*
responsibilities: return the element stored at the given index position
post-condition: the list is unchanged
throws: index out of bounds exception if pre-condition is not met
returns: element at position index

indexOf (*Type* target)
pre-condition: none
responsibilities: determine index of the first occurrence of target in the list
post-condition: list is unchanged
returns: the index of the first occurrence of target in the list if found, or −1 if not found

lastIndexOf (*Type* target)
pre-condition: none
responsibilities: determine index of the last occurrence of target in the list
post-condition: list is unchanged
returns: the index of the last occurrence of target in the list if found, or −1 if not found

listIterator (int index)
pre-condition: $0 \leq$ index $\leq$ *size*
responsibilities: create a ListIterator object to access the elements in the list in sequence in forward and reverse orders. Index is the index of the first element that would be returned by the iterator via a call to the ListIterator next() operation.
post-condition: a ListIterator is created, the list is unchanged
throws: index out of bounds exception if pre-condition is not met
returns: a ListIterator

remove (int index)
pre-condition: $0 \leq$ index $<$ *size*
responsibilities: remove element at position index
post-condition: element at position index is removed from the list
size is decremented by 1
tail position is decremented by 1; *tail* is null if the list is empty
head refers to null if the list is now empty, else the element in the first position

| throws: | index out of bounds exception if pre-condition is not met |
| returns: | the element removed |

set (int index, *Type* newElement)

pre-condition:	$0 \le$ index $<$ *size*
responsibilities:	replace the element at position index with newElement
post-condition:	the element previously at index is replaced by newElement
	size, *tail*, and *head* are unchanged
throws:	index out of bounds exception if pre-condition is not met
returns:	the element that had previously been at position index

sublist (int fromIndex, int uptoIndex)

pre-condition:	$0 \le$ fromIndex $\le$ *size*
	$0 \le$ uptoIndex $\le$ *size*
	fromIndex $\le$ uptoIndex
responsibilities:	provide a sublist ("view") of this list containing the elements in the positions from fromIndex to uptoIndex -1 inclusive. The sublist is backed by this list, so changes made to the sublist change this list. Operations on the sublist are undefined if the list is structurally modified in any way except through the sublist.
post-condition:	this list is unchanged
throws:	index out of bounds exception if pre-conditions are not met
returns:	a List object referencing the elements from this list in the positions fromIndex to uptoIndex -1, inclusive

External operations

The indexOf() and lastIndexOf() operations require that *Type* provide an equals() operation to test for equality of elements.

The purpose and descriptions of most of the operations are straightforward, but a few features should be discussed.

The range of list indices is specified as 0 to *size* $- 1$.[2] This choice is based on the fact that languages such as Java begin indexing at 0. Alternatively, the indexing can range from 1 to *size*. Of course, an application can provide a view of a list that uses a different range, mapping it to the range supported by the List ADT.

We should clarify the pre-conditions for some of the operations that take an index argument since they are an easy source for off-by-one errors. I often approach this by asking simple "Why?", "What?", and "Where?" questions. Asking these kinds of questions (and answering them!) is a good problem solving technique that will help you avoid problems later and is especially important in the early stages when you have only a vague idea of what an operation is supposed to do.

---

[2]Remember, *size* is the number of elements actually in the list and is not the capacity of the list.

For example: Where can I safely add a new element? The add operation takes as its first argument the index where the new element is to be inserted. The list invariants specify that all elements must be logically adjacent in the list and that the range of element *indices* is 0 to *size* – 1. So the range of available indices for inserting a new element is 0 (the first element) to *size* (the index of the last element's successor) inclusive. Any index below 0 is clearly invalid—no such position will ever exist. Anything beyond *size* is also invalid because it would violate the element adjacency invariant. Finally, while there is no element at position *size*, this position is valid since it is adjacent to the last element in the list at position *size* – 1. Figure 5.1 illustrates the possibilities.

Where can I safely access (`get()`, `set()`, or `remove()`) an element? These operations also take an integer argument specifying the index of the target element. Here, the purpose is to act on an *existing* element. Again, through the adjacency invariant we know that all elements in the list occupy indices in the range from 0 to *size* – 1, so the integer argument must be in this range. There is no element with an index less than 0, nor are there elements beyond *size* – 1.

The note about external operations at the end of the ADT description highlights the fact that a collection may place requirements on the element type the collection stores. These need to be explicitly stated in the ADT description. In this case, the `indexOf()` and `lastIndexOf()` operations need to be able to test elements for equality.

The `sublist()` operator returns a *view* of some part of the underlying list. What does that mean? The sublist created is a list that has its own set of indices and supports all the `List` operations. However, any changes made to the sublist are reflected in the underlying list. Figure 5.2(a) illustrates the view we are given when we send a `sublist(2,6)` message to a `List` object. Note that the elements are also a part of the original list. Part (b) of that figure shows what happens when the sublist is modified with a remove operation, and part (c) illustrates a nifty use of `sublist()`.

Figure 5.1 Insertion and access indices in a list of size = 5.

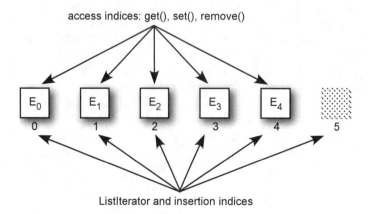

Figure 5.2 Creating and modifying the "view" of a list.

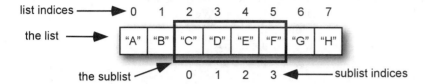

(a) Sublist created by `List<String>subl = list.sublist(2, 6);`

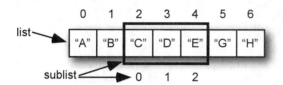

(b) List and sublist after executing `subl.remove(3);`

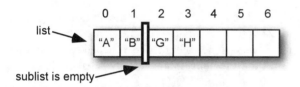

(c) List and sublist after executing `list.sublist(2, 6).clear();`

The `listIterator()` operation returns a "list iterator." As suggested in the Consequences section of the Iterator design pattern presented in Chapter 4, the `ListIterator` is an iterator specialized for lists. As you now know, a distinguishing characteristic of a list is that we can associate an *index* with each of its elements and, as a consequence, each element of the list (save the first and last) has a built-in notion of predecessor and successor. This allows you to begin the iteration at an arbitrary position within the list *and* to move both forward (to a successor) and backward (to a predecessor) through the list.

`ListIterator` is an iterator specialized for lists

As we did with the iterator, we move the cursor between the logical gaps that are between the list's elements. It is possible to move forward and backward within the same iteration. The iteration can begin at the following:

■ Index 0 (the gap before the first element), allowing a forward traversal. This is equivalent to the general iterator presented in the last chapter

■ At index `list.size()` (the gap *after* the last element), allowing a backward traversal (see Figure 5.1)

■ Anywhere in the interior of the list

The following ADT gives a specification of the `ListIterator` ADT. You should look at the pre-conditions and post-conditions very closely, because there are a number of dependencies between the methods and a complete understanding of them is essential to correctly implementing and using a `ListIterator`. Since `ListIterator` is a specialization of `Iterator` and includes all the `Iterator` methods, `hasNext()` and `next()` are not included in the specification.

The ListIterator ADT

Description
Provide access to the elements of a list starting from a given position in the list. Movement through the list may be forward or backward.

Properties
1. Iteration can begin with an element in the range 0 to list.*size*.
2. The underlying list over which the ListIterator iterates may not be structurally changed (an element added or deleted) by non-ListIterator methods while an iteration is in progress. Doing so generates a concurrent modification exception.

Attributes

cursor:	position marker that keeps track of where the iterator is in the iteration; *cursor* resides in the gap between the elements, with the element to its right being the element to be returned by the next call to next() and the element to its left the element to be returned by the next call to previous().
nextIndex:	index of the element to be returned by the next call to next(); if hasNext() is false, this is the list's *size*
previousIndex:	index of the element to be returned by the next call to previous(); −1 if hasPrevious() is false

Operations: (some operations from the Iterator ADT are not repeated)

ListIterator(int index)

pre-condition:	0 ≤ index ≤ list.size()
responsibilities:	constructor—initialize the iterator attributes so that a call to next() would return the element at position index
post-condition:	*cursor* is set to the gap *before* the element for the given index; *previousIndex* is index −1; *nextIndex* is set to index
returns:	nothing
throws:	index out of bounds exception if the pre-condition is not met

hasPrevious()

pre-condition:	none
responsibilities:	determine if the underlying collection has any more elements at positions below *cursor*
post-condition:	the iterator and underlying collection are unchanged
returns:	true if *cursor* is *not* in the first gap of the iteration sequence

previous()
    pre-condition: hasPrevious() is true
    responsibilities: return the element that precedes *cursor* in the list
    post-condition: *cursor* is moved to the gap to the left in the sequence *nextIndex* and *previousIndex* are decremented by 1
    returns: the previous element in the sequence
    throws: no such element exception if the pre-condition is not met

nextIndex()
    pre-condition: none
    responsibilities: return the index of the element that would be returned by the next call to next() or list.*size* if hasNext() is false
    post-condition: the iterator is unchanged
    returns: *nextIndex*

previousIndex()
    pre-condition: none
    responsibilities: return the index of the element that would be returned by the next call to previous() or -1 if hasPrevious() is false
    post-condition: the iterator is unchanged
    returns: *previousIndex*

add(*Type* newElement)
    pre-condition: no concurrent modification
    responsibilities: add newElement between the elements that would be returned by previous() and next()
    post-condition: newElement is inserted at the position immediately below *cursor* so that a call to previous() would return newElement
                            nextIndex, previousIndex are incremented
    returns: nothing
    throws: concurrent modification exception if the pre-condition is not met

remove()
    pre-condition: no concurrent modification
                            next() or previous() has been called at least once; either next() or previous() has been called since the last call to remove() or add()
    responsibilities: remove the element returned by the last call to next() or previous()
    post-condition: the last element returned by next() or previous() is removed; *nextIndex* and *previousIndex* are decremented if the element deleted was at a position below *cursor*
    returns: nothing
    throws: concurrent modification exception if first pre-condition is not met; illegal state exception if the second pre-condition is not met

set(*Type* newElement)
    pre-condition: neither remove() nor add() have been called since the last call to next() or previous()

responsibilities:	replace the element returned by the last call to next() or previous() with newElement
post-condition:	the element in the list returned by the last call of next()/previous() is replaced with newElement
returns:	nothing
throws:	illegal state exception if the pre-condition is not met

The pre-conditions for the `ListIterator`'s mutator methods are based on the fact that it is calls to `next()` and `previous()` that supply the element from the iteration sequence that is to be mutated. If no such call has been made, there is no element to mutate. A consequence of this is that once a call has been made to one of `set()`, `remove()`, or `add()`, a call must be made to `next()` or `previous()` to supply another list element before `set()`, `remove()`, or `add()` can be called again.

Important ListIterator details

CHECKPOINT

5.1 What is true about a list when the *head* and *tail* refer to the same position?

5.2 What values will the state variables have when the list is empty?

5.3 Explain each of the pre-conditions to `ListIterator.remove()`.

■ 5.3 The `List` Interface in the Java Collections Framework

The JCF provides a `List` interface that extends the `Collection` interface, so all the methods in `Collection` are also to be found in `List` (see the UML diagram in Figure 5.3). `List` adds the following:

- ■ The ability to access elements by index (e.g., `add(int index, E element)`)
- ■ A `listIterator()` method returning a `ListIterator` object that can begin the iteration at any position in the List and is bidirectional

As we saw with the `Collection` interface, the optional methods in the `List` interface (see Table 5.1) are those that would modify the list in some way. An implementing subclass must implement the required methods and any of the optional methods it needs for its specialization, leaving the rest of the optional methods with an implementation that throws `UnsupportedOperationException`, as we did with `BasicCollection` in the last chapter.

5.3.1 The `java.util.List` Interface

The `List` operations described in the `List` ADT are a subset of the methods defined in the JCF `List` interface. The contracts of the operations in the `List` ADT match their counterparts in the JCF's `java.util.List<E>` interface.

Figure 5.3 The `java.util.List<E>` interface hierarchy in the JCF (UML class diagram).

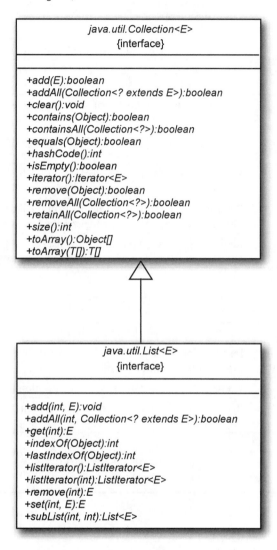

A close examination of the methods specified by `List` and those inherited from `Collection` reveals an unfortunate inconsistency. The `List.add(int, E)` method is a `void` method. But `Collection.add(E)` returns a `boolean`, indicating whether or not the collection structure was modified as the result of the add (if duplicates are not allowed, `add()` would return false if its argument were already in the collection). Consistency in naming and behavior is important—as stated in the first chapter, we expect similar things to behave in similar ways. Variations in behavior like this force the programmer to have to remember more rules, which can lead to errors. You should keep this in mind when you design your own interfaces.

Similar things should behave similarly

Table 5.1 The `java.util.List<E>` interface.

Required Methods

`boolean equals(Object o)`	Compares the specified object with the list for equality. (Overridden method from `Object`)
`E get(int index)`	Returns the element at the specified position in the list.
`int hashCode()`	Returns the hash code value for the list. (Overridden method from `Object`)
`int indexOf(Object o)`	Returns the index in the list of the *first* occurrence of the specified element, or −1 if the list does not contain the element.
`int lastIndexOf(Object o)`	Returns the index in the list of the *last* occurrence of the specified element, or −1 if the list does not contain the element.
`ListIterator<E> listIterator()`	Returns a list iterator of the elements in the list (in proper sequence).
`ListIterator<E> listIterator (int index)`	Returns a list iterator of the elements in the list (in proper sequence), starting at the specified position in this list.
`List<E> subList(int fromIndex,           int uptoIndex)`	Returns a view of the portion of the list between `fromIndex` (inclusive) and `uptoIndex` (exclusive).

Optional Methods

All optional methods not supported by a `List` implementation must throw an `UnsupportedOperationException`.

`void add(int index,E element)`	Inserts the specified element at the specified position in the list.
`boolean addAll(int index, Collection<? extends E> c)`	Inserts all of the elements in the specified collection into the list at the specified position.
`E remove(int index)`	Removes the element at the specified position in the list.
`E set(int index, E element)`	Replaces the element at the specified position in the list with the specified element.

Methods Inherited from `Collection`

`contains(),containsAll(),isEmpty(),iterator(), size(), toArray(),`
`add(),addAll(),clear(),remove(),removeAll(), retainAll()`

The `equals()` and `hashCode()` methods are defined in `Object`, but are included in the `List` interface because the contract for `java.util.List` requires these methods to have overridden implementations specialized for a `List`.

5.3.2 The `java.util.ListIterator<E>` Interface

The `ListIterator` interface (see Table 5.2) extends `Iterator` (see the UML diagram in Figure 5.4) and, as we saw in the previous section, adds functionality in four areas:

ListIterator methods use `List` indexing

■ An iterator can be constructed to begin at any position in the list from 0 to List.*size*.

Table 5.2 The `ListIterator<E>` interface.

Required Methods

`boolean hasNext()`	Returns true if this list iterator has more elements when traversing the list in the forward direction.
`boolean hasPrevious()`	Returns true if this list iterator has more elements when traversing the list in the reverse direction.
`E next()`	Returns the next element in the list.
`int nextIndex()`	Returns the index of the element that would be returned by a subsequent call to `next()`, or `size()` if there are none.
`E previous()`	Returns the previous element in the list.
`int previousIndex()`	Returns the index of the element that would be returned by a subsequent call to `previous()`, or -1 if there are none.

Optional Methods

All optional methods not supported by a `ListIterator` implementation must throw an `UnsupportedOperationException`.

`void add(E o)`	Inserts the specified element into the list at the current position of the iterator.
`void remove()`	Removes from the list the last element returned by `next()` or `previous()`.
`void set(E o)`	Replaces the last element returned by `next()` or `previous()` with the specified element.

Figure 5.4 The `java.util.ListIterator<E>` interface hierarchy in the JCF.

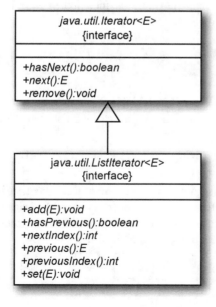

- Directionality is added to the iteration. You now have the ability to move backward and forward in the sequence, reflecting the fact that a list is a linear construction with a notion of predecessor and successor.

- Consistent with the support for positional indexing found in lists, ListIterator includes methods to return the index of the element that would be returned by next() and previous().

- The optional methods are mutator methods to add a new element to the list, replace an element at some position with another element, and remove an element.

5.3.3 Examples of List Operations

Figure 5.5 illustrates the behavior of many of the List methods. Listing 5.1 gives a complete example showing several ways to use a list iterator. The program creates a LinkedList object, adds some elements to it, uses a list iterator to traverse and print out the elements of the list in reverse order using an iterator in a while loop (lines 21–24), then prints the elements in forward order using the special for loop designed for iterators (lines 28–29). It next uses another list iterator to make changes to the list using another while loop (lines 34–41), and finally outputs the list using an iterator in a standard for loop (lines 46–47). The output from the program follows Listing 5.1.

SUMMING UP

The List ADT is a specialized kind of collection that supports indexing of its elements. ListIterator is a specialized kind of Iterator for lists that allows iterations to begin at any position in a list and to move forward and backward within a list. java.util.List<E> is a generic collection in the JCF and is a subinterface of java.util.Collection<E>. As in Collection, the methods specified in List are grouped into required and optional methods.

CHECKPOINT

5.4 Why *must* the remove() method from Iterator be optional?

5.5 Which optional methods would you implement to create a list that only allows replacing existing elements?

5.6 What would be the effect of the following code (iter is a ListIterator object)? iter.next(); iter.previous();

5.7 The following diagram shows the state of a ListIterator object iter that is iterating over a list. You can assume that cursor reached its current position via iter.previous(). Using the diagram as the starting point, what would the list look like and where would cursor be after each of the following?

a. iter.add("E5");

b. iter.remove();

Figure 5.5 Behavior of some `List` operations.

Method	Purpose	Object State	Return Value
List<String> list = new LinkedList<String> ()	To create an empty list.	*size* = 0 *head* = *tail* = null	a LinkedList object for Strings
list.add (0, "A")	To add "A" to the list at position 0. Tests adding to an empty list.	*size* = 1 *head* = 0; *tail* = 0 "A" 0	
list.add(1, "B")	To add "B" to the list at position 1. Tests adding at the end of the list; index check at size().	*size* = 2 *head* = 0; *tail* = 1 "A" "B" 0 1	
list.add(0, "B")	To add "B" to the list at position 0. Tests adding in the front of a non-empty list.	*size* = 3 *head* = 0; *tail* = 2 "B" "A" "B" 0 1 2	
list.indexOf("A")	To get the index of the *first* occurrence of "A" in list.		1
list.lastIndexOf("B")	To get the index of the *last* occurrence of "B" in list.		2
list.get(1)	To get the element in position 1.		"A"
ListIterater <String> iter = list.listIterator(list.size())	To get a list iterator, starting the iteration at the last element.	"B" "A" "B" 0 1 2 Δ	ListIterator object for Strings starting at the end of the list
iter.nextIndex()	To get the index of the element that would be returned by next().		3
iter.previousIndex()	To get the index of the element that would be returned by previous().		2
String s = iter.previous()	To get the previous element.	"B" "A" "B" 0 1 Δ 2	"B"
iter.remove()	To remove the last element returned by next()/previous().	*size* = 2 *head* = 0; *tail* = 1 "B" "A" 0 1 Δ	
iter.hasPrevious()	To see whether there are more elements in the iteration sequence moving backward.		true
s = iter.previous()	To get the previous element.	"B" "A" 0 Δ 1	"A"
iter.set("Z")	To set the value of the last element returned by previous().	*size* = 2 *head* = 0; *tail* = 1 "B" "Z" 0 Δ 1	*(continues)*

Figure 5.5 Behavior of some `List` operations (continued)

Method	Purpose	Object State	Return Value
s = iter.previous()	To get the previous element.	"B" "Z" Δ 0 1	"B"
iter.previousIndex()	To verify an operation when there is no previous element to get.		−1
iter.nextIndex()	To get the index of the next() element.		0
s = iter.next()	To get the next element and see if we can move forward once the beginning of the list is reached.	"B" "Z" 0 Δ 1	"B"

Listing 5.1 An example of the use of `ListIterator`.

```
1    import java.util.List;
2    import java.util.ListIterator;
3    import gray.adts.list.*;
4
5    import java.util.List;
6    /**
7     * Illustrate the use of a list iterator on a List.
8     */
9
10   public class ListIteratorEx {
11
12       public static void main(String[] args) {
13           List<String> movies = new LinkedList<String>();
14           movies.add( 0, "Cinema Par" );
15           movies.add( 1, "Lilies of the Field" );
16           movies.add( 2, "In the Heat of the Night" );
17
18           System.out.println( "Here are the film titles in the " +
19                               "collection\nin a backward traversal:" );
20           // create an iterator to do a backward traversal
21           ListIterator<String> iter =
22                               movies.listIterator( movies.size() );
23           while ( iter.hasPrevious() )
24               System.out.println("    " + iter.previous());
25
```

```
26              // now print them with a forward traversal
27              System.out.println( "\n... and in a forward traversal:" );
28              for ( String movie : movies )
29                  System.out.printf( "%s  \n", movie );
30
31              System.out.println("\n==============");
32              // use ListIterator's set() and remove() methods to change
33              // the list do a forward traversal this time
34              iter = movies.listIterator();     // need another iterator
35              while ( iter.hasNext() ) {
36                  String str = iter.next();
37                  if ( str.equals( "Cinema Par" ) )
38                      iter.set(new String( "Cinema Paradiso" ));
39                  else if ( str.indexOf( "of" ) != -1 )
40                      iter.remove();
41              }
42
43              System.out.println( "\nAfter fixing the title errors and " +
44                  "removing all\ntitles containing \"of\", " +
45                  "here is the list:" );
46              for( iter = movies.listIterator( movies.size() );
47                  iter.hasPrevious();   )
48              System.out.println( "    " + iter.previous() );
49          }
50      }
```

OUTPUT

```
Here are the film titles in the collection
in a backward traversal:
    In the Heat of the Night
    Lilies of the Field
    Cinema Par

. . . and in a forward traversal:
Cinema Par
Lilies of the Field
In the Heat of the Night


==============


After fixing the title errors and removing all
titles containing "of", here is the list:
    Cinema Paradiso
```

■ 5.4 Designing a Test Plan

The approach we take to design a test plan for our `List` implementation is the same approach we took for `BasicCollection` in the last chapter. Here we will look at the following:

- Reusing test plans
- Tests unique to `List` and `ListIterator`
- Checking for unmet pre-conditions

We can quickly dispense with the test cases for the methods `List` inherits from `Collection`. All the test cases developed for `BasicCollection` in Chapter 4 can be applied here with one simple modification: We use a `List` variable in place of a `Collection` variable. Test Case 5.1, for example, is the test case for the `add(E)` method from Chapter 4, adapted for `List`.

Reusing the tests is convenient and is perfectly acceptable *as long as List has not changed the semantics of the tested methods*. In our case, the contract for `List.add(E)` stipulates that the element be *appended* to the list. The `contains()` method will verify that the element was added to the list, but what we really need to verify is that it was added at the *end* of the list. There are two methods in `List` that can do this for us: `get()` and `indexOf()`. It makes sense to use them both since that will provide a test of their behavior as well.

Reusing tests from `BasicCollection`

Testing `add(E)`

The approach taken for `add(E)` suggests a test case for the indexed version: `add(int, E)`. How should adding a new element at a particular position in a list affect the list's state? If you insert a new element at some position *i*, the element should be retrievable from that position, and the element that had previously been in position *i* and all the elements in higher positions should have had their indices incremented by one. Anything else? We should do some bounds checking. According to the pre-condition for `add(int, E)`, the index should be in the range 0 to `list.size()`, so we should check at the bounds and somewhere in the list interior. This gives us Test Case 5.2.

Testing `add(int, E)`

Developing a test plan for the `set()` method is straightforward, but be sure to verify that you can access the list at the bounds of the method's index range. Instead of looking at testing `set()` for a *valid* index, let's develop a plan to see what `set()` should do when it gets an *invalid* parameter. Remember, a method that accepts invalid data is as bad as one that rejects valid data.

A method that accepts invalid data is as bad as one that rejects valid data

If we know what the valid values are for a parameter, we know what the invalid values are. According to the pre-condition for `set()`, the index must be in the range of 0 to `size()` − 1. So our test plan will use an invalid index (see Test Case 5.3). What value should we use? One that has a reasonably good chance of appearing. That is, of course, one generated by an off-by-one error.

We must also develop test plans for the `ListIterator`. To begin, let's talk generally about what must be tested and develop some representative plans. Here are four areas where testing should be done:

Testing the `ListIterator`

1. Since a `ListIterator` can begin anywhere in a list, we should test the constructor at the boundaries (first and last gaps) and in the interior of the list.

Test Case 5.1 Testing the append add method: `List.add(E)`.

Method	Purpose	Object State	Expected Result
List<String> list = new LinkedList<String>()	To create an empty list.	*size* = 0 *head* = *tail* = null.	a LinkedList object for Strings
list.add ("A")	To add to an empty list.	*size* = 1 *head* = *tail* = 0 "A" 0	true
list.contains("A")	To verify the list state with respect to the insertion.		true
list.get(list.size() −1)	To verify get() and add().		"A"
list.indexOf("A")	To verify indexOf() and add().		0
list.lastIndexOf("A")	To verify lastIndexOf() and add().		0
list.add("B")	To add to the list. The new element should be appended.	*size* = 2 *head* = 0 *tail* = 1 "A" "B" 0 1	true
list.contains("B")	To verify the list state with respect to the last insertion.		true
list.get(list.size() − 1)	To verify add() and get().		"B"
list.indexOf("B")	To verify indexOf() and add().		1
list.add("C")	To add to the end of the list.	*size* = 3 *head* = 0 *tail* = 2 "A" "B" "C" 0 1 2	true
list.contains("C")	To verify list state with respect to the last insertion.		true
list.get(list.size() − 1)	To verify add().		"C"
list.indexOf("C")	To verify indexOf() and add().		2
list.size()	To verify list state.		3
list.isEmpty()	To verify list state.		false
list.contains("Missing")	To verify contains() operation on an element not in the list.		false

2. We should also verify that the constructor rejects invalid initial positions (e.g., −1 and size() + 1).

3. The mutator methods have a number of restrictions, which should be checked (e.g., `next()`/`previous()` must have been called prior to `add()`, `set()`, or `remove()`).

Test Case 5.2 Testing the indexed add method: `List.add(int, E)`.

Method	Purpose	Object State	Expected Result
List<String> list = new LinkedList<String>()	To create an empty list.	*size* = 0 *head* = *tail* = null	a LinkedList object for Strings
list.add (0, "A")	To add an element at the beginning and end of list (that is, to add to an empty list!).	*size* = 1 *head* = *tail* = 0 "A" 0	
list.indexOf("A")	To verify add(int, E).		0
list.add(1, "B")	To add to the end of the list; *upper* bound test.	*size* = 2 *head* = 0 *tail* = 1 "A" "B" 0 1	
list.indexOf("B")	To verify add(int, E).		1
list.add(1, "C")	To add to the interior of the list; *interior* test.	*size* = 3 *head* = 0 *tail* = 2 "A" "C" "B" 0 1 2	
list.indexOf("C")	To verify add(int, E).		1
list.indexOf("B")	To verify an index shift after add.		2
list.add(0, "Z")	To verify add at beginning of a non-empty list; *lower lower* bound test.	*size* = 4 *head* = 0 *tail* = 3 "Z" "A" "C" "B" 0 1 2 3	
list.indexOf("Z")	To verify add(int, E) at lower bound.		0

Test Case 5.3 Catching an illegal index argument to `set()`.

Method	Purpose	Object State	Expected Result
List<String> list = new LinkedList<String>()	To create an empty list.	*size* = 0 *head* = *tail* = null	a LinkedList object for Strings
list.add (0, "A")	To add an element to an empty list.	*size* = 1 *head* = *tail* = 0 "A" 0	
list.add(1, "B")	To add an element to the end of the list.	*size* = 2 *head* = 0 *tail* = 1 "A" "B" 0 1	
list.set(list.size(), "C")	To verify that an illegal index is caught—test at upper bound + 1.		IndexOutOf-BoundsException

4. Verify that concurrent modification is caught.

Test Case 5.4 verifies that a list iteration sequence can begin at the first gap of the sequence.

Test Case 5.5 examines most aspects of using `ListIterator.remove()`.

Tests for variants of these test cases and the remaining methods are left as exercises.

Test Case 5.4 ListIterator methods for an iteration sequence begun in the first gap.

Method	Purpose	Object State	Expected Result
List<String> list = new LinkedList<String>()	To create an empty list.	*size* = 0 *head* = *tail* = null	a LinkedList object for Strings
list.add (0, "A")	To add an element to an empty list.	*size* = 1 *head* = *tail* = 0 "A" 0	
list.add(1, "B")	To add an element.	*size* = 2 *head* = 0 *tail* = 1 "A" "B" 0 1	
list.add(2, "C")	To add an element.	*size* = 3 *head* = 0 *tail* = 2 "A" "B" "C" 0 1 2	
ListIterator<String> iter = list.listIterator(0)	To start the iteration sequence in the first gap.	"A" "B" "C" Δ 0 1 2	a ListIterator object for Strings starting at the head of the list
iter.previousIndex()	To verify method and starting position.		−1
iter.nextIndex()	To verify method.		0
iter.hasPrevious()	To verify method.		false
iter.hasNext()	To verify method.		true
strings = iter.next()	To advance cursor and test next().	"A" "B" "C" 0 Δ 1 2	"A"
iter.previousIndex()	To verify method.		0
iter.nextIndex()	To verify method.		1
iter.hasPrevious()	To verify method.		true
iter.hasNext()	To verify method.		true

Test Case 5.5 Testing different requirements for `ListIterator.remove()`.

Method	Purpose	Object State	Expected Result
List<String> list = new LinkedList<String>()	To create an empty list.	$size = 0$ $head = tail = $ null	a LinkedList object for Strings
list.add (0, "A")	To add an element to an empty list.	$size = 1$ $head = tail = 0$ "A" 0	
list.add(1, "B")	To add an element.	$size = 2$ $head = 0$ $tail = 1$ "A" "B" 0 1	
list.add(2, "C")	To add an element.	$size = 3$ $head = 0$ $tail = 2$ "A" "B" "C" 0 1 2	
ListIterator<String> iter = list.listIterator(0)	To start the iteration sequence in the first gap.	"A" "B" "C" Δ 0 1 2	a ListIterator object for Strings
strings = iter.next()	To advance cursor.	"A" "B" "C" 0 Δ 1 2	"A"
iter.previousIndex()	To get the previous index.		0
iter.nextIndex()	To get the next index.		1
iter.remove()	To remove an element returned by last call to next().	$size = 2$ $head = 0$ $tail = 1$ "B" "C" Δ 0 1	
iter.previousIndex()	To verify the previous index update.		-1
iter.nextIndex()	To verify the next index update.		0
list.size()	To verify that an element was removed.		2
list.contains("A")	To verify that the element was removed.		false
iter.next()	To get the next element.	"B" Δ "C"	"B"
iter.remove()	To remove the element returned by the last call to next().	$size = 1$ $head = tail = 0$ "C" Δ 0	
iter.remove()	To verify the removal pre-condition: next()/previous() must be called to supply an element to remove.		IllegalStateException

SUMMING UP

Because `List` is a subinterface of `Collection` and inherits all of the `public` and `protected` methods from `Collection`, the test code developed for `BasicCollection` (our concrete implementation of `java.util.Collection` in the last chapter) can be used to help test our implementation of `List`. As long as our `List` implementation doesn't change the meaning of the methods it inherits from `Collection`, we can use the `BasicCollection` test methods unchanged. However, if the subclass places additional constraints on the method, you must adjust the tests accordingly.

Much of the additional testing for `List` is focused on `List`'s specialization, indexing of its elements, with special emphasis on catching off-by-one errors. Careful description of the expected behavior of each method pays dividends when designing test cases and during implementation.

INVESTIGATE The `Serializable` Interface—Adding Persistence to the Courier Application

Description

(*Note*: This Investigate extends this chapter's Focus on Problem Solving, which can be found on the Website.) Currently, the courier slips you enter are only stored in the computer's memory and are lost when the application exits. This is inconvenient and is not how a typical application behaves. You expect to be able to save your work before exiting the application and to be able to reload it later. This is called **persistence** because the data persists beyond the runtime of the application. The chief objective of this *Investigate* is to add persistence to the courier application; that is, to add the ability to save and restore courier slips to and from a file.

Persistent data

The problem statement for the courier slip program now includes the following additional requirement. The Design section will fill in details. The application should support loading courier slips from a file and saving courier slips to a file.

Additional courier requirement

A number of technical questions naturally arise, the first being in what format should the entries be stored? It would be nice to maintain the structure found in our class diagram. One possibility is to write the data out as a collection of strings, with the data fields separated by a special delimiter character. This would require some special handling on input and output. We want to avoid that if we can.

Another, simpler, possibility is to make use of Java's serializing capability. **Serializing** is the ability to take an object, possibly with fields that are themselves objects, and "flatten" or serialize it, converting the data from a representation that is logically multidimensional to a one-dimensional stream of bytes suitable for traveling over any byte stream (e.g., to/from a file, pipe, socket, etc.). **Deserializing** is the reverse of serializing—it takes a stream of bytes and reconstitutes the object.

Serializing

Deserializing

Objectives

■ Understand the requirements of Java's serializing capability

■ Use a marker interface

■ Add persistence to the courier slip application

■ Develop familiarity with the Java I/O classes

■ Use a GUI component to handle selecting a file for loading/saving

Visualization

Figure 5.6 illustrates serializing a single courier slip. The entry is shown as a two-dimensional data object. The serializer is an output byte stream pipeline.

Identify the Necessary Classes

The figure shows an I/O pipeline connecting the application to a file, suggesting that we need support in two areas: serialization/deserialization and getting the name of the file to load/save. We will deal with these separately.

Serialization/Deserializing. There are many useful interfaces and classes in the java.io package. One of these interfaces supports serialization. Using the Java online documentation, answer the following questions.

1. The java.io.Serializable interface defines no methods and is another example of a "marker" interface in that it marks the implementing class or interface as having a certain capability.

   a. How does a class indicate that it is serializable?

   b. What capability does implementing the Serializable interface provide?

   c. Is serialization recursive? That is, if a class is defined using composition such that some of its data fields are references to other objects, are those objects also serialized? Are there restrictions?

Figure 5.6 Serializing a CourierSlip.

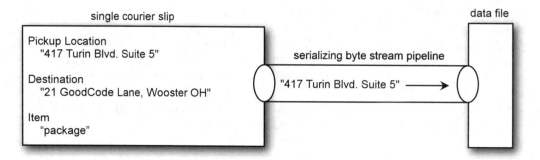

    d. What happens when there is an attempt to serialize a class that does not implement `java.io.Serializable`?

2. The *See Also* section of `Serializable`'s description contains a link to `java.io.ObjectOutputStream`.

    a. What is the purpose of `ObjectOutputStream`?

    b. A data field may be marked transient. How does `ObjectOutputStream` treat such fields? What other fields are treated similarly?

    c. The constructor for `ObjectOutputStream` takes what kind of argument?

    d. How would you make an I/O pipeline with an `ObjectOutputStream` object and a `FileOutputStream` object?

    e. Which method from the `ObjectOutputStream` class do you use to output an object to the stream? What exceptions can this method throw and under what circumstances?

3. The *See Also* section of the `Serializable` description also has a link to `java.io.ObjectInputStream`.

    a. What is the purpose of `ObjectInputStream`?

    b. What does `ObjectInputStream` do with transient and static fields?

    c. What kind of argument does the constructor for `ObjectInputStream` take?

    d. How would you make a pipeline with an `ObjectInputStream` object and a `FileInputStream` object?

    e. Which method from the `ObjectInputStream` class do you use to input an object from the stream? What exceptions can this method throw and under what circumstances?

4. What is the relationship between data written using an `ObjectOutputStream` object and the data read using an `ObjectInputStream` object?

5. Applying the information just gained, make a list of the changes you will need to make (your task list) to each class from the Courier application to support serialization.

Getting the Filename via a Dialog Box. The `java.awt` package provides a GUI component for getting the name of a file for reading or writing. Using the Java online documentation for the `FileDialog` class in the `java.awt` package, answer the following questions.

1. According to the documentation, `FileDialog` is a *modal* dialog box. What does this mean?

2. Describe the arguments to the constructor `FileDialog(Frame parent, String title, int mode)`.

3. What methods would you call to get the directory name and file name for the selected file?

4. `FileDialog` has `Component` as an ancestor and inherits several useful methods from it. What do the `setSize(int, int)` and `setVisible(boolean)` methods from `Component` do? How will your `FileDialog` object use these methods?

Design

What needs to be saved to disk? Serialization applies to objects, so we need to iden-tify which object will be serialized and written to a file. This will also be the object that is reconstituted when we load courier slips from a file. Where are the slips stored in the application? They are stored in an object of type List, which is a data field in a CourierModel object. Your first inclination might be to write the List object to the file, since that is where the courier slips are physically stored in the application, but from a system perspective, the slips are stored inside the CourierModel (look at the UML diagram again). The fact that the model stores the slips inside a List, instead of an array or linked list as in Chapter 3, is not relevant from the system perspective. So it is the CourierModel as a whole that we will save and restore.

Which component has the responsibility for loading/saving the CourierModel object from/to a file? Since the Model is stored inside the View, it will be CourierView's responsibility to load/save the CourierModel object from/to a file.

CourierModel Changes

1. Your review of the documentation from the first part of this *Investigate* should tell you how to identify the classes that need to implement java.io.Serializable. For example,

```
public class CourierSlip implements java.io.Serializable
```

CourierView Changes

1. The File menu needs two additional entries:

    a. "Open File. . ." allows the user to load a saved CourierModel.

    b. "Save As. . ." allows the user to save the CourierModel object to a file.

2. CourierView will need three more methods to support the I/O. Here we iden-tify the methods and provide pseudocode.

    a. Get the name of the file for the load/save.

    > **Pseudocode: String getFilename(String title, int mode)**
    > *create a file dialog box with the given arguments*
    > *set its size and make it visible*
    > *return the file name supplied by the dialog box*

    b. Load a saved CourierModel from a file (the deserializer).

    > **Pseudocode: void restoreFromFile(String filename)**
    > *// Steps 1 and 2 create an input pipeline for reading objects from a file*
    > *open an input stream for reading from the input file*
    > *attach an object input stream object to the file input stream*
    > *read a CourierModel object from the pipeline*
    > *close in the input pipeline*

    > **IMPORTANT:** This method creates a *Model* with input from a file. It does *not* update the *View*. You will have to do this separately by fetching the slips from the model one at a time and adding them to the view.

c. Save the `CourierModel` to a file (the serializer).

Pseudocode: void saveToFile(String filename)
// Steps 1 and 2 create an output pipeline for writing objects to a file
open a file output stream connected to the output file
attach an object output stream to the file output stream
write the CourierModel object to the pipeline
close the output pipeline

Implementation

Implementation requires converting the design into Java code. Here are the specific steps.

1. Add menu item objects for "Open File..." and "Save As..." to the File menu of `CourierView`.

2. Add an `ActionListener` for these new menu objects. Like the other menu items, the `ActionListener` object will be `this`.

3. Update `CourierView.actionPerformed()` to handle the two new menu items.

   Pseudocode: to handle "Open File..." selection.
   get the name of the input file (via getFilename())
   load the saved CourierModel (via restoreFromFile())
   update the view with the slips in the CourierModel

   Pseudocode: to handle "Save As..." selection.
   get the name of the output file (via getFilename())
   save the CourierModel to the file (via saveToFile())

   Look at the code for the original solution to help you with steps 1 through 3.

4. Implement the methods written in pseudocode in the Design section and add them to the `CourierView` class.

Testing

At this point we assume that the underlying list data structure has been tested and is in good working order, so you can focus your attention on the code related to persistence. Here are a few general questions you should answer before trying them out with your modified courier slip application.

1. When you load a `CourierModel` from disk, what should the view look like? What should be in the list and details text fields?

2. How can you verify that the `CourierModel` was correctly saved to a file?

SUMMING UP

Persistence means that the data manipulated by an application continues to exist after the application has terminated by saving the data to a file. Serializing refers to the ability to take an object, possibly with fields which are themselves objects, and "flatten," or serialize it, into a one-dimensional stream of bytes suitable for transmission over a byte stream. Deserializing is the reverse of serializing—it takes a stream of bytes and reconstitutes the object.

`java.io.Serializable` is a marker interface that marks an implementing class as having the ability to serialize/deserialize itself. Serializing is done with methods from `java.io.ObjectOutputStream` and deserializing with methods from `java.io.ObjectInputStream`.

◼ 5.5 A Linked List Implementation of the List ADT

In this section we develop our own implementation of List using a doubly linked structure. You should review the List ADT and ListIterator ADT specifications. Our class will be compatible with other classes in the JCF, so we will first look at what the framework provides that might assist us. In developing the implementation you will extend your understanding of the following:

1. Important OO techniques such as inheritance, and working with interfaces and abstract classes

2. Sequential access data structures, specifically doubly linked lists

3. Building within the constraints of an existing software framework

5.5.1 The JCF `AbstractList` and `AbstractSequentialList`

In the last chapter, we saw that there are no concrete implementations of `Collection` in the JCF. Instead, an abstract class, `AbstractCollection`, is provided as a foundation for defining various kinds of collection classes, and we based our construction of `BasicCollection` on it.

In fact, as you can see from Figure 5.7, the JCF includes a hierarchy of abstract classes that mirrors its interface hierarchy. This is a common OO design technique—identify types and specify APIs through interfaces and either provide concrete implementations of the interfaces or abstract classes from which concrete classes can easily be built. This is the approach taken in the JCF:

OO techniques:
◼ design with interfaces
◼ build on abstract classes

- `AbstractCollection` implements the `Collection` interface. It makes no assumption about the backing store that would be used by a concrete implementation. In Chapter 4, `BasicCollection` extended `AbstractCollection` and used an array as the backing store.

- `AbstractList` extends `AbstractCollection` and implements the `List` interface. `AbstractList` assumes a *random* access implementation. The concrete class `ArrayList` extends `AbstractList` and uses an array as the backing store.

- `AbstractSequentialList` also extends `AbstractList`, but assumes a *sequential access* data structure to represent the list. In the JCF, `java.util.LinkedList` is the concrete implementation of `AbstractSequentialList` and uses a linked list as the backing store. Our class will also be called `LinkedList` and will also extend `AbstractSequentialList`.

Figure 5.7 Interfaces and abstract classes in the JCF that support the `List<E>` type.

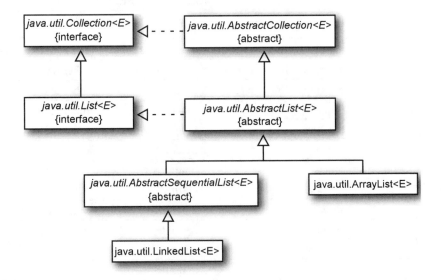

The name given in the `package` statement is what will distinguish our class from the class defined in `java.util`. Remember, it is the fully qualified name that distinguishes two classes of the same name: *java.util.LinkedList* and *gray.adts.list.LinkedList*.

Using the notation established in Chapter 4, Table 5.3 shows where the `List` methods are implemented. Our `LinkedList` class will implement all the required methods from `Collection` and `List`, as well as the following optional methods:

- `Collection.add(E)`
- `Collection.remove(E)`
- `List.add(int, E)`
- `List.addAll(int, Collection<? extends E>)`
- `List.remove(int)`
- `List.set(int, E)`

Optional methods to support from `Collection` and `List`

Other optional methods remain unsupported and throw an exception if invoked.

There are some useful OO lessons to be learned by looking at the implementation of some of the methods in `AbstractSequentialList`.

When considering the implementation of a class, you should step back and take a look at the big picture to see what is involved. In our case this means looking carefully at the interfaces involved: `Collection`, `List`, `Iterator`, and `ListIterator`.

As a first example, `Iterator` and `ListIterator` look and behave a lot alike. In fact, we know that `ListIterator` is a subinterface of `Iterator`. Do I really want to build, test, and maintain separate `Iterator` and `ListIterator` classes? No! I'm basically lazy, and if I can find a way to avoid work but still get the job done properly, I'll do it. Thinking carefully about the behavior of the two iterator types, I

Table 5.3 How `List` methods are supported in `AbstractList` and `AbstractSequentialList`.

	Implementing Classes		
List Methods	**java.util.-** **AbstractList**	**java.util.-** **Abstract-** **SequentialList**	**gray.adts.-** **list.LinkedList**
`equals(Object)`	overridden from `Object`	inherited	inherited
`hashCode()`	overridden from `Object`	inherited	inherited
`indexOf(Object)`	concrete	inherited	inherited
`lastIndexOf(Object)`	concrete	inherited	inherited
`subList(int, int)`	concrete	inherited	inherited
`listIterator()`	concrete	inherited	inherited
`listIterator(int)`	concrete	*abstract*	concrete
`size()`	*abstract*	inherited	inherited
`get(int)`	*abstract*	concrete	inherited
`add(int, E)`	optional	overridden	inherited
`add(E)`	concrete	inherited	inherited
`addAll(int, Collection` `        <? extends E>)`	concrete	overridden	inherited
`remove(int)`	optional	overridden	inherited
`remove(Object)`	optional	inherited	inherited
`set(int, E)`	optional	overridden	inherited

realize that an `Iterator` sequence over a list is the same as a one-way `ListIterator` sequence that starts at position 0. This suggests the implementation of `iterator()` in Listing 5.2.

This works because a `ListIterator` "is a kind of" `Iterator` and the substitution principle from Chapter 1 tells us that instances of a subclass can be accessed through superclass references. Furthermore, although it is a `ListIterator` object that is created, because an `Iterator` reference is returned, only `Iterator`-defined messages can be sent to the object.[3] Using this OO trick, I only need a `ListIterator` class: I don't need to code a separate `Iterator` class. Very nice!

Listing 5.2 Implementation of `List.iterator()`.

```
1  public Iterator<E> iterator(){
2      return this.listIterator(0);
3  }
```

---

[3]Of course, if the client knows that we returned a `ListIterator` object, the client could cast the `Iterator` reference back to a `ListIterator` reference, but because the details of the implementation are hidden from the client, this is not an issue.

What else can we do? Looking at the interfaces, are there any methods that do similar work? If so, perhaps they can be combined in some way. Here is a very simple example. The `listIterator()` method returns a `ListIterator` object that begins its iteration with the element in position 0. This is easily implemented using the `ListIterator(int)` method shown in Listing 5.3.

Here is a more sophisticated example. What is involved in the `add()` methods? For `List.add(int index, E 0)`, I need to

> get a reference to the node at position index
> insert the new element

Okay, now what is involved in the `ListIterator.add(E)` method? Take a quick look at the ADT description for `ListIterator`. The list iterator's *cursor* will reference a specified position in the list and the new element will be inserted there. Is there any common work here? Why not use the indexed `listIterator(int)` method to get a reference to the desired insertion point in the list and then use `ListIterator.add(E)` to do the insertion? We took the same approach implementing `Collection.remove()` using `Iterator.remove()` in the last chapter. Listing 5.4 shows the implementation of `List.add()` using a `ListIterator`.

An annotated UML sequence diagram for this method is shown in Figure 5.8. A *self-call* is a call from a method in an object to another method within the *same* object; in this case `List.add()` calls `List.ListIterator()`. The `LinkedListIterator` object, iter, is free for garbage collection once the `List.add()` method is returned.

UML sequence diagrams: self-calls

The use of `ListIterator` methods simplifies handling of the `List` optional methods in another way. In looking at Table 5.3, you might have wondered how `AbstractSequentialList` can provide *concrete* implementations of the *optional* methods, when it should be up to a concrete subclass to decide which optional methods to support. The answer is rather neat. By building the optional methods on top of the `ListIterator` methods, we leave it to the implementation of

---

Listing 5.3 Implementation of `List.listIterator()`.

```
1   public ListIterator<E> listIterator(){
2       return this.listIterator(0);  // start iteration at position 0
3   }
```

Listing 5.4 Implementation of `List.add(int, E)` using `ListIterator`.

```
public void add( int index, E element ){
```
get a reference to the node at position index
```
    ListIterator<E> iter = this.listIterator( index );
```
insert the new element
```
    iter.add( element );
}
```

Figure 5.8 Using a `ListIterator` to implement `List.add(int, E)`
(UML Sequence diagram).

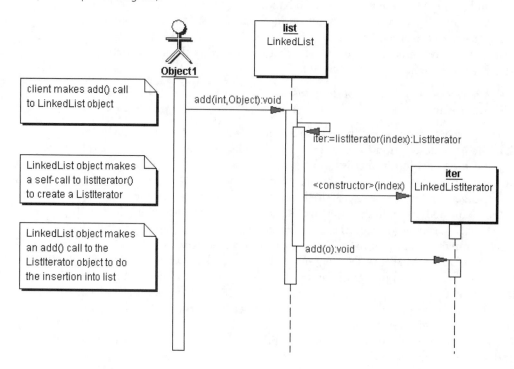

`ListIterator` to determine whether or not an optional method is fully supported. If the optional method is not supported, the `ListIterator` method will throw the exception. If, on the other hand, we want to support an optional method, all we need to do is provide the necessary implementation in one place—the `ListIterator` class. For example, the `List.add()` method can be implemented secure in the knowledge that all these decisions have been delegated to `ListIterator.add()`. What we have done is use existing capabilities to implement another capability. The other optional methods can easily be implemented in a similar fashion.

SUMMING UP

The JCF provides a hierarchy of abstract classes that mirrors the hierarchy of collection types. These abstract classes provide a foundation for defining various kinds of concrete collection classes. This is a common OO design technique—identify types and specify APIs through interfaces and either provide concrete implementations of the interfaces or abstract classes from which concrete classes can easily be built.

CHECKPOINT

5.8 Using the examples given in this section, show a likely implementation for the following methods:

a. `E get( int )`

b. `E remove( int )`

5.9 How are `AbstractList` and `AbstractSequentialList` the same? How are they different?

5.5.2 The `LinkedList` Class

We now turn to an implementation of our `LinkedList` class within the JCF. Our class will implement the `List` interface, extending `AbstractSequentialList`. We will approach this by creating a task list, enumerating the tasks we need to complete:

Task list for creating the <code>LinkedList</code> class

1. Define attributes, including deciding on the backing store for the List's elements.

2. Provide implementations for the only method left abstract in `AbstractSequentialList.listIterator(int)`.

3. Define a class, `LinkedListIterator`, that implements the `ListIterator` interface.

4. Provide support for the optional methods `Collection.add(E)`, `Collection.remove(E)`, `List.add(int, E)`, `List.addAll(int, Collection<? extends E>)`, `List.remove(int)`, and `List.set(int, E)`. Actually, a look at Table 5.4 as well as at the last section will tell you that this has been done for us by the abstract classes we are building on. Once the `LinkedListIterator` class has been implemented, these optional methods will be fully supported. Cool!

An ongoing task will be to check the contracts for the abstract classes to make sure that the methods implemented in our `LinkedList` class meet all the obligations laid out by an ancestor.

The remainder of this section focuses on the *process* involved in completing the items on the task list. The complete `LinkedList` class can be found on the CD accompanying this book.

5.5.3 `LinkedList` Task 1: Define `List` attributes

Since `LinkedList` extends `AbstractSequentialList`, we know that the backing store will be a sequential access data structure. We studied two sequential data structures in Chapter 3: singly and doubly linked linear structures.

Recall that the singly linked structure is unidirectional—each node contains only a single link, which "points to" the next node in the structure. A doubly linked structure, though, is bidirectional, because each node maintains links to its predecessor and successor in the structure, making it possible to easily move forward and backward in the structure.

Since the `ListIterator` requires bidirectionality, it is clear that the doubly linked structure is the better choice. We will reuse the `DLNode<E>` class defined in Chapter 3. Also, since they were so effective in our implementations in Chapter 3, we will use dummy `head` and `tail` nodes to mark the beginning and end of the list. The `head`'s `successor` field plays the role of the *head* attribute from the specification and `tail`'s `predecessor` field the role of the *tail* attribute. The *size* attribute can be stored as an integer. `LinkedList` also has access to the `modCount` field inherited from `AbstractList`. As we saw in the implementation of the `Iterator` class in `BasicCollection`, this field is used to check for concurrent modifications. This gives us Table 5.4.

Backing store: a doubly linked structure using dummy nodes

5.5.4 `LinkedList` Task 2: Implement Abstract Method `listIterator(int)`

According to Table 5.3, the only method left abstract from `Abstract-SequentialList` is `listIterator(int)`. It just creates and returns an instance of the `LinkedListIterator` class that we discuss next.

The integer argument is the position in the list where the iteration is to begin and should be in the range $0 \leq position \leq size$. It is important to establish whose responsibility it is to validate the input. In this case, the method leaves it up to the `LinkedListIterator` constructor (see Listing 5.5).

Whose job is it to validate input?

5.5.5 `LinkedList` Task 3: Define the `ListIterator` Class: `LinkedListIterator`

By far the most challenging task is the development of a class that implements the `ListIterator` interface. We will use the experience gained developing the `BasicIterator` class in the last chapter, but `ListIterator` supports several additional methods and is more complicated, so requires more careful planning. We'll create a separate task list for `LinkedListIterator`.

Table 5.4 Mapping of `List` attributes to `LinkList` data fields.

Attribute	LinkedList data field
head	`DLNode<E> head.succcessor()`
tail	`DLNode<E> tail.predecessor()`
size	`int size`

Listing 5.5 Implementation of `List.list Iterator`.

```
1  public ListIterator<E> listIterator( int position ) {
2      // let LinkedListIterator constructor validate position
3      return new LinkedListIterator<E>( position );
4  }
```

1. Map the components of the logical model to the `List` implementation as a doubly linked list.

2. Identify the `LinkedListIterator` data fields.

3. Implement the `LinkedListIterator` required methods.

4. Implement the `LinkedListIterator` optional methods.

5.5.6 `LinkedListIterator` Task 1: Map Logical Model to Doubly Linked List

In part, the logical model of an iterator developed in Section 4.2.2 applies to a list iterator. The differences are that a *list* iterator can

■ move forward and backward through the iteration sequence

■ begin with the cursor in *any* of the gaps in the iteration sequence

■ provide the index of the previous or next element to be returned in the sequence

Consequently, our logical model for iterating over a list is somewhat different than it was for the simpler, one-way iterator presented in the last chapter. For example, a list iteration can begin with cursor in the gap between E_1 and E_2 (see Figure 5.9). A call to next() would move cursor to the gap between E_2 and E_3, returning E_2. Alternatively, a call to previous() would move cursor to the gap between E_0 and E_1, returning E_1.

A forward iteration is complete when cursor is in the last gap and a backward iteration is complete when cursor is in the first gap.

As before, we need to determine the order in which the elements of the list are to be returned by the list iterator. The key characteristic that distinguishes a `List` from a `Collection` is that a `List` defines an ordered sequence—each element is in an indexable position. A `ListIterator` must honor this sequence.

Figure 5.9 A logical model of the elements in a list iteration sequence. A list iteration can begin with cursor in any of the gaps.

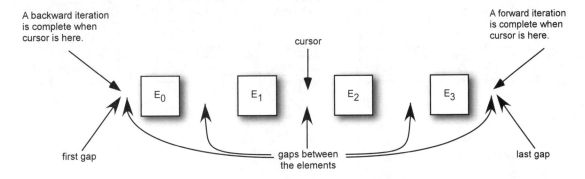

ListIterator<SomeType> iter = list.listIterator(2);

Our next step is to map the components of our logical model from Figure 5.9 onto the concrete implementation of `List` as a doubly linked list. Our logical view of the iteration sequence had gaps in it, with cursor residing in the gap between the elements to be returned by `previous()` and `next()`. Since linked lists don't have gaps between their elements that we can reference, we need to establish a software equivalent. Table 5.5 gives this mapping and Figure 5.10 is a visualization of the mapping for an iteration begun in position 0.

5.5.7 `LinkedListIterator` Task 2: Identify Data Fields

As the table and the diagram indicate, the `ListIterator` will maintain a variable cursor, which will always reference the node storing the `element` to be returned by `next()`. A call to `next()` should retrieve the `element` stored in cursor's node, *then* advance cursor to its successor.

Since `next()` and `previous()` are inverses of each other, we would reverse this order for a call to `previous()`—move cursor to its predecessor, *then* return the `element` stored in the cursor's node.

Table 5.5 Mapping of components of the `ListIterator` logical model to the concrete implementation.

Logical Model	Concrete Implementation
first gap	head's successor node
last gap	tail dummy node
cursor	a reference to any node from head's successor to tail, inclusive

Figure 5.10 `ListIterator` components mapped to a doubly linked list at the start of an iteration begun at position 0 of the list. Also see Table 5.5.

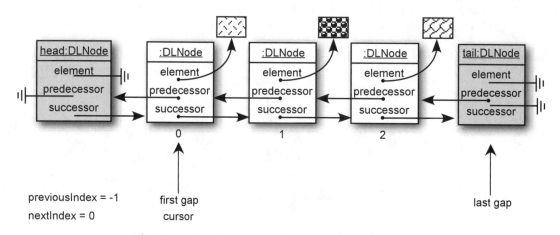

```
ListIterator<SomeType> iter = list.listIterator(0);
```

Of course, this assumes there are more elements to retrieve. How do we know when there are no more elements in the forward direction? When cursor is in the last gap—that is, cursor references the tail node (cursor == tail). How do we know when there are no more elements in the backward direction? When cursor is in the first gap—cursor references head's successor (cursor == head.getSuccessor()).

ListIterator also supports methods to get the index of the element that would be retrieved by the next call to next() or previous(). You might be tempted to define two integer data fields, nextIndex and previousIndex, to store these values, but it isn't necessary. Since our design so far has been based on next()'s behavior, we can maintain a single integer index, nextIndex, which stores the index of the next element to be returned by next(). According to our description, this will be the index of the node referenced by cursor. A call to next() that moves cursor to its successor in the sequence, would *increment* nextIndex.

cursor and nextIndex move together

We can now treat previousIndex as a *synthesized attribute* that can be computed using nextIndex. By the description of previous() given above, previousIndex will always be nextIndex − 1. Hence, a call to previous(), which moves cursor to its predecessor, would *decrement* nextIndex.

previousIndex is a synthesized attribute

Looking at the contract for ListIterator, we see that the set() and remove()methods operate on the element returned by the last call to next() or previous(), whichever was called most recently. So we need a variable, lastNodeReturned, to keep track of this, updating it every time next() and previous() are called. Figure 5.11 makes clear that there can only be one "last node" returned, and that it will be different depending on whether next() or previous() was called last.

lastNodeReturned references the last node returned by next()/ previous()

Finally, as we did for the BasicIterator developed in the last chapter, LinkedListIterator will maintain the data field expectedModCount to detect concurrent modifications and okToRemove to determine when it is valid for ListIterator.remove() to be called.[4]

We will make our list iterator class an inner class within LinkedList. Here are the data field declarations.

```
1   // inner class within LinkedList
2   public class LinkedListIterator<E> implements ListIterator<E> {
3       // invariant: cursor should always reference a node from
4       // head's successor to tail inclusive.
5       private DLNode<E> cursor;
6       private int nextIndex;                    // index of node returned by next()
7                                                 // previousIndex = nextIndex − 1
8       private boolean okToRemove;
9       private int exptectedModCount;
10      private DLNode<E> lastNodeReturned;   // by next()/previous()
```

---

[4]You are invited to explore an alternative implementation in the Exercises.

Figure 5.11 Identifying the last node returned by `next()` and `previous()`.

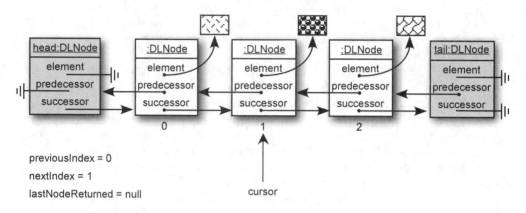

previousIndex = 0
nextIndex = 1
lastNodeReturned = null

cursor

(a) Partial state of a list iteration.

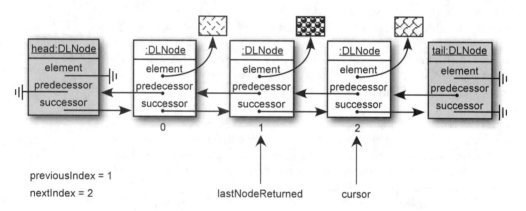

previousIndex = 1
nextIndex = 2

lastNodeReturned   cursor

(b) State of (a) after: `Object o = iter.next();`

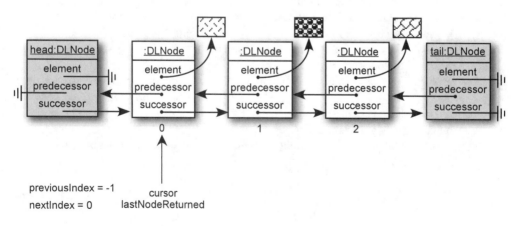

previousIndex = -1   cursor
nextIndex = 0   lastNodeReturned

(c) State of (a) after: `Object o = iter.previous();`

5.5.8 `LinkedListIterator`
Task 3: Implement Required Methods

Correctly implementing `ListIterator` methods requires a thorough understanding of how the state of a `ListIterator` object is represented and how the `ListIterator`'s methods change the object's state. Most of this information was described in the first two `LinkedListIterator` tasks.

The constructor is pretty straightforward, but there is one aspect worth mentioning. The integer argument is the position on the list where the iteration is to begin. This can be anywhere from 0 to *size*. The interesting bit is to remember that a doubly linked list is bidirectional. Imagine a 100-element linked list and that the iteration is to begin in position 92. Since a linked list is a sequential access structure, we can't just jump to the node in position 92. But we can be clever about this and start at the end that is *closest to* the target. In our case, starting at the `head` means traversing 93 links (including the `head` link) to get to the target. But if I start at the `tail`, I only need to follow eight links. With this approach, I never have to follow more than *size*/2 links to get to the starting point of an iteration. The larger the list is, the greater the benefit can be.

We will work through two representative required methods to get a sense for what is involved.

The first is the accessor method `previousIndex()`, which returns the index of the element that would be returned by the next call to `previous()`. The pseudocode is shown in Listing 5.6. Note that, as much as is reasonable, the pseudocode is couched in terms of `ListIterator` *attributes*. For example, the fact that `previousIndex` is realized as a synthesized attribute of `nextIndex` is an implementation detail—the purpose of the pseudocode is to identify the logical steps to take and the order in which to take them.

One other item to point out: Where did the −1 come from on line 6 of Listing 5.6? From the contract for `previousIndex()` in `ListIterator`. You must always make sure that your implementation meets the contract specified in the documentation.

Now we look at the mutator method `previous()`, which returns the next element in the sequence moving "backward." This is a mutator method because it updates almost all of the object's state variables. Note that lines 9 and 10 of the code in Listing 5.7 cannot be reversed.

> The constructor: minimizing the cost of getting to the starting point of the iteration

> Check the method's contract

5.5.9 `LinkedListIterator`
Task 4: Implement Optional Methods

There are three optional methods. Since these are all mutator methods, we know they will change the state of the object, so we should begin by determining how each method will affect the state variables. I find it helpful to phrase this as a question; for example, "Where should `nextIndex` be after `remove()` has removed a node?" I would do this for each of the state variables. If it helps, I draw pictures of what should happen.

Of the three methods, `remove()` is the most complicated, so we will look at it. The pseudocode and Java implementation are given in Listing 5.8. `remove()`

Listing 5.6 Implementation of `ListIterator.previousIndex()`.

```
public int previousIndex() {
```
if there has been concurrent modification generate an exception
```
    checkForConcurrentModification();
```
if there is a predecessor in the sequence
```
    if ( hasPrevious() )
```
return previousIndex
```
        return nextIndex - 1;
```
else return –1
```
    else return -1;
}
```

Listing 5.7 Implementation of `ListIterator.previous()`.

```
public E previous() {
```
if there has been concurrent modification generate an exception
```
    checkForConcurrentModification();
```
if there is no predecessor in the sequence generate an exception
```
    if ( ! hasPrevious() )
        throw new NoSuchElementException();
```
indicate it is okay to remove an element
```
    okToRemove = true;
```
update previousIndex attribute
```
    nextIndex--;
```
get cursor's predecessor in the sequence
```
    cursor = cursor.getPredecessor();
```
indicate this is the last node returned
```
    lastNodeReturned = cursor;
```
return cursor's element
```
    return cursor.getElement();
}
```

removes the node referenced by `lastNodeReturned`. Consider parts (b) and (c) of Figure 5.11 and you see that there are two cases to check for. This is what makes `remove()` trickier than `get()` and `add()`.

Let's use visualization to help us identify what has to be done and how the state variables are affected. Figure 5.12(b) shows the state of an iteration following a call

Case 1: next()

Listing 5.8 Implementation of `ListIterator.remove()`.

```
public void remove() {
```

if there has been concurrent modification generate an exception

```
    checkForConcurrentModification();
```

if there is no element to remove generate an exception

```
    if ( ! okToRemove )
        throw new IllegalStateException();
```

indicate it is not okay to remove an element

```
    okToRemove = false;
```

if last node was returned by previous()
    advance cursor to its successor
else last node was returned by next()
    decrement nextIndex and previousIndex

```
    if ( cursor == lastNodeReturned )
        cursor = cursor.getSuccessor();     // move cursor forward
    else                                    // removing item returned by a next() call
        nextIndex--;                        // move nextIndex backward
```

unlink the node and cleanup

```
    lastNodeReturned.getPredecessor().setSuccessor(
                            lastNodeReturned.getSuccessor() );
    lastNodeReturned.setSuccessor( null );
    lastNodeReturned.setPredecessor( null );
    lastNodeReturned.setElement( null );
    lastNodeReturned = null;
```

indicate size is smaller by 1

```
    size--;                                 // update LinkedList data field
```

indicate a structural modification made

```
    modCount++;                             // update AbstractList data field
    expectedModCount = modCount;
}
```

to next(). Part (c) of the figure shows the new state after the element referenced by lastNodeReturned is removed. Notice that cursor has not moved—it still references the node storing "C". However, nextIndex has been decremented.

Now, Figure 5.13(b) shows the state of an iteration following a call to previous(). Part (c) of the figure shows the new state after the element referenced by lastNodeReturned is removed. In this case, nextIndex remains unchanged, but cursor moved to its successor.

Case 2: `previous()`

Figure 5.12 Behavior of `ListIterator.remove()` when the node to be deleted was supplied by `ListIterator.next()`.

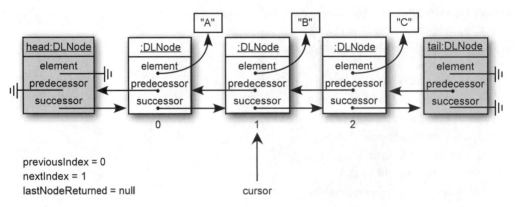

previousIndex = 0
nextIndex = 1
lastNodeReturned = null   cursor

(a) State before call to `iter.next();`

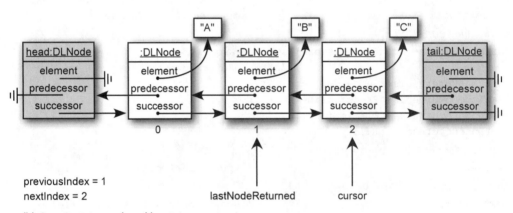

previousIndex = 1
nextIndex = 2   lastNodeReturned   cursor

(b) Case 1: state produced by `Object o = iter.next();`

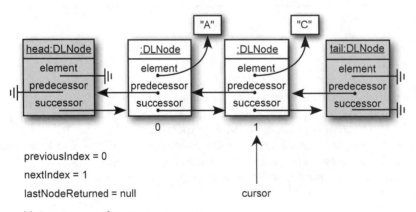

previousIndex = 0
nextIndex = 1
lastNodeReturned = null   cursor

(c) Case 1: state after `iter.remove();`

Figure 5.13 Behavior of `ListIterator.remove()` when the node to be deleted was supplied by `ListIterator.previous()`.

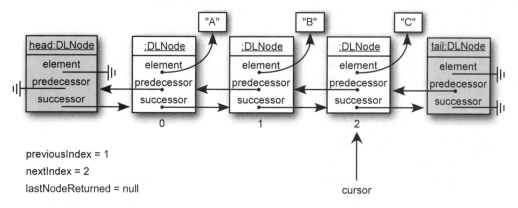

previousIndex = 1
nextIndex = 2
lastNodeReturned = null

cursor

(a) State before call to `iter.previous();`

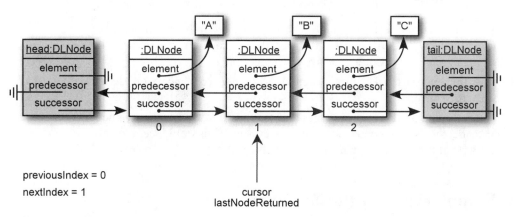

previousIndex = 0
nextIndex = 1

cursor
lastNodeReturned

(b) Case 2: state produced by `Object o = iter.previous();`

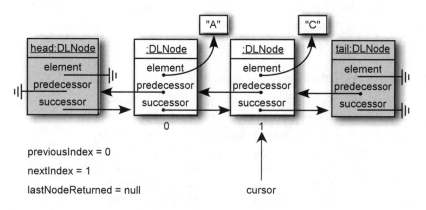

previousIndex = 0
nextIndex = 1
lastNodeReturned = null

cursor

(c) Case 2: state after `iter.remove();`

In both cases `lastNodeReturned` is set to `null` after the remove because the node it referenced no longer exists. As discussed earlier, but not shown in the diagram, `okToRemove` would be set to `false`. Finally, since the list has been structurally modified, we would update `modCount` and `expectedModCount`.

Okay, now you know how `ListIterator.remove()` works, but that wasn't really why we went over it. The more important lesson is the following process we used:

■ Read the documentation to make sure you understand what the methods in the class are to do.

■ Use a logical model to identify the attributes involved and how they interact.

■ Produce a task list identifying what you have to do.

■ Draw pictures to clarify your understanding.

■ Write pseudocode and check it with your model and pictures before coding.

CHECKPOINT

5.10 How would we have written `contains()` if we wanted to begin the search at the end of the list? If we cut and pasted this code to use in defining `lastIndexOf()`, what would we have to change?

5.11 Using the approach taken for designing `ListIterator.remove()`, design `ListIterator.add()`.

5.12 Look at the end of `ListIterator.remove()`. Why do we bother to increment `modCount`, then set `expectedModCount` to `modCount`? This would seem to have no effect for the `ListIterator` object, so why do it?

■ 5.6 Implementing the Test Plan

Testing of the `LinkedList` class needs to be done in three areas:

1. Test the methods implemented from the `List` ADT described in the `java.util.List` interface.

2. Test the `ListIterator` developed based on the `ListIterator` ADT and the `java.util.ListIterator` interface.

3. Verify that `LinkedList` can work with other classes in the JCF.

Test plans for the first two items were developed in Section 5.4. Writing the test code with JUnit follows closely from these plans.

For the third item, we need to confirm that our `LinkedList` class works within the JCF. The acid test is whether we can successfully pass instances of our `LinkedList` class around as a `Collection` and, conversely, have a `LinkedList` object access other kinds of `Collections` as objects of type `Collection`. Listing 5.9 is not test code, but it shows how collections of different types may by combined. The output is given in Figure 5.14.

Listing 5.9 Demonstrate how `LinkedList` can work with other `Collection` types within the Java Collections Framework.

```
1    /**
2     *  Demonstrate how LinkedList can work with other Collection
3     *  types within the Java Collections Framework.
4     */
5    import java.util.*;  // we use lots of classes from this package
6
7    public class CollectionTester {
8       static void printAnyCollection( Collection<?> collection ){
9          for ( Object element : collection )
10            System.out.println( element );
11       }
12
13       public static void main(String[] args) {
14       List<String> arrayList = new ArrayList<String>();
15       arrayList.add( 0, "cpi.doc" );
16       arrayList.add( 1, "prog1.txt" );
17       arrayList.add( 2, "p1.dat" );
18
19       System.out.println( "Elements in the ArrayList object: " );
20       printAnyCollection( arrayList );
21
22       System.out.println( "\nElements in a LinkedList object " +
23           "populated using addAll( arrayList )" );
24       // note use of fully qualified name here to avoid
25       // confusing with java.util.LinkedList
26       List<String> linkedList =
27                          new gray.adts.list.LinkedList<String>();
28       linkedList.addAll( arrayList );
29       printAnyCollection( linkedList );
30
31       System.out.println( "\nElements in a TreeSet object " +
32           "populated using new TreeSet( linkedList )" );
33       Set<String> set = new TreeSet<String>( linkedList );
34       printAnyCollection( set );
35       }
36    }
```

The `printAnyCollection()` method was developed in the last chapter, but there is a twist here worthy of comment. The method's argument is of type `Collection<?>`. Recall that we said in the last chapter that the unbounded wildcard allows us to pass in `Collections` of any *element type*. What is new here are the kinds of *collections* we are passing in: `java.util.ArrayList`, `java.util.TreeSet`, and

Figure 5.14 Output from program in Listing 5.9.

```
Elements in the ArrayList object:
cpi.doc
prog1.txt
p1.dat

Elements in a LinkedList object populated using addAll( arrayList )
cpi.doc
prog1.txt
p1.dat

Elements in a TreeSet object populated using new TreeSet( linkedList )
cpi.doc
p1.dat
prog1.txt
```

gray.adts.list.LinkedList. This works because they are all descended from Collection and, using the substitution principle from Chapter 1, we can pass in instances of subclasses to a superclass reference.

■ 5.7 Analysis and Measurement

There are two implementations of the List ADT (array– and linked list–based) that can be used interchangeably as long as you adhere to methods defined in their parent, List. The question naturally arises as to which implementation is "better." In this section we will compare the implementations in terms of their time and space complexities and we will see an oft-repeated theme: There is a tradeoff of flexibility for efficiency.

The space requirement of the array-based implementation is $\Theta(m)$, where m is the capacity of the list—that is, the maximum number of elements we can store in the list before it is full. In this sense we can say that the unused space in the array implementation is the space overhead incurred for using arrays. If you have made a good guess as to your space needs, then the array should be almost full, reducing the cost of this overhead. The more you *over*estimate your needs, the greater the cost of the overhead. In systems where space is at a premium, this is an important consideration. On the other side, if you have guessed poorly and have *under*estimated your space needs, your program probably cannot run to a successful completion unless the implementation provides a way, as java.util.ArrayList does, of providing a larger array; but we have seen that this, too, has a cost. This is where the flexibility of linked lists is realized.

Space complexity for arrays

The space overhead for the linked list version is the cost of the link fields (predecessor and successor), which is $\Theta(n \cdot 2 \cdot \text{size of a reference})$. One issue here is how big the rest of the object is in comparison to the size of the references. If we

Space complexity for linked lists

think of the object referenced by the `element` field of a linked list node as the payload of the node, and everything else as overhead, then the smaller the element object is, the larger the percentage of the overall space is attributable to overhead. This cost has to be considered against the flexibility linked lists provide.

The conclusion, then, is that if you have a good idea of how large your list needs to be, the array implementation will require less space than the linked list implementation. If you are unsure how many elements will be in the list, or if the number might fluctuate a great deal, the linked list version is going to be more efficient.

When considering the time complexity of the implementations, we are most interested in operations that alter the list and traverse it. First, we know that arrays are random-access data structures that allow us to move to any position in an array by first calculating the address of the target cell, then doing a single memory access. Linked lists, on the other hand, are sequential access data structures. To get to a particular position we must sequentially move from some starting position (typically the head of the list) to the target position, one element at a time. Each advance requires a memory lookup to extract the `successor` field from the node, then a second memory lookup to get the node `successor` points to. While we would call this an O(1) operation in asymptotic terms, in real terms it is a good deal more expensive than calculating the address of a cell in an array.

Time complexity

Because the lists are unsorted, the cost of `contains()` and `indexOf()` is O(n) for both implementations, since we cannot be sure where in the list the target may be (if it is in the list at all) and have to examine all the list's elements. In practice, the cost of the array's address calculations will be less than the cost of the linked list's additional memory accesses. An important point we should take from this is that any operation that requires traversal of the list is going to have an O(n) cost, at a minimum, just for the traversal. However, the real cost for traversing a linked list will be significantly higher than for an array because of the additional memory accesses.

Traversals cost O(n)

The `add()` and `remove()` operations involve similar concerns, so we can consider their analysis together. Because arrays and linked lists have different access characteristics, we need to distinguish between add/remove at the head, interior, and tail of a list.

The cost of inserting an element at the head of an `ArrayList` is $\Theta(n)$ since *all* the elements in the list must be shifted to the right one position to make room for the new element. Insertion in the interior of `ArrayList` is O(n), since *at most n* elements will have to be shifted right. Inserting at the tail of `ArrayList` is O(1) because we simply need to increment `tail`, then insert the element. The analysis of the deletion operation is similar, except that we are shifting elements to the *left* (or "down") one position to fill the gap created by the deleted element.

By contrast, inserting at the head or tail of a `LinkedList` is O(1)—our implementation maintains references to these two points in the list, so there is no traversing of the list. We just allocate a new `DLNode`, set its link and data fields, then insert it at the `head` or `tail`.[5] Although this requires more steps than we needed for

---

[5]For the sake of completeness it should be said that this assumes the allocation of an object can be done in constant time. This is an issue in the management of the heap, which is beyond the scope of this book.

`ArrayList`, it is still a fixed number of operations, so it is also $O(1)$. Remember also that with linked lists there is never a need to shift any elements since they are not adjacent in memory. Inserting in the interior of a linked list requires traversing the linked list to the insertion point, which we have already established has a cost of $O(n)$. However, in our implementation we made use of the fact that we can traverse the list in either a forward or backward direction. The `LinkedListIterator` constructor starts at the end that is closest to the index we seek, so it never has to traverse more than $n/2$ links. While this is still $O(n)$, it is a measurable improvement over the worst-case time to traverse n links. Analysis of deletions in a linked list is similar. Table 5.6 summarizes the discussion so far.

Table 5.6 shows that the two implementations have the same run time for several operations, but we have already said that the cost of an address calculation is less than that of a memory reference, so it is reasonable to wonder whether the asymptotic analysis is reflected in actual behavior.

Table 5.7 gives the time per iteration for a program that builds random-access (`ArrayList`) and sequential-access (`LinkedList`) lists of the same size, populates them, and uses an iterator to walk through them. As the table shows, doubling the size of the list pretty nearly doubles the time required to iterate over the list.

Table 5.6 Time complexity for the List ADT operations for the array and linked list implementations.

Operation	ArrayList	LinkedList
add()/remove()		
at head	$\Theta(n)$	$O(1)$
at tail	$O(1)$	$O(1)$
in interior	$O(n)$	$O(n)$
contains()/indexOf()	$O(n)$	$O(n)$
get()	$O(1)$	$O(n)$
listIterator(int)	$O(1)$	$O(n)$
size()/clear()	$O(1)$	$O(1)$

Table 5.7 Comparison of traversals of `ArrayList` and `LinkedList` (in seconds).

	Time per Iteration	
n	Array	Linked List
20,000	02.44	05.50
40,000	04.80	11.00
60,000	07.33	16.40
80,000	10.40	23.00
100,000	13.70	27.60

However, the results also show that the time needed for the linked list-based implementation is consistently twice that for the array-based implementation, confirming our suspicion that while traversal operations may be $O(n)$ for both implementations, in reality the sequential access implementation is much slower.

CHECKPOINT

5.13 If the asymptotic cost of traversing a list is $O(n)$ for both the array and linked list implementations, why should the actual cost be so much higher for linked lists?

5.14 If the cost of updating the links for an insertion or deletion is really just $O(1)$ (because this is a guaranteed fixed number of operations), why is the cost of insertions and deletions overall given as $O(n)$?

5.15 Why is insertion at the head of `ArrayList` $\Theta(n)$, but insertion in the interior is $O(n)$?

5.7.1 A Last Comment on `Lists` in the JCF

The JCF provides two concrete implementations of `List` using two data structures: an array and a doubly linked list. As we know, these data structures have different strengths and weaknesses. The JCF designers built these considerations into the two `List` implementations.

As shown in Figure 5.15, in addition to the methods specified by the `List` interface, `java.util.LinkedList` provides methods that accentuate the strengths of a doubly linked list—accesses to the head and tail. These extra methods do not *extend* the functionality defined by `List`; rather, they are convenience methods that simplify certain operations that a linked list version of `List` can perform efficiently. Look at the methods added to `LinkedList`, for example, and you will see that these are operations that could be carried out via `add(index, element)`, `get(index)`, and `remove(index)`, respectively.[6] The problem with using these methods is that it makes it impossible to switch to a different implementation of `List`. For example, if your code uses a `LinkedList` object and makes use of, say, `getFirst()`, you cannot switch to the `ArrayList` implementation because `getFirst()` is not in the API for `ArrayList`. If this kind of flexibility is important, you should only write code using the methods from the `List` interface. You should also keep this kind of problem in mind when you design your own interfaces and classes.

Write to the interface

---

[6]This is akin to the notion of syntactic sugar—a construct that adds nothing new, but makes it easier to carry out commonly needed operations. The switch and for statements in Java are examples. Every switch statement could be replaced with cascaded if-else statements and every for statement can be implemented as a while loop.

Figure 5.15 LinkedList and ArrayList specializations.

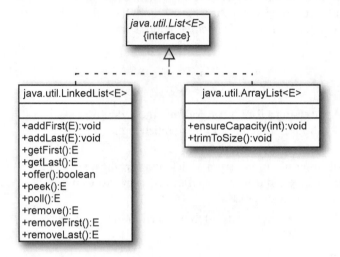

java.util.List<E>
{interface}

SUMMING UP

The JCF includes two concrete implementations of java.util.List: ArrayList, which uses an array to store the list's elements, and LinkedList, which uses a linked list to store its elements. Each of these classes defines a few additional methods that are specific to the backing store used to store the elements. Code that makes use of these specialized methods precludes switching between the implementations. The general rule is to write to the interface, guaranteeing that classes implementing the interface are interchangeable.

The time complexity of the methods for the two implementations reflects the backing store used—accesses are faster for the array-based implementation than for the linked list implementation. The cost of traversing all the elements is $O(n)$ for both implementations, but traversals of a linked list will be slower than for an array due to the extra memory accesses inherent in a linked list representation.

EXERCISES

Paper and Pencil

1. Give the values of the List attributes after each of the following operations.

```
List<String> ex = new LinkedList<String>();
ex.add("Pooh");
ex.add(1, "Tigger");
ex.add(1, "Piglet");
ex.add(0, "Owl");
List<String> exView = ex.sublist(1,4);
exView.clear();
```

2. Which optional methods would you support for a list that, once initialized, can have elements removed but none added?

3. What is the complexity of the addAll() operation?

4. Prepare a test case for the ListIterator.add() method.

5. Redraw Figure 5.16 after iter.add("Coffee") has executed.

6. Redraw Figure 5.16 after iter.remove() has executed.

7. Fill in the blank entries for the following table.

Method	Object State	Returned Value
`List<String> list =` `    new LinkedList<String>()`		
`list.add ("peach")`		
`list.add(0, "apple")`		
`list.contains("orange")`		
`list.isEmpty()`		
`list.add(1, "banana")`		
`List<String> l2 =` `    new ArrayList<String>( list )`		
`l2.add(0, "grape")`		
`l2.add(2, "pear")`		
`l2.remove("apple")`		
`l2.remove("grape")`		
`ListIterator<String> iter =` `    list.listIterator()`		
`iter.hasNext()`		
`String s = iter.next()`		
`iter.add("date");`		
`s = iter.next()`		
`iter.remove()`		
`iter.hasNext()`		
`list.remove("peach")`		
`s = iter.next()`		

Figure 5.16 A sequence for ListIterator object iter.

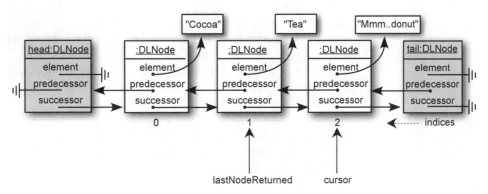

Testing and Debugging

Identify and fix the errors with the following code. Assume the doubly linked implementation presented in this chapter.

1.
```
public E remove( E target ) {
    DLNode<E> node = head.getSuccessor();

    while ( ! node.getElement().equals(target) )
        node = node.getSuccessor();
    node.setSuccessor( node.getSuccessor () );
    return node.getElement();
}
```

2.
```
public void remove( int index ) {
    ListIterator<E> iter = this.ListIterator( index );
    iter.remove();
}
```

3.
```
static public main() {
    List<String> ex = new ArrayList<String>(10);
    ex.add("Pooh");
    ex.add("Tigger");
    ex.add("Piglet");
    ex.add("Owl");
    Iterator<String> iter = ex.iterator();
    while ( iter.hasNext() )
        System.out.println( iter.next() );
    ex.add("Roo");
    while ( iter.hasNext() )
        System.out.println( iter.next() );
}
```

4. During a bit of careless typing (thinking?) when putting together the ADT for List, the boundary condition for uptoIndex in List.sublist() was given as uptoIndex < size. Below is the specification with the mistake. What are the implications of this? Why is this wrong?

sublist (int fromIndex, int uptoIndex)

pre-condition:	$0 \leq$ fromIndex $<$ *size*
	$0 \leq$ uptoIndex $<$ *size*
	fromIndex $\leq$ uptoIndex
responsibilities:	provide a sublist ("view") of this list containing the elements in the positions from fromIndex to uptoIndex − 1 inclusive. The sublist is backed by this list, so changes made to the sublist change this list. Operations on the sublist are undefined if the list is structurally modified in any way except through the sublist
post-condition:	this list is unchanged
throws:	index out of bounds exception if pre-conditions are not met
returns:	a List object containing the elements in the positions fromIndex to uptoIndex − 1, inclusive.

Modifying the Code

For each of the exercises in this section you must prepare the pre- and post-conditions and determine how you will test the method.

Also, in grade school we would take a short test and then exchange our answers with a neighbor to grade them. For some of these exercises you could do something similar—add functionality to someone else's code and evaluate their code on the basis of how easy it was to modify it.

- How difficult was it to understand the methods you had to modify? What features made the modifications especially difficult or easy?

- Were good and consistent naming conventions used? How about formatting conventions?

- How difficult was it to produce a test suite for this code?

- Was the documentation helpful? Was it accurate?

1. Add a method `reverse()` to our `LinkedList` class that reverses the elements of a list.

2. Re-implement `LinkedList` using a single dummy node whose successor field references the first node in the list and whose predecessor link references the last node in the list. That is, redo `LinkedList` as a circularly linked list, as outlined in Section 3.6.

3. The `LinkedListIterator` class uses `okToRemove` to determine when it is valid to call the list iterator's `remove()` and `set()` methods. The element to remove/set is referenced by `lastNodeReturned`. Re-implement `LinkedListIterator` to use only `lastNodeReturned` to determine when it is valid to remove or set an element.

4. Calling a constructor to create a new node for a linked list takes time. One optimization is to put nodes that have been freed via one of the `List` remove operations onto a list of free `DLNodes` to be reused. Now, when an element is to be added to the list and a `DLNode` is needed, it can come from the free list. If the free list is empty, then a new `DLNode` is instantiated. Implement this variation in `LinkedList`.

5. Provide an implementation of `List` that disallows `null` elements and duplicates.

6. Define your own `ArrayList` class that extends `java.util.ArrayList` and add the methods found in the UML diagram for `java.util.LinkedList` in Figure 5.15 so that there is an array-based implementation of `List` that has all of the methods of the linked list-based implementation found in the JCF.

7. Some applications keep a list of most recently used items. A word processor, for example, might keep track of the four most recently accessed documents and fonts, with the most recently used item in the first position on the list, the second most recently used item in the second position, and so on. Design and implement a class `MruItems` (**M**ost **r**ecently **u**sed **Items**) that stores some number of most recently used items in an object of type `List`. When an element is

added to a full Mru list, the oldest item is removed. The constructor to the class should take an integer argument indicating the maximum number of items to be stored in the list. The class should allow a client to do as follows:

- Add new items, discarding the oldest elements when the Mru list becomes full
- Clear the Mru list of all items
- Get an element from some position in the Mru list

You should also write a sample application that demonstrates the use of MruItems.

8. Big Movie Video is a chain of stores that rents videos, DVDs, and video games. It is putting new computer systems in its stores nationwide and wants a new software system to manage its rentals. Your task is to create a system that will associate rental items with a customer. Each customer has a name, address, phone number, unique customer ID, a balance due, and list of items currently checked out. A rental item can be any of those listed above. All rental items have a title, type (Video, DVD, Game), and a rental category (New Release, Special Offer, Regular Release). You need to be able to add new customers, let a customer check out an item and return an item, and display all the items held by a particular customer.

ON THE WEB

Additional study material is available at Addison-Wesley's Website at http://www.aw.com/cssupport. This material includes the following:

- Focus on Problem Solving: CourierModel Revisited

    Problem: The Courier application developed in Chapter 3 has been released and is now in the maintenance phase of the software lifecycle when updates and fixes are made. Barking Dogs Software has hired an intern and assigned her the task of re-implementing the application using a List to store the courier slips.

    Solution: Because the Model-View design pattern was used to develop the original solution, you will see that only the CourierModel class that stores the courier slips needs to be modified. All the other classes will work "as is"; a neat example of the power of thoughtful design.

- Study Guide Exercises
- Answers to CheckPoint Problems
- Additional exercises

The Stack Abstract Data Type

6

CHAPTER OUTLINE

A stack's behavior is described very nicely by the stack of trays commonly found in cafeterias. In our cafeteria, trays are placed in a spring-loaded container with only the topmost tray accessible, so that a student needing a tray always takes the topmost tray. The tray below that is then automatically moved up to the topmost position ready for the next student. When clean trays are added to the stack, they are pushed onto the top of the tray stack so that the *last* tray put *into* the stack becomes the topmost tray, and will be the *first* tray taken *out* of the stack when the next student comes along. It is this characteristic behavior that identifies a stack as a *last-in/first-out* (LIFO) collection.

A stack is a last-in/first-out (LIFO) data structure

A stack is a very simple kind of collection, and, like many simple things, has a wide variety of useful applications.

Stacks have many practical uses

■ All browsers have a "Back" button that allows you to return to the last URL you visited. When you follow a link on a page, the current URL is pushed onto the top of a URL stack before the browser follows the link. When you hit the "Back" button, the topmost entry on the URL stack is the most recently visited URL. It is popped off the stack and reloaded into the browser.

Stacks are good for reversing things

■ A feature commonly found in editors is an undo button that lets you undo changes you made to your document. The editor keeps track of changes to the state of your document by pushing the current state onto an undo stack, then updating the document with your changes. When you hit the undo button, it returns your document to the last saved state (which is on top of the saved state stack). By keeping a history of such changes on an undo stack, you can back out of a series of changes you made to a document in the *reverse* order in which you made them.

■ With programming languages, support for subroutines (method, function, procedure) must handle storage of the subroutine's parameters, local variables, and other state information. This is conveniently handled by placing these items in a **call frame** when the subroutine is invoked and pushing the call frame onto the top of the **process stack** where it can easily be accessed. *Each* call to a subroutine results in a call frame being pushed onto the process stack. A frame is popped off the stack and ceases to exist when the subroutine that created it exits. We look more closely at call frames and the process stack in Chapter 8 where we examine recursion.

■ Operand stacks are used to evaluate arithmetic expressions given in postfix form (this is done by some calculators and the Java Virtual Machine). The operands are pushed onto the operand stack as they are encountered in a left to right scan of the expression. When an operator is found, its operands are popped from the stack, applied to the operator, and the result is pushed back onto the stack. When the end of the expression has been reached, the top of the stack holds the result of the expression's evaluation. We look at expression evaluation in this chapter's Focus on Problem Solving (on the Website).

■ 6.1 Stack Description

A stack is a last-in/first-out (LIFO) data structure. All accesses to the stack are restricted to the topmost element, referenced through an attribute called **top**. An insertion to the stack is done via a push operation, which always inserts the new element on top of the stack. The stack *top* is then moved "up" one element to reference the newly inserted element. A deletion from the stack is done via a pop operation, which always removes and returns the element referenced by *top*. The element exposed by removing the top element becomes the new top element. The peek operation returns the element referenced by *top*, but does not remove it.

All stack accesses are done via the *top* attribute

A stack may be static and have a capacity that is established when the stack is created, or it may be dynamic and logically unlimited in its capacity.

■ **6.2** Stack Specification

The ADT specification is quite simple. There are only five operations in addition to the constructor.

The Stack ADT

Description
This ADT describes a dynamic stack (*size* is not fixed) whose element type is left unspecified.

Properties
1. Stacks are LIFO data structures. All accesses are done to the element referenced by *top*.
2. The *top* always refers to the topmost element in the stack.
3. Insertions are done "above" the top element.

Attributes

size:	The number of elements in the stack: *size* $> = 0$ at all times.
top:	The topmost element of the stack, refers to null, a special value indicating *top* doesn't reference anything in the stack when the stack is empty.

Operations

Stack()
pre-condition:	none
responsibilities:	constructor—initialize the stack attributes
post-condition:	*size* is 0
	top refers to null (a special value not part of the stack)
returns:	nothing

push(*Type element*)
pre-condition:	none
responsibilities:	push element onto the top of the stack
post-condition:	element is placed on top of the stack
	size is incremented by 1
	top refers to the element pushed
returns:	nothing

pop()
pre-condition:	isEmpty() is false
responsibilities:	remove and return the element at *top*
post-condition:	the top element is no longer in the stack
	size is decremented by 1
	top refers to the element below the previous topmost element or null if the stack is empty

returns:	the element removed
throws:	empty stack exception if pre-condition is not met

peek()
pre-condition:	isEmpty() is false
responsibilities:	return the element at *top*
post-condition:	the stack is unchanged
returns:	the element referenced by *top*
throws:	empty stack exception if pre-condition is not met

size()
pre-condition:	none
responsibilities:	determine the number of elements in the stack
post-condition:	the stack is unchanged
returns:	the number of elements in the stack

isEmpty()
pre-condition:	none
responsibilities:	determine if the stack has any elements in it
post-condition:	the stack is unchanged
returns:	true if the stack is empty (size() = = 0), false otherwise

CHECKPOINT

6.1 Browsers also have a "Forward" button that undoes the most recent Back action, and editors frequently include a redo button which "undoes" the action taken by the most recent undo action. How might these be implemented?

6.2 What is the effect of the following for a *Stack* s? What would the stack look like?
```
s.push( "www.nsf.gov" );
s.push("smithsonian.org");
s.pop();
```

6.3 How would the ADT change if we wanted to specify a stack that has a fixed capacity?

■ 6.3 The `stack` Interface

Listing 6.1 gives a Java interface for the `Stack` ADT specification. The `pop()` and `peek()` methods throw an `EmptyStackException` if they are called when the stack is empty.

Figure 6.1 illustrates the behavior of the `Stack` operations.

Listing 6.1 The Stack interface.

```
 1   package gray.adts.stack;
 2
 3   /**
 4    * A stack provides last-in-first-out behavior. All access
 5    *  operations on a stack are done at its <tt>top</tt>.
 6    */
 7
 8   public interface Stack<E> {
 9
10       /**
11        * Determine if the stack is empty.
12        * @return <tt>true</tt> if the stack is empty,
13        * otherwise return <tt>false</tt>.
14        */
15       public boolean isEmpty();
16
17       /**
18        * Return the top element of the stack without removing it.
19        * This operation does not modify the stack.
20        * @return topmost element of the stack.
21        * @throws EmptyStackException if the stack is empty.
22        */
23       public E peek();
24
25       /**
26        * Pop the top element from the stack and return it.
27        * @return topmost element of the stack.
28        * @throws EmptyStackException if the stack is empty.
29        */
30       public E pop();
31
32       /**
33        * Push <tt>element</tt> on top of the stack.
34        * @param element the element to be pushed on the stack.
35        */
36       public void push( E element );
37
38       /**
39        * Return the number of elements currently stored in the stack.
40        * @return the number of elements in this stack.
41        */
42       public int size();
43   }
```

Figure 6.1 The behavior of `Stack`'s methods.

Method	Purpose	Object State	Return Value
Stack<String> s = new LinkedStack<String>()	To create an empty stack s.	*size* = 0 *top* = null	a LinkedStack object for Strings
s.push ("A")	To add "A" to stack s.	*size* = 1 "A" *top*	
s.push ("B")	To add "B" to stack s.	*size* = 2 "A" "B" *top*	
String str = s.peek()	To peek at the top element of stack s.		"A"
str = s.pop()	To pop top element from stack s.	*size* = 1 "A" *top*	"B"
s.isEmpty()	To see if the stack s is empty.		false
str = s.pop()	To pop top element from stack s.	*size* = 0 *top* = null	"A"
s.isEmpty()	To see if the stack s is empty.		true
str = s.peek()	To peek at the top element of stack s.		exception

SUMMING UP

A stack is a last-in-first-out collection. A stack is accessed through its *top* attribute. Stacks have many applications in computing, including: back buttons on browsers, undo buttons in editors, expression evaluation, and runtime support for subroutine invocation.

■ 6.4 Designing a Test Plan

To emphasize some important points, we begin the design of our stack test plan by answering a few general questions.

■ *What are the bounds?* The bounds to check would include operations on an empty stack, a stack with only one element in it, and, if the stack supports an upper bound on its capacity, similar operations when the stack is full (is at its capacity) and is one element short of its capacity.

■ *How does each operation change the state of the stack?* The responsibilities and post-conditions provided with each operation in the ADT specification should provide this information. When creating the test plan, if you are not able to clearly determine how an operation affects the object's state, you have not provided a complete specification and must provide more detail. Remember that one outcome of developing the test plan at this point is that you have a much clearer idea about the expected behavior of the ADT.

■ *What are the invalid conditions that must be caught?* This is provided by the operation's pre-conditions and further clarified in the throws field (if present) of each operation's description.

Test Case 6.1 checks two things:

1. That a stack object is correctly instantiated
2. That the pre-conditions for `peek()` and `pop()` are properly handled.

Test Case 6.2 verifies that pushes are done properly. When a new element is pushed onto the stack, it should become the topmost element. We can confirm this with `peek()`. Also, the size of the stack should increase by one, which can be confirmed using `size()`.

Test Case 6.1 Stack instantiation.

Method	Purpose	Object State	Expected Result
Stack\<String\> s = new ListStack\<String\>()	To create an empty stack.	*size* = 0 *top* = null	a ListStack for Strings
s.size()	To verify empty stack state.		0
s.isEmpty()	To verify empty stack state.		true
String str = s.peek()	To verify operation pre-condition.		exception
str = s.pop()	To verify operation pre-condition.		exception

Test Case 6.2 Pushing elements onto a stack.

Method	Purpose	Object State	Expected Result
Stack\<String\> s = new ListStack\<String\>()	To create an empty stack.	*size* = 0 *top* = null	a ListStack for Strings
s.push("www.nps.gov")	To push onto an empty stack.	*size* = 1 *top* = "www.nps.gov"	
s.size()	To verify new stack state.		1
s.isEmpty()	To verify new stack state.		false
String str = s.peek()	To verify new stack state.		"www.nps.gov"
s.push("www.nasa.gov")	To push onto a nonempty stack.	*size* = 2 *top* = "www.nasa.gov" "www.nps.gov"	
s.size()	To verify new stack state.		2
str = s.peek()	To verify new stack state.		"www. nasa.gov"
s.push("www.bls.gov")	To push onto a nonempty stack.	*size* = 3 *top* = "www.bls.gov" "www.nasa.gov" "www.nps.gov"	
s.size()	To verify new stack state.		3
str = s.peek()	To verify new stack state.		"www.bls.gov"

Test Case 6.3 Popping elements to create an empty stack.

Method	Purpose	Object State	Expected Result
Stack<String> s = new ListStack<String>()	To create an empty stack.	*size* = 0 *top* = null	a ListStack for Strings
s.push("www.nps.gov")	To push onto an empty stack.	*size* = 1 *top* = "www.nps.gov"	
s.push("www.nasa.gov")	To push onto a nonempty stack.	*size* = 2 *top* = "www.nasa.gov" "www.nps.gov"	
s.push("www.bls.gov")	To push onto a nonempty stack.	*size* = 3 *top* = "www.bls.gov" "www.nasa.gov" "www.nps.gov"	
String str = s.pop()	To pop from a nonempty stack.	*size* = 2 *top* = "www.nasa.gov" "www.nps.gov"	"www.bls.gov"
str = s.peek()	To verify new stack state.		"www.nasa.gov"
s.size()	To verify new stack state.		2
str = s.pop()	To pop from a nonempty stack.	*size* = 1 *top* = "www.nps.gov"	"www.nasa.gov"
str = s.peek()	To verify new stack state.		"www.nps.gov"
s.size()	To verify new stack state.		1
s.isEmpty()	To verify new stack state.		false
str = s.pop()	To pop from a nonempty stack.	*size* = 0 *top* = null	"www.nps.gov"
s.size()	To verify new stack state.		0
s.isEmpty()	To verify new stack state.		true

Finally, we need to know that pops work properly. Test Case 6.3 proceeds in much the same way as Test Case 6.2. We begin by pushing a number of elements on, and then pop them. Each pop() should decrease the size attribute by one and should produce a new top of stack element. When all the elements have been popped, the stack should be empty.

SUMMING UP

A good place to begin development of a test plan is with bounds and off-by-1 tests. As has been pointed out many times now (but bears repeating), developing the tests *prior* to implementation provides a check on the quality of the specification and will help avoid time-consuming errors during implementation. Be sure to include tests that verify your code checks method pre-conditions.

■ **6.5** Stack Implementation: `ListStack`— Using the Adapter Design Pattern

We turn now to a discussion of the stack ADT's implementation. As we have done before, we first ask if there is any *existing* code we could reuse in our implementation.

From the stack description it seems reasonable (sort of) to say that a Stack "is a kind of" List that has the specialization that all accesses are made at only one end of the list. It would seem natural, then, to create a stack by *extending* a class that implements the `List` interface. As shown in Figure 6.2, this is precisely what is done for the implementation of Stack within the JCF. This is code reuse through inheritance.

Unfortunately, in using inheritance to implement Stack, the JCF designers violated a rule of OOP that says do not allow operations on or accesses to a data type beyond those provided by the type's expected API—in our case, the basic Stack operations from the Stack ADT. However, because `java.util.Stack` extends `Vector`, which implements `List`, *all* the methods from the `List` and `Collection` APIs are available. This means, for example, that I could push several elements onto a stack, then display them all using an iterator, or access them from the *bottom* of the stack *up* using `get(int index)`. This is decidedly non-Stack behavior, but it is possible because of how `Stack` is implemented in the JCF.

Code reuse through inheritance

This misuse of inheritance is an example of an *antipattern*. Where a design pattern is a good, general solution to a commonly encountered problem, an antipattern is a solution that *looks like* it will work for a problem, but actually is incorrect. In our case, we were initially misled by characterizing a Stack as "a kind of" List, which naturally suggested an inheritance relationship to us.

An antipattern describes a solution that is commonly misapplied to a problem

It is disappointing that inheritance is not really practical in this case, especially because it is clear that a `List` really can provide the behavior of a stack, albeit through a different API. But maybe all is not lost—maybe *composition* can help us where inheritance could not. In fact, this is precisely the case, and the problem we are faced with is so common it is described in a design pattern.

Code reuse through composition

6.5.1 The Adapter Software Design Pattern[1]

Name

Adapter

Problem

We need to create a class that implements the API defined in an interface we are given. We know of an *existing* class that offers some or all of the functionality *described by* the target interface we need to implement, but the existing class has a *different* API. Still, we would like to reuse this code if at all possible. We could copy and paste what we need from the existing class into our new class, but this is a really clumsy way to promote code reuse and it assumes we have access to the source.

---

[1]*Design Patterns: Elements of Reusable Object-Oriented Software* by Erich Gamma, Richard Helm, Ralph Johnson, John Vlissides. Addison Wesley Professional, 1994.

Figure 6.2 The Stack class in the JCF.

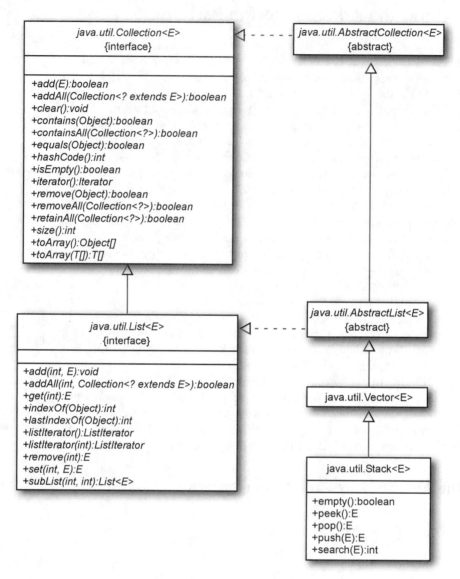

Solution

The Adapter design pattern solves this problem by *adapting* the API of the existing class to that of the target interface. The basic steps are as follows (see Figure 6.3).

- We define an adapter class, (here called AdapterClass, but the actual name doesn't matter) that implements the target interface.
- Methods in the target interface are matched with counterparts in the existing class (called ExistingClass here) that provide the same general behavior.

Figure 6.3 The Adapter design pattern.

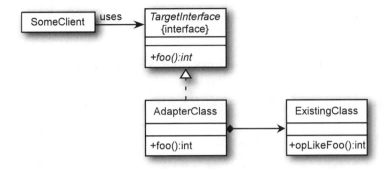

- An *instance of* `ExistingClass` is included in `AdapterClass` through *composition*.
- The methods in `AdapterClass` simply forward the message to the corresponding method in `ExistingClass`. This is called **message forwarding**.

Message forwarding

`TargetInterface` provides the interface that a client expects to be able to use.

`SomeClient` is the client class; it expects to have access to methods conforming to the API defined by `TargetInterface`.

`ExistingClass` provides most or all of the behavior defined by `TargetInterface`, but using a different API (e.g., `opLikeFoo()` from `ExistingClass` provides the same semantics as `foo()` from `TargetInterface`).

`AdapterClass` implements `TargetInterface` and includes an instance of `ExistingClass` through composition. The method implementation in `TargetInterface` simply forwards the message to the corresponding method from `ExistingClass` for processing. For example, Adapter's implementation of `foo()` will contain a call to `ExistingClass.opLikeFoo()`and can, if it wants, return the result provided by `opLikeFoo()`.

Consequences

- The adapter pattern allows you to quickly implement a new class by reusing an existing class that provides at least some of the behavior needed, but through a different API. This is especially useful for rapid development of prototypes, when execution speed is not an issue.
- There is a performance cost. The indirection introduced by the message forwarding from the `AdapterClass` object to the `ExistingClass` object requires additional time.
- The API of `ExistingClass` is visible only to `AdapterClass` and is completely hidden from the client.

6.5.2 Building a Stack from a List Using the Adapter Design Pattern

The List API can provide the *behavior* of the Stack API, but the two are clearly different. So we will follow the Adapter design pattern and adapt List to implement Stack.

Here are the tasks we must complete to implement a Stack using a List as the backing store:

Task list to create Stack from List

1. Determine whether a field from List can take on the responsibility of an attribute or method from Stack.

2. Determine which methods from List can provide the behavior defined by methods from Stack.

3. Implement the Stack methods using the information gathered in the first two tasks.

6.5.3 ListStack Task 1: Map Stack Attributes to List Attributes/Methods

We normally think of an attribute as something stored as a data field, but it can also be synthesized (*computed* from other information). Stack's *size* attribute is precisely matched to the *size* attribute of List, which we can access through List's size() method.

size = list.size()
A synthesized attribute

The *top* attribute is slightly trickier. In using List to represent a stack, we are mapping the elements of the stack to positions in a list. We can treat either end of a list as the logical top of a stack. That is, we can do all our insertions and deletions at the *head* of a list or at the *tail* of a list.

We know from the last chapter that the linked list implementation of a List has efficient accesses at the *head* and *tail*, and from Chapter 3 we know that the array-based implementation of List is much better at accesses at the *tail* than at the *head*, so we'll treat the *tail* of the List as the logical *top* of Stack. This will allow us to use either the array or the linked implementation of List.

Use what you know about the characteristics of array and linked data structures

Furthermore, because we want the freedom to switch between the array and linked list implementations of List, we must use *only* operations they have in common—those found in the List interface. This means, for example, that we cannot use any of the specialized methods found in either ArrayList or LinkedList, such as addLast(), getLast(), and removeLast() from java.util.LinkedList.

The List ADT describes *tail* as being the index of the last position in the list. The range of indices for list elements is 0 to size() − 1; so *tail* logically refers to the last element in the list at position size() − 1. Thus anytime we want to access the top element of our stack, we must access position size() − 1 of the list (see Figure 6.4). Table 6.1 shows the mapping of Stack attributes to List attributes/methods.

top = list.size () − 1

Figure 6.4 The position of Stack's *top* attribute in a list.

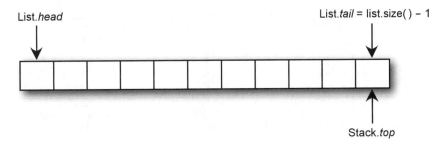

Table 6.1 Mapping of `Stack` attributes to `List` attributes/methods.

Stack Attribute	List Equivalent
top	size() − 1
size	size()

6.5.4 `ListStack` Task 2: Map `Stack` Methods to `List` Methods

Given the results of Task 1, a push() operation on a stack corresponds to *appending* an element to a list. We learned in Chapter 4 that insertions at the end of the list will occur at position size(). When we push an item onto a stack, it goes *on top of* the topmost element (remember the tray analogy from the beginning of the chapter), with *top* then referencing that element. Where is this in a list? It is one position beyond the *tail* of the list, giving us

size() − 1	+ 1	= size()
tail of list	next position beyond *tail*	location to "push" the new stack element

So, a push() operation on a stack will be the equivalent of an add() operation at the end of a list. Table 6.2 shows the `List` operations we will use to handle each `Stack` operation.

Table 6.2 `Stack` operations and their equivalent `List` operations.

Stack Operation	List Operation Equivalent
push(element)	add(size(), element)
E pop()	E remove(size() − 1)
E top()	E get(size() − 1)
int size()	int size()
boolean isEmpty()	boolean isEmpty()

Figure 6.5 Design of the `ListStack` class using the Adapter design pattern.

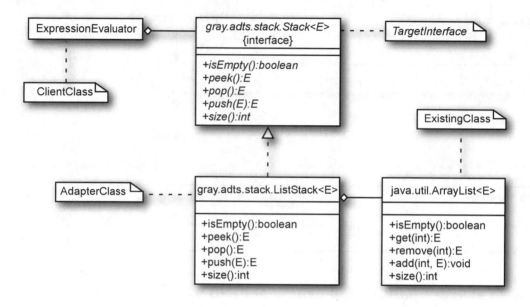

Listing 6.2 The `ListStack` class implemented using the Adapter design pattern and a `List`.

```
1    package gray.adts.stack;
2
3    import java.util.LinkedList;
4    import java.util.List;
5    import java.util.EmptyStackException;
6
7    /**
8     * An implementation of the Stack interface using a list as the
9     *   underlying data structure.
10    */
11   public class ListStack<E> implements Stack<E> {
12        private java.util.List<E> stack;
13        // the top of stack is represented by position
14        //    size() - 1 in the list.
15
16        /**
17         * Create an empty stack.
18         */
19        public ListStack() {
20             stack = new LinkedList();
21        }
22
```

```
23          /**
24           * Determine if the stack is empty.
25           * @return <tt>true</tt> if the stack is empty,
26           * otherwise return <tt>false</tt>.
27           */
28          public boolean isEmpty()
29          {
30              return stack.isEmpty();
31          }
32
33          /**
34           * Return the top element of the stack without removing it.
35           * This operation does not modify the stack.
36           * @return topmost element of the stack.
37           * @throws EmptyStackException if the stack is empty.
38           */
39          public E peek()
40          {
41              if ( stack.isEmpty() )
42                  throw new EmptyStackException();
43              return stack.get( stack.size() - 1 ) ;
44          }
45
46          /**
47           * Pop the top element from the stack and return it.
48           * @return topmost element of the stack.
49           * @throws EmptyStackException if the stack is empty.
50           */
51          public E pop()
52          {
53              if ( stack.isEmpty() )
54                  throw new EmptyStackException();
55              return stack.remove( stack.size() - 1 );
56          }
57
58          /**
59           * Push <tt>element</tt> on top of the stack.
60           * @param element the element to be pushed on the stack.
61           */
62          public void push( E element)
63          {
64              stack.add( stack.size(), element );
65          }
66
67          /**
68           * Return the number of elements currently stored in the stack.
69           * @return topmost element of the stack.
```

```
70          */
71          public int size()
72          {
73                return stack.size();
74          }
75      }
```

Figure 6.5 shows the UML diagram of our solution using the `ExpressionEvaluator` class we developed as the client class in this chapter's Focus on Problem Solving (on the Website).

It is important to note that using composition instead of inheritance completely hides the `List` methods from the client. Indeed, the client need not even know that a `List` is involved in the implementation at all. The only methods from `List` shown here are those that are needed to complete the adaptation of `List` to meet the needs of `Stack`. Compare this figure with Figure 6.3 given with the Adapter description.

6.5.5 `ListStack` Task 3: Implement `Stack` Methods Using `List` and the Adapter Pattern

The implementation of `ListStack` using the Adapter pattern is given in Listing 6.2. As promised, the `Stack` methods just forward the message to the corresponding method from `List`. It is remarkably simple! Note on line 5 that we use the `EmptyStackException` class from `java.util`. We'll create a custom exception class in the next chapter.

SUMMING UP

Inheritance and composition are two ways to reuse code. The Adapter design pattern uses composition to provide a simple way to quickly implement a new class using attributes and behavior supplied by an existing class. A stack can be implemented this way using an implementation of `List`. An antipattern is the opposite of a pattern—it is a solution that looks like it applies, but does not.

■ 6.6 Stack Implementation: `LinkedStack`— Using a Linked Data Structure

The Adapter design pattern made it quite easy to implement the `Stack` ADT using a `List` as the backing store. In this section we will take a different approach, implementing the `Stack` ADT from scratch using a linked list as the backing store. We do this in order to revisit some design decisions suggested in earlier chapters.

After considering what has to be done, we can identify three tasks to be completed, in the following order.

Task list for the linked list implementation of the Stack ADT

1. Decide which linked structure representation to use: singly linked list or doubly linked list.

2. Map the Stack ADT attributes to a linked list implementation. In doing this we will identify the data fields our class will need.

3. Implement the Stack ADT operations as methods in our class.

6.6.1 `LinkedStack` Task 1: Decide Which Linked Structure Representation to Use

The first decision we have to make is whether to use a singly or a doubly linked list. In Chapter 5, we used a doubly linked structure to implement the List ADT because we needed to be able to move forward and backward through the list.

Since all access to a stack is restricted to the top (one end of the linear structure), we have no need to move forward *and* backward through the stack. Indeed, *traversals* of a stack aren't even supported by the ADT, so we do not need the flexibility (and associated complexity) of the doubly linked structure (`DLNode`), and can settle instead for the simplicity of the singly linked structure (`SLNode`) developed in Chapter 3. In creating this linked implementation, we want to be sure to draw on our experience using linked structures in Chapter 3, particularly Section 3.4.3, which described the `SinglyLinkedList`. We will reuse `SLNode`, making it an inner class of `LinkedStack`.

Should we use a singly or a doubly linked list?

6.6.2 `LinkedStack` Task 2: Map `Stack` ADT Attributes to a Linked List Implementation?

In Section 6.5.2, we let the *tail* of a `List` represent the *top* of the `Stack` because accesses to the *tail* were efficient for both the array and linked list implementations of `List`.

However, since we are now restricting ourselves to a singly linked list implementation, it makes much more sense to let the *top* of the stack be represented by the first node of the linked list, since insertions and deletions can be done very efficiently there.

Let top be the first node in the linked list, represented by a dummy node

Also, we saw in Chapter 3 that the use of a dummy node to represent the *head* of the linked list simplified the coding, so we'll make use of that trick again and let the *top* attribute of `Stack` reference an instance of `SLNode` whose `element` field is always `null`.[2]

When the stack is empty, top's `successor` field will be `null`; otherwise top's `successor` field references the topmost element in the stack. Since all accesses to the stack will be at one end of the linked list, we have no need for a dummy node at the tail of the linked list.

Representing an empty stack

To avoid any nasty surprises, we want to be sure that the `successor` field of the last node in the linked list (the bottommost node in the stack) is always `null`. Logically this should be the case—the `successor` fields always refers to the *successor*

---

[2]The Exercises give you an opportunity to contest the claim that a dummy node simplifies the Stack implementation.

node in the linked list, but since the last node in the linked list has no successor, its successor field really should be null to clearly mark the end of the linked list. We make this an implementation invariant.

Implementation invariant: The linked list is terminated by a null successor field

So, the Stack ADT's attributes will be represented by two data fields with the understanding that *top* is implemented as described above.

```
public class LinkedStack<E> implements Stack<E> {
    private int size;
    private SLNode<E> top;
    ...
```

6.6.3 LinkedStack Task 3: Implement the LinkedStack Methods

The Default Constructor

Instantiating LinkedStack means initializing the two data fields. The default constructor for SLNode ensures that its element and successor fields are set to null (see Listing 6.3). The result, of course, is an empty stack, which is illustrated in Figure 6.6.

LinkedStack()

Pushing an Element onto the Stack

Pushing an element onto the stack can be done very efficiently because we already have a reference to the *top* of the stack. The pseudocode is shown in Listing 6.4. The first step is to create a new SLNode object that will store the element to be pushed. Then we must link the new node into the linked list so that it is the new *top* of stack. Finally, we need to update *size* because the stack is now larger by one element. The labeled steps in the pseudocode correspond to the labeled statements in the code and to the parts of Figure 6.7.

push(E)

Listing 6.3 Constructor for LinkedStack.

```
1  public LinkedStack() {
2      size = 0;
3      top = new SLNode<E>();
4  }
```

Figure 6.6 An empty LinkedStack.

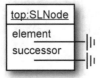

Listing 6.4 Implementation of `LinkedStack.push(E)`.

```
1    public void push( E element ) {
```
Create a new SLNode and   *Figure 6.8(a)*
Set the new node's successor field to be the same as top's successor field   *Figure 6.8(b)*
```
2        SLNode newNode = new SLNode<E>( element, top.getSuccessor() );
```
Set top's successor field to reference the node   *Figure 6.8(c)*
```
3        top.setSuccessor( newNode );
```
Increment size by 1
```
4        size++;
5    }
```

Figure 6.7 Pushing an element onto an empty stack.

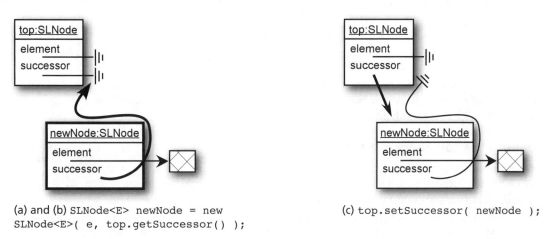

(a) and (b) `SLNode<E> newNode = new`   (c) `top.setSuccessor( newNode );`
`SLNode<E>( e, top.getSuccessor() );`

As we saw with `SinglyLinkedList` in Chapter 3, the advantage of the dummy node is that it simplifies the coding. For example, with `top` referencing a dummy node, pushing an element onto an empty stack is the same as pushing onto a non-empty stack. Compare (a) and (b) of Figure 6.7 to (a) and (b) of Figure 6.8.

There is a subtle point here. When the stack is constructed, the `successor` field of the `top` node is made `null`. The way `push()` is implemented, the new node's `successor` field is set to whatever `top`'s `successor` field is. Since `top`'s `successor` field starts out `null`, the `successor` field of the first node added to the linked list (pushed onto the stack) will also be `null`. This guarantees the implementation invariant that the last node in the linked list clearly indicates that it has no successor by setting its `successor` field to `null`.

Ensure the implementation invariant is honored

Peeking at the Top Element of the Stack

E peek()

This is a nondestructive *read* operation. If the stack is empty, we throw an exception; otherwise we simply get and return the `element` field of the topmost entry in

Figure 6.8 Pushing an element onto a nonempty stack.

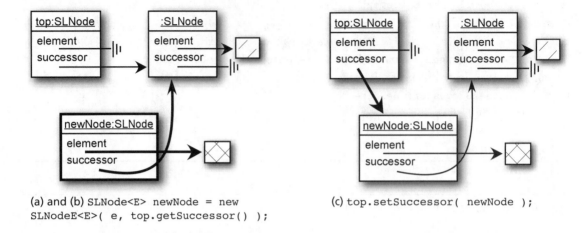

(a) and (b) `SLNode<E> newNode = new`
`SLNodeE<E>( e, top.getSuccessor() );`

(c) `top.setSuccessor( newNode );`

the stack (see Listing 6.5). The only tricky part is making sure that we don't return the `element` field of `top`, since it is a dummy node. The first data node is found by following `top`'s successor field.

Popping the Top Element off the Stack

`E pop()`

Unlike `peek()`, this is a *destructive* read operation. If the stack is empty, an exception is thrown; otherwise we *remove* the topmost entry in the stack and return its `element` field (see Listing 6.6). Note that we are careful to sever the popped node's connection to the data element and to the rest of the linked list.

The `size()` and `isEmpty()` methods are straightforward and are not shown.

Listing 6.5 Implementation of `LinkedStack.peek()`.

```
1    /**
2      * Return the element at top.
3      * @return the element at the top of the stack
4      */
5    public E peek() {
6        if ( isEmpty() )
7            throw new EmptyStackException();
8        return top.getSuccessor().getElement();
9    }
```

Listing 6.6 Implementation of `LinkedStack.pop()`.

```
1   /**
2    * Remove and return the element at top.
3    * @return the element at the top of the stack.
4    * @throws EmptyStackException if the stack is empty.
5    */
6   public E pop() {
7       if ( isEmpty() )
8           throw new EmptyStackException();
9       SLNode<E> t = top.getSuccessor();
10      E e = t.getElement();
11      top.setSuccessor( t.getSuccessor() );
12      // sever the node's connection to the element and
13      // the rest of the linked list
14      t.setElement( null );
15      t.setSuccessor( null );
16      size--;
17      return e;
18  }
```

SUMMING UP

A singly linked data structure is superior to a doubly linked data structure in implementing a stack because singly linked data structures are simpler, have less overhead, and we don't need the additional flexibility doubly linked data structures provide. Accesses at the head of the linked list are very efficient, so it is used as the *top* of the stack.

■ 6.7 Implementing the Test Plan

The test plan developed based on the Stack ADT applies, of course, to both of our Stack implementations and should produce the same results. We should ask now whether, for each of our implementations, there are any special cases that should be tested that are not covered by the test plan.

One of the advantages of using the Adapter design pattern is that we get to use software that has already been tested, so most of the Stack testing is reduced to seeing that we have used the representation data structure (List) properly. This testing must focus, then, on the associations we made between Stack attributes and methods, and how they are represented using the List (e.g., Stack's *top* and List's size()). The test plan seems sufficient.

As for the linked list implementation, we need to be certain that elements are inserted so that the LIFO protocol is observed. The test plan does this. We might

Listing 6.7 Implementation of test method `testPopEmpty()`.

```
1    public void testPopEmpty() {
2        Stack s = new ListStack();
3
4        try {
5            s.pop();
6        } catch ( EmptyStackException ex ) {
7            return;   // this is what we expect
8        }
9        // if we get here — the test failed :-(
10       fail("testPopEmpty should have raised an EmptyStackException here");
11   }
```

also be concerned that empty stacks are handled correctly so that we don't get any `NullPointerExceptions`. Again, the test plan meets our needs. I'll say a little about coding the test plan using JUnit and leave the rest to you.

The `pop()` and `peek()` operations in Test Case 6.1 *should* generate exceptions, since trying to look at the *top* of an empty stack is meaningless. This presents a bit of a problem in implementing the test case since throwing an exception will terminate a test method. There are a few ways around this, but the simplest is to create a separate `testXXX()` method for each test case in which you are expecting an exception to be thrown (indeed, that is what we are testing for in this case).

In Listing 6.7 an empty stack is created, followed by an attempt to pop its topmost element. If an exception is thrown (as expected), the catch clause just returns us from the method. This is what we want to happen because it means that `pop()` will have correctly spotted the attempt to pop from an empty stack. It is bad news if no exception is thrown. In this case the test fails, which is communicated by the `fail()` statement at line 10, which will only be executed if the `pop()` call does *not* generate an exception.

SUMMING UP

The test plan developed based on the ADT description is pure black-box testing—it focuses on the expected behavior as specified by the ADT. Once the implementation is complete, additional tests may suggest themselves based on the specifics of the implementation. When using the Adapter design pattern, you should make sure that the attributes of the target interface are correctly mapped to the attributes/methods of the existing class.

■ 6.8 Evaluation of the Implementations

Since we are using the Adapter design pattern, the runtime cost of `ListStack` is really based on the runtime cost of the underlying data structure and the overhead

Table 6.3 The cost of `Stack` operations for the Adapter implementation using a `List`.

Stack Operation	**List** Operation	Cost
push(element)	add(size(), element)	O(1)
pop()	remove(size() − 1)	O(1)
top()	get(size() − 1)	O(1)

of the message forwarding. The actual cost of message forwarding is the topic of this chapter's *Investigate*.

Clearly the cost of the accessor methods `size()` and `isEmpty()` is O(1) since that is their cost for `List` and we have just increased the size of the constant with the message forwarding. The more interesting analysis comes from those methods that have to access the list: `push()`/`add()`, `pop()`/`remove()`, and `peek()`/`get()`, which include the cost of the equivalent `List` operations. We carefully chose to let the *tail* of the list represent the *top* of the stack in the Adapter implementation since the cost of accesses to the tail is O(1) for both the array and linked implementations of list. Table 6.3 shows the asymptotic costs of the methods.

The cost of the stack operations for the singly linked list implementation is also O(1). Again, we carefully chose to do all accesses at the head of the singly linked list where the cost is O(1) (we could have used tail instead, of course, at the same cost). This nicely illustrates the importance of knowing the cost of the backing store operations.

CHECKPOINT

6.4 What problem does the Adapter design pattern solve?

6.5 Why would having the logical *top* of the stack represented by the head of a list pose a problem when using the `ArrayList` implementation?

6.6 What do I need to do to adapt the API of one class to match the API of a target interface?

INVESTIGATE Measuring the Cost of Using an Adapter

Description

In Section 6.5 we saw how easy it was to implement the Stack ADT by adapting one of the `List` implementations to provide the needed stack behavior. But we also saw that one of the consequences of using the Adapter design pattern was the cost of the message forwarding done by the adapter class. It is natural to wonder how significant this cost is. In this *Investigate*, we try to get a handle on the cost of message forwarding.

Objectives

- Gain more experience implementing classes using the Adapter design pattern.
- Determine the cost of the message forwarding when using the Adapter design pattern.
- Work with timing measurement.

Visualization

Because we already have a class (`ListStack`) that uses the adapter strategy, the most obvious way to approach this is to measure the time it takes to send messages to one or more methods in a `ListStack` object (playing the role of the `AdapterClass` from Figure 6.3) and then do the same for the equivalent methods of a `List` object (playing the role of the `ExistingClass` from Figure 6.3). The problem with this is that we would be measuring the processing time for the method's *behavior* as well as the time it takes to send the message and return the result. What we are interested in, though, is the cost of the *overhead* of the message forwarding, so we need to try something different.

To more accurately measure the cost of message forwarding, you will create another collection of classes following the Adapter design pattern. Figure 6.9 shows the interface and classes we will create for this *Investigate* and their relationship to one another. Compare the structure of this diagram with that of the Adapter design pattern given in Figure 6.3. The only difference is that `ExistingClass`, which provides the behavior *used by* the adapter class, `AdapterClass`, is also used directly by the client class, `TimerClient`. The reason for this organization is that to determine the cost of the message forwarding, we need to compare the cost of sending messages to `opLikeFoo()`.

- *directly* through `ExistingClass`
- *indirectly* through `AdapterClass.foo()`, which forwards the message to `opLikeFoo()` in the `ExistingClass` object.

TargetInterface is the interface the client expects to use for this data type.

ExistingClass provides the behavior needed by `AdapterClass`, but using a different API. In this case, `AdapterClass`'s `foo()` corresponds to `ExistingClass`'s `opLikeFoo()`.

AdapterClass implements `TargetInterface` and includes an instance of `ExistingClass` through composition. The method `foo()` in `AdapterClass` forwards its message to the corresponding method (`opLikeFoo()`) in `ExistingClass` for processing.

TimerClient is the client class responsible for tracking time. This class will include instances of both the adapter and the existing classes, so that calls to `opLikeFoo()` can be made directly through the `ExistingClass` object and indirectly through the `AdapterClass` object. The figure may give the appearance that `TimerClient` and `AdapterClass` share a reference to a *single* `ExistingClass` object, but that is not what the diagram means, nor is it what we will do. A UML class diagram illustrates the *static* structure of a system. To be clear, the `AdapterClass` and `TimerClient` classes will each create *their own* `ExistingClass` objects.

Figure 6.9 identifies the classes we have to create and their relationship to one another. Using that diagram and the description of the Adapter design pattern from Section 6.5, answer the following.

1. Why does `foo()` have to be in the `AdapterClass` class?

2. What method has to be in `ExistingClass`?

3. Does the name of the method in `ExistingClass` that will supply the behavior needed by `foo()` from `AdapterClass` matter?

4. Does the signature of the method `opLikeFoo()` that will supply the needed behavior matter?

5. Would it be permissible that the behavior needed by an `AdapterClass` method be supplied by calling two (or more) methods from the `ExistingClass`?

Design

The broad design of the solution has been given in Figure 6.9. With the exception of the client class that collects the timings, there is almost no code to write.

Implementation

In general outline, the first four steps are the ones you would follow when creating a set of related classes according to the Adapter design pattern. See the class description in Figure 6.9 for the signatures of the methods described below.

1. Write an interface, `TargetInterface`, with only the method `foo()` defined in it.

2. Write `ExistingClass` with only `opLikeFoo()` defined in it. The method body should just return an integer.

3. Implement the adapter class `AdapterClass`, which extends `TargetInterface`. Its single instance variable should be of type `ExistingClass`. The constructor should create an instance of `ExistingClass`. The single method, `foo()`, should contain a single line that forwards the message to `opLikeFoo()` in the `ExistingClass` object.

Figure 6.9 The classes to create for this *Investigate*.

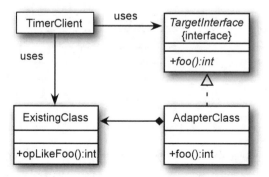

4. Implement the `AdapterClassTimer` class.

  a. Initially the class should only create a single instance, `nullAdapter`, of the `AdapterClass` class.

  b. Add timing loops following the approach presented in Chapter 2. The main action of the inner loop will be to call `nullAdapter.foo()`.

  c. Add statements after the timing loops to output the timing information gathered.

  Don't move on to step 5 until all of step 4 works.

5. Create an instance of `ExistingClass`, then add code to time calls to the `ExistingClass` object by repeating steps (a) through (c) of step 4 for the `ExistingClass` object. This code can follow the code developed in step 4, but be sure to reinitialize your timing variables.

  As always, when running your timing code, don't give your computer anything else to do! Close all other applications, don't wiggle the mouse and don't type on the keyboard.[3]

Execution

1. What average time do you get for calls to the method in the adapter class?

2. What average time do you get for calls to the method in the existing class?

3. What is the source of this overhead? Look up the documentation on the Java Virtual Machine and briefly describe the process undertaken when a method is invoked.

EXERCISES

Paper and Pencil

1. Fill in the blank entries for the following table.

Method	Object State	Return Value
`Stack<String> s =` `   new ListStack<String>();`		
`s.push( "C" );`		
`s.push( "A" );`		
`s.push( "M" );`		
`s.peek();`		
`s.pop();`		
`s.peek();`		
`s.isEmpty();`		

---

[3]Okay, asking you not to do these things is like putting up a "Don't touch. Wet Paint." sign—you feel compelled to try it and see for yourself. So . . . what happens to your timing output when you move the mouse around? Better yet, try launching another application or following a link in a browser while your timing application is still running.

Method	Object State	Return Value
s.pop();	_____	_____
s.pop();	_____	_____
s.peek();	_____	_____
s.pop();	_____	_____

2. As mentioned at the beginning of the chapter, a browser stores the current URL on a stack when you follow a new link. When you press the "Back" button, the most recently visited URL is popped from the stack and reloaded into the browser. Can the "Forward" button also use a stack? Try this out and draw a diagram illustrating what happens when you use the forward and back buttons.

Testing and Debugging

1. Complete the JUnit tester class for the test cases given in Section 6.4.

2. The code that accompanies this text includes class `FawltyStack`. Using the test plan outlined in Section 6.4, find and correct the error(s) in this implementation.

3. Write a test program that verifies that methods from the `Collection` and `List` interfaces are accessible through `java.util.Stack`.

4. Redo the timing from the *Investigate* in this chapter, using methods from `ListStack` and `List`. How do your measurements compare with what you discovered during the *Investigate*?

5. Is the following implementation of `testPopEmpty()` equivalent to that shown in Listing 6.2?

```
1    public void testPopEmpty() {
2        Stack s = new ListStack();
3
4        try {
5            s.pop();
6            fail("testPopEmpty EmptyStackException expected");
7        } catch ( EmptyStackException ex ) {
8            return;   // this is what we expect
9        }
10   }
```

Using a Stack

1. Stacks can be used to pair program elements such as parentheses, braces, brackets, and so on. As the input is scanned from left to right, left symbols (e.g., '(', '{', '[', '<') are pushed onto a stack. When a right symbol is found (e.g., ')', '}', ']', '>'), the top element of the stack is popped and examined to see if it is the mate for the current symbol. For example, if the element just read is ')', the top of stack should be '('. If the stack is empty or the symbol on top is not the mate, there is an error and the rest of the input string is abandoned. If the end of the input string is reached with no mismatches found *and* the symbol stack is empty, the input string was properly balanced. For example, [{()}] is a properly

balanced string, as is [[((<>))]]. But ({)} is not properly balanced, even though the *number* of left and right symbols agrees. Nor is ({{ properly balanced, since (will still be on the stack when the end of the input string is reached. Two versions of a symbol balancer using a stack are described.

Version 1 Write an application that performs symbol matching as described above for the following pairs of symbols: () [] {} <> "". If your application is console-based, the string to be parsed comes from the keyboard and is terminated by an end-of-line character. If the application is GUI-based, the input comes from a text field as a `String`.

Version 2 Allow the user to specify the pairs of symbols to be matched. The pairs should be given in a string with no whitespace separating the pairs and with a left symbol immediately followed by its right symbol mate. Here are two examples: ()[]<> and "ab\/. Note in the second example that we are saying that an 'a' is matched by 'b' and '\' by '/'.

2. A palindrome is a string that is the same when read forward and backward (skipping whitespace characters and punctuation, and ignoring differences in case). For example, "pap," "Madam I'm Adam," and "Able was I ere I saw Elba" are all palindromes. Write an application that takes an input string from the user and uses a stack to determine whether the string is a palindrome.

3. Use a stack to reverse the elements of a list.

4. *Traversing a maze*: If you have ever been through a maze you know that one approach to finding a solution involves backtracking. You follow a path until it either gets you to a solution or it becomes a dead end. If you reach a dead end, you backtrack (go back) to a point in the maze where there is an unexplored path, which you follow. You keep doing this until you find a solution or have explored all possible paths, in which case there is no solution (and you ask for your money back). A key aspect of taking this approach to solve a maze on a computer is keeping track of the points to which you will backtrack when you hit a dead end. An obvious possibility is to store your current location whenever you reach a point in the maze where there are multiple unexplored paths you can explore. If you hit a dead end, you simply restart at one of these saved points.

Write an application that solves a maze following the approach described above using a stack to store the backtrack points. The maze can be represented as a two-dimensional array of asterisks, with blanks indicating paths that can be followed. The starting point for the maze is identified with the character S and the ending point with the character E. A simple example is shown below for a 5-by-7 maze. The initial state is shown by the maze on the left. The middle maze shows us partway through. The periods show paths we have explored (and don't wish to explore again!). The maze on the right shows the final result.

```
**S****        **S****        **S****
**   *E*       **..*E*        **..*E*
*  ** *        * .** *        * .**.*
** ** *        ** ** *        **.**.*
**    *        **    *        **....*
```

Support some/all of the following features:

a. Allow the user to create the maze. This could be done through editing a text field of a GUI or by loading an existing maze from a file.

b. Randomly generate a maze to be searched. This is a nice feature since it is a little painful to create the mazes by hand, but it tends to produce a lot of unsolvable mazes.

c. Update the maze as each step is taken (instead of showing the completed maze at the end).

Modifying the Code

1. A problem from CheckPoint 6.1 asked what changes you would have to make to the Stack ADT to support a stack that has a fixed upper bound on the number of elements that can be pushed onto it.

    a. Revise the Stack ADT to reflect these changes.

    b. Define a Java interface that includes these changes. The new interface should extend the `Stack` interface given in this chapter.

    c. Provide a test plan that covers the additional methods.

    d. Implement and test the new ADT. Think about which tests from this chapter can be reused and which must be redone.

2. Add descriptions to the Stack ADT for the following methods, then develop test plans for the methods, add them to both the `ListStack` and `LinkedStack` classes, and run the tests from the test plan.

    a. `void clear()` removes all elements from the stack, returning it to its initialized state.

    b. `Stack( Collection c )` creates an instance of a stack initialized to contain the elements from the `Collection` c.

    c. `Collection toCollection()` creates and returns a `Collection` object that contains the elements of this stack. The stack should not be modified by this operation.

3. In Section 6.6 it was decided that a dummy node would be used to represent the Stack *top* because that made the implementation simpler. Re-implement Stack using a single linked list and no dummy node for *top*. Provide an analysis of your implementation compared to that provided in Section 6.6, focusing on the advantage, or not, of the dummy node in this case.

ON THE WEB

Additional study material is available at Addison-Wesley's Website http://www.aw.com/cssupport. This material includes the following:

■ Focus on Problem Solving: Evaluation of Postfix Expressions

Problem: An infix arithmetic expression places a binary operator *between* its operands (e.g., 7 + 2). A postfix arithmetic expression places the operator *after*

its operands (e.g., 7 2 +). Write an application that evaluates postfix expressions. These expressions can contain any combination of the binary operators +, −, *, and /. A binary operator has two operands. All operands are to be integers. This application is to be console-based. Operators and operands are to be separated by at least one blank, with the end of the line marking the end of the expression. A blank input line signifies there are no more expressions to evaluate and terminates the application.

Solution: The access characteristics of the Stack ADT are ideal for evaluating postfix expressions. Parsing a postfix expression from left to right, we push operands onto the stack until we find an operator, then we pop the operator's operands from the stack, apply the operator to them, and push the result. The Java Virtual Machine uses a stack to evaluate expressions in exactly this fashion.

■ Study Guide Exercises

■ Answers to CheckPoint Problems

■ Additional exercises

The Queue Abstract Data Type

7

CHAPTER OUTLINE

The behavior of a queue is familiar to us from everyday experience. We wait in lines (queues) at the bank, in grocery store checkout lines, on planes sitting on the runway before take off, and when we want to talk to a "customer service representative" on the phone. An important characteristic of queues is that they maintain the order in which items are inserted into them—the *first* thing to go *into* a queue is the *first* thing to come *out* of the queue. It is this characteristic behavior that identifies a queue as a *first-in/first-out* (FIFO) collection. This behavior has wide use in computing:

A queue is a first-in/first-out data structure

▪ Operating systems use queues in a number of areas. One is the scheduling of processes in a multi-tasking system. Using a strategy known as **round-robin scheduling**, the operating system gives each process a small amount of time, called a **time-slice**, to execute. When the time-slice expires, the operating system suspends the process, puts it at the rear of a queue of processes that are ready to run (called the **ready queue**), then takes the process that is at the front of the ready queue and gives it to the processor to run for a time-slice.

▪ A printer spooler accepts requests to print a document, putting the requests into a queue. As the printer becomes available, the spooler provides a print job from the front of its print queue. When a new job arrives at the spooler, it is inserted at the end of the print queue. Eventually that job will make its way to the front of the queue and be printed.

▪ Networks use queues to buffer data. For example, **bursty data** means that packets of information arrive at a machine at a very irregular rate – sometimes there are many packets arriving, sometimes only a few. The **leaky bucket algorithm** uses a queue to buffer packets that arrive in bursts at a machine, sending the packets out on their next hop at a more regular rate. The Focus on Problem Solving for this chapter explores this idea.

Uses of queues

■ 7.1 Queue Description

A queue is a first-in/first-out (FIFO) collection that obeys a first-come, first-served protocol. The front and rear of a queue are accessed through attributes called, appropriately, *front* and *rear*. An insertion to a queue is done via an enqueue operation and the new element is always inserted at the *rear*. A deletion is done via a dequeue operation and the element is always removed from the *front*. The peek operation returns, but does not remove, the element at the *front* of the queue.

A queue can have a fixed capacity that is established when the queue is created, or it may be logically unlimited in its capacity.

■ 7.2 Queue Specification

So far, all of our collection ADTs (Collection, List, and Stack) have been dynamic— they could grow in size as needed, so we never needed to worry about the collection becoming full (beyond the unavoidable problem of running out of memory).

This time our ADT will have a fixed capacity that determines the maximum number of elements that can be inserted into it. From the perspective of learning about collection ADTs, working with a fixed size data structure is important for the following reasons:

▪ It will provide some variety to your design and programming experience – dealing with upper bounds introduces additional constraints.

■ As a practical matter, some applications need to place an upper bound on capacity, for example, to meet constraints on memory usage or to avoid overwhelming processing capacity.

Before reading the discussion that follows, you may find it helpful to review the ADT specification for the Stack ADT, which has *no* upper bound on its capacity.

The constraint on the upper bound on the capacity of the queue requires additional attributes and operations, and it changes how we view some of the other attributes and operations.

Compare the Stack ADT specification to the Queue ADT specification with respect to *capacity*

Attributes and operations to support a fixed capacity

■ A *capacity* attribute will hold the maximum number of elements that can be stored in the collection. The ADT should specify a *default capacity*. An implementation can decide what actual value is appropriate.

■ The default constructor now has a little more work to do: It must initialize *size* and *capacity*.

■ There is also a need for an overridden constructor that takes the queue's capacity as an argument. The constructor must verify that this value is sensible (greater than 0).

■ There must be an accessor operation for the *capacity* attribute.

■ Having a *capacity* attribute changes the constraints on the *size* attribute. When capacity is unbounded, *size*'s only constraint is that it must be greater than or equal to zero. Now there is the additional constraint that *size* must be less than or equal to *capacity*.

■ Because these constraints are ADT invariants, we must re-examine the pre-conditions and post-conditions of the Queue ADT operations, particularly those that insert elements. There is only enqueue() to consider. Its pre-condition now must include that the queue is not already full.

■ We need a method to determine whether or not the queue is full. This is required so that a client of the ADT can verify the pre-condition to the enqueue()operation. It is important that a client have a way to verify that it is meeting the pre-conditions of an ADT's operations. When these pre-conditions involve attributes of the ADT, it is the ADT's responsibility to provide the necessary operations.

The Queue ADT

Description
A Queue is a linear collection that supports insertions at the rear of the queue and deletions from the front of the queue. A Queue is mutable, allows duplicates, and has a fixed capacity. The Queue element type is left unspecified.

Properties

1. Queues are FIFO data structures. All insertions are done at the rear and all deletions at the front.
2. The front always refers to the first element in the queue.
3. The rear always refers to the position where the next element is to be inserted in the queue.
4. The queue has a fixed upper bound (capacity) on the number of elements it can store.

Attributes

DEFAULT_CAPACITY:	A constant—the default value used for *capacity*.
capacity:	The maximum number of elements that can be in the queue at one time.
size:	The number of elements in the queue: $0 \leq size \leq capacity$ at all times.
front:	The first element of the queue or a null, a special value indicating front doesn't reference anything in the queue.
rear:	The position in the queue where the next element is to be inserted or a null value when the queue is empty.

Operations

Queue()

pre-condition:	none
responsibilities:	constructor - initialize the queue attributes
post-condition:	*size* is set to 0
	capacity is set to *DEFAULT_CAPACITY*
	front refers to a null value (a special value not part of the queue)
	rear refers to the position where the first insertion is to be made
returns:	nothing

Queue(int maxElements)

pre-condition:	maxElements > 0
responsibilities:	constructor—initialize the queue attributes
post-condition:	*size* is set to 0
	capacity is set to maxElements
	front refers to a null value
	rear refers to the position where the first insertion is to be made
returns:	nothing
throws:	invalid argument exception if pre-condition is not met

enqueue(*Type* element)

pre-condition:	isFull() is false
responsibilities:	insert element at the *rear* of the queue
post-condition:	element is placed at the *rear* of the queue
	size is incremented by 1
	rear is advanced to the position where the next element will be inserted or some null value if the queue is full
returns:	nothing
throws:	full queue exception if pre-condition is not met

dequeue()
    pre-condition: isEmpty() is false
    responsibilities: remove and return the element at *front*
    post-condition: the *front* element is no longer in the queue
                            size is decremented by 1
                            front refers to the element that followed the previous *front* element or null if the queue is empty
    returns: the element removed
    throws: empty queue exception if pre-condition is not met

peek()
    pre-condition: isEmpty() is false
    responsibilities: return the element at *front*
    post-condition: the queue is unchanged
    returns: the element referenced by *front*
    throws: empty queue exception if pre-condition is not met

size()
    pre-condition: none
    responsibilities: determine the number of elements in the queue
    post-condition: the queue is unchanged
    returns: *size*

capacity()
    pre-condition: none
    responsibilities: determine the capacity of the queue
    post-condition: the queue is unchanged
    returns: *capacity*

isEmpty()
    pre-condition: none
    responsibilities: determine if the queue has any elements in it
    post-condition: the queue is unchanged
    returns: true if the queue is empty (`size() == 0`), false otherwise

isFull()
    pre-condition: none
    responsibilities: determine if the queue has room in it for more elements
    post-condition: the queue is unchanged
    returns: true if the queue is full (`size() == capacity()`), false otherwise

clear()
    pre-condition: none
    responsibilities: empty the queue of elements
    post-condition: there are no elements in the queue
                            size is 0
                            front refers to a null value
                            rear refers the position where the first insertion is to be made
    returns: nothing

■ 7.3 The Queue Interface

The JCF includes neither an interface nor a class supporting the Queue ADT, so we provide our own. Listing 7.1 gives a Java interface that corresponds to the Queue ADT. The dequeue() and peek() methods throw an EmptyQueueException if they are called when the queue is empty. Similarly, enqueue() throws a FullQueueException if it is called and the queue is full. We'll need to create these exception classes.

Figure 7.1 illustrates the behavior of the Queue operations.

Listing 7.1 The Queue interface

```
 1    package gray.adts.queue;
 2
 3    /**
 4     * Interface for the Queue ADT with a fixed upper bound on
 5     * the number of elements that can be stored in the queue.
 6     */
 7    public interface Queue<E> extends java.io.Serializable {
 8
 9        /**
10         * The default number of entries in a Queue.
11         */
12        static final int DEFAULT_CAPACITY = 100;
13
14        /**
15         * Return the upper bound on the number of elements this
16         * Queue can store.
17         * @return the capacity of this queue.
18         */
19        public int capacity();
20
21        /**
22         *  Empty the queue of all elements.
23         */
24        public void clear();
25
26        /**
27         * Add <tt>element</tt> to the rear of the queue.
28         * @param element The element to add to thie rear of this queue
29         * @throws FullQueueException if the queue is full
30         */
31        public void enqueue( E element);
32
```

```
33        /**
34         * Remove and return the element at the front of the queue.
35         * @return this queue's front element
36         * @throws EmptyQueueException if the queue is empty
37         */
38        public E dequeue();
39
40        /**
41         * Determine if this queue has any elements.
42         * @return <tt>true</tt> if this queue has  no elements
43         *        (<tt>size() == 0</tt>); <tt>false</tt> otherwise.
44         */
45        public boolean isEmpty();
46
47        /**
48         * Determine if this queue has room for more elements.
49         * @return <tt>true</tt> if this queue has room for more
50         *    elements (<tt>size() == capacity()</tt>);
51         *    <tt>false</tt> otherwise.
52         */
53        public boolean isFull();
54
55        /**
56         * Return the element at the front of this queue. This
57         * operation does not change the state of this queue.
58         * @return the element at the front of this queue
59         * @throws EmptyQueueException if the queue is empty
60         */
61        public E peek();
62
63        /**
64         * Determine the number of elements stored in this queue.
65         * @return the number of elements in this queue
66         */
67        public int size();
68    }
```

SUMMING UP

A queue is a First-In-First-Out collection. Queues have many applications in computing, including ordering requests for services in a first-come-first-served order and buffering of network traffic. Changing the nature of the collection from dynamic to static such that the collection's *size* is bounded by a capacity requires additional methods and rethinking the pre-conditions of operations.

Figure 7.1 The behavior of Queue's methods.

Method	Purpose	New Object State	Returned Value
Queue<String> q = new LinkedQueue<String>()	To create an empty Queue q.	*capacity*= 5 *size*= 0 *front*= null *rear*= 1st queue slot	a LinkedQueue object for Strings using the default capacity
q.enqueue ("A")	To add an element to an empty queue.	*size*= 1 "A" *front*= "A" *rear*= 2nd queue slot	
q. enqueue ("B")	To add an element to a non-empty queue.	*size*= 2 "A" "B" *front*= "A" *rear*= 3rd queue slot	
q.isFull()	To see if q is full.		false
q. enqueue ("C")	To add "C" to q.	*size*= 3 "A" "B" "C" *front*= "A" *rear*= 4th queue slot	
String str = q.peek()	To peek at the front element of q.		"A"
str = q.dequeue()	To delete the front element from q.	*size*= 2 "B" "C" *front*= "B" *rear*= 3rd queue slot	"A"
q.isEmpty()	To see if q is empty.		false
str = q.dequeue()	To delete front element from q.	*size*= 1 "C" *front*= "C" *rear*= 2nd queue slot	"B"
str = q.dequeue()	To delete front element from q and produce an empty queue.	*size*= 0 *front*= null *rear*= 1st queue slot	"C"
q.isEmpty()	To see if q is empty.		true
str = q.peek()	To peek at the front element of q and check peek() pre-condition.		empty queue exception

■ **7.4** Designing a Test Plan

The majority of the test plan will test for the kinds of things we have looked for before:

- correct instantiation
- that accessor methods return the correct values
- that insertions really do insertions and in the right place
- that deletions really do deletions and return the correct element

What is different for us now is the bounds testing. When capacity wasn't an issue, the only bounds test was for lower bounds: an empty structure and a structure with only a single element (look at the test plan for `Stack` in Chapter 6 and its description for a recent example).

Now, of course, we have an upper bound to test as well, but the principle is the same as testing for lower bounds. We need to

- instantiate a queue with a small capacity.
- verify that there is no problem inserting and accessing elements up to the queue's capacity, paying special attention to when the queue is at its capacity and when it is one element short of capacity.
- verify that an attempt to insert into a full queue generates the expected error.

The last two tests (accessing/inserting when *size* == *capacity* − 1 and *size* == *capacity*) check for those pesky off-by-one errors. As before, we use the queue's accessor operations to provide state information, which we can use to verify the correctness of the Queue ADT operations.

Test Case 7.1 shows how we might test for inserting up to the queue's capacity. The other test cases can easily be created using the `Stack` test cases as a model. Note in Test Case 7.1 that once the queue is full, the *rear* attribute is null. This is because, at this point, there is nowhere to do another insertion.

SUMMING UP

Experience building test cases for other collection ADTs helps identify and create test cases for new ADTs. It is important, though, to be aware of the differences between the collection ADTs and to focus additional testing on those differences. Building test cases for upper bounds is very similar to building test cases for lower bounds and is as important.

Test Case 7.1 Enqueueing elements into a queue up to *capacity*.

Method	Purpose	Object State	Expected Result
Queue<String> q = new LinkedQueue<String>(3)	To create an empty Queue with a fixed capacity of 3.	*capacity*= 3 *size*= 0 *front*= null *rear*= 1st queue slot	a LinkedQueue object for Strings with a capacity of 3
q.enqueue("A")	To enqueue into empty queue.	*size*= 1 "A" *front*= "A" *rear*= 2nd queue slot	
q.enqueue("B")	To enqueue into a nonempty queue.	*size*= 2 "A" "B" *front*= "A" *rear*= 3rd queue slot	
q.enqueue("C")	To enqueue into a nonempty queue and reach the queue's capacity.	*size*= 3 "A" "B" "C" *front*= "A" *rear*= null	
q.size()	To verify queue state.		3
q.isEmpty()	To verify queue state.		false
q.isFull()	To verify queue state.		true
q.peek()	To verify queue state.		"A"
q.enqueue("oops")	To verify test for pre-condition for enqueue().		FullQueueException

CHECKPOINT

7.1 Why don't we provide a mutator method for the *capacity* attribute?

7.2 How does making the Queue size fixed change the design of Queue compared to having Queue be dynamic?

7.3 What will the queue look like after the insertions are done from the following code segment? What will the queue look like after the dequeue() operation executes? (with thanks to Scott Adams)

```
Queue<String> q = new LinkedQueue<String>(5);
q.enqueue("Wally");
q.enqueue("Alice");
q.enqueue("Dogbert");
q.front();
q.dequeue();
```

■ 7.5 List Implementation Using the Adapter Design Pattern

We will look at two ways to implement the Queue ADT. The first makes use of the Adapter design pattern again, but with a small complication. The second uses an array, but with a slight twist (more like a bend really).

For our first implementation of `Queue` we will make use of the Adapter design pattern and, as we did for `Stack`, will use an implementation of `List` to provide the needed behavior. This gives you more experience working with `List` and will strengthen your appreciation for the access characteristics of an ADT and of the fundamental data structures.

For the most part, our task list addresses mapping `List` to `Queue`:

Task list for implementing `Queue` using `List`

1. Choose which implementation of `List` is most appropriate for representing `Queue`.

2. Decide which attributes from `List` will play the roles of the `Queue` attributes.

3. Select methods from `List` that will provide the behavior needed for the `Queue` API.

4. Decide how to support `Queue` behavior or attributes not supported by `List`.

5. Define the exception classes `FullQueueException` and `EmptyQueueException`.

7.5.1 `ListQueue` Task 1: Choose Which Implementation of `List` Is Most Appropriate for Representing a Queue

A queue, like a stack, is a linear collection. Unlike a stack, which only allows operations at one end of the linear structure, a queue requires operations to be carried out at both ends. This seemingly small difference has a big impact on our decision making at this point.

If we choose `ArrayList` as the data structure to implement `Queue`, then, depending on which end of the list we call the *head* and which the *tail*, either insertions will be efficient and deletions expensive, or the other way around. However, we have seen that a doubly linked list can very efficiently do insertions and removals at either end (assuming the list maintains references to both ends of the queue, as our linked-list implementation of `List` from Chapter 5 does). It is modifications to the middle of the list that are inefficient for linked lists, but since we never access a queue in the middle, this is not a problem.

`LinkedList` is better than `ArrayList` for accesses at both ends of the list

7.5.2 `ListQueue` Task 2: Decide Which Attributes from `List` Will Play the Roles of the `Queue` Attributes

`Queue` has four attributes that must be accounted for either directly in `Queue` or indirectly through `List`: *size, front, rear,* and *capacity*.

The *size* attribute of `Queue` is nicely matched by the *size* attribute of `LinkedList` and is accessible through `List.size()`.

size attribute

There are two possibilities for finding matches for *front* and *rear*. We can either have the *front* of the queue correspond to the *head* of List with Queue's *rear* matching List's *tail*, or the other way around. Since the former is more intuitive, we will use it.

front and *rear* attributes

Finally, *capacity* has no analog, or associated attribute, in List, so it must be handled directly by Queue.

capacity attribute

Table 7.1 summarizes the four attributes.

7.5.3 ListQueue Task 3: Select Methods from List That Will Provide the Behavior Needed for the Queue API

Finding methods from List that match the behavior of methods from Queue requires looking at the specification of Queue, the documentation for List, and the attribute mappings from Table 7.1. As you might have guessed, we'll use the same methods from List to implement Queue that we used to implement Stack. What will change, of course, are the method arguments.

With that in mind, it is important to remind you that we cannot precisely define the arguments to the List methods until the question of attribute associations has been settled. For example, we need to have decided that the *rear* attribute of Queue would correspond to the position at List's *tail* attribute before we can say that Queue's enqueue(element) matches add(list.size(), element) from List. Table 7.2 gives the Queue and List operation associations.

When using the Adapter pattern, identify analogs for attributes first, *then* find analogs for the methods

7.5.4 ListQueue Task 4: Decide How to Support Queue Behavior or Attributes Not Supported by List

When we used the Adapter pattern to adapt a List to implement a Stack, all of the behavior we needed was provided by the List implementation. As can be seen from Table 7.2, not all of the Queue methods have counterparts in List. This is not surprising since we are implementing Queue with a fixed capacity, while LinkedList implements an unbounded list and so has no notion of, nor support for, *capacity*.

But that doesn't mean that the Adapter pattern doesn't apply. It simply means that we will have to provide the unsupported behavior in our Queue class directly. In using the Adapter pattern, we have made good use of the principle of code reuse, but will still have to write some code of our own. We can live with this.

Table 7.1 Attribute associations between Queue and List.

Queue Attribute	List Attribute or Method
size	size()
front	*head*—position 0 of the list
rear	*tail*—position size() of the list
capacity	none

Table 7.2 Queue operations and the equivalent List operations assuming the attribute associations of Table 7.1.

Queue Operation	List Operation
void enqueue(element)	void add(list.size(), element)
E dequeue()	E remove(0)
E front()	E get(0)
int size()	int size()
boolean isEmpty()	boolean isEmpty()
void clear()	void clear()
boolean isFull()	*none*
capacity()	*none*

The design of our ListQueue class using the Adapter pattern with LinkedList as the backing store for our queue is shown in Figure 7.2. You should compare this with the Adapter design pattern in Figure 6.4 and the design of ListStack in Figure 6.6.

The implementation for the class is shown in Listing 7.2. It is remarkably short and easy. The class uses two exception classes, EmptyQueueException and FullQueueException, which are presented in the last task.

7.5.5 ListQueue Task 5: Define the Exception Classes FullQueueException and EmptyQueueException

You can easily define your own exception class by extending an existing exception class, either one provided by Java or one you have already created. The only decision you must make is whether the exception should be checked or unchecked.[1]

Recall from Chapter 2 that if the exception is to be checked, you extend Exception or some class descended from Exception other than RuntimeException. If the exception is to be unchecked, you extend RunTimeException or some class descended from RuntimeException.

Checked and unchecked exceptions

The custom exception class only needs to provide two constructors. Everything else that is needed is inherited from the superclass. EmptyQueueException in Listing 7.3 is shown as an example.

---

[1]As a reminder, the compiler will check that any method that generates a checked exception either is in a try-catch block or the invoking method throws the exception again. Unchecked exceptions are much more relaxed. The compiler doesn't check that you have handled them, leaving it to the programmer to decide what to do.

Figure 7.2 Design of the `ListQueue` class using the Adapter design pattern.

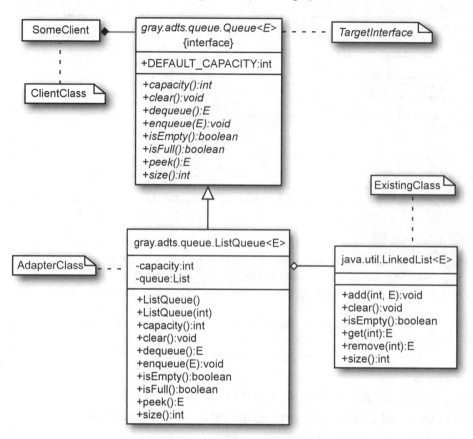

Listing 7.2 The `ListQueue` class implemented using the Adapter design pattern.

```
1    package gray.adts.queue;
2
3    import java.util.LinkedList;
4    import java.util.List;
5    import java.lang.IllegalArgumentException;
6
7    /**
8     *  Queue ADT implemented using the Adapter design pattern and
9     *  java.util.LinkedList as the storage data structure. This
10    *  version of Queue assumes an upper bound on the number of
11    *  elements that can be stored in the queue.
12    */
13   public class ListQueue<E> implements Queue<E> {
14     private List<E> queue;
```

```
15        private int capacity;
16
17        /**
18         * Default constructor. Create an empty queue with the
19         * default capacity.
20         */
21        public ListQueue() {
22            this( DEFAULT_CAPACITY );
23        }
24
25        /**
26         * Create a queue with a capacity of <tt>maxElements</tt>.
27         * @param maxElements int must be greater than 0.
28         * @throws IllegalArgumentException if <tt>maxElement</tt>
29         * is less than or equal to 0.
30         */
31        public ListQueue(int maxElements) {
32            this.queue = new LinkedList<E>();
33            if ( maxElements <= 0 ) {
34                throw new IllegalArgumentException();
35            }
36            this.capacity = maxElements;
37        }
38
39        /**
40         * Return the upper bound on the number of elements this
41         * Queue can store.
42         * @return the capacity of this queue.
43         */
44        public int capacity() {
45            return this.capacity;
46        }
47
48        /**
49         *  Empty the queue of all elements.
50         */
51        public void clear() {
52            this.queue.clear();
53        }
54
55        /**
56         * Remove and return the element at the front of the queue.
57         * @return this queue's front element
58         * @throws EmptyQueueException if the queue is empty
59         */
60        public E dequeue() {
61            if (this.queue.isEmpty()) {
```

```
62                   throw new EmptyQueueException("The queue is empty");
63              }
64          return this.queue.remove(0);
65      }
66
67      /**
68       * Add <tt>element</tt> to the end of the queue.
69       * @throws FullQueueException if the queue is full
70       */
71      public void enqueue(E element) {
72          if ( this.isFull() ) {
73              throw new FullQueueException("The queue is full");
74          }
75          this.queue.add(this.queue.size(), element);
76      }
77
78      /**
79       * Return the element at the front of this queue. This
80       * operation does not change the state of this queue.
81       * @return the element at the front of this queue
82       * @throws EmptyQueueException if the queue is empty
83       */
84      public E peek() {
85        if ( this.queue.isEmpty() ) {
86          throw new EmptyQueueException("The queue is empty");
87        }
88        return this.queue.get(0);
89      }
90
91      /**
92       * Determine if this queue has any elements.
93       * @return <tt>true</tt> if this queue has no elements
94       *     (<tt>size() == 0</tt>); <tt>false</tt> otherwise.
95       */
96      public boolean isEmpty() {
97          return this.queue.isEmpty();
98      }
99
100      /**
101       * Determine if this queue has room for more elements.
102       * @return <tt>true</tt> if this queue has no room for more elements
103       * (<tt>size() == capacity()</tt>); <tt>false</tt> otherwise.
104       */
105      public boolean isFull() {
106          return this.queue.size() == this.capacity;
107      }
108
```

```
109        /**
110         * Determine the number of elements stored in this queue.
111         * @return The number of elements in this queue.
112         */
113        public int size() {
114            return this.queue.size();
115        }
116    }
```

Listing 7.3 `EmptyQueueException`—a custom exception class.

```
1    package gray.adts.queue;
2
3    /**
4     * Thrown when there is an attempt to access the front
5     * of an empty queue.
6     */
7    public class EmptyQueueException extends RuntimeException {
8
9        public EmptyQueueException() {
10            super();
11        }
12
13        public EmptyQueueException( String errMsg ) {
14            super(" " + errMsg );
15        }
16    }
```

SUMMING UP

With the Adapter design pattern, the existing class need not provide *all* the behavior required by the target interface. The first step in applying the Adapter pattern is always to match attributes of the target interface to attributes/methods from the existing class. Then you can meaningfully determine which methods in the existing class provide behavior needed by methods in the target interface. Understanding the access characteristics of candidate data structures is essential to making good implementation decisions.

CHECKPOINT

7.4 When applying the Adapter pattern, why is it important to identify analogs for the attributes *before* analogs for the methods?

7.5 Describe how we could get an off-by-one error if we made a mistake in either Table 7.1 or Table 7.2.

7.6 Is there anything wrong with implementing `front()` as follows, assuming we used our Adapter pattern and a `List` to store the queue elements?

```
public E front() {
    if ( this.isEmpty() )
        throw new EmptyQueueException( "The queue is empty" );
    return queue.get( 0 );
}
```

■ 7.6 `ArrayQueue`: Implementing Queue Using an Array

When we discussed the relative merits of `ArrayList` and `LinkedList` as the data structure to use in implementing `ListQueue`, we quickly decided that `ArrayList` was inappropriate because arrays provide poor performance for accesses at the head of the list.

While using the array implementation of a `List` (`ArrayList`) for our `Queue` didn't seem to work for us earlier, that doesn't mean that we have to give up completely on arrays and the advantages they offer. Let's re-examine the problem more closely.

There are two obvious ways we can map the elements of a queue to an array.

The problem with arrays

1. Have `Queue`'s *front* always be at index 0 of the array, with `Queue`'s *rear* moving toward the right end of the array as insertions are made. Supporting insertions at the end of an array can be done very efficiently—all we need to do is insert the new element at array index *rear* and then advance *rear*. It is deletions at the front of the queue (index 0) that are expensive because they require us to shift all the elements down one cell so that the element that is to be the new front of the queue is always at index 0 (see Figure 7.3 (a)).

2. Alternatively, we can have `Queue`'s *rear* always be at index 0 of the array, with `Queue`'s *front* toward the right end of the array. This orientation makes deletions efficient, since we just have to return the element at position *front* and then decrement *front*. Now it is insertions that are expensive, since we need to shift all the queue elements up one position to make room for the new element inserted at *rear*, fixed at index 0 of the array (see Figure 7.3 (b)).

Clearly neither of these orientations works particularly well for us, so we need to use what we have learned and *think differently* about how we might represent a Queue using an array. Let's assume that we want to use something like the first orientation described above. To begin, why insist that the front of the queue be fixed at index 0? Why not let *front*'s value change to match the storage of elements in the array (queue), rather than making the storage of elements in the array change (via a series of element move operations) to match the fixed position of the queue *front*? Hmm . . . looks promising.

Idea: instead of moving the data to the front, move front to the data

Figure 7.3 Two possibilities for implementing a queue using an array.

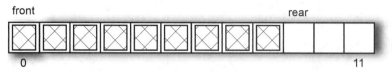

(a) Queue.*front* is always at 0—shift elements *left* on dequeue().

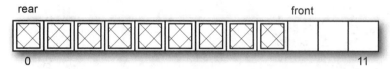

(b) Queue.*rear* is always at 0—shift elements *right* on enqueue().

A problem with this idea is that *front* and *rear* will move toward, and eventually reach, the end of the array, and the queue will report that it is out of room, even though there will be many empty places in the queue to the left of the advancing *front*. The dilemma is illustrated in Figure 7.4. It begins to look like using an array is still not practical after all.

Part of our problem is that we have been viewing the array in the same way we would logically view a queue—as a linear collection. What if we maintain the *logical* view of a queue as linear, but treat the array representing the queue as *circular* so that when *front* or *rear* arrive at the end of the array, they automatically wraparound to the actual front of the array? The result is shown in Figure 7.5. In this view, *front* and *rear* keep moving around and around the circular array. This neatly solves the problems described above and lets us use an array to efficiently represent a queue. Cool! Be willing to explore alternatives!

Idea: Treat the array as circular

As we have done several times now, we list the tasks we must complete:

1. Map Queue ADT attributes to a circular array implementation.

2. Implement the Queue ADT operations as methods.

Figure 7.4 Letting *front* advance through the array.

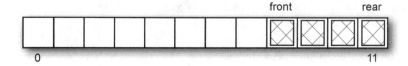

Figure 7.5 A circular view of a queue.

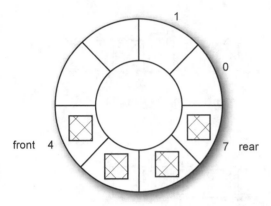

7.6.1 `ArrayQueue` Task 1: Map Queue ADT Attributes to a Circular Array Implementation

The four Queue ADT attributes are realized directly as data fields in ArrayQueue. The fifth data field is the array that will be storing the queue's elements and is specific to this implementation of the Queue ADT.

```
public class ArrayQueue<E> implements Queue<E> {
    private E[] queue;
    private int capacity;
    private int size;
    private int front;
    private int rear;
```

There are still several issues we must address.

What Should the Initial Values for *Front* and *Rear* Be?

This is really important because a number of operations in the ADT rely on these attributes and all operations must be in agreement about both the *meaning* of the attributes and their actual representation within the class.

Since *rear* will reference the place in the queue where the *next* insertion is to be done, it makes sense to initialize it to 0 so the first element of the queue will be the first element of the array. As an aside, based on this description we can establish that the enqueue() operation will do the insertion at position *rear* and *then* increment *rear* so that it is in the correct position for the next insertion. Note that this is consistent with the view developed earlier of inserting at position size() of a list.

Initialize *rear* to 0

The initial value for *front* is a little more problematic. The specification says that when the queue is empty, *front* should reference a "null" value, which we have always taken to mean "a reference to something that can't be part of the collection." One purpose of this would be to signify that the queue is empty.

One possibility is to initialize the attribute to -1, which is clearly outside the bounds of any array, so meets the criteria outlined above. Unfortunately, while this approach will work, it will complicate the code with tests for special cases. I'll back this claim up with an example shortly, but first let's consider a simpler alternative.

We need not rely on *front* to test for an empty queue since a test for the attribute *size*== 0 does this much more simply and intuitively. Also, we can put other checks in place to guarantee that we don't inadvertently access the queue when it is empty. For example, the pre-condition for `dequeue()` and `peek()` is that the queue is not empty, which we can explicitly check. This frees us up to choose a more convenient initial value for *front*. Since *rear* == 0 is where the first element will be inserted, it makes sense to start *front* at 0 too, since the first insertion will be at index 0, making this the first element to be removed. The safeguards just described will guarantee that *front* is not accessed until there is a meaningful value there.

Initialize *front* to 0

This description immediately suggests the default constructor in Listing 7.4. Line 3 of the constructor requires some explanation. `ArrayQueue<E>` is a generic collection type with type parameter `E`. So it makes sense that, if we are going to store the elements in an array, the element type of the array will be `E`. That is what happens. But Java will not allow you to do

```
this.queue = new E[ capacity ];
```

An explanation would require a complicated discussion that is beyond the scope of this book. The solution, which you see on line 3, is to create an array of the most general type Java can create, `Object[]`, and cast it to be an array of type `E[]`. This will generate a warning from the compiler saying there is an unchecked type conversion (from `Object[]` to `E[]`), which you can safely ignore (indeed, there isn't much you can do about this).

How Should *Front* and *Rear* Be Updated for the `dequeue()` and `enqueue()` Operations?

Since we have established that *front* holds the index of the first element of the queue, doing a deletion means extracting the value at position *front* in the array, then incrementing *front* (with wraparound as described below). Similarly, since *rear* holds the index in the array where the next insertion will be made, we'll do the insertion and then increment *rear* (with wraparound), so that it is ready for the next `enqueue()` operation.

Updating *front* and *rear*

Listing 7.4 Constructor for array-based implementation of a circular queue.

```
1    public ArrayQueue<E> () {
2        this.capacity = DEFAULT_CAPACITY;
3        this.queue = (E[]) new Object[ capacity ];
4        this.size  = 0;
5        this.front = 0;
6        this.rear  = 0;
7    }
```

What Do We Do When *Front* and *Rear* Reach the End of the Array? That Is, How Do We Handle the Wraparound?

The index of the last element in the array is *capacity* − 1. When either *front* or *rear* reach this index and need to advance, we need them to wraparound to the beginning of the array (index 0). There are two possibilities. Let's use *front* as an example. The logic would be the same for *rear*.

Wraparound for front and rear

First, we can increment *front* and then test to see if it is at index *capacity*. If so, we reset it to 0; otherwise *front* has the correct value and we do nothing, as follows:

```
front++;
if ( front == capacity ) // do wraparound
    front = 0;
```

Alternatively, we can do the increment and apply the modulus operator to the result as follows:

```
front = (front + 1) % capacity;
```

The result will always be a value in the range 0 to *capacity* − 1, with the wraparound to 0 occurring automatically when (*front* + 1) is equal to *capacity*, which is what we need. For example, assume *capacity* is 10. When *front* is in the range 0 to 8 and we add 1, we get a new value in the range 1 to 9. When we apply % *capacity* to this value, we get the value back (for example, 1 % 10 is 1 and 9 % 10 is 9). But when *front* is 9 and we add 1, we have 10 % 10, which is 0. This is elegant.

7.6.2 `ArrayQueue` Task 1: Implement the Queue ADT Operations as Methods

In the rest of this section we'll look at some of the more interesting aspects of implementing the Queue ADT using a circular array.

7.6.3 Determining Whether the Queue Is Empty

The simplest and most intuitive way to determine whether the queue is empty is to see if its *size* is 0 (see Listing 7.5).

isEmpty()

Listing 7.5 Array-based implementation of `Queue.isEmpty()`.

```
1   /**
2    * Determine whether the queue is empty.
3    * @return <tt>true</tt>, if the queue is empty, <tt>false</tt>
4    * otherwise
5    */
6   public boolean isEmpty() {
7       return this.size == 0;
8   }
```

Now, this looks pretty easy, so why present it? The method `isEmpty()` relies on the enqueue, dequeue, and `clear` operations to properly update the *size* attribute. While this is an obvious thing to point out, it is an easy mistake to make. It is common for programmers to be careful and focused when dealing with code they perceive to be tricky, but to be less diligent when working with code they perceive to be simple and obvious. This leads to bugs and headaches later on.

So:

1. Be careful—even with the "easy" stuff.
2. Understand how each method *changes* the attributes.
3. Understand how each method *uses* the attributes.

Understand the relationship between attributes and operations

7.6.4 Inserting an Element into a Queue

By definition, all insertions are done at the rear of the queue. The pre-conditions and responsibilities tell us what we have to do. The only tricky part is making sure the order in which we use and update *rear* is correct, so we pseudocode the method first (see Listing 7.6).

enqueue(E)

Steps 2 and 3 in the pseudocode cannot be switched. This is a very good example of the importance of being *very clear* about what the ADT attributes mean and

---

Listing 7.6 Array-based implementation of `Queue.enqueue()`.

```
/**
 * Insert element at the rear of the queue.
 * @param element the element to be inserted
 * post       element is placed at the rear of the queue
 *            size is incremented by 1
 *            rear is position where the next element will be inserted
 * @throws   FullQueueException if isFull() is true
 */
public void enqueue( E element )
                throws FullQueueException{
```

1. if the queue is full throw a FullQueueException
```
    if ( this.isFull() )
        throw new FullQueueException();
```
2. put element at the rear of the queue
```
    this.queue[rear] = element;
```
3. advance rear with wraparound
```
    this.rear = (this.rear + 1 ) % this.capacity;
```
4. increment size by 1
```
    this.size++;
}
```

---

how they will be implemented. I was deliberately careful above to explain that *rear* represents the location where the new element is to be inserted. Confusion or carelessness about these details will lead to some frustrating (but well-deserved!) bugs.

In the discussion about the initial value to assign to *front*, we suggested that -1 was a possibility, but that it would complicate the code. Now that you have seen how simple the code is when you use 0 as the initial value for front, you can meaningfully compare it to what the code would look like if you used -1 instead. The code is the same (see Listing 7.7) except for the additional test to see whether the queue is empty. If the queue is empty, *front* must be -1 and you have to set it back to 0 before you can proceed. You also reset *rear* to 0 to make sure that *front* and *rear* are in agreement about where the new first element of the queue will be. You need to reset *rear* because you can't be sure about the value it had when the queue became empty.

What is especially irksome about this approach is that the test has to be done for every insertion, but will only be "useful" when the queue is empty.

7.6.5 Clearing the Queue

To really clear a queue we need to make all the occupied cells of the array `null`. Since `dequeue()` does this for each element that is removed, we just keep calling it until the queue is empty. Then we re-initialize the queue's attributes to the values they had when the queue was first created, as shown in Listing 7.8. The Exercises have you take a second look at this method.

`clear()`

Listing 7.7 Alternative implementation of `Queue.enqueue()` assuming attribute *front* is -1 when the queue is empty.

```
 1    // if we use -1 as the starting point for front
 2    public void enqueue( Object element ) throws FullQueueException {
 3        if ( this.isFull() )
 4            throw new FullQueueException( "The queue is full" );
 5
 6        if ( this.isEmpty() ) {   // front is -1
 7            this.front = 0;
 8            this.rear = 0;          // make sure front and rear agree
 9        }
10
11        this.queue[rear] = element;
12        this.rear = (this.rear + 1) % this.capacity;
13        this.size++;
14    }
```

Listing 7.8 Implementation of `Queue.clear()`.

```
1    /**
2     * Empty the queue of elements.
3     */
4    public void clear() {
5       // empty the queue, making all the array cells null
6       while ( !this.isEmpty() )
7          this.dequeue();
8       // loop post-condition: this.size is 0
9
10      this.front = 0;
11      this.rear = 0;
12   }
```

SUMMING UP

Recognizing that the `Queue` attributes *front* and *rear* represent the logical first element and next insertion slot of a queue and not necessarily any fixed position in an array was a first step to developing an efficient solution using arrays. The second step was realizing that we can view an array as circular—we don't have to live with it as linear.

CHECKPOINT

7.7 What are the essential characteristics of the circular array implementation that make it practical as a representation for a queue?

7.8 Could we have initialized *front* and *rear* to any value in the range 0 to *capacity* – 1?

7.9 What would happen if the pseudocode steps labeled 2 and 3 in `ArrayQueue`'s implementation of `enqueue()` were switched?

■ **7.7** Testing the Implementation

The implementation of the test plan from Section 7.3 is left as an exercise; it is quite straightforward if you use the test code developed for any of the collection types we have examined so far.

Remember that, once you have implemented the test plan for, say, `ListQueue`, all you need to do to test the array implementation is change one line so that it instantiates an `ArrayQueue` object instead. Both implementations should provide *exactly* the same behavior, so you should see no changes in the output.

There is one other consideration with respect to the array-based implementation. Since we went to some pains to determine the initial values to use for *front* and *rear*, how to advance them and handle the wraparound, we should write a separate test plan for this. In particular, when testing the implementation using the circular array, we need to be sure that we do enough insertions and deletions so that the *front* and *rear* attributes get wrapped around to the beginning of the array. We should also test that queue accesses at and around the boundaries 0 and *capacity* work properly. One possibility for such a test plan is given in Test Case 7.2.

SUMMING UP

As we saw in the last chapter, the test plan developed based on the ADT description is pure black box testing—it focuses on the expected behavior as specified by the ADT. Once the implementation is complete, additional tests may suggest themselves based on the specifics of the implementation.

■ 7.8 Evaluation of the Implementations

The two implementations use different backing stores, so we must provide two analyses.

Since we used the Adapter design pattern to implement `ListQueue`, the cost of its operations are really based on the runtime cost of the backing store (`LinkedList`) and the overhead of the message forwarding. Consequently, it should not be surprising that the analysis of `ListQueue` is almost identical to that of `ListStack`.

The cost of the accessor methods `size()` and `isEmpty()` is O(1) because that is their cost for `List`. The accessor methods unique to `ListQueue`, `capacity()` and `isFull()`, will also be O(1) because all they do is return the value stored in a data field.

Recall that we chose the linked-list implementation of `List` as the backing store for our first implementation because it is very efficient at doing accesses at the *head* and *tail* of the list (*front* and *rear* of a queue). The cost for these operations is also O(1) (review the analysis discussion from Chapter 3 if you don't recall why this is so). `LinkedList`'s `clear()` method simply updates the two link fields of its dummy header to make the list empty, so it has a fixed cost as well. Table 7.3 shows the asymptotic costs of the methods.

The accessor methods of `ArrayQueue` are all O(1) because they merely return a value. The `peek()` method must do an array access, but this also has a fixed cost. The mutator methods that insert and remove single elements have a cost of O(1) because they also have a fixed number of steps that is independent of the queue's size. The implementation of `clear()` empties the queue by removing the elements

Test Case 7.2 Checking wraparound for the circular array implementation of the Queue ADT.

Method	Purpose	Object State	Expected Result
Queue<String> q = new ArrayQueue<String>(3)	To create an empty Queue q with capacity to store 3 elements.	*capacity* = 3 *size* = 0 *front* = null *rear* = 1st queue slot	an ArrayQueue object for Strings
q.enqueue("A")	To enqueue into an empty queue.	*size* = 1 "A" *front* = "A" *rear* = 2nd queue slot	
q.enqueue("B")	To enqueue into a non-empty queue.	*size* = 2 "A" "B" *front* = "A" *rear* = 3rd queue slot	
q.enqueue("C")	To enqueue into a non-empty queue and reach the queue's capacity.	*size* = 3 "A" "B" "C" *front* = "A" *rear* = undefined null	
q.size()	To verify queue state.		3
q.isFull()	To verify queue state.		true
q.dequeue()	To remove front element.	*size* = 2 "B" "C" *front* = "B" *rear* = 3rd queue slot	"A"
q.enqueue("D")	To test wraparound on insert.	*size* = 2 "B" "C" "D" *front* = "B" *rear* = undefined null	
q.dequeue()	To remove front element.	*size* = 2 "C" "D" *front* = "C" *rear* = 3rd queue slot	"B"
q.dequeue()	To remove front element.	*size* = 1 "D" *front* = "D" *rear* = 2nd queue slot	"C"
q.dequeue()	To test wraparound on delete.	*size* = 0 *front* = null *rear* = 1st queue slot	"D"

one by one using `dequeue()`. In the worst case, the queue is full to capacity, making the cost $O(n)$ where n is the *capacity* of the queue. Table 7.4 shows the asymptotic costs of the methods for `ArrayQueue`.

Table 7.3 The cost of `ListQueue` operations.

`ListQueue` Operation	List Operation	Cost
enqueue(element)	add(size(), element)	O(1)
dequeue()	remove(0)	O(1)
peek()	get(0)	O(1)
clear()	clear()	O(1)

Table 7.4 The cost of `ArrayQueue` operations.

`ArrayQueue`	Operation Cost
enqueue(element)	O(1)
dequeue()	O(1)
peek()	O(1)
clear()	$O(n)$

INVESTIGATE A First Look at Priority Queues

Description

Like queues, priority queues restrict access to the collection's elements. Unlike queues, which follow a FIFO protocol, priority queues maintain an ordering of the elements based on some externally defined priority, so that the *highest priority* element *in* the priority queue is the *first* element *out* of the queue. This makes a priority queue a *highest-priority-in/first-out* (HPIFO) collection. From this perspective, a queue is a priority queue in which an element's priority is determined by its arrival time, with the oldest item in the queue having the highest priority.

A priority queue is a highest-priority-in/first-out data structure

The application of priority to the elements of a queue has many uses, in and out of computing:

■ We frequently make To Do lists in which we enumerate the things we have to do and the order in which we need to do them. This ordering is determined by some set of criteria (due date, closing time, fun (!), appointment time, etc.). When a To Do item is completed, we move to the next most important item on the list. A complication in computing as well as in everyday life, is that new tasks can arrive that change the order of the items already in the To Do list.

Uses of priority queues

■ Emergency rooms are a very good example of priority queues. When an ill or injured person arrives at the emergency room, the order in which that person is treated depends on the severity of the problem and the status of patients already waiting to be seen. The patient with the greatest medical need receives the highest priority in receiving attention.

■ Priority queues abound in computing. Operating systems, for example, maintain many prioritized task queues:

A **process Ready Queue** keeps references to all the processes in the system that are ready to run and are waiting on access to the cpu. These processes can be ordered based on a priority. For example, administrative jobs might be regarded as the most important, followed by faculty jobs, and finally, alas, student jobs. When the processor becomes free, the highest priority process in the queue is removed and assigned to the cpu.

A **printer queue** can order print jobs based the priority of the sender (administration, faculty, students), or, perhaps, on the size of the print job and how long it has been sitting in the printer queue, or some combination of these could be used.

An **I/O request queue** contains a collection of requests to do some I/O, to a hard disk, for example. The priority of a request can be based on a number of criteria: fairness, throughput, response time, or something else entirely.

The main objective of this *Investigate* is to look at issues in code reuse via inheritance and composition in an OO language. We will revisit priority queues in Chapter 10, where we will take a quite different approach. At that point you will see that the approach taken here is flawed.[2]

Objectives

- Introduction to the behavior of priority queues.
- Compare using composition and inheritance to build a new class from existing classes.
- Use inheritance with interfaces and classes.
- Implement a `PriorityQueue` class.

Design

Our first step is to provide a specification for the PriorityQueue ADT. A priority queue observes the protocol that the highest priority element in the queue is the first element out (HPIFO). The priority of an element is determined externally and is dependent on the application. It is this priority that determines which element is the next to be removed from the priority queue. Inserting an element into a priority queue is done via an `enqueue` operation and a deletion is done via a `dequeue` operation that always removes the element with the highest priority. We'll assume for now that *priority* is represented as an integer and that the lower the number, the higher the priority.

The PriorityQueue ADT

Description
A priority queue is an HPIFO collection. This ADT describes a priority queue with unbounded capacity and whose element type is left unspecified.

---

[2] I won't tell you what the flaw is now, but I will tell you there are valuable lessons to be learned in looking at an approach that seems to be right, but doesn't make the cut.

Properties

1. The next element returned from the priority queue is the element with the highest priority.
2. Priority is represented as an integer, the lower the integer, the higher the priority.

Attributes

size:	The number of elements in the priority queue: $0 \leq size$ at all times.

Operations

PriorityQueue()
pre-condition:	none
responsibilities:	constructor—initialize the priority queue attribute
post-condition:	*size* is set to 0
returns:	nothing

enqueue(*Type* element)
pre-condition:	element has the lowest priority of all elements in the priority queue
responsibilities:	insert element into the priority queue such that all other elements have higher priority
post-condition:	element is placed in the priority queue
	size is incremented by 1
returns:	nothing

enqueue(int priority, *Type* element)
pre-condition:	none
responsibilities:	insert element into the priority queue with the given priority
post-condition:	element is placed in the priority queue
	size is incremented by 1
returns:	nothing

dequeue()
pre-condition:	isEmpty() is false
responsibilities:	remove and return the element with the highest priority
post-condition:	the element is no longer in the queue
	size is decremented by 1
returns:	the element removed
throws:	empty priority queue exception if pre-condition is not met

peek()
pre-condition:	isEmpty() is false
responsibilities:	return the element with the highest priority
post-condition:	the queue is unchanged
returns:	the element with the highest priority
throws:	empty queue exception if pre-condition is not met

size()
pre-condition:	none
responsibilities:	determine the number of elements in the priority queue
post-condition:	the priority queue is unchanged
returns:	*size*

isEmpty()
> pre-condition: none
> responsibilities: determine if the priority queue has any elements in it
> post-condition: the priority queue is unchanged
> returns: true if the priority queue is empty (size()== 0), false otherwise

clear()
> pre-condition: none
> responsibilities: empty the queue of elements
> post-condition: there are no elements in the queue
> *size* is 0

Given the apparent similarities between Queue and PriorityQueue, it is natural to ask if we can use an implementation of Queue to implement PriorityQueue. We know of two approaches to create a new class from existing classes: composition and inheritance. The following questions explore these possibilities:

1. Write the Java interface, PriorityQueue, based on the ADT specification.

2. Independently of how PriorityQueue is implemented, it will have to be tested.

   a. How much, if any, of the test plan created for Queue can be applied to PriorityQueue?

   b. Provide a complete test plan for PriorityQueue.

3. *Building using composition.* Assume we want to use composition to create a PriorityQueue class using Queue; that is, the PriorityQueue class contains ("has a") Queue as a data field. This sounds like the Adapter design pattern. Let's see if this is feasible.

   a. Using the material from Section 7.5 as a model, map the attributes and methods of PriorityQueue to Queue.

   b. Following Figure 7.2, draw the UML diagram showing the relationship between your PriorityQueue class and some implementation of Queue.

   c. What method from PriorityQueue has no counterpart in Queue?

   d. What access do you need to the Queue implementation's attributes to implement the methods identified in the last question? How is this done in Java?

   e. What is your opinion of this approach? Does it seem appropriate? That is, will it work? Are there risks or potential complications?

4. *Building using inheritance.* Given the descriptions of and interfaces for Queue and PriorityQueue, it seems intuitive to say that a PriorityQueue "is a kind of" Queue.

   a. Assume this is so and draw the UML diagram showing the inheritance relationship between Queue and PriorityQueue.

   b. Add class diagrams for ListQueue (implements Queue) and ListPriorityQueue (implements PriorityQueue and extends ListQueue) to your UML diagram.

c. Based on your understanding of Queue and PriorityQueue, will any of the methods PriorityQueue inherits from Queue need to be overridden? If so, which ones and why?

d. The method enqueue(int priority, E element) will have to be implemented in PriorityQueue. What access do you need to ListQueue's attributes to do this? How is this done in Java?

e. What is your opinion of this approach? Does it seem appropriate? That is, will it work? Are there risks or potential complications?

5. How do the composition and inheritances approaches compare?

Implementation

Using one of the two approaches explored in the Design section, try to provide an implementation for PriorityQueue.

Testing

1. Using JUnit, implement the test plan created for PriorityQueue.
2. Find and fix any bugs.

SUMMING UP

A priority queue inserts elements in such a way that the next element dequeued is always the element with the highest priority. OO languages encourage the creation of new classes using inheritance and composition. It is possible to define a PriorityQueue class using a Queue class through inheritance and composition, but this requires looking carefully at the access modifiers for the Queue attributes. Each OO language handles this slightly differently. It is important to learn the meaning of a language's access modifiers, how they can be used, and what the possible risks are.

EXERCISES

Paper and Pencil

1. Queue: Fill in the blanks for the following table.

Method	Object State	Returned Value
Queue<String> q = new LinkedQueue<String>();		
q.enqueue("C");		
q.enqueue("A");		
q.enqueue("M");		
q.peek();		
q.dequeue();		

Method	Object State	Returned Value
q.peek();	_____	_____
q.isEmpty();	_____	_____
q.dequeue();	_____	_____
q.dequeue();	_____	_____
q.peek();	_____	_____
q.dequeue();	_____	_____

2. Queue: Explain how a queue is a priority queue in which arrival time determines priority.

3. PriorityQueue: Assuming a priority queue is implemented using List as the backing store, what is the cost of doing an insertion if the list is implemented using an array? Using a linked list? Provide an explanation.

Testing and Debugging

1. ArrayQueue: Two approaches were given for dealing with the wraparound of the attributes *front* and *rear* in ArrayQueue. Which do you think is faster? Can this be quantified? Explain.

2. Queue: Consider the following mechanism to handle the wraparound for *front*. Do they all work? If so, what do you think of them as implementations?
   a. *front* = (front == capacity) ? 0 : front++;
   b. *front* = front++ % capacity;
   c. *front* = ++front % capacity;

3. Queue: What are the implications of forgetting to include an isFull() method for a type whose size is static (e.g., the Queue implementations)?

4. The implementation of ArrayQueue.clear()is simple to write and test, but it is inefficient because of the method calls to dequeue(). Provide an alternative implementation that clears the array directly. Perform timing measurements to see what the improvement in speed is.

Design

1. Implement PriorityQueue using the Adapter pattern with List as the backing store.

2. Re-implement PriorityQueue assuming that the higher the number, the higher the priority. This is the opposite of what was implemented in the *Investigate* section. How does this affect the implementation and your test plan?

3. Re-implement CourierModel using a PriorityQueue.

4. What should happen if an element to be inserted into a priority queue had the same priority as an element already in the priority queue? In a case like this we want the element already in the priority queue to be removed before any other element of the same priority that was inserted later. One way to handle this is to implement the priority queue as a linked list of queues, with a separate queue for each priority. When an element is to be added to the priority queue, it goes to the back of the queue for its priority (in fact operating systems can employ

such a scheme for prioritizing processes). This guarantees that elements of the same priority leave the priority queue in the order in which they arrived. Design, implement, and test `PriorityQueue` using this approach.

Using the ADT

1. Redo the maze problem from Chapter 6 using a queue to store the path options. How does using a queue change the order in which path options are investigated?

2. Redo the palindrome problem from Chapter 6 using both a stack and a queue. The idea is to store each character of the input string (skipping blanks and punctuation again) in both the stack and the queue. Since a stack and a queue will provide the stored characters in the opposite order, you can easily confirm or disprove that a string is a palindrome.

Modifying the Code

1. Change the TDM networking simulation such that one input line is twice as fast as the others and so gets two slots in the output frame instead of one.

2. Change the TDM networking simulation (developed in the Focus on Problem Solving on the Web) so that it is asynchronous. In **asynchronous TDM**, any input device can fill any slot in a TDM frame. That is, input lines take turns filling the TDM frame slots until all the slots are filled or all the queues are empty. The advantage of this is that if one or more input lines have no data blocks to send, the slots they would have used in the TDM frame can be used by another input line. Consequently we make better use of the network's capacity since the only time a slot won't be used is if the queues for all the input lines are empty.

Because the slots are no longer permanently assigned to a particular input line, there needs to be some additional addressing information carried in each TDM frame slot that identifies the input line that provided the data block in the slot. Figure 7.6 illustrates the problem. Modify the solution to the synchronous TDM problem to make it asynchronous. You should output the same values and compare them to the results of synchronous TDM.

Figure 7.6 An example illustrating asynchronous TDM. Input lines take turns filling the TDM frame slots until all the slots are filled.

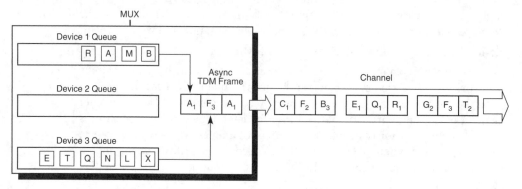

ON THE WEB

Additional study material is available at Addison-Wesley's Website http://www.aw.com/cssupport. This material includes the following:

■ Focus on Problem Solving: The Leaky Bucket Algorithm

Problem: At a low level, traffic travels over a computer network in frames. Each frame carries user data (the frame's "payload") and administrative information such as the address of the frame's destination and a checksum for error handling. Frames make their way from their source to their destination through a series of switches. Frames arrive at a switch on one port and exit on another port, as determined by the frame's destination address.

A network has a limited capacity to transfer information. Highways provide a simple analogy. There is no problem when traffic is light (well below the highway's capacity), but congestion can occur when there is a sudden increase in traffic, particularly at places where merging occurs. Highways work better when the traffic is evenly distributed along its length and insertion of additional traffic can be controlled. So it is with networks. Unfortunately, some applications produce data in bursts – there are periods where little data is sent and periods when lots of data is sent. It is best for the network overall if bursty data can be held at a switch temporarily, with a fixed number of frames released at regular intervals, producing a more regular flow of traffic "downstream."

One technique for handling bursty data is the leaky bucket algorithm. With a leaky bucket, water is poured in at an irregular rate, and exits through the holes at a regular rate. If too much water is poured in, it spills over the side and is lost. We can apply this idea to frames arriving at a network switch. As frames arrive at a switch, they are placed in the queue (leaky bucket) for an outgoing port. If the queue is full, the arriving frames are discarded. The switch releases a fixed number of frames at regular intervals, thus producing more regular network traffic.

Write an application that simulates bursty network traffic arriving at a switch in the network. The traffic should be managed via the leaky bucket algorithm. The simulation takes several parameters:

■ the size of the bucket (in frames)

■ the number of frames to release at the end of each time unit

■ the probability of a burst of frames arriving at the switch in the current time unit

■ the number of frames in a frame burst

■ the length of the simulation (number of time units)

When the simulation ends, the application should display the following statistics:

■ an echo of the input parameters

- the number of frames
  - □ arriving at the switch
  - □ released from the switch
  - □ discarded by the switch due to insufficient space
- the average time that a frame waits in the switch before being released

Solution: A switch implementing the leaky bucket algorithm must maintain the FIFO ordering of the arriving frames; that is, the switch is not allowed to change the *order* in which the frames leave, only the *rate* at which they leave. The access characteristics of the Queue ADT nicely maintain this FIFO ordering, so the switch uses a Queue to buffer the frames as they await release through a port. Again, the solution's design uses the Model-View pattern. The View presents the user with a simple GUI for manipulating the simulation, which is stored in the Model.

The presentation of the solution proceeds through Analysis (discussion of simulator inputs and outputs and the layout of the simulator interface), Design (identification of classes with their responsibilities and collaborators, visualized through a UML class diagram), and Implementation of the classes.

- Study Guide Exercises

- Answers to CheckPoint Problems

- Additional exercises

Recursion 8

■ **8.1** What Is Recursion?

A recursive definition is one in which the thing being defined is part of the definition. Although this may sound unpromising, it has tremendous expressive power and wide application in computing.

For example, recursion is used to specify elements of programming languages, and the structure of ADTs and associated algorithms. In programming, recursion is another way to do iteration and provides very elegant solutions to programming problems. What is especially nice is that once a problem has been specified recursively, its implementation usually follows the recursive definition quite closely.

■ 8.2 Recursive Definitions

8.2.1 Programming Languages

Every programming language includes rules for how the words of the language are to be constructed. These rules are used during compilation by the **scanner**, which does **lexical analysis**, assembling characters into words, called **lexemes**, which are valid according to the language. For example, `replyButton`, `159`, `>=` and `new` are all valid words in Java. Every programming language also has rules governing how these words can be combined to form grammatically correct sentences in the language. This is the language's syntax or grammar. During compilation, the **parser** requests words from the scanner and tries to build sentences with them using rules from the grammar. An arithmetic expression, an if-statement, and a while-statement are examples. This is called **syntactic analysis**. The specification of a programming language regularly makes use of recursive definitions to specify the rules for the construction of the language's lexical elements (words) and syntactic elements (sentences).[1] We will look at two examples from Java: identifiers and simple arithmetic expressions.

The scanner does lexical analysis during compilation

The parser does syntactic analysis during compilation

The Lexical Specification of an Identifier (Direct Recursion)

You know the rules for constructing an identifier in Java—it must begin with an underscore or letter and can be followed by zero or more instances of a letter, digit, or underscore. Table 8.1 gives a recursive definition for a Java identifier using Backus Normal Form (BNF).

Table 8.1 BNF definition of an identifier.

Rule Number	Term		Rule Definition
1	\<underscore\>	::=	_
2	\<letter\>	::=	a | b | c | d | e | f | g | h | i | j | k | l | m | n | o | p | q | r | s | t | u | v | w | x | y | z | A | B | C | D | E | F | G | H | I | J | K | L | M | N | O | P | Q | R | S | T | U | V | W | X | Y | Z
3	\<digit\>	::=	0 | 1 | 2 | 3 | 4 | 5 | 6 | 7 | 8 | 9
4	\<identifier\>	::=	\<letter\> |
5			\<underscore\> |
6			\<identifier\> \<letter\> |
7			\<identifier\> \< digit\> |
8			\<identifier\> \<underscore\>

[1]Compiler tools such as lex and yacc can build scanners and parsers from specially formatted rules, some of which are recursive.

BNF is a **meta-language** used to describe the elements of a language. In BNF, a **non-terminal** is a language element that can be expanded to produce zero or more other language elements. A non-terminal is identified by the brackets that surround the term being defined or used, for example <letter> and <identifier> in Table 8.1.

A **terminal** is a language element that cannot be expanded further; for example, '_' (the underscore), the letter 'd', and the digit '2' are terminals in Table 8.1. A **rule** associates a **term**, representing a single non-terminal, with its **definition**. The left side of each rule gives the term being defined and the right side of the rule specifies how it is to be constructed. These rules are often called **productions** because, by applying the right side of each rule, you can produce an instance of the element given on the left side of the rule. The pipe symbol (|) that appears on the right-hand side of some rules means logical OR. By rule 2, for example, a <letter> can be a OR b OR c OR . . . OR z OR A OR B or . . . OR z. Similarly, by rule 3, a <digit> can be any of the digits 0 to 9.

Rules 6 to 8 are **self-referential**—the lexical element we are defining, <identifier>, appears in its own definition, so the definition refers to itself. A self-referential definition is said to be **recursive**. A lexical analyzer would use these rules to determine whether a string of characters from the input was a legal identifier.

Figure 8.1 shows a derivation of ir2_D2 working backward from the last character ('2') to the first ('i'). At each step, a single non-terminal is expanded using a rule from Table 8.1. The number above the arrows indicates the rule being applied. Starting from the top left of Figure 8.1,

- By rule 7, an <identifier> is expanded to an <identifier> followed by a <digit>.
- By rule 3, the non-terminal <digit> can be replaced by the terminal '2', producing the following:

Non-terminals expand to other language elements

Terminals are literal values and cannot be expanded

A self-referential definition is recursive

Characters in the definition matched with characters from the word.

ir2_D | 2

<identifier> | 2

Now we need to see if we can expand the definition of <identifier> to match ir2_D.

Figure 8.1 The derivation of ir2_D2 using the rules of Table 8.1.

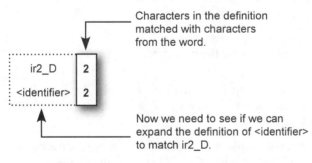

<identifier> $\xrightarrow{7}$ <identifier><digit> $\xrightarrow{3}$ <identifier>2 $\xrightarrow{6}$ <identifier><letter>2

$\xrightarrow{2}$ <identifier>D2 $\xrightarrow{8}$ <identifier><underscore>D2 $\xrightarrow{1}$ <identifier>_D2

$\xrightarrow{7}$ <identifier><digit>_D2 $\xrightarrow{3}$ <identifier>2_D2 $\xrightarrow{6}$ <identifier><letter>2_D2

$\xrightarrow{2}$ <identifier>R2_D2 $\xrightarrow{4}$ <letter>R2_D2 $\xrightarrow{2}$ iR2_D2

You see that we have used the rules to match the last character in the identifier, '2'. We now have a smaller version of the original problem to solve: to expand <identifier> to match the remaining unmatched characters: `ir2_D`.

■ By rule 6, <identifier> can be expanded to an <identifier> followed by a <letter>

■ By rule 2, <letter> can be replaced by the terminal character 'D', producing the following:

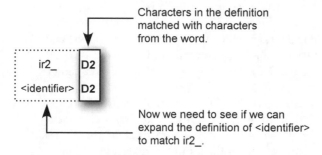

Characters in the definition matched with characters from the word.

Now we need to see if we can expand the definition of <identifier> to match ir2_.

This continues until all non-terminals have been replaced by terminals.

Rules 4 and 5 are not recursive. They generate a single <letter> or a single <underscore>. But they also serve another, very important, purpose—they do not involve reapplication of the definition of <identifier>. That is, they are *not* recursive. Without them, an <identifier> would have infinite length since, with only rules 6, 7, and 8 to use, we would have no way to terminate the string of characters being generated (try an expansion without rules 4 and 5 if you don't believe me).

This gives us an important insight into recursive definitions. Every recursive definition contains two parts:

■ A *base case*, which is *non*recursive and, consequently, terminates the recursive application of the rule. Rules 4 and 5 provide the base cases for <identifier> in Table 8.1.

■ A *recursive case*, which reapplies a rule. In BNF, these are the rules for non-terminals whose definition is self-referential. Rules 6, 7, and 8 provide the recursive cases for <identifier> in Table 8.1.

Elements of a recursive definition:
■ base case(s)
■ recursive case(s)

The specification of an identifier in Table 8.1 provides examples of **direct recursion**, since the definition of <identifier> directly invokes itself in rules 6, 7, and 8. This is illustrated in Figure 8.2 for rule 7. Compare this to Figure 8.4, which shows an example of indirect recursion.

Direct recursion

Figure 8.2 An illustration of direct recursion in a recursive definition (rule 7 of Table 8.1).

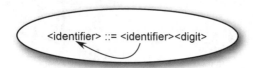

The Syntactic Specification of an Arithmetic Expression (Indirect Recursion)

The syntax (grammar) of a language can also be described using BNF. For example, an arithmetic expression can be the following:

■ A numeric literal (base case)

■ An identifier of some numeric type (base case)

■ An arithmetic expression contained in parentheses (recursive case)

■ A pair of arithmetic expressions separated by a binary arithmetic operator (recursive case).

A BNF specification for simplified arithmetic expressions is given in Table 8.2.

Consider the expression 5 * (a − 2). How can 5, 2, and a be <expr>s? By rule 8, the identifier a is a <factor>, and by rule 9, the numbers 5 and 2 are <factor>s. By rule 6, a <factor> is a <term> and by rule 3 a <term> is an <expr>. Following from this, the subexpression a − 2 is an expression by rule 2, and so on for the rest of the expression (try it!).[2] Figure 8.3 shows the derivation of 5 * (a − 2) by applying the rules of Table 8.2.

Where is the recursion? It is *indirect*, as illustrated in Figure 8.4.   **Indirect recursion**

How does the recursion end? Where is the base case? The recursion ends when all the syntactic elements (<expr>, <term>, <factor>) are eventually expanded to either an <identifier> or a <number>, which expand to terminals and so do not generate any further syntactic elements.

Table 8.2 BNF definition for the syntax of simple arithmetic expressions.

Rule Number	Term		Definition
1	<expr>	::=	<term> + <term> |
2			<term> − <term> |
3			<term>
4	<term>	::=	<factor> *<factor> |
5			<factor> / <factor> |
6			<factor>
7	<factor>	::=	(<expr>) |
8			<identifier> |
9			<number>

---

[2]The entire definition of <expr> no doubt looks unnecessarily complex. The problem with the much simpler definition

<binop> ::= − | + | * | /
<expr> ::= <identifier> | <number > | (<expr>) | <expr> <binop> <expr>

is that it gives all the binary operators the same level of precedence so that a * b + c could be interpreted as *either* (a * b) + c *or* a * (b + c). Only one of these can be correct. The more complex definition ensures that * and / are done before + and −, unless modified by parentheses.

Figure 8.3 Derivation of 5 * (a − 2) using the rules of Table 8.2 and applying Table 8.1 to handle the identifier a. *NS* means the definition is not shown in Table 8.2.

$$\langle expr \rangle \xrightarrow{3} \langle term \rangle \xrightarrow{4} \langle factor \rangle * \langle factor \rangle \xrightarrow{7} \langle factor \rangle * (\langle expr \rangle)$$

$$\xrightarrow{2} \langle factor \rangle * (\langle term \rangle - \langle term \rangle) \xrightarrow{6} \langle factor \rangle * (\langle term \rangle - \langle factor \rangle)$$

$$\xrightarrow{9} \langle factor \rangle * (\langle term \rangle - \langle number \rangle) \xrightarrow{NS} \langle factor \rangle * (\langle term \rangle - 2)$$

$$\xrightarrow{6} \langle factor \rangle * (\langle factor \rangle - 2) \xrightarrow{8} \langle factor \rangle * (\langle identifier \rangle - 2)$$

$$\xrightarrow{NS} \langle factor \rangle * (a - 2) \xrightarrow{9} \langle number \rangle * (a - 2) \xrightarrow{NS} 5 * (a - 2)$$

Figure 8.4 An illustration of indirect recursion in which the recursive application of a definition may be separated from the definition by one or more intervening definitions (rules 3, 6, and 7 from Table 8.2).

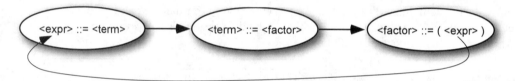

CHECKPOINT

8.1 Give a derivation for a + b / c using the rules from Table 8.2.

8.2 Explain the difference between the base case and the recursive case in a recursive definition. What role does each play?

8.3 How are direct and indirect recursion the same? How are they different?

8.2.2 Data Structures and ADTs

Recursive definitions can also be used to describe the *structure* of common data structures and ADTs. This is particularly useful for nonlinear ADTs such as trees (as we will see later) and graphs. We will look first at an old acquaintance, the linked data structure.

The Linked Data Structure

Consider the recursive definition of a singly linked list in Table 8.3.

The recursive definition of a linked list makes it relatively easy to think about recursive methods for accessing the elements of the structure. The important idea here is that a recursive definition leads more naturally to recursive applications.

Table 8.3 A BNF definition of a singly linked data structure.

Rule Number	Term		Definition
1	<LinkedList>	::=	null |
2			<SLNode>
3	<SLNode>	::=	<DataField> < Successor >
4	<Successor>	::=	<LinkedList>

According to Table 8.3, a linked list is either empty (rule 1) or consists of <SLNode> (rule 2). Rule 3 tells us that <SLNode> consists of a <DataField> and a <Successor>, while rule 4 states that <Successor> is a <LinkedList> (this is another example of indirect recursion).

In data structure terms, rule 3 tells us what data fields must appear in an SLNode class. This corresponds exactly to the definition of SLNode given in Chapter 3 (see Listing 8.1).

Rules 1, 2, and 4 tell us how to construct a linked list from individual nodes. The linked list is terminated by a null successor. This is the base case that ends, or terminates, the recursive application of the definition. When the successor is not null, it references an SLNode, which is the first node in another linked list (representing the recursive case).

In Figure 8.5, A is the head of the entire linked list. Its successor is non-null and references the head (B) of another linked list. Similarly for B, whose successor references a linked list headed by C. The last SLNode in the linked list is D, whose successor is null (an empty list), ending the linked list and the application of the recursive definition of a linked list.

In a sense, what we have done in Figure 8.5 is to break a linked list down into a collection of sub-lists, each of which is smaller than the list of which it is a part, but which has the same organization as the entire list. This idea, that the part is smaller than the whole, but has the same organization as the whole, will be a refrain throughout the rest of this chapter.

> Linked List:
> base case:
> null successor
> recursive case:
> non-null successor
>
> Recursive view of a linked list
>
> In recursive structures, the substructures have the same organization as the whole structure, but are smaller than the whole structure

Listing 8.1 Java class corresponding to rule 3 of Table 8.3.

```
1   /**
2    *  A single node in a singly linked structure.
3    */
4   public class SLNode<E> {
5       private E      dataField;
6       private SLNode successor;  // Recursive part of the definition
7       . . .
8   }
```

Figure 8.5 A singly linked list viewed from a recursive perspective.

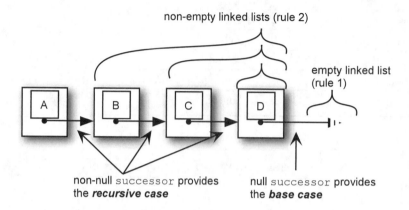

The Tree ADT

Trees are discussed in more detail starting in Chapter 10. Here we want to look at the recursive definition of the structure of a binary tree. It is in describing and accessing nonlinear types that recursion is most useful and, perhaps, most intuitive.

A tree is a hierarchical type (everything else we have seen so far has been linear) consisting of tree nodes connected by edges. The successors to a node are called its **children** and a node's predecessor is called its **parent** (there can only be one). One node has the special designation as the **root** of the tree. The root has no parent. A node with no children is called a **leaf**.

A **binary tree** is a tree with the constraint that each node in the tree can have 0, 1, or 2 children where the children are ordered as left child and right child. Figure 8.6 shows a binary tree labeled with our tree terminology.

Tree ADT terminology

Binary tree—a tree in which a node can have 0, 1, or 2 children

Figure 8.6 A binary tree labeled with tree terminology.

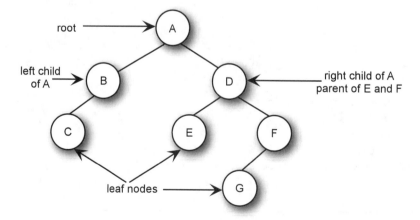

We can break a tree down into a collection of subtrees—each child of a node is the root of a subtree, which is smaller than and has the same general organization as the whole tree. Figure 8.7(a) shows a tree with one node and two empty subtrees (children). Figure 8.7(b) shows four nonempty trees. The largest of the trees has A as its root. A's left child is a subtree consisting of just B. A's right child is a two-node subtree with C as its root. C's right child is a one-node subtree with D as its root.

This description and the illustrations suggest the recursive definition of a binary tree in Table 8.4. A binary tree is either empty or has two children, each of which is a binary tree. Note the similarity in structure to the recursive definition of a singly linked list.

A subtree has the same organization as the whole tree, but is smaller than the whole tree

Figure 8.7 Subtrees have the same organization as the whole tree. Thus a tree can be recursively defined as consisting of a collection of subtrees.

(a) Tree with one node and two empty subtrees.

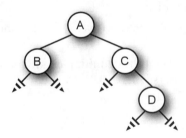

(b) A tree is composed of subtrees.

Table 8.4 A BNF definition of a binary tree.

			Rule
Rule Number	Term		Definition
1	<BinaryTree>	::=	null |
2			<BinaryTreeNode>
3	<BinaryTreeNode>	::=	<DataField> <LeftChild> <RightChild>
4	<LeftChild>	::=	<BinaryTree>
5	<RightChild>	::=	<BinaryTree>

The base case occurs when a <BinaryTree> is null (empty). Conversely, the recursive case occurs when a <BinaryTree> produces a <BinaryTreeNode>. Following the model established by the recursive definition of a linked list and the Java class definition of an SLNode, the BNF definition of a <BinaryTree> suggests the Java class for a <BinaryTreeNode> shown in Listing 8.2.

SUMMING UP

Recursive definitions provide a succinct and intuitive way to define many things. They are commonly used to describe the elements of a programming language as well as common data structures and ADTs. Every recursive definition has two components: a **base case** that ends the recursive application of the definition and a **recursive case** that reapplies the definition. If the base case is missing, the recursion is infinite. The recursive case always involves an instance of the original problem that is closer to the base case than the original problem.

CHECKPOINT

8.4 Explain how the organization of a sublist is the same as that for the entire list. How does this relate to recursive definitions?

8.5 Explain how the definition of <BinaryTree> is recursive. Be sure to identify the base and recursive cases.

8.6 Draw a figure similar to that in Figure 8.4 for the definition of either a singly linked list (see Table 8.3) or a binary tree (see Table 8.4).

Listing 8.2 Java class corresponding to rule 3 of Table 8.4.

```
1   /**
2    *  A single tree node in a binary tree.
3    */
4   public class BinaryTreeNode<E> {
5       private E                 dataField;
6       private BinaryTreeNode<E> leftChild;   // Recursive part of definition
7       private BinaryTreeNode<E> rightChild;  // Recursive part of definition
8       . . .
9   }
```

■ 8.3 Problem Definitions and Recursive Programming

A recursive definition is also a natural choice for many programming problems. Not only does it provide a clear and concise definition of the problem to be solved, it also usually leads to a clear and concise implementation of a method in a programming language. We will look at three examples to demonstrate this and will explore more in later sections when we examine the relationships between recursion and iteration and look at the cost of recursion. The next chapter, on sorting, will make use of recursion again.

8.3.1 The Factorial Function

The classic example of a recursive function is the factorial function (n!), which provides a conceptually gentle introduction to recursive methods. First, some examples:

$$
\begin{aligned}
5! &= 5 * \underline{4 * 3 * 2 * 1} => 120 = 5 * \mathbf{24} \\
4! &= \underline{4 * 3 * 2 * 1} => \mathbf{24} = 4 * \mathbf{6} \\
3! &= \underline{3 * 2 * 1} => \mathbf{6} = 3 * \mathbf{2} \\
2! &= 2 * 1 => \mathbf{2} = 2 * \mathbf{1} \\
1! &= => \mathbf{1}
\end{aligned}
$$

Looking at the examples, we can deduce the following recursive $n!$ definition for $n > 0$:

$$
n! = \begin{cases}
1, \text{ if } n == 1 & \textit{base case} \\
n\,(n-1)!, \text{ if } n > 1 & \textit{recursive case}
\end{cases}
$$

The base case always results in a direct answer (1), which is returned to the caller and combined with other answers. The recursive case is always a reapplication of the problem definition to a smaller version of the original problem, $(n-1)!$. As we have already seen, it is essential that a recursive definition includes at least one base case and that each recursive case take the problem's input closer to the base case; otherwise, the recursive calls will never end. Failure to obey this simple rule leads to infinite recursion.

A key characteristic of recursive problem solving, evident from the factorial example, is that each recursive application of the definition deals with a subproblem that

Key characteristics of recursive problem solving

■ has the same organization as the original problem.

■ is closer to the base case than the original problem.

In the factorial example, the subproblem is just a smaller version of the original problem. Remember, we saw this with the recursive definition of data structures.

A binary tree is composed of subtrees. Each subtree is constructed in the same manner as the whole tree and each subtree is smaller than the whole tree of which it is a part.

Recursive programming finds a way to partition a large problem into smaller versions of the same problem (the recursive calls). Once the base case is met, the recursion is said to **unwind**, during which the solutions to the subproblems are combined until eventually there is a solution to the original problem.

In the factorial problem, the subproblem is always to compute $(n - 1)!$. Eventually $n - 1$ reaches 1, the base case, producing a solution to the smallest factorial subproblem $(1!)$. When this result is returned, it is used in the expression $n \times (n - 1)!$ from the previous call, to produce the result $n!$. This is illustrated in Figure 8.8 for 4!.

Listing 8.3 shows the elements of a recursive definition side by side with its implementation as a Java method. Notice how easy the transition is.

What is the runtime cost of the factorial function? The original input is n and each recursive call reduces the input size by only 1, so the cost is $\Theta(n)$. This is a bit misleading because, in practice, the overhead of the method call can be pretty high in relation to the amount of work done in the method body. We'll return to this issue in a later section to look at alternatives.

Figure 8.8 Application of the recursive factorial definition to compute 4!.

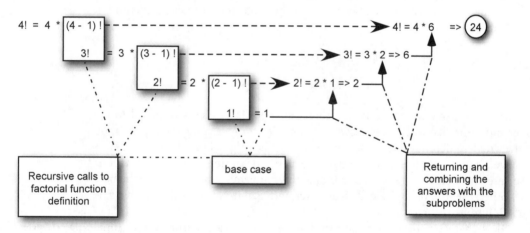

Listing 8.3 The recursive definition of factorial and the equivalent Java method.

Recursive Definition		**Recursive Method**	
$n!$	function	1	`long factorial( int n ) {`
if n is 1, then $n! = 1$	base case	2	`    if ( n == 1 ) return 1;`
if $n > 1$, then $n! = n \times (n-1)!$	recursive case	3	`    return n * factorial( n - 1 );`
		4	`}`

8.3.2 Recursive Searching: The Linear and Binary Search Algorithms

The use of recursion as a divide-and-conquer technique is more dramatic (and satisfying) when applied to the problem of finding an element in an ordered collection of sorted elements.

Recursion uses a divide-and-conquer strategy

But first, consider the problem of finding an element (the target) in an indexed, *unordered* collection of elements. A simple and effective technique is to picture the collection as partitioned into two parts: a searched part (that we have looked through, so we know our target isn't in this part) and an unsearched part (that we have not yet looked through, so we don't know yet if our target is in this part).[3] Initially, the searched part is empty and the unsearched part is the entire collection.

Sequential search on an unordered collection

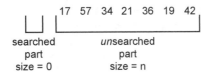

Sequential search proceeds by comparing the target against the first element in the unsearched part. If there is a match, we are done. If there is no match, we "move" the compared element from the unsearched part to the end of the searched part. This increases the size of the searched part by 1 and decreases the size of the unsearched part by 1, as shown below.

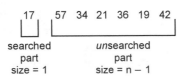

After a failed comparison, the search begins anew on the unsearched part of the collection. Note that the nature of the problem has not changed. We are still looking for a target element in a collection of elements. What has changed is that with each element comparison, we have reduced the size of the problem (the unsearched part) by 1. The search ends when either the target is found or the size of the unsearched part becomes 0. This suggests the following recursive definition for a sequential search on an unordered collection of n elements.[4] The Java implementation is in Listing 8.4.

SequentialSearch(collection, first, last, target)
$\begin{cases} \text{failure, if first > last} & \textit{base case} \\ \text{success, if collection(first) is equal to the target} & \textit{base case} \\ \text{SequentialSearch(collection, first + 1, last, target)} & \textit{recursive case} \end{cases}$

where:
   collection – the collection of elements to search
   first   – the index of the first element in the unsearched part
   last   – the index of the last element in the unsearched part
   target   – the element we are searching for

---

[3]We will reuse this idea in the next chapter on sorting when we will view a collection as having a sorted part and an unsorted part.

[4]The Exercises ask you to revisit this problem assuming the input is ordered.

Listing 8.4 The recursive definition of SequentialSearch and the equivalent Java method.

Recursive Definition			Recursive Method
SequentialSearch(collection, first, last, target)	function	1	`int sequentialSearch( int[] collection,`
		2	`int first, int last, int target ){`
if first > last return failure	base case	3	`if ( first > last ) return −1; // failure`
if collection(first) is equal to the target,	base case	4	`if ( collectionl[first] == target )`
return success		5	`return first;          // success`
SequentialSearch(collection, first +1, last, target)	recursive case	6	`return sequentialSearch( collection,`
		7	`first + 1,`
		8	`last, target);`
		9	`}`

This algorithm meets the criteria of a recursive definition. It has a base case (two of them actually, one for success and one for failure) that terminates the search, and a recursive case that continues the search on a smaller instance of the original problem. Thus each comparison that does not produce a match reduces the searched part of the input by 1.[5] So, for a collection of 1,000 elements, in the worst case the algorithm does 1,000 comparisons. Ugh! We can do better than that!

SequentialSearch runtime complexity is O(n)

We can greatly improve on the runtime complexity of `SequentialSearch` if we know the input is sorted in ascending order and we are a bit more clever about how much work we get out of each comparison.

The idea behind binary search is familiar to you from a game you will have played. I have a number between 1 and 1,000. What is it? If your guess is wrong, I'll tell you if my number is lower or higher than your number. Clearly, unless you are clairvoyant, your best first guess is 500, because when I tell you my number is lower, you know you have eliminated everything from 500 to 1,000 from consideration. With a single guess, you have eliminated half of the unsearched part of the collection! Furthermore, the *structure* of your problem is still the same: guess a number from a collection of values. All that has changed is that the *size* of the problem is reduced by about half. The strategy behind your solution remains the same as well —find the midpoint of the remaining collection of candidates and do a comparison of the target against the value there. When is the game over? Either when you guess the correct number or the entire collection has been eliminated (in which case I cheated and owe you a hot fudge sundae). This suggests the following recursive definition for BinarySearch. The implementation is shown in Listing 8.5.

Let's play a guessing game

---

[5]The reasoning here is identical to that of the factorial function. In each case a recursive call reduces the size of the problem by one. So if the original input size is n, the "worst" case will always require $O(n)$ recursive calls.

$$
\text{BinarySearch (collection,} \left\{ \begin{array}{ll}
\text{failure, if first > last} & \textit{base case} \\
\text{success, if collection(mid) is equal to the target} & \textit{base case} \\
\text{BinarySearch(collection, first, mid} - 1, \text{target),} & \\
\qquad \text{if target < collection(mid)} & \textit{recursive case} \\
\text{BinarySearch(collection, mid} + 1, \text{last, target),} & \\
\qquad \text{if target > collection(mid)} & \textit{recursive case}
\end{array} \right.
$$

where:
- collection – the collection of elements to search
- first – the index of the first element in the unsearched part
- last – the index of the last element in the unsearched part
- mid – (first + last) / 2
- target – the element we are searching for

In general, how many comparisons will be done in the worst case for a collection of n elements? Since each comparison to the value at the midpoint eliminates about *half* the unsearched collection, you end up doing about $\log_2 n$ comparisons. So, for a list of 1,000 elements, in the worst case you will do only 10 comparisons. This is *much* better than the 1,000 required for linear search in the worst case.

Figure 8.9 illustrates this for a collection of eight elements. The top part of the figure shows the comparisons that would be made if the target were either the largest value in the collection or larger than the largest value (so, it is not in the collection). Similarly, the bottom part of the figure shows what would happen if we were looking for the smallest value or a value not in the collection that is smaller than the smallest value in the collection.

As you will see in the next chapter, other algorithms attempt to split the input in half with each recursive call to get this nice $\log_2 n$ behavior.

> BinarySearch run-time complexity is $O(\log_2 n)$ because each comparison reduces the problem size by *half*

Listing 8.5 The recursive definition of BinarySearch and the equivalent Java method.

Recursive Definition		Recursive Method
BinarySearch(collection, first, last, target)	function	1 public static int binarySearch(int[]collection, int first, 2 int last, int target) {
failure, if first > last	base case	3 int mid = (first + last) / 2; 4 if (first > last) 5 return -1; // failure − base case

success, if collection (mid) == target	base case	6 if (collection[mid] == target)
		7 return mid; // success − base case
		8

if target < collection (mid) BinarySearch(collection, first, mid − 1, target)	recursive case	9 // recursive cases 10 if (collection[mid] < target) 11 return binarySearch(collection, 12 first, mid - 1, target);
if target > collection (mid) BinarySearch(collection, mid + 1, last, target)	recursive case	13 else 14 return binarySearch(collection, 15 mid + 1, last, target); 16 }

Figure 8.9 Counting the number of calls made to BinarySearch. There is one call made for each comparison of the target to an element in the collection.

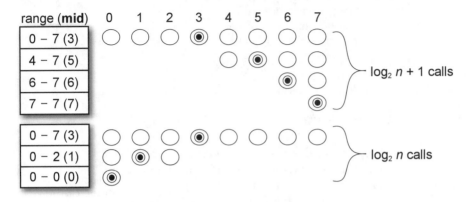

8.3.3 Finding the kth Smallest Value of an Array

The last problem we will look at is to find the kth smallest item in an array. This is a generalization of the problem of finding the median value in a collection and is useful in a variety of applications. The problem is also interesting in that we can certainly describe an elegant recursive solution, but it doesn't have some of the nice time complexity properties that algorithms like BinarySearch have. We'll see why after we look at the algorithm. We will reuse the algorithm developed here when we look at the QuickSort algorithm in the next chapter, and we revisit it again when we look at binary search trees.

First, if the array is already sorted, we would find the kth smallest element in position k − 1 (remember, indexing begins at 0). This is shown in Figure 8.10, where we find the seventh smallest element in position 6.

The kth smallest element is in position k − 1 in a sorted array

Well, that was too easy. What if the input isn't sorted? An obvious solution is to sort the input first, then fetch the element in position k − 1. While this would certainly do, it is more work than we need (or want) to do. But it does give us an idea —do just enough sorting so that the kth smallest element ends up in position k − 1 (which is where we would find it if the array were completely sorted).

Idea: Do a partial sort so that the kth smallest value is in position k − 1

Figure 8.10 The seventh smallest element in an array of 10 sorted elements is in position 6.

11	17	25	34	52	79	81	85	90	95	elements
0	1	2	3	4	5	6	7	8	9	indices

A solution that "sort of" sorts sounds improbable, but it works just fine. Here is the outline of the solution. We select an element from the array, called the **pivot**, and rearrange the other elements in the array so that the following occurs.

elements < pivot	pivot	elements >= pivot

This is called **partitioning** because it partitions (splits) the collection of elements into two partitions such that all the elements that are less than the pivot are to its left and all the elements greater than or equal to the pivot are to its right. This defines a **partial ordering** of the array's elements—the left and right partitions may not be sorted internally, but they *are* sorted with respect to the pivot. Consequently, *the pivot is in the position it would be in if the array were fully sorted.*

This last point is critical for us. If, after partitioning, the position of the pivot is k − 1, we are done and can return the pivot as the kth smallest value. Whether the rest of the array is sorted or not doesn't matter. This is shown in Figure 8.11 (b) where we are looking for the sixth smallest value of the unsorted array in Figure

Partitioning around the pivot value

The key idea: After partitioning, the pivot is in the position it would be in if the array were fully sorted

---

Figure 8.11 The fourth smallest element in an array of 10 unsorted elements is in position 3.

79	85	52	81	11	34	90	17	95	25	elements
0	1	2	3	4	5	6	7	8	9	indices

(a) An unsorted array using the elements from the array in Figure 8.10.

elements < pivot					pivot	elements >= pivot				
34	25	52	17	11	79	90	81	95	85	elements
0	1	2	3	4	5	6	7	8	9	indices

(b) The array after partitioning around the pivot value 79.

< pivot			pivot	>= pivot						
17	25	11	34	52	79	90	81	95	85	elements
0	1	2	3	4	5	6	7	8	9	indices

(c) The array after repartitioning around the pivot value 34 using only the left partition of the array from (b).

8.11 (a). Note that the elements to the left of the pivot are all less than the pivot *and* that, while they are not sorted with respect to each other, they *are* sorted with respect to the pivot. Similarly, all the values to the right of the pivot are greater than or equal to it, so they are also sorted with respect to the pivot. Since we know that the value 79 is in its final "sorted" position (index 5) and we are looking for the sixth smallest value, which will be in position 5, we are done!

Cool! But what happens when the position of the pivot after partitioning is not the position we are looking for? The answer is that we determine whether k − 1 is in the left or the right partition and reapply the algorithm on that partition (we can safely ignore the other partition since we know our value can't be in it). Say, for example, that our target is the fourth smallest value (which would be found in position 3). After the first partition (see Figure 8.11 (b)), the pivot ended up in position 5. Since our target, 3, is less than 5, we know that the fourth smallest value must be in the left partition. So we apply the partitioning step to the left partition and ignore the right partition because all its indices are greater than our target (3).

Figure 8.11(c) shows the result of repartitioning the elements in positions 0 to 4 using 34 as the pivot. This time the pivot ended up in position k − 1 (3), so we are done and can return 34 as the fourth smallest value. If you have doubts about this, look at Figure 8.10, which is the sorted version of the array we began with in Figure 8.11 (a). In Figure 8.10 you will see that, indeed, 34 is the fourth smallest value.

This description suggests the following recursive solution to finding the kth smallest value in an array:

$$
\text{kthSmallest(k,} \quad
\begin{cases}
\text{array[pivotPosition], if pivotPosition is equal to k} - 1 & \textit{base case} \\
\text{array,} \quad \text{kthSmallest(k, array, first, pivotPosition} -1) \text{ , if k} - 1 < \text{pivotPosition} & \textit{recursive case} \\
\text{first,} \quad \text{kthSmallest(k, array, pivotPosition} +1, \text{last) , if k} - 1 > \text{pivotPosition} & \textit{recursive case} \\
\text{last)}
\end{cases}
$$

where
    pivotPosition is the index of the pivot after partitioning
    first   is the index of the first element of the region of the array to examine
    last   is the index of the last element of the region of the array to examine

The pseudocode for `kthSmallest()` follows very closely from the definition:

Pseudocode: kthSmallest(k, array, first, last)
let pivotPosition be the position of pivot after partitioning the array (first to last)
if pivotPosition is equal to k − 1   // base case
    return the element at position pivotPosition in the array
if k − 1 is less than pivotPosition   // recursive case – look at left partition
    kthSmallest(k, array, first, pivotPosition − 1)
else   // recursive case – look at right partition
    kthSmallest(k, array, pivotPosition + 1, last)

Now we have to consider how the pivot value is chosen and how the partitioning is really done.

Choosing the Pivot

Actually, I just took the first element of the portion of the array to be partitioned as the pivot—this was 79 in Figure 8.11 (a) to get to (b), and 34 in (b) to get to (c). Since I don't know in advance what value is in this position, it may be a good choice or a bad choice.

What makes a good pivot value? Think back to the BinarySearch algorithm. What made it so successful is that each repetition *halved* the size of the input, giving us that nice $\log_2 n$ behavior. I want a pivot that is close to the median value in the array so that after partitioning I have about half of the remaining values in the left partition and half in the right partition, as shown in Figure 8.12.

What can go wrong? If the pivot value is close to the smallest or largest value in the array, the left and right partitions will be grossly unequal in size. Consider Figure 8.13. In (a) you see that if the pivot is the smallest value, then after partitioning, the left partition is empty and the right partition has $n - 1$ elements. Not good.

What makes a good pivot? One that splits the input in half

Figure 8.12 A good pivot choice splits the array into two equal partitions.

~(n – 1)/2 elements	pivot	~(n – 1)/2 elements

Figure 8.13 Maximum and minimum pivot values produce poor partitioning of the array.

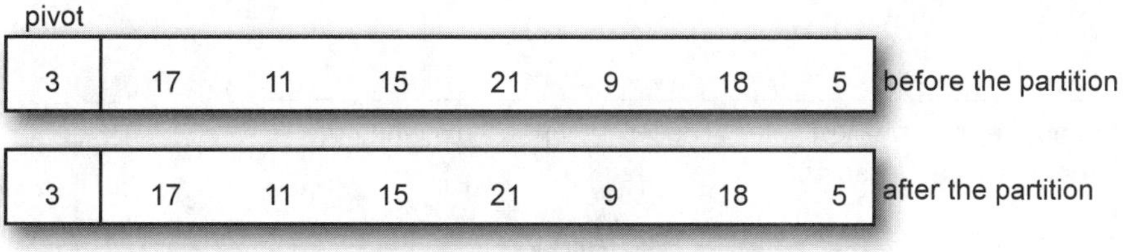

pivot

3	17	11	15	21	9	18	5	before the partition

3	17	11	15	21	9	18	5	after the partition

(a) Partitioning when pivot is the *smallest* value in the array.

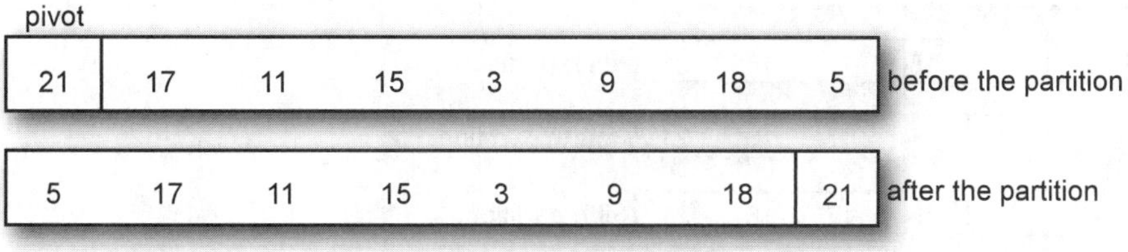

pivot

21	17	11	15	3	9	18	5	before the partition

5	17	11	15	3	9	18	21	after the partition

(b) Partitioning when pivot is the *largest* value in the array.

The situation is reversed in (b), where the pivot is the largest value in the array. Clearly neither of these has split the array into two roughly equal partitions.

To emphasize the point, let's consider the worst case. Imagine that you want to find the sixth smallest value in an array and it turns out (although you didn't know it) that the array is sorted in ascending order.

The worst case occurs when the array is sorted

Figure 8.14 illustrates the sequence of partitions that will be created to find the sixth smallest value if the first element of the unexamined partition is used as the pivot. We haven't looked at the partitioning process yet, but you can be sure it isn't free, so having to do all these (almost useless) partitions is expensive.

You might be thinking, "Just use the median value. That will guarantee an even split every time!" But how do we find it? It is the $(n/2)$th smallest value in the array and we could use our algorithm to find it. Wait . . . no, that's silly! The exercises discuss a simple and inexpensive tweak that improves our chances of avoiding a bad pivot.

The Partition Step

For the partition step, we'll assume that the pivot is the element in the first position of the section of the array to be partitioned.

First, let's try to capture the flavor of what partitioning does. Very generally, it *moves* elements less than the pivot value into positions below the pivot's *final* (or *sorted*) position (this will always move these elements left), and it *moves* elements greater than or equal to the pivot into positions above the pivot's *final* position (this will always move these elements right).

The idea behind the partitioning process

To do this we maintain two scanners (int variables storing array indices). The scanner variables are named after the *direction in which they will move* in the array. So, the *right* scanner will start just to the right of the pivot at the left end of the array and will move *right* looking for a value that is *greater than or equal to the pivot*.

Figure 8.14 Partitions to find the sixth smallest value. The worst case occurs when the input is in order (pivots are shaded).

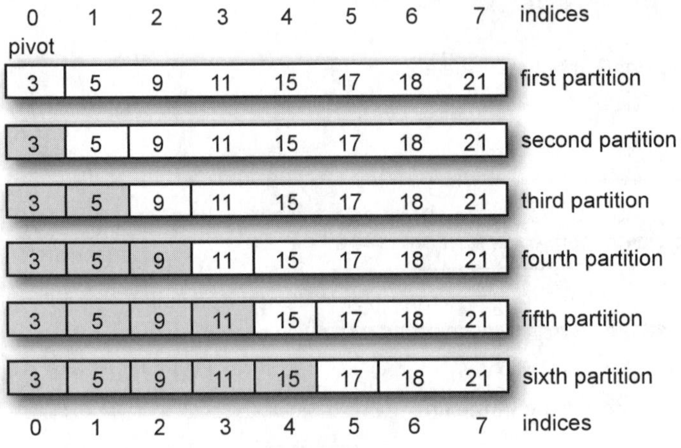

Similarly, the *left* scanner will begin at the last position in the array and will move *left* looking for a value that is *less than the pivot*. This is illustrated in Figure 8.15 (a).

The values at the right and left scanner positions are then swapped, so that the smaller value is moved down the array and the larger value is moved up, thus achieving the objective outlined above of moving values greater than the pivot above the pivot's *sorted* position and smaller values below the pivot's *sorted* position. The swap is shown in Figure 8.15 (b).

After the swap, we resume the two scans. Figure 8.15 (c) shows the next stopping point for the scans and (d) shows the result of the swap that follows.

When are we done scanning? When the scanners cross one another. This terminating condition maintains the two scanner invariants—we know that everything to the right of the left scanner is greater than or equal to the pivot, and everything to the left of the right scanner is smaller than the pivot (except, of course, for the pivot value in the first position), as shown in Figure 8.15 (e). This is important to our ability to reason about the correctness of the algorithm.

Right scanner invariant: All values to the left are < pivot

The last step is to swap the pivot with the value in the position where the *left* scanner ended up. The result, shown in Figure 8.15 (f), is an array partitioned around the pivot and note that it maintains the scanner invariants. Compare this to Figure 8.11 (b).

Left scanner invariant: All values to the right are ≥ pivot

Here is high-level pseudocode for the partition process just described:

Partition pseudocode

Pseudocode: partition()
start the right scanner one position above the pivot
start the left scanner at the last position
while the left and right scanners haven't crossed
    scan right looking for a value >= the pivot
    scan left looking for a value < the pivot
    if the scanners haven't crossed
        swap the values at the right and left scanner positions
    // loop invariant: all values to the left of the right scanner are < pivot
    //   all values to the right of the left scanner are >= pivot

swap the pivot with the value in the left scanner position

// post-condition: all values to the left of the pivot's position are < pivot
//   all values to the right of the pivot's position are >= pivot

Before looking at the time and space complexities of the algorithms, let's consider a subtle aspect of the partitioning algorithm that can lead to an off-by-one error. Considering problems like this is important to developing better problem solving skills and coding habits.

Caution: Subtle point being presented. Read carefully!

There is an important relationship between the terminating condition of the main loop and the step after the loop in which we move the pivot value into its sorted position. The key to getting it right is in knowing what we expect to be true after the pivot swap: All the values to the pivot's left are to be less than the pivot and all the values to its right are to be greater than or equal to the pivot. Note that this is included as a post-condition comment in the pseudocode. Doing this should help

Figure 8.15 Scanning and swapping while partitioning an array.

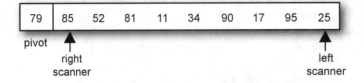

(a) Array after first scan with right and left scan markers.

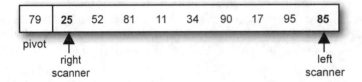

(b) Array after swapping the values at the right and left scan markers.

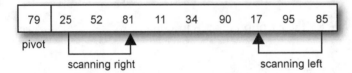

(c) Continuing the right and left scans.

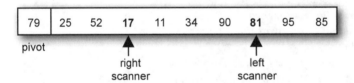

(d) Array after swapping the values at the right and left scan markers.

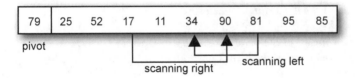

(e) Scanning ends when the scanning indices cross.

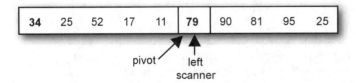

(f) The array after swapping the pivot with the value in the position of the left scanner.

you *avoid* making mistakes when you are doing design and when you convert your pseudocode into code. Consequently, to complete the partitioning it is the value in the *left* scanner position that we want to swap with the value in the pivot position.

The cost of the kth smallest algorithm depends on `partition()`, where most of the work is done, and how many times `partition()` is called. We'll count the number of comparisons that are done. We don't need to look at the code to figure this out. If the partition is to work correctly, the pivot must be compared to all other elements in the partition.

In the worst case, each partition step produces one empty partition, and the rest of the elements (except the pivot) are in the other partition. Thus each partition decreases the amount of work to be done by only one element, giving us

kth smallest *time complexity*:
avg case: O(n)
worst case : O(n^2)

$$\sum_{i=1}^{n} i = 1 + 2 + \dots + n = \frac{n(n+1)}{2} = O(n^2)$$

If, however, each partition halves the size of the input, there will be $\log_2 n$ calls to partition and the size of each partition will be half the size of the last partition, giving us (for *n* a power of 2):

$$n + \frac{n}{2} + \frac{n}{4} + \dots + \frac{n}{n} = \sum_{i=0}^{\log_2 n} 2^i = 2^{(\log_2 n)+1} - 1 = 2n - 1 = O(n)$$

Thus in the average case, our kth smallest algorithm is linear in *n*. Pretty neat.

As we have seen already, the space complexity is determined by the number of recursive calls made. The time complexity analysis above tells us that in the average case there will be O($\log_2 n$) calls (activation records) and in the worst case there will be O(n) calls (activation records).

kth smallest *space complexity*:
avg case: O($\log_2 n$)
worst case : O(n)

SUMMING UP

Recursion is a form of divide-and-conquer problem solving. A problem is solved by splitting it into subproblems until each subproblem is small enough to be solved easily. The solutions to the subproblems are combined to provide a solution to the entire problem.

Like recursive definitions of language elements and data structures, recursive definitions of programming problems consist of a base case and a recursive case. In the recursive case, the subproblem to be solved is smaller than, but has the same organization as, the original problem input.

Recursion provides elegant and intuitive solutions to many computational problems, but the cost of recursive method calls can be high in time and space.

CHECKPOINT

8.7 What are the key characteristics of a recursive solution to a problem?

8.8 How does the selection of the pivot affect the run time of the kth smallest algorithm?

■ **8.4** Recursion as Iteration

As you have probably realized by now, recursion is just another way to do iteration (looping). In this section we gain more insight into recursion by looking at its relationship to looping. We start by looking at the components of a loop and reviewing some loop terminology.[6]

*recursion ==
iteration*

loop entry condition   Also called the *continuation condition*; this condition determines if the loop body is to be executed.

loop exit condition   The condition under which the loop exits; the inverse of the entry condition.

loop control variable (LCV)   The variable in the loop entry condition that determines if the loop terminates or executes again; the LCV must be updated so that eventually the exit condition is met.

loop body   The block of code that executes each time the loop entry condition is met.

Table 8.5 shows the relationship between the essential components of a loop and a recursive definition.

Listing 8.6 shows two factorial methods side by side. One uses good old-fashioned looping and the other our powerful new tool, recursion.

*Execution of loops
and recursive
methods*

- If the loop exit condition/base case is met, execution ends and the result is returned.

- If the continuation/recursive case is met, another iteration occurs and the loop/method body is reentered.

- When the loop/method body is repeated, the LCV/method input is closer to the exit condition/base case.

Table 8.5 Comparison of elements of a loop and a recursive function.

Loop	Recursive Method
loop control variable	method input
loop exit condition	base case
loop entry condition	recursive case
loop body	method body

---

[6]It must be pointed out, however, that not every recursive method has a simple iterative solution.

Listing 8.6 The iterative and recursive implementations of the factorial function.

```
long factorial ( int n ) {          1  long factorial ( int n ) {
   long f = 1;                       2
   while ( n > 1 ) {                 3     if ( n == 1 )  // base case met;
   // entry condition met; iterate again   4        return 1;   // return a result
   f = f * n;                        5     else
   n = n - 1;        // update LCV to get   6     // recursive case met: update method
                     // closer to exit condition   7   // input to get closer to base case
                     // and iterate again   8     // and iterate again
   }                                 9
   // exit condition: iteration ends   10
   // return a result f is n! for n >= 0   11
   return f;                         12       return n * factorial( n - 1 );
}                                    13  }
```

8.4.1 Recursion, Activation Records, and the Runtime Stack

To understand how recursion works in a computer, we need to introduce some terminology. In operating system parlance, a **process** is a program that is executing. Each process gets a **process stack** to store data and other information. This stack exhibits the same behavior as the Stack ADT presented in Chapter 6.

When a method is called, an **activation record** is allocated on top of the process stack. The activation record is used to store variables local to the invoked method, the parameters passed to the method, the method's return value, and some administrative information necessary to restore the runtime environment of the call*ing* method when the call*ed* method returns (see Figure 8.16). This is called **stack dynamic allocation** because the memory is allocated on the stack at runtime when it is needed (making it dynamic).

The use of stacks in recursion is further examined in this chapter's *Investigate*. Every invocation of a method causes an activation record to be created and pushed on the stack, so that the activation record on the top of the stack is associated with the currently active (executing) method. The topmost activation record is popped from the stack when the method call that created it exits.

Figure 8.17 shows the growth of the stack to compute `factorial(4)` to the point where the base case is met (top right of the figure), followed by the reduction of the stack as the recursion unwinds and the computed values are returned.

Figure 8.16 Contents of an activation record.

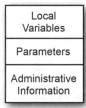

Figure 8.17 State of the process stack and activation records for an initial call to `factorial(4)` (also see Listing 8.6).

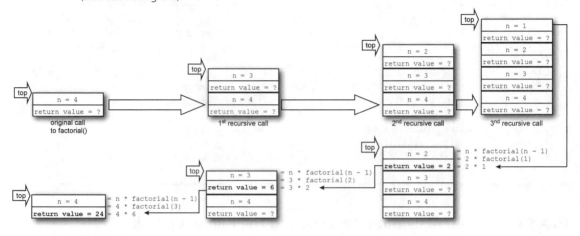

Given Figure 8.17, can you make a reasoned guess about the space complexity for `factorial()`? The only space needed is in the activation records created for each recursive call. The number of calls made determines the number of activation records.

How many activation records are on the stack when the base case for `factorial()` is met?

8.4.2 Tail Recursion

A recursive method call is **tail recursive** if the recursive call is the last statement to be executed before the method returns. Such methods are of interest because they can easily be converted to use a loop to do the iteration. Why bother? Because tail recursive methods are particularly inefficient in their use of space. Let's look at an example.

The `printArray()` method in Listing 8.7 is a tail recursive method because the very last statement is the recursive call. The method recursively prints the contents of an array from the first element to the last. The method first checks (lines 3–4) that we aren't at the end of the array. This is the base case and it means we have printed

In a tail recursive method, the recursive call is the last statement executed

Listing 8.7 A simple tail recursive method.

```
1    // print the elements of values in order from 0 to values.size - 1
2    void printArray( int[] values, int n ) {
3        if ( n == values.length )              // base case
4            return;
5        System.out.println( values[n] );
6        n++;
7        printArray( values, n );               // recursive case
8    }
```

out the entire array, so there is no more work to be done and the recursive calls end. How many activation records are on the stack at this point? One for each cell of the array that has been printed, plus one for the base case (`values.length + 1`).

If the base case is not met, we print out the value stored in position *n*, update *n* to take us closer to the base case, then make the recursive call to print the next entry in the array (lines 5–7). This recursive call is the very last thing done in `printArray()`, which means that the data values stored in the activation record for this call won't be needed again, yet we cannot release the activation records (pop them from the stack) until the method calls that created them exit, which means we have memory allocated that we don't need anymore. This is the source of the space inefficiency we want to remove.

Tail recursion: The wasted space is in the activation records

This is illustrated in Figure 8.18, which shows part of the stack where the recursion ends. There are four activation records, one for each of the calls to `printArray()`. Each activation record stores the parameters (the index of the element to print and a reference to the array), and the administrative information necessary to restore the environment of the caller. However, none of these hold any data that will be used as the calls return and the recursion unwinds.

What can we do about this? Do the iteration using a loop instead of recursion. Listing 8.8 shows the tail-recursive and looping versions of `printArray()` side by side for comparison. The `if` statement that checks for the base case in the recursive solution is converted into a `while` loop. Earlier in this section we saw the relationship between loops and recursion, so you know that the `while` loop also replaces the recursive call. Notice that the conditional test done in the `if` statement of the recursive version (line 2) is inverted in the `while` statement of the iterative version.

Convert tail recursive methods into looping methods

Figure 8.18 The (partial) process stack created by the call `printArray( a, 0 )` for a = {17, 32, 44}.

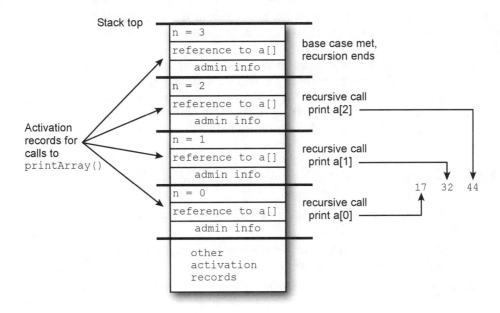

Listing 8.8 Recursive and nonrecursive versions of `printArray()`.

Recursive Version	Iterative Version (Tail Recursion Removed)

```
void printArray( int[] values, int n ) {
   if ( n == values.length )  // base case
      return;
   System.out.println( values[n] );
   n++;
   printArray( values, n ); // recursive case
}
```

```
1  void printArray( int[] values, int n ) {
2     while ( n != values.length ){
3        System.out.println( values[n] );
4        n++;
5     }
6  }
```

The `BinarySearch()` method is also tail recursive. The fact that there are two calls in `BinarySearch()` (see Listing 8.5) doesn't mean it isn't tail recursive, because only one of the recursive calls in the `if-else` statement will execute and it will always be the last statement in the method to execute.

SUMMING UP

Because recursion is another way to do iteration, it has characteristics in common with loops: There is a value used in a condition to determine whether another iteration will occur and the iteration body updates that value so that eventually the iteration ends.

Recursion is supported by **activation records**. An activation record is allocated on top of the **process stack** each time a method (recursive or not) is called. The activation record stores data (parameters and local variables) to be used by the method invocation and administrative information to restore the environment of the calling method on return. An activation record is popped from the stack when the method returns. The activation records can contribute significantly to the space complexity of a recursive method.

In a **tail recursive method**, the last statement to execute in the method is the recursive call. Such recursive implementations are inefficient in space since the activation records that have been allocated are no longer needed but cannot be released until the methods return. Tail recursive methods can easily be converted to looping methods, eliminating both the space and time overhead of recursive calls.

CHECKPOINT

8.9 Describe the components of a loop and how they relate to the components of a recursive method.

8.10 What information is stored in an activation record? When and where are activation records created? When are they freed?

8.11 What makes a method tail recursive? Why do you want to remove the tail recursion?

■ 8.5 Evaluating Recursion

Recursion provides elegant, clear solutions to many problems, but this comes at a cost in time and space. In this section we look at these costs, then consider some alternatives that try to minimize them. Actually, what we will be doing is looking at tradeoffs—trading time for space, space for time, and, sometimes, coding complexity for space/time.

8.5.1 Space and Time

Every method invocation, recursive or nonrecursive, results in an activation record being pushed on the process stack. That activation record remains on the stack until the invocation that produced it returns. As you saw in Figure 8.17, with recursive methods there may be many activation records on the stack at one time. How much space these activation records require depends on two factors:

Tradeoffs are made based on competing needs

1. the size of the activation record, which depends on how many parameters and local variables there are

2. the depth of the recursion; that is, how many calls will be made before the base case is met, at which point no more recursive calls are made.

Each method invocation takes a certain amount of time, independently of the processing time needed to execute the method's body. The relative cost of this overhead increases as the processing time for the body decreases. This is illustrated in bar-graph form in Figure 8.19. As we will see shortly, we can trade time for space to reduce the cost of this overhead.[7]

8.5.2 Dynamic Programming and the Fibonacci Numbers

Occasionally, part of the problem is that while a recursive definition provides a nice, clear decomposition of a problem, as an implementation it results in duplication of effort. Given our druthers, sometimes we would prefer to compute something once

Figure 8.19 The "cost" of the method invocation goes up as the execution time of the body goes down.

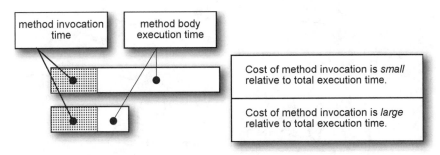

---

[7]This issue of the cost of overhead relative to the overall cost of the operation is a common theme in computer science (and in life in general).

and save the value for reuse later rather than recompute it each time it is needed. This is a source of the space-for-time tradeoff.

The recursive Fibonacci function illustrates both the space and time problems that recursive methods can have. It is not, by any means, the only recursive function that exhibits this behavior, but it has the merit of being easy to understand and to visualize.

Here are the first eight Fibonacci numbers: 0, 1, 1, 2, 3, 5, 8, 13. Looking at the sequence, you can see that each number after the first two is computed by adding its two predecessors. This suggests that a Fibonacci number can be defined recursively, as follows.

$$fib_n \begin{cases} 0, \text{if } n == 0 & \textit{base case} \\ 1, \text{if } n == 1 & \textit{base case} \\ fib_{n-1} + fib_{n-2}, \text{if } n > 1 & \textit{recursive case} \end{cases}$$

Note that there are two base cases here and that the function is doubly recursive—each call to Fibonacci results in two recursive calls: fib_{n-1} and fib_{n-2}.

Now consider the calling tree for computing fib(6) in Figure 8.20. Table 8.6 tells us how many times we computed fib(i) for i from 1 to 6. The results are discouraging. For larger values of n, there would be more repetition, requiring relatively more time.

The Recursive Approach column of Table 8.7 lists timings for computing several Fibonacci numbers (the rightmost column will be explained shortly—looks intriguing, doesn't it?!). As the table shows, we don't get very far before the time

---

Figure 8.20 Call tree for computing the sixth Fibonacci number.

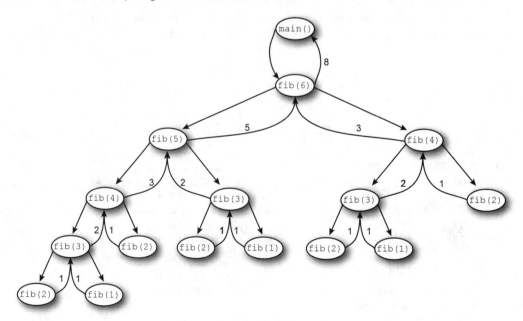

Table 8.6 Count of number of times a Fibonacci number is computed while computing fib(6).

n	Number of Times fib(n) Is Called to Compute fib(6)
1	3
2	5
3	3
4	2
5	1
6	1

Table 8.7 Timings to compute several Fibonacci numbers (in milliseconds).

n	fib(n)	Time (in milliseconds)	
		Recursive Approach	**Dynamic Approach**
25	75025	5	0
26	121393	11	0
27	196418	22	0
28	317811	27	0
29	514229	44	0
30	832040	77	0
31	1346269	116	0
32	2178309	192	0
33	3524578	307	0
34	5702887	500	0
35	9227465	808	0
36	14930352	1301	0
37	24157817	2110	0
38	39088169	3410	0
39	63245986	5520	0
40	102334155	8931	0
41	165580141	14423	0
42	267914296	23343	0
43	433494437	37773	0
44	701408733	61082	0
45	1134903170	98811	0

becomes noticeably large (a millisecond is a thousandth of a second, so it took 98.811 seconds to compute fib(45)!). Listing 8.9 shows the code used to generate the Recursive Approach column of timings in Table 8.7.

Typically, when we know that a computed value will be needed several times, we compute it once and store the result in memory, preferring to do a memory lookup instead of a recomputation when we need the value again. We will explore this idea, which is a component of an advanced problem solving technique called **dynamic programming**.

Listing 8.10 shows the code for the dynamic programming solution and Listing 8.11 illustrates its use. When the method `getFib(n)` computes a Fibonacci number, it stores it in an array (`fibs`) of Fibonacci numbers (lines 32–33 of Listing 8.10). Subsequently, if the nth Fibonacci number is needed, we fetch it from `fibs[n]`. Since we have replaced computation with a lookup, the method is no longer recursive. As the timings in the last column of Table 8.7 plainly show, this approach is *much* faster than recomputing the values.[8]

> Dynamic programming: Look up a stored result instead of recomputing it

---

Listing 8.9 Naïve recursive version of the Fibonacci function. This is the code used to generate the Recursive Approach column of timings in Table 8.7.

```
1    public class FibonacciEx {
2        public static long fibonacci( int n ) {
3            if ( ( n == 0 ) || ( n == 1 ) )
4                return n;
5            return fibonacci( n - 1 ) + fibonacci ( n - 2 );
6        }
7
8        public static void main( String[] args ) {
9            long start, end, fib = 0, time = 0;
10
11           System.out.println("\n\nn    Fib(n)    time (in milliseconds)");
12           for ( int i = 41; i <= 45; i++ ) {
13               time = 0;
14               for ( int j = 0; j < 10; j++ ) {   // get avg of 10 calls
15                   start = System.currentTimeMillis();
16                   fib = fibonacci( i );
17                   end = System.currentTimeMillis();
18                   time += end - start;
19               }
20               System.out.println( i + "\t" + fib + "     \t\t" +
21                                   ( time / 10 ) );
22           }
23       }
24   }
```

---

[8]You might be wondering why the column is entirely zeros. The answer is that the time required for the computation is less than the resolution of the clock—it is too small to measure. While saying the time is zero is not quite accurate (but would make good marketing copy), it does convey that the algorithm is lots faster than the simple recursive solution.

Listing 8.10 Dynamic programming version of the Fibonacci function.

```
1    /**
2     * Dynamic programming version of the Fibonacci function.
3     */
4
5    public class DynamicFibonacci {
6        private long[] fibs;
7        private int lastComputedFib;
8        private int capacity;
9
10       public DynamicFibonacci ( int size ) {
11           capacity = size;
12           fibs = new long[ capacity + 1 ];
13           fibs[0] = 0; fibs[1] = 1; fibs[2] = 1;
14           lastComputedFib = 2;
15       }
16
17       public long getNextFib() {
18           if ( lastComputedFib > capacity )
19               return -1;
20           lastComputedFib++;
21           fibs[lastComputedFib] = fibs[lastComputedFib - 1] +
22                                   fibs[lastComputedFib - 2];
23           return fibs[lastComputedFib];
24       }
25
26       public long getFib( int n ) {
27           int i;
28           if ( n > capacity )
29               return -1;
30           lastComputedFib++;
31           for ( ; lastComputedFib <= n; lastComputedFib++ )
32               fibs[lastComputedFib] = fibs[lastComputedFib - 1] +
33                                       fibs[lastComputedFib - 2];
34           // undo the last ++ from the last iteration of the for loop
35           lastComputedFib--;
36           return fibs[lastComputedFib];
37       }
38   }
```

How does it compare in its space requirements? At first glance the dynamic programming approach appears to be more expensive because you can *see* the array declaration that is used for the lookups (so it is evident that the space complexity of our nonrecursive version is $\Theta(n)$), while the recursive implementation only has the single int parameter. However, this ignores the space cost of all the activation records that recursion stacks up. To compute fib(n) nonrecursively would require an array of at least size n, while the recursive implementation would have that many

Space complexity for the simple and dynamic programming solutions to the Fibonacci function

---

Listing 8.11 Using the dynamic version of the Fibonacci function. This is the code used to generate the second set of timings in Table 8.7.

```
1    /**
2     * Using the DynamicFibonacci class to compute some
3     * Fibonacci numbers.
4     */
5
6    public class DynamicFibonacciEx {
7
8        public static void main(String[] args) {
9            DynamicFibonacci dynoFib = new DynamicFibonacci( 45 );
10           long start, end, time, f = 0;
11
12       System.out.println("\n\nn    Fib(n)   time (in milliseconds)");
13           for( int i = 25; i <= 45; i++ ) {
14               time = 0;
15               for ( int j = 0; j < 10; j++ ) {
16                   start = System.currentTimeMillis();
17                   f = dynoFib.getFib( i );
18                   end = System.currentTimeMillis();
19                   time = end - start;
20               }
21               System.out.println( i + "\t" + f + "    \t\t" +
22                                  ( time / 10 ) );
23           }
24       }
25   }
```

---

activation records on the stack at the point the base case is met and the recursion ends. So we would say that both implementations are $\Theta(n)$ in their space complexity. As a practical matter, though, each cell of the array need store only a single long, while each activation record will require space for the int argument plus several memory locations for administrative information, making it larger. Since the computer is more concerned with real needs, this is good to know.

8.5.3 Smart Recursion—Exponentiation

As with most things, with recursion there are good and bad solutions. We saw this with computing Fibonacci numbers, and powering, or exponentiation, gives us another example. The problem we will consider is to compute x^n. An example will suggest an iterative and a simple recursive solution.

$$x^5 = x \cdot x \cdot x \cdot x \cdot x = x \cdot x^4$$
$$x^4 = x \cdot x \cdot x \cdot x = x \cdot x^3$$
$$x^3 = x \cdot x \cdot x = x \cdot x^2$$
$$x^2 = x \cdot x = x \cdot x^1$$
$$x^1 = x = x$$

This looks like the structure of the factorial example given in Section 8.3.1, so it should be no surprise that the recursive definition has the same structure.

$$x^n = \begin{cases} x, \text{ if } n == 1 & \textit{base case} \\ \\ x \cdot x^{n-1}, \text{ if } n > 1 & \textit{recursive case} \end{cases}$$

This characterization has all the elements we need to produce a naïve recursive implementation, which is shown side by side with an iterative solution in Listing 8.12.

The iterative solution executes in $\Theta(n)$ time, as does the recursive version. Unfortunately, the recursive version will actually take longer due to the overhead of the recursive calls. Also, the space complexity of the recursive version is $\Theta(n)$, since there will be that many activation records on the stack when the base case is met. Compare this to the $O(1)$ space complexity of the iterative solution due to the single activation record needed.

The time complexity of naïve recursive and iterative solutions is $\Theta(n)$

The $\Theta(n)$ time complexity is discouraging, but by thinking about the nature of the problem, we can do much better. Let's take what we know about exponentiation and see if we can design a smarter, more efficient solution.

Use what you know to produce more elegant solutions

Consider computing 2^8. As shown in the example below, we can do this by multiplying 2 by itself seven times to get 2^8.[9] But I can get the same result by computing 2^2 by itself only three times to get $(2^2)^4 = 2^8 = 4^4$. This is less than half the work of the original problem. Carrying on with this idea, I can do $(4^2)^2 = 16^2$ in about a quarter of the time it would take to compute 2^8.

$$\begin{array}{ll} 2 \cdot 2 \cdot 2 \cdot 2 \cdot 2 \cdot 2 \cdot 2 \cdot 2 & = 2^8 \\ 4 \cdot 4 \cdot 4 \cdot 4 & = (2^2)^{8/2} \quad = 4^4 \\ 16 \cdot 16 & = (4^2)^{4/2} \quad = 16^2 \\ 256 & = (16^2)^{2/2} = 256^1 \end{array}$$

Listing 8.12 Iterative and naïve recursive functions to compute x^n.

```
double power( double x, int n ) {      1    double power( double x, int n ) {
    double p = x;                      2
    while ( n > 1 ) {                  3    if ( n == 1 )   // base case; recursion ends
        // entry condition; iterate again   4        return x;   //   return a result
        p = p * x;                     5    else
        n = n - 1;  // update LCV to get 6        // recursive case: update input size to
            // closer to exit condition  7        // get closer to base case and
    }                                  8        // iterate again
    // exit condition: iteration ends  9        return x * power( x, n - 1 );
    // return a result                 10   }
    return p;                          11
}                                      12
```

---

[9]Let's be sure we understand this because it looks a little odd. If I multiply 2 by itself once, I have 2 * 2, which is 2^2. It is the number of multiplies that we are counting.

What if n is odd, for example x^7? This is elegantly handled by converting into a problem we know how to solve (powering with even exponents): $x \cdot x^6$

Generalizing, we have the following:

- If n is even, we compute $1 \cdot x^n$
- If n is odd, we compute $x \cdot x^{n-1}$

When are we done computing? When $n < 2$

These ideas lead us to the following recursive definition. Listing 8.13 shows the resulting recursive method.

$$x^n = \begin{cases} \text{factor, if } 0 \le n < 2 & \textit{base case} \\ \text{factor} \cdot (x^2)^{n/2}, \text{ if } n \ge 2 & \textit{recursive case} \end{cases}$$

$$\text{where factor} = \begin{cases} 1, \text{ if } n \text{ is even} & \textit{// even exponent} \\ x, \text{ if } n \text{ is odd} & \textit{// odd exponent} \end{cases}$$

How expensive is this in time? When we looked at the BinarySearch method, we saw that halving the size of the input with each recursive call resulted in about $\log_2 n$ calls. Our `power()` method exhibits the same behavior (it is a good idea to look for these sorts of things). Look at the recursive case; it invokes `power()` with an exponent that is half the size of its input. So `power()`'s run time is $\Theta(\log_2 n)$, which is a great deal better than the $\Theta(n)$ for both the iterative and the naïve recursive ver-

`power()`'s space and time complexities are $\Theta(\log_2 n)$

Listing 8.13 The "smart" recursive power method.

```
1    /**
2     *   Calculate x to the n.
3     *   @param x — the base
4     *   @param n — the exponent
5     *   @returns x raised to the power of n
6     */
7    double power( double x, int n ) {
8        double factor;
9
10       if (( n % 2 ) == 0 )
11           factor = 1.0;            // even exponent
12       else
13           factor = x;             // odd exponent
14       if ( n < 2 )
15           return factor;          // base case
16
17       return factor * power( x * x, n / 2 ); // recursive case
18   }
```

sions. The space complexity for power() is also $\Theta(\log_2 n)$ since there will be $\log_2 n$ activation records on the stack when the base case is met.

SUMMING UP

Recursive solutions are usually simple and elegant, but have an added cost in time due to the method calls, and in space, due to the activation records allocated with each method call.

Dynamic programming trades space for time—recomputation of a value is avoided by storing a computed value and looking it up when it is needed. The Fibonacci function is an example of a function that can take advantage of this approach.

Sometimes we can produce a more efficient recursive solution at the cost of additional complexity in the code, but looking for shortcuts requires having a good understanding of the function being implemented.

CHECKPOINT

8.12 How does dynamic programming trade space for time?

8.13 How does the depth of recursion affect an algorithm's space complexity?

8.14 What "trick" is used in the smart powering algorithm?

INVESTIGATE Simulating Recursion Using Loops and a Stack

Description

When a recursive method is called, an activation record for it is created and pushed on top of the process's stack. The contents of the activation record include memory for variables declared locally to the method, parameters passed to the method, the return value, and administrative information necessary to return execution control to the caller when the method returns.

Older languages, such as Cobol and Fortran 77, did not support the dynamic creation of activation records on top of a process stack, so recursion was only possible through looping and simulation of a process stack. In this *Investigate*, we will use loops and an instance of the Stack ADT described in Chapter 6 to simulate recursion. We will do this in two parts. In Part A you will get a feel for the overhead associated with recursion by simulating what goes on with activation records. In Part B, you redo the problem from Part A, using the practical approach that you will need in later chapters.

To allow us to better focus on our objectives, we will re-implement the very simple factorial function. The exercises invite you to simulate other recursive algorithms. Later chapters will also use a stack to simulate recursion.

As a reminder, here is the recursive definition of factorial.

$$n! = \begin{cases} 1, \text{if } n == 1 & \textit{base case} \\ n\,(n-1)!, \text{if } n > 1 & \textit{recursive case} \end{cases}$$

Objectives

■ Simulate recursion using a stack.

■ Replace recursion with looping.

■ Directly analyze the space complexity of a recursive algorithm.

Part A: Simulating Recursion with Activation Records

To clearly understand what you will need to do, let's reconsider what happens when the recursive factorial method is called. Consider Figure 8.17 again, which shows the growth of the process stack to compute 4!. Activation records are pushed on the stack until the base case is met. Note that, up to the time the base case is met, the "Return value" field of each activation record is '?', indicating that a factorial value has not been computed and assigned to it yet. This makes sense, since we cannot know a factorial value until the base case is met and the recursion unwinds.

When the base case is met, the "Return value" field of the activation record on top of the stack is assigned 1 (top right of Figure 8.17), and, as the method returns and its activation record is popped, this value is returned to the *caller* to be used in its calculation (bottom right of Figure 8.17). This continues, so that, as the recursive calls are unwinding, a method calculates a factorial value using the value returned to it and stores the computed value in the "Result field" of its *own* activation record. This process continues until a final result is computed, the last factorial activation record is popped and its "Return value" field is the result returned.

Design

From the discussion above we can identify several requirements of the simulation:

1. Create a stack.
2. Push an activation record onto a stack.
3. Pop an activation record from a stack.
4. Create an activation record.
5. Put a parameter in an activation record.
6. Get a parameter from an activation record.
7. Put a return value in an activation record.
8. Get a return value from an activation record.

The stack Class

Requirements 1, 2, and 3 require a stack to play the role of the per-process stack that every process has. We already have a stack class, so there is no additional work needed here.

The Activation Record Class

Requirements 4 through 8 require a class playing the role of an activation record. From Figure 8.17 we see that we need two `int` fields: one to store the input parameter that would be passed in during a method call and the other to store the return value from the method call. We can combine requirements 4 and 5 by having the class's constructor take the value n as its argument. Requirements 6 through 8 can be handled either by making the data fields `public` and allowing a client to access them directly, or by supplying accessor and mutator methods for them. You do not need to store the administrative information kept in real activation records.

Simulating the Recursion

You need to simulate pushing activation records onto the stack until the base case is met. Then you need to simulate unwinding the recursion by popping the activation records and using the popped value until the stack is empty and the final result is computed.

Since you aren't using recursion to do the iteration, you will have to use two loops. Here is an outline of the simulated recursive factorial method:

1. The first loop simulates the recursive method *calls*. Each iteration of this loop simulates a single recursive call by creating an activation record using the current value for n as the argument and pushing the activation record onto a stack.

   ■ What should you do with n to take you closer to the loop terminating condition (the base case)?

   ■ When does this loop terminate? *Hint*: Look at the top right of Figure 8.17.

   Assign a return value to the topmost activation record. Once the first loop has terminated, the base case has been met and there are activation records on the stack for n down to 1. Now the recursion unwinds. The first step of the unwinding is to assign a return value to the top activation record.

   ■ What should this value be according to the recursive definition of factorial?

2. The second loop simulates the method *returns* from all the simulated calls. On each iteration of this loop:

   ■ The top activation record must be popped and its return value extracted. This is the value factorial$(n - 1)$ in the formula $n \times$ factorial$(n - 1)$. Where is the value n? *Hint*: Look carefully at the bottom part of Figure 8.17.

   ■ A return value will have to be computed and put in the "Return value" field of the top activation record on the stack.

   ■ When should this loop terminate?

   Once this loop terminates, the last activation record left on the stack represents the original (nonrecursive) call and its result field stores the value you need to return.

Pseudocode

■ Write the interface for the activation record class and name the data fields.

■ Write pseudocode for the nonrecursive method outlined in the Design section.

■ Deskcheck your pseudocode with 3!.

Implementation

- Create a class `FactorialAR` to represent the factorial activation record according to the interface developed in the Design section.

- Create a main class called `StackFactorialExample`. The class will contain three methods:

    1. `factorial()`—the recursive implementation of the factorial function, as shown in Listing 8.6, to be used for comparison to the simulated recursive method.

    2. `stackFactorial()`—a nonrecursive version of `factorial()` that simulates recursion by using its own stack. This is the method you wrote pseudocode for in the Design section.

    3. `main()`—should call the recursive and nonrecursive methods for several values of *n*, outputting the results to the screen for comparison.

- Like its recursive cousin, `stackFactorial()` takes a single argument *n* of type `int` and calculates *n*!.

- Implement your pseudocode. Include a statement between the two loops that prints out the size of the stack after the "recursive" calls have ended (the base case is met).

- Run the program, comparing the values returned by `factorial()` and those returned by `stackFactorial()`. What does the size of the stack at this point tell you about the space complexity of the recursive factorial method?

Part B: Simulating Recursion without Activation Records

In this part, you repeat Part A, but only push onto the stack `Integer` objects representing the diminishing values for *n*. That is, don't bother with the bulky `FactorialAR` objects.

First, I want to address a question you undoubtedly have—why simulate recursion? There will be times when a problem's solution is very elegantly described recursively and you want your code to reflect this simplicity without using recursion. Simulating the recursion, as you are about to do, is the solution.

Also, in some cases the nature of the problem really requires some of the characteristic behavior we see with recursion. Let me explain a bit more. It is helpful to think of recursive problems, such as factorial, as traveling from a starting point to a destination with all the points visited along the way stored on a stack as they are visited. Often the actual work is done on the return trip from the destination back to the starting point. In the recursion example, the starting point is *n* and the destination is 1. The "points in between" that are stored on the stack are the integers from *n* down to 1. The computation of factorials actually occurs on the return trip going from 1 back to *n*. Figure 8.17 shows this nicely. Although simulating recursion for computing factorials is trivial and inefficient, it does illustrate the idea of moving from a starting point to a destination and back again nicely. There will be more useful application of this idea later.

Figure 8.21 Only the integer arguments to factorial need to be pushed and popped.

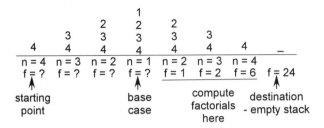

Visualization

Figure 8.21 illustrates our new approach. We repeatedly push smaller values of n until n is 1 (the base case is met), then repeatedly pop values, computing a factorial with the popped value, until the stack is empty.

Design and Implementation

■ Is it necessary to push the last value ($n== 1$) onto the stack?

■ If not, what is the terminating condition for pushing values onto the stack?

■ What is the terminating condition for popping values from the stack?

■ What has to happen in the loop that pops values from the stack?

Implementation

■ Recode the two loops from Part A so that only the value for n is pushed and popped.

EXERCISES

Paper and Pencil

1. Briefly explain the following terms: BNF, terminal, non-terminal, rule, production, and derivation.

2. Applying the rules from Tables 8.1 and 8.2, produce derivations for the following:
   a. _bnum2
   b. b2l
   c. a_Num
   d. a * b − c / d
   e. (a + b) * c

3. For each of the following, draw the method call tree for `BinarySearch` assuming the input array is
   ```
   int[] array = {300, 301, 302, 303, 304, 305, 306, 307, 308, 309}
   a. binarySearch( array, 0, 9, 301 );
   b. binarySearch( array, 0, 9, 311 );
   ```

4. What does the following method do for the call `printArray(a, a.length)` for the array a = { 54, 23 36 }? What is wrong with this method? Fix the problem, if you can.

```
void printArray( int[] values, int n ) {
    if ( n < 0 )
        return;
    n--;
    printArray( values, n );
    System.out.print( values[n] );
}
```

Testing and Debugging

1. Lori first coded recursive `binarySearch()` as follows. Where did she go wrong?

```
public static int binarySearch( int[]coll, int target ) {
    int first = 0,
        last = target.length,
        mid = ( first + last ) / 2;
    if ( first > last )     return -1;  // failure – base case
    if ( coll[ mid ] ==   target )      // success – base case
        return mid;
    if ( coll[ mid ] < target ) {       //  recursive cases
        last = mid – 1;
        return binarySearch( coll, target );
    }
    else {
        first = mid + 1;
        return binarySearch( coll, target );
    }
}
```

2. What does the output statement in `main()` print out? What is wrong with the implementation of `factorial()` in this class?

```
public class BadFactorial {
    private int n;
    public static long factorial () {

        if ( n == 1 )       // base case; recursion ends
            return 1;       //   return a result
        else {
            // recursive case: update input size to
            // get closer to base case and iterate again
            n = n – 1;
            return n * factorial();
        }
    }
}
```

```
    public static main() {
        n = 4;
        System.out.println("factorial 4 is " + factorial() );
    }
}
```

Design and Implement

1. Give a recursive definition for SequentialSearch, assuming the collection to be searched is sorted in ascending order. What are the worst-case and average-case time complexities for this algorithm?

2. Write a recursive method that prints out the elements of a linked list in forward order (from the first node to the last).

3. Remove the tail recursion from BinarySearch to provide an iterative solution.

4. Re-implement the recursive factorial function to use dynamic programming as we did for the Fibonacci function.

5. Redo the kth smallest algorithm using List as the collection type.

6. Provide a nonrecursive implementation of uncover() from the MineSweeper application. (See Chapter 8's Focus on Problem Solving on the Website.) How does it compare with the recursive version in terms of coding complexity? Which do you think is easier to read and understand?

ON THE WEB

Additional study material is available at Addison-Wesley's Website http://www.aw.com/cssupport. This material includes the following:

■ Focus on Problem Solving: Cell Identification in MineSweeper

Problem: MineSweeper is a popular computer game played on a grid of cells, some of which hide mines. Uncovering a mine explodes it and you lose the game.

The goal of the game, then, is to find the hidden mines without getting blown up. You accomplish this through a process of elimination by identifying cells that do not hide mines. Barking Dogs Software has been hired to write a Java version of the MineSweeper game for a new generation of tablet computer by Lunar Microsystems.

The game will run in a fixed grid size of 16 by 16 cells and there will always be 20 mines hidden in the grid. A menu should provide the user the ability to reveal what lies beneath every cell, start a new game, or exit. When run, the game will present its grid with the mines already hidden. A user must be able to uncover a cell with a left mouse click or place a flag on an uncovered cell with a right mouse click. Flags can be removed by right clicking on them a second time. Every time a flag is placed, the number of mines remaining is decremented. But placing a flag on a cell does not necessarily mean that the cell contains a mine. The game is won only when every cell is either uncovered or has a flag on it. This can only happen if you placed the flags correctly.

Solution: The process of discovering mine locations is aided by clue cells that hold an integer indicating how many adjacent cells contain a mine. Uncovering an empty cell automatically uncovers every adjacent cell that is either empty or contains a clue. This uncovering step is handled very elegantly using recursion.

The presentation of the solution proceeds through Analysis (discussion of game inputs and outputs and the layout of the game interface), Design (identification of classes with their responsibilities and collaborators, visualized through a UML class diagram), and Implementation of the classes.

■ Study Guide Exercises

■ Answers to CheckPoint Problems

■ Additional exercises

Sorting and Searching

9

CHAPTER OUTLINE

I n this chapter we look at several algorithms for sorting and at support for sorting and searching in the Java Collections Framework. Sorting is an important topic that has many applications. As we saw with Binary Search in the last chapter, searching is more efficient on a sorted collection than on an unsorted collection. Sorting is also very important in data views. For example, I can view the contents of the folders on my computer by name, type, size, or date. Changing the view requires resorting the folder contents. The e-mail software I use will let me sort a mailbox by sender, send date, subject, priority, and so on. Switching from one order to another requires resorting the messages in the mailbox.[1]

To allow us to focus on the ideas behind the algorithms, we will first look at sorting arrays of integers. These algorithms would work equally well for other primitive types. Then we will look at the object-oriented issues involved in sorting

---

[1]This is also a nice example of the Model-View pattern.

objects. This will lead to a discussion of the important topics of polymorphism and generic programming. For each algorithm presented we will

■ discuss the main idea behind the algorithm

■ illustrate its behavior with an example

■ develop pseudocode and provide an implementation

■ determine the algorithm's time and space complexities

The two operations that dominate the work of sorting are comparing elements and moving elements. Clearly the fewer of these an algorithm does, the less expensive it will be. An important question is how sensitive the algorithm is to the ordering (sorted, reverse sorted, random) of the input. Ironically, some algorithms do *more* work when the input is already ordered than when it is random.

Comparing and moving elements dominate the cost of sorting

■ 9.1 Sorting Terminology

When someone says that something is "sorted," we assume they mean it is sorted in "increasing" order. We need to be clear about our terms, so here are the definitions we will use.

sort key. The sort key is the value used to sort the elements of a collection. If each element of the collection is a simple type, such as an integer, the element's value is the key. But if the elements are of a composite type (a type composed of multiple fields), then one of the fields is identified as the key and the ordering is based on it. For example, when you display the contents of a folder sorted by file size, the key is the size of the file. You could change the key to be the file name and display the files alphabetically, say. In a more sophisticated ordering, you would use primary and secondary keys. The files might be sorted first by file type (the primary key) and files of the same type would then be sorted lexicographically by name (the secondary key).

total ordering. Assume we have operations "equals to" (denoted ==) and "less than or equal to" (denoted ≤) defined on the elements of a collection. The elements of the collection are said to be totally ordered if, for any elements x, y, and z from the collection, the following conditions are met:

reflexive: $x == x$
transitive: if $x \leq y$ and $y \leq z$, then $x \leq z$
antisymmetric: if $x \leq y$ and $y \leq x$, then $x == y$
total: either $x \leq y$ or $y \leq x$

For example, this defines a total ordering of the integers:

$$\ldots -1 \leq 0 \leq 1 \leq 2 \leq 3 \leq 4 \ldots$$

increasing order (also called sorted or ascending order). The elements in the sorted collection are unique (no duplicates) and are ordered such that $e_1 < e_2 < e_3 < \ldots < e_n$. For example: $2 < 5 < 16 < 21$

nondecreasing order. The elements in the sorted collection may contain duplicates and are sorted such that $e_1 \leq e_2 \leq e_3 \leq \ldots \leq e_n$. For example: $2 \leq 5 \leq 5 \leq 21$

decreasing order (also called reverse sorted or descending order). The elements in the sorted collection are unique (no duplicates) and are ordered such that $e_1 > e_2 > e_3 > \ldots > e_n$. For example: $21 > 16 > 5 > 2$

nonincreasing order. The elements in the sorted collection may contain duplicates and are sorted such that $e_1 \geq e_2 \geq e_3 \geq \ldots \geq e_n$. For example: $21 \geq 5 \geq 5 \geq 2$

stable sort. Duplicates from the unsorted collection appear in the same relative order in the sorted collection. That is, if $e_i == e_j$ and $i < j$, then e_i will appear before e_j in the sorted sequence. In the following example, the subscripts to **5** show their relative order in the unsorted sequence.

Unsorted collection:	$\mathbf{5}_1$	2	6	$\mathbf{5}_2$	4
Sorted, stable:	2	4	$\mathbf{5}_1$	$\mathbf{5}_2$	6
Sorted, not stable:	2	4	$\mathbf{5}_2$	$\mathbf{5}_1$	6

in-place sort. The *extra* space required to store the data during the sort is independent of the size of the input. The space complexity of such an algorithm is $O(1)$.

Finally, the following piece of apparently obvious information will come in handy on several occasions: A collection of size 1 is always sorted.

A collection of size 1 is always sorted

■ **9.2** Sorting Primitive Types in an Array

When we looked at linear and binary search in the last chapter, we viewed the input array as having two parts: a searched part and an unsearched part. As the search algorithms progressed, the searched part became larger and the unsearched part smaller. We will start our discussion of sorting algorithms by taking a similar approach. Initially at least, we will view the input array as logically split into a sorted part and an unsorted part. A step in the sorting algorithm will increase the size of the sorted part by 1 and decrease the size of the unsorted part by 1.

Sorted and unsorted parts of the input

9.2.1 Selection Sort

Figure 9.1 (a) shows the initial configuration for a simple sorting algorithm called **selection sort**. The algorithm is so named because we *select* the largest item in the *un*sorted part of the array and move it to the *front* of the sorted part.[2] This step repeats until the size of the unsorted part is 1.

The idea behind selection sort

The first pass through the unsorted part of the array will find the largest element in the array. This becomes the first element in the sorted part (see Figure 9.1 (b)). Since this element is the largest in the array, it must be the case that all the elements remaining in the unsorted part are less than or equal to it. The next pass through the unsorted part will again find the largest element in the unsorted part. This element cannot be larger than the element already in the sorted part or we would have found it in the first pass. Consequently, when this element is prepended

How do we know this works?

---

[2]The exercises explore an alternative approach: looking for the smallest value in the unsorted part and moving it to the *rear* of the sorted part.

Figure 9.1 The first three passes of selection sort.

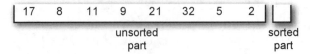

(a) Initial configuration for selection sort. The input array is logically split into an unsorted part and a sorted part.

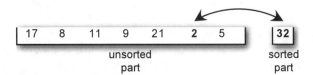

(b) The array after the largest value from the unsorted part has been moved to the front of the sorted part (first pass).

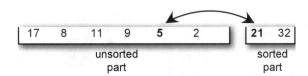

(c) The array after the largest value from the unsorted part has been moved to the front of the sorted part (second pass).

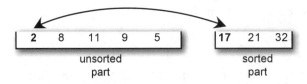

(d) The array after the largest value from the unsorted part has been moved to the front of the sorted part (third pass).

to the sorted part, we know that the elements in the sorted part are in nondecreasing order and that all the elements left in the unsorted part are less than or equal to the smallest element in the sorted part (see Figure 9.1 (c) and (d)).

When does the algorithm stop? When the size of the unsorted part is 1. By the reasoning above, the single element left in the unsorted part must be less than or equal to the smallest value in the sorted part, so it is already in its final, sorted position and we needn't do anything more with it.

The description and the illustration of the algorithm's behavior in Figure 9.1 give a general idea of what the algorithm should look like. Here is the high-level pseudocode.

Pseudocode: selectionSort(SomeType [] array)

1. *while the size of the unsorted part is greater than 1*
2. *find the position of the largest element in the unsorted part*
3. *move this largest element into the first position of the sorted part*
4. *decrement the size of the unsorted part by 1*
5. *// invariant: all elements from the first position to the last position of the*
6. *//   sorted part are in non-decreasing order*

> Including invariants helps you to think about your code

This is pretty high-level, but I like to begin at this level because it allows me to really focus on what has to be done instead of how it will be done in some language. I can worry about details as I refine the algorithm, which I do next for the first two steps in the loop.

The first step in the loop (*find the position of the largest element in the unsorted part*) is just the findMax() method developed in Chapter 2. It simply walks through the unsorted part of the array looking for the position of the largest value.

Pseudocode: finding the largest value in the unsorted part—step 2 of selectionSort()

let max be the position of the first element of the unsorted part
let current position be the second element of the unsorted part
while there are still elements to examine in the unsorted part
    if the value at the current position is greater than the value in max position
        let max be the current position
    advance current position

An issue not addressed yet is how we know the bounds of the sorted and unsorted parts. We will look at this next.

In step 3 of selectionSort() (*move this largest element into the first position of the sorted part*), we move the value found in the first step into the first position of the sorted part. But where is this in the array? The view presented in Figure 9.1 is a logical view we adopted to more easily understand the behavior of the algorithm. How do we determine the actual index of the "front" of the "sorted part" of the array? Look at the swaps done in Figure 9.1 and note that the "front" of the sorted part is actually the last element in the *unsorted* part.

The three passes from Figure 9.1 are shown again in Figure 9.2, this time with the array indices included. Here you can more easily see that the index of the "front"

> The "front" of the unsorted part of the array

Figure 9.2 The index to move the selected value to is always the size of the unsorted part of the array minus the number of the pass through the array.

0	1	2	3	4	5	6	7	indices
17	8	11	9	21	2	5	**32**	1st pass: index = 8 - 1 = 7
17	8	11	9	5	2	**21**	32	2nd pass: index = 8 - 2 = 6
2	8	11	9	5	**17**	21	32	3rd pass: index = 8 - 3 = 5

of the sorted part is always the size of the array minus the number of passes through the unsorted part. The implementation is given in Listing 9.1 and includes the high-level pseudocode as comments (in fact, I start by turning the pseudocode into comments and let them guide my coding).

I don't show this method as part of a class, but of course it is. The method is declared `static` and is one of several useful methods to be found in the class `gray.utils.ArrayUtils`. The other array-sorting algorithms presented here can also be found there.

Listing 9.1 The Java implementation of selection sort on an array of integers.

```
 1   /**
 2    * Sort an array of integers in ascending order using
 3    * selection sort.
 4    * @param a the array of integers to sort
 5    * @param n the number of elements to sort in <tt>a</tt>;
 6    * <tt>n</tt> must be less than or equal to <tt>a.length</tt>
 7    * @throws NullPointerException if the array object is null
 8    * @throws IndexOutOfBoundsException if <tt>n</tt> is
 9    *    greater than <tt>a.length</tt>
10    */
11   public static void selectionSort( int[] a, int n ) {
12       if ( a == null )
13           throw new NullPointerException();
14       if ( n > a.length )
15           throw new IndexOutOfBoundsException();
16
17       // while the size of the unsorted section is > 1
18       for ( int unsortedSize = n; unsortedSize > 1; unsortedSize-- ) {
19
20           // find the position of the largest element in
21           //   the unsorted part
22           int maxPos = 0;
23           for ( int pos = 1; pos < unsortedSize; pos++ )
24               if ( a[pos] > a[maxPos] )
25                   maxPos = pos;
26           // post-condition: maxPos is the position of the largest
27           //                 element in the unsorted part
28
29           // Swap the largest value with the last value in the
30           // unsorted part
31           int temp = a[unsortedSize - 1];
32           a[unsortedSize - 1] = a[maxPos];
33           a[maxPos] = temp;
34       }
35   }
```

What is the time complexity of selection sort? We will count the number of comparisons that are made as the measure of the algorithm's time complexity.[3] One comparison is done each time the inner loop iterates. The inner loop executes on each iteration of the outer loop. So the number of comparisons done is

time complexity:
Count the number of comparisons done

$$1 \quad * \quad \frac{\text{\# iterations of the inner loop per}}{\text{iteration of the outer loop}} \quad * \quad \text{\# iterations of the outer loop}$$

How many times will the outer loop iterate? The entry condition to the loop gives us a clue: The outer loop exits when the size of the unsorted part is 1. Because the initial size of the unsorted part is n and each iteration of the outer loop decreases this size by 1, we know that the outer loop will execute $n - 1$ times, which is $O(n)$.

How many times does the inner loop iterate? Its purpose is to find the largest value in the unsorted part of the array, which we know gets smaller by 1 for each iteration of the outer loop. On the first iteration of the outer loop then, the inner loop must look at n elements, and on the second iteration of the outer loop, the inner loop must look at $n - 1$ elements, then $n - 2$, and so on down to just 1 element. So, in asymptotic terms, the cost of the inner loop is $O(n)$. Plugging into the time complexity formula above we have

$$1 * O(n) * O(n) = O(n^2)$$

Selection sort's time complexity is $O(n^2)$

What is the space complexity of selection sort? We don't count the size of the array itself, only the additional space needed to do the sort. The algorithm requires space for local variables to index through the array and to do the swap. These needs are fixed and independent of the size of the array, so the array could contain 10 elements or 10,000 elements and the additional space needs would be the same. So selection sort's space complexity is $O(1)$, and it is an in-place sort.

Selection sort's space complexity is $O(1)$—it is an *in-place* sort

Before moving on we need to discover whether selection sort is sensitive to the ordering of the input. The inner for loop must examine every element in the unsorted part, looking for the largest element in it. These comparisons will be done no matter what the ordering of the unsorted part is. The swap that is done after the inner loop exits will also always be done, which means the initial ordering doesn't affect it either. So we can conclude that selection sort is *not* sensitive to the ordering of the input.

Selection sort is not sensitive to the ordering of the input

9.2.2 Insertion Sort

Like selection sort, **insertion sort** can view the input as split into sorted and unsorted parts, and each step in the algorithm increases the size of the sorted part by 1 while decreasing the size of the unsorted part by 1. However, as shown in Figure 9.3 (a), we begin selection sort with the sorted part on the *left* of the array and it already contains one element.[4]

---

[3]We will revisit this shortly to look at the cost in terms of data moves.

[4]We could also start at the right end of the array and build the sorted part as we move toward the beginning of the array. Hmm. . .might make a good exercise!

Figure 9.3 The first three passes of insertion sort.

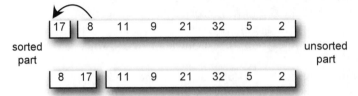

(a) Initial configuration for insertion sort. The input array is logically split into a sorted part (starting with one element) and an unsorted part.

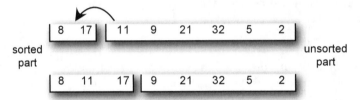

(b) The array after the first value from the unsorted part has been inserted in its proper position in the sorted part (first pass).

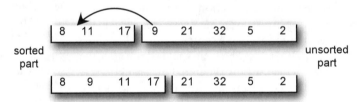

(c) The array after the first value from the unsorted part has been inserted in its proper position in the sorted part (second pass).

(d) The array after the first value from the unsorted part has been inserted in its proper position in the sorted part (third pass).

The idea behind insertion sort is that we take the first element (the *target*) of the unsorted part and look through the sorted part to find the position where this new element is to be inserted (hence the name of the algorithm) such that the sorted part remains sorted. Figure 9.3 shows several passes of the algorithm, illustrating its behavior.

The idea behind insertion sort

The sorted part starts with a single element. Because a collection of size 1 is always sorted, we know the "sorted part" is indeed sorted when the algorithm begins. The next step is to determine where the first element (the target) of the unsorted part should go in the sorted part and put it there. If we do this step correctly, the sorted part is larger by one element and remains sorted. This step is repeated until the unsorted part is *empty*, at which point all the elements have been inserted into their sorted position in the sorted part of the array.

The search for the insertion position stops when either an element less than or equal to the target is found (see Figure 9.3(c) and (d)) or the beginning of the array is reached (see Figure 9.3(b)). Here is the high-level pseudocode for insertion sort:

Pseudocode: insertionSort (SomeType [] array)
while the size of the unsorted part is greater than 0
      let the target element be the first element in the unsorted part
      find target's insertion point in the sorted part
      insert the target in its final, sorted position
      // invariant: the elements from position 0 to (size of the sorted part − 1)
      //   are in nondecreasing order

The second step in the loop is where the bulk of the work is done and needs refining. Since we need to make room in the sorted part of the array for the target, each time we find an element that is greater than the target we shift the element up a position.

Pseudocode: finding the insertion point for the target in the sorted part
get a copy of the first element in the unsorted part
while (there are elements in the unsorted part to examine AND
      we haven't found the insertion point for the target)
      move the sorted element up a position // make room for the target

The Java implementation of this pseudocode is given in Listing 9.2.

To determine the time complexity of insertion sort, we again count the number of times the target is compared with an element of the array. One comparison is done each time the inner loop iterates and the inner loop executes on each iteration of the outer loop. So the number of comparisons done is

Time complexity: count the number of comparisons done

$$1 \; * \; \begin{array}{c} \text{\# iterations of the inner loop per} \\ \text{iteration of the outer loop} \end{array} \; * \; \text{\# iterations of the outer loop}$$

How many times will the outer loop iterate? Each iteration of the outer loop results in one more element being moved into the sorted part. Since the algorithm begins with $n-1$ unsorted elements (look again at Figure 9.3(a)), the outer loop will execute $n-1$, or $O(n)$ times.

How many times will the inner loop iterate? The inner loop is responsible for finding the insertion point for the target in the sorted part of the array. In the worst case, the element to insert is the smallest seen so far and the inner loop will be forced to look at *all* the elements in the sorted part. How many are there? Recall that the size of the sorted part starts at 1 and grows by 1 with each iteration of the *outer* loop. So, in the worst case, the first time through the outer loop, one comparison will be done in the inner loop, the second time through two comparisons will be done, and so on up to $n-1$, which is $O(n)$. Plugging into the time complexity formula we get

$$1 * O(n) * O(n) = O(n^2)$$

Insertion sort's time complexity is $O(n^2)$

Listing 9.2 The Java implementation of insertion sort on an array of integers.

```
1   /**
2    * Sort an array of integers in ascending order using
3    * insertion sort.
4    * @param a the array of integers to sort
5    * @param n the number of elements to sort in <tt>a</tt>;
6    * <tt>n</tt> must be less than or equal to <tt>a.length</tt>
7    * @throws NullPointerException if the array object is null
8    * @throws IndexOutOfBoundsException if <tt>n</tt> is
9    *   greater than <tt>a.length</tt>
10   */
11  public static void insertionSort( int[] a, int n ) {
12      int target;    // the element we want to insert
13      int targetPos; // position of element we want to insert
14      int pos;
15
16      if ( a == null )
17          throw new NullPointerException();
18      if ( n > a.length )
19          throw new IndexOutOfBoundsException();
20
21      // while the size of the unsorted section is greater than 0
22      // when targetPos reaches n,
23      //     there are no more unsorted elements
24      for ( targetPos = 1; targetPos < n; targetPos++ ) {
25          // get a copy of the first element in the unsorted part
26          target = a[targetPos];
27
28          // while there are elements in the unsorted section to part
29          // AND we haven't found the insertion point for target
30          for ( pos = targetPos - 1; pos >= 0 && a[pos] > target; pos-- )
31
32              // element at pos is > target; move it up in the array
33              a[pos + 1] = a[pos];
34          // loop post-condition: pos == -1 or a[pos] <= target,
35          //                      so pos + 1 is the new home for target
36
37          // insert target in its final sorted position
38          a[pos + 1] = target;
39      }
40  }
```

Thus the time complexity for insertion sort is the same as for selection sort. What is the space complexity of insertion sort? There are local variables to walk through the array and to do the swaps, but that is all that is needed and, like selec-

Insertion sort's space complexity is O(1)— it is an *in-place* sort

tion sort, these space needs are independent of the size of the input array. So insertion sort is an in-place sort, and its space complexity is O(1).

This analysis might lead you to believe that the two algorithms do roughly the same amount of work. If we just consider comparisons, this would be true. But keep in mind the other important, and more expensive, operation that sorting algorithms do: moving elements around in the array. These moves aren't free, so we would like to do as few of them as possible.

What if we count element move operations instead of comparisons?

How do the two algorithms compare in terms of number of moves? The answer to this provides some neat insights into the differences between the two algorithms.

Selection sort always knows *where* the next element is going to go (the first position in the sorted part), but it doesn't know *which* element this is going to be (it has to find the largest element in the unsorted part). Consequently, selection sort only swaps two elements for each element that is moved to the sorted part of the array. At most this will be $n-1$ element swaps.[5]

Selection sort knows where to insert, but not what to insert

On the other hand, insertion sort knows *which* element to insert into the sorted part (the target, which is the first element in the unsorted part), but it doesn't know *where* in the sorted part it will go (it has to find the insertion point). Since the insertion point could be anywhere in the sorted part and we are using an array, it is necessary to move elements to make room for the element to be inserted. In the best case the input is already in order. In this case, the inner loop will do one comparison and then exit, so there would be no extra element movement.

Insertion sort knows what to insert, but not where to insert

In the worst case, the array is in descending order and every insertion will require *every* element of the sorted part to be moved up a position. The first time an insertion is done, one move would be needed. The second would require two moves, and so on up to $n-1$ moves for the last element inserted, giving

$$1+2+\ldots+n-1 \approx \frac{n^2+n}{2} = O(n^2)$$

So insertion sort is sensitive to the initial order of the input.

Well, $O(n^2)$ sounds like a lot of work and we long ago established that we would prefer to do as little work as possible. The next two sections look at two recursive sort algorithms, quick sort and merge sort, which can sort in $O(n\log_2 n)$ time.

CHECKPOINT

9.1 What are the essential differences between how selection sort and insertion sort do the sorting?

9.2 Why are selection sort and insertion sort in-place sorts?

9.3 Why is insertion sort sensitive to the order of the input?

---

[5]An exercise has you consider an alternative implementation in which unnecessary moves are avoided.

9.2.3 Quick Sort

In Chapter 8 we looked at a recursive algorithm to find the kth smallest element of an array. Recall that our solution was based on the idea that we only needed to do a partial sort of the input to find the kth smallest element. To do this we used a partition algorithm that partitioned the input around a pivot value. Once a partition is complete, we know the following (also summarized in Figure 9.4): **pivot and *partition*() revisited**

- The pivot is in its sorted position and won't need to move again.
- The values in the left partition are all less than the pivot and still need to be sorted.
- The values in the right partition are all greater than or equal to the pivot and still need to be sorted.

So each partition produces one more sorted element (the pivot), although these sorted elements (the pivots) may not always be contiguous to the other sorted elements as occurs with selection sort and insertion sort.

If this sounds like it could be the basis for a sorting algorithm, you are right, because if we can find a way to sort the left and right partitions, we will have a completely sorted array.

Hmm ... the `partition()` method provides a partial sort of a collection of elements. If we keep calling it on the unsorted partitions, will it eventually provide a complete sort? Yep!

Also, if you look closely at the nature of the problem, you will see that we have all the components of a neatly defined recursive solution to the problem of sorting. **Quick sort is naturally recursive** The partitioning algorithm puts one element into its final, sorted position and splits the original problem into two smaller problems—namely sorting the left and right partitions. This is the recursive case for a recursive sort algorithm. What is the base case? We know that a collection of size 1 is always sorted (I told you that would come in handy) and that an empty collection obviously requires no work, so when the size of a partition is less than or equal to 1, we are done sorting it. This description suggests the following recursive solution to sorting a linear collection of n elements.

$$
\text{QuickSort(collection, first, last)} \begin{cases} \text{collection, if size(collection)} \leq 1 & \text{// base case} \\ \text{QuickSort(collection, first, pivotPosition } - 1 \text{)} & \text{// recursive case — sort left partition} \\ \text{QuickSort(collection, pivotPosition } + 1, \text{ last)} & \text{// recursive case — sort right partition} \end{cases}
$$

if size(collection) > 1

where
  collection   the collection to be sorted
  first   the index of the first element of *collection*
  last   the index of the last element of *collection*
  pivotPosition = partition(collection, first, last)

As shown in Listing 9.3, the pseudocode and implementation follow quite nicely from the definition.

Figure 9.4 The result of partitioning around a pivot. The pivot is in its final, sorted position and will not move again.

elements < pivot	pivot	elements >= pivot

Listing 9.3 Pseudocode and Java implementation of the `quickSort()` method.

Pseudocode from Definition		Recursive Implementation
QuickSort (collection, first, last)	function	```void quickSort (int [] array,``` ``` int first, int last) {```
if size(collection) <= 1 return	base case	``` if (first >= last)``` ``` return;```
let pivotPosition be the position of the pivot returned by partition(collection, first, last)		``` int pivotPosition =``` ``` partition (array, first, last) ;```
// recursively sort the left partition QuickSort(collection, first, pivotPosition – 1)	recursive case	``` // recursive case: sort left partition``` ``` quickSort (array, first, pivotPosition – 1)```
// recursively sort the right partition QuickSort(collection, pivotPosition + 1, last)	recursive case	``` // recursive case: sort right partition``` ``` quickSort (array, pivotPosition+1, last);```
		```}```

Figure 9.5 shows the sequence of calls that would be made to sort an array (for purposes of comparison, this is the same array sorted with selection sort in Figure 9.1 and insertion sort in Figure 9.3). A few comments on the example will help to explain the action.

1. `partition()` uses the technique outlined in the exercises of the previous chapter to try to pick a good pivot. In this case, it examined the values in the first position (index 0), last position (index 7), and midpoint position (index 3), and picked the median of the values at those positions. It then swapped the chosen value into the pivot position (index *first*).

2. This is the result of the first partition. The left partition occupies the indices 0 to 2, and the right partition occupies indices 4 to 7.

3. This is the first recursive call. It will sort the left partition created by the first call to `partition()` (the result commented on in Note 2).

4. This recursive call meets the base case—remember that a collection of size 1 is always sorted.

Figure 9.5 A quick sort example. The partition steps are boxed. Pivots (the sorted elements) are shown in **boldface**.

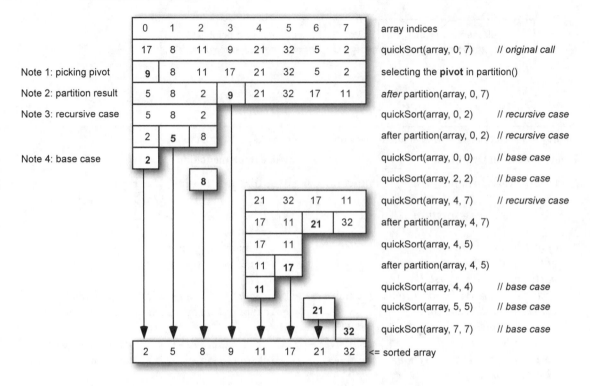

The cost of quick sort depends on the cost of partition() and on how many times it is called. In the last chapter we established that the cost of partition() is $O(n)$, since every element in the area being partitioned must be compared to the pivot. But let's look at this in the context of quick sort to be sure we are clear about the source of the algorithm's cost.

Figure 9.6 shows the partitions that are created in the average case. The first time partition() is called, it is looking at the whole collection, so there are clearly $n-1$ comparisons done, which is $O(n)$. The result is the collection partitioned into two roughly equal parts (each containing about $n/2$ elements). Quick sort will then be called recursively on each of these partitions, and each partition will require about $n/2$ comparisons, for a total of $O(n)$ comparisons for the pair. So at each level in Figure 9.6 there are $O(n)$ comparisons done. As the figure also illustrates, when the pivot evenly splits the input array, there are $\log_2 n$ levels, so the cost of quick sort in the average case is $O(n) * O(\log_2 n) = O(n\log_2 n)$.

Is quick sort sensitive to the ordering of the input? From the last chapter we know that the worst case for partition() occurs when it uses either the smallest or the largest value as the pivot, resulting in one empty partition and the other partition with $m-1$ elements, where m is the size of the input partition and $m \leq n$. The cost of each call to partition() is still $O(n)$, but now the number of calls to

Quick sort time complexity: average case is $O(n\log_2 n)$

Quick sort time complexity: Worst case is $O(n^2)$

Figure 9.6 The number of comparisons made when `partition()` evenly splits the input is $O(n\log_2 n)$: $O(n)$ comparisons at each level and $O(\log_2 n)$ levels.

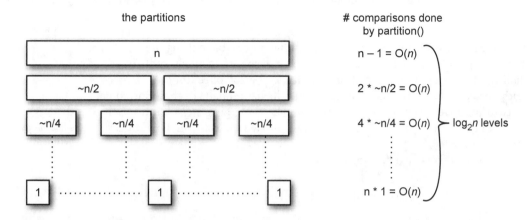

partition() shoots up to $O(n)$ (see Figure 9.7), producing a time complexity of $O(n) \times O(n) = O(n^2)$! So, yes, quick sort is *very* sensitive to the input ordering and in the worst case has the same time complexity as selection sort and insertion sort.

Quick sort uses a few indexing and swap variables, but these are independent of the size of the input. However, as with most recursive methods, the space complexity of quick sort is determined by the number of activation records on the stack when the base case is met. In the average case this is $O(\log_2 n)$ (see Figure 9.6). In the worst case, there are $O(n)$ calls producing $O(n)$ activation records on the stack (see Figure 9.7). So, quick sort is *not* an in-place sort.

Quick sort space complexity: Avg: $O(\log_2 n)$ Worst: $O(n)$

Quick sort is not an in-place sort

Figure 9.7 The number of comparisons made when `partition()` produces one empty partition and another with $n - 1$ elements is $O(n^2)$: $O(n)$ comparisons at each level and $O(n)$ levels.

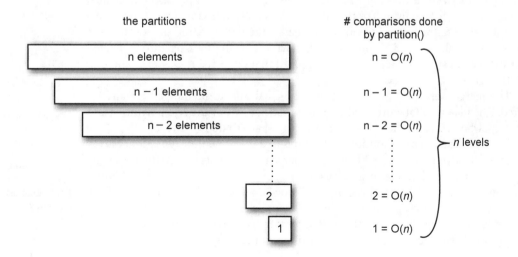

9.2.4 Merge Sort

Quick sort works well most of the time, but it is very sensitive to the initial order of the input. Recall that the key to the quick sort $O(n\log_2 n)$ runtime is evenly splitting the input.

Quick sort sorts while *splitting* partitions

The **merge sort** algorithm guarantees that the split is even. Unlike quick sort, the sorting in merge sort is not done as part of the process of splitting the input (via quick sort's `partition()` method). Instead, merge sort continually splits its input in half until the size of each partition is 1 (remember, a collection of 1 element is already sorted). Merge sort then merges (hence its name) pairs of these sorted partitions to produce a larger, sorted partition. These merging steps continue until there is only a single partition left (the entire sorted collection). This process is shown in Figure 9.8.

Merge sort sorts while *merging* partitions

Here is the recursive definition:

$$\text{MergeSort(collection, first, last)} \begin{cases} \text{collection, if size(coll) } \leq 1 & \textit{// base case} \\ \text{MergeSort(collection, first, midpoint} - 1) & \textit{// recursive case — sort left partition} \\ \text{MergeSort(collection, midpoint, last)} & \textit{// recursive case — sort right partition} \\ \text{merge (collection, first, midpoint, last)} & \textit{// merge left and right partitions} \end{cases}$$

— if size(collection) > 1

where
- *collection*   the collection to be sorted
- *first*   the index of the first element of *coll*
- *midpoint*   (first + last + 1) / 2
- *last*   the index of the last element of *coll*

Conceptually this is easy to understand. The implementation, however, is somewhat tricky (and trying to explain it is harder still, so bear with me). The tricky part is the merging step. The most intuitive approach is presented first, then a more efficient (but more complex) solution is given.

First, remember that, as with quick sort, when we partition the array, we are not creating two *separate* arrays to be merged. This is only a logical partition. In reality, the partitions just take up different ranges of indices in the same array. For example, in Figure 9.8, the two partitions created after the first splitting step occupy the ranges 0 through 3, and 4 through 7 in the array, and the four partitions created after the second splitting step occupy the index ranges 0 to 1, 2 to 3, 4 to 5, and 6 to 7 in the array.

The merge step relies on the fact that the partitions to be merged are already sorted. The idea is to take the smaller of the first element of the two partitions and put it . . . where? This is the rub—we need extra space to do the merge.

Merge sort needs extra space for the merging step

The simplest and most intuitive solution is to create an empty, temporary array the size of the two partitions to be merged, merge the elements into it, then copy the temporary array back to the original array.

Simple solution: Merge sorted partitions into a temporary array

This approach is shown in Figure 9.9. Notice that we need to keep track of the "front" element of each partition. When a "front" element from one of the partitions is copied to the temporary array, its successor becomes the "front" element. We also need to keep track of the insertion position in the temporary array.

Figure 9.8 Merge sort follows a series of splitting steps with a series of merging steps which produce sorted partitions.

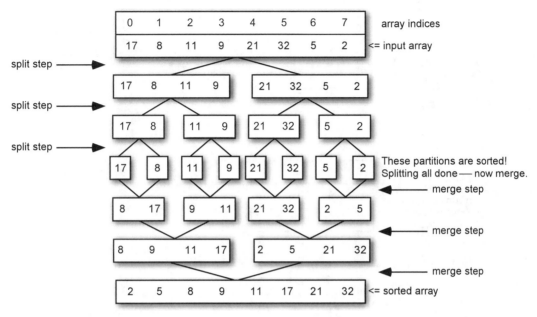

Also note that when one of the partitions is "empty" (has had all its elements copied to the temporary array), the elements left in the other partition can be copied to the temporary array without doing any comparisons. We'll make good use of this shortly.

The problem with this simple solution is the extra space and element move operations required. The temporary array is always the size of the two partitions, which is always ≤ *n*, so the space complexity for the merge alone is O(*n*) (this doesn't count the cost of the activation records on the stack).

Since the merging is done into the temporary array, there are at most *n* element moves from the partitions to the temporary array, where *n* is the number of elements in the partitions to be merged. After the merge is complete, the temporary array has to be copied back to the input array for a total cost of 2*n* = O(*n*) element moves.

At the cost of a little more complexity, we can about halve the cost of the merge. Let's think about this a bit. Here is what we know (don't discount the trivial!):

■ The two partitions to be merged are already sorted.

■ The merged partition will be the combined size of the two partitions to be merged.

■ Once merged, the smallest elements from the two partitions will occupy the lower part of the merged partition, and the larger elements will be in the upper partition.

The idea is to use the *input array* to do the merge. To make room for the merging, a temporary array the size of the *lower* partition is created and the lower parti-

Better solution: Merge into the input array

Figure 9.9 In the simple merge, a temporary array the size of the two partitions to be merged is used to merge their elements. Then the temporary array is copied back to the input array.

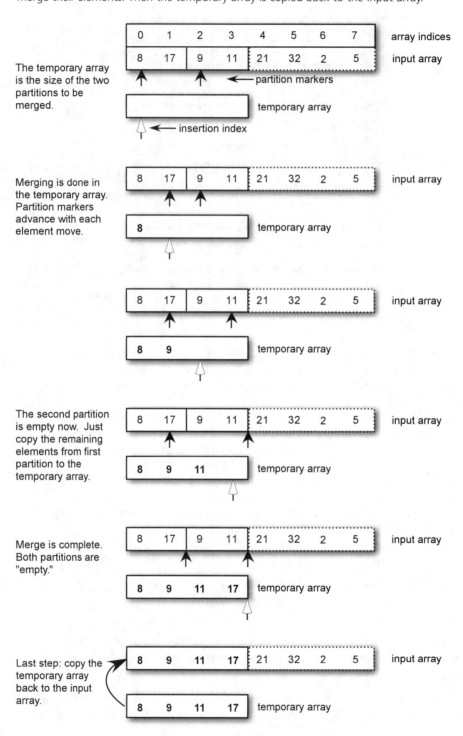

The temporary array is the size of the two partitions to be merged.

Merging is done in the temporary array. Partition markers advance with each element move.

The second partition is empty now. Just copy the remaining elements from first partition to the temporary array.

Merge is complete. Both partitions are "empty."

Last step: copy the temporary array back to the input array.

tion is copied to it (so now the size of the temporary array is at most *n*/2, half the size of the temporary array used in our simpler solution). Now the temporary array and the upper partition of the input array are the sources for the merge and the input array from the first position of the lower partition to the last position of the upper partition is the destination for the merge (see Figure 9.10 (a)).

Figure 9.10 In the more efficient merge, the temporary array is a copy of the first partition and the merging is done in the input array.

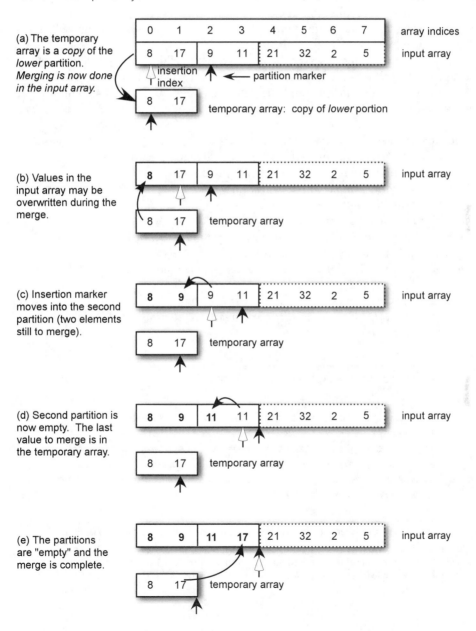

The merging proceeds as shown in Figure 9.10. At most there will be *n* additional data movements during this merge. This occurs if all the elements in the upper partition are less than or equal to the smallest element in the lower partition. If we are lucky, however, all the elements in the lower partition are less than or equal to the smallest element in the upper partition and there will only be an additional *n*/2 moves as the temporary array is copied back to the lower partition. The elements in the upper partition will already be in place.

One more point of improvement. I have assumed that the two versions of merge discussed allocate the temporary array *inside* the merge method. While it is true the array is freed on exit from the merge method and, presumably, garbage collected when necessary, we should avoid the overhead of these allocations if we can. The solution, of course, is to allocate the temporary array once outside the merge method and reuse it by passing it in as a parameter.

Next improvement: Reuse the temporary array

How big should this temporary array be if we are just to allocate it once? Since merge sort guarantees to split the input in half,[6] the largest partition to be merged will be $\lceil n / 2 \rceil$ in size. The complete implementation is shown in Listing 9.4.[7] The implementation of merge is based on the following pseudocode.

Pseudocode: merge(inputArray, tempArray, first, mid, last)
// the lower partition is in the input array from first to mid − 1
// the upper partition is in the input array from mid to last
// the merged partition is in the input array from first to last
copy the lower partition to the temp array
while neither partition is empty
     merge the partitions into the input array from positions first to last
// loop post-condition: one of the partitions is empty
// if the lower partition is empty, just return since the upper partition is
// already in the input array
if the second partition is empty
     copy the remainder of the lower partition from the temp array into
        the input array

Listing 9.4 The Java implementation of the merge sort algorithm.

```
1    /**
2     * The recursive merge sort algorithm to sort the elements from
3     * <tt>first</tt> to <tt>last</tt> in <tt>inputArray</tt>
4     * using <tt>tempArray</tt> as a temporary space to do the merging.
5     * @param inputArray Array containing the elements to be sorted
6     * @param tempArray Temporary array to use during the merge phase
7     * @param first Index of first element of the partition to be sorted
```

---

[6]If the size of the input is odd, the upper partition will have one more element than the lower partition.

[7]I have included comments for `internalMergeSort()` and `merge()` using the javadoc style. They will be ignored by the javadoc tool because the methods are private, so these comments are for the programmer. I use the javadoc style for consistency. You could choose a different style; the important thing is to include the comments.

```
8      * @param last Index of last element of the partition to be sorted
9      * @pre   The array arguments are not null.
10     * @pre   first and last are within the bounds of the inputArray.
11     * @post The inputArray is sorted in non-decreasing order.
12     */
13    private static void internalMergeSort( int[] inputArray,
14                                           int[] tempArray,
15                                           int first, int last ){
16        if ( ( last - first + 1) <= 1 )
17            return;    // base case - partition size is 1
18
19        // find the mid point of the partition from first to last
20        int mid = ( ( first + last + 1 ) / 2 );
21        internalMergeSort( inputArray, tempArray, first, mid - 1 );
22        internalMergeSort( inputArray, tempArray, mid, last );
23        merge( inputArray, tempArray, first, mid, last );
24    }
25
26    /**
27     * Sort the array of integers using the merge sort algorithm.
28     * @param inputArray The array of integers to be sorted.
29     * @throws NullPointerException if the argument is null.
30     */
31    public static void mergeSort( int[] inputArray ){
32        if ( inputArray == null )
33            throw new NullPointerException();
34
35        int tempArray[] = new int[inputArray.length / 2];
36        internalMergeSort( inputArray, tempArray, 0,
37                          inputArray.length - 1 );
38    }
39
40    /**
41     * The merge algorithm merges the elements from the two
42     * partitions in the input array. The lower partition is
43     * in positions <tt>first</tt> to <tt>mid - 1</tt> and
44     * the upper partition is in <tt>mid</tt> to <tt>last</tt> in
45     * <tt>inputArray</tt>. <tt>tempArray</tt> is used as a
46     * temporary space to do the merging.
47     * @param inputArray Array containing the elements to be sorted
48     * @param tempArray Temporary array to use during the merge phase
49     * @param first Index of the first element of the lower partition
50     * @param mid Index of first element of upper partition
51     * @param last Index of the last element of the upper partition
52     * @pre   The array arguments are not null
53     * @pre   first, mid and last are within the bounds of inputArray
54     * @post inputArray from first to last is sorted in non-decreasing
55     *          order
56     */
```

```
57     private static void merge( int [] inputArray, int[] tempArray,
58                                 int first, int mid, int last){
59         int tempSize = last - first + 1,
60             insertIndex          = first,
61             firstPartitionIndex  = 0,
62             secondPartitionIndex = mid;
63
64         // copy the lower partition to the temp array
65         System.arraycopy( inputArray, first, tempArray, 0,
66                                 mid - first);
67
68         // while neither partition is empty
69         while ( ( firstPartitionIndex < ( mid - first ) ) &&
70                   ( secondPartitionIndex <= last ) ) {
71             // merge the partitions into the input array from positions
72             //    first to last
73             if ( tempArray[firstPartitionIndex] <
74                                     inputArray[secondPartitionIndex] ){
75                 inputArray[insertIndex] = tempArray[firstPartitionIndex];
76                 firstPartitionIndex++;
77             }
78             else {
79                 inputArray[insertIndex] = inputArray[secondPartitionIndex];
80                 secondPartitionIndex++;
81             }
82             insertIndex++;
83         }
84         // postcondition: one of the partitions is empty
85
86         // if the lower partition is empty, just return since the upper
87         //    partition is already in the input array
88
89         // if the second partition is empty, copy the remainder of the
90         // lower partition from the temp array into the input array
91         while ( firstPartitionIndex < ( mid - first ) ) {
92             inputArray[insertIndex] = tempArray[firstPartitionIndex];
93             firstPartitionIndex++;
94             insertIndex++;
95         }
96     }
```

SUMMING UP

Selection sort and insertion sort are nonrecursive algorithms for sorting elements in an indexed linear collection. Selection sort sorts by selecting the largest unsorted element and prepending it to a sorted collection. Insertion sort sorts by taking the first unsorted element and inserting it at its sorted position in a sorted collection. Both algorithms have a time complexity of $O(n^2)$ and are in-place sorts.

Table 9.1 The time and space complexities of the sorting algorithms.

Algorithm	Time Complexity		Space Complexity	
	Average Case	Worst Case	Average Case	Worst Case
Selection sort	$O(n^2)$	$O(n^2)$	$O(1)$	$O(1)$
Insertion sort	$O(n^2)$	$O(n^2)$	$O(1)$	$O(1)$
Quick sort	$O(n\log_2 n)$	$O(n^2)$	$O(\log_2 n)$	$O(n)$
Merge sort	$O(n\log_2 n)$	$O(n\log_2 n)$	$O(n)$	$O(n)$

Quick sort and merge sort are recursive sorting algorithms. Quick sort sorts while splitting the input, since each partitioning step places one value (the pivot) in its final, sorted position. Merge sort sorts while merging sorted partitions. Quick sort's time complexity is $O(n\log_2 n)$ in the average case, but $O(n^2)$ in the worst case. Its space complexity is $O(\log_2 n)$ in the average case, but $O(n)$ in the worst case. Merge sort is $O(\log_2 n)$ with a space complexity of $O(n)$ due to the extra space needed to do the merge (see Table 9.1).

CHECKPOINT

9.4 Why is quick sort sensitive to the initial ordering of the input?

9.5 How does merge sort guarantee that it evenly splits the input every time? Why can't quick sort do that?

9.6 Why are quick sort and merge sort not in-place sorts?

■ **9.3** Comparing Objects

What if we want to sort an array of objects instead of an array of primitive types? With only a few changes, the algorithms developed in the last section will work beautifully. More importantly, making the necessary changes will illustrate generic programming through polymorphism—one of the true advantages of OOP.

The central issue is how element comparisons are done on objects. The relational operators we used to compare integers in the last section won't do the same duty for objects—they'll compare the object *references* instead of the object *values*. Instead, we need each class to provide a method that can compare two instances of itself. To guarantee uniformity in how this is done, Java defines the generic interface Comparable<T> (see Listing 9.5), which specifies a single method: int compareTo(T).

For two objects obj1 and obj2, of the same type T, a method call obj1.compareTo(obj2) returns

Relational operators cannot be used on objects to compare their values

Use Comparable<T>'s compareTo()to compare object values

■ a negative integer if obj1 is "less than" obj2

■ a positive integer if obj1 is "greater than" obj2

■ zero if obj1 is "equal to" obj2

Listing 9.5 The `java.lang.Comparable< T >` interface.

```
1    public interface Comparable<T> {
2        int compareTo( T o );
3    }
```

Table 9.2 shows the equivalent test to make using `compareTo()` for each of the relational operators, and the program in Listing 9.6 illustrates some of these uses for the `Integer` class.[8] Note that we still need the relational operators to compare the method's result with 0 (lines 10, 13, and 16 of Listing 9.6 and in Table 9.2).

There are two things we need to do to get our sorting methods to sort objects.

1. Modify the sorting methods to use `Comparable.compareTo()` to compare the objects stored in the input array.

2. See how to customize our own classes to implement `Comparable<T>`.

9.3.1 Modifying the Sort Methods to Use `Comparable<T>`

We'll modify the implementation of selection sort as an example. Modifications to the other sort algorithms follow easily from this. Actually, there are very few changes that need to be made to support sorting objects using `Comparable`. They involve how the element comparisons are done in the sort method and defining a generic method header.

Modifying selectionSort to use Comparable<T>

How to Do the Comparison of Objects Using `compareTo()`

We need to change the line that compares array elements. In the `int[]` implementation, we directly compared two elements of the `int` array using the relational operator `>`, as follows:

```
if ( a[currentPos] > a[maxPos] )
    maxPos = currentPos;
```

Table 9.2 Semantics of `Comparable.compareTo()` in terms of the relational operators.

Test Using **compareTo()** to Compare Objects	Equivalent Relational Operation to Compare Primitives
`a.compareTo( b ) < 0`	$a < b$
`a.compareTo( b ) > 0`	$a > b$
`a.compareTo( b ) == 0`	$a == b$
`a.compareTo( b ) != 0`	$a != b$
`a.compareTo( b ) <= 0`	$a <= b$
`a.compareTo( b ) >= 0`	$a >= b$

---

[8]The wrapper classes for the Java primitive types all implement `Comparable` as do `String` and `Date`.

Listing 9.6 A simple illustration of the use of `Comparable.compareTo()` on `Integer` objects. The output follows the listing.

```
1   /**
2    * Illustrate the use of Comparable.compareTo() on Integers.
3    */
4   public class IntegerCompareToEx {
5       public static void main(String[] args) {
6           Integer int5 = new Integer( 5 );
7           Integer int7 = new Integer( 7 );
8           Integer int5Dup = new Integer( 5 );
9
10          if ( int5.compareTo( int7 ) < 0 )
11              System.out.println( int5 + " is less than " + int7 );
12
13          if ( int5.compareTo( int5Dup ) == 0 )
14              System.out.println( int5 + " is equal to " + int5Dup );
15
16          if ( int7.compareTo( int5 ) > 0 )
17              System.out.println( int7 + " is greater than " + int5 );
18      }
19  }
```

OUTPUT

```
5 is less than 7
5 is equal to 5
7 is greater than 5
```

Table 9.2 tells us how to use `compareTo()` to get the semantically equivalent behavior for `Comparable` objects. If the object in `a[currentPos]` is "greater than" the object in `a[maxPos]`, `compareTo()` will return a positive integer. Here is the change:

Comparing objects using `Comparable`'s `compareTo()`

```
if ( a[currentPos].compareTo(a[maxPos]) > 0 )
    maxPos = currentPos;
```

Updating the `selectionSort()` Method Header

The second change we need to make is to the method header. We really do not want to have to provide separate `selectionSort()` methods for every class we want to be able to sort. For example, we don't want to have to provide

Don't do this!

```
void selectionSort( Integer[] a, int n )
void selectionSort( Float[] a, int n )
void selectionSort( Date[] a, int n )
void selectionSort( String[] a, int n )
etc.
```

Instead, we want to provide a single generic method that will sort any array whose elements are comparable using `compareTo()` from `Comparable`. So what should the array type be?

Your first thought might be to define a generic method for some type `T`. Recall that a generic method has a formal type parameter section that appears before the method return type. The type variable from the type parameter section can appear as the method's return type, in the parameter list, and as the type of local variables. So a first attempt might look like

```
public static <T> void selectionSort( T[], int n)
```

where `T` represents the array element type. This is a good first attempt but falls short of what we need. The problem is that the method doesn't know enough about the actual type that will map to `T`. We need to be sure that whatever type `T` ends up being, its elements are `Comparable` to one another. Achieving our goal will require introducing some new generics syntax. We'll do this in two steps.

In the first step, let's see how we can make sure that the elements are `Comparable`. What do the classes specified in the `selectionSort()` method headers above have in common? They all implement the `Comparable` interface (you can check the documentation on this). This is illustrated in the UML inheritance diagram in Figure 9.11. Here are some of the corresponding class headers:

```
// The Integer class declares that it implements
// the Comparable interface so that an instance of
// itself can be compared to another Integer.
public class Integer implements Comparable<Integer>
```

```
// The String class declares that it implements
// the Comparable interface so that an instance of
// itself can be compared to another String.
public class String implements Comparable<String>
```

Note the use of a specific type in the type parameter field

In these class headers the `T` in `Comparable<T>` has been replaced by the type that an instance of the class wants to compare to itself. So, for example, class `Integer` needs to be comparable to `Integers`; class `String` needs to be comparable to `Strings`; and so on. We'll look at this again shortly when we make some of our own classes comparable.

Figure 9.11 The relationship between some Java classes and `Comparable` (UML class diagram).

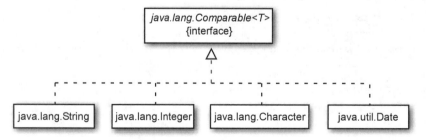

What is important to us here is that this means we can say that all these types *are subtypes of* Comparable (an Integer object "is a kind of" Comparable object; a Date object "is a kind of" Comparable object; and so on). Now what we need for our generic method is a way to say that instances of the actual type passed in for T are comparable to one another. Our second attempt at the method header now looks like this:

```
public static <T extends Comparable<T>> void selectionSort( T[] a, int n )
```

which means that selectionSort() can sort instances of any type T that implements Comparable.

The use of extends here is potentially confusing because it can also mean that one class extends another (e.g., public class Square extends Rectangle) or that one interface will extend another (e.g., public interface ListIterator<E> extends Iterator<E>). Likewise, implements can mean that a class will implement an interface (e.g., public class Integer implements Comparable<Integer>). However, the purpose of extends in the context of type parameters means the two *types* are related to each other. Consequently, the expression "S extends T" means that S is a subtype of T. If T is an interface (as in this case), it means that S implements T.

> Think of "S extends T" as saying that S is a *subtype* of T

The header <T extends Comparable<T>> is pretty generic, but we can do better. In the second step to introducing new generic syntax, we can make the header even more generic. Indeed we have to because if we don't, some objects that are comparable will be rejected by the compiler as being of the wrong type. The problem is that <T extends Comparable<T>> means the class we provide for T must implement Comparable *itself*: It cannot have *inherited* the compareTo() method from a superclass that implemented Comparable.

For example, consider the inheritance diagram in Figure 9.12. Class SuperType implements Comparable and defines the compareTo() method. Class SubType extends SuperType, so inherits the implementation of compareTo(). Let's assume that how SuperType compares instances of itself also works for SubType. In other words, the compareTo() method inherited by SubType can be used to compare SubType objects. It would make sense, then, that an array of SubType objects could be sorted using the header for selectionSort() given above. However, this is not the case. For our second attempt at the selectionSort() header above, the call

```
selectionSort( arrayOfSubType, arrayOfSubType.length );
```

will generate a compiler error—something like "void selectionSort(SuperType, int) cannot be applied to selectionSort(SubType, int)."

What we need now is a way to say either that T implements Comparable itself, or that some *supertype* of T implements Comparable (in which case T will inherit that class's compareTo() method). In Chapter 4 we used the ? wildcard with extends to indicate a type upper bound (e.g., <? extends T> describes the family of types bounded above by T). Here we will use the wildcard with the keyword super to specify a type *lower bound* (e.g., <? super T> describes a family of types bounded *below* by T). Our header is now

> Specifying a type *lower* bound for a generic type

```
<T extends Comparable<? super T>> void selectionSort( T[], int n )
```

Figure 9.12 Instances of SubType inherit compareTo() from SuperType, but cannot be sorted using <T extends Comparable<T>> selectionSort(T[], int) because SubType does not implement Comparable.

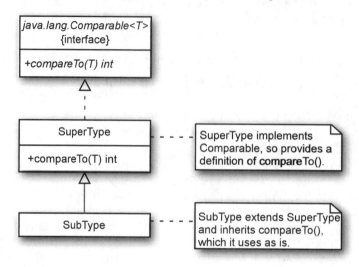

This means the method accepts an array of any type T (the lower bound) that implements Comparable or has a supertype (ancestor) that implements Comparable. This is as generic as we can get and is, perhaps, a little more understandable when you realize that after the compiler has done type erasure on the method, the header will look this:

```
public static void selectionSort( Comparable [] a, int n )
```

The int and generic Comparable array implementations are shown side by side in Listing 9.7, with the affected lines highlighted in boldface. Note that the only message sent to any object in the input array is compareTo(). This is just as well, since it is almost the only method that we can be sure is defined on every object in the array (how can we be sure of that?). So, our new selectionSort() does not care if it is sorting Integer, Address, Employee or WorkOrder objects. All it cares about is that the objects in the array are comparable to one another using compareTo().

This is pretty cool. We have a *generic* sorting algorithm that can sort an array of any type that has access to a compareTo() method (i.e., a class that either implements Comparable itself or has an ancestor that implements it). Listing 9.8 shows how our new implementation is used to sort an array of String objects and an array of Date objects.

How does this work? First, when the compiler sees a call to selectionSort(), it will verify that the array's element type has access to Comparable's compareTo() method. If not, a syntax error is generated. Second, once the program compiles and is running, the Java runtime system knows the actual type of the objects being stored in the array that is passed to the sort method. Also, recall that when we intro-

Listing 9.7 The `int` and `Comparable` implementations of `selectionSort()` with the modified parts shown in **boldface**.

```
/**
 * Sort the array elements in ascending order
 *    using selection sort.
 * @param a the array of integers to sort
 * @param n the number of elements in a to sort
 * @throws NullPointerException if a is null
 * @throws IndexOutOfBoundsException if <tt>n</tt>
 *    is greater than <tt>a.length</tt>
 */
static void selectionSort( int[a], int [n] ) {

   if ( a == null )
      throw new NullPointerException();

   if ( n > a.length )
      throw new IndexOutOfBoundsException();

   // while the size of the unsorted part is > 1
   for ( int unsortedSize = n;
         unsortedSize > 1; unsortedSize-- ) {
      // find the position of the largest
      // element in the unsorted section
      int maxPos = 0;
      for (int pos = 1; pos < unsortedSize; pos++)
         if ( a[pos] > a[maxPos] )
            maxPos = pos;
      // postcondition: maxPos is the position
      // of the largest element in the unsorted
      // part of the array

      // Swap largest value with the last value
      // in the unsorted part
      int temp = a[unsortedSize − 1] ;
      a[unsortedSize − 1] = a[maxPos] ;
      a[maxPos] = temp;
   }
}
```

```
/**
 * Sort the array elements in ascending order
 *    using selection sort.
 * @param a array of Comparable objects to sort
 * @param n the number of elements in a to sort
 * @throws NullPointerException if a is null
 * @throws IndexOutOfBoundsException if <tt>n</tt>
 *    is greater than <tt>a.length</tt>
 */
static <T extends Comparable<? super T>>
            void selectionSort( T[] a, int n )
   if ( a == null )
      throw new NullPointerException() ;

   if ( n > a.length )
      throw new IndexOutOfBoundsException() ;

   // while the size of the unsorted part is > 1
   for ( int unsortedSize = n;
         unsortedSize > 1; unsortedSize-- ) {
      // find the position of the largest
      // element in the unsorted section
      int maxPos = 0;
      for (int pos = 1; pos < unsortedSize; pos++)
         if ( a[pos].compareTo (a[maxPos]) > 0)
            maxPos = pos;
      // postcondition: maxPos is the position
      // of the largest element in the unsorted
      // part of the array

      // Swap largest value with the last value
      // in the unsorted part
      T temp = a[unsortedSize − 1];
      a[unsortedSize − 1] = a[maxPos] ;
      a[maxPos] = temp;
   }
}
```

duced polymorphism in Chapter 1, we said that at runtime the system would dynamically bind the method call (`compareTo()` in this case) to the correct object. That is, it will determine the actual type of the object in the array and then send the message to *that* object.

Polymorphism and dynamic binding

A word of caution before we move on. Just because two classes implement the `Comparable` interface doesn't mean that instances of those two classes can be compared to one another. For example, it would not be very sensible to write

Objects compared with `Comparable` must be of the same type

```
String apples = new String("It won't work!");
Integer oranges = new Integer( 6 );
int badCompare  = apples.compareTo( oranges );
```

Listing 9.8 Using a generic `selectionSort()` to sort an array of `String` objects and an array of `Date` objects (the output follows the listing).

```
 1    /**
 2     * Illustrate sorting based on Comparable.compareTo().
 3     */
 4    import gray.util.ArrayUtils;
 5    import java.util.Date;
 6    import java.util.Calendar;
 7
 8    public class ComparableEx {
 9
10        public static void main( String[] args ) {
11            // First, sort a bunch of String objects
12            String[] c = new String[5];
13
14            System.out.println("\nFirst, sort some String objects");
15            c[0] = new String( "In the Heat of the Night" );
16            c[1] = new String( "The Dish" );
17            c[2] = new String( "Farewell My Concubine" );
18            c[3] = new String( "Tea with Mussolini" );
19            c[4] = new String( "My Life as a Dog" );
20
21            System.out.println("The unsorted Strings (movie titles):");
22            ArrayUtils.print( (Object[])c , 0, c.length - 1 );
23            ArrayUtils.selectionSort( c, c.length );
24            System.out.println("\nThe sorted Strings:");
25            ArrayUtils.print( (Object[])c , 0, c.length - 1   );
26
27            // Now sort a bunch of Date objects
28            Date[] dates = new Date[5];
29            Calendar calendar = Calendar.getInstance();
30
31            System.out.println("\n\nNow, sort some Date objects");
32            //  Set a date                      Put the date in the array
33            calendar.set( 1957, 11, 4 );        dates[0] = calendar.getTime();
34            calendar.set( 2001, 10, 4 );        dates[1] = calendar.getTime();
35            calendar.set( 2001, 0, 1 );         dates[2] = calendar.getTime();
36            calendar.set( 1957, 10, 1 );        dates[3] = calendar.getTime();
37            calendar.set( 1952, 6, 15 );        dates[4] = calendar.getTime();
38
39            System.out.println("The unsorted Dates:");
40            ArrayUtils.print( dates , 0, dates.length - 1 );
41            ArrayUtils.selectionSort( dates, dates.length );
42            System.out.println("\nThe sorted Dates:");
43            ArrayUtils.print( dates , 0, dates.length - 1   );
44        }
45    }
```

OUTPUT (in two columns)

```
First, sort some String objects        Now, sort some Date objects
The unsorted Strings (movie titles):   The unsorted Dates:
In the Heat of the Night               Wed Dec 04 12:41:11 EST 1957
The Dish                               Sun Nov 04 12:41:11 EST 2001
Farewell My Concubine                  Mon Jan 01 12:41:11 EST 2001
Tea with Mussolini                     Fri Nov 01 12:41:11 EST 1957
My Life as a Dog                       Tue Jul 15 12:41:11 EDT 1952

The sorted Strings:                    The sorted Dates:
Farewell My Concubine                  Tue Jul 15 12:41:11 EDT 1952
In the Heat of the Night               Fri Nov 01 12:41:11 EST 1957
My Life as a Dog                       Wed Dec 04 12:41:11 EST 1957
Tea with Mussolini                     Mon Jan 01 12:41:11 EST 2001
The Dish                               Sun Nov 04 12:41:11 EST 2001
```

If we were to compile this code, we would get an error saying that we cannot apply compareTo(String) to compareTo(Integer). This actually makes sense. Go back to the inheritance hierarchy in Figure 9.11 and the sample class headers for Integer and String. The class header for Integer says that it implements Comparable<Integer>, meaning that we can *only* compare an Integer to an Integer using its compareTo() method. Keep this in mind as we discuss implementing Comparable in some classes of our own.

9.3.2 Customizing a Class to Be Comparable

The next task is to see how to make a class Comparable so that instances of it can be compared and sorted. To begin, when implementing an interface, we must look at the interface's contract carefully so that we are clear about the requirements the implementation must meet.

Understand the interface's contract!

Comparable defines a total ordering on the objects of a class that implements it. This is called the class's *natural ordering* and the compareTo() method of a class is called its *natural comparison method*. Also, although it is not required by the contract, it is considered good practice to make sure x.equals(y) for all objects for which x.compareTo(y)== 0.[9] As we will see, this has implications beyond the implementation of Comparable.

compareTo() defines a class's natural ordering

Next, we need to decide what integer compareTo() will return. The contract only says that for objects x and y, x.compareTo(y) must return the following:

compareTo()
== → return 0
< → return −1
> → return +1

■ A negative integer if x is "less than" y

■ A positive integer if x is "greater than" y

■ Zero if x is "equal to" y

---

[9]Recall that equals() is inherited from the class Object and that the default implementation compares the references of the objects involved and not their values.

But the contract doesn't say *which* integer to return for "less than" and "greater than." We will use −1 and +1, respectively.

Example 1: the `Name` class

We will develop two examples to make this more concrete. First, we'll create a `Name` class to store a person's name. Such a class has use in many applications. The class will store first and last names as `String`s and will provide the usual accessor and mutator methods. Of course, it will implement `Comparable`, so it must have a `compareTo()` method. In looking at the contract for `Comparable`, we see there is more we should do.

As outlined earlier, it is desirable that `equals()` return `true` for any two objects for which `compareTo()` returns 0, so we also need to override the `equals()` method inherited from `Object`. Wait! There's more! As we saw in Chapter 1, by the contract for `equals()`, we must also override `hashCode()` (also inherited from `Object`) so that for any two objects for which `equals()` returns `true`, `hashCode()` returns the same integer value. Figure 9.13 shows the relationship in a UML diagram.

Is this a hassle? Well, it is more work to be sure, but the (much more) important point is that a client of any class you implement has an expectation that you will honor the terms of *all* contracts involved. In some cases, this has implications beyond the interface you want to implement, as you are seeing in the implementation of `Comparable` in the `Name` class. Your class cannot be reliably used if you don't follow through on all aspects of all the contracts involved.

A class must honor all aspects of an interface's contract

While the implementation of `compareTo()` will obviously be unique to the needs of each implementing class (type), we can pseudocode its general structure across types:

Pseudocode: compareTo(Type other)
verify argument other is not null
compare the fields in the desired sort order and return the result

General structure of `compareTo()` in pseudocode

Figure 9.13 Relationship between `Name`, `Object`, and `Comparable` (UML class diagram).

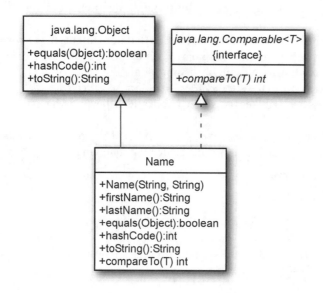

The natural sort order for names is lexicographical by last name, then first name. The code is shown in Listing 9.9. Note in the class header on line 4 that we make Name the type parameter to Comparable. This says that instances of Name will be Comparable to each other. Also, because we gave Name as the type parameter to Comparable in the class header, we must use Name as the argument type to compareTo(*Name*) (see line 47 and look again at Comparable in Listing 9.5).

Listing 9.9 The Name methods provided to implement Comparable.

```
1    /**
2     * The <tt>Name</tt> class stores a person's first and last name.
3     */
4    public class Name implements Comparable<Name> {
5
6        private String firstName;
7        private String lastName;
8
9        // CONSTRUCTORS, ACCESSORS, AND MUTATORS NOT SHOWN
10
11       /**
12        * Determine if this name is equal to the given argument.
13        * @param o The <tt>Name</tt> object to which we are to compare
14        *        this <tt>Name</tt>
15        * @return true if both the first and last names of this
16        *   <tt>Name</tt> match the first and last names of the given
17        *   argument; otherwise return false.
18        */
19       public boolean equals( Object o ) {
20           if ( o instanceof Name )
21               return this.compareTo( (Name)o ) == 0;
22           return false;
23       }
24
25       /**
26        * Return the hashcode for this <tt>Name</tt>.
27        * @return  The hashcode for this name.
28        */
29       public int hashCode(){
30           return 31 * this.lastName.hashCode() +
31               this.firstName.hashCode();
32       }
33
34       /**
35        * Compare this <tt>Name</tt> to the <tt>Name</tt> supplied in
36        * the argument.
37        * @param o The <tt>Name</tt> to which to compare this
```

```
38       *   <tt>Name</tt>.
39       * @return  -1 if this name is lexicographically less than the
40       *       other name.<BR>
41       * 0 if they are equal<BR>
42       * 1 if this name is lexicographically greater than the
43       *  other name
44       * @throws <tt>IllegalArgumentException</tt> if
45       *   <tt>other</tt> is <tt>null</tt>
46       */
47      public int compareTo( Name other ){
48
49         if ( other ==  null )
50            throw new IllegalArgumentException();
51
52         int result = 0;
53         if ( this.lastName.compareTo( other.lastName() ) < 0 )
54            result = -1;
55         else if (this.lastName.compareTo( other.lastName() ) == 0)
56            result = this.firstName.compareTo( other.firstName() );
57
58         return result;
59      }
60   }
```

We guarantee that equals() (lines 11–23) is consistent with the **equals()**
compareTo()notion of equality by letting compareTo() do the actual comparison
and returning true if the result is 0 (line 21). You are probably wondering why the
argument to compareTo() is of type Name, but the argument to equals() is of type
Object. The equals() method is overridden from class Object, which specifies that
the parameter type is Object. If we implement equals(Name) instead, we are defining a *new* method, not overriding the equals() method from Object.
Consequently, we need first to check that the Object reference being passed in to
equals() is, in fact, of type Name (line 20), and cast it as a Name (line 21) before
sending it to compareTo(). If the argument is *not* of type Name and we failed to do
the check, a ClassCastException would be thrown when we tried to access the
object as if it was an instance of Name. Note also that if the type test on line 20 fails,
false is returned (line 22); two objects of different types cannot be "equal."

The implementation of hashCode() (lines 25–32) is included for completeness.
Hashing is discussed in detail in Chapter 12.

For a second example, we will build a WorkOrder class that implements   **Example 2: the**
Comparable. (We'll revisit this class again later in the chapter.) Many businesses   **WorkOrder class**
have a department responsible for building maintenance. When something needs
fixing or adjusting, a work order is created documenting the request. For our purposes, a WorkOrder includes the name of the person submitting the work order
(Name); the date the work order was submitted (Date); the department to bill for the

work (String); and a description of the work to be done (String). We will say that the natural ordering for WorkOrders sorts by looking at the fields in the following order:[10]

1. Name of requester

2. Date of submission

3. Department to be billed

4. Work order description

This order is reflected in the implementation in Listing 9.10. You should observe that the structure of WorkOrder.compareTo() (lines 43–77) is identical to that of Name.compareTo(), as outlined by the pseudocode given earlier.

Listing 9.10 The WorkOrder class.

```
1    /**
2     * A <tt>WorkOrder</tt> is a request for work to be done.
3     * Every request has a person who submits the request, a date
4     * on which the request was submitted and a department for
5     * which the work is to be done.
6     * <p>Work orders are ordered by the name of the requester.</p>
7     */
8    import java.util.Date;
9
10   public class WorkOrder implements Comparable<WorkOrder> {
11       private Name requester;
12       private Date dateSubmitted;
13       private String department;
14       private String workDescription;
15
16       // CONSTRUCTOR, ACCESSORS AND MUTATORS NOT SHOWN
17
18       /**
19        * Determine if this <tt>WorkOrder</tt> is equal to <tt>o</tt>.
20        * @param o The <tt>WorkOrder</tt> object to which we are to
21        * compare this <tt>WorkOrder</tt>.
22        * @return true if the two <tt>WorkOrders</tt> are equal (have
23        * the same requester, same department and the same day
24        * submitted.
25        */
26       public boolean equals( Object o ){
27           if ( o instanceof WorkOrder )
28               return this.compareTo( (WorkOrder)o ) == 0;
29           return false;
```

---

[10]If this seems unnatural to you, don't worry; we will explore a mechanism to get other orderings in this chapter's *Investigate*

```
30          }
31
32          /**
33           * Return the hashcode for this WorkOrder.
34           * @return  The hashcode for this WorkOrder.
35           */
36          public int hashCode() {
37              return 17 * this.requester.hashCode() + 31 *
38                  this.dateSubmitted.hashCode() +
39                  11 * this.department.hashCode() +
40                  this.workDescription.hashCode();
41          }
42
43          /**
44           * Compare this <tt>WorkOrder</tt> to the <tt>WorkOrder</tt>
45           * supplied in the argument.
46           * @param wo the <tt>WorkOrder</tt> to which to compare this
47           * <tt>WorkOrder</tt>. The comparison is done on the fields
48           * in the following order:
49           * <OL>
50           * <LI>  name of requester
51           * <LI> date of submission
52           * <LI> department to be billed
53           * <LI> work order description
54           * </OL>
55           * @returns -1 if this <tt>WorkOrder</tt> is less than the
56           * <tt>WorkOrder</tt> passed in.<BR>
57           * 0 if they are equal.<BR>
58           * 1 if this <tt>WorkOrder</tt> is greater than the
59           * <tt>WorkOrder</tt> passed in.
60           * @throws IllegalArgumentException if <tt>wo</tt> is null
61           */
62          public int compareTo( WorkOrder wo ){
63              if ( wo == null )
64                  throw new IllegalArgumentException();
65              int nameCmp, dateCmp, deptCmp;
66
67              nameCmp = this.requester.compareTo( wo.requester() );
68              if ( nameCmp != 0 ) return nameCmp;
69
70              dateCmp = this.dateSubmitted.compareTo( wo.dateSubmitted() );
71              if ( dateCmp != 0 ) return dateCmp;
72
73              deptCmp = this.department.compareTo( wo.department() );
74              if ( deptCmp != 0 ) return deptCmp;
75
76              return this.workDescription.compareTo( wo.workDescription() );
77          }
78      }
```

SUMMING UP

The relational operators cannot be used to compare the values of objects. Instead, a class can implement the `Comparable` interface, making instances of the class comparable. `Comparable.compareTo()` provides a total ordering and is called the class's natural ordering.

Polymorphism is the ability to use the same block of code on different types. What makes this possible is that the objects have a common ancestor and the polymorphic code relies only on methods from the common ancestor. The modified `selectionSort()` method is a nice example of generic code—it can sort an array of any type that has `Comparable` as an ancestor.

When specifying a type parameter for a generic method, you often want to specify a family of types bounded by some specific type. `<? extends T>` provides a family of types that is bounded *above* by `T`—this will match any type for `T` or any of `T`'s *descendants*. Similarly, `<? super T>` provides a family of types that is bounded *below* by `T`—this will match any type for `T` or any of `T`'s *ancestors*.

CHECKPOINT

9.7 Assuming a and b are instances of a class that implements `Comparable`, how would you test for a > = b using `compareTo()`?

9.8 The wrapper classes `Integer` and `Float` both implement `Comparable`. So why won't the following work?

```
Integer i = new Integer( 7 );
Float f = new Float( 7.0 );
int cmpResult = i.compareTo( f );
```

■ 9.4 Sorting Lists and Linked Lists

So far we have only looked at sorting arrays. What if the elements are stored in a list or a linear linked list? This possibility raises some interesting issues.

First, as we saw in Chapter 3, sequential access structures (e.g., linear linked lists) are more complicated and require more code support than random access structures (e.g., arrays). To provide the necessary support for sorting a linked list would require developing a class around a linked list to supply such operations as getting a value at a particular position, inserting at and deleting from a position, etc.

We already have such a class, `LinkedList`, which implements the `List` interface. So unless our needs are special, we wouldn't roll our own linked structure methods; we would just used `LinkedList`. Is there a performance penalty for using a ready-made class such as `LinkedList` instead of creating a custom class for performance? Sure, but as the *Investigate* in Chapter 6 showed, the cost is minimal, and it does not generally outweigh the productivity advantage we gain by using something already available and tested. Also, there is a really neat trick to speed up sorting elements stored in a `LinkedList`.

In the JCF, `java.util.Arrays` provides methods to sort arrays of primitive types and arrays of objects, but it has no equivalent for the linear linked structure. Instead, the JCF also provides the `java.util.Collections` class, which includes a `sort()` method that takes a `List` as an argument and does a modified merge sort on it. The `List` can be implemented using an array or a linear linked list.

What is interesting about the sort implementation in `Collections` is that it completely sidesteps the difficulties of sorting a linked list by converting the `List` to an array! A commented version of the implementation from the JCF is shown in Listing 9.11. The `toArray()` method is mandated by the `Collection` interface, so every collection type descended from `Collection` must provide it.

Once the `List` has been converted to an array (line 3), one of the methods from `java.util.Arrays` is used to do the sort (line 4). Then the `List` is recreated from the array (lines 7–11).

Clearly this is not an in-place sort. What is the runtime cost? The breakdown is shown in Table 9.3. Despite the cost of converting from a `List` to an array at the beginning of the method and back again at the end, the algorithm still has a cost of $O(n\log n)$. There is an $O(n)$ cost to move from the linked list to an array and back again, but the predominant cost is due to the sort.

Listing 9.11 `java.util.Collections.sort()` converts the `List` to an array before doing the sort.

```
1    public static <T extends Comparable<? super T>>
2           void sort( List<T> list ) {
3       Object[] a = list.toArray();      // convert this List to an array
4       Arrays.sort( a );                 // sort the array
5
6       // recreate the List from sorted array
7       ListIterator<T> i = list.listIterator();
8       for ( int j=0; j < a.length; j++ ) {
9           i.next();
10          i.set( (T)a[j] );
11      }
12   }
```

Table 9.3 The cost for converting between a `List` and `array` (and back again) does not change the asymptotic cost of `Collections.sort()`.

Operation	Cost	Line Numbers
Convert `List` to an array	$O(n)$	line 3
Sort the array	$O(n\log_2 n)$	line 4
Convert array back to `List`	$O(n)$	lines 7–11
Total	$O(n) + O(n\log_2 n) + O(n) = O(n\log_2 n)$	

Table 9.4 Timings for the optimized `sort()` method for `List`s supplied in the JCF and a (slower) traditional version.

Algorithm	Time to Sort 5000 `Integer` Objects
`Collections.sort()` (Listing 9.11)	71 milliseconds
`mergeSortList()`	7129 milliseconds

You would think that the `List`-array conversions would make the method unbearably slow and that directly sorting the `List` or the underlying linked list would have to be faster. But this isn't the case.

This is another example of asymptotic analysis not telling the full story. Table 9.4 gives timings for the JCF implementation of sorting a `List` and a traditional implementation of merge sort on a `LinkedList` using only `List` methods.

You might argue that by using high-level `List` methods we were almost guaranteeing we would get bad timings. The exercises invite you to re-implement (and time) merge sort for `LinkedList` by directly accessing the internal linked list. (Have fun ☺.)

What you will see is that it isn't the overhead of the method calls that slow us down so much as that sequential access data structures are *inherently* slow for some operations. This confirms a lesson learned in Chapter 3: while linked structures are more flexible than arrays and offer better performance for some operations, they are clearly not ideal for all operations. The important insight here is that sometimes the cost of moving between array and linked list implementations really pays off.

Consider converting a linked list into an array for some operations

SUMMING UP

Sequential access data structures are slower than arrays for some operations. The data access and manipulation required by merge sort make it very slow on linear linked lists. The JCF avoids this time penalty by converting a `LinkedList` into an array (a random access data structure), sorting the array, then recreating the `LinkedList` from the array.

CHECKPOINT

9.9 Why is merge sort on a linear linked list so slow?

9.10 How do you convert a `List` to an array? Where is this method specified?

9.11 Why didn't the `private` methods include code to check that the values of the parameters met the method's pre-conditions?

INVESTIGATE Using Comparators to Sort WorkOrders

Description

There are two problems with Comparable. The first is that the Comparable-based sorting algorithms we developed won't work for classes that don't implement Comparable. The second problem is that sometimes we want to sort objects based on some criteria other than the type's natural ordering. We have seen two examples of this—sorting the contents of a folder by name, file type, size, and so forth, and sorting the contents of a mail folder by sender, arrival time (most recent first or oldest first), subject, sender, and the like.

The solution to both problems is to pass the sorting method a specialized comparator that compares two objects based on some programmer-specified ordering. In this way, you can create a comparator class for each ordering you might need. The java.util.Comparator<T> interface specifies the necessary methods and guarantees uniformity in how comparators look.

This *Investigate* is done in two parts. In Part A, you will implement (and test!) a Comparator class that will allow you to use the date of submission as the primary key for sorting WorkOrder objects. In Part B, you will modify one of the sorting algorithms from this chapter to make use of the comparator developed in Part A.[11]

Objectives

■ Build a Comparator class to provide an alternative ordering for the WorkOrder class.

■ Design a test plan to verify the correctness of the comparator.

■ Build a generic method that sorts based on the ordering defined by some comparator.

Background

You need to become more familiar with Comparator's interface and how it is used by sorting methods. In the Java online documentation, look up java.util.Comparator and java.util.Collections.

1. What methods are specified by Comparator?

2. How does Comparator's method for doing a comparison differ from Comparable's?

3. What does Comparator's comparison method return and what does the return value mean?

4. What constraints, if any, are there on Comparator's comparison method?

5. What exception does this method throw and under what circumstances?

6. How are the two Collections.sort() methods different?

7. What is the collection type passed to the sort() methods in Collections?

---

[11]You will find the information and examples from Section 9.3 an Comparable useful here.

Part A: Building a Comparator to Sort `WorkOrders` by Date

In this part we will build a `Comparator` for `WorkOrders` using the date the work order was submitted as the primary sort key. As in the `compareTo()` method created in Section 9.3, your comparison must produce a total ordering. So the complete comparison order is as follows:

1. Date of submission (`Date`)
2. Name of the person requesting the work (`Name`)
3. Department to bill for the work (`String`)
4. Description of the work to be done (`String`)

Design

1. Design a test plan for the `compare()` method of your comparator. Carefully consider the sort order specified above.

   a. Why are you creating the test plan before creating the comparator?

   b. How is this useful?

2. Choose an integer value to return for the less-than and greater-than relationships.
3. What will you return in `compare()` for the equals relationship?
4. Pseudocode `compare()`.
5. Deskcheck your pseudocode using the test plan you created in step 1.
6. Pseudocode `equals()`. Since the comparator has no state information that can be compared, the only meaningful test for equality of comparators is to see if the argument is an instance of this kind of comparator.

Implementation

1. Create a class `WorkOrderByDate` that implements `Comparator` based on the work done in the Design section. Be sure to include javadoc comments explaining the ordering the comparator provides, the exceptions thrown, and so forth.
2. Create a JUnit test program based on your test plan.

   a. Use `Collections.sort(List, Comparator)` to test your comparator. This means, of course, that you will have to store the `WorkOrders` specified in your test plan in a `List` object.

   b. How can you check that the `List` of `WorkOrders` is properly sorted without printing the elements out and visually checking the order?

3. Why are you testing the comparator now using `Collections.sort()`? Why not wait until the end of Part B when you will have a sorting algorithm modified to work with your comparator?

Part B: Modifying a Sorting Method to Use a Comparator

In this part you will modify one of the sorting algorithms developed in this chapter to use a comparator to determine the ordering of the objects stored in an *array*. As you saw when you converted the `int`-based sorting algorithms to be `Comparable`-based, there will be very few changes to make them `Comparator`-based.

Design

1. Decide which sorting algorithm from the chapter you want to modify and make a copy of it.

2. What should the type of the array in the parameter list be? (*Hint*: Look at the searching and sorting methods from `java.util.Collections`.) Why should it *not* be `Comparable`?

3. Which statements in the method are affected by the use of a `Comparator` object?

4. Will the test plan developed in Part A apply to testing your modified sorting algorithm?

Implementation

1. Add a `Comparator` as a parameter to the sorting method.

2. Change the line in the algorithm that does the comparison of objects to use the `Comparator.compare()` method instead of `Comparable.compareTo()`.

3. Using the JUnit testing program developed in Part A as a model, create a JUnit test program to test your modified sorting algorithm.

SUMMING UP

The `Comparable` interface has two limitations. First, not all classes implement it, which means that we need some other mechanism for comparing instances of a class. Second, `Comparable` only allows a single sort order—the class's *natural ordering*. Sorting objects using any other ordering calls for a different mechanism. The object-oriented solution is to provide a separate comparator class that encapsulates the desired ordering. Generic sort methods can take as an argument a collection to be sorted *and* a comparator that defines the sort order. In Java, a comparator class is built by implementing the `Comparator` interface. `Comparator.compare()` defines a total ordering and its return value has the same semantics as `Comparable.compareTo()`.

■ 9.5 Searching for Objects

The basic algorithms for searching were presented in the previous chapter. More will be presented in Chapters 11 and 12 when we look at binary search trees and hash tables.

The mechanisms used to sort objects, `Comparable` and `Comparator`, apply equally well to searching for objects in a collection. We can modify the search algorithms from Chapter 8 to search for objects just as in this chapter we adapted sort algorithms for primitive types to sort objects:

1. Change the line that does the comparison of elements to use `Comparable.compareTo()` or `Comparator.compare()`.

2. Change the method header.

Listing 9.12 shows the implementation of the binary search algorithm for objects that are comparable. This method is part of gray.util.ArrayUtils. Note that this is a generic method and that the type parameter is identical to the type parameter for our selectionSort() algorithm.

Listing 9.12 The binary search algorithm modified to search for a target in an array of comparable elements.

```
1    /**
2     * Searches <tt>array</tt> for <tt>target</tt> using the binary
3     * search algorithm. The array must be sorted into ascending order.
4     * If it is not sorted, the results are undefined. If the array
5     * contains multiple elements equal to <tt>target</tt>, there is
6     * no guarantee which one will be found.
7     * @param array the array to search, must be sorted in ascending
8     * order
9     * @param first index of the first element in the search space;
10    *    must be in the bounds of the array
11    * @param last index of the last element in the search space;
12    *    must be in the bounds of the array
13    * @param target the data item we are looking for
14    * @return the index of <tt>target</tt> in the array if found,
15    *    -1 otherwise
16    * @throws IndexOutOfBoundsException if <tt>first</tt> or
17    * <tt>last</tt> is less than 0 or greater than or equal to
18    * <tt>array.length</tt>
19    */
20   public static <T extends Comparable< ? super T > >
21        int binarySearch( T[] array, int first, int last, T target ){
22       if ( first > last )
23          return -1;              //  Base case - failure
24
25       if ( ( first < 0 ) || ( first >= array.length ) ||
26            ( last < 0 ) || ( last >= array.length ) )
27          throw new IndexOutOfBoundsException();
28
29       int mid = ( first + last ) / 2;
30       if ( array[ mid ].compareTo( target ) ==  0 )
31          return mid;        // Base case - success
32
33       // recursive cases
34       if ( array[ mid ].compareTo( target ) < 0 )
35          return binarySearch( array, mid + 1, last, target );
36        else
37          return binarySearch( array, first, mid - 1, target );
38   }
```

The JCF supports searching for objects. Actually, we looked at this already when we looked at `Collection.contains( Object )` and `List.indexOf( Object )`. The classes `java.util.Arrays` and `java.util.Collections` contain a variety of search methods.

EXERCISES

Paper and Pencil

1. Show the first two partitions that would be created by quick sort on the following arrays.

9	18	51	39	15	45	14	5
51	45	39	18	15	14	9	5

2. Show the first three merge steps done by merge sort for the following array.

9	18	51	39	15	45	14	5

Testing and Debugging

1. A classmate of yours has coded the following version of `selectionSort()`. Will it work? Explain.

```java
/**
 * Sort the array elements in ascending order
 * using selection sort.
 * @param a the array of Objects to sort
 * @throws NullPointerException if a is null
 */
static void selectionSort( Object[] a ) {
    if ( a == null )
        throw new NullPointerException();
    // while the size of the unsorted part is > 1
    for ( int unsortedSize = a.length; unsortedSize > 1; unsortedSize-- ) {
        // find the position of the largest
        // element in the unsorted section
        int maxPos = 0;
        for ( int pos = 1; pos < unsortedSize; pos++ )
            if ( a[pos] > a[maxPos] )
                maxPos = pos;
        // postcondition: maxPos is the position
        // of the largest element in the unsorted
        // part of the array
        // Swap largest value with the last value
        // in the unsorted part
        Object temp = a[unsortedSize - 1];
        a[unsortedSize - 1] = a[maxPos];
        a[maxPos] = temp;
    }
}
```

2. Kenta coded the following `compareTo()` method for the `Name` class. Is this okay? Explain.

```
public int compareTo( Object o ){

    if ( !( o instanceof Name ) )
        throw new ClassCastException();

    Name other = (Name)o;
    return lastName.compareTo( other.lastName() );
}
```

Design and Code

1. Rewrite insertion sort so that, instead of building the sorted part at the beginning of the array, it builds it at the end of the array (so the unsorted part will always be to the left of the sorted part instead of the other way around). What are the time and space complexities for this implementation? Explain.

2. Redo insertion sort to sort in nonincreasing order.

3. Modify the selection sort algorithm so it avoids the element move step if the element is already in the correct position. On what basis would you decide that the cost of this extra check outweighs the cost of not doing the check?

4. Another improvement that can be made to quick sort and merge sort is to use a nonrecursive algorithm such as selection sort when the size of the partitions is below some threshold. Make this change to the algorithms. How will you decide what the threshold should be?

5. Reimplement one of the array merge sort algorithms to replace recursion with looping and a stack. See the *Investigate* from Chapter 8 for ideas.

6. Write a program to do timings of the sort methods presented in this chapter. The program should take timings for different sizes of collections and for different orderings:
   - ■ sorted ascending
   - ■ sorted descending
   - ■ random

7. Write a small program to determine the value actually returned by `Comparable.compareTo()` for several wrapper types (e.g., `Integer`, `Float`, `Byte`).

8. Store several strings in an instance of `java.util.Stack`. Try to sort the stack using `Collections.mergeSort()` and output the result. Explain what happened.

9. An e-mail tool allows a user to sort e-mails in a mailbox in a variety of ways. Create a simple `Email` class with the following fields (your instructor may add others).
   - ■ date sent
   - ■ sender

- priority (1 – 10 with 1 = high priority and 10 = low priority)
- subject line
- read/unread

The `Email` class should implement `Comparable` with the natural sort order being the order in which the fields were given. Develop a test plan to verify that the ordering is done correctly.

10. Reimplement the searching algorithms from the last chapter to search for elements in a `List`.

ON THE WEB

Additional study material is available at Addison-Wesley's Website http://www.aw.com/cssupport. This material includes the following:

- Focus on Problem Solving: External Sorting

  Problem: The ACME Security Company sells computer-monitored access control systems. In such a system every door in a building is locked. To unlock a door an employee must swipe an access card in a card reader. A central computer determines whether the employee has sufficient clearance to enter through the door; if so, the system unlocks the door.

  Every time a card is swiped, an entry is made in a log file. Here is a sample entry (the first line simply clarifies the spacing of the data fields, as described next):

  ```
  01234567890123456789012345678901234567890123456789012345678901
  345667 20020902  09:32  GOOD  RM-3455 Accounting Dept
  511143 20020902  09:33  BAD   RM-3455 Accounting Dept
  ```

  From left to right, each record consists of a six-character employee number, an eight-character date code (year, month, day), a five-character time (for a 24-hour clock), a four-character result code (either GOOD or BAD), a seven-character room code, and a 21-character room description. There are always two spaces between each field. The records are set up this way to simplify the printing process and so that inexpensive printers can be used. There could be hundreds of entries in the log file in a day.

  A new client has requested custom programming to analyze the movements of its employees over any arbitrary period of days. You have been assigned to the programming team at Barking Dogs Software and given the specific task of writing a program that will take the log file from a period of time and sort it using the employee number, date, and time as the sorting key. Other members of the team will use this sorted file to perform the analysis.

  Thinking to the future when this application may be used at large companies and the file size may exceed the capacity of the computer's memory, you decide that an external merge sort is the most appropriate approach.

Solution: Occasionally, the amount of data to be sorted is too large to fit in the computer's memory at one time and an external sorting algorithm is required to do the sort. The sort by merging characteristic of MergeSort makes it ideal for sorting data "externally" by incrementally bringing chunks into memory to be merged, then written back to disk. Repeated application of this idea, which is exactly what MergeSort does, produces a sorted data set.

The presentation of the solution proceeds through Analysis (a discussion and visualization of how external MergeSort works; the inputs and outputs to the application; and the layout of the application interface), Design (identification of classes with their responsibilities and collaborators, visualized through a UML class diagram), and Implementation of the classes.

■ Study Guide Exercises

■ Answers to CheckPoint Problems

■ Additional exercises

Trees 10

CHAPTER OUTLINE

So far we have studied several types of linear collections (list, stack, queue) in which there is a one-to-one relationship between the elements in the collection—each element except the first has a unique predecessor and each element except the last has a unique successor (see Figure 10.1 (a)).

Linear collections: one to one

In this chapter we look at a **hierarchical collection** called a **tree** that supports a one-to-many relationship between the collection's elements—every element in the collection except the first has a unique predecessor and every element except the last may have many successors (see Figure 10.1 (b)).

Hierarchical collections: one to many

We will look at binary trees in this chapter. In the next chapter, we continue the discussion and look at trees specialized for searching: binary search trees, AVL trees, and splay trees.

Figure 10.1 Linear and hierarchical (tree) collections.

(a) A linear collection. Each element except the first has a unique predecessor, and each element except the last has a unique successor.

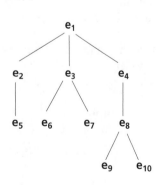

(b) Hierarchical collection. Moving from the top down, each element except the first (e_1) has a unique predecessor, and each element except the last can have many successors.

■ **10.1** Tree Terminology

A tree is a hierarchical structure consisting of a collection of **nodes**, one of which has the special designation **root**. The nodes are connected by edges such that each node except the root has a unique predecessor called the **parent**, and zero or more successors called **children** (this is the one-to-many relationship—a parent can have zero or more children). A node with no children is called a **leaf** or **external node**, and a node with one or more children is an **internal node**. Nodes with a common parent are called **siblings**. The **degree of a node** is the number of children it has. A leaf always has a degree of 0. The **degree of a tree**, also called its **arity**, is the largest degree of all its nodes. These terms are illustrated in Figure 10.2.

Figure 10.2 A sample tree and some tree terminology.

root: e_1
internal nodes: e_1, e_2, e_3, e_4, e_8
leaves: e_5, e_6, e_7, e_9, e_{10}

e_1 is the parent of e_2, e_3, e_4, so e_2, e_3, e_4 are **siblings** and are **children** of e_1.

The **degree** of e_1 is 3. The degree of e_3 is 2 and the degree of e_9 is 0.

The **arity** of the tree is 3—e_1 has 3 children and no other node in the tree has more children.

A **path** is a sequence of unique, connected nodes. The **path length** is the number of nodes it contains. There is a unique path from the root to every node in a tree. The **depth of a node** in a tree is the length of the path from the tree's root to the node[1] and can be defined recursively for any node n:

$$\text{depth}(n) = \begin{cases} 1, \text{ if } n \text{ is the root of the tree} & \textit{base case} \\ 1 + \text{depth}(n\text{'s parent}), \text{ if } n \text{ is not the root} & \textit{recursive case} \end{cases}$$

A tree can also be viewed as having **levels**, and the depth of a node is also its level.

The **height of a node** is the length of the longest path from the node to a leaf descendant. The height of a tree is the number of levels it has. The **width of a tree** is the number of nodes in its widest level. The **size of a tree** is the number of nodes it contains. An empty tree has a size of 0.

As you will have noticed by now, tree terminology borrows a great deal from genealogy. This includes notions of ancestors and descendants (see Figure 10.3). The **ancestors** of a node n can be succinctly defined recursively as follows:

$$\text{ancestor}(n) = \begin{cases} \text{empty, if } n \text{ is the root of the tree} & \textit{base case} \\ n\text{'s parent} + \text{ancestor}(n\text{'s parent}), \text{ if } n \text{ is not the root} & \textit{recursive case} \end{cases}$$

The **descendants** of a node n are all the nodes for which n is an ancestor.

Figure 10.3 A sample tree and more tree terminology.

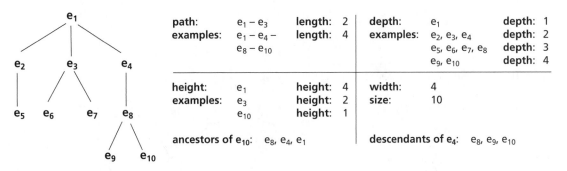

path:	$e_1 - e_3$	length: 2	depth:	e_1	depth: 1
examples:	$e_1 - e_4 -$	length: 4	examples:	e_2, e_3, e_4	depth: 2
	$e_8 - e_{10}$			e_5, e_6, e_7, e_8	depth: 3
				e_9, e_{10}	depth: 4

height:	e_1	height: 4	width:	4
examples:	e_3	height: 2	size:	10
	e_{10}	height: 1		

ancestors of e_{10}: e_8, e_4, e_1 descendants of e_4: e_8, e_9, e_{10}

---

[1]There is not universal agreement on this. In some books you will see that the root has a depth of 0 and the length of the path is the number of edges it contains.

CHECKPOINT

10.1 For the tree shown to the right, answer the following questions.

a. List the descendants of e_7.

b. List the ancestors of e_3.

c. What is the arity of the tree?

d. What is the height of the tree?

e. What is the width of the tree?

f. List the leaves and internal nodes of the tree.

g. What is the depth of e_5? e_6? e_4? e_{10}?

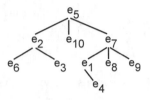

■ 10.2 Binary Tree Description

As its name suggests, a **binary tree** is a tree with an arity of 2—a node may have 0, 1, or 2 children. As first presented in Chapter 8, the definition is recursive—a child is also a binary tree. Leaves form the base case since they have zero children. The two children are ordered and are designated as the left child and the right child.

A **full binary tree** of height h is one in which all nodes from level 1 to level $h-1$ have two children. A **complete binary tree** of height h is one in which all nodes from level 1 to $h-2$ have two children and all the children of nodes at level $h-1$ are contiguous and to the left of the tree. A full tree is also a complete tree (see Figure 10.4).

10.2.1 Binary Tree Properties

There are several properties of binary trees that are important to understand as we make use of binary trees. You can visually verify these properties with the trees in Figure 10.5.

Figure 10.4 Full and complete binary trees.

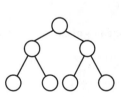

(a) A full binary tree of height 3.

(b) Complete binary trees of height 3 and 4.

Figure 10.5 Two binary trees with seven nodes.

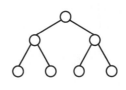

(a) A highly unbalanced binary tree with $n = 7$ and $h = 7$.

(b) A full binary tree with $n = 7$ and $h = 3$.

Property 10.1   A full binary tree of height h has $2^h - 1$ nodes.

Property 10.2   The height of a full binary tree with n nodes is $\lceil \log_2 n \rceil$. Necessarily this is also the length of the longest path in a full binary tree.

Property 10.3   The height of a binary tree with n nodes is at least $\lceil \log_2 n \rceil$ and at most n (this occurs when no node has more than 1 child). This is also the length of the longest path.

SUMMING UP

A hierarchical collection allows an element to have zero or more successors and predecessors. A tree is a kind of hierarchical collection that allows an element to have zero or one predecessor, called the parent, and multiple successors, called children. A binary tree is a tree in which an element can have zero to two children. Binary trees have some well-defined properties that make it easy to determine the cost of algorithms that manipulate them.

10.2.2 Tree Traversals

Just as we supported a way to traverse, or iterate, over the elements of a `List`, so we need a way to traverse over the elements of a binary tree. The `ListIterator` supported two traversal orders for visiting a list's elements: forward and backward. Binary trees typically support four traversal orders: preorder, inorder, postorder, and level-order.

Binary trees have four traversal orders

Three actions are performed on a node during a traversal. The order in which these actions are carried out is determined by the traversal order. The three actions are as follows:

1. The node is visited, meaning that something is done with the value stored in the node. For example, you could print out the value or perform a computation using the value.

2. The node's left child is traversed.

3. The node's right child is traversed.

First, let's look at what happens during the four traversal orders; then we can consider different ways to implement them for a binary tree. Table 10.1 illustrates the behavior of the four traversal orders on a sample binary tree. Notice that three of the traversal orders are elegantly described using recursion and rely on the LIFO

Table 10.1 Behavior of the four binary tree traversal orders

Traversal Order	Order in Which the Nodes Are Visited

preorder(node)
    if node is not null
        visit this node
        preorder(node's left child)
        preorder(node's right child)
	preorder(root) visits the nodes in the following order: A B D E C F G

inorder(node)
    if node is not null
        inorder(node's left child)
        visit this node
        inorder(node's right child)
	inorder(root) visits the nodes in the following order: D B E A F C G

postorder(node)
    if node is not null
        postorder(node's left child)
        postorder(node's right child)
        visit this node
	postorder(root) visits the nodes in the following order: D E B F G C A

levelorder(node)
    if node is not null
        add node to a queue
        while the queue is not empty
            get the node at the head of the queue
            visit this node
            if the node has children
                put them in the queue in left to right order
	levelorder(root) visits the nodes in the following order: A B C D E F G

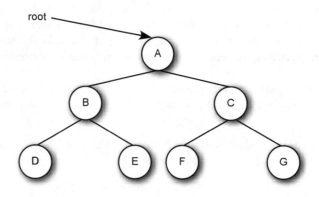

properties of a stack, while the fourth, level-order, relies on the FIFO properties of a queue.

There are two approaches we can take to handle traversing the elements of a tree: **tree iterators** and **visitors**. What they have in common is that every node in the tree is visited in some defined order. What separates them is who has responsibility for controlling the traversal: the tree object or the client object. We will look at both approaches and adopt one for our implementation, leaving the other for the Exercises.

10.2.3 Tree Traversals Using an Iterator

You are familiar with the idea of a collection providing an iterator that gives access to the elements of the collection in some well-defined order. We looked at a simple iterator for `BasicCollection` in Chapter 4, then an iterator specialized for `List`s in Chapter 5. With the iterator approach

- The collection provides the client with an iterator to walk through the elements of the collection.
- The client controls the iteration via the iterator object.
- The client applies some code to each element as it is "visited" (returned by the iterator).

Using this model we can describe a tree iterator. A binary tree would supply a tree iterator object to a client, which the client would use to access the elements of the tree in one of the four traversal orders. Figure 10.6 illustrates this approach. In this scenario, the client controls the iteration and decides what is to be done with each element as it is "visited" (returned by the iterator).

The following ADT describes Tree Iterator. In Java, such an ADT could be created by implementing the `Iterator` interface and leaving the optional `remove()` method unsupported. Binary Tree Node is specified in the ADT in Section 10.3.

Figure 10.6 With the iterator approach, the collection object supplies an iterator to the client, which is responsible for managing the traversal.

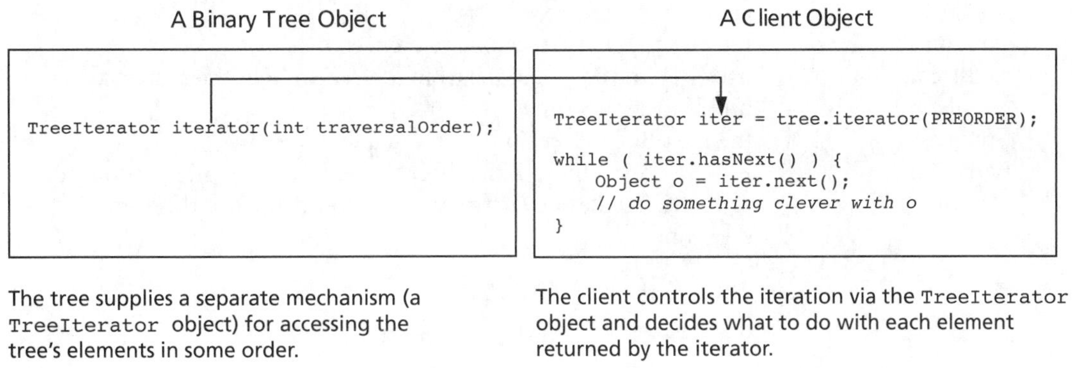

A Binary Tree Object

A Client Object

```
TreeIterator iterator(int traversalOrder);
```

```
TreeIterator iter = tree.iterator(PREORDER);

while ( iter.hasNext() ) {
    Object o = iter.next();
    // do something clever with o
}
```

The tree supplies a separate mechanism (a `TreeIterator` object) for accessing the tree's elements in some order.

The client controls the iteration via the `TreeIterator` object and decides what to do with each element returned by the iterator.

The TreeIterator ADT

Description

This ADT describes an iterator for a binary tree. The order in which the nodes of the tree are visited is determined by the implementation; for example, preorder, inorder, postorder or level-order. The iterator returns nodes in the tree, not the elements stored in the nodes.

Properties

The behavior of the iterator is undefined if the tree it is traversing is structurally modified while an iteration is in progress.

Attributes

cursor:	The BinaryTreeNode to be returned by the next call to next(); a null value if there are no more BinaryTreeNodes to visit in this traversal.

Operations

BinaryTreeIterator()

pre-condition:	none
responsibilities:	constructor—initialize the BinaryTreeIterator
post-condition:	*cursor* is set to the BinaryTreeNode to be returned by the first call to next(). This is determined by the traversal order.
returns:	a BinaryTreeIterator

hasNext()

pre-condition:	none
responsibilities:	determine if the BinaryTree has any more BinaryTreeNodes to visit in this iteration
post-condition:	the iterator and underlying BinaryTree are unchanged
returns:	true if there are more BinaryTreeNodes in the iteration sequence, false otherwise

next()

pre-condition:	hasNext() is true the tree has not been structurally modified since this iterator's creation
responsibilities:	return the BinaryTreeNode referenced by *cursor*
post-condition:	*cursor* is moved to the next BinaryTreeNode in the sequence, or null if there are none
returns:	the next BinaryTreeNode in the sequence
exception:	if there are no more BinaryTreeNodes in this iteration sequence or if the tree has been structurally modified since this iterator's creation

10.2.4 Tree Traversals with a Visitor

An alternative to the tree iterator is to have the *tree* control the traversal and require the client to provide the code to be applied to each node as it is visited. This scenario is illustrated in Figure 10.7. It is a simplified version of the software design pattern called, appropriately, Visitor. With the visitor approach:

- The *collection* controls the traversal through a traversal method.
- The client provides the tree with a visitor object that contains the code the client wants applied to the nodes of the tree.
- The tree's traversal method takes a visitor object, which it applies to each node of the tree as the node is visited in the traversal.

We developed the iterator approach when working with lists, so for contrast, we will develop the visitor approach in this chapter.

SUMMING UP

Binary trees typically support four traversal orders: preorder, inorder, postorder, and level-order. There are two approaches we can take to handling traversing the elements of a tree: tree iterators and tree traversals with a visitor. With the iterator approach, the binary tree supplies an iterator object to the client, which is responsible for managing the traversal. With the visitor approach, the client supplies a visitor object to the binary tree to apply to each node visited during the traversal, which is managed by the collection.

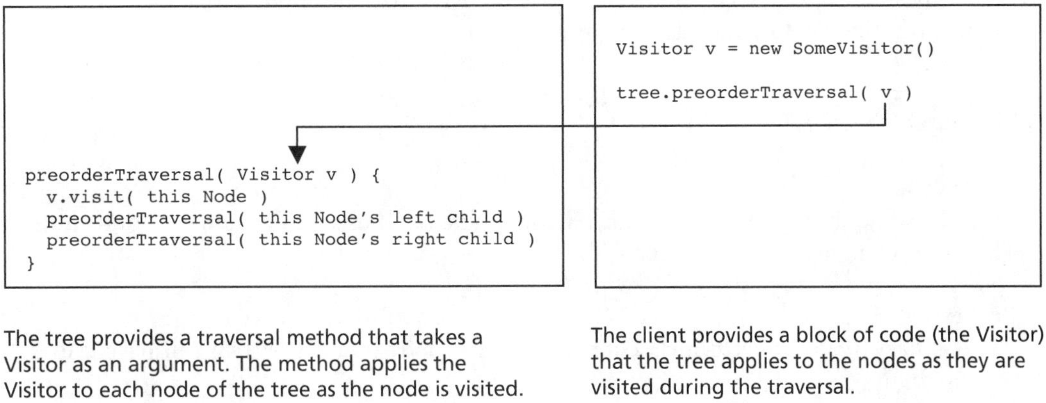

Figure 10.7 With the visitor approach, the client supplies a Visitor object to the collection to apply to each node visited during the traversal. The traversal is managed by the collection.

```
Visitor v = new SomeVisitor()

tree.preorderTraversal( v )
```

```
preorderTraversal( Visitor v ) {
  v.visit( this Node )
  preorderTraversal( this Node's left child )
  preorderTraversal( this Node's right child )
}
```

The tree provides a traversal method that takes a Visitor as an argument. The method applies the Visitor to each node of the tree as the node is visited.

The client provides a block of code (the Visitor) that the tree applies to the nodes as they are visited during the traversal.

CHECKPOINT

10.2 Show the order in which the nodes of the tree to the right are visited for

   a. level-order

   b. post-order

   c. preorder

   d. inorder

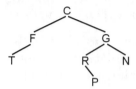

10.3 Explain the key difference between doing a traversal with an iterator and with a visitor.

◼ 10.3 Binary Tree Specification

The JCF does not contain any tree ADTs (although it uses specialized trees as the backing store for other types of collections), so we are free to create our own interface. The ADT developed here is somewhat minimal. You are invited to add operations in the exercises.

Let's consider the kinds of operations that are needed at a minimum. We need to be able to:

- Add a node at some position in the tree
- Remove a node and its descendants from a tree
- Traverse a tree
- Navigate around the tree by getting to a node's parent and children
- Get an element from a node

We'll divide these responsibilities over two ADTs: The BinaryTree ADT will cover the first three operations and the BinaryTreeNode ADT will cover the last two.

The specification for the BinaryTree ADT is given in ADT 10.2. It supports four traversal methods that take a visitor as an argument.[2]

The BinaryTree ADT

Description
This ADT describes a binary tree whose element type is left unspecified and cannot be null. The tree is composed of BinaryTreeNodes.

Properties
  1. A BinaryTree is a hierarchical data structure. A node in a BinaryTree can have 0 to 2 children.

---

[2]You are invited to evaluate an alternative design in the Exercises.

2. The *root* is the access point to a BinaryTree and never has a parent.
3. Insertions and deletions may be done at any position in a BinaryTree.

Attributes

size: The number of nodes in this BinaryTree.

root: The root of this BinaryTree; a null value not part of the tree when the BinaryTree is empty.

Operations

BinaryTree()

pre-condition:	none
responsibilities:	constructor—create an empty BinaryTree
post-condition:	*size* is set to 0
	root is set to a null value not part of the tree
returns:	nothing

BinaryTree(*Type* element)

pre-condition:	element cannot be null
responsibilities:	constructor—create a BinaryTree with element stored in the root
post-condition:	*size* is set to 1
	root is set to the node created to store element
returns:	nothing
exception:	if element is null

BinaryTree (BinaryTree leftTree, *Type* element , BinaryTree rightTree)

pre-condition:	element cannot be null
responsibilities:	constructor—create a BinaryTree with element stored in the root and leftTree and rightTree as its left and right children.
post-condition:	*root* refers to the node created to store element
	root's left child is set to leftTree
	root's right child is set to rightTree
	size is set to the size of the two subtrees + 1
returns:	BinaryTreeNode—the root of this tree
exception:	if element is null

makeRoot(*Type* element)

pre-condition:	the tree is empty
element	cannot be null
responsibilities:	create a BinaryTreeNode to store element and make it the root of the tree
post-condition:	*root* is set to the new node
	size is set to 1
returns:	BinaryTreeNode—the root of this tree
exception:	if the tree is not empty or if element is null

makeLeftChild(BinaryTreeNode parent, *Type* element)
    pre-condition: parent is not null
                                 parent has no left child
    responsibilities: create a BinaryTreeNode to store element and make this the left child of parent
    post-condition: parent has a non-null left child
                                 size is incremented by 1
    returns: BinaryTreeNode—the new left child
    exception: if element is null or if parent has a left child already

makeRightChild(BinaryTreeNode parent, *Type* element)
    pre-condition: parent is not null
                                 parent has no right child
    responsibilities: create a BinaryTreeNode to store element and make this the right child of parent
    post-condition: parent has a non-null right child
                                 size is incremented by 1
    returns: TreeNode – the new right child
    exception: if element is null or if parent has a right child already

remove(BinaryTreeNode node)
    pre-condition: node is not null
    responsibilities: remove the specified node from this tree
    post-condition: the node is removed from the tree; its position is filled by one of its leaf descendants
                                 size is decreased one
    returns: nothing
    exception: if node is null

root()
    pre-condition: none
    responsibilities: return a reference to the root of this tree; null if the tree is empty
    post-condition: the tree is unchanged
    returns: the root of this tree or null if the tree is empty

contains(*Type* target)
    pre-condition: none
    responsibilities: determine if target is stored in this tree
    post-condition: the tree is unchanged
    returns: true if target is found in this tree, false otherwise

preOrderTraversal(Visitor visit)
    pre-condition: visit is not null
    responsibilities: perform a preorder traversal of this tree applying the Visitor to each node
    post-condition: determined by the Visitor
    returns: the result of the traversal
    exception: if visit is null

inOrderTraversal(Visitor visit)
    pre-condition: visit is not null
    responsibilities: perform an inorder traversal of this tree applying the Visitor to each node
    post-condition: determined by the Visitor
    returns: the result of the traversal
    exception: if visit is null

postOrderTraversal(Visitor visit)
    pre-condition: visit is not null
    responsibilities: perform a postorder traversal of this tree applying the Visitor to each node
    post-condition: determined by the Visitor
    returns: the result of the traversal
    exception: if visit is null

levelOrderTraversal(Visitor visit)
    pre-condition: visit is not null
    responsibilities: perform a level-order traversal of this tree applying the Visitor to each node
    post-condition: determined by the Visitor
    returns: the result of the traversal
    exception: if visit is null

Not shown: isEmpty(), size(), clear()

A binary tree is composed of binary tree nodes. A binary tree node has four attributes:

1. the element to be stored in the node
2. the left child
3. the right child
4. the parent

Because a client of a binary tree should only be able to alter a tree through tree operations, `BinaryTreeNode` provides a mutator for only the element attribute. Access to a binary tree node's other attributes must be done under the control of the tree to which the node belongs. How this is done is up to the implementation. An implementation can decide to provide accessors and mutators, or could choose to implement the attributes as `protected` fields, accessible by name.

The BinaryTreeNode ADT

Description
This ADT describes a node in a binary tree. The element type stored in each node of the tree is left unspecified and cannot be null.

Properties
1. A BinaryTreeNode can have 0 to 2 children.
2. A BinaryTreeNode can have 0 or 1 parent.

Attributes

element:	The value stored by this BinaryTreeNode.
parent:	The parent of this BinaryTreeNode.
leftChild:	The left child of this BinaryTreeNode.
rightChild:	The right child of this BinaryTreeNode.

Operations

BinaryTreeNode(*Type* element)

pre-condition:	element cannot be null
responsibilities:	constructor—creates a BinaryTreeNode storing element
post-condition:	*element* is set to element
	parent, *leftChild* and *rightChild* are set to a null value
returns:	nothing
exception:	if element is null

element()

pre-condition:	none
responsibilities:	return the *element* stored in this BinaryTreeNode
post-condition:	the node is unchanged
returns:	the *element* stored in this BinaryTreeNode

parent()

pre-condition:	none
responsibilities:	return the *parent* of this BinaryTreeNode
post-condition:	the node is unchanged
returns:	*parent* of this BinaryTreeNode

leftChild()

pre-condition:	none
responsibilities:	return the *leftChild* of this BinaryTreeNode
post-condition:	the node is unchanged
returns:	*leftChild* of this BinaryTreeNode

rightChild()

pre-condition:	none
responsibilities:	return *rightChild* of this BinaryTreeNode
post-condition:	the node is unchanged
returns:	*rightChild* of this BinaryTreeNode

setElement(*Type* newElement)

pre-condition:	newElement is not null
responsibilities:	*element* is set to newElement
post-condition:	*element* refers to newElement

returns:	nothing
exception:	if newElement is null

isInternal()
pre-condition:	none
responsibilities:	determine if this node is an internal BinaryTreeNode
post-condition:	the node is unchanged
returns:	true if this node is an internal node, false otherwise

10.3.1 The `BinaryTree` and `BinaryTreeNode` Interfaces

The Java interface corresponding to the Binary Tree ADT is given in Listing 10.1. The constructors described in the ADT specification don't appear in the interface, but would be supported by an implementation of the interface (which we do shortly).

Listing 10.1 The `BinaryTree` Interface.

```
1   package gray.adts.binarytree;
2
3   /**
4    * The interface for a binary tree. Nodes in a binary tree
5    * may have 0, 1 or 2 children.  The children are distinguished
6    * as the left child and the right child.
7    */
8
9   public interface BinaryTree<E> {
10
11      /**
12       * Create a node to store <tt>element</tt> and make it
13       * the root of the tree. The tree must be empty to be able
14       * to create a new root for it.
15       * @param element The element to add to the tree; cannot be
16       *      <tt>null</tt>.
17       * @return The root of this tree.
18       * @throws TreeException If the tree is not empty.
19       * @throws IllegalArgumentException If <tt>element</tt>
20       *      is <tt>null</tt>.
21       */
22      public BinaryTreeNode makeRoot( E element );
23
24      /**
25       * Create a node in the tree to store <tt>element</tt> and
26       * make it the left child of <tt>parent</tt>.
```

```
27          * @param parent The parent of the node to be added;
28          *     cannot be <tt>null</tt>.
29          * @param element The element to be stored in the new node;
30          *     cannot be <tt>null</tt>.
31          * @return The new left child.
32          * @throws TreeException If <tt>parent</tt> is <tt>null</tt>
33          * or has a left child, or if <tt>element</tt>
34          * is <tt>null</tt>.
35          */
36         public BinaryTreeNode<E> makeLeftChild(
37                         BinaryTreeNode<E> parent, E element );
38
39         /**
40          * Create a node in the tree to store <tt>element</tt>
41          * make it the right child of <tt>parent</tt>.
42          * @param parent The parent of the node to be added;
43          *     cannot be <tt>null</tt>.
44          * @param element The element to be stored in the new node;
45          *     cannot be <tt>null</tt>.
46          * @return The new right child.
47          * @throws TreeException If <tt>parent</tt> is <tt>null</tt>
48          * or has a right child, or if <tt>element</tt>
49          * is <tt>null</tt>.
50          */
51         public BinaryTreeNode<E> makeRightChild(
52                         BinaryTreeNode<E> parent, E element );
53
54         /**
55          * Remove the specified node from the tree. The target's
56          * position is replaced by a leaf descendant.
57          * @param target The node to remove; cannot be <tt>null</tt>.
58          * @throws TreeException If <tt>node</tt> is <tt>null</tt>.
59          */
60         public void remove( BinaryTreeNode<E> node );
61
62         /**
63          * Return the root of this tree.
64          * @return The root of this tree or <tt>null</tt> if the tree
65          * is empty.
66          */
67         public BinaryTreeNode<E> root();
68
69         /**
70          * Look for <tt>target</tt> in this tree. If it is found,
71          * return the <tt>BinaryTreeNode</tt> that contains it,
72          * else return <tt>null</tt>. Uses <tt>equals()</tt> to
```

```
73          * compare the target against object stored in this tree.
74          * @param target The object we wish to find.
75          * @return <tt>true</tt> if <tt>target</tt> if found in this
76          *    tree, <tt>false</tt> otherwise.
77          */
78         public boolean contains( E target );
79
80         /**
81          * Perform a preorder traversal of this tree applying the
82          * <tt>Visitor</tt> to each node.
83          * @param visit The <tt>Visitor</tt> to apply during the
84          * traversal.
85          */
86         public void preOrderTraversal( Visitor<E> visit );
87
88         /**
89          * Perform an inorder traversal of this tree applying the
90          * <tt>Visitor</tt> to each node.
91          * @param visit The <tt>Visitor</tt> to apply during the
92          * traversal.
93          */
94         public void inOrderTraversal( Visitor<E> visit );
95
96         /**
97          * Perform a post-order traversal of this tree applying the
98          * <tt>Visitor</tt> to each node.
99          * @param visit The <tt>Visitor</tt> to apply during the
100         * traversal.
101         */
102        public void postOrderTraversal( Visitor<E> visit );
103
104        /**
105         * Perform a level-order traversal of this tree applying the
106         * <tt>Visitor</tt> to each node.
107         * @param visit The <tt>Visitor</tt> to apply during the
108         * traversal.
109         */
110        public void levelOrderTraversal( Visitor<E> visit );
111
112        /**
113         * Return the number of nodes in this <tt>BinaryTree</tt>.
114         * @return The number of nodes in this tree.
115         */
116        public int size();
117    }
```

The Java interface corresponding to the Binary Tree Node ADT is given in Listing 10.2. As before, the constructors described in the ADT specification don't appear in the interface, but would be supported by an implementation of the interface.

Listing 10.2 The `BinaryTreeNode` Interface.

```
1    package gray.adts.binarytree;
2
3    /**
4     * A <tt>BinaryTreeNode</tt> is a node in a binary tree.
5     * Each node stores a single object and may have 0 to 2
6     * children and 1 parent.
7     */
8
9    public class LinkedBinaryTreeNode<E> implements BinaryTreeNode<E> {
10       private   E                        element;
11       protected LinkedBinaryTreeNode<E>  parent;
12       protected LinkedBinaryTreeNode<E>  leftChild;
13       protected LinkedBinaryTreeNode<E>  rightChild;
14
15       /**
16        * Creates an empty <tt>BinaryTreeNode</tt>.
17        */
18       public LinkedBinaryTreeNode(){
19           this( null );
20       }
21
22       /**
23        * Creates a <tt>BinaryTreeNode</tt> storing
24        * <tt>theElement</tt>.
25        * @param theElement the element to store in this node when
26        *  it is created
27        */
28       public LinkedBinaryTreeNode( E theElement ){
29           this.parent = null;
30           this.leftChild = null;
31           this.rightChild = null;
32           this.element = theElement;
33       }
34
35       // ****************** ACCESSOR METHODS
36       /**
37        * Return the parent of this node.
38        * @return a reference to the parent node, null if this node
39        * has no parent
40        */
41       public BinaryTreeNode<E> parent(){
```

```
42              return this.parent;
43          }
44
45          /**
46           * Return a reference to the left child of this node.
47           * @return the left child of this node, null if there is
48           * no left child
49           */
50          public BinaryTreeNode<E> leftChild(){
51              return this.leftChild;
52          }
53
54          /**
55           * Return a reference to the right child of this node.
56           * @return the right child of this node, null if there is
57           * no right child
58           */
59          public BinaryTreeNode<E> rightChild(){
60              return this.rightChild;
61          }
62
63          /**
64           * Return the element stored in this node.
65           * @return the element stored in this node
66           */
67          public E element(){
68              return this.element;
69          }
70
71          // ******************  MUTATOR METHODS
72          /**
73           * Replaces the element stored in this node with the
74           * specified element.
75           * @param theElement the new element to be stored by this node.
76           */
77          public void setElement( E theElement ){
78              this.element = theElement;
79          }
80
81          /**
82           * Determine if this node is an internal node (has a child).
83           * @return true if node is an internal node, false otherwise
84           */
85          public boolean isInternal(){
86              return ( this.leftChild != null) ||
87                      ( this.rightChild != null );
88          }
89      }
```

Figure 10.8 illustrates the use of some of these methods in the construction of a parse tree for an arithmetic expression. The example makes use of Java's autoboxing feature, thus the compiler converts new LinkedBinaryTree<Char>('+'); into new LinkedBinaryTree<Char>(new Char('+')); for us (saves typing!).

10.3.2 Designing a Test Plan for BinaryTree

Our testing strategy follows the approach taken with all the other ADTs we have tested so far:

■ The accessor methods are tested as they are used to verify the mutator methods.

■ Methods that throw exceptions are invoked in such a way that pre-conditions are violated and an exception is thrown.

Figure 10.8 The construction of a binary tree to store the expression a * b + c using the methods from the BinaryTree interface.

Operation	Resulting Tree
`BinaryTree<Char> tree =` `    new LinkedBinaryTree<Char>( '+' );`	 +
`BinaryTreeNode<Char> root = tree.root();`	
`lchild = tree.makeLeftChild( root, '*' );`	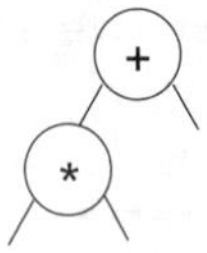 + with left child *
`tree.makeRightChild( root, 'c' );`	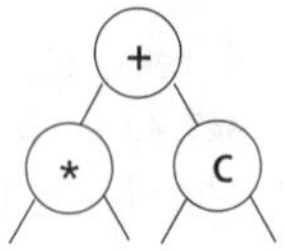 + with left child *, right child c
`tree.makeLeftChild( lchild, 'a' );`	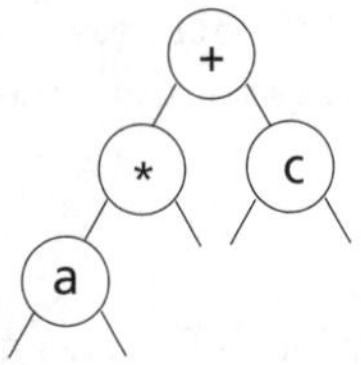 + with left child *, right child c; * with left child a
`tree.makeRightChild( lchild, 'b' );`	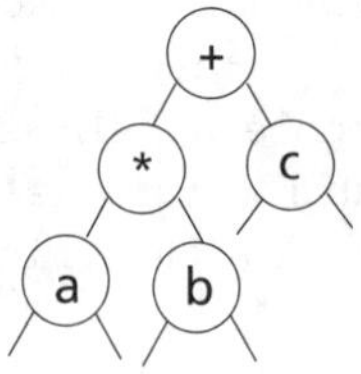 + with left child *, right child c; * with left child a, right child b

A simple way to verify that the addition and removal of nodes is done correctly is to dump the tree to a `List` using a tree traversal and compare what the traversal produces against what is expected. Some tests are developed here and the rest are left as exercises. Note that in Test Cases 10.1 and 10.2, the element type stored in the `BinaryTree` is `Integer`. The example also makes use of Java's autoboxing feature. The compiler converts `tree.makeRoot(2)` into `tree.makeRoot(new Integer(2))` for us.

Test Case 10.1 Creating an empty binary tree and adding nodes to it.

Method	Purpose	Object State	Expected Result
BinaryTree<Integer> tree = new LinkedBinaryTree <Integer>()	To create an empty binary tree using the default constructor.	*size* = 0 *root* = **null**	LinkedBinaryTree for Integers
tree.root()	To verify tree is empty.		null
tree.size()	To verify tree is empty.		0
root = tree.makeRoot(2)	To create a root node in an empty tree.	*size* = **1** *root* = **Integer(2)** *root*.**leftChild** = **null** *root*.**rightChild** = **null**	BinaryTreeNode containing Integer(2)
tree.size()	To verify a node was added.		1
tree.makeLeftChild(root, 1)	To add a left child to this tree's root.	*size* = **2** *root* = Integer(2) *root*.**leftChild** = **Integer(1)** *root*.rightChild = null	BinaryTreeNode containing Integer(1)
BinaryTreeNode<Integer> lchild = root.leftChild()	To verify left child was added.		BinaryTreeNode containing Integer(1)
lchild.element()	To verify contents of left child.		Integer(1)
lchild.parent()	To verify child connected to root.		*root*
tree.size()	To verify a node was added.		2
tree.makeRightChild(root, 3)	To add a right child to this tree's root.	*size* = **3** *root* = Integer(2) *root*.leftChild = Integer(1) *root*.**rightChild** = **Integer(3)**	BinaryTreeNode containing Integer(3)
BinaryTreeNode<Integer> rchild = root.rightChild()	To verify right child was added.		BinaryTreeNode containing Integer(3)
rchild.element()	To verify contents of right child.		Integer(3)
rchild.parent()	To verify child connected to root.		*root*
tree.size()	To verify a node was added.		3

Test Case 10.2 Verify that violation of method pre-conditions is caught.

Method	Purpose	Object State	Expected Result
BinaryTree<Integer> tree = new LinkedBinaryTree<Integer> (null)	To verify violation of pre-condition is caught.		exception
BinaryTree<Integer> tree = new LinkedBinaryTree(2)	To create a binary tree with an Integer element at the root.	*size* = 1 *root* = **Integer(2)** *root*.**leftChild** = **null** *root*.**rightChild** = **null**	LinkedBinaryTree object
tree.makeRoot(2)	To verify violation of pre-condition is caught.		exception
tree.makeLeftChild(tree.root(), null)	To verify violation of pre-condition is caught.		exception

CHECKPOINT

10.4 Draw the tree that is created by the following sequence of operations.

```
BinaryTree<Char> t = new LinkedBinaryTree<Char>( 'B' );
BinaryTreeNode<Char> c = t.makeLeftChild( t.root(), 'C' );
t.makeRightChild( c, 'G' );
t.makeRightChild( t.root(), 'P' );
```

10.5 Give a sequence of operations to create the following binary tree.

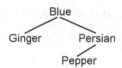

■ **10.4** Implementations of the Binary Tree ADT

In implementing a binary tree, we need to decide how the tree's elements will actually be stored. Here we consider two possible backing stores: an array and a linked structure.

10.4.1 Array Implementation

A binary tree is a **hierarchical collection** and an array is a **linear data structure**, so implementing a binary tree using an array as the backing store might not seem like a good idea, but it is easily done and, as we will see later in this chapter, is an ideal combination in some situations.

What makes this possible is that a binary tree has a regular structure—every node can have zero to two children, which allows us to define a mapping of the nodes of a *full* binary tree of height h to an array of length $2^h - 1$.

The nodes of a binary tree are laid out in the array in a top-to-bottom, left-to-right order (a level-order traversal). Figure 10.9 shows a full binary tree and its layout in an array.

There are simple formulas to determine the location of a node's parent and children in the array. For a node in position i, its

■ Left child is in position $2 \times i + 1$
■ Right child is in position $2 \times i + 2$
■ Parent is in position $\lfloor (i-1)/2 \rfloor$

Also, for a full tree with n nodes, the interior nodes of the tree are all found in positions 0 to $\lfloor n/2 \rfloor - 1$, and the leaves are found in positions $\lfloor n/2 \rfloor$ to $n - 1$.

What if some nodes in the tree don't have the full complement of two children? That is, what if the tree is not full? We can still use an array, but the cells that correspond to the missing children must store some value that indicates the cell doesn't store a tree node. Figure 10.10 shows such a situation.

Finally, if the tree is sparse (has lots of missing children), using an array is inefficient, as suggested in Figure 10.11, where fewer than half the cells of the array store tree nodes. The tree shown in the figure has a height h of 3, so requires an array of size $7 = 2^h - 1$, but less than half the cells are occupied.

As we have seen several times now, the advantage of using an array as the backing store is the access time; using the parent and left- and right-child formulas, we can efficiently get to any node in the tree. The disadvantage is the space inefficiency due to missing children.

Figure 10.9 A full binary tree and its layout in an array. A binary tree of height h will require an array of length $2^h - 1$.

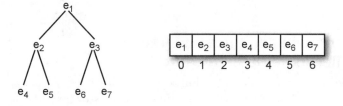

Figure 10.10 Array cells must still be allocated for nodes missing from a tree. These cells must store a value that indicates the node is missing.

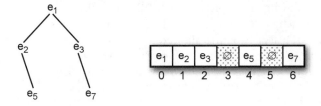

Figure 10.11 A tree of height *h* requires an array of length $2^h - 1$, regardless of how many elements there are in the tree.

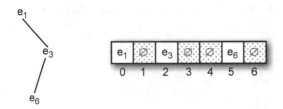

However, if we know the tree will be complete and if quick access to parents and children is important, then using an array as the backing store is a good choice. We will see an instance of this when we look at heaps in Section 10.5.

CHECKPOINT

10.6 Show the array contents for the following tree.

10.7 Show the binary tree for the following array.

10.4.2 Linked Implementation and the `BinaryTreeNode` Class: Another Recursive Data Structure

When we created doubly linked lists, each node in the linked list had links to its predecessor and successor. A node in a binary tree can have a single predecessor (its parent) and up to two successors (its children), suggesting that every linked binary tree node will have three link fields.

> Having parent and child links makes moving up and down the tree easier

Remembering that at one point we used singly linked lists in which each node only needed a single link to connect it to its successor, you might be wondering why we include a link from a node to its parent. Why not save on links and only maintain connections to the children? Drawing some pictures helps. Figure 10.12 (a) illustrates a four-node tree in which each node has a parent link. Figure 10.12 (b) is the same tree without the parent links. Just as two links allowed us to move forward and backward in a doubly linked linear list, maintaining both parent and child links will allow us to move up and down the tree easily, which will be quite convenient for some operations. The downside is the additional complexity inherent in making sure all links are always properly updated.

Figure 10.12 A Binary Tree with and without parent links.

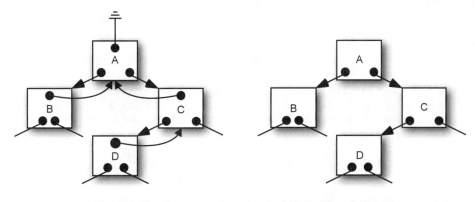

(a) The parent link makes it easy to move up the tree.

(b) A tree without the parent link is a one-way data structure: top to bottom.

LinkedBinaryTreeNode

The data fields of our `LinkedBinaryTreeNode` class will look like this:

```
public class LinkedBinaryTreeNode<E>    implements BinaryTreeNode<E> {
    protected E                         element
    protected LinkedBinaryTreeNode<E>   parent;
    protected LinkedBinaryTreeNode<E>   leftChild;
    protected LinkedBinaryTreeNode<E>   rightChild;
```

Recall that when we were describing the BinaryTree ADT, we said that we wanted to ensure that a client could only change the structure of a tree through tree methods. A client can, however, change the element stored in a `LinkedBinaryTreeNode`, so the only mutator method provided by `LinkedBinaryTreeNode` is `setElement()`. A consequence of this is that the link fields in `LinkedBinaryTreeNode` must be `protected` (not `private`) so that classes in the same package as `LinkedBinaryTreeNode` can access them directly.

Make the data fields **protected** if you don't provide accessors or mutators

The implementation of the methods follows from their javadoc descriptions and is straightforward. The `element` field has both an accessor and a mutator, so it could have been made `private`.

LinkedBinaryTree

A `LinkedBinaryTree` is composed of a collection of `LinkedBinaryTreeNodes`. The Binary Tree ADT described the attributes and operations to be supported for a Binary Tree. The two attributes, *size* and *root*, will be represented as data fields. Here we develop three of the methods. As we have done before, the work to be done is presented as a sequence of tasks:

1. Implement a constructor that creates a tree from an element and two subtrees.
2. Implement `remove()` to remove a node from the binary tree.
3. Implement `preorderTraversal()` using a Visitor.

10.4.3 `LinkedBinaryTree` Task 1: Constructor to create a binary tree from an element and two subtrees

```
/**
 * Create a <tt>BinaryTree</tt> with <tt>element</tt>
 * stored in the root and <tt>leftTree</tt> and <tt>rightTree</tt>
 * as its left and right children.
 * @param leftTree the root of the new tree's left subtree
 * @param element the element to store in the root of the new tree
 * @param rightTree the root of the new tree's right subtree
 * @throws NullPointerException if <tt>element</tt> is null
 */
public LinkedBinaryTree( BinaryTree<E> leftTree, E element,
                         BinaryTree<E> rightTree );
```

This constructor builds a new tree from two existing trees and a root element. The only pre-condition is that the element to be stored in the root node cannot be null. We will have to check for this. When you look at the code, note that the `LinkedBinaryTreeNode` data fields are accessed directly (that is, a mutator method is not used).

There are a few spots where we have to be careful. What is the size of the new tree? It will be one (for the root) plus the size of the left and right subtrees. It would be easy to have an off-by-one error here and forget to include the root.

Another issue is how much pseudocoding is enough. Often, as in Listing 10.3, pseudocode is written in pretty broad terms. But sometimes, as the saying goes, "The devil is in the details." For example, the pseudocode might suggest we could do something like this:

Issues in pseudo-coding detail

```
// make size = 1 + size of the left subtree + size of the right subtree
size = 1 + leftTree.size() + rightTree.size();
```

This seems innocent enough, but it assumes that `leftTree` and `rightTree` are not null. We need to check for this first (lines 7 and 15 in Listing 10.3).

Also, the pseudocode statement "*make leftTree the root's left subtree*" leaves out how this is done. To correctly code this we need to be clear about what is involved in linking two nodes in a parent-child relationship. As the Java code shows, the relationship between pseudocode and implementation is not always one-to-one. Again, drawing pictures can be a big help. Figure 10.13 shows three possible arguments to the constructor and the relationships in the tree that is constructed. Drawing the picture helps me to see that the child links of the root of the new tree must refer to the roots of the left and right subtrees *and* that the parent links of the subtree roots must be updated to refer to their new parent.[3]

Of course, any mistake you make translating your pseudocode to code should be caught by your thorough testing! You get in trouble when your pseudocode is very high level, but your coding from it isn't careful and your test plan is weak. As you gain more experience, you should occasionally rethink your position on the roles played by planning, coding, and testing in producing error-free code.

Reflect on what makes you successful

---

[3]As mentioned before, this example suggests that having the parent link actually complicates the code. You get to evaluate this further in the Exercises.

Listing 10.3 A constructor for `LinkedBinaryTree` to create a new tree given an element for the root and two (possibly empty) subtrees.

```
1    public LinkedBinaryTree ( BinaryTree<E> leftTree,
2                              E element, BinaryTree<E> rightTree ){
```

check the pre-conditions
```
3        if ( element == null )
4            throw new NullPointerException();
```

create a new LinkedBinaryTreeNode to store element and
  make this new node the root of this tree
```
5        root = new LinkedBinaryTreeNode<E>( element );
```

make size = 1+ size of the left subtree + size of the right subtree
```
6        size = 1;
```

make leftTree the root's left subtree
```
7        if ( leftTree != null ) {
8            size += ((LinkedBinaryTree<E>)leftTree).size();
9            root.leftChild =
10               (LinkedBinaryTreeNode<E>)((LinkedBinaryTree<E>)leftTree).root();
11           root.leftChild.parent = root;
12       }
13       else
14           root.leftChild = null;
```

make rightTree the root's right subtree
```
15       if ( rightTree != null ) {
16           size += ((LinkedBinaryTree<E>)rightTree).size();
17           root.rightChild =
18               (LinkedBinaryTreeNode<E>)((LinkedBinaryTree<E>)rightTree).root();
19           root.rightChild.parent = root;
20       }
21       else
22           root.rightChild = null;
23   }.
```

10.4.4 `LinkedBinaryTree` Task 2: Implement `remove()`

The second method we design and build is `remove()`, which removes the specified node from the tree. Removing a leaf is straightforward. Removing an internal node is a little tricky. For example, in Figure 10.14(a), what do we do with A's children if we remove A? The solution we will adopt is to replace the node to be removed with

Figure 10.13 The construction of a Binary Tree given a root element and left and right subtrees. It is important to remember to complete all child and parent links.

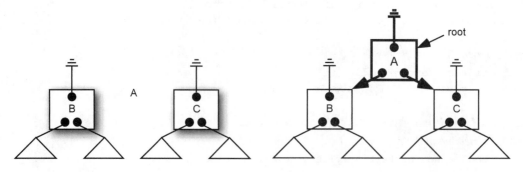

(a) The three arguments to the constructor: left subtree, element A, right subtree.

(b) A `LinkedBinaryTreeNode` has been created to store A and becomes the root of the tree linked to its subtrees.

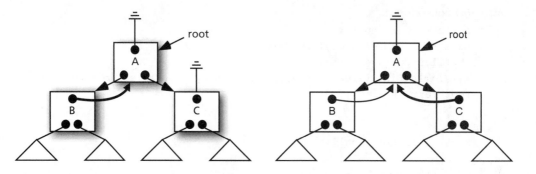

(c) The left subtree is linked to its new parent.

(d) The right subtree is linked to its new parent.

a leaf descendant. To make things even simpler, we won't actually move the leaf node. Instead we'll replace the target node's element with the leaf's element. Then we just detach the leaf node, which is easy to do. This is a handy approach we will reuse. The result is shown in Figure 10.14(b). The javadocs for remove() must describe how the tree is restructured by the remove.

Listing 10.4 shows the pseudocode we started with and the resulting Java method. Some of the higher-level pseudocode statements turned into utility methods, which are shown in Listing 10.5.

Before we move on, let's look at Figure 10.15, which shows before and after pictures for a call to remove() on a leaf. The illustration helps make it clear that we need to cut *all* the links between the node and its parent: the link from the node to its parent *and* the link from the parent to the node. Note that the way the code is written in detachFromParent(), it is important to not lose the connection to the

Figure 10.14 Removing an internal node from a binary tree.

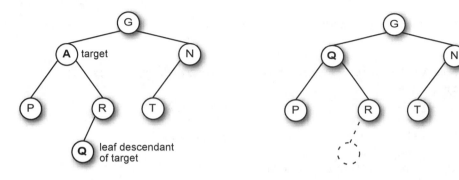

(a) Target node A is an internal node.

(b) Replace target's element with the element from a leaf descendant; remove the leaf.

Listing 10.4 The `LinkedBinaryTree.remove()` method.

```
 1    public void remove( BinaryTreeNode<E> target ) {
```
if target is null there is nothing to do so return
```
 2        if ( target == null )
 3            return;        // nothing to remove
 4        LinkedBinaryTreeNode<E> node = (LinkedBinaryTreeNode<E>) target;
```
if target is internal
```
 5        // If this is an internal node, we need to get another
 6        // node (a leaf descendant) to put in its place
 7        if ( node.isInternal () ) {
```
get a leaf descendant of target; move leaf's element into target and detach the leaf
```
 8            LinkedBinaryTreeNode<E> leaf = getaLeafDescendant( node );
 9            node.setElement( leaf.element() );
10        }
```
else target is a leaf and needs to be detached
```
11        else
12            detachFromParent( node );
```
decrement tree's size by 1
```
13        size--;
14    }
```

parent before the parent's child link has been updated. Disconnect the node from its parent *after* the parent disconnects from the child. This sort of mistake is easy to make.

Listing 10.5 Utilities methods used in support of remove().

```
1    /**
2     * Detach this leaf node from the tree.
3     * @pre <tt>node</tt> is a leaf (not checked)
4     */
5    private void detachFromParent( LinkedBinaryTreeNode<E> node ){
6        if ( node.parent == null )
7           return;                          // nothing to do
8
9        LinkedBinaryTreeNode<E> parent = node.parent;
10       node.parent = null;
11       if ( parent.leftChild == node )
12          parent.leftChild = null;
13       else
14          parent.rightChild = null;
15   }
16
17   /**
18    * Get a descendant of node that is a leaf. Preference is for
19    * the rightmost child, but we'll go left if we have to.
20    * @pre node is not null (not checked)
21    * @pre node has at least one child (not checked)
22    * @post the node returned is detached from its parent.
23    */
24   private LinkedBinaryTreeNode<E> getaLeafDescendant(
25                                       LinkedBinaryTreeNode<E> node ){
26       // if there is a right child, go that direction
27       if ( node.rightChild != null )
28          return getaLeafDescendant( node.rightChild );
29
30       // if there is no right child, try going left
31       else if ( node.leftChild != null )
32          return getaLeafDescendant( node.leftChild );
33       // no right or left children, so this is the node we want.
34       // Detach it from its parent and return it.
35       else {
36          detachFromParent( node );
37          return node;
38       }
39   }
```

Figure 10.15 Removing a leaf from a tree. All connections between the node to be removed and its parent must be severed.

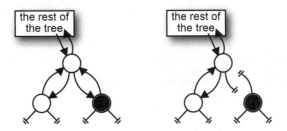

10.4.5 `LinkedBinaryTree` Task 3: Implement `preorderTraversal()` using a Visitor

The last method we examine is `preorderTraversal()` using a Visitor. First, we'll look at the `Visitor` interface, then implement `preorderTraversal()`. Finally, we'll create a `ListVisitor` class that puts the elements of a binary tree in a list. What we will see is that the traversal method is very straightforward and most of the complexity is in the visitor.

The traversal method is completely independent of what is done with each node as it is visited. A visitor object that encapsulates the code to be applied to the tree nodes is passed to the traversal method. The only method specified in the visitor interface is `visit(BinaryTreeNode)`—see Listing 10.6.

The public version of `preOrderTraversal()` in Listing 10.7 calls a private recursive method that does the work. This organization is necessary because the

Listing 10.6 The `Visitor` interface.

```
1    package gray.adts.binarytree;
2
3    /**
4     * Implementation of the Visitor design pattern.
5     */
6    public interface Visitor<E> {
7
8        /**
9         * Visit the specified node.
10        * The implementation determines what, if anything, will
11        * be done with the node.
12        * @param node The node to visit.
13        */
14       public void visit( BinaryTreeNode<E> node );
15   }
```

Listing 10.7 The Binary Tree `preOrderTraversal()` method.

```
1    void preOrderTraversal( Visitor<E> visitor ) {
2        doPreOrderTraversal( this.root(), visitor );
3    }
```

preorder(node)

```
4    void doPreOrderTraversal( BinaryTreeNode<E> node, Visitor<E> visitor ){
```

if the node is null return

```
5    if ( node == null )         // base case
6        return;
7    // node is not null - recursive case
8    LinkedBinaryTreeNode<E> thenode = (LinkedBinaryTreeNode<E>) node;
```

visit this node

```
9        visitor.visit( thenode );
```

preorder(node's left child)

```
10        doPreOrderTraversal( thenode.leftChild (), visitor );
```

preorder(node's right child)

```
11        doPreOrderTraversal( thenode.rightChild(), visitor );
12   }
```

recursive method needs to pass the current node, as well as the visitor, as arguments, and the public method only allows the Visitor argument.

The base case for the recursive method is that the node passed in is `null` (clearly if a node is `null`, there is nothing to visit). The recursive case occurs when the node is non-null, in which case there is a node to visit and child links to recursively traverse.

Class `ToListVisitor` implements the `Visitor` interface. Since its purpose is to store the elements of the tree in a list, the class must have a `List` data field (line 13 of Listing 10.8). It will also need an accessor to make the completed list available to its client (lines 23–29). The `visit()` method (lines 31–36) need only append the method's argument to the `List`. The complete (very short!) class is shown in Listing 10.8.

Separating *how* the traversal is done from *what* is done during the traversal is a pretty neat idea. Listing 10.9 gives an example that demonstrates that this works. The example shows the result of using all four traversal orders when applying `ToListVisitor`. As a second example, Listing 10.10 shows the application of `NodeCountVisitor`, a `Visitor` class that counts the nodes in a tree. These examples nicely illustrate that the traversal methods are completely independent of what the `Visitor` class does.

The visitor approach allows you to separate *how* the traversal is done from *what* is done

Listing 10.8 The `ToListVisitor` class.

```
1    package gray.adts.binarytree;
2
3    import java.util.List;
4    import java.util.ArrayList;
5
6    /**
7     * A Visitor class for converting a tree into a <tt>List</tt>.
8     * The order in which the elements of the tree are placed in the
9     * list is determined by the tree traversal used. This class
10    * implements the Visitor design pattern.
11    */
12   public class ToListVisitor<E> implements Visitor<E> {
13       private List<E> list;
14
15       /**
16        * Create an empty list into which <tt>visit</tt> will
17        * append the tree's elements.
18        */
19       public ToListVisitor(){
20           list = new ArrayList<E>();
21       }
22
23       /**
24        * Return the list of elements.
25        * @return A list of the elements from a tree.
26        */
27       public List<E> list(){
28           return this.list;
29       }
30
31       /**
32        * Appends the specified node to the end of the list.
33        */
34       public void visit( BinaryTreeNode<E> node ){
35           list.add( node.element() );
36       }
37   }
```

Listing 10.9 Using the `ToListVisitor` class.

```
1     import gray.adts.binarytree.*;
2     import java.util.List;
3     import java.util.Iterator;
4
5     /**
6      * Example usage of the ListVisitor.
7      */
8     public class ToListVisitorEx {
9
10       public static void main(String[] args) {
11           BinaryTree<String> tree = new LinkedBinaryTree( "A" );
12           BinaryTreeNode<String> root = tree.root();
13           tree.makeLeftChild( root, "B" );
14           tree.makeRightChild( root, "C" );
15           BinaryTreeNode<String> child = root.leftChild();
16           tree.makeLeftChild( child, "D" );
17           tree.makeRightChild( child, "E" );
18           child = root.rightChild();
19           tree.makeLeftChild( child, "F" );
20           tree.makeRightChild( child, "G" );
21
22           System.out.println("preorder traversal: ");
23           ToListVisitor<String> listMaker =
24                                   new ToListVisitor<String>();
25           tree.preOrderTraversal( listMaker );
26           List<String> list = listMaker.list();
27
28           for( String s : list )
29               System.out.print( "\t" + s + " " );
30           System.out.println();
31
32           System.out.println("\ninorder traversal: ");
33           listMaker = new ToListVisitor<String>();
34           tree.inOrderTraversal( listMaker );
35           list = listMaker.list();
36
37           for( String s : list )
38               System.out.print( "\t" + s + " " );
39           System.out.println();
40
41           System.out.println("\npostorder traversal: ");
42           listMaker = new ToListVisitor<String>();
43           tree.postOrderTraversal( listMaker );
44           list = listMaker.list();
45
```

```
46              for( String s : list )
47                  System.out.print( "\t" + s + " " );
48              System.out.println();
49
50              System.out.println("\nlevelorder traversal: ");
51              listMaker = new ToListVisitor();
52              tree.levelOrderTraversal( listMaker );
53              list = listMaker.list();
54
55              for( String s : list )
56                  System.out.print( "\t" + s + " " );
57              System.out.println();
58          }
59      }
```

OUTPUT

```
preorder traversal:
A      B      D      E      C      F      G
inorder traversal:
D      B      E      A      F      C      G
postorder traversal:
D      E      B      F      G      C      A
levelorder traversal:
A      B      C      D      E      F      G
```

Listing 10.10 Using the NodeCountVisitor class.

```
1   import gray.adts.binarytree.*;
2   import java.util.*;
3
4   /**
5    * Example usage of the NodeCounterVisitor.
6    */
7   public class NodeCountVisitorEx {
8       public static void main(String[] args) {
9           BinaryTree<String> tree =
10                          new LinkedBinaryTree<String>( "A" );
11          BinaryTreeNode<String> root = tree.root();
12          tree.makeLeftChild( root, "B" );
13          tree.makeRightChild( root, "C" );
14          BinaryTreeNode child = root.leftChild();
15          tree.makeLeftChild( child, "D" );
16          tree.makeRightChild( child, "E" );
17          child = root.rightChild();
18          tree.makeLeftChild( child, "F" );
```

```
19              tree.makeRightChild( child, "G" );
20
21              NodeCountVisitor<String> nodeCounter =
22                              new NodeCountVisitor<String>();
23              tree.preOrderTraversal( nodeCounter );
24              System.out.println( "preorder traversal count is " +
25                              nodeCounter.count() );
26
27              nodeCounter = new NodeCountVisitor<String>();
28              tree.inOrderTraversal( nodeCounter );
29              System.out.println( "inorder traversal count is " +
30                              nodeCounter.count() );
31
32              nodeCounter = new NodeCountVisitor<String>();
33              tree.postOrderTraversal( nodeCounter );
34              System.out.println( "postorder traversal count is " +
35                              nodeCounter.count() );
36
37              nodeCounter = new NodeCountVisitor<String>();
38              tree.levelOrderTraversal( nodeCounter );
39              System.out.println( "levelorder traversal count is " +
40                              nodeCounter.count() );
41          }
42      }
```

OUTPUT

```
preorder traversal count is 7
inorder traversal count is 7
postorder traversal count is 7
levelorder traversal count is 7
```

10.4.6 Testing the Implementations

In Section 10.3.2 we saw that one way to test for correct addition and deletion of elements is by dumping the contents of a tree to a list. With ToListVisitor we now have a tool for doing this. The JUnit test code fragment in Listing 10.11 inserts a number of elements into a tree (some in setUp() and others in the test method testMergeTrees()). To verify the elements were in fact inserted *in the correct place*, we dump the tree to a List and use the List comparison method equals() to verify the order.[4]

---

[4]*Hint*: You should look up the meaning of List.equals() in the javadocs.

Listing 10.11 JUnit fragment to test insertions into a tree.

```
1    /**
2     * Sets up the text fixture.
3     * Called before every test case method.
4     */
5    protected void setUp() {
6       tree = new LinkedBinaryTree<Integer>();
7       tree2 = new LinkedBinaryTree<Integer>( 2 );
8       tree3 = new LinkedBinaryTree<Integer>( 2 );
9       BinaryTreeNode<Integer> lchild = tree3.makeLeftChild(tree3.root(), 1 );
10      BinaryTreeNode<Integer> rchild = tree3.makeRightChild(tree3.root(), 3 );
11      tree3.makeLeftChild( lchild, 4 );
12      tree3.makeRightChild( lchild, 5 );
13      tree3.makeLeftChild( rchild, 6 );
14      tree3.makeRightChild( rchild, 7 );
15
16      expectedTree3List = new ArrayList();
17      expectedTree3List.add( 1 );
18      expectedTree3List.add( 2 );
19      expectedTree3List.add( 3 );
20      expectedTree3List.add( 4 );
21      expectedTree3List.add( 5 );
22      expectedTree3List.add( 6 );
23      expectedTree3List.add( 7 );
24   }
25
26   public void testMergeTrees(){
27      BinaryTree<Integer> mergedTree =
28         new LinkedBinaryTree<Integer>(tree2, 0, tree3);
29      assertEquals( mergedTree.size(), 9 );
30
31      List<Integer> expectedTreeList = new ArrayList<Integer>();
32      expectedTreeList.add( 0 );
33      expectedTreeList.add( 2 );
34      expectedTreeList.add( 2 );
35      expectedTreeList.add( 1 );
36      expectedTreeList.add( 4 );
37      expectedTreeList.add( 5 );
38      expectedTreeList.add( 3 );
39      expectedTreeList.add( 6 );
40      expectedTreeList.add( 7 );
41
42      ToListVisitor<Integer> treeVisitor = new ToListVisitor<Integer>();
43      mergedTree.preOrderTraversal( treeVisitor );
44      assertTrue( treeVisitor.list().equals( expectedTreeList ) );
45   }
```

10.4.7 Evaluation of Implementations

The cost of traveling from the root of a complete binary tree to a leaf is $O(\log_2 n)$, the height of the tree. In the worst case, the tree is very unbalanced, and the time needed to travel from the root to a leaf is linear in n ($O(n)$). The add and remove operations involve a few link updates, so they are $O(1)$. But if you include the time to find the insertion or deletion point, they are $O(n)$, in the worst case.

When the binary tree is stored in an array, the trip from the root to leaf involves finding the location of each node's child, which takes a number of computations, and a single memory lookup to get to the leaf. In the linked implementation, each of these computations is replaced by a memory lookup.

There are three links maintained for each node, so the space complexity is $O(n)$. Having the parent link simplifies the code in some places, but complicates it in others.

SUMMING UP

The elements of a binary tree can be stored in either an array or a linked structure. The array implementation has the advantage of fast access, but at the cost of some wasted space if the tree is not full. The linked implementation can grow or shrink according to its needs, but this flexibility is gained at the cost of slower access time (memory lookups for links in place of index computations for an array) and memory for the links in each node.

■ 10.5 Heaps and Binary Trees

A **heap** is a special kind of binary tree that has the following properties

Property 10.4   The heap's binary tree is a complete binary tree.

Property 10.5   A heap is either a **minheap** or a **maxheap**, which can be defined recursively as follows:

minheap—The element in a node is *less than* or equal to the elements in its children. Each child is the root of a minheap.

maxheap—The element in a node is *greater than* or equal to the elements in its children. Each child is the root of a maxheap.

A **valid heap** is one that has both heap properties. An **invalid heap** has one or both heap properties violated. A binary tree of only one element is clearly a valid heap. Figure 10.16 shows valid and invalid minheaps.

10.5.1 Heap ADT Specification and Java Interface

The **read** access point of a heap is its *top*, which is the root of the complete binary tree and which stores the smallest/largest value in the heap. A heap supports add and remove operations. Unlike the ADTs we have seen so far in which an element is added to a collection at some position, the placement of a new element in a heap

Figure 10.16 Examples of valid and invalid minheaps.

(a) A valid minheap.

(b) An invalid minheap (violates the complete binary tree property; 21's left child is missing).

(c) An invalid minheap (violates the minheap property: P is greater than B).

depends on its value. The remove operation, called top(), removes the top element of the heap, which will always be the smallest element in a minheap and the largest element in a maxheap. This is a value-oriented operation in that the value returned is always the smallest/largest value in the heap.

Accesses to a heap are value-oriented, not position-oriented

Because where an object is added in a heap depends on its value, the objects must be comparable. As we saw in the chapter on sorting, one approach to enforcing this constraint is to require that the type of an object added to a heap be `Comparable`. The problem with this approach, though, is that relying on `Comparable` means the heap can only support one ordering of the elements (whatever the implementation of `Comparable` provides). Supporting alternative orderings would mean re-implementing the type's implementation of `Comparable.compareTo()`. Clearly that is clunky.

Heap elements must be comparable

The solution that we used when we looked at sorting algorithms was to provide the sort routine with a separate `Comparator` object. If we wanted to change the way the elements were sorted, we just provided a different `Comparator` that defined the desired sort order. The sort routine did not need to be changed at all. The same solution can be applied to heaps. Since this is the more flexible solution, we will adopt it for our heap—a `Comparator` will be provided when a heap is constructed.

The Heap ADT gives the specification of the Heap ADT. It does not specify if this is a minheap or a maxheap, leaving that to the implementation. A corresponding Java interface is given in Listing 10.12.

The Heap ADT

Description
A heap stores a collection of comparable elements and allows the smallest (minheap) or largest (maxheap) element to be read and removed from the collection.

Attributes
comparator: The Comparator to use to compare elements of the heap.
size: The number of elements in the heap.
top: The top element of the heap—the root of a complete binary tree.

Properties
1. A heap is always a complete binary tree.
2. If this is a minheap, the value in each node is less than or equal to the values of its children.
3. If this is a maxheap, the value in each node is greater than or equal to the values of its children.

Operations

heap (Comparator compare)

pre-condition:	compare is not null
responsibilities:	constructor—create an empty heap. The ordering of elements in the heap will be defined by the Comparator compare.
post-condition:	*size* is 0
	top is null
	comparator is set to compare
returns:	nothing
exception:	if compare is null

heap(Collection c, Comparator compare)

pre-condition:	the Collection and Comparator are not null
	the elements in the collection are comparable using compare
responsibilities:	constructor—create a valid heap from the elements in the given collection
post-condition:	the heap stores the elements of c
	size is the number of elements in the collection c
	top refers to the largest (maxheap) or smallest (minheap) element in the heap
	comparator is set to compare
returns:	nothing
exception:	if the Collection or Comparator are null or if c's elements are not comparable using the Comparator

add(*Type* element)

pre-condition:	element is not null and is comparable to the other elements in the heap using *comparator*
responsibilities:	insert element into the heap such that the heap properties are maintained
post-condition:	element is in the heap
	size is incremented by 1
	top refers to the largest (maxheap) or smallest (minheap) element in the heap
returns:	nothing
exception:	if element is null

top()

pre-condition:	the heap is not empty
responsibilities:	remove and return the *top* element of the heap

post-condition:	*size* is decremented by 1
	top refers to the largest (maxheap) or smallest (minheap) element remaining in the heap
returns:	the previous *top* element of the heap
exception:	if the heap is empty

peek()

pre-condition:	the heap is not empty
responsibilities:	return the *top* element of the heap
post-condition:	the heap is unchanged
returns:	the *top* element of the heap
exception:	if the heap is empty

Not shown: size(), clear() and isEmpty()

Listing 10.12 The Heap Interface.

```
1   package gray.adts.heap;
2
3   /**
4    * <p>The interface for the Heap ADT.</p>
5    * <P>
6    * This interface can describe either a minheap or a maxheap.
7    * <UL>
8    * <LI> <B>minheap</B> - the element at the root of a heap is
9    * less than or equal to the elements in its children, which
10   * are also the roots of heaps.</LI>
11   * <LI><B>maxheap</B> - the element at the root of a heap is
12   * greater than or equal to the elements in its children, which
13   * are also the roots of heaps.</LI>
14   * </UL>
15   */
16  public interface Heap<E> {
17      /**
18       * Insert the given element into the heap.
19       * @param element The element to add to the heap.
20       * @throws NullPointerException if <tt>element</tt>
21       * is null
22       */
23      public void add( E element );
24
25      /**
26       * Remove and return the top element of the heap.
27       * @return The top element of the heap.
28       * @throws EmptyHeapException if the heap is empty.
```

```
29              */
30          public E top();
31
32          /**
33           * Removes all of the elements from this heap.
34           */
35          public void clear();
36
37          /**
38           * Return the element at the top of this heap without
39           * removing it.
40           * @return The top element of the heap.
41           * @throws EmptyHeapException if the heap is empty.
42           */
43          public E peek();
44
45          /**
46           * Return the number of elements stored in this heap.
47           * @return The number of elements in this heap.
48           */
49          public int size();
50
51          /**
52           * Determine if this heap is empty.
53           * @return <tt>true</tt> if this heap is empty
54           * (<tt>size() == 0</tt>), otherwise return <tt>false</tt>.
55           */
56        public boolean isEmpty();
57    }
```

10.5.2 Heap Implementation

Before considering how to store the elements of a heap, let's look at what is involved in the add() and top() operations, and the construction of a heap from a collection of elements. While we will talk about minheaps in the rest of this section, the concepts apply generally to a maxheap.

Adding an Element to a Minheap

When an element is added to or removed from a heap, the heap properties may be violated, requiring restructuring to make the heap valid again. Clearly we want to do this in the simplest and most efficient manner possible.

Consider the binary tree in Figure 10.17(a). If we add the element as the new rightmost leaf (where the circle is), we can guarantee that the tree is still a complete binary tree (heap property 10.4). However, it is possible that this will violate the minheap property (heap property 10.5). This is shown in Figure 10.17(b), where the

Figure 10.17 Adding an element to a heap: heap.add(6).

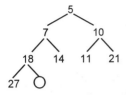

(a) A minheap prior to adding an element. The circle is where the new element will be put initially.

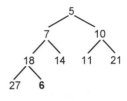

(b) Add the element as the new rightmost leaf. This maintains a complete binary tree, but may violate the minheap property.

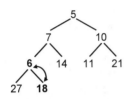

(c) Starting with the new element, if the child is less than the parent, swap them. This moves the new element up the tree.

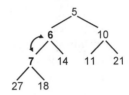

(d) Repeat the step described in (c) until the parent of the new element is less than or equal to the new element. The minheap property has been restored.

element 6 has been inserted as a new, rightmost leaf. The new element is smaller than its parent, so we have some repairing to do.

Making the heap valid again is simple: We move the new element up the tree through a series of exchanges between a parent and child until the minheap property is restored. Note that a child-parent exchange does not change the structure of the tree, so if the tree was already a complete binary tree, these exchanges won't violate that property. Also note that we only need to look at the new element and its parent. We never have to look at the new element's sibling as the new element moves up the heap. Why not? Because if the tree rooted at the parent was a valid minheap prior to adding the new element, it must be true that the new element's sibling is greater than or equal to the parent. The new element will only be swapped with its parent if it is less than the parent. Consequently the sibling (which becomes the child of the new element after the swap) must be greater than the new element if a swap was done. The examples in this section illustrate this useful fact. Figures 10.17(c) and (d) show the exchanges that are made.

The description and illustration suggest the following pseudocode for the add() operation.

Pseudocode: add(element)
insert the new element as the new rightmost leaf
increment size by 1
while the new element has a parent and the new element is less than its parent
  swap the parent and child elements

The cost of the add() operation is bounded by the distance the new element can travel. Since the new element starts as a leaf and the highest it can climb is to the root, this bound is the height of the tree. By Property 10.2, we know this to be $\lceil \log_2 n \rceil$, so the cost of add() is $O(\lceil \log_2 n \rceil)$.

Removing the Top Element from a Minheap

The top() operation always removes and returns the top element of the heap, creating a gap there. The gap is easily filled by moving the last element in the heap (the rightmost leaf) into the top position (the root of the tree). This guarantees that the tree is still a complete binary tree, but it will almost certainly violate the minheap property. The solution is to move the top value down the tree through a series of parent-child exchanges until the minheap property is restored.

The solution relies on the following observation: Before the rightmost leaf was swapped into the top position, the heap was valid. Consequently, after the rightmost leaf was swapped into the top position, the top element and its two children may not be a valid heap, but it is guaranteed that the heaps rooted at top's children are still valid heaps—they were valid heaps before the swap and the swap does not change that. This is the case in Figure 10.19 (a) after the rightmost leaf has been moved to the top. The heap rooted at the top (18) is invalid, but the heaps roots at its children (6 and 10) are valid.

When fixing a heap rooted at some node *n*, you first find the smaller of *n*'s children (not *n*'s descendants, just *n*'s immediate children). This smallest element is

If the parent's element is greater than its children's elements, swap the parent's element with the smallest of its children

---

Figure 10.18 Fixing a heap means swapping the smaller of the children with the parent, if the parent is larger than either child.

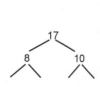

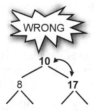

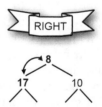

(a) The heaps rooted at 8 and 10 are valid. The heap consisting of 17, 8, and 10 is invalid.

(b) Promoting the larger child can produce an invalid heap at the sibling.

(c) Promoting the smaller child means the triple (8, 17 10) is a valid heap and only the swapped child (17) needs to be further examined.

Figure 10.19 Fixing the heap following a `top()` operation.

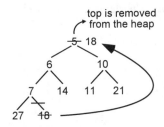

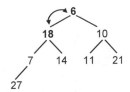

(a) Moving the rightmost leaf to the top of the heap to fill the gap created when the top element (5) was removed. This is a complete binary tree, but the minheap property has been violated.

(b) Swapping top with the smaller of its two children leaves top's right subtree a valid heap. The subtree rooted at 18 still needs fixing.

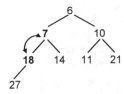

(c) Swapping top with the smaller of its two children leaves top's right subtree a valid heap. The subtree rooted at 18 still needs fixing.

compared to n's element. If n's element is smaller or equal, then n and its children form a valid heap. Since n's children are the roots of valid heaps, the entire heap rooted at n is valid. If, however, n's element is greater than that of its *smallest* child, they swap elements. Figure 10.18 illustrates these ideas.

Figure 10.19 (a) shows the result of moving the rightmost leaf to the top of the heap. Figure 10.19 (b) shows the top element (18) swapped with the smaller of its two children (6). This step is repeated until the value is less than or equal to both of its children (see Figure 10.19 (c)), at which point the entire heap is valid again.

We will reuse the code for fixing the heap shortly when we look at building a heap from a collection of elements, so we pseudocode `top()` and `fixHeap()` separately.

Pseudocode: top() // remove and return the top element of the heap
extract the top element from the heap and store it in oldTop
move the rightmost leaf into top
decrement size by 1
fixHeap(top) // fix the heap starting at the top
return oldTop

Pseudocode: fixHeap(node) // fix the heap rooted at node

let cursor reference node
while the cursor has a child and the cursor's element is greater than the element in either child
// invariant: the cursor's children are roots of valid heaps
    swap the cursor's element with the element of the smaller of cursor's children
    // invariant: the cursor and its children are a now valid heap
    move cursor to the swapped child
// loop post-condition: the binary tree rooted at node is a valid heap

The cost of removing the top element, like that of adding a new element, is bounded by how far an element can move as the heap is fixed. This bound is the height of the tree, so the cost of removing the top element is the same as that of adding an element: $O(\log_2 n)$

Building a Heap from a Collection of Elements

One of the overloaded heap constructors builds a heap from a collection of elements supplied as an argument. Using `fixHeap()`, the steps to building the heap are short and simple. First the elements of the collection are mapped to a complete binary tree, as shown in Figure 10.20 (this should look familiar to you from the section on Binary Trees; we will discuss it again shortly). Now we need to fix it so it satisfies the minheap property. To do this we start near the bottom of the tree and work our way toward the root level by level, fixing subheaps as we go.

Constructing the heap relies on the same observation we made when looking at fixing the heap after removing the top element: as we visit interior nodes of the binary tree, the heap rooted at that node may be invalid, but the heaps rooted at its children will always be valid. This leads us to a shortcut.

Since a leaf is already a valid minheap (a heap of size 1 is always a valid heap), we start the heap construction with the rightmost *interior* node. Note that this node's

---

Figure 10.20 A list of elements mapped to a heap structure. The heap violates the minheap property and must be fixed.

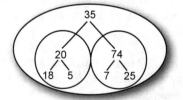

(a) A collection of random elements.

(b) The collection mapped to a Binary Tree. The circled subtrees are heaps that must be fixed. The leaves are also heaps, but a heap of size 1 is always valid.

children are valid heaps—they must be because they are leaves. We use `fixHeap()` on the rightmost interior node to turn it into a valid heap. Then we move to its left neighbor on the same level and repeat the process.[5] When all the nodes on a level have been visited in this fashion, we move up a level and repeat this process, moving right to left. This is just a level-order traversal of the tree in reverse—bottom up, right to left instead of top down and left to right (see Figure 10.21).

Pseudocode: buildHeap(Collection c)
move the elements of c into a complete binary tree rooted at top
let cursor be the rightmost interior node
// invariant: the children of cursor are valid heaps
while there are heaps to fix
        fix the heap rooted at cursor
        move cursor to the next rightmost unvisited interior node

---

Figure 10.21 Building a heap from a collection of elements.

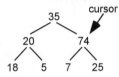

(a) Start with cursor at the rightmost interior node. Invariant: cursor's children are always valid heaps.

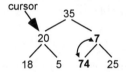

(b) When the heap is fixed by swapping the parent's value with the smaller of its children, move cursor to the next node.

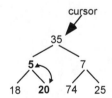

(c) When all the nodes on a level have been visited, move cursor up a level, starting at the right side, moving left. Note that cursor's children are the roots of valid minheaps.

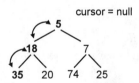

(d) Fixing the heap starting at the top required two swaps. After this, cursor is `null`, indicating there are no more heaps left to fix.

---

[5]We could move left to right on each level instead of right to left, but we will see shortly that moving left to right is easily implemented.

The cost of this algorithm is easy to establish – `fixHeap()` costs $O(\log_2 n)$ and is called about $n/2$ times, giving a cost of $O(n\log_2 n)$.

Application: `HeapSort`

One application of a heap is to sort a collection of elements. If we wanted to sort the elements of a collection in nondecreasing order using a heap, we would start by creating a minheap from an unsorted collection of elements, then keep peeling off the smallest element from the top of the heap, appending it to the end of a list, until the heap was empty. Listing 10.13 shows the pseudocode and corresponding generic Java method for creating a sorted list using the `heapSort()` method.

The call to the overloaded constructor, `ArrayMinHeap( Collection<? extends T>, Comparator<? super T> )` on line 5 will result in a call to `buildHeap()` at a cost of $O(n\log_2 n)$. The `while` loop (lines 8–10) executes until the heap is empty, so there will be n iterations of the loop. The body of the loop calls `top()` to remove the top element and append it to the list. The cost of `top()` is $O(\log_2 n)$ and the cost of appending to the end of the list is $O(1)$, so the cost of the `while` loop becomes $O(n\log_2 n)$. The runtime complexity of heapSort is therefore $O(n\log_2 n)$, putting it in the same complexity class as quick sort and merge sort. As `heapSort()` is written here, its space complexity is $O(n)$ due the extra space for the list that holds the sorted elements. The exercises discuss an in-place version for creating a sorted array.

Listing 10.13 A generic `heapSort()` method.

```
heapSort( Collection c )
  1    <T> List<T> heapSort( Collection<? extends T> collection,
  2                          Comparator<? super T> comparator ){
if the collection is empty or null
  3        if ( collection == null || comparator == null )
return null
  4            return null;
create a heap from a collection
  5        Heap<T> heap = new ArrayMinHeap<T>( collection, comparator );
create an empty list
  6        List<T> list = new ArrayList<T>();
while the heap is not empty
  7        while ( !heap.isEmpty() ) {
get the top element from the heap
  8            T e = heap.top();
append it to the list
  9            list.add( e );
 10        }
 11        return list;
 12    }
```

Implementing a Heap Using an Array

As discussed in Section 10.4.1, an array is a good data structure for storing the elements of a binary tree because it provides fast access to a node's parent and children. It also makes finding the rightmost interior node and the rightmost leaf easier:

■ The rightmost leaf is always in position *size* − 1 of the array

■ The rightmost interior node is always in position $\lfloor size/2 \rfloor - 1$ of the array, for *size* > 1.

Finally, doing a "reverse" level-order traversal, which is needed for `buildHeap()`, is as easy as walking backward through the array from $\lfloor size/2 \rfloor - 1$ down to 0.

SUMMING UP

A heap is a complete binary tree such that the element in a node is always less than or equal to (for a minheap) or greater than or equal to (for a maxheap) the elements in its children. All heap operations are bounded by the height of the tree, $O(\log_2 n)$.

CHECKPOINT

10.8 Show the construction of a minheap for the elements 12, 5, 7, 10, 3, and 4.

10.9 Using the heap constructed above, show the heap after a `top()` operation.

INVESTIGATE A Second Look at Priority Queues

Description

In the Chapter 7 *Investigate*, we took a first look at priority queues, operating under the belief that a priority queue was just a special kind of queue. While that *Investigate* should have taught you a few things about composition and inheritance, on the whole it may have been an unsatisfactory experience because priority queues and queues actually have little in common (except the misleading similarity in names). In this *Investigate* you take a much sounder approach, using some tools that were not available to you in Chapter 7.

As a reminder, a priority queue observes the protocol that the highest priority element in the queue is the first element out (HPIFO). Inserting an element into a priority queue is done with an enqueue operation. A deletion is done with a dequeue operation, which always removes the element with the highest priority. It is this use of a priority to determine which element is removed next that makes priority queues quite different from queues. The assignment of priority is not the priority queue's concern and is determined by the application setting up the priority queue. The evaluation that determines an item's priority can occur either when the element is inserted into the priority queue *or* when it is removed. One way to think

A priority queue is a highest-priority-in/ first-out data structure of the difference between queue and priority queue is that the queue operations enqueue() and dequeue() are *position*-oriented, while priority queue's enqueue() and dequeue() operations are *value*-oriented.

Priority queue's enqueue() and dequeue() operations are value-oriented

Objectives

- ▪ Learn more about priority queues.
- ▪ Work with the Adapter Design Pattern again.
- ▪ Use inheritance with interfaces and classes.
- ▪ Implement and use a Priority Queue class.
- ▪ Work with Comparators.

Design

The first step is to update the priority queue specification, which you will do as follows.

1. Rewrite the priority queue ADT from Chapter 7 so that instead of relying on a priority that is explicitly provided as a method argument, the priority queue uses a Comparator supplied when the priority queue is instantiated.

   a. Identify the operations in the ADT that are affected by this change.

   b. Remove unnecessary operations.

   c. Rewrite the description of affected operations you need to keep. Make sure that the ADT invariants are honored and look at how the changes you made affect other operations in the ADT.

   d. Do any operations need to be added?

2. Write the Java interface, PriorityQueue, based on your new ADT specification. Be sure to include javadocs.

3. Compare your ADT and interface with those of other students in your class. Do they look the same? If they don't, how do you account for the differences? There should be no differences in the semantics.

4. Create a test plan for PriorityQueue based on the ADT specification and the interface.

Implementation

As you were working on your modifications to the priority queue ADT you may have had the feeling that a priority queue behaves a lot like a heap. Indeed, while their interfaces are different, their behavior appears to be identical, suggesting that you could implement a priority queue with a heap using the Adapter Design Pattern.

1. Using the material from Section 7.6 as a model, produce two tables showing the mapping of attributes and methods from PriorityQueue to Heap.

2. Using Figure 7.8 as a model, draw the UML diagram showing how class HeapPriorityQueue can implement the PriorityQueue interface using Heap as the backing store.

3. Implement this design.

Testing

1. Using JUnit, implement the test plan created in the design phase.
2. Run the test plan and fix any bugs.

Application

Extend the `WorkOrder` class from Chapter 9 so that `WorkOrders` can be stored in a priority queue.

EXERCISES

Paper and Pencil

1. Show the maxheap that is constructed by adding the following elements in the order shown: 10, 5, 8, 2, 7, 21 9.
2. Is an array sorted in nondecreasing order always a minheap? Can the opposite be said—that the elements of a minheap are always sorted in nondecreasing order? Explain.
3. Is heap sort stable? Explain with an example. If it is not stable, can it be made stable?
4. One of the marginal comments states: "The visitor approach allows you to separate *how* the traversal is done from *what* is done." Is this not also true of the iterator approach?

Testing and Debugging

1. Kim created the following interface for `Heap`. Any comments?

```
public interface Heap<E> {
    public void add( Comparable<E> element );
    public void setComparator( Comparator<E> c );
    public E top();
    public E peek();
    public void clear();
    public int size();
    public boolean isEmpty();
}
```

2. Here is a JUnit method Anna used to test removing the root. It kept reporting failure, but Anna could see nothing wrong with `remove()`'s implementation. After a frustrating hour of trying to solve the problem, Anna was floored when Opal walked by and pointed immediately to the mistake. What did Opal see?

```
public void testRemoveRoot(){
    BinaryTreeNode<Integer> root = tree3.root();
    integer target = root.element();
    // remove target from tree3 and the list of elements
    // we expect to see in tree3
```

```
        expectedTree3List.remove( target );
        tree3.remove( root );
        assertTrue( !tree3.contains( target ) );
        ToListVisitor<Integer> treeVisitor = new ToListVisitor<Integer>();
        tree3.preOrderTraversal( treeVisitor );
        assertTrue( expectedTree3List.equals( treeVisitor.list() ) );
    }
```

Modifying the Code

1. Re-implement `LinkedBinaryTree` with the parent link removed from `LinkedBinaryTreeNode`. Make sure to test your implementation. Evaluate the two implementations from the perspective of coding complexity and debugging effort.

Note: Questions 2 and 3 refer to the Focus on Problem Solving on the Web.

2. Extend the Huffman compress application to include a Huffman decompress utility. The GUI should have compress and decompress buttons. The user first selects a file, then selects one of the buttons.

3. The team that reviewed the implementation of Huffman coding doesn't like that the bit codes are first built in strings within the interior nodes of the tree, then converted to binary format at the leaves. They believe that codes should have been constructed in binary form from top to bottom. Unfortunately, the guy who did the original implementation has left and you have been asked to make this change. Smile. Be happy.

4. Implement the Heap ADT using an array as the backing store.

5. Jenna claims that she can provide a single implementation of a heap and make it a minheap or a maxheap simply by creating a new heap object with a different `Comparator`. If you agree, demonstrate that this is possible. If you disagree, explain why providing a different `Comparator` isn't enough.

6. One way to make heap sort in-place is to use a maxheap with an array as the backing store and as the elements are removed from the heap, they are placed back in the array, beyond the range of indices being used by the heap. Implement this version of heap sort.

7. Write a method that sorts elements in decreasing order using a minheap.

8. Ben thinks that the four traversal operations in the Binary Tree ADT should be reduced to a single operation, traverse(), that takes an integer argument indication which traversal order to use and a Visitor object to apply to each node. Do you agree with Ben? Make this change to the ADT, then update the test cases and implementation. What is your opinion of this change after all the work has been done?

Using the ADTs

1. Construct the parse tree for the following arithmetic expressions. What traversal order is needed to evaluate your parse trees? Write an application that

builds the parse tree for arithmetic expressions containing the binary operators
+, −, * /, and %. The data can be integer or real literals.

   a. 8 * 3 + 4 / 2

   b. (15 − 4) / 3 * 2

   c. 32 % 7 * (2 + 9)

2. Write an application that evaluates parse trees according to the meaning assigned by Java to the arithmetic operators.

3. We have established that it isn't quite right to implement a priority queue as a queue, but can we go the other way? That is, can we implement the queue interface using a priority queue? If this can be done, show how; if not, explain why not.

4. Assume you were able to successfully implement a queue using a priority queue in the last problem. Your intuition tells you it should be a relatively simple matter to implement a `Stack` using a priority queue. Has your intuition failed you? If not, explain what the implementation would look like.

ON THE WEB

Additional study material is available at Addison-Wesley's Website at http://www.aw.com/cssupport. This material includes the following:

■ Focus on Problem Solving: Data Compression Using Huffman Trees

Problem: In talking to its clients about its sorting application for security log files (see the Focus on Problem Solving section for Chapter 9), ACME Security Company representatives have heard complaints about the size of the log files. Once the files are generated, they are used for a while, but are rarely accessed after that. However, they must be kept for several years, depending on the content of the file. Unfortunately, these files take up considerable space. ACME's marketing department sees this as an opportunity to add to the suite of software tools it sells.

Barking Dogs Software has been contracted to write a compression program so that inactive files can be saved in a more space-efficient manner, and we've been given the assignment.

The application must get the name of the text file to compress from the user. Once the file has been compressed, the application should

■ remind the user of the compressed file's name. The compressed file will have the same name as the input file, but with an .hfc extension.

■ tell the user how big the compressed file is and how much smaller it is than the original file.

Solution: There are a variety of techniques to do file compression. One technique that can be used on text files is Huffman coding, which takes advantage of variations in the frequency of occurrence of characters in a file.

The presentation of the solution begins with the ideas behind Huffman compression and the algorithm for uncompressing the result. This discussion naturally suggests the use of the Binary Tree and Heap ADTs and makes use of Comparators. The solution includes Analysis (discussion of the inputs and outputs to the application, and the layout of the application interface), Design (identification of classes with their responsibilities and collaborators, visualized through a UML class diagram), and Implementation of the classes.

- Study Guide Exercises
- Answers to CheckPoint Problems
- Additional exercises

Binary Search Trees 11

CHAPTER OUTLINE

When you look for something, usually you want to find it quickly. Our experience has been that searches are more efficient if the information is sorted. Compare, for example, linear searches on ordered and unordered sequences. Better still, consider a binary search on an ordered array. In this chapter we continue our examination of trees by looking at **search trees**. A search tree provides an ordering of its elements that facilitates searching. First, we'll look at simple Binary Search Trees (BSTs), then we will look at two BST variations, AVL and splay trees that offer better performance.

■ **11.1** The Binary Search Tree ADT

11.1.1 Binary Search Tree Description

A **binary search tree** is a binary tree whose elements are ordered such that

- For any node in the tree, all the elements in the node's left subtree are less than the node's element and all the elements in its right subtree are greater than the node's element. We will refer to this as the **binary search tree property**. This ordering implies that duplicates are not allowed.
- The left and right subtrees are binary search trees.

A consequence of this is that an inorder traversal of a BST will produce an ordered sequence of the tree's elements, as shown in Figure 11.1.

11.1.2 Binary Search Tree Specification

We need to be able to add, remove, and find elements in a BST, so one approach to designing the BST ADT is to extend the binary tree ADT from the last chapter. After all, a binary search tree is just an ordered binary tree, isn't it? Well, yes and no.

The essential difference between the two is that accesses to a binary tree are by position, whereas accesses to a BST are by value. This explains why the operations in the BinarySearchTree ADT differ from those in the binary tree ADT in the previous chapter. Also, since a BST provides an ordering of its elements, it is necessary that the elements be comparable to one another.

Binary trees are *position*-oriented

BSTs are *value*-oriented

BST elements must be comparable

■ **The BinarySearchTree ADT**

Description
This ADT describes a binary search tree (BST) whose element type is left unspecified. The ordering of the tree's elements is according to their "natural" ordering. Duplicates are not allowed.

Figure 11.1 An inorder traversal of a BST produces an ordered sequence of its elements.

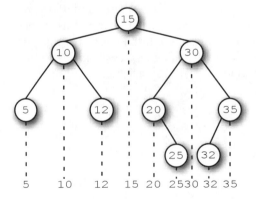

Properties

1. A BST is a hierarchical data structure. A node in a BST can have 0 to 2 children.
2. The root is the access point to a BST.
3. Elements are inserted such that all the elements in the node's left subtree are less than the node's element and all the elements in the node's right subtree are greater than the node's element. This is called the binary search tree property.
4. The elements of a BST must be comparable to one another.

Attributes

size:	The number of nodes in this BinarySearchTree.
root:	The root of this BinarySearchTree; a null value not part of the tree when the tree is empty.

Operations

BinarySearchTree ( )

pre-condition:	none
responsibilities:	constructor—create an empty BinarySearchTree
post-condition:	*size* is set to 0
	root is set to a null value
returns:	nothing

BinarySearchTree (*Type* element)

pre-condition:	element is not null
responsibilities:	constructor—create a BinaryTree with element stored in the root
post-condition:	*size* is set to 1
	root is set to the node created to store element
returns:	nothing
exception:	if element is null

add (*Type* element)

pre-condition:	element is not null, is not already in the tree and is comparable to the other elements in the tree
responsibilities:	add an element to the tree such that the BST properties are maintained
post-condition:	*size* is incremented by 1
	element is added to the tree
returns:	nothing
exception:	if element is null, is already in the tree or is not comparable to other elements in the tree

remove(*Type* element)

pre-condition:	element is not null and is comparable to the other elements in the tree
responsibilities:	remove element from the tree such that the BST properties are maintained. If the target is not in the tree, nothing happens and the tree is not changed
post-condition:	*size* is decremented by 1, if element was in the tree element is removed from the tree
returns:	nothing

contains(*Type* target)
     pre-condition: target is not null
     responsibilities: determine if target is stored in this tree
     post-condition: the tree is unchanged
     returns: true if target is found in this tree, false otherwise
     exception: if target is null

iterator ()
     pre-condition: none
     responsibilities: create and return an Iterator for this tree. The iterator performs
                                  an inorder traversal of this tree's elements
     post-condition: the tree is unchanged
     returns: an Iterator for this tree

size(), isEmpty() and clear() are not shown

11.1.3 The `BinarySearchTree` Interface

The Java Collection Framework (JCF) does not provide a BST interface or class, so we must provide our own. Listing 11.1 gives a Java interface corresponding to our BinarySearchTree ADT. The `add()` and `contains()` methods throw a custom `SearchTreeException` when their pre-conditions are not met. For this implementation we use `Comparable` to provide an ordering of the elements. As discussed in the last chapter, we want to accept a family of types with the constraint that either generic type `E` or one of its ancestors implements the `Comparable` interface. This is what the type parameter on line 10 says. The interface also extends `java.lang.Iterable`, which mandates an `iterator()` method. This is needed so that we can use Java's shortened `foreach` loop.

Listing 11.1 The `BinarySearchTree` interface.

```
1    package gray.adts.binarysearchtree;
2
3    /**
4     * A binary tree with the property that for each node in the tree,
5     * the value in the node's left child is less than the parent's
6     * value, the value in the node's right child is greater than the
7     * parent's value, and the left and right children are the roots
8     * of a binary search tree.
9     */
10   public interface BinarySearchTree<E extends Comparable<? super E>>
11                        extends java.lang.Iterable<E> {
12
13       /**
14        * Add an element to the tree such that the BST properties
15        * are maintained.
16        * @param element the element to add to the tree;
17        *    <tt>element</tt> should not be <tt>null</tt> and should
```

```
18          *      not already be in the tree
19          * @throws SearchTreeException if element is <tt>null</tt>
20          *    or is already in the tree
21          */
22         public void add( E element );
23
24         /**
25          * Remove element from the tree such that the BST properties
26          * are maintained. If the target is not in the tree, nothing
27          * happens. The tree is not changed.
28          * @param element the element to remove from the tree
29          */
30         public void remove( E element );
31
32         /**
33          * Determine if element is in the tree.
34          * @param target the element to look for; can't be <tt>null</tt>
35          * @return <tt>true</tt> if found, <tt>false</tt> otherwise
36          * @throws SearchTreeException if <tt>target</tt> is
37          *   <tt>null</tt>.
38          */
39         public boolean contains( E target );
40
41         /**
42          * Returns an iterator over the elements in this collection.
43          * The iterator provides this tree's element in an inorder
44          * sequence.
45          * @return an <tt>Iterator</tt> over the elements in this tree
46          */
47         public java.util.Iterator<E> iterator();
48
49         /**
50          * Determine if this tree is empty or not.
51          * @return true if there are no elements in this tree
52          */
53         public boolean isEmpty();
54
55         /**
56          * Return the number of nodes in this
57          *   <tt>BinarySearchTree</tt>.
58          * @return the number of nodes in this tree.
59          */
60         public int size();
61
62         /**
63          * Removes all the elements from this
64          * <tt>BinarySearchTree</tt>.
65          */
66         public void clear();
67    }
```

11.1.4 The Tree Iterator

In the last chapter we observed that traversing a tree could be done via a traversal method controlled by the tree or by an iterator controlled by the client. The binary tree class we developed in the last chapter took the traversal approach—the client supplied the tree with a visitor object that the traversal method would apply to each node of the tree.

In this chapter we will take the iterator approach—the tree provides the client with an iterator object. The client controls the iteration in exactly the same way we did for lists in Chapter 5. Our iterator will implement the `java.util.Iterator` interface and will perform an inorder traversal of the tree. Handling iterations for the other traversal orders is left as an exercise.

As a reminder, the `java.util.Iterator` interface is shown in Listing 11.2. The optional method `remove()` will not be implemented, so will throw `UnsupportedOperationException` if invoked.

As we saw in the last chapter, an inorder traversal is elegantly accomplished recursively.

Recursive algorithm for inorder traversal

Pseudocode: inorder(*node*)
if node is not null   // *base case*
    inorder(*node's left child*)   // *recursive case—left*
    visit this node   // *do something with this node*
    inorder(*node's right child*)   // *recursive case—right*

Unfortunately, our iterator cannot use this recursive approach because it does not provide a way for the client to control the progress of the iteration.[1] However, if we simulate the recursion by maintaining our own stack of tree nodes still to be visited, we get the elegance of the recursive approach while allowing the client to control the pace of the iteration.[2]

Let's be clear about why a stack is appropriate here. The tricky part is to keep track of which nodes have been returned to the client and which are still to be seen. A moment's reflection and a quick look at the stack under the recursive approach reveal why a stack is ideal for this problem.

Simulating recursive inorder traversal with a stack

Applying the recursive algorithm above to the tree in Figure 11.2 (a) would produce the stack shown in Figure 11.2 (b) at the point where the base case is first met—when we visit 5's null left child.

At this point, we have gone as far left from the root as we can. This is equivalent to *recursive case—left* in the pseudocoded recursive algorithm when starting at the root of the tree. Now we pop the top node from the stack and visit it (*do something with this node* in the recursive algorithm).

When a node is popped from the stack, we know that we have visited all its left-child descendants, but we still have the node's right subtree to examine. In a fashion that replicates the recursive algorithm's behavior, the node's right child (if it exists) is pushed onto the stack, followed by all its left-child descendants (*recursive*

---

[1]The recursive approach was appropriate in the last chapter because we had the tree object controlling the iteration, applying a Visitor object supplied by the client to each node of the tree.

[2]This is an application of the material presented in the Chapter 8 *Investigate*.

Listing 11.2 The `java.util.Iterator` interface.

```
public interface Iterator<E> {
    /**
     * Returns <tt>true</tt> if the iteration has more elements.
     * (In other words, returns <tt>true</tt> if <tt>next</tt>
     * would return an element rather than throwing an exception.)
     * @return <tt>true</tt> if the iterator has more elements.
     */
    boolean hasNext();

    /**
     * Returns the next element in the iteration.
     * @return the next element in the iteration.
     * @throws NoSuchElementException iteration has no more
     * elements.
     */
    E next();

    /**
     * Removes from the underlying collection the last element
     * returned by the iterator (optional operation).  This method
     * can be called only once per call to <tt>next</tt>.  The
     * behavior of an iterator is unspecified if the underlying
     * collection is modified while the iteration is in progress
     * in any way other than by calling this method.
     *
     * @throws UnsupportedOperationException if the
     *             <tt>remove</tt> operation is not supported by
     *             this Iterator.
     * @throws IllegalStateException if the <tt>next</tt> method
     *             has not yet been called, or the <tt>remove</tt>
     *             method has already been called after the last
     *             call to the <tt>next</tt> method.
     */
    void remove();
}
```

case–right in the recursive algorithm. This suggests the following pseudocode for
our tree iterator.

> **Pseudocode: TreeIterator**()
> *create the stack*
> *node = this tree's root*
> *while node is not null*   *// check for base case*
>   *push node onto the stack*   *// recursive case—left*
>   *node = node's left child*

Figure 11.2 The stack when 5's left child has been found during an inorder traversal.

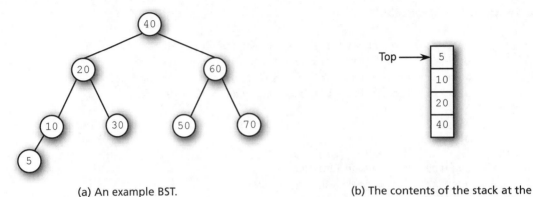

(a) An example BST.

(b) The contents of the stack at the point where 5 has been pushed.

Pseudocode: hasNext()
true if the stack is not empty false otherwise

Pseudocode: next()
if the stack is empty
    throw an exception
node = popped stack item
value is node's element
node = node's right child   // recursive case—right
while node is not null   // check for base case
    push node onto the stack
    node = node's left child
// loop post-condition: base case met—found a null left child
return value

SUMMING UP

A binary search tree is a binary tree whose elements are ordered. For any node X in the tree, all the elements in X's left subtree are less than X's element, and all the elements in X's right subtree are greater than X's element. It is in this sense that BSTs are value-oriented—where an element is inserted and found depends on its value and the values already in the BST.

As it did for linear collections, ordering the elements in a hierarchical collection makes searches faster.

CHECKPOINT

11.1 Show the BST that would be created from the following elements, added in the order given.

    a. 20 25 17 22 1 5

    b. 17 22 3 1 25 5 20

11.2 Show the contents of the stack during an iteration of the trees created above after 5 has been visited.

11.1.5 Designing a Test Plan for `BinarySearchTree`

The general idea behind the test plan follows the approach taken many times now. Two test cases will be presented.

The approach for `add()` is straightforward—when an element is added to the tree, we should be able to verify that the tree really does contain the new value and that an inorder traversal produces an ordered sequence of all the tree's elements. It would make sense to add elements such that both subtrees of the root are touched. Of course, we should check that adding duplicate and null elements produces the expected exception. Some of this is shown in Test Case 11.1. Borrowing an idea from the last chapter, we can dump the contents of a BST to a `List` using the tree iterator (that is what the utility method `toList( tree )` in Test Case 11.1 does) and compare this list of elements against an expected list of ordered elements. Note that `expectedList` is sorted before we attempt to compare it to `actualList` produced by utility method `toList()`. This is necessary because the contract for `List.equals()` specifies that the two lists must have the same number of elements and must match in an element-by-element comparison. So the order of the elements in each list matters.

A similar approach is clearly appropriate for the `remove()` operation. Obvious cases to check are removing a leaf, removing an internal node, and removing the root. We should also check that trying to remove an element that is not in the tree does not generate an exception and does not affect the tree (see Test Case 11.2).

The `contains()` and `size()` operations can be used to confirm the `add()` and `remove()` operations.

■ **11.2** Linked Implementation of `BinarySearchTree`

Looking ahead, we want to produce an implementation that we can extend to support AVL and splay trees. Figure 11.3 shows the interfaces and classes we will construct, and their relationships.[3]

---

[3]Splay Tree is presented in this chapter, but not implemented. You get to decide where it fits in this hierarchy and how to implement it.

Test Case 11.1 Testing the `BST add()` method.

Method	Purpose	Object State	Expected Result
BinarySearchTree<Integer> tree = new LinkedBST<Integer>()	To create an empty binary search tree using default constructor.	*size* = 0 *root* = **null**	LinkedBST object to store Integers
tree.size()	To verify tree is empty.		0
tree.add(10) // *expectedList is a List object* expectedList.add(10)	To add to an empty tree.	*size* = 1 *root* = **Integer(10)** *root*.**leftChild** = **null** *root*.**rightChild** = **null**	
tree.size()	To verify size() and add() to an empty tree.		1
tree.contains(10)	To verify contains() and add() to an empty tree.		true
tree.add(5) expectedList.add(5)	To add to left subtree.	*size* = 2 *root* = Integer(10) *root*.**leftChild** = **Integer (5)** *root*.rightChild = null	
tree.size()	To verify an element was added.		2
tree.contains(5)	To verify contains() and add() to left subtree.		true
tree.add(15) expectedList.add(15)	To add to right subtree.	*size* = 3 *root* = Integer(10) *root*.leftChild = Integer(5) *root*.**rightChild** = **Integer(15)**	
tree.size()	To verify an element was added.		3
tree.contains(15)	To verify contains() and add() to right subtree.		true
List<Integer> actualList = toList(tree) Collections.sort(expectedList) actualList.equals(expectedList)	To verify elements of the tree are in the correct order. Compare expected and actual lists.		true
tree.add(null)	To check pre-condition for null elements.		SearchTreeException
actualList = toList(tree) actualList.equals(expectedList)	To verify the tree is unchanged.		true
tree.add(10)	To check pre-condition for duplicate elements.		SearchTreeException
actualList = toList(tree) actualList.equals(expectedList)	To verify the tree is unchanged.		true

Test Case 11.2 One test of the BST `remove()`method to remove the root (assumes the tree created in Test Case 11.1).

Method	Purpose	Object State	Expected Result
tree.remove(5) expected.remove(5)	To test removing the root of the tree.	size = **2** **root** = **Integer(10)** **root**.**leftChild** = **null** *root*.rightChild = Integer(15)	
tree.size()	To verify tree size updated.		1
tree.contains(5)	To verify element was removed.		false
List actualList = toList(tree) actualList.equals(expectedList)	To verify remaining elements of the tree are in the correct order.		true

Figure 11.3 Binary search tree classes and their relationships (UML class diagram).

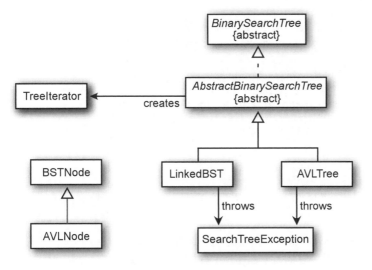

Our implementation of `BinarySearchTree` relies on the class that defines the nodes of a tree, so we'll start with a description of `BSTNode`. Then we'll skip ahead to `LinkedBST`, the concrete implementation of `BinarySearchTree`. Finally we look at what is in `AbstractBinarySearchTree`. The reason for this ordering of presentation will become clear at that time.

11.2.1 Class BSTNode

A bare bones BSTNode class is shown in Listing 11.3. Some explanation is in order. First, as indicated with BinarySearchTree, the elements stored in the tree must be comparable to one another, consequently BSTNode has the same type parameter as BinarySearchTree (line 7 in Listing 11.3).

Listing 11.3 The BSTNode class.

```
1    package gray.adts.binarysearchtree;
2    /**
3     * A binary search tree is composed <tt>BSTNode</tt>'s.
4     * The element stored in must be comparable with other
5     * elements in the BST.
6     */
7    public class BSTNode<E extends Comparable<? super E>> {
8        protected BSTNode<E> parent;
9        protected BSTNode<E> leftChild;
10       protected BSTNode<E> rightChild;
11       protected E element;
12
13       /**
14        * Constructor. Create an instance of BSTNode storing data.
15        * Parent and child links are null.
16        * @param data the data to store in this node.
17        * @throws IllegalArgumentException if data is null.
18        */
19       public BSTNode( E data ){
20           if ( data == null )
21               throw new java.lang.IllegalArgumentException();
22
23           this.element = data;
24           this.parent = null;
25           this.leftChild = null;
26           this.rightChild = null;
27       }
28
29       /**
30        * Constructor. Create an instance of BSTNode storing
31        * data. Parent and child links are set to the given
32        * parameters.
33        * @param data the data to store in this node
34        * @param p the parent of this node
35        * @param lChild the left child of this node
36        * @param rChild the right child of this node
37        * @throws IllegalArgumentException if data is <tt>null</tt>
38        */
39       public BSTNode( E data, BSTNode<E> p,
40                           BSTNode<E> lChild, BSTNode<E> rChild ) {
```

```
41                  if ( data == null )
42                     throw new java.lang.IllegalArgumentException();
43
44                  this.element = data;
45                  this.parent = p;
46                  this.leftChild = lChild;
47                  this.rightChild = rChild;
48          }
49      }
```

Second, the situation with a BST is different from that of binary tree in the last chapter. The client's view of a binary tree was that it consisted of a collection of nodes that stored elements and occupied positions in a binary tree. So in the last chapter, clients of binary tree had access to the node objects, and through the nodes a client had access to the elements.

Since a BST is accessed by value, clients will never see the nodes that store the elements. Consequently, we can take an approach to their implementation different from that in the last chapter. As far as a client of a BST is concerned, a BST stores values, so instead of providing `private` data fields with corresponding accessor and mutators, the data fields in `BSTNode` are `protected`, and so are directly accessible in other classes in the same package and by any class that extends `BSTNode`.

In taking this approach, we gain some efficiency by avoiding the overhead of accessor/mutator method calls. But we do this at the expense of losing the protection provided by `private` data members that are accessible only through accessor and mutators. We now have the additional burden of making sure that the accessing code behaves properly!

Using protected is a tradeoff of protection for efficiency

11.2.2 Class `LinkedBST`

First, as the UML diagram in Figure 11.3 makes clear, `LinkedBST` extends `AbstractBinarySearchTree` which implements `BinarySearchTree`. Class `LinkedBST` has a single data field:

```
public class LinkedBST<E extends Comparable<? super E> >
                             extends AbstractBinarySearchTree<E> {
    private BSTNode<E> root;
```

Now for the BST operations. It is in the nature of a binary search tree that many of its operations can be succinctly and elegantly described recursively. Therefore, we'll also implement them recursively, starting with the simplest and most intuitive.

11.2.3 Method `contains()`: Finding an Element in a `LinkedBST`

The recursive `contains()` method ideally behaves much like the recursive binary search method discussed in Chapter 8 (we'll revisit this idea when we look at AVL trees). We start the search at the root. If the value there is not equal to our target, we start over again with the root's left subtree if the target is less than root's element, or with the root's right subtree if the target is greater than root's element. This suggests the following recursive definition.

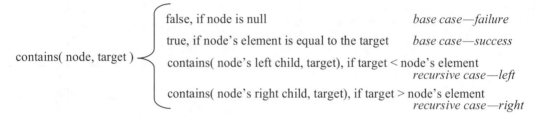

where:
    node   the root of the subtree to search (initially the root of the tree)
    target the element for which we are searching

The `public` method calls a `protected` utility method to carry out the search. Once again, notice how easily the code follows from the recursive definition.

As shown in Figure 11.4, the search progresses down the tree. When one of the base cases is met, either false (failure—line 15 in Listing 11.4) or true (success—line 23) is returned to the caller. In a sense, as the recursion unwinds, this result is passed back up the tree such that the current invocation is returning a value that is an indication of whether the current node *or any of its descendants* contained the target. For example, on the left side of Figure 11.4, when the target is found, true is returned to the invocation for its parent (30), which is returned to its parent (20) and so on up to the root of the tree, where the search began.

Similarly for failure, when a null link is reached, this failure is reported to its parent, which returns this result to its parent and so on up to the root, as shown on the right side of Figure 11.4.

Recursive contains()—the result is passed back up the tree as the recursion unwinds

---

Figure 11.4 Call and return paths for successful and unsuccessful `contains()` calls.

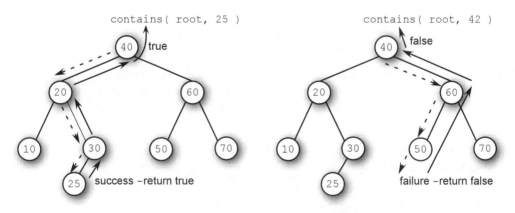

Listing 11.4 Methods from `AbstractBinarySearchTree` to determine if a tree contains an element

```
1   /**
2    * Determine if <tt>target</tt> is in the tree.
3    * @param target the element to look for; can't be <tt>null</tt>
4    * @return <tt>true</tt> if found, <tt>false</tt> otherwise
5    * @throws SearchTreeException if <tt>target</tt> is <tt>null</tt>
6    */
7   public boolean contains( E target) {
8       if ( target == null )
9           throw new SearchTreeException();
10      return contains( this.root(), target );
11  }
12
13  protected boolean contains( BSTNode<E> node, E target ){
14      if ( node == null )                 // base case — failure
15          return false;
16
17      int compareResult = target.compareTo( node.element );
18      if ( compareResult < 0 )            // recursive case — left
19          return contains( node.leftChild, target );      ◄──────
20      else if ( compareResult > 0 )  // recursive case — right    Note direct access to
21          return contains( node.rightChild, target );     ◄────── node's data fields.
22      else
23          return true;                    // base case — success
24      }
25  }
```

11.2.4 Method `add()`: Inserting a Node into a `LinkedBST`

When an insertion is done, the new node will either be the root of the tree if the tree had been empty, or it will become the left or right child of some node already in the tree. That is, insertions will always be done at a leaf. To see why, let's look at an example.

Insertions will always be done at a leaf

In Figure 11.5 (a), we want to insert the value 17. Starting at the root of the tree, we see that 17 is less than the value at the root, so 17 will have to go in the root's left subtree to maintain the BST property. Similarly at the node storing 15, we go to the right subtree. Then at the node storing 20, we go to the left subtree, which is `null`. Obviously we cannot go any further down the tree, so 20's left child is the insertion point, producing the tree in Figure 11.5 (b).

Putting these ideas together, we add an element by adding it to the root. If the tree is empty, the new element becomes the root of the tree. If the root is not `null`, depending on the element's value, we recursively add the element to the root's left or right subtree. This suggests the following recursive definition of a method for adding an element to a BST.

$$\text{add (node, element)} = \begin{cases} \text{BSTNode(element, this, this), if node is null} & \textit{// base case—success—do insertion} \\ \text{exception, if element == node.element} & \textit{// base case—failure—no duplicates} \\ \text{node.leftChild = add(node.leftChild, element) if element < node.element} \\ \qquad\qquad\qquad\qquad\qquad\qquad\qquad\qquad\qquad\qquad \textit{// recursive case—left} \\ \text{node.rightChild = add(node.rightChild, element) if element > node.element} \\ \qquad\qquad\qquad\qquad\qquad\qquad\qquad\qquad\qquad\qquad\qquad \textit{// recursive case—right} \end{cases}$$

where:

node	the root of the subtree to add (initially it is the root of the tree)
element	the element to be added to the tree

The Java implementation follows closely from the recursive definition. In Listing 11.5 note the code to throw an exception if a duplicate is found (lines 30–31), as required by the specification.

The argument list includes parent, which is a reference to node's parent in the tree. These two references walk down the tree so that when the insertion point is found node is null and parent is a reference to the node that will be the new node's parent. The child-to-parent link is made on line 21. The reciprocal parent-to-child link will be made in the caller on line 26 or line 28.

In fact, this parent-to-child link will be *re*-established for each node as the recursion unwinds. Consider again adding 17 to Figure 11.5 (a). The left side of Figure 11.6 shows a stylized version of the sequence of recursive calls that are made. Note that in *each* case the value returned by a call to add() is assigned as the "new" left or right child of the current node. However, only the insertion of the new node will create a new child link. The right side of Figure 11.6 shows the node references that are returned as the recursion unwinds.

Figure 11.5 Before and after views of a binary search tree to which 17 is added.

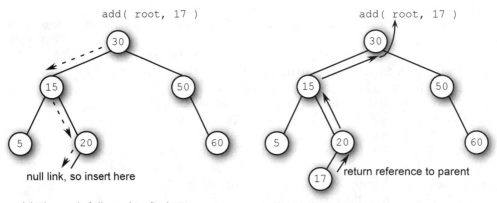

(a) The path followed to find 17's insertion point.

(b) The new node is always inserted at a leaf position.

Listing 11.5 Methods to add an element to a binary search tree. The public `add()` is in `AbstractBinarySearchTree` and the utility `add()` is in `LinkedBST`.

```
1    /**
2     * Add an element to the tree such that the BST properties
3     * are maintained.
4     * @param element the element to add to the tree;
5     *    <tt>element</tt> should not be <tt>null</tt> and should
6     *    not already be in the tree
7     * @throws SearchTreeException if element is <tt>null</tt>
8     *    or is already in the tree
9     */
10   public void add( E element ) {
11       if ( element == null )
12           throw new SearchTreeException();
13       setRoot( add( null, this.root(), element ) );
14       size++;
15   }
16
17   protected BSTNode<E> add( BSTNode<E> parent, BSTNode<E> node,    ⎤ parent is the parent
18                            E element ){                            ⎦ of node
19       if ( node == null )  {              // base case            ⎤ create a link from
20           node = new BSTNode<E>( element );                       │ the new node to its
21           node.parent = parent;                                   │ parent
22       }                                                           ⎦
23       else {  // recursive cases
24           int compareResult = element.compareTo( node.element );
25           if ( compareResult < 0 )         // recursive case – left
26               node.leftChild = add( node, node.leftChild, element );
27           else if ( compareResult > 0 )    // recursive case – right
28               node.rightChild = add( node, node.rightChild, element );
29           else
30               throw new SearchTreeException( "Duplicate element: " +
31                                              element.toString() );
32       }                                                           ⎤ create a link from
33       return node;                                                │ the parent to the
34   }                                                               ⎦ left/right child
```

Working from the bottom to the top, the new node for 17 is created and returned to its caller, which makes the new node the *new* left child of 20's node (look again at Figure 11.5 (b)). At this point in the recursive calls, the current node is 20, which gets returned to its caller and becomes the right child of 15's node. Similarly, 15's node is returned to become the left child of 30's node. Finally, 30's node is returned to the originating invocation to become the root of the tree (see line 13 of Listing 11.5). You will see this behavior in some of the other recursive BST algorithms we will present.

Figure 11.6 Establishing the parent-child link as the recursion unwinds.

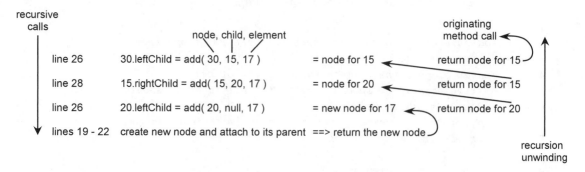

11.2.5 Method `remove()`: Removing a Node from a Binary Search Tree

Removing an element from a binary search tree is slightly more complicated than either searching or adding because after the element's node is deleted, the tree must remain connected and still honor the binary search tree property. In the simplest case the target is a leaf, and there is no extra work to be done. If the target is an internal node, some rearranging of the tree would appear to be required, but we'll use an old trick to make the problem easier to handle.

> Removing a leaf is easy; removing an internal node requires some work

There are three cases to consider, the first two of which are easily handled; the third requires a little insight into the nature of binary search trees.

Case 1. The node to remove is a leaf.

As illustrated in Figure 11.7, removing a leaf node just requires updating its parent's child link to be `null`.

Case 2. The node to remove is an internal node with one child.

When the target has only a single child, that child simply takes its parent's place in the tree. This only requires updating the target's parent's child link to reference the new child, as shown in Figure 11.8. It doesn't matter whether the child is the left or right child of the target.

Figure 11.7 Removing a leaf node from a binary search tree.

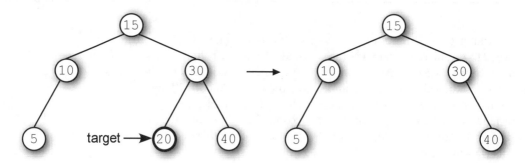

Figure 11.8 Removing a node with one child from a binary search tree—move the single child into the parent's position.

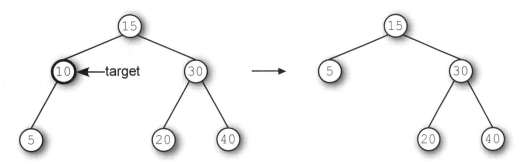

Case 3. The node to remove is an internal node with two children.

Before looking at the solution to Case 3, let's first consider the defining characteristic of a binary search tree: The elements are ordered. That is, an inorder traversal of a BST produces an ordered sequence of its elements, as was shown in Figure 11.1.

Remember, each element of an ordered sequence except the first has a unique predecessor, and each element except the last has a unique successor. The rules for finding an element's predecessor and successor in an ordered tree are simple:

Predecessors and successors in a BST

predecessor   The predecessor of an internal node is the *right*most node in its *left* subtree. In Figure 11.1, 15's predecessor is 12, and 30's predecessor is 25.

successor   The successor of an internal node is the *left*most node in its *right* subtree. In Figure 11.1, 15's successor is 20, and 30's successor is 32.

Another important observation is that an element's predecessor or successor in the tree will always have at most one child. This must be the case because if the node has two children, we have not yet found the rightmost/leftmost node in the target's left/right subtree.

Consequently, the solution for Case 3 is to replace the targeted element with either its successor or predecessor (it doesn't matter which). In Figure 11.9, element 15 is removed and is replaced by its successor, 20.

Note that, as we did in the previous chapter, it will be much simpler to just move the value 20 into 15's node rather than deleting the 15 node and moving the 20 node into its place. Once this replacement has been done, the replaced node (20 in our example) must be removed. But also note that since the replacement element will never have more than one child, removing it becomes a matter of Case 1 or Case 2, as described above. Easy!

Here is the simplifying trick

The resulting recursive definition and method follow.

$$
\text{remove (node, element) =}
\begin{cases}
\text{node.element = successor(node).element , if node.element == target} \\
\text{remove(successor(node))} \qquad\qquad \textit{// base case—success} \\[1em]
\text{null , if node == null} \qquad\qquad\qquad \textit{// base case—failure,} \\
\qquad\qquad\qquad\qquad\qquad\qquad\qquad\qquad\qquad \textit{element not found} \\[1em]
\text{node.leftChild = remove(node.leftChild, element) if element < node.element} \\
\qquad\qquad\qquad\qquad\qquad\qquad\qquad\qquad \textit{// recursive case} \\[1em]
\text{node.rightChild = remove (node.rightChild, element) if element > node.element} \\
\qquad\qquad\qquad\qquad\qquad\qquad\qquad\qquad \textit{// recursive case}
\end{cases}
$$

where:
node	the root of the subtree to remove from (initially the root of the tree)
element	the element to be removed from the tree
successor	provides the node of the successor element

Figure 11.9 Removing a node with two children from a binary search tree—replace it with its successor.

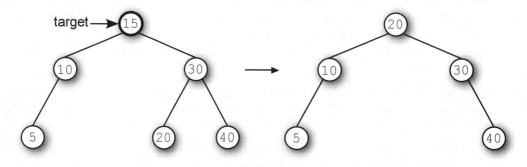

As we saw with `add()`, each recursive call returns a node reference (line 43 of Listing 11.6) which becomes the left child (line 19) or right child (line 21) of some parent node as the recursion unwinds and the last node returned becomes the root of the tree (line 10). You should trace the removal of a node for each of the three cases to be sure you understand how the recursion keeps the tree's nodes linked properly and maintains the BST properties.

11.2.6 Method `iterator()`: Providing the Client with an Iterator

The `iterator()` method just creates and returns an instance of the `TreeIterator` class. Coding of `TreeIterator`, which implements `java.util.Iterator`, is straightforward based on the pseudocode presented earlier and is left as an exercise. The iterator should be fail fast. That is, if the tree is structurally modified while an iteration is in progress, the iterator should throw an exception when one of its methods is next called. Revisit the implementation of `ListIterator` in Chapter 5 for an example.

Listing 11.6 The `LinkedBST.remove()` methods from `AbstractBinaryTree`.

```
1    /**
2     * Remove element from the tree such that the BST properties
3     * are maintained. If the target is not in the tree, nothing
4     * happens and the tree is not changed.
5     * @param element the element to remove from the tree
6     */
7    public void remove( E element ) {
8        if ( element == null )  // ignore null elements
9            return;
10       setRoot( remove( this.root(), element ) );
11   }
12
13   protected BSTNode<E> remove( BSTNode<E> node, E target ){
14       if ( node == null )   // element isn't in the tree :
15           return null;      // base case — failure
16
17       int compareResult = target.compareTo( node.element );
18       if ( compareResult < 0 )        // recursive case — left
19           node.leftChild = remove( node.leftChild, target );
20       else if ( compareResult > 0 )   // recursive case — right
21           node.rightChild = remove( node.rightChild, target );
22       else {    // found it!             // base case — success
23           this.size--;
24
25           // handle the case of two children first
26           if ( ( node.leftChild != null ) &&
27                ( node.rightChild != null ) ) {
28               BSTNode<E> replacement = successor( node );
29               node.element = replacement.element;
30
31               // now deal with removing the replacement
32               BSTNode<E> newChild = replacement.leftChild == null ?
33                       replacement.rightChild : replacement.leftChild;
34               if ( replacement == replacement.parent.leftChild )
35                   replacement.parent.leftChild = newChild;
36               else
37                   replacement.parent.rightChild = newChild;
38           }
39           else // Collapse the cases of no children and 1 child
40               node = ( node.leftChild == null ) ?
41                       node.rightChild : node.leftChild;
42       }
43       return node;
44   }
```

11.2.7 AbstractBinarySearchTree—an Abstract Class Implementation of BinarySearchTree

We can now present AbtractBinarySearchTree, which is shown in Listing 11.7. You will have noticed before that the recursive methods all take two arguments: a node and a target element. This is necessary because what happens in the recursive case always depends on the combination of the value at the current position (node) in the tree and the target element (that is, in the recursive case we will either go left of the current node or go right).

However, the BinarySearchTree interface specifies that the public add(), remove(), and contains() methods only supply a target as an argument.

As shown in the implementation of AbtractBinarySearchTree, this is easily handled by having the public method call an internal utility method using the tree's root as the starting point.

There is one other thing to point out about AbtractBinarySearchTree. The abstract class needs to be able to access and set the tree's root, but it cannot commit to the root's type, which will be determined by the subclass. The solution, as we saw when we looked at AbstractCollection in Chapter 4 and AbstractList in Chapter 5, is to use abstract methods that the subclasses will implement once the details are known.[4]

Listing 11.7 The AbstractBinarySearchTree abstract class.

```
1    package gray.adts.binarysearchtree;
2
3    public abstract class
4            AbstractBinarySearchTree<E extends Comparable<? super E>>
5            implements BinarySearchTree<E> {
6
7        protected int size;
8
9        public void add( E element ) {
10           if ( element == null )
11               throw new SearchTreeException();
12           setRoot( add( null, this.root(), element ) );
13           size++;
14       }
15
16       public void remove( E element ) {
17           if ( element == null )  // ignore null elements
18               return;
19           setRoot( remove( this.root(), element ) );
20       }
21
```

---

[4]Abstract classes are really handy, so you should become comfortable using and designing with them. We'll see a really neat use of AbstractCollection in the next chapter.

```
22          public boolean contains( E target ) {
23              if ( target == null )
24                  throw new SearchTreeException();
25              return contains( this.root(), target );
26          }
27
28          public java.util.Iterator<E> iterator(){
29              return new TreeIterator<E>();
30          }
31
32          /**
33           * Perform an inorder traversal of this tree applying
34           *   the Visitor to each node.
35           * @param visitor the visitor to apply to each node of
36           * this tree
37           */
38          public void inOrderTraversal( Visitor<E> visitor ){
39              doInOrderTraversal( this.root(), visitor );
40          }
41
42          public boolean isEmpty(){
43              return this.size() == 0;
44          }
45
46          public int size() {
47              return this.size;
48          }
49
50          public void clear() {
51              setRoot( null );
52              this.size = 0;
53          }
54
55          // UTILITY METHODS
56          protected abstract void setRoot( BSTNode<E> newRoot );
57
58          protected abstract BSTNode<E> root();
59
60          /**
61           * Internal method to do the add. Called by public add().
62           * @throws SearchTreeException if node is found in the tree
63           */
64          protected abstract BSTNode<E> add( BSTNode<E> parent,
65                                             BSTNode<E> node,
66                                             E element );
67
68          /**
```

```
 69          * Internal method to do the remove. Called by public remove().
 70          * @throws SearchTreeException if node is found in the tree
 71          */
 72         protected abstract BSTNode<E> remove( BSTNode<E> node,
 73                                                   E element );
 74
 75         /**
 76          * The recursive method for doing an inorder traversal of
 77          * the tree rooted at node, applying visitor to each node
 78          * of the tree.
 79          * @param node the node to visit; not null (no check done)
 80          * @param visitor the code to apply to the node; is not null
 81          *   (no check done)
 82          */
 83         protected void doInOrderTraversal( BSTNode<E> node,
 84                                                   Visitor<E> visitor ){
 85             if ( node != null ){
 86                 doInOrderTraversal( node.leftChild, visitor );
 87                 visitor.visit( node );
 88                 doInOrderTraversal( node.rightChild, visitor );
 89             }
 90         }
 91
 92         protected boolean contains( BSTNode<E> node,
 93                                         E target ){
 94             // Code shown in Listing 11.4
 95         }
 96
 97
 98         protected BSTNode<E> successor( BSTNode<E> node ){
 99             node = node.rightChild;
100             while ( node.leftChild != null )
101                 node = node.leftChild;
102             return node;
103         }
104
105         class TreeIterator<E extends Comparable<? super E> >
106                     implements java.util.Iterator<E> {
107             // Implementation left as an excercise :-)
108     }
```

SUMMING UP

Making the data fields of BSTNode class protected is a tradeoff. It allows the fields
to be efficiently accessed directly by its subclasses and other classes in the same
package, but it lacks the safeguards provided by accessors and mutators, thus requir-

ing more disciplined programming. Of course, careful programming combined with responsible testing will improve the soundness of your code.

A binary search tree can be elegantly described recursively, as can most of its methods. Usually a recursive implementation follows naturally from the recursive definition, producing short and simple methods. All operations must maintain the tree as a BST.

CHECKPOINT

11.3 Following the example in Figure 11.5, trace the execution to add 15 to the tree below.

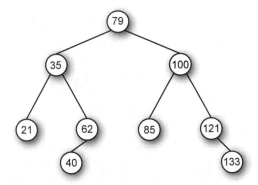

11.4 Following the examples in Figures 11.7, 11.8, and 11.9, trace the execution of the following remove operations.

a. remove(85)

b. remove(35)

c. remove(10) // *10 is not in the tree; the tree structure should not change*

■ **11.3** The Need for a Balanced Search Tree

At the beginning of this chapter we explained the need for BSTs by pointing out that searches on ordered collections are faster than searches on unordered collections.

The problem with a plain BST is that while it will always be ordered, it could become very unbalanced (lopsided). Indeed, as shown in Figure 11.10 (a), in the worst case a BST can become a linear ordered collection with an $O(n)$ access time. Much preferable is a perfectly balanced tree in which all leaves are on the same or on two adjacent levels, such as the BST in Figure 11.10 (b). Why? Because the worst case for a search becomes O(tree height), which is $O(\log_2 n)$ for a perfectly balanced tree of n elements (Property 10.2).

> A badly balanced BST has access time equivalent to a linear collection: $O(n)$

> A balanced BST has $O(\log_2 n)$ access time

We saw this nice $O(\log_2 n)$ behavior when we looked at the binary search as an example of a recursive algorithm. Recall that a binary search compares the target against the midpoint of the ordered linear collection. If the value at the midpoint is

---

Figure 11.10 A badly unbalanced binary search tree and its equivalent balanced binary search tree.

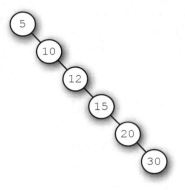

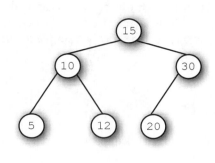

(a) An unbalanced BST has O(*n*) access time.   (b) A balanced BST has O(log₂*n*) access time.

not the target, we only have to look in the lower or upper half of the collection, thus halving the search space with each comparison.

You may also recall that implementing a binary search was effective for a direct access data structure such as an array, but not for a linear sequential access data structure such as a linear linked list, due to the cost of finding the midpoints of the sublists still to be searched. The point here is that a BST implemented as a hierarchical linked structure neatly solves this problem, because in a balanced BST each child link references the midpoint of its side of the remaining data items. Thus each comparison against the element in the root of a subtree will halve the remaining search space.

Search a balanced BST behaves like binary search

For example, in Figure 11.10 (b), element 15 partitions the tree into two almost equal parts, while its left child, 10, equally partitions all of the elements in the tree that are less than 15.

SUMMING UP

Binary search trees maintain an ordering of their elements, but provide no guarantee on the tree's height. In the pathological case, a binary search tree can degenerate into a linear linked list with O(*n*) access time.

A perfectly balanced BST in which all leaves are on at most two adjacent levels provides O(log₂*n*) access time per operation because the tree's height is guaranteed to be $\lceil \log_2 n \rceil$.

■ 11.4 AVL Tree: A Balanced Binary Search Tree

A perfectly balanced tree is the ideal. For example, a complete binary tree with *n* nodes has a height of $\lceil \log_2 n \rceil$ (Property 10.2). Unfortunately, an add() or remove()

done on a complete binary tree will change the tree's structure and a great deal of work may have to be done to restore it as a complete binary tree. When the costs outweigh the benefits, we must consider alternatives.

If we cannot easily create a perfectly balanced tree, perhaps we can settle for a close approximation of it. One alternative is the AVL tree, so named in honor of its inventors, Adel'son-Vel'skii and Landis.[5]

An AVL tree is a BST with the following additional constraints:

- The height of a node's left and right subtrees differ by no more than 1.
- The left and right subtrees are AVL trees.

It turns out that this approach is cost effective and guarantees that the height of the tree is a small multiple of $\log_2 n$, so it still provides $O(\log_2 n)$ access time, and, as we will see, the cost of keeping a BST AVL-balanced is affordable. Figure 11.11 shows an AVL tree labeled with balance (b) and height (h) information. You should note the following:

Computing heights and balances in an AVL tree

- Calculating heights and balances is done from the leaves up.
- An empty subtree has a height of 0.
- A leaf always has a balance of 0 and a height of 1.
- An internal node's height is the height of its taller subtrees plus 1: node.height = (height of taller of two subtrees) + 1.
- An internal node's balance is the height of its left subtree minus the height of its right subtree: node.balance = height left subtree − height right subtree.

11.4.1 Specification

An AVL tree is a BST with a guarantee on the height, so the AVL tree operations are those of the BinarySearchTree ADT.

Figure 11.11 An AVL tree with balancing (b) and height (h) information.

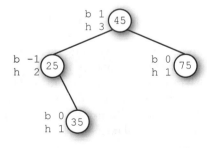

---

[5]G. M. Adel'son-Vel'skii and E. M. Landis. "An algorithm for the organization of information," English translation: Soviet Math. Report 3, pages 1259–1263, 1962.

As the UML diagram in Figure 11.3 shows, AVLNode extends BSTNode, so it inherits the BSTNode's child, parent, and element data fields. AVLNode adds two more attributes: height and balance.[6]

Class AVLTree

Like LinkedBST, AVLTree is an implementation of BinarySearchTree that extends AbstractBinarySearchTree. Again, note that the type we expect the tree to store comes from a family of types that are Comparable. AVLTree has a single data field.

```
public class AVLTree<E extends Comparable<? super E>>
                            extends AbstractBinarySearchTree<E> {
    private AVLNode<E> root;
```

11.4.2 Rotations to Rebalance a BST Tree

When an add() or remove() operation is done, the tree is changed structurally; consequently, the nodes on the path from the point of insertion or deletion up to the root must have their balances and heights recomputed. During this process, a node may be discovered whose balance is 2 or -2, indicating that the tree has gone out of balance at that node. Figure 11.12 illustrates this recomputation process following an add() operation and the identification of an imbalance.

Figure 11.12 (a) shows an AVL tree before the add() is done. Note that the balance values confirm the tree is AVL-balanced. In Figure 11.12 (b), 22 has been added to the tree. Since a new node will always be a leaf, the new node's height is 1 and its balance is 0. In Figure 11.12 (c) we begin to work back up the tree, recomputing heights and balances, and looking for an imbalance. Node 20's height becomes 2 and its balance becomes -1, reflecting that its right subtree is one deeper than its left subtree. But the tree rooted at 20 is AVL-balanced. In Figure 11.12 (d), the recomputation reveals an imbalance at 25. The subtree rooted at 25 is not an AVL tree because the height of its left subtree ($h = 2$) differs by more than one from the height of the right subtree ($h = 0$). Thus 25's balance becomes 2, reflecting that its left subtree is the source of the imbalance and the subtree rooted at 25 requires rebalancing.

Imbalances are discovered bottom-up during height/balance recomputation

Rebalancing is achieved by rotation(s) of subtrees rooted at the unbalanced node. The effect of the rotation(s) is to shorten the deeper of the two subtrees, producing a rebalanced subtree. All imbalances can be identified as belonging to one of four cases, and each imbalance case has its own rebalancing rotation.

Since the recomputation of heights and balances is done in a bottom-up fashion, any imbalanced node discovered must be the lowest such node in the path from the insertion or deletion point to the root. Let X be the lowest unbalanced node in the tree. This node is the root of the tree that requires rebalancing.

If the balance at X is 2, the tree must be unbalanced to the left. We need to look at the subtree rooted at X's left child because the deeper of its two subtrees is the

Left-imbalanced AVL trees

---

[6]The Exercises look at making these synthesized instead of stored attributes.

Figure 11.12 Recomputation of balance and height following an `add()` operation. The values of the node being recomputed are shown boxed.

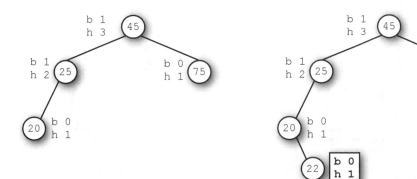

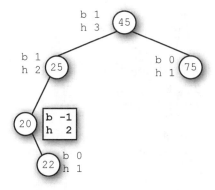

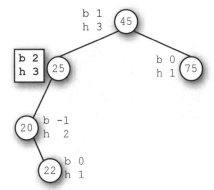

(a) The AVL tree before add (22).

(b) The AVL tree after add (22). Now begin recomputing heights and balances.

(c) The recomputation occurs moving up the tree.

(d) An imbalance is created at 25, where balance becomes 2.

problem. How can we know which is taller? The information is already at hand—it is the balance at X's left child.

Case LL   The balance at X's left child, X_L, is 1, so the **Left** child's **Left** subtree, rooted at X_{LL}, is taller (see Figure 11.13 (a)).

Case LR   The balance at X's left child, X_L, is −1, so the **Left** child's **Right** subtree, rooted at X_{LR}, is taller (see Figure 11.13 (b)).

The right-imbalanced cases are the mirror images of the left-imbalanced cases. If the balance at X is −2, the tree must be unbalanced to the right. We need to look at the subtree rooted at X's right child because the deeper of its two subtrees is the source of the imbalance.

Right-imbalanced AVL trees

Figure 11.13 Abstract representation of four types of imbalances in an AVL tree..

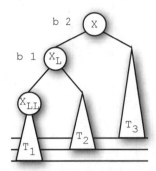

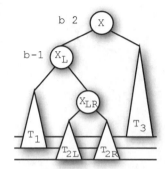

(a) Case LL—balance at X_L is 1, so the subtree rooted at X_{LL} is deepest.

(b) Case LR—balanced at X_L is −1, so the subtree rooted at X_{LR} is deepest.

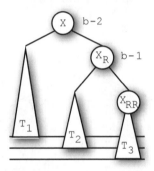

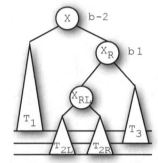

(c) Case RR—balance at X_R is −1, so the subtree rooted at X_{RR} is deepest.

(d) Case RL—balance at X_R is 1, so the subtree rooted at X_{RL} is deepest.

Case RR	The balance at X's right child, X_R, is −1, so the **R**ight child's **R**ight subtree, rooted at X_{RR}, is taller (see Figure 11.13 (c)).
Case RL	The balance at X's right child, X_R, is 1, so the **R**ight child's **L**eft subtree, rooted at X_{RL}, is taller (see Figure 11.13 (d)).

Again, note that Cases LL and RR are mirror images of each other, as are Cases LR and RL. Consequently, we will only look at Cases LL and LR in detail.

Case *LL*—The *Left* Subtree of X's *Left* Child Is Tallest

The solution is to make a single right (clockwise) rotation around X by moving the tree rooted at X_L up a level such that

- X becomes X_L's right child.
- X_L's right child (T_2) becomes X's left child.
- X_L is the new root of the subtree.

As shown in Figure 11.14 (b), this combination of changes moves T_1 up a level, T_2's level remains unchanged, and T_3 moves down a level, restoring the balance at X_L, which becomes the new root of the subtree.

Some rotations produce a new root to the subtree

What may not be so obvious is that the BST property is retained. That is, if we assume that the unbalanced tree in Figure 11.14 (a) is a BST, the rotation producing the balanced tree in Figure 11.14 (b) is also a BST. Briefly, T_2 and X_L are moved relative to X, and what we know about the values in T_2 is this:

$$X_L < \text{values in } T_2 < X$$

Thus T_2 must be between X_L (on the left) and X (on the right) in a BST. This is true of both trees in Figure 11.14, so the rebalanced tree is still a BST.

Figure 11.15 gives an example of an LL imbalance and its restoration.

The example in Figure 11.15 also makes clear that the rebalanced subtree is part of a larger tree and that, after X_L becomes the new root of the subtree, it must be connected to the rest of the tree (X's old parent, 45 in Figure 11.15).

Figure 11.14 Case LL requiring a right (clockwise) rotation to restore the AVL property.

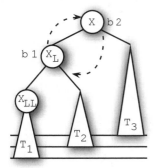   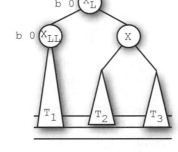

(a) An LL imbalance at X.

(b) Balance is restored by a right (clockwise) rotation.

Figure 11.15 Example of Case LL requiring a right rotation to restore the AVL property.

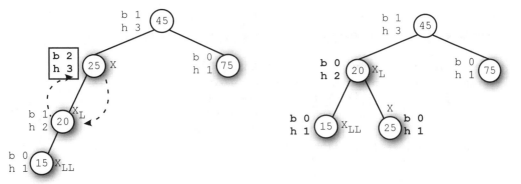

Method `rightRotation()` is shown in Listing 11.18, along with the utility method `updateBalanceAndHeight()` used to update a node's `balance` and `height` attributes. Note in `rightRotation()` that once all the links are changed, the structure of the subtree has changed, so the balance and height values in the affected nodes must be updated (lines 18–19).

The initializing assignment to `newRoot` on line 7 requires a cast because `parent`, `leftChild`, and `rightChild` are all defined as `BSTNodes`. You will see this sort of thing throughout the `AVLTree` code.

Lastly, since `rightRotation()` does a fixed number of operations, its runtime cost is O(1).

Listing 11.8 The `AVLTree` `rightRotation()` and `updateBalanceAndHeight()` methods.

```
1    /**
2     * Perform a right (clockwise) rotation at <tt>x</tt>.
3     * @param x the lowest unbalanced node found in this tree.
4     * @return The new root of the balanced subtree.
5     */
6    private AVLNode<E> rightRotation( AVLNode<E> x ){
7        AVLNode<E> newRoot = (AVLNode<E>)x.leftChild;
8        newRoot.parent = x.parent;
9        x.parent = newRoot;
10       x.leftChild = newRoot.rightChild;
11       // newRoot is guaranteed to have a left child, but
12       //   we can't be sure it has a right child
13       if ( newRoot.rightChild != null )
14           newRoot.rightChild.parent = x;
15       newRoot.rightChild = x;
16
17       // lastly: do updates from the bottom up
18       updateBalanceAndHeight( x );
19       updateBalanceAndHeight( newRoot );
20       return newRoot;
21   }
22
23   /**
24    * Update the balance and height properties of <tt>node</tt>.
25    */
26   private void updateBalanceAndHeight( AVLNode<E> node ){
27       int leftHeight = height( (AVLNode<E>)node.leftChild );
28       int rightHeight = height( (AVLNode<E>)node.rightChild );
29       node.height = ( leftHeight > rightHeight ?
30                               leftHeight: rightHeight ) + 1;
31       node.balance = leftHeight − rightHeight;
32   }
```

Case *LR*—X's *L*eft Child's *R*ight Subtree Is Tallest

Again the imbalance is at X and X_L is X's left child. As shown in Figure 11.16 (a), it is X_L's right subtree that is tallest. In this case, a single rotation will not rebalance the tree.

First, a left (counterclockwise) rotation of X_{LR} is done around X_L. This moves X_L's right child, X_{LR}, up the tree. X_{LR}'s left subtree (T_{2L}) becomes the right subtree of X_L. X_{LR}'s right subtree (T_{2R}) moves up the tree with X_{LR}. The result of this left rotation is shown in Figure 11.16 (b). As you can see, this does not restore the balance at X.

Figure 11.16 Case RL requires a left-right double rotation to restore the AVL property.

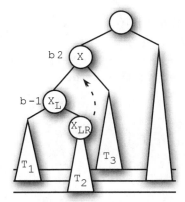

(a) Original unbalanced tree. The dotted arc indicates that a left (counterclockwise) rotation of X_{LR} around X_L will be done to produce the tree in (b).

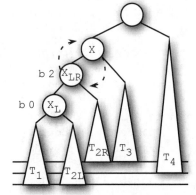

(b) The tree is still unbalanced at X. The dotted arc shows the right (clockwise) rotation of X_{LR} around X to produce the balanced trree in (c).

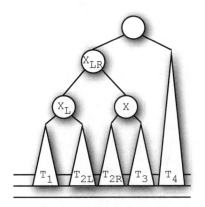

(c) The tree is AVL balanced.

We now do a right (clockwise) rotation around X. As we saw in the LL case, this moves X's left child up the tree a level while moving X down a level. The resulting rebalanced tree is shown in Figure 11.16 (c).

The rebalancing maintains the BST property. A quick examination of Figures 11.16 (a) and (c) will show that nodes and subtrees touched by the rotations still maintain the following relationships:

$$X_L < \text{values in } T_{2L} < X_{LR} < \text{values in } T_{2R} < X$$

Method `leftRotation()` is shown in Listing 11.9 along with the `rebalance()` method responsible for identifying the imbalance case and performing the necessary rotations to restore balance. The rebalancing method identifies the imbalance using the technique outlined in this chapter's Focus on Problem Solving on the Web.

Like its right-side counterpart, `leftRotation()` has an O(1) runtime cost.

Listing 11.9 The `AVLTree` `leftRotation()` and `rebalance()` methods.

```
1    /**
2     * Perform a left (counter-clockwise) rotation at <tt>x</tt>.
3     * @param x the lowest unbalanced node found in this tree.
4     * @return The new root of the balanced subtree.
5     */
6    private AVLNode<E> leftRotation( AVLNode<E> x ){
7        AVLNode<E> newRoot = (AVLNode<E>)x.rightChild;
8        newRoot.parent = x.parent;
9        x.parent = newRoot;
10       x.rightChild = newRoot.leftChild;
11
12       // newRoot is guaranteed to have a right child, but
13       //  we can't be sure it has a left child
14       if ( newRoot.leftChild != null )
15           newRoot.leftChild.parent = x;
16       newRoot.leftChild = x;
17
18       // lastly: do updates from the bottom up
19       updateBalanceAndHeight( x );
20       updateBalanceAndHeight( newRoot );
21       return newRoot;
22   }
23
24   /**
25    * On entry, <tt>x</tt> is the root of a subtree that has
26    * violated the balance properties of an AVL tree, so
27    * requires rebalancing.
28    * @param x the root of the tree to be rebalanced.
29    * @return The new root of the balanced subtree.
30    */
```

```
31    private AVLNode<E> rebalance( AVLNode<E> x ){
32        AVLNode<E> newRoot = null; // new root of  balanced subtree
33
34        // LL case — new node inserted into left subtree of
35        //          last unbalanced node's left child
36        if ( x.balance == 2 ) // left subtree is unbalanced
37            // Check for LL CASE
38            if ( ((AVLNode<E>)x.leftChild).balance == 1 ) {
39                newRoot = rightRotation( x );
40            }
41            else  {// LR CASE
42                x.leftChild = leftRotation( (AVLNode<E>)x.leftChild );
43                newRoot = rightRotation( x );
44            }
45        else
46            if ( x.balance == -2 ) // right subtree is unbalanced
47                // Check for RR CASE
48                if ( ((AVLNode<E>)x.rightChild).balance == -1 ) {
49                    newRoot = leftRotation( x );
50                }
51                else {  // LR case
52                    x.rightChild =
53                            rightRotation( (AVLNode<E>)x.rightChild );
54                    newRoot = leftRotation( x );
55                }
56        return newRoot;
57    }
```

11.4.3 Method `add()`—Adding an Element to an AVL Tree

The insertion of a new node into an AVL tree is done pretty much as it was for LinkedBST. We recursively descend the tree until the base case occurs—a null link is found. The new node is created and inserted, then the recursion unwinds and the algorithm walks back up the tree, retracing the path, in reverse, that it took from the root to the leaf to do the insertion.

Finding the insertion point

The only difference in AVLTree.add() is that we recompute each node's height and balance with updateBalanceAndHeight() as the recursion unwinds and we back up the tree. If a subtree is out of balance, we rebalance it with rebalance(). This is all done in the utility method fixSubtreeRootedAt() (called on line 27; defined on lines 32–43 in Listing 11.10). Once the rebalancing is complete, the new subtree root is returned to add(), where it is attached to the rest of the tree (lines 17 and 19–20).

Recompute heights and balances as the recursion unwinds

Method `remove()`—Removing an Element from an AVL Tree

Removing a node is slightly more complicated than adding one. First, let's look at the part that is analogous to add(). It makes sense that the nodes in the path from

Listing 11.10 The `AVLTree` `add()` and `fixSubtreeRootedAt()` methods.

```
1    /**
2     * Add <tt>element</tt> to the tree.
3     * @param parent parent of  <tt>node</tt>
4     * @param node root of subtree to which element is to be added
5     * @param element the element to be added to the tree
6     * @throws SearchTreeException if node is found in the tree
7     */
8    protected BSTNode<E> add( BSTNode<E> parent, BSTNode<E> node,
9                              E element ){
10       if ( node == null )  {    // base case
11           node = new AVLNode( element );
12           node.parent = parent;
13       }
14       else {  // recursive case
15           int compareResult = element.compareTo( node.element );
16           if ( compareResult < 0 )
17               node.leftChild = add(node, node.leftChild, element);
18           else if ( compareResult > 0 )
19               node.rightChild =
20                                 add( node, node.rightChild, element );
21           else
22               throw new SearchTreeException( "Duplicate element: " +
23                                            element.toString() );
24
25           // now do height/balance updates and possible
26           //  subtree fixes
27           node = fixSubtreeRootedAt( (AVLNode<E>)node );
28       }
29       return node;
30   }
31
32   /**
33    * Make sure subtree rooted at <tt>node</tt> is an AVL tree.
34    * @param node the root of the subtree to be fixed.
35    * @return the root of the subtree. The root will be different
36    * from <tt>node</tt> if the subtree required rebalancing.
37    */
38   private AVLNode<E> fixSubtreeRootedAt( AVLNode<E> node ) {
39       updateBalanceAndHeight( node );
40       if ( ( node.balance == 2 ) || ( node.balance == -2 ) )
41           node = rebalance( node );
42       return node;
43   }
```

the point of removal up to the root will need to have their heights and balances checked. As done in `add()`, this is easily handled with a call to `fixSubtreeRootedAt()` following each recursive call (lines 14 and 18 in Listing 11.11).

Recall from the implementation of `remove()` in `LinkedBST` that when the target to be removed is an internal node with two children, we actually replace the target with its successor, then remove the successor's node from the tree. This is the source of the complication since it means that the nodes in the path from the *successor*'s node to the *target*'s node must also have their heights and balances checked. Unfortunately, we cannot do this as part of the recursion unwinding since in this case the recursive calls to find the target will not have taken us down to the successor node. For example, in Figure 11.17, if we do `remove(20)`, the recursive calls will take us down to the node storing 20. We replace 20 with the value of its successor, 25, then remove 25's node from the tree. As you can see, the nodes between the target (20) and its successor (25) need to have their heights and balances updated.

One solution, implemented in `updatePath()`, is to start at the target node and recursively move down the tree to the successor node's parent (lines 63 to 74— remember, the successor's node will have been removed from the tree). When the successor node's parent is found, we just back up the tree, checking each node with `fixSubtreeRootedAt()` (lines 68 and 73). The resulting code is shown in Listing 11.11.

Find the target

Replace target with successor

Update from target to root as recursion unwinds

Update from successor to target

Complication: When the target has two children, the target is replaced by its successor

SUMMING UP

The cost of keeping a BST perfectly balanced is prohibitive and outweighs the access time guarantees it provides. AVL trees offer a compromise that provides access times within a small multiple of $\log_2 n$ with acceptable maintenance costs. In an AVL tree, the heights of a node's left and right subtrees can differ by no more than 1. Imbalances in the tree caused by additions and removals are rebalanced through subtree rotations at the point of the imbalance.

CHECKPOINT

11.5 After a change to the tree, why must balances and heights be recomputed from the bottom up?

11.6 Provide balance and height values for the tree shown here. If it is unbalanced, identify the case and perform the necessary rotation(s) and recalculate the balances and heights.

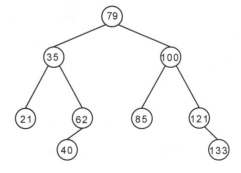

Figure 11.17 The nodes between the target (20) and its successor (25) need to have
their heights and balances updated.

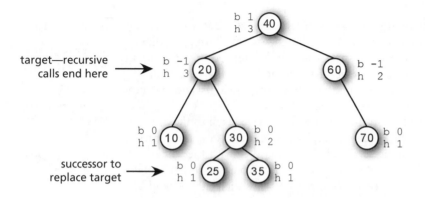

(a) The recursive calls to remove ( ) will reach
the target node (20). The target's successor
(25) is below the target in the tree.

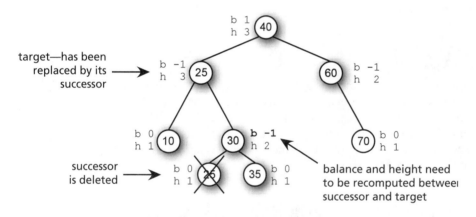

(b) A separate mechanism is needed to adjust
the tree between the successor (following its
removal) and the target.

Listing 11.11 The `AVLTree` `remove()` and `updatePath()` methods.

```
1    /**
2     * Remove element from this tree.
3     * @param node the root of the subtree from which to remove
4     *   element.
5     * @param element the element to remove.
6     */
```

```
7   protected BSTNode<E> remove( BSTNode<E> node, E target ){
8       if ( node == null ) // element isn't in the tree
9           return null;
10
11      int compareResult = target.compareTo( node.element );
12      if ( compareResult < 0 ) {
13          node.leftChild = remove( node.leftChild, target );
14          node = fixSubtreeRootedAt( (AVLNode<E>)node );
15      }
16      else if ( compareResult > 0 ) {
17          node.rightChild = remove( node.rightChild, target );
18          node = fixSubtreeRootedAt( (AVLNode<E>)node );
19      }
20      else {    // found the target!
21          this.size--;
22          // handle the case of two children first
23          if ( ( node.leftChild != null ) &&
24               ( node.rightChild != null ) ) {
25              BSTNode<E> replacement = successor( node );
26              node.element = replacement.element;
27
28              // now deal with removing the replacement
29              BSTNode<E> newChild = replacement.leftChild == null ?
30                      replacement.rightChild : replacement.leftChild;
31              if ( replacement == replacement.parent.leftChild )
32                  replacement.parent.leftChild = newChild;
33              else
34                  replacement.parent.rightChild = newChild;
35
36              // now fix the height/balance from the replacement's
37              //  parent to node. If, along the way, we find a
38              //  subtree unbalanced, rebalance it
39              node = updatePath( (AVLNode<E>)node,
40                                    replacement.parent.element  );
41          }
42          else // Collapse the cases of no children and 1 child
43              node = ( node.leftChild == null ) ? node.rightChild :
44                                                node.leftChild;
45      }
46      return node;
47  }
48
49  /**
50   * Update the path from node down to the node containing
51   * element. Since it is guaranteed there is a path between
52   * these two arguments, node should never become null.
53   * @param node the root of some subtree, originally the root
54   *   of the subtree whose node was removed.
55   * @param element the element stored at the end of the path
```

```
56        * to be updated. This element was the parent to the value
57        * that supplied the replacement value for a node during a
58        * remove() operation.
59        */
60       private AVLNode<E> updatePath( AVLNode<E> node, E element ){
61           int compareResult = element.compareTo( node.element );
62
63           if ( compareResult == 0 )    // reached the end of the path
64               node = fixSubtreeRootedAt( node );
65           else if ( compareResult < 0 ) {
66               node.leftChild = updatePath( (AVLNode<E>)node.leftChild,
67                                            element );
68               node = fixSubtreeRootedAt( node );
69           }
70           else if ( compareResult > 0 ) {
71               node.rightChild = updatePath( (AVLNode<E>)node.rightChild,
72                                            element );
73               node = fixSubtreeRootedAt( node );
74           }
75           return node;
76       }
```

11.4.4 Analysis

As pointed out earlier, a rotation consists of some link assignments followed by balance updates, so the cost of a rotation is fixed: $O(1)$.

The cost to add and remove is bounded by the height of the tree: $O(\log_2 n)$. An add() will always descend to the bottom of the tree (to an empty link) and then unwind to the root, possibly doing a rotation along the way. The trip down and up is $O(\log_2 n)$, and the rotation just adds a constant cost, so add() is an $O(\log_2 n)$ operation.

As we have seen, remove() behaves very much like add() and has the same time complexity.

The space complexity for all the recursive methods is $O(\log_2 n)$, the number of activation records on the process stack when the base case is met.

11.4.5 Designing a Test Plan

The test plan for BST can be used for AVL trees to test that ordering is maintained. However, we need additional tests to ensure that balance is maintained. The method in Listing 11.12 does this and should be used in testing after methods that access (add, find, remove) a tree element. For example, a test method for remove() might do:

```
avlTree.remove( target );
assertTrue( !avlTree.contains( target ) );
assertTrue( checkHeightAndBalance ( avlTree, (AVLNode)avlTree.root() ) );
```

Listing 11.12 The `AVLTree` `checkHeightAndBalance()` method for verifying that a tree is AVL-balanced.

```
 1    private boolean checkHeightAndBalance( AVLTree<Integer> t,
 2                                           AVLNode<Integer> node ) {
 3        if ( node == null ) return true;
 4
 5        boolean leftCheck =
 6                checkHeightAndBalance( t, (AVLNode)node.leftChild );
 7        boolean rightCheck =
 8                checkHeightAndBalance( t, (AVLNode)node.rightChild );
 9        int leftHeight = t.height( (AVLNode)node.leftChild );
10        int rightHeight = t.height( (AVLNode)node.rightChild );
11        int checkedHeight =  (leftHeight > rightHeight ?
12                                          leftHeight : rightHeight) + 1;
13        int checkedBalance = leftHeight - rightHeight;
14        boolean thisCheck = ( checkedHeight == node.height ) &&
15                            ( checkedBalance == node.balance) ;
16        if ( !leftCheck ) {
17            System.out.println( "left check failed on " +
18                                (AVLNode)node.leftChild );
19            System.out.println( "Expected: Balance: " +checkedBalance +
20                                " Height: " + checkedHeight );
21        }
22        if ( !rightCheck ) {
23            System.out.println( "right check failed on " +
24                                (AVLNode)node.rightChild );
25            System.out.println( "Expected: Balance: " +checkedBalance +
26                                " Height: " + checkedHeight );
27        }
28        if ( !thisCheck ) {
29            System.out.println( "this check failed on " +
30                                (AVLNode)node );
31            System.out.println( "Expected: Balance: " +checkedBalance +
32                                " Height: " + checkedHeight );
33        }
34        return leftCheck && rightCheck && thisCheck;
35    }
```

INVESTIGATE ## Finding the kth Smallest Element in a Binary Search Tree

Description

In Chapter 8 we looked at the problem of finding the kth smallest element in a collection. At the time, we observed that if the elements were stored in a linear, ordered collection starting at 0, the kth smallest element was always in position $k-1$. Thus, the combination of an ordered and indexable collection made it easy to find the kth smallest element.

BSTs are ordered, but not indexable, so it is not immediately obvious how we would find the kth smallest element in a BST. However, intuition tells us that since BSTs are ordered, finding the kth smallest element should be possible (and not all that difficult). The purpose of this *Investigate* is to develop a method that will find the kth smallest element of a BST without making any changes to the way a BST is implemented.

Objectives

- Solve the kth smallest problem for BSTs.
- Work with recursive definitions and methods.
- Introduce the notion of rank.
- Work with BSTs some more.

Visualization

An element's **rank** in a sequence is the number of elements in the sequence that are less than it.[7] In an ordered sequence, then, the first element's rank will always be 0 and the nth element's rank will be $n - 1$.

11	17	25	34	52	79	81	85	90	95	elements
0	1	2	3	4	5	6	7	8	9	indices

1. Create a relatively balanced BST from the elements in the array above and label each element with its rank.

2. What is the rank of the kth smallest element for the following values of k?
   $k = 1$ (element is 11)? $k = 7$ (element is 81)? $k = 5$ (element is 52)?

3. What is the relationship between k and rank?

The relationship between k and rank suggests that if we can determine an element's rank, we can use that information to find the kth smallest element. For example, if $k = 5$ and the rank of the node we are examining is 10, we know we need to continue our search in this node's left subtree. Whereas if $k = 5$ and the current node's rank is 3, we need to continue with this node's right subtree. This suggests the following first attempt at a recursive definition:

$$
\text{kthSmallest(node, k)}
\begin{cases}
\text{node's element, if } k - 1 == \text{node's rank} & \textit{// base case} \\
\text{kthSmallest(node's left child, k), if } k - 1 < \text{node's rank} \\
& \textit{// recursive case—left subtree} \\
\text{kthSmallest(node's right child, k), if } k - 1 > \text{node's rank} \\
& \textit{// recursive case—right subtree}
\end{cases}
$$

where:
   k   find the kth element
   node   the root of the subtree being searched

---

[7]This definition assumes there are no duplicates. If duplicates are allowed, the definition is amended as follows: An element's rank in a sequence is the number of elements in the sequence that are less than it plus the number of elements of equal value at lower ranks.

But how can we determine a node's rank? Let's look at what we know about the relative position of elements in a BST. Figure 11.18 shows four elements of a BST and their relative ranks (which, of course, is a reflection of their relative values). We can compute the ranks of X_R and X_{RL} as follows (look at this carefully!):

$$\text{rank}(X_R) = \text{rank}(X) + \text{size of } X_R\text{'s left subtree} + 1$$

$$\text{rank}(X_{RL}) = \text{rank}(X) + \text{size of } X_{RL}\text{'s left subtree} + 1$$

4. Create an example BST. Assign X, X_R, X_{RL}, and X_{RR} to the appropriate nodes of the BST you created and verify these equations.

5. Using the equations above as a model, give the equations to compute the rank of X_{RR} and X_{RLL} (the left child of X_{RL}).

Your answers to these questions and the recursive definition suggest that as we recursively descend the tree, moving *right* out of a node X, we are "passing over" all the elements that are less than or equal to X's element. Thus X's rank establishes a confirmed lower bound on the rank of our target (the kth smallest element). Note that X's right child will need to know X's rank so that it can compute its own rank.

To complete the picture, when you move left out of a node, the lower bound on rank is still that of the last node from which we followed a right link. Initially this value is 0. This suggests the following equation for computing the rank of a node:

This bit is tricky. Look at it carefully

$$\text{rank of node X} = \text{rank lower bound} + \text{size of X's left subtree} + 1$$

For example, when looking for the 5th smallest element from the tree in Figure 11.19, we start with rankLowerBound = 0 at 40, the root of the tree. Since 40's rank is 6, we move left to node 30. Because we moved left in the tree, no additional nodes have been passed over, so rankLowerBound is still 0. Since 30's rank is 3, we next move right to 35 and rankLowerBound becomes 3. The rank for 35 is 5 (rank of 20's node plus the size of 35's left subtree = 5), so we move left to 32. Since this is a left move, no additional nodes are passed over and rankLowerBound stays at 3. Applying our formula, we get a rank of 4 for 32, making it the 5th smallest element in the tree.

Looking for the 5th smallest element in Figure 11.19.

6. Use this new approach to compute the rank of 50 for the tree in Figure 11.19.

7. Modify the recursive definition given above to include the rankLowerBound information as a parameter.

Figure 11.18 Abstract representation of the ranks of four elements in a BST.

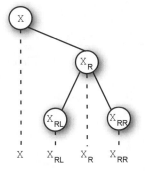

Figure 11.19 Sample tree to examine rank.

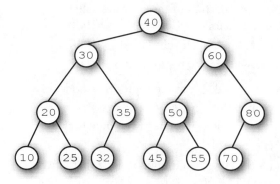

8. Verify the new recursive definition by tracing the search for the 1st, 8th, and 13th smallest values in Figure 11.19.

Design

1. Based on the recursive description, pseudocode a recursive method `kthSmallest()`.
2. Provide a recursive definition to compute the size of a subtree rooted at some node.

$$\text{size(node)} \begin{cases} \text{What is the base case?} \\ \text{What is the recursive case?} \end{cases}$$

3. Pseudocode the `size()` method based on your recursive definition.
4. Provide a test plan for the `kthSmallest()` method.

Implementation

1. Implement the methods pseudocoded in the Design section.
2. Implement and run the test plan.

Discussion

1. Does your algorithm rely on the tree being balanced? Explain.
2. What are the runtime and space complexities of your algorithm? Think about this in relation to the previous question.
3. Briefly describe the relationship between the recursive definition here for the kth smallest element and that given in Chapter 8.

■ 11.5 Splay Tree: A Self-Adjusting Binary Search Tree

What if accesses to the tree were not evenly distributed over its elements? That is, what if there was a pattern of accesses to the tree's elements? It would be nice if our collection was flexible and could provide improved performance based on the access pattern. Alas, height-balanced trees such as an AVL tree can do nothing to help. By design, an AVL tree is required to keep the tree height-balanced, even if that means that the most commonly accessed element is at the bottom of the tree. What we get in return for this inflexibility is that the tree guarantees an $O(\log_2 n)$ access time for every access.

An alternative approach is to forego this guarantee of uniform access time and to tolerate an occasional costly, $O(n)$, access time in return for a larger number of very efficient, $O(1)$, accesses, so that over time the average access cost is comparable to that of height balanced trees, $O(\log_2 n)$.

Splay trees are self-adjusting binary search trees adapted to changing access patterns. The simple mechanism for achieving this is to always move the most recently accessed element to the root under the assumption that it will be accessed again in the near future. If this turns out to be the case, subsequent accesses will be very efficient. However, splay trees make no promises about height or balance. Indeed, in the pathological case, it is possible that the tree degenerates into a linear structure, so the worst case access time for an individual access is $O(n)$. This doesn't sound very promising, but, as you will see, it can work out nicely.

Splay trees are self-adjusting binary search trees

11.5.1 Specification

Splay trees are a particular implementation of binary search trees, so `SplayTree` will implement the `BinarySearchTree` interface, with the following modifications.

`add( element )`	The node containing element becomes the root of the tree.
`contains( target )`	Success: The node containing target becomes the root of the tree.
	Failure: The last node whose element was compared to the target becomes the root of the tree.
`remove( target )`	Success: The parent of target becomes the root of the tree. If target was at the root, the left child becomes the root; the right child becomes the root if the left child does not exist.
	Failure: The last node whose element was compared to the target becomes the root of the tree.

11.5.2 Designing a Test Plan

Because a splay tree is a binary search tree, all of the BST tests apply. Additional tests address the unique characteristics of splay trees.

■ After an `add()` and successful `contains()`, verify that the accessed node is the root.

- After a `remove()`, verify that the target's parent is moved to the root. If the target was already in the root position, verify that the correct child was promoted.
- After an unsuccessful `contains()` or `remove()`, verify that the last node touched has become the root (see Test Case 11.3).

For each of these tests, we should verify that the tree is still a BST and that no elements have been lost (no subtrees have become detached).

Test Case 11.3 Testing movement of most recently accessed element to the root a splay tree.

Method	Purpose	Object State	Expected Result
BinarySearchTree<Integer> tree = new SplayTree<Integer>()	To create an empty splay tree using the default constructor.	*size* = 0 *root* = **null**	SplayTree object to store Integers
tree.size()	To verify tree is empty.		0
tree.add(10) //expected is a List object expectedList.add(10)	To add to an empty tree.	*size* = 1 *root* = **Integer (10)** *root*.**leftChild** = **null** *root*.**rightChild** = **null**	
tree.size()	To verify size() and add() to an empty tree.		1
tree.contains(10)	To verify contains() and add() to an empty tree.		true
tree.add(5) expectedList.add(5)	To add to left subtree.	*size* = 2 *root* = **Integer(5)** *root*.**leftChild** = **null** *root*.**rightChild** = **Integer(10)**	
tree.root().element()	To verify new value is at root.		Integer(5) object
tree.size()	To verify 5 was added.		2
tree.find(5)	To verify contains() and add().		true
tree.add(7) expectedList.add(7)	To add to tree.	*size* = 3 *root* = **Integer(7)** *root*.**leftChild** = **Integer(5)** *root*.**rightChild** = **Integer(10)**	
tree.root().element()	To verify new value is at root.		Integer(7) object
tree.size()	To verify 7 was added.		3
tree.find(7)	To verify contains() and add().		true
List<Integer>actualList = toList(tree) Collections.sort(actualList) actualList.equals(expectedList)	To verify elements of the tree are in the correct order.		true

Note the use of the `protected` method `root()` to gain access to the root element. This assumes that the test plan will be implemented within the same package as the other binary search tree classes.

11.5.3 Splay Rotations

The purpose of a rotation in an AVL tree is to restore balance to a subtree while keeping the tree a BST. A side effect, which we noted at the time, is that some nodes will move up the tree. We make use of that here—a splay tree moves the target node up to the root using repeated rotations. Of course, after any rotation, the tree must still be a BST.

There are two 1-level splay cases and four 2-level splay cases. The 1-level splay rotations are used when the target is the left or right child of the root, thus the goal of the 1-level rotation is to move the target up one level into the root. Figure 11.20 shows the case when the target is the left child (the L case). This is handled with a single right (clockwise) rotation of the target around its parent. The figure shows the tree relatively balanced, but that need not be the case since splay trees make no guarantees about balance. The R case is symmetric to the L case.

The four 2-level cases are shown in Figure 11.21. Notice the structure of the four AVL tree rotation cases. The goal of a 2-level rotation is to move the target up the tree two levels. Which 2-level rotation to apply is determined by the relationship between the target and its grandparent.

The rotations for the LR and RL splay cases are identical to the LR and RL AVL cases. The LR case is shown in Figure 11.22.

The rotations for the LL and RR cases are similar to their AVL counterparts. In the LL case, shown in Figure 11.23, we do two right rotations instead of the single right rotation done for AVL trees. As shown in the figure, this double rotation has the desired effect—it moves the target up the tree two levels and maintains the tree as a BST.

Figure 11.20 The L-splay rotation for splay trees.

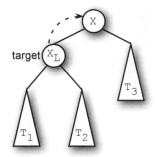

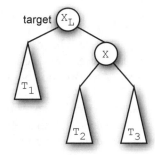

(a) The target is the root's left child.

(b) The target is moved to the root position.

Figure 11.21 The four 2-level splay cases.

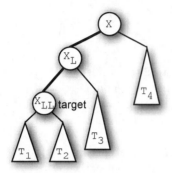

(a) Splay Case LL—target is
the left child of a left child.

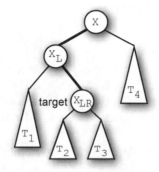

(b) Splay Case LR—target is
the right child of a left child.

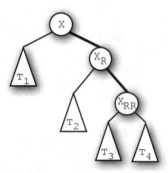

(c) Splay Case RR—target is
the right child of a right child.

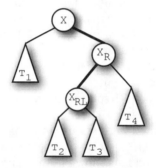

(d) Splay Case RL—target is
the left child of a right child.

11.5.4 Implementation

A `splay()` method moves the target up to the root and maintains the tree as a BST.
As long as the target's depth is greater than two, one of the 2-level rotations is
applied. If the target's depth is one, the appropriate 1-level rotation is applied.

Our BST implementation is easily modified to support splay trees. The only
methods affected are those that access an element: `add()`, `remove()`, and
`contains()`. (The sticky problem of what to do about the iterator has been left as
an exercise.)

The simplest approach is to just have these methods do what they would usually do (add an element, remove an element, find an element), then call `splay()` at
the end of the method to move the target to the root.

Figure 11.22 The LR splay case.

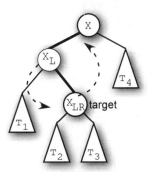

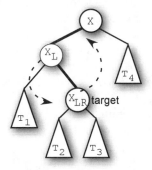

(a) Step 1: Do a left (counterclockwise) rotation of X_{LR} around X_L.

(b) Step 2: Do a right (clockwise) rotation of X_{LR} around X.

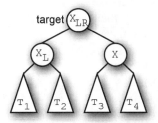

(c) LR splay complete; target has moved up two levels.

Figure 11.23 The LL splay case.

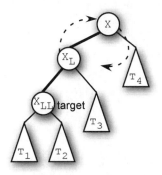

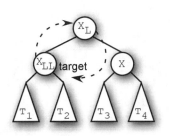

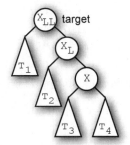

(a) Step 1: Do a right (clockwise) rotatation of X_L around X.

(b) Step 2: Do a right rotation of X_{LL} around X_L.

(c) LL splay complete; target is moved up two levels.

11.5.5 Amortization Analysis

Although the runtime complexity of an individual access to a splay tree is $O(n)$, it can be shown that a sequence of m accesses will have a cost of $O(m\log_2 n)$, giving an *amortized* cost of $O(\log_2 n)$ per access. Amortized analysis is used in cases where the implementation goal is not to provide a guaranteed maximum on a *single* operation, but for a *series* of operations.

Some operations may be quite costly, but ideally they are laying the groundwork that will make operations in the near future very efficient. In a sense, then, amortization allows you to distribute the cost of an expensive operation over a sequence of subsequent cheaper operations.

SUMMING UP

Splay trees offer a different take on how a tree's elements can be organized to provide good access time. Since the depth of an element in a tree determines its actual access cost, clearly the shallower the element (the higher up in the tree it is), the lower the cost. If the element is in the root, the cost is $O(1)$. Splay trees always move the referenced element to the root under the assumption that it will be accessed several more times before a different element in the tree is accessed. A splay tree may become unbalanced, so the worst-case access time for an operation is $O(n)$.

In amortized analysis we are interested not in the cost of an individual operation, but in the cost of a series of operations. It can be shown that the cost of m splay tree operations is $O(m\log_2 n)$, giving an amortized cost of $O(\log_2 n)$ per operation. Simply, the frequent inexpensive operations help to "pay for" the occasional expensive operation.

CHECKPOINT

11.7 Identify the splay case for the following operations applied to the tree shown here.

a. contains(25)

b. add(20)

c. remove(85)

d. contains(133)

11.8 What assumption is behind splay tree design?

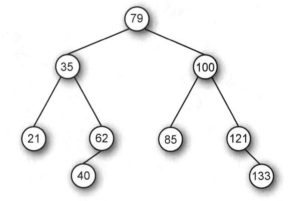

EXERCISES

Paper and Pencil

1. For each search tree type below, show the tree that would be built by adding the following elements in the order shown: 50, 40, 50, 20, 10, 30, 100, 80.
   a. binary search tree
   b. AVL tree
   c. splay tree

2. Provide the balance and height information for the nodes in the AVL tree from Exercise 1.

3. Using the trees constructed in Exercise 1, show the binary search, AVL, and splay trees after a `remove( 40 )` operation. For the AVL and splay trees, identify the rotations involved.

4. Draw an illustration of the AVL tree RL rotation.

5. Trace the `kthSmallest()` algorithm for $k = 6$ for one of the search trees created in Exercise 1.

6. Draw an illustration of the splay tree RR rotation.

7. Draw an illustration of the splay tree RL rotation.

8. Describe a pattern of access to a splay tree that would provide excellent performance. Now describe an access pattern that would provide poor performance.

Testing and Debugging

1. Provide test cases similar to Test Case 11.2 to test `BST.remove()` on a leaf and an internal node that is not the root.

2. Provide Test Cases for BST to test for exceptional conditions.

3. Explain how lines 39–42 of Listing 11.6 collapse the cases of removing a node in a BST when the target has 0 or 1 children. Include illustrations with your explanation and provide test cases to verify the code behaves as you have explained it.

4. Update the BST test cases to work for AVL trees. How will you use the method from Listing 11.14?

5. Provide test cases for splay tree's `contains()` and `remove()` operations.

Modify the Code

1. Complete the implementation of `LinkedBST` and apply our completed test plan (see the Exercises under Testing and Debugging) to it.

2. What do you think of these implementations in terms of coding complexity and understandability, and runtime and space costs?

3. Add a `replace( oldValue, newValue )` method to the `BinarySearchTree` interface and implement it in one or more of the tree classes. The method replaces the element `oldValue` with `newValue`.

4. Implement the `TreeIterator` class. Make sure that it is fail fast.

5. Re-implement the recursive methods of `LinkedBST` to be nonrecursive.

6. Add a constructor to `AVLTree` and `SplayTree` that takes a `Collection` as an argument and populates the tree with the collection's elements.

7. Add a method to `AVLTree` and `SplayTree` that provides the elements stored in the tree as a `Collection`.

ON THE WEB

Additional study material is available at Addison-Wesley's Website at http://www.aw.com/cssupport. This material includes the following:

■ Focus on Problem Solving: A Modifiable Spell Checker

Problem: Lunar Microsystems, the company that makes the tablet computer and contracted for a version of MineSweeper a few weeks ago, now envisions a number of related products that will involve text processing of some kind. They believe that a single spell checker could be used as a component in each of these products. They were so pleased with the MineSweeper app that they have turned again to Barking Dogs Software to make the spell checker prototype and to demonstrate its use with a simple graphical front end. We have been given the job of designing this prototype and have been told that the spell checker should be able to

■ look up a word and return the status of the search (found or not found)

■ add a word to the spell checker's dictionary

■ delete a word from the spell checker's dictionary

■ save the dictionary to a file

Solution: The ability to search for a word quickly is important in these applications. A balanced BST is a good choice to store the spell checker's dictionary. In this case we use the AVL ADT.

The solution includes Analysis (discussion of the inputs and outputs to the application, and the layout of the application interface), Design (identification of classes with their responsibilities and collaborators, visualized through a UML class diagram), and Implementation of the classes.

■ Study Guide Exercises

■ Answers to CheckPoint Problems

■ Additional exercises

The Map ADT 12

CHAPTER OUTLINE

■ 12.1 The Map ADT

So far, all the collection types we have considered viewed the element stored in a collection as a data value. For example, while we stored an element by position in a list, stack, or queue, and by value in a binary search tree, in each of these cases, it was the value itself we were interested in.

However, there are many applications in which *two* pieces of information are associated and we use one piece of information, the **key**, to lead to the other piece, the **value**. Here are some examples:

■ Concordance—A concordance is a tool used for analysis of texts (the Bible and works of Shakespeare, for example). It consists of the words that appear in the text, in alphabetical order, along with how frequently the word appears in the text and the line numbers on which it appears.

■ Book index—An index is an ordered collection of key words and the numbers of the pages on which the word appears in a text. Subentries of a key word consist of related words and the page numbers where they appear.

■ Symbol table—A compiler uses a symbol table to keep track of the identifiers that appear in a program. An entry in a symbol table consists of the identifier and its type, size, and relative memory address.

■ Command-line processor—Every executable program resides in a directory (folder) somewhere in the operating system's file system. The absolute path for an application is the sequence of directories you pass through to get to the executable from the root (top) of the file system hierarchy down to the executable (for example, /usr/local/bin/javac under a UNIX system or C:\JavaTools\jdk1.5.1\bin\javac under Microsoft Windows). To quickly find the path for a particular command, command-line processors maintain a table of <command, path> pairs. Given a command, the table produces the path to its executable, which is used to launch the program.

A **map** (also called a *dictionary*) is a collection type that stores <**key, value**> pairs. In such a key-based collection, there is no sense of "where" a value is stored. Instead, a value is retrieved by supplying the map with the associated key. This idea is shown in Figure 12.1. It is in this sense that we say that a map maps keys to values.

There are several useful variations of maps. In a map, the relationship between a key and a value is one-to-one. In a **multimap**, the relationship is one-to-many, so a multimap entry would store a single key and one or more values associated with that key. The entries in a map are not ordered, but, as we have seen, ordering is sometimes useful. An **ordered map** can provide its entries in a sequence ordered by key. The concordance and book index examples would use yet another variant, an **ordered multimap**.

> Map variations:
> ■ multimap
> ■ ordered map
> ■ ordered multimap

12.1.1 Map Specification

A map stores **entries**, also called **associations**, consisting of <key, value> pairs. A map entry establishes an association between a key and a value. While the keys in a map must be unique, there may be duplicate values. Entries are not stored in any particular order in a map. Typically a map can grow to any size.

Figure 12.1 A map is a *key-based* collection. Given a key, the map produces an associated value.

The Map ADT

Description
A map stores <key, value> pairs. Given a key, a map provides the associated value. The types of the key and value are not specified, but it must be possible to test for equality among keys and among values.

Properties
1. Duplicate keys are not allowed.
2. A key may be associated with only one value.
3. A value may be associated with more than one key.
4. Keys can be compared to one another for equality; similarly for values.
5. Null keys and values are not allowed.

Attributes
size:	The number of <key, value> pairs in this map.

Operations

Map( )

pre-condition:	none
responsibilities:	constructor—create an empty map
post-condition:	*size* is set to 0
returns:	nothing

put(KeyType key, ValueType value)

pre-condition:	key and value are not null
	key can be compared for equality to other keys in this map
	value can be compared for equality to other values in this map
responsibilities:	puts the <key, value> pair into the map. If key already exists in this map, its value is replaced with the new value
post-condition:	*size* is increased by one if key was not already in this map
returns:	null if key was not already in this map, the old value associated with key otherwise
exception:	if key or value is null or cannot be compared to keys/values in this map

get(KeyType key)

pre-condition:	key is not null and can be compared for equality to other keys in this map
responsibilities:	gets the value associated with key in this map
post-condition:	the map is unchanged
returns:	null if key was not found in this map, the value associated with key otherwise
exception:	if key is null or cannot be compared for equality to other keys in this map

remove(KeyType key)

pre-condition:	key is not null and can be compared for equality to other keys in this map
responsibilities:	remove the value from this map associated with key
post-condition:	*size* is decreased by one if key was found in this map
returns:	null if key was not found in this map, the value associated with key otherwise
exception:	if key is null or cannot be compared for equality to other keys in this map

containsValue(ValueType value)

pre-condition:	value is not null and can be compared for equality to other values in this map
responsibilities:	determines if this map contains an entry containing value
post-condition:	the map is unchanged
returns:	true if value was found in this map, false otherwise
exception:	if value is null or cannot be compared for equality to other values in this map

containsKey(KeyType key)

pre-condition:	key is not null and can be compared to other keys in this map
responsibilities:	determines if this map contains an entry with the given key
post-condition:	the map is unchanged
returns:	true if key was found in this map, false otherwise
exception:	if key is null or cannot be compared for equality to other keys in this map

values()

pre-condition:	none
responsibilities:	provides a Collection view of all the values contained in this map. The Collection supports element removal, but not element addition. Any change made to the Collection is reflected in this map and vice versa
post-condition:	the map is unchanged
returns:	a Collection providing a view of the values from this map

Not shown: clear(), isEmpty(), and size()

A few operations deserve some comment. First you should note the semantics of the put() operation. It says that if the key for a <key, value> pair already exists in the map, then the value supplied in the put() operation replaces the value associated with key already in the map, and the old value is returned (see Figure 12.2).

Next, the values() operation is interesting for what it provides and how. We'll look at "what" it provides here, leaving the issue of "how" for the discussion of implementation in Section 12.2.5.

The values() operation provides what is called a Collection **view** of the map. Here is the description from the JavaDocs for `java.util.HashMap.values()`:

Figure 12.2 The behavior of Map's put() operation.

Returns a collection view of the values contained in this map. The collection is backed by the map, so changes to the map are reflected in the collection, and vice versa. If the map is modified while an iteration over the collection is in progress, the results of the iteration are undefined. The collection supports element removal, which removes the corresponding mapping from the map, via the `Iterator.remove`, `Collection.remove`, `removeAll`, `retainAll`, and `clear` operations. It does not support the `add` or `addAll` operations.

Collection view

The documentation says that the `Collection` object returned is "backed by" the map, so any changes that are made to the map are reflected in the collection and vice versa. We saw something similar when we looked at the sublist() operation from the List ADT in Chapter 5. Figure 12.3 illustrates what is going on. The `Collection` returned by `Map.values()` just gives us a different way to view the values stored in the map. Any change made to the map entries through one view will be seen in the other view, since both views are looking at the same collection of map entries. The program in Listing 12.1 and its output demonstrate that, indeed, changes to the collection affect the map and vice versa.

12.1.2 The Map Interface

The `Map` interface in Listing 12.2 corresponds to the Map ADT 12.1 and is a subset of the methods found in `java.util.Map` in the JCF.

12.1.3 Designing a Test Plan for a Map

As we have done before, we use the predicate and accessor methods to verify state changes resulting from the mutator methods. We look at a few examples here. The map properties and the specification of `put()` suggest several separate tests:

■ If we put a <key, value> pair in an empty map, we should be able to get the value back, given the key, and to determine that the map contains the key and the value. This is shown in Test Case 12.1.

Figure 12.3 A Collection view is a different way to "view" the entries stored in the map.

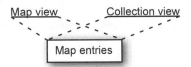

Listing 12.1 Program illustrating the meaning of a collection view of a map. The output is shown following the listing.

```
1    package mapviewex;
2
3    import gray.adts.map.*;
4    /**
5     * Description: Example of the Collection view of a map.
6     */
7    public class CollectionMapViewEx {
8        public static void main(String[] args) {
9            HashMap map = new HashMap<String, String>();
10
11            map.put( new String( "Hound" ), new String( "Ginger" )  );
12            map.put( new String( "Dog" ), new String( "Blue" )  );
13            map.put( new String( "Cat" ), new String( "Pepper" ) );
14            map.put( new String( "Bird" ), new String( "Persian" ) );
15            map.put( new String( "Fish" ), new String( "Penny" ) );
16            map.put( new String( "Turtle" ), new String( "Tensy" ) );
17
18            System.out.println( "Here are the values from the map" +
19                                " that we can see in the collection." );
20            java.util.Collection<String> collection = map.values();
21            for ( String s : collection )
22                System.out.println( "pet is " + s );
23
24            System.out.println( "\nRemoving \"Penny\" from " +
25                                "the collection." );
26            collection.remove( new String( "Penny" ) );
27            System.out.println( "Is \"Penny\" still in the map? " +
28                                map.containsValue( "Penny" ) );
29            System.out.println( "\nDoes the collection contain " +
30                    "\"Albert\"? " + collection.contains( "Albert" ) );
31            System.out.println( "Adding (Snake, Albert) to the map.");
32            map.put( new String( "Snake" ), new String( "Albert" ) );
33            System.out.println( "Now does the collection contain " +
34                    "\"Albert\"? " + collection.contains( "Albert" ) );
35
36            collection.clear();
37            System.out.println( "\nMap's size after clearing through" +
38                                " the collection view is " + map.size() );
39        }
40    }
```

OUTPUT

```
Here are the values from the map that we can see in the collection.
pet is Pepper
pet is Persian
```

```
pet is Ginger
pet is Tensy
pet is Penny
pet is Blue

Removing "Penny" from the collection.
Is "Penny" still in the map? false

Does the collection contain "Albert"? false
Adding (Snake, Albert) to the map.
Now does the collection contain "Albert"? true

Map's size after clearing through the collection view is 0
```

Listing 12.2 The Map Interface.

```java
1    package gray.adts.map;
2
3    /**
4     * A Map associates keys with values in map entries. Given a key,
5     * the map produces the associated value. Duplicate keys are not
6     * allowed and a key can be associated with only a single value.
7     * However, duplicate values are allowed, so a value may be
8     * associated with multiple keys.
9     */
10   public interface Map<K, V> {
11
12       /**
13        * Removes all the entries from this map.
14        */
15       public void clear();
16
17       /**
18        * Determines if the map contains an entry containing
19        * <tt>key</tt>.
20        * @param key the key to search for in the map.
21        * @return <tt>true</tt> if <tt>key</tt> was not found
22        * in the map, <tt>false</tt> otherwise.
23        * @throws <tt>IllegalArgumentException</tt> if <tt>key</tt>
24        * is <tt>null</tt>.
25        */
26       public boolean containsKey( K key );
27
28       /**
29        * Determines if the map contains an entry containing
30        * <tt>value</tt>.
31        * @param value the value to search for in the map.
32        * @return <tt>true</tt> if <tt>value</tt> was not found
33        * in the map, <tt>false</tt> otherwise.
34        * @throws <tt>IllegalArgumentException</tt> if
```

```
35          * <tt>value</tt> is <tt>null</tt>.
36          */
37         public boolean containsValue( V value );
38
39          /**
40          * Gets the value associated with <tt>key</tt> from this map,
41          *  if it exists.
42          * @param key the key to use to search the map; cannot be
43          *  <tt>null</tt>.
44          * @return <tt>null</tt> if <tt>key</tt> was not found in the
45          * map; the value associated with <tt>key</tt> otherwise.
46          * @throws <tt>IllegalArgumentException</tt> if <tt>key</tt>
47          * is <tt>null</tt>.
48          */
49          public V get( K key );
50
51          /**
52          * Determine if this map is empty.
53          * @return <tt>true</tt> if there are no values in this map.
54          */
55         public boolean isEmpty();
56
57          /**
58          * Puts the (<tt>key</tt>, <tt>value</tt>) pair into this
59          * map. If an entry with this <tt>key</tt> already exists in
60          * the map, its <tt>value</tt> is replaced with the new
61          * <tt>value</tt> and the old <tt>value</tt> is returned.
62          * @param key the key for this map entry; cannot be
63          *  <tt>null</tt>.
64          * @param value the value for this map entry; cannot
65          *  be <tt>null</tt>.
66          * @return <tt>null</tt> if the <tt>key</tt> was not already.
67          * in the map; the old value associated with <tt>key</tt>
68          * otherwise.
69          * @throws <tt>IllegalArgumentException</tt> if <tt>key</tt>
70          * or <tt>value</tt> are <tt>null</tt>.
71          */
72         public V put( K key, V value );
73
74          /**
75          * Remove the element from this the map associated with
76          * <tt>key</tt>. If a <tt>value</tt> with this <tt>key</tt>
77          * exists in the map, it is returned, otherwise <tt>null</tt>
78          * is returned.
79          * @param key remove the entry identified by <tt>key</tt>;
80          * cannot be <tt>null</tt>.
81          * @return <tt>null</tt> if <tt>key</tt> was not found in the
82          * map, the <tt>value</tt> associated with <tt>key</tt>
83          * otherwise.
84          * @throws <tt>IllegalArgumentException</tt> if <tt>key</tt>
85          * is <tt>null</tt> or cannot be compared to other keys in
```

```
86              * the map.
87              */
88            public V remove( K key );
89
90              /**
91              * Return the number of entries in this map.
92              * @return the number of entries in this map.
93              */
94            public int size();
95
96              /**
97              * Provides a <tt>Collection</tt> view of all the values
98              * contained in this map.
99              * @return a <tt>Collection</tt> view of the values
100             * stored in this map.
101             */
102           public java.util.Collection<V> values();
103      }
```

Test Case 12.1 Verify `put()` for a unique key.

Method	Purpose	Object State	Expected Result
map.put (k, v)	To put the entry (k, v) into a map.	*size*: 1 *map*: (k, v)	null
map.size()	To verify that the entry has been added to the map.		1
map.get(k)	To verify the put() operation.		v
map.isEmpty()	To verify the put() operation.		false
map.containsKey(k)	To verify the put() operation.		true
map.containsValue(v)	To verify the put() operation.		true

- If we put a <key, value> pair in an empty map, then put in another pair using the same key but a different value, the original value should be returned. The specification for put() says that attribute size should only be increased if a new entry was put in the map. Also, attempts to see if the original value is still in the map should return false, while an attempt to see if the map contains the key and the new value should return true. These checks are shown in Test Case 12.2.

- A value can be associated with more than one key. In Test Case 12.3, two pairs that have the same value are put in the map. The map should regard these as separate entries, so attribute size should be 2. Contains operations should verify that the map contains the two keys and the value, and get() on the two keys should return equal values.

Test Case 12.2 Verify put() for a duplicate key.

Method	Purpose	Object State	Expected Result
map.put(k, v1)	To put entry (k, v1) into empty map.	*size*: 1 *map*: (k, v1)	null
map.put(k, v2)	To verify that key k exists in the map, and to replace its value with v2.	*size*: 1 *map*: (k, v2)	v1
map.size()	To verify that the replaced value doesn't affect the size attribute.		1
map.get(k)	To verify that v2 replaced v1 for key k.		v2
map.isEmpty()	To verify the put() operation.		false
map.containsKey(k)	To verify the put() operation.		true
map.containsValue(v1)	To verify that the previous value was replaced.		false
map.containsValue(v2)	To verify that the new value is in the table.		true

Test Case 12.3 Verify put() for duplicate values.

Method	Purpose	Object State	Expected Result
map.put(k1, v1)	To verify that no entry in the map has key k1, and to put entry (k1, v1) into the map.	*size*: 1 *map*: (k1, v1)	null
map.put(k2, v1)	To verify that no entry in the map has key k2, and to put entry (k2, v1) into the map.	*size*: 2 *map*: (k1, v1) (k2, v1)	null
map.size()	To verify that unique entries have been inserted.		2
map.containsKey(k1)	To verify the put() operation.		true
map.containsKey(k2)	To verify the put() operation.		true
map.containsValue(v1)	To verify that the common value is in the table.		true
Object o1 = map.get(k1)	To verify the value associated with k1.		v1
Object o2 = map.get(k2)	To verify the value associated with k2.		v1
o1.equals(o2)	To verify that both keys have the same value.		true

Testing the values() operation presents a new challenge. Briefly, we need to be sure that the values in the Collection view are all the values in the map and that any change to the map is reflected in the Collection view and vice versa. Here is an outline for `values()`, which is implemented in the JUnit test method in Listing 12.3.

A test plan for
Map.values()

1. As <key, value> pairs are put to the map, also add the value to a `Collection`, `expectedValues`.

2. All the values in `expectedValues` should be contained in the `Collection` view and vice versa.

3. Adding a <key, value> pair to the map should make the new value visible in the `Collection` view.

4. Removing a value from the `Collection` view should also remove the value and its associated value from the map.

5. Removing a value (via its key) from the map should also remove it from the `Collection` view.

Listing 12.3 A JUnit test method for `Map.values()`.

```
 1   public void testValues(){
 2       // Step 1: add elements - remember setUp() will have been called already
 3       map1.put( key5, value1 );
 4       map1.put( key10Duplicate, value2 );
 5       map1.put( key7, value5 );
 6       List<String> expectedValues = new ArrayList<String>();
 7       expectedValues.add( value0 );
 8       expectedValues.add( value1 );
 9       expectedValues.add( value2 );
10       expectedValues.add( value5 );
11
12       // Step 2: see if values() produces all values in the map
13       java.util.Collection<String> actualValues = map1.values();
14       assertTrue( actualValues.containsAll( expectedValues ) );
15
16       // Step 3: add a (key,value) pair to map; see if it is in the view
17       map1.put( key4, value7 );
18       assert( actualValues.contains( value7 ) );
19
20       // Step 4: remove a key from the view; see if it is still in the map
21       actualValues.remove( key10Duplicate );
22       assert( !map1.containsValue( value2 ) );
23
24       // Step 5: remove a key from the map; see if it is still in the view
25       map1.remove( key5 );
26       assert( !actualValues.contains( value1 ) );
27   }
```

SUMMING UP

A map associates values with keys and stores <key, value> pairs. These pairs are stored in no particular order. A value is retrieved by supplying the map with the corresponding key.

Variations on the map allow multiple values to be associated with a single key (multimap) and to retrieve the keys in a map in order (ordered map).

A `Collection` view allows a client to look at the values stored in a map from the perspective of a collection. The view is backed by the map, so any changes made to the view are reflected in the map, and any changes to the map are reflected in the view.

CHECKPOINT

12.1 Fill in the empty cells of the following table.

Method	Object State	Return Value
map.put(k1, n)		null
	size: 2 *map*: (k1, n), (k2, m)	null 1
map.containsKey(k2)		
map.get(k1)		n
	size: 2 *map*: (k1, p), (k2, m)	n
map.containsValue(n)		
	size: 1 *map*: (k2, m)	p
map.remove(k2)		
map.containsValue(m)		

■ **12.2** Hashing and Hash Tables

Indexed access in a collection is only fast when you know the index of your target. Without the index, you have to search, comparing elements from the collection against the target. If the collection is ordered with direct access, binary search will find the target in $O(\log_2 n)$ time. Similarly, for an ordered, hierarchical balanced collection such as an AVL tree, the result can be found in $O(\log_2 n)$ time.

It would be nice if we could do better, but this can only happen if we can somehow use the search key (the target) as an index into the collection to take us directly to the value. This idea is the basis for hashing.

A **hash table** is an indexable collection. Each position in the hash table is called a **bucket** and can hold one or more entries. A **hash function** converts an entry's key

Goal: improving on $O(\log_2 n)$ search time

Figure 12.4 Indexing into a hash table with a hash function.

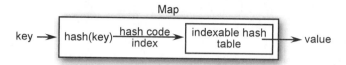

into an index that is used to access a bucket in the hash table. Figure 12.4 illustrates the role of the hash function for inserting an entry into a hash table and for finding it within the table.

Hashing idea: Use the key as an index into a table

If each key maps to a unique position in the hash table, then most hash table operations (insertion, removal, and retrieval) will have a run time of $O(1)$. Can't beat that! But to guarantee that each key hashes to a unique position in the hash table, the table would have to have as many buckets as there are possible keys. Since the range of keys may be quite large (think of nine-digit Social Security numbers, 10-digit telephone numbers, or seven-digit university ID numbers), this is usually not practical.

Instead, as we have done before, we work with an approximation to the ideal. The hash table will be a manageable size of m buckets (where m may be significantly smaller than the range of keys) and the hash function may hash more than one key to the same bucket. When this happens, we have a **collision**.

Collision—when two or more keys hash to (collide at) the same bucket

First, we look at strategies for dealing with collisions. Then we look at some representative hashing functions. After that we will be ready to look at a hash table implementation of the map ADT.

12.2.1 Collision Resolution Strategies

Collision resolution strategies are broadly grouped into open and closed addressing. The essential difference between them is in the capacity of the bucket. In **open addressing**, each bucket can contain only a single entry. Consequently, when a collision occurs, we must find a bucket at another position in the table to store the entry. With open addressing, then, we "open up" the table and allow the entry to be stored in a bucket *other than* the one to which it originally hashed (its primary hash index). We will look at one simple open addressing collision strategy called **linear probing** (also called **open linear addressing**).

Open addressing: one key for multiple buckets

In contrast, in **closed addressing**, an entry *must* be stored at the position (bucket) to which it originally hashed. The strategy here is to allow the bucket capacity to be greater than 1. In other words, each bucket is itself a collection (hopefully small). We will look at a widely used closed address strategy called **chaining**.

Closed addressing: one key for one bucket

12.2.2 Open Addressing: Linear Probing

When a collision occurs at position i and a different bucket must be found, a very simple approach is to try the position at $(i + 1)$. This is called **linear probing** because it results in walking through the table position by position, wrapping around to the first position when we hit the end of the table.

Inserting entries using linear probing

While the idea is simple, it has some complicated side effects. Let's start by looking at how linear probing works for the insertion and retrieval operations.

For simplicity's sake, we use a very naïve hash function that takes a person's name (the key) as an argument and uses the first letter of the name to generate an index. So "Alan" hashes to 0, "Boris" to 1, "Carol" to 2, and so on. Here is the sequence of operations to insert entries into the hash table:

1. We start with an empty table into which we insert("Bill"), which hashes to location 1—as shown in Figure 12.5 (a).

2. Then we insert("Boris")—see Figure 12.5 (b). Since "Boris" hashes to the same location as "Bill", we have a collision. With linear probing we simply move to the next bucket to see if it is free. Since position 2 is free, "Boris" is inserted there.

3. Now we insert("Bing"). The primary hash position for "Bing", 1, is occupied, as is the next bucket, so "Bing" is put in position 3—see Figure 12.5 (c).

Clustering occurs when several adjacent buckets are filled. In particular, the phenomenon here is known as **primary clustering**, which occurs when several keys hash to the *same* position and end up occupying adjacent buckets. Primary clustering

Now when we insert("Carol") and insert("Dora"), we get the situation in Figure 12.5 (d). Although "Carol" is the first key to hash *directly* to position 2, we are forced to move down to position 4 before we find a free bucket. Similarly, "Dora" is the first key to hash *directly* to position 3, but because of earlier collisions, "Dora" is placed in position 5.

This is called **secondary clustering** and occurs when a key collides with other keys that have spilled over from collisions at their primary hash positions. What makes clustering even worse is that anytime you insert a new entry and hash into a cluster, you will make that cluster larger by one. Secondary clustering

Clusters are self-aggravating

Now let's look at how a search would proceed. We'll look at both successful and unsuccessful searches. The approach is almost identical to that for inserting a new

Figure 12.5 Resolving collisions with linear probing.

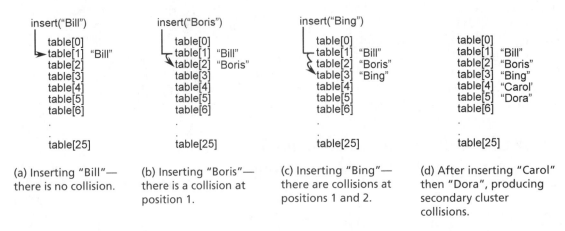

(a) Inserting "Bill"— there is no collision.

(b) Inserting "Boris"— there is a collision at position 1.

(c) Inserting "Bing"— there are collisions at positions 1 and 2.

(d) After inserting "Carol" then "Dora", producing secondary cluster collisions.

entry: Hash to the primary location and probe until either a match is found (success), an empty bucket is discovered (failure), or all buckets have been examined with no match (failure).

1. If we were looking for "Bill" (the target), we would hash to position 1, do a comparison of our target against the entry stored at that position, and get a match.

2. If we are looking for "Bing", again we would hash to position 1 (Bill's primary hash index), but this time the comparison would not find a match because "Bing" ≠ "Bill". Using linear probing we would try the entry stored in position 2. This too would fail ("Bing" ≠ "Boris"), so we would try position 3, where we would get a match. See Figure 12.6 (a).

3. If the target is "James", we hash to position 9 and find it empty, so we know "James" is not in the table and would return failure quickly.

4. Lastly, if the target is "Betsy", we hash to position 1, where we don't get a match. In this case, linear probing will walk us along doing (failed) comparisons at each position until we get to position 6, which is empty, so we return failure (the target was not found). See Figure 12.6 (b).

Before moving on, if you look at the description of insertions and failed searches, you will see that the sequence of probes is identical. For example, if we were to now insert "Betsy", we would examine exactly the same positions as we did in the failed search above.

The details are saved for later, but clearly clustering affects the performance of insertions and searches. Clusters also complicate deletions. The problem is that linear probing relies on the elements of the cluster being continuous from the cluster's entry point (the position of the first entry in the cluster) to the last element in the cluster. There are two cases to worry about.

Case 1: If the first element in the cluster is removed, the cluster's entry point is lost. For example (look at Figure 12.5 again):

1. "Bill" is removed from the table and position 1 is made empty.

2. A search for "Boris" hashes to position 1. Since 1 is empty, we conclude that "Boris" is not in the table and mistakenly return failure.

Figure 12.6 Searching a hash table using linear probing.

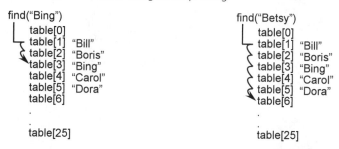

(a) Finding "Bing" requires three probes before succeeding.

(b) Finding "Betsy" requires six probes before failing.

Case 2: If an element in the cluster's interior is removed, the cluster is split in two and continuity is lost. For example:

1. "Bing" is removed from the table and position 3 is made empty.

2. A search for "Carol" hashes to position 2. Since "Carol" ≠ "Boris", we probe at position 3. Since position 3 is empty, we conclude that "Carol" is not in the table and mistakenly return failure. See Figure 12.7 (a).

The solution is to maintain the continuity of the cluster by replacing a removed entry with a bridge. An insertion can replace a bridge with a new element. A search simply crosses the bridge to get to the rest of the cluster and resume the probe, as shown in Figure 12.7 (b).

> Solution: Removed entries are replaced by a bridge that maintains the continuity of the cluster

Analysis of Linear Probing

Before looking at chaining, we should consider the time complexity of linear probing. As the examples we walked through might have suggested to you, the cost of hash operations is dependent on how full the table is. The **load factor, λ,** of a hash table is the number of entries the table stores divided by the number of buckets in the table.

> Load factor:
> $\lambda = n / m$, where:
> n is the number of entries in the table
> m is the number of buckets in the table

Since all operations depend on the cost of searching, we will focus on that. As the description of the search operation suggests, the cost of an unsuccessful search is different from that for a successful search. What the equations below make clear is that the cost is dependent on the load factor.

$$U_n \approx \frac{1}{2}\left(1 + \frac{1}{(1-\lambda)^2}\right) \qquad \text{Unsuccessful search}$$

$$S_n \approx \frac{1}{2}\left(1 + \frac{1}{1-\lambda}\right) \qquad \text{Successful search}$$

Figure 12.7 Using a bridge to fill the gap in a cluster created when an entry is removed.

(a) With "Bing" deleted, there is a gap at position 3, so a probe beginning in position 2 fails when it encounters the gap.

(b) With a bridge in the place "Bing" occupied, the probe correctly advances to position 4.

With open addressing, λ cannot exceed 1. In fact, once λ reaches about .70, the table should be resized. This means creating a larger table (typically twice the size of the old table) and rehashing all the elements from the old table into the new, larger table.

12.2.3 Closed Addressing: Chaining

With closed addressing, we allow each bucket to store more than one entry. In chaining, the entries that hash to a bucket are chained together. Figure 12.8 shows what the entries from Figure 12.5 look like under chaining. From the figure you can see that the problem of secondary clustering is completely eliminated—collisions at a bucket have no affect on other buckets. Primary clustering can still pose a problem, which emphasizes the importance of having a hash function that uniformly distributes the keys over the table's index range.

Insertion is an O(1) operation if we hash to a bucket and make the entry the first link in the chain. However, looking ahead to when we will use a hash table to implement a map, we see that an insertion must be preceded by a search operation since we need to ensure that there are no duplicate keys.

If the entries on a chain are kept in ascending order by key, we can shorten the average search time for an entry on a chain. It could be argued that since we expect the chains to be short, it isn't worth the effort to keep them ordered. However, the need to do a search to check for a duplicate key during insertions hides the additional cost of determining where a new entry would be inserted in the chain.

Deletion requires a search followed by an unlinking of the entry. The cost of unlinking, like that of linking, is O(1), so it is the search time that also dominates the cost of deletion.

Analysis of Chaining

With chaining, the cost of an access depends on the length of a bucket's chain. In the worst case, all n keys in the table hash to the same bucket, giving an O(n) access time. If the keys are distributed evenly over the table, intuitively we expect the length of a chain to be the number of keys divided by the number of buckets, which is $\lambda = n/m$. For an unsuccessful search, all keys on a chain must be examined, so the number of comparisons for an unsuccessful search is λ. For a successful search, on

---

Figure 12.8 Hashing using chaining.

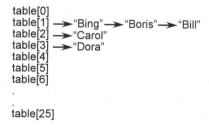

```
table[0]
table[1] ──▶ "Bing" ──▶ "Boris" ──▶ "Bill"
table[2] ──▶ "Carol"
table[3] ──▶ "Dora"
table[4]
table[5]
table[6]
    ·
    ·
table[25]
```

average we expect to look at half the keys on a bucket's chain, requiring $1 + \lambda/2$ comparisons.

$$U_n = \lambda \qquad \qquad \text{Unsuccessful search}$$

$$S_n = 1 + \frac{\lambda}{2} \qquad \qquad \text{Successful search}$$

Lastly, note that with open addressing $\lambda \leq 1$, but with closed addressing, λ can be greater than 1.

CHECKPOINT

12.2 Assuming a table with 26 buckets, the simple first-letter hashing scheme used in this section, and linear probing, show the hash table after the following operations:

```
insert( "John" )
insert( "Kevin" )
insert( "Mosan" )
insert( "Kia" )
insert( "Joe" )
remove( "Kia" )
insert( "Jackie" )
```

12.3 Repeat Problem 12.2 for chaining.

12.2.4 Hashing Functions

A hash function has three important requirements:

Hash function requirements

1. Deterministic—A hash function must always produce the same hash value each time it is given the same key.

2. Efficient—Every access to the table requires hashing a key, so it is important to the table's performance that the hash value be simple to compute.

3. Uniform—The treasured $O(1)$ access time is only realized if the hash function distributes the keys uniformly over the hash table. A poor hash function will promote clustering, which hurts performance.

Converting a String into an Integer

Unfortunately, not all keys are of an integer type that is easily converted into a value suitable for indexing into an array. Strings are a good example of a common non-integer key and provide a convenient way to introduce the problems inherent in producing good hash values.

A very simple method to convert a string to an integer is to sum the integer values of the characters in the string. Unfortunately, this approach has several drawbacks. First, unless the table is small or the string quite long, the sums will tend to

Idea: Just sum the integer values of the characters

cluster at the lower end of the table's index range. Second, because addition is commutative, all permutations of a string will hash to the same value. For example, "abc", "bca", "cab", "cba", "bac", and "acb" will all hash to 294 (as will a number of other character combinations).

One solution to this problem is to treat each character as a digit in a base the size of the character set. ASCII characters require seven bits ($2^7 = 128$), so we could convert each ASCII character to its integer equivalent and treat it as a base-128 digit. As an example, "Java" would become

> **Idea:** Treat the characters as digits in base 128

$$\begin{matrix} J & a & v & a \\ 74 * 128^3 + & 97 * 128^2 + & 118 * 128^1 + & 97 * 128^0 \end{matrix}$$

Since 128 is a power of 2, the powering and multiplication can be done very efficiently using shifting. Using J as an example

$$74 * 128^3 = 74 * (2^7)^3 = 74 * 2^{21} = 74 << 21$$

That is good news, but if you ponder this for a moment, you will see a problem. Assuming we are dealing with 32-bit unsigned integers, if the string is longer than five characters ($2^5 = 32$), the bits representing the characters from the sixth position on will be shifted off the left end of the result, so will play no role in determining the hash value. Hmm . . . not so good.

$$Char_5 * 128^4 = Char_5 * (2^7)^4 = * 2^{28} = Char_5 << 28$$
$$Char_6 * 128^5 = Char_6 * (2^7)^5 = * 2^{35} = Char_6 << 35$$

The obvious solution to this problem is to multiply the integer value of each character by a smaller prime number raised to the power of the character's position. Java uses 31, giving us

> **Java uses "base" 31**

$$\begin{matrix} J & a & v & a \\ 74 * 31^3 + & 97 * 31^2 + & 118 * 31^1 + & 97 * 31^0 \end{matrix}$$

The bad news is that 31 is not a power of 2, so our shifting trick won't work here. But all is not lost: The exercises suggest an improvement.

Mid-square Hash Technique

In the mid-square approach, the key is first converted into an integer, then squared. The index is formed from a group of b bits from the middle of the resulting integer such that $2^b = m$, the number of buckets in the table (see Figure 12.9).

Figure 12.9 Selecting b bits as the hash value from the interior of an integer.

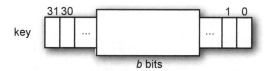

Folding Hash Technique

The key is broken up into same-sized groups. These groups are then folded together using addition, multiplication, or a logical operator (AND, OR, or XOR). Here is a simple example[1] for the string "Winchester" with three-character groupings and each character treated as a base 256 (Extended-ASCII) integer.

Step 1: Fold					Step 2: Convert back to base 10:
		1	1		$1 * 256^3 + 46 * 256^2 +$
Win		87	105	110	$70 * 256^1 + 270 = 19{,}810{,}062$
che	+	99	104	101	
ste	+	115	116	101	
r	+	0	0	114	
		1 46	70	170	
		(base 256)			

Hashing for a Collection

Providing a hash value for a collection is a little different from providing a hash value for an individual element. The problem rests with the notion of equality. Recall that the contracts for `Object.equals()` and `Object.hashCode()` say that if two objects are considered equal, they should produce the same hash code. We have seen that the comparisons produced by `Comparable` and `Comparator` should also be consistent with `equals()` and `hashCode()`.

The problem is, when are two collections equal? Is it when they store the same elements, or when they store the same elements with the same internal structure? Generally we want to leave structure out of it and only consider the elements in the collection. This suggests that an iteration over the collection's elements that sums their individual hash values should be sufficient. However, they must be the same *kind* of collection. Would we want to say that a list and an AVL tree that store the same elements are equal?

When are two collections equal?

Hashing in Java

In Java, each object is responsible for generating its own hash value. The `hashCode()` method defined in `Object` meets this need. Subclasses are expected to override the method to provide a type-appropriate implementation.

There are two remaining issues. First, `hashCode()` may produce a negative integer (as a result of overflow), which, of course, is no good for indexing into an array. Second, since an object does not know the size of the hash table, it cannot guarantee that the value its `hashCode()` method returns is within the table's index range. The hash table can handle both of these problems easily by checking for negative results and dividing the hash value by the capacity of the table and taking the remainder:

```
hashIndex = someObject.hashCode();
if ( hashIndex < 0 )
    hashIndex = -hashIndex;
hashIndex = hashIndex % tableCapacity;
```

---

[1]Note that this is a variation on the idea of summing the integer values of each of the string's characters.

Here is how some common Java classes generate a hash value:

- `Character`—the character's underlying integer representation
- `Float`—the bits that represent the floating-point number interpreted as an integer
- `Integer`—the `Integer`'s int value
- `String`—folding; the sum of the int values of each character in the `String` multiplied by 31, raised to the power of the character's position in the `String`
- `ArrayList`—folding; the sum of the hash values of each element in the `List` multiplied by 31 raised to power of the element's position in the `List`

SUMMING UP

A **hash table** is an indexable collection. Each position in the hash table is called a **bucket** and can hold one or more entries. A **hash function** converts (hashes) an entry's key into an integer index that is used to access a bucket in the hash table. The goal of hashing is to provide O(1) access time by converting a key into an index where the associated value is stored.

A **collision** occurs when more than one key hashes to the same bucket. Two popular collision resolution strategies are **open addressing using linear probing** and **closed addressing using chaining**. In open addressing, each bucket can contain only a single entry, so collisions are resolved by finding a bucket at another position in the table to store the entry. In **closed addressing**, an entry *must* be stored at the position to which it originally hashed, so collisions are resolved by allowing the bucket capacity to be greater than 1. In chaining the entries for a bucket are chained together.

The **load factor**, λ, of a hash table is the number of entries the table stores divided by the number of buckets in the table. The load factor impacts hash table performance; as the load factor goes up, performance goes down.

Hash functions must be deterministic, efficient to compute, and uniformly distribute the keys over the table.

CHECKPOINT

12.4 What is the load factor for a table with 117 buckets and 62 entries?

12.5 What is the hash value for "Mississippi" using folding?

12.6 What hash value would Java compute for "Blog"?

12.7 Why does a hash function have to be deterministic?

◼ 12.3 `HashMap`: A Hash Table Implementation of Map

A hash table implementation of a map will provide O(1) access time for key-based searching (assuming we have a uniform hashing function). Here we look at the more interesting aspects of the implementation, which are presented as a series of tasks.

12.3.1 `HashMap` Task 1: Representing an Entry in a Map with `Entry` and `LinkEntry`

A <key, value> pair is stored in an `Entry` class (see Listing 12.4). Since a client may want to store an instance of a map to a file using serialization (as we will do with customer information in the pizza delivery problem in the Focus on Problem Solving Section on the Web.), `Entry` must implement the `Serializable` interface. Recall that this is a marker interface. It specifies no methods; only that instances of `Entry` can be serialized using `ObjectOutputStream.writeObject()`. The *key* and the *value* attributes are stored and have accessor methods. There is a mutator method for the *value* attribute, but none for the *key* attribute. Why not?

Since our implementation will use a chained hash table to store the entries, we extend `Entry` to include the necessary link fields. This is done in class `LinkEntry`, which must also implement `Serializable` (see Listing 12.5). The chains are implemented as a singly linked list of `LinkEntrys`.

An entry in a bucket's chain.

Listing 12.4 The `Entry` class.

```
1    package gray.adts.map;
2
3    public class Entry<K, V> implements java.io.Serializable {
4        private K key;
5        private V value;
6
7        public Entry(){
8            key = null;
9            value = null;
10       }
11
12       /**
13        * Create an entry for key <tt>k</tt> and value <tt>v</tt>.
14        * @param k the key for this entry
15        * @param v the value associated with key <tt>k</tt>
16        *     for this entry
17        * @throws <IllegalArgumentException> if either <tt>k</tt> or
18        *     <tt>v</tt> is <tt>null</tt>
19        */
```

```
20          public Entry( K k, V v ) {
21              if ( ( k == null ) || ( v == null ) )
22                  throw new IllegalArgumentException( "null argument" );
23              this.key = k;
24              this.value = v;
25          }
26
27          /**
28           * Return the <tt>key</tt> for this entry.
29           * @return the <tt>key</tt> for this entry
30           */
31          public K key(){
32              return this.key;
33          }
34
35          /**
36           * Return the <tt>value</tt> for this entry.
37           * @return the <tt>value</tt> for this entry
38           */
39          public V value(){
40              return this.value;
41          }
42
43          /**
44           * Set the <tt>value</tt> field for this entry to
45           *    <tt>newValue</tt>.
46           * @param newValue the new value for this entry
47           * @return the old <tt>value</tt> for this entry
48           */
49          public V setValue( V newValue ){
50              if ( newValue == null )
51                  throw new IllegalArgumentException( "null argument" );
52              V tempValue = this.value;
53              this.value = newValue;
54              return tempValue;
55          }
56
57          /**
58           * Overridden method from <tt>Object</Code>.
59           * @return <tt>String</tt> representation of this entry.
60           */
61          public String toString(){
62              return "Key: " + this.key + "\nValue: " + this.value ;
63          }
64  }
```

Listing 12.5 The LinkEntry class.

```
1    package gray.adts.map;
2
3    /**
4     *  A linked-list implementation of the <tt>Entry</tt>
5     *  class used to create a chained hash table.
6     */
7    public class LinkEntry<K, V> extends Entry<K, V>
8                          implements java.io.Serializable {
9
10       private LinkEntry<K, V> successor;
11
12       /**
13        * Create an entry for key <tt>k</tt> and value <tt>v</tt>.
14        * @param k the key for this entry
15        * @param v the value associated with key <tt>k</tt>
16        *      for this entry
17        * @param n the link to the successor entry in this chain
18        * @throws <IllegalArgumentException> if either <tt>k</tt> or
19        *      <tt>v</tt> is <tt>null</tt>
20        */
21       public LinkEntry( K k, V v, LinkEntry<K, V> n ) {
22           super( k, v );
23           this.successor = n;
24       }
25
26       /**
27        * Return a reference to the successor to this link entry.
28        * @return the successor to this link entry
29        */
30        public LinkEntry<K, V> successor(){
31           return this.successor;
32        }
33
34       /**
35        * Reset the successor to this entry in the chain.
36        * @param newSuccessor the new link to the successor entry
37        *   in this chain
38        */
39       public void setNext( LinkEntry<K, V> newSuccessor ){
40            this.successor = newSuccessor;
41       }
42    }
```

12.3.2 `HashMap` Task 2: Identify `HashMap` Data Fields

Listing 12.6 shows the data fields needed for the implementation. The fields are well commented, so there are only a few remarks.

▪ Fields marked `transient` won't be serialized.

▪ `MAX_LOAD_FACTOR` is the maximum load factor the table can support before performance really degrades and the table is resized.

▪ The first time `values()` is called, a `Collection` object will be created for that view and returned to the caller. Since the `Collection` is backed by the map, subsequent calls to `values()` will return the existing `Collection` view. That is, we don't create a new `Collection` view for *each* call. This will become clearer once you have looked at Task 5.

▪ The iterator constants are used to identify the kind of iterator that is created. This is presented in Task 6, but the basic idea is that we can implement a single iterator that can be configured at the time of instantiation to return different kinds of map entities.

Listing 12.6 Data fields for `HashMap`.

```
 1   package gray.adts.map;
 2
 3   import java.util.Collection;
 4   import java.util.ConcurrentModificationException;
 5   /**
 6    * Hash table implementation of the <tt>Map</tt> interface. This
 7    * implementation does not allow either the key or the value to
 8    * be <tt>null</tt>.
 9    */
10   public class HashMap<K, V>
11                         implements Map<K, V>, java.io.Serializable {
12
13       /**
14        * Fields used to determine the type of iterator created.
15        * Depending on the type, an iterator will return an entry,
16        * an entry's key or an entry's value.
17        */
18       private static final int KEY_ITERATOR   = 0;
19       private static final int VALUE_ITERATOR = 1;
20       private static final int ENTRY_ITERATOR = 2;
21
22       /**
23        * The default capacity of the table. To facilitate uniform
24        * distribution of keys over the table, capacity should be
```

```
25          * a prime number.
26          */
27         private static final transient int DEFAULT_CAPACITY = 11;
28
29         /**
30          * The maximum load factor the table will sustain before
31          * resizing.
32          */
33         private static final transient float MAX_LOAD_FACTOR = .70f;
34
35         /**
36          * The hash table.
37          */
38         private LinkEntry<K, V> table[];
39
40         /**
41          * The actual number of buckets in this hash table. This value
42          * will change over time if the table is resized.
43          */
44         private int capacity;
45
46         /**
47          * The number of entries stored in this hash table.
48          */
49         private int size;
50
51         /**
52          * This is the <tt>Collection</tt> view of this map.
53          */
54         private Collection<V> collectionView = null;
55
56         /**
57          * The number of add and remove operations performed on this
58          * collection. This information is used by the iterator to
59          * provide a fail-fast iterator. Any operation that changes the
60          * size of this collection should add 1 to <tt>modcount</tt>
61          * for <it>each</it> change made.
62          */
63         protected transient int modCount;
```

12.3.3 HashMap Task 3: HashMap.put()— Inserting an Entry into the Map

The put() method takes a <key, value> pair as an argument, creates a LinkEntry object to store them, and puts the LinkEntry in the map.

If the hash table's load factor has exceeded the threshold MAX_LOAD_FACTOR (lines 20–21 in Listing 12.7), the hash table has to be resized before the new entry can be inserted.

Utility method getHashIndex()(defined on lines 62–75) is called on line 27 and is responsible for getting an index for the key that is within the index range of the hash table.

Since duplicates keys are not allowed, put() needs to make sure there is no entry in the map with the given key. We could use Map.get() or Map.containsKey() to see if the key is already in the map, but the contract for put() says that if the key is already in the map, the value currently in the map is replaced by the new value, so it isn't enough to know *if* the key is in the table; we also need to know *where* it is.

Utility method find() (defined on lines 47–60) is called on line 28 and does this for us. Given a bucket, it simply walks down the bucket's chain, looking for a match for its key argument. If it finds one, it returns the entry. If find() gets to the end of the chain without finding a match, it returns null, indicating failure. The

---

Listing 12.7 The HashMap.put() method (with utility methods find() and getHashIndex()).

```
 1      /**
 2       * Puts the (<tt>key</tt>, <tt>value</tt>) pair into this
 3       * map. If an entry with this <tt>key</tt> already exists in
 4       * the map, its <tt>value</tt> is replaced with the new
 5       * <tt>value</tt> and the old <tt>value</tt> is returned.
 6       * @param key the key for this map entry; cannot be
 7       *    <tt>null</tt>.
 8       * @param value the value for this map entry; cannot
 9       *    be <tt>null</tt>.
10       * @return <tt>null</tt> if the <tt>key</tt> was not already
11       *    in the map, the old value associated with <tt>key</tt>
12       *    otherwise.
13       * @throws <tt>IllegalArgumentException</tt> if <tt>key</tt>
14       *    or <tt>value</tt> are <tt>null</tt>.
15       */
16      public V put( K key, V value ) {
17          if ( ( key == null ) || ( value == null ) )
18              throw new IllegalArgumentException( "null argument" );
19
20          if ( ( (float) this.size / this.capacity ) >=
21                  this.MAX_LOAD_FACTOR ) {
22              this.resize();
23          }
24
25          this.modCount++;
26
27          int hashIndex = getHashIndex( key );
```

```
28            LinkEntry<K, V> entry = find( this.table[hashIndex], key );
29
30            // if we hit the end of the chain, the key isn't already
31            // in the table, so put this new entry at the head of
32            // the chain
33            if ( entry == null ) {
34                entry = new LinkEntry<K, V>( key, value,
35                                                 this.table[hashIndex] );
36                this.table[hashIndex] = entry;
37                this.size++;
38                return null;
39            }
40            else { // key is in the table, so replace its value field
41                V tempValue = entry.value();
42                entry.setValue( value );
43                return tempValue;
44            }
45        }
46
47        /**
48         * Utility method to locate an entry in the hash table.
49         * @param current the entry point to a hash chain
50         * @param targetKey the key we are search for
51         * @return null if the key was not found, a reference to its
52         * entry otherwise
53         */
54        private LinkEntry<K, V> find( LinkEntry<K, V> current,
55                                          K targetKey )  {
56            while ( ( current != null ) &&
57                    ( !current.key().equals( targetKey ) ) )
58                current = current.successor();
59            return current;
60        }
61
62        /**
63         * Compute a hash index for <tt>key</tt> in the range 0 to
64         *   <tt>this.capacity - 1</tt>
65         * @param <tt>key</Code> the key for which we want a hash
66         * index - cannot be null (not checked)
67         * @return an integer in the range 0 to this.capacity - 1
68         */
69        private int getHashIndex( K key ){
70            int hashIndex = key.hashCode();
71            if ( hashIndex < 0 )
72                hashIndex = -hashIndex;
73            hashIndex = hashIndex % this.capacity;   // get it in range
74            return hashIndex;
75        }
```

implementation shown in Listing 12.7 makes the new entry the head of the bucket's chain (lines 33–39). Observe that in put() we only increment attribute size (line 37) if the entry is new to the map.

12.3.4 HashMap Task 4: `HashMap.containsKey()` and `HashMap.containsValue()`

Since a map is a key-based collection, the method containsKey() is straightforward. You just hash on the key to get to a bucket and then use the utility method find() to search the bucket. Simple.

Because a map is a key-based collection there is no *direct* way to access the map (the hash table) given a value. Instead, we are forced to look through the hash table bucket by bucket. It would be really convenient if we had an iterator that would help us walk through the map. It turns out that values() will need an iterator as well, so we will assume the existence of a HashTableItererator class and use it (we'll develop the iterator in Task 6).

The body of Listing 12.8 should look familiar. It uses an Iterator to iterate over the collection looking for a match for target.

12.3.5 HashMap Task 5: `HashMap.values()`— Providing a `Collection` View of the Values Stored in a Map

Recall that values() provides a Collection view of the values in a map; that is, it returns a Collection that is backed by the map such that changes made to the map

---

Listing 12.8 The `HashMap.containsValue()` method.

```
 1   /**
 2    * Determines if the map contains an entry containing
 3    * <tt>value</tt>.
 4    * @param value the value to search for in the map.
 5    * @return true if <tt>value</tt> was not found in the map,
 6    *   false otherwise
 7    * @throws <tt>IllegalArgumentException</tt> if <tt>value</tt>
 8    *   is <tt>null</tt>
 9    */
10   public boolean containsValue( V target ) {
11       java.util.Iterator iter =
12                   new HashTableIterator( VALUE_ITERATOR );
13       while ( iter.hasNext() ) {
14           V value = (V)iter.next();
15           if ( value.equals( target ) )
16               return true;
17       }
18       return false;
19   }
```

are reflected in the `Collection` and vice versa. How do you create a `Collection` that uses the map as the backing store? The answer is pretty cool and uses quite a bit of the material we looked at way back in Chapters 4 (`AbstractCollection`) and 5 (sublists).

What we do is create and return an anonymous class that extends `AbstractCollection`. Recall that only four methods from `AbstractCollection` are abstract: `clear()`, `contains()`, `size()`, and `iterator()`. The implementation of the first three is simply forwarded to the corresponding map methods and the result returned. The `iterator()` method just creates and returns an instance of `HashMapIterator` configured to return values (we look at this in the next task).

Now, you might be wondering how it is possible to remove elements from the map by calls on the collection. This is another cool part of the implementation of `AbstractCollection`. The `AbstractCollection` methods that can remove elements (`remove()`, `removeAll()`, `retainAll()`) do so through an iterator! As an example, Listing 12.10 shows the `AbstractCollection.remove()` method. When the iterator on line 15 in Listing 12.9 is created, it is actually an instance of `HashMapIterator` that is instantiated, so when `e.remove()` is called on lines 7 and 14 of Listing 12.10, it is `HashMapIterator.remove()` that is invoked. In fact, all the methods in `AbstractCollection` that access elements in the collection do so through an iterator. Since that iterator is an instance of `HashMapIterator`, the collection is actually accessing the entries stored in the map. That is how the map can be the backing store for the `Collection` and changes to one affect the other. Pretty cool!

Listing 12.9 The `Map.values()` method returns an anonymous instance of a class that extends `AbstractCollection`.

```
1    /**
2     * Provides a <tt>Collection</tt> view of all the values
3     *   contained in this map.
4     * @return a <tt>Collection</tt> containing all the entries
5     * from this map.
6     */
7    public Collection<V> values() {
8        // if there is already a Collection object for this map,
9        // return it
10       if ( collectionView == null ) {
11           // otherwise, create one ...
12           collectionView = new java.util.AbstractCollection<V>(){
13               // ... and fill in the missing (abstract) methods
14               public java.util.Iterator iterator() {
15                   return new HashTableIterator( VALUE_ITERATOR );
16               }
17
18               public int size() {
19                   return HashMap.this.size();
```

```
20                    }
21
22                    public boolean contains( Object target ) {
23                        return containsValue( (V)target );
24                    }
25
26                    public void clear() {
27                        HashMap.this.clear();
28                    }
29                };
30            }
31        return collectionView;
32    }
```

Listing 12.10 The `AbstractCollection.remove()` method uses the `remove()` method from its iterator.

```
1    // this method is from java.util.AbstractCollection
2    public boolean remove( Object o ) {
3        Iterator<E> e = iterator();
4        if (o == null) {
5            while ( e.hasNext() ) {
6                if ( e.next() == null ) {
7                    e.remove();
8                    return true;
9                }
10           }
11       } else {
12           while ( e.hasNext() ) {
13               if ( o.equals( e.next() ) ) {
14                   e.remove();
15                   return true;
16               }
17           }
18       }
19       return false;
20   }
```

12.3.6 HashMap Task 6: `HashMapIterator`—Providing an Iterator That Can Return Values, Keys, or Entries

What is special about `HashMapIterator` is that there is the need to iterate over the map from three perspectives: values, keys, and entries. We don't want to make three iterators, so what do we do? Fortunately, two aspects of iterating over a map work in our favor:

■ Independently of what we want to return (values, keys, or entries), an iterator must still walk through the map *entry by entry*.

■ What gets returned by an iterator can be isolated within the next() method, since it is that method that is responsible for returning an object reference to the caller.

The idea is simple. When an iterator is created, an argument to the constructor specifies what type of iterator is wanted: value, key, or entry. You have already seen this in the implementation of some of the map methods. Then, as each entry is grabbed by next(), we return the entry, the entry's value field, or the entry's key field, depending on the iterator's type. That's it!

The other aspect of the iterator that requires some thought is determining whether next() or hasNext() has the responsibility of advancing cursor (the iterator's reference to the next entry to be visited in the iteration) to the next entry to visit. This is a nice example of two methods dividing the labor and coordinating their activities.

In Listing 12.11, I chose to put the complexity in hasNext(). It is responsible for advancing cursor to the next entry to return. If it finds such an entry, hasNext() returns true; otherwise it returns false. Note that advancing cursor may mean moving down the array to a nonempty bucket or down a chain within a bucket.

The next() method (lines 100–120) is fairly simple. After checking to make sure that a call to next() is valid, the next() method updates some iterator attributes, then returns either a value, a key, or an entry, depending on the iterator's type (lines 111–118).

Much of the rest of the implementation is devoted to checking for concurrent modification using the approach we have taken before, and making sure that all calls to the iterator's remove() method have been preceded by a call to next() (lines 107 and 140 to 141).

Listing 12.11 The HashMapIterator class.

```
 1   /**
 2    * This iterator is used as a utility in support of the
 3    * containsValue() and values() methods. It returns Entries,
 4    * leaving it to the caller to extract the fields needed.
 5    */
 6   private class HashTableIterator
 7                       implements java.util.Iterator {
 8       /**
 9        * The bucket number of the current chain being
10        * iterated over.
11        */
12       private int bucket;
13
14       /**
15        * Reference to the entry to be returned by the next call
```

```
16          * to next(); next() makes cursor null when the entry has
17          * been iterated over and hasNext() advances it to the
18          * next entry to be returned.
19          */
20         private LinkEntry<K, V> cursor;
21
22         /**
23          * Reference to the last entry returned by next(). Use
24          * this to advance through the chain for the bucket at
25          * table[bucket].
26          */
27         private LinkEntry<K, V> last;
28
29         /**
30          * Provides fail-fast operation of the iterator. For each
31          * call to an iterator method, expectedModcount should be
32          * equal to the collection's modCount, otherwise an
33          * intervening change (concurrent modification) to the
34          * collection has been made and we cannot guarantee that
35          * the iterator will behave correctly.
36          */
37         private int expectedModcount;
38
39         /**
40          * The contract of remove() says that each call to remove()
41          * must have been preceded by a call to next() (they are
42          * paired). So if there has been NO call to next() prior to
43          * a remove() or if there were two remove() calls without
44          * an intervening next() call, it is NOT ok to try to
45          * remove an item.
46          */
47         private boolean okToRemove;
48
49         /**
50          * The iterator type determines what kind of iterator
51          * this is, which determines what is returned by next():
52          *  a key, a value or an entry.
53          */
54         private int iteratorType;
55
56         public HashTableIterator( int theType ){
57             iteratorType = theType;
58             bucket = -1;
59             cursor = last = null;
60             expectedModcount = modCount;
61             okToRemove = false;
62         }
```

```
63
64        public boolean hasNext() {
65            // check for concurrent modification
66            if ( expectedModcount != modCount )
67                throw new ConcurrentModificationException();
68
69            if ( bucket == capacity )
70                return false;
71
72            // see if client has consumed last entry found by
73            // hasNext()
74            if ( cursor != null )
75                return true;
76
77            // see if there are more entries in the current chain
78            if ( last != null ) {
79                // get to next entry in the chain, if it exists
80                cursor = last.next();
81                if ( cursor != null )   // got an entry
82                    return true;
83                else    // exhausted this chain; advance in table
84                    last = null;
85            }
86
87            // exhausted the last chain, advance to the next
88            // non-empty bucket
89            bucket++;
90            while (( bucket < capacity ) && ( table[bucket] == null ))
91                    bucket++;
92            if ( bucket >= capacity )
93                return false;
94            // at least one more entry to return
95            cursor = table[bucket];
96
97            return true;
98        }
99
100       public Object next(){
101           if ( !this.hasNext() ) throw new NoSuchElementException();
102
103           // check for concurrent modification
104           if ( expectedModcount != modCount )
105               throw new ConcurrentModificationException();
106
107           okToRemove = true;
108           last = cursor;
109           cursor = null;
```

```
110              Object o = null;
111              switch ( iteratorType ) {
112                  case KEY_ITERATOR :   o = (Object)last.key();
113                                        break;
114                  case VALUE_ITERATOR : o = (Object)last.value();
115                                        break;
116                  case ENTRY_ITERATOR :
117                                        o = (Object)last;
118              }
119              return o;
120          }
121
122          /**
123           * Remove the element returned by the last call to
124           * <tt>next()</tt>.
125           * @throws <tt>ConcurrentModificationException</tt> if this
126           * collection has been modified by a method outside of this
127           * iterator.
128           * @throws <tt>IllegalStateException</tt> if there has been
129           *  no call to <tt>next()</tt> for this iteration or if two
130           * calls to <tt>remove()</tt> have been made with no
131           * intervening call to <tt>next()</tt>.
132           */
133          public void remove() {
134              // check for concurrent modification
135              if ( expectedModcount != modCount )
136                  throw new ConcurrentModificationException();
137
138              // check that there has been a next() message to
139              // provide an element to remove
140              if ( !okToRemove )
141                  throw new IllegalStateException();
142
143              expectedModcount++;
144              okToRemove = false;
145              HashMap.this.remove( last.key() );
146          }
147      }
```

12.3.7 Testing `HashMap`

The test plan described for the map interface should be applied to any implementation of `Map`. Knowing the details of the `HashMap` implementation, particularly the use of chaining and the resizing of the table, we can identify several additional tests that should be run.

- Insert entries whose keys hash to the same index. This will test that chaining is working properly. I used `Integer` as the key type to simplify figuring out appropriate hash values (e.g., for a table capacity of 11 values, 6 and 17 will hash to position 6). You should verify that accesses to bucket 0 and bucket *capacity* – 1 work properly.

- Remove an entry from a bucket whose chain length is 1. The bucket should be empty afterward.

- Remove an entry from a bucket whose chain length is greater than 1 to make sure the chain is not broken. Removing items from the head, interior, and tail of a chain should be done.

- Insert enough elements to ensure that the table is resized, then make sure that the new table contains all the elements. You could do this by calling `values()`, but since `values()` simply walks through the array and chains entry by entry, you also need to make sure that you can still access individual entries by hashing on their keys.

SUMMING UP

A hash table is often used as the backing store for a map. If a good hash function is used, `HashMap` can provide O(1) access time for most operations. Making the table size a prime number can help the hash function uniformly distribute the keys over the table.

For `HashMap` to be serializable, `HashMap`, `Entry`, `LinkEntry`, and the key and value fields must all implement `java.io.Serializable`.

Although the public interface of `Map` does not include an iterator method, several other methods make use of one. Rather than create three iterators to return entries, values, and keys, a single iterator can be implemented whose constructor takes an argument identifying the iterator's type: entry, key, or value. Since the iterator must access entries in the table, it is a simple matter for `next()` to return the entry or extract the entry's key or value field to return.

The `values()` method provides a `Collection` view of `HashMap` that is backed by the `HashMap` (the hash table). This is accomplished by providing an implementation of `AbstractCollection`. The abstract `Collection.iterator()` method is implemented to return an instance of `HashMap`'s iterator. Since `Collection`'s methods access the collection's elements through its iterator, the `Collection` view is actually accessing elements in the `HashMap`.

INVESTIGATE Radix Sort

Description

We have looked at algorithms for sorting n things that had run times of $O(n^2)$—selection sort and insertion sort—and $O(n\log_2 n)$—quick sort and merge sort. It turns out that with the use of some ideas and techniques from hashing, we can sort in O(n) time with an algorithm called radix sort. This seems rather remarkable and you might wonder why we didn't begin and end our discussion of sorting by covering radix sort. By the end of this *Investigate* you will understand why, and you will have a fresh appreciation for the value of considering alternative points of view on how something can be done.

Objectives

■ Design and implement the radix sort algorithm.

■ Work with ideas and techniques from hashing.

■ Work with queues.

■ Broaden your perspective on how to view problems.

Visualization

The sorting algorithms we have seen so far compared data values as if they were atomic; that is, as if they couldn't be broken down and compared based on *parts* of each data value. This is radix sort's novelty. The algorithm gets its name from the fact that it sorts *integers* (which we usually think of as atomic) by looking at them from the perspective of data values composed of digits in some radix (base).

Radix = base

Figure 12.10 illustrates a radix 10 example. The data structure used to do the sort is a simplified hash table. The number of digits in the base determines the number of buckets in the table. Base 10 has 10 digits, 0 through 9, so our hash table has 10 buckets. The index to each bucket is the digit itself, so digit 0 will hash to table[0] and digit 5 will hash to table[5]. Each bucket will contain a list,[2] possibly empty, of

---

Figure 12.10 Radix sort example for radix = 10 on five 3-digit numbers. The digit being examined in the current pass is <u>underscored</u>. The numbers in `table` are sorted based on the digits in *italics*.

	original unsorted sequence	sequence after Pass 0	sequence after Pass 1
	72<u>3</u>,27<u>4</u>,24<u>3</u>,54<u>1</u>,32<u>1</u>	5<u>4</u>1,3<u>2</u>1,7<u>2</u>3,2<u>4</u>3,2<u>7</u>4	<u>3</u>21,<u>7</u>23,<u>2</u>43,<u>5</u>41,<u>2</u>74
	Pass 0 (1's digit)	Pass 1 (10's digit)	Pass 2 (100's digit)
table[0]		table[0]	table[0]
table[1]	54*1* 32*1*	table[1]	table[1]
table[2]		table[2] 3*2*1 7*2*3	table[2] *2*43 *2*74
table[3]	72*3* 24*3*	table[3]	table[3] *3*21
table[4]	27*4*	table[4] 5*4*1 2*4*3	table[4]
table[5]		table[5]	table[5] *5*41
table[6]		table[6]	table[6]
table[7]		table[7] 2*7*4	table[7] *7*23
table[8]		table[8]	table[8]
table[9]		table[9]	table[9]

Sorted sequence after
the last pass.
243, 274, 321, 541, 723

---

[2]The collection need not be a list. It could be a queue or even a simple linked list. The only requirement is that as integers are added, they must go to the rear of the collection.

the integers that hash to that bucket. The key to radix sort is how the integers are moved into the buckets.

Through a succession of passes (see Figure 12.10), the input integers are examined digit by digit, starting from the right with the least significant digit and moving to the left to the most significant digit. Continuing our base 10 example, in pass 0, we examine the digit in the 1's position ($10^0 = 1$) for each input integer; in pass 1 we examine the digit in the 10's position ($10^1 = 10$), and so on. The hash function keeps track of the pass number and uses it to determine which digit position to extract from the input number. The extracted digit is the number's hash value for this pass.[3]

1. Give an equation that will extract the desired digit from an integer for a given pass number.

    Again, when an integer is added to a bucket, it is always *appended* to the bucket's list.

    A pass ends when all the input integers have been entered in the table. At the end of a pass, we iterate over the table, starting with the bucket for the first digit in the base. As each bucket is traversed, the integers it holds are extracted from its collection, starting at the front, and are *appended* to a temporary list. (To save space, the original list can be used instead.) When all the integers have been moved from the table to the temporary list, the next pass can begin. Between passes, each bucket in the table must be reinitialized with a new instance of the collection that will store the bucket's integers.

    What each pass is doing is ordering the integers *based on the digits seen so far*. For example, after pass 1 has completed, the algorithm has looked at the two least significant digits of all the integers. At this point the bucket for table[4] in Figure 12.10 contains the integers 5**41**, 2**43**. Looking only at the digits the algorithm has examined to this point (the two low-order digits shown in **bold italics**), the sequence is ordered. If you look at the entire sequence generated after pass 1 (top of the third column in Figure 12.10), you will see that it is ordered based on the two low order digits.

    Each pass provides an ordering of the input based on the digits seen so far

$$3\mathbf{21}, 7\mathbf{23}, 5\mathbf{41}, 2\mathbf{43}, 2\mathbf{74}$$

    Pass 2 will reorder this sequence by looking at the digit in the second position (the 100's digit), completing the sort.

2. Create a list of five 4-digit integers. Using the description above and the example in Figure 12.10 as a model, sort your list of integers.

3. What is the time complexity of
    a. initializing the table before each pass?
    b. inserting the integers from the list into the table?
    c. extracting the integers from the table and moving them to the list?

---

[3]It is here that the use of hashing terminology breaks down a bit. For a given input, a hash function should always return the same hash value. But the idea of generating an index through some manipulation of an input value and using that index to access a table where the input value will be stored is the idea behind hashing. So we are in the same ballpark, and one of the goals of this *Investigate* is to encourage you to look for relationships between things that are not obviously related and to reuse ideas. Sometimes it really pays off.

4. Based on the example in Figure 12.10 and your experience sorting your list of four-digit integers, how does the range of integers affect the number of passes required to complete the sort?

5. What is the time complexity for radix sort? Explain.

6. What is the space complexity of radix sort? Explain.

7. Should anything special happen when the extracted digit is 0?

8. What should happen if you are sorting m-digit integers and the current integer has only $m - 2$ significant digits? For example, what happens when $m = 5$, the current integer is 217, and this is pass 3?

9. Does the algorithm sort properly if any of the integers are negative? Explain your answer. If your answer is no, give a counter example to illustrate.

Design

1. From the description in the Visualization section and your experience tracing the execution, pseudocode the radix sort algorithm for radix = 10 (the Exercises explore other possibilities).

2. Verify your pseudocode by walking through it with a different collection of integers.

3. Describe a test plan for your algorithm.

Implementation and Evaluation

1. Implement the algorithm pseudocoded in the Design section.

2. Implement and run your test plan.

3. Time your implementation sorting an array of 5,000 integers that are in the range of 0 to 99,999 (that is, they are five-digit integers).

4. Redo your timing to sort 5,000 10-digit integers.

5. Explain the source of the difference in the timings.

6. Do these timings confirm the asymptotic analysis for radix sort? Explain.

7. Time a merge sort for the integer arrays you used above. How do these timings compare to that of radix sort?

Discussion

1. Is radix sort a stable sort?

2. Will radix sort work on strings? Generalizing on radix sort, try sorting the following list of strings: tom, sue, tim, sol.

3. Why can't the individual values (letters or digits) be scanned from left to right? Give an example where scanning from left to right results in a sequence that is *not* ordered.

4. Are there other types of data that can be sorted using the ideas behind radix sort?

We need not confine ourselves to base 10 and can take advantage of the binary representation of unsigned integers to work in bases that are powers of 2. In Figure 12.11, a 32-bit unsigned integer is treated as a base-16 value. A base-16 digit requires 4 bits to represent so a 32-bit unsigned integer contains eight base-16 digits. Since the radix hash table must contain a bucket for each digit in the base, we now need a 16-bucket table.

5. How many passes are required if a 32-bit unsigned integer is treated as a base-16 number?

6. Draw a picture similar to Figure 12.11 assuming a base-256 number.

7. How many buckets are required now?

8. Give the time and space complexities for base-16 and base-256 radix sort.

9. Write a paragraph describing the space-time tradeoffs involved.

10. Can we compromise and use 5- or 6-bit groupings? Explain.

11. Does radix sort work for signed integers? Explain.

■ **12.4** Ordered Map

A map makes no promises about the ordering of its elements. There may be times, though, when we would like to retrieve a map's values in order by their keys. The concordance and book index problems given at the beginning of the chapter are good examples.

The ordered map ADT extends the map ADT by specifying that its keys can be provided in an inorder fashion. The only significant change in the ADT operations is that operation keys() now provides a collection of keys that are ordered according to their natural ordering. That is, an iteration over the collection will provide the ordered map's keys in order.

An obvious requirement is that the key must provide a way to compare itself with other keys to provide the ordering. A map only required the ability to test for equality. As we have seen before, Java provides two mechanisms, Comparable and Comparator, for doing ordering. As you can see from the ADT description, both are supported.

If the default constructor is used, it is assumed that the keys are Comparable to one another. Alternatively, a Comparator can be supplied through a constructor.

Figure 12.11 A 32-bit unsigned integer treated as eight base-16 digits.

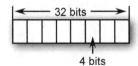

The OrderedMap ADT

Description
An OrderedMap stores <key, value> pairs ordered by key. A difference between Map and OrderedMap is that the keys() operation returns a Collection view of the keys in the OrderedMap such that an iteration over the Collection provides the keys in order. The ordering is either the key type's natural ordering as defined by Comparable or one defined by a Comparator supplied when an OrderedMap is created.

Properties
1. Duplicates keys are not allowed.
2. A key may be associated with only one value.
3. A value may be associated with more than one key.
4. Null keys and values are not allowed.

Attributes
size:	The number of <key, value> pairs in this OrderedMap.
comparator:	The comparator to use to order the keys. If no comparator is provided, the keys are ordered based on the key type's natural ordering as defined by Comparable.

Operations
OrderedMap()

pre-condition:	none
responsibilities:	constructor—create an empty OrderedMap. Keys will be ordered based on their natural ordering as defined by the key's implementation of Comparable
post-condition:	*size* is set to 0
	comparator is null
returns:	nothing

OrderedMap(Comparator comparator)

pre-condition:	comparator cannot be null
responsibilities:	constructor—create an empty OrderedMap. Keys will be ordered based on comparator
post-condition:	*size* is set to 0
	comparator is set to comparator
returns:	nothing
exception:	if comparator is null

Implementing OrderedMap is a simple matter of choosing a backing store that provides ordering. A hash table is clearly inappropriate since its elements are *not* ordered. That is the price we pay for the nice O(1) search time.

One possibility is to store the `Entrys` in some implementation of `BinarySearchTree`. For example, we could have `AVLMap` and use an AVL tree as the backing store. This is another example of using the Adapter design pattern.

■ 12.5 MultiMap

A map defines a one-to-one relationship between a key and a value; for each key there is a single (not necessarily unique) value. Thus the `Entry` class created for the implementation of `Map` had `Object` data fields `key` and `value`.

A MultiMap allows a one-to-many relationship between a key and a collection of values. The concordance and book index problems presented at the beginning of the chapter illustrate the need for storing more than one value associated with a key.

We can extend the map ADT to specify a MultiMap, redefining some of the map operations and supplying a few new operations.

The MultiMap ADT

Description
A MultiMap allows more than one value to be associated with a single key. A MultiMap stores <key, collection> pairs.

Properties
1. Duplicates keys are not allowed.
2. A key is associated with one or more values.
3. A value may be associated with more than one key.
4. Duplicate values associated with a key are not allowed.
5. There is no guarantee on the ordering of the keys or values.
6. Null keys and values are not allowed.

Attributes

size: The number of <key, collection> pairs in this Map.

Operations

MultiMap( )
    pre-condition: none
    responsibilities: constructor—create an empty MultiMap
    post-condition: *size* is set to 0
    returns: nothing

put(KeyType key, ValueType value)
    pre-condition: key and value are not null and are comparable for equality to other keys/values in this MultiMap
    responsibilities: puts the <key, value> pair into this MultiMap

post-condition:	*size* is increased by one if key was not already in this MultiMap. If key already exists in the map, value is added to the collection of values associated with key assuming value isn't a duplicate
returns:	null if the key was not in the map, the value if it was already associated with key
exception:	if key or value is null or either cannot be compared for equality with keys/values in this MultiMap

get(KeyType key)

pre-condition:	key is not null and is comparable for equality to other keys in this MultiMap
responsibilities:	gets the first value from this MultiMap in the collection of values associated with key
post-condition:	the MultiMap is unchanged
returns:	null if the key was not found in this MultiMap, the first value in the collection associated with key otherwise
exception:	if the key is null or cannot be compared for equality to other keys in this MultiMap

getValues(KeyType key)

pre-condition:	key is not null and is comparable for equality to other keys in this MultiMap
responsibilities:	gets the collection of values associated with key in this MultiMap, if key exists in the MultiMap
post-condition:	the MultiMap is unchanged
returns:	null if the key was not found in the map, the collection associated with key otherwise
exception:	if the key is null or cannot be compared for equality to other keys in this MultiMap

remove(KeyType key)

pre-condition:	key is not null and is comparable for equality to other keys in this MultiMap
responsibilities:	remove the collection of values from this MultiMap associated with key. If a collection of values with this key exists in the map, it is returned, otherwise null is returned
post-condition:	*size* is decreased by one if there was a value in this MultiMap with the given key
returns:	null if the key was not found in this MultiMap, the value associated with key otherwise
exception:	if the key is null or cannot be compared to other keys in this MultiMap

remove(KeyType key, ValueType value)

pre-condition:	key and value not null and are comparable for equality to other keys and values in this MultiMap
responsibilities:	remove from this MultiMap the value associated with key

post-condition:	*size* is decreased by one if value was the only value associated with key in this MultiMap. In this case, key is removed as well.
returns:	null if the key was not found in this MultiMap, the value associated with key otherwise
exception:	if the key or value is null or cannot be compared to other keys/values in this MultiMap

values()
pre-condition:	none
responsibilities:	provides a Collection view of all the values contained in this MultiMap. The Collection supports element removal, but not element addition. Any change made to the Collection is reflected in this map and vice versa
post-condition:	the MultiMap is unchanged
returns:	a Collection containing all the entries from this MultiMap. Each element of the collection is itself a Collection

EXERCISES

Paper and Pencil

1. What is the load factor for a table with 97 buckets and 35 entries?

2. What is the hash value for "Mockingbird" using folding?

3. Following the form shown in Figure 12.10, use a radix sort to sort the integers 49, 127, 82, 251, and 402.

4. Briefly describe a problem, other than those presented in this chapter, that can be represented by a
   a. map
   b. MultiMap
   c. ordered map
   d. ordered MultiMap

Testing and Debugging

1. Produce a graph comparing linear probing and chaining for successful and unsuccessful searches for load factors in the range 0 to 1.

2. A member of your programming team suggests that your rehash() method first convert the key to a String using its toString() method, then hash on the resulting string. Evaluate this idea. Be sure to justify your claims.

3. Ari understands the importance of a hash function uniformly distributing the keys over the hash table. Someone suggested that Ari incorporate random number generation into the hash function to ensure that each index in the table has an equal probability of being generated. Should Ari follow through with this idea?

4. Provide a test plan for a MultiMap.

Modify the Code

1. Try different collection types for the bucket in open addressing.

2. Use a priority queue as the backing store for the `Orders` in `PizzaOrderModel`, ordered by `Date`. (See the Focus on Problem Solving section on the Web.) Update the system to allow an order to be canceled after it has been submitted.

3. Redo the *Investigate* problem to sort strings.

4. Performance under chaining might be improved if the chains were ordered in ascending order by key. Implement this variation and do a timing comparison against the implementation given in this chapter. Was this a worthwhile change to make?

5. If the last entry in a cluster is removed, it doesn't need to be replaced with a bridge. Outline how this might be implemented and discuss the advantages and disadvantages of making this change to answer the question: Is it worth the effort?

6. In the implementation of `HashMap` in this chapter, the `put()` and `get()` methods used a utility method, `find()`, to locate an entry with a given key. The `remove()` method also needs to find an entry with a given key, but we cannot use `find()` because `remove()` needs a reference to the target's predecessor in a chain so that the chain can be reconnected once the target entry has been removed. If the chains were implemented as a doubly linked list, `put()`, `get()`, and `remove()` could all use `find()`. Would it be worth it to change the implementation along these lines?

7. The `Map` interface in `java.util` has a method that returns a `Set<K>keySet()` that returns a `Set` view of the keys contained in the map. See if you can use the implementation of `values()` as a model to add this method to our implementation of the Map ADT. You will need to look at the documentation for `java.util.Set` in the JCF.

8. A map is often called a *dictionary* for the fairly obvious reason that we can think of a word as the key and the definition as the value. However, a word can have multiple definitions (meanings), which would seem to violate the unique key property of maps. If you were implementing an online dictionary using a map, how would you handle this?

9. Implement a MultiMap.

10. Implement an ordered map.

11. Implement an ordered MultiMap.

ON THE WEB

Additional study material is available at Addison-Wesley's Website at http://www.aw.com/cssupport. This material includes the following:

■ Focus on Problem Solving: A Pizza Ordering System

Problem: A friend of yours, Guido, opened a small pizzeria, and while the response has been very positive, he would like to do better. A friend with a business major told Guido that he can better compete with the chain pizza places if he offers home delivery (something Guido initially didn't feel he needed to do), so Guido's Pizzeria is going to start home delivery. But Guido cannot afford the expensive software systems that keep track of home delivery customer information, so he turns to you (a former intern with Barking Dogs Software) to design a simple system that will see him through to when he can afford something more powerful.

Having ordered a few pizzas in our time, we know what a pizza place asks for when we order a pizza and after a short talk with Guido, we decide the job shouldn't be too hard (the free pizza while we write programs also motivates you).

Solution: The application needs to quickly and uniquely identify a customer calling for a home delivery pizza. Phone numbers fit the bill, so customer information is stored in an implementation of the Map ADT as <phone number, customer information> pairs.

The solution includes Analysis (discussion of the inputs and outputs to the application, and the layout of the application interface), Design (identification of classes with their responsibilities and collaborators, visualized through a UML class diagram), and Implementation of the classes.

■ Study Guide Exercises

■ Answers to CheckPoint Problems

■ Additional exercises

Index